MAGILL'S AMERICAN FILM GUIDE

MAGILL'S AMERICAN FILM GUIDE

VOLUME 2
CO-I WA
777-1560

Edited by

FRANK N. MAGILL

Associate Editors

STEPHEN L. HANSON

PATRICIA KING HANSON

A Salem Softbacks Book
SALEM PRESS
Englewood Cliffs, N.J.

LIBRARY OF CONGRESS CATALOG CARD NUMBER: 82-61666

Complete Set: ISBN 0-89356-250-5
Volume 2:   ISBN 0-89356-251-1

Most of this material has appeared previously under the
title *Magill's Survey of Cinema.*

PRINTED IN THE UNITED STATES OF AMERICA

LIST OF TITLES IN VOLUME TWO

MAGILL'S
AMERICAN
FILM
GUIDE

THE COUNTY CHAIRMAN

Released: 1935
Production: Edward W. Butcher for Twentieth Century-Fox
Direction: John Blystone
Screenplay: Sam Hellman and Gladys Lehman; based on an original story by
  George Ade
Cinematography: Hal Mohr
Editing: no listing
Running time: 85 minutes

Principal characters:
Jim Hackler	Will Rogers
Ben Harvey	Kent Taylor
Lucy Rigby	Evelyn Venable
Elias Rigby	Berton Churchill
Mrs. Rigby	Louise Dresser
Sassafras Livingston	Stepin' Fetchit
Hy Cleaver	Frank Melton
Abigail	Jan Duggan
Riley Cleaver	Charles B. Middleton
Wilson Prewitt	Erville Alderson
Uncle Eck	William V. Mong
Freckles	Mickey Rooney

To describe Will Rogers as merely a movie star is tantamount to calling
Jesus of Nazareth only a carpenter—and to many people just as sacrilegious.
For a generation of Americans, Will Rogers was almost a saint. His radio
broadcasts were listened to religiously each week. His sayings—the most
famous of which is, of course, "I never met a man I didn't like"—have become
part of American folklore. He was a homespun American philosopher who
dabbled in many crafts, including vaudeville, revue, journalism, and film
acting.

Between 1918 and 1935, the year in which he died in a plane crash, Rogers
starred in more than sixty features and shorts. The silent films did little to
add to his success, but in the twenty-one sound features that he made for
Fox, and later Twentieth Century-Fox, he created a screen persona which
was peculiarly his own, and along the way he became the cinema's number-
one box-office star. All of Rogers' films were natural subjects for him; he
played a basic screen character, that of a simple small-town or rural man
righting minor wrongs which mirror the major wrongs in American society
in a simple fashion. He ad-libbed much in his films, using them as propaganda
machines for his Democratic philosophies, a number of which, unfortunately,
seem a little racist by today's standards.

In *They Had to See Paris* (1929 and Rogers' first talkie), Rogers plays a small-town fellow from Claremore, Oklahoma (his actual birthplace), who strikes oil and is taken by his family to Paris, where he shows the French that there is more honest sophistication in Claremore than in their capital city. In *So This Is London* (1930), he cements Anglo-American relations by pointing out that "God Save the King" and "My Country 'Tis of Thee" both have the same tune. In *A Connecticut Yankee* (1931), Rogers brings his affable simplicity to the Court of King Arthur in the film based on Mark Twain's story. In *Ambassador Bill* (1931), he is a most undiplomatic ambassador; in *State Fair* (1933), he is a farmer whose one interest in life, outside of his family, is a prize pig; and in *Doubting Thomas* (1935), he demonstrates the phoniness of small-town sophisticates. Only the three films that Rogers made for director John Ford—*Dr. Bull* (1933), *Judge Priest* (1934), and *Steamboat 'round the Bend* (1935)—are in any way removed from the usual Rogers style, probably because Ford proved more strong-willed than his star, and as such these films should not be considered typical Rogers vehicles.

The County Chairman, released in the last year of Rogers' life, is a perfect example of a typical Rogers production, containing all the classic elements that appeared in most of the star's films. It is not particularly well-known, despite its excellent direction by John Blystone (a man usually and unfortunately associated with the films of Laurel and Hardy). Were his name not on the credits, one could well surmise that *The County Chairman*'s director was John Ford. The film has the look of a Ford production, which is quite simply explained by its being made by Ford's studio. If ever an example could be used to disprove the *auteur* theory it is *The County Chairman*, which, viewed with any of Ford's Fox productions, proves that the *auteur* of a film is not the director but the studio.

The film is based on a classic story by George Ade about small-town politics in Wyoming of the 1890's. Rogers plays a local attorney named Jim Hackler who has adopted and brought up Ben Harvey (Kent Taylor), his candidate for public prosecutor; Harvey is fighting a political battle with Elias Rigby (Berton Churchill), an obvious blustering phoney who can only corrupt politics. To complicate matters, Harvey is in love with Rigby's daughter, Lucy (Evelyn Venable). Her mother (Louise Dresser) meanwhile, is an old girl friend of Jim Hackler. In the end, of course, Harvey wins both the girl and the election. Unlike reality, the best man always succeeds in a Rogers film; romance always triumphs and the American political machinery—sometimes with a spot of finagling by Rogers—always elects the honest man. It is life as Rogers the philosopher would wish it to be, and as his millions of devoted admirers hoped it would be under President Franklin D. Roosevelt. As *Variety* (January 22, 1935) wrote, "Story is simple, but the production, direction and histrionisms surmount everything to impress *County Chairman* for box-office satisfaction."

The County Chairman boasts a host of members of the Will Rogers company of character players. Venable and Taylor are perfectly solid, dull, and attractive in a small-town way as the young lovers. Dresser is the bosomy screen mother, understanding and tolerant of everything. Churchill is the blustering villain—although villain is too strong a word—whose eloquence cannot hide his basic fraudulent nature. He continually denies he is running for office, in the true American political tradition, leading Rogers to comment, "That's just the kind of men we want in politics in this country—men who are not candidates." Other Rogers film regulars include Ford's brother Francis, Frank Melton, Charles B. Middleton, William V. Mong, and Russell Simpson.

The quintessential Rogers' black and the cinema's most famous stereotyped black, Stepin' Fetchit, is also in *The County Chairman*. Generally, he does not have anything to do with the plot, but in this case he does add a touch of suspense to the ending by announcing the wrong winner in the race for state prosecutor. As Sassafras Livingston, Fetchit's chief function is to amble slowly around the film, muttering almost indecipherable comments. He is slow in speech, movement, and in thought. To some he is a racist slur, but to many others he is the character he is portraying. In *The County Chairman*, Fetchit uses the pretense of the continuing births of new children to gain dollars from white people for the honor of having the new offspring named after them. Only Rogers sees through the fraud, but he is too kind to expose Fetchit, particularly when his own political rivals are ever willing to pay out dollars to the black. Fetchit's lethargic actions somehow seem an integral part of Rogers' small-town America.

The films of Rogers reflect the man's beliefs, tolerance, and moral stance. As such they succeed. Behind Rogers' humor there is a seriousness of purpose which the philosopher never sets aside. His films may appear dated—even quaint—but they stand as living testaments to his philosophies and ideals. Few filmmakers can make such a claim.

Anthony Slide

THE COURT JESTER

Released: 1956
Production: Norman Panama and Melvin Frank for Dena Enterprises; released by Paramount
Direction: Norman Panama and Melvin Frank
Screenplay: Norman Panama and Melvin Frank
Cinematography: Ray June
Editing: Tom McAdoo
Song: Sylvia Fine and Sammy Cahn
Running time: 101 minutes

> *Principal characters:*
> Hawkins .... Danny Kaye
> Maid Jean .... Glynis Johns
> Sir Ravenhurst .... Basil Rathbone
> Princess Gwendolyn .... Angela Lansbury
> King Roderick .... Cecil Parker
> Griselda .... Mildred Natwick
> Sir Griswold .... Robert Middleton
> Black Fox .... Edward Ashley
> Giacomo .... John Carradine

In a long line of screen comedians, Danny Kaye was probably the one with the most impact in the 1940's and early 1950's. During that period, he made a short but impressive series of movies, many of which contained little of value other than Kaye's comic talents. *The Court Jester* is probably the best of this series.

Born Daniel David Kaminsky in Brooklyn, Kaye had his first success on Broadway in 1940 in *Lady in the Dark* with Gertrude Lawrence. A number entitled "Tchaikovsky" in which Kaye named fifty-four Russian composers in thirty-nine seconds, brought him attention and typified the verbal alacrity and rubber-faced delivery which were to become Danny Kaye's trademark.

Soon after this success, Samuel Goldwyn put Kaye under contract. Agonizing over Kaye's features, Goldwyn recommended a nose job. Kaye refused, but did become a blond on Goldwyn's advice. Kaye's wife, Sylvia Fine, who wrote his specialty songs, was also signed.

Unbeknownst to Goldwyn, Danny Kaye had already done some film work in two-reel comedies for Educational Pictures in Astoria, with actors Imogene Coca, June Allyson, and Hank Henry. Under contract, however, Goldwyn produced a series of vehicles for Kaye, among them *Wonder Man* (1945), *A Song Is Born* (1948), and *The Secret Life of Walter Mitty* (1947). Kaye's character was generally patterned after Harold Lloyd—shy and inept, but nevertheless winning the girl, usually played by Virginia Mayo, in the end.

Unfortunately, these early films were, for the most part, merely showcases for Danny Kaye's musical spoofery. Logic was not their strong point, as the naïve Kaye was set into unusual situations and forced to make the best of them. General weaknesses in plot and characterization caused a lack of audience empathy for Kaye's character.

After an erratic film career, which added *The Inspector General* (1949), *On the Riviera* (1951), and *Hans Christian Andersen* (1952) to his list of earlier credits, Danny Kaye and Sylvia Fine formed their own production company for the purpose of creating films which would be more tailored to Kaye's talents. The writing/directing/producing team of Norman Panama and Melvin Frank, comedy writers for Goldwyn, whose combined efforts would produce such successes as *My Favorite Blonde* (1942), *Mr. Blandings Builds His Dream House* (1948), and several of the Bob Hope/Bing Crosby "Road" pictures, were hired. Individually, Norman Panama would go on to do *The Maltese Bippy* (1969), a "Laugh-In" product, while Melvin Frank would direct *A Funny Thing Happened on the Way to the Forum* (1966), and, continuing his tradition as a writer/director/producer, would create *A Touch of Class* (1973).

Under Panama and Frank's careful handling, Kaye's character achieved something it had not had before: believability. Comedy was combined with a realistic character, one who could be credible as a romantic lead or a hero, while retaining his clownish aspect. The first efforts of the new production team yielded Kaye's two best pictures, *Knock on Wood* (1954) and *The Court Jester* (1956). This period, from 1954 to 1956, marked the highlight of Danny Kaye's career.

The critics were wildly enthusiastic about *The Court Jester*; in praising the film, a spoof on swashbucklers and Robin Hood types, they were quick to comment on the expertise and talent of the film's creators. The most expensive screen comedy of that time, filmed at a cost of four million dollars, *The Court Jester* was a lavish costume spectacle. Kaye is cast as Hawkins, the inept pot boy for a raffish band of Merry Men type outlaws and nursemaid to an infant deposed king, the Purple Pimpernel. Trying hard to earn the admiration of his hero, the Black Fox (Edward Ashley), leader of this underground movement, Hawkins becomes involved with a plot to return the Purple Pimpernel to his throne.

Involved also is Maid Jean (Glynis Johns), tough but lovely leader in the absence of the Black Fox, and a tender and credible romance begins to develop between Hawkins and her. While trying to smuggle the royal baby into the castle, Maid Jean is caught and carried off to the unlawful King Roderick (Cecil Parker). Hawkins, meanwhile, has donned the costume of Giacomo (John Carradine), "King of Jesters and Jester to the King," in order to establish contact with the king and steal the key to an underground passage allowing for the entry of the Black Fox's men. Hawkins is unwittingly thrown into an impossible and seemingly hopeless situation, but his character is believable and sympathetic, and carries along the film's overabundant plot.

Sylvia Fine's specialty songs are an additional benefit.

Once inside the castle, Hawkins falls prey to the advances of Princess Gwendolyn (Angela Lansbury), whose old nursemaid, the witch Griselda, is trying to prevent the forced marriage of Gwendolyn and Sir Griswold. Spying Hawkins as the solution to the dilemma, Griselda (Mildred Natwick) casts a spell on him, whereby, at the snap of a finger, he becomes a dashing, courageous lover. An additional snap, however, changes him back to his usual cautious and inept self. Thus, the stage for comedy is set. The twists and turns which the plot now takes, in attempting to reunite Hawkins and Maid Jean and to restore the Purple Pimpernel, are numerous to the point of absurdity. The film handles these convolutions with wit and sparkle, as the plot moves at a breathtaking pace.

Among the highlights is Hawkins' duel with Sir Ravenhurst, played by Basil Rathbone with his usual elegance and wit in a gentle spoof of the characters he played so well throughout the 1940's. The dual is a hilarious contrast between Hawkins as himself and as a bold swordsman, as these two natures are rapidly alternated by the continual snapping of fingers. In what must surely be a take-off on *The Mark of Zorro* (1940), and suggested, perhaps, by Rathbone, who also appeared in that film, Ravenhurst slices off the tip of a candle with his saber and challenges Hawkins to match him. Hawkins, with a marvelously smug countenance, strides cooly over to an entire candelabra and slashes at it. As the candles continue to burn, Ravenhurst emits a derisive laugh, but is soon silenced as Hawkins blows at the candelabra, whereupon all the tips fall off and he laughs derisively in his turn.

Other occurences befalling the unhappy Hawkins are his incredibly swift induction into knighthood in order to qualify to fight a duel against Sir Griswold (Robert Middleton) and the duel itself. Customarily, the contestants are required to drink a preliminary toast on the field of battle, but one is poisoned, and Hawkins is warned beforehand that, "The pellet with the poison's in the vessel with the pestle; the chalice with the palace has the brew that is true." As a flagon with a dragon is introduced, Hawkins' panic and confusion increase. Having successfully eluded the toast, Hawkins is faced with combat with the enormous and powerful Sir Griswold. Nervously arming himself with every weapon available, Hawkins enters the arena. A fortuitous lightning bolt strikes him, magnetizes his armor, and saves the day. Eventually, an army of dwarfs enters the palace, catapulting the enemies out, restoring the Purple Pimpernel to his throne, and bringing the film to a happy close.

Primarily notable for Kaye's comic qualities, *The Court Jester* also contains the polished performances of an illustrious supporting cast, including Rathbone, Angela Lansbury, Cecil Parker, Mildred Natwick, Robert Middleton, John Carradine, and Glynis Johns.

Rathbone, himself considered Hollywood's best swordsman, was greatly impressed by Kaye's talent. Commenting that he combined this talent with a prodigious amount of work, Rathbone stated that Kaye could as easily make an audience cry as laugh, and that this was the mark of a truly great comedian. With his quick reflexes and his extraordinary sense of mime, which enabled him to imitate easily anything seen once, Kaye could outfence Rathbone after a few weeks of instruction. Trusting to his own talent, Kaye refused to have anything doubled for him, and even went so far as to learn to play the cornet for the film *The Five Pennies* (1959), a musical biography of Red Nichols.

The number of Kaye's films is small, as Kaye has refused to make more than one film a year in order to leave time for recording and for radio and stage performances; he always has been more concerned with the performance than with becoming a star. Although many of his films have been enormously popular, it generally has been felt that Kaye is a stage performer and entertainer rather than a screen performer, and he comes across to audiences much more vibrantly in person. Because of his incredible rapport with his audiences, Kaye has enjoyed great success on the London stage, which has led to a Royal Command performance. Kaye was recognized with a special Academy Award in 1954 "for his unique talents, his service to the industry and the American people." *The Court Jester* remains a prime example of Danny Kaye at his best.

Grace Anne Morsberger

CRAIG'S WIFE

Released: 1936
Production: Edward Chodorov for Columbia
Direction: Dorothy Arzner
Screenplay: Mary C. McCall, Jr.; based on the play of the same name by
George Kelly
Cinematography: Lucian Ballard
Editing: Viola Lawrence
Running time: 85 minutes

Principal characters:
Harriet Craig .... Rosalind Russell
Walter Craig ....John Boles
Mrs. Harold .... Jane Darwell
Mrs. Frazier .... Billie Burke
Miss Austen .... Alma Kruger
Ethel Landreth .... Dorothy Wilson
Professor Gene Fredericks ....Robert Allen

Originally a Pulitzer Prize-winning play, *Craig's Wife* has been successfully filmed three times. The first version was a silent film starring the beautiful and sadly forgotten Irene Rich. In 1936, Rosalind Russell appeared for Columbia in what is considered the definitive version; and in 1952, Joan Crawford turned Craig's wife into a total villain who thinks more of her carpets than of her husband. The Crawford version, entitled *Harriet Craig*, depicted the original play's disturbed yet human heroine without a trace of sympathy.

Craig's Wife is the ultimate woman's picture. Rather than a typical soap-opera like most pictures made specifically for female audiences, it is an intelligent analysis of the social and economic aspects of the institution of marriage. Although written in 1925, the film's message is still appropriate today: marriage should be for love, not for financial security. Harriet Craig married her husband so that she could have a beautiful home; once she had her home, she found her husband merely a necessary nuisance.

The film opens with Harriet Craig, against her better judgment, having left the home she loves to go to Albany because she has received word that her sister is seriously ill, a fact which Mrs. Craig will not believe. In her absence the servants breath easier, but Mrs. Harold (Jane Darwell), the housekeeper, keeps everything immaculate and ready for her mistress, in case she might suddenly return. It is Mrs. Harold's opinion that if Mrs. Craig should get an idea that there is a pin out of place, she will take the first train out of Albany. Mrs. Harold has long ago learned that the only way to live peacefully is to keep at least a day ahead of a woman like Mrs. Craig. There is more than a pin out of place, however, for the newspaper headlines announce a recent scandalous murder mystery in which the bodies of the J. Fergus Passmores have been discovered dead in the Passmore library—and Fergus Passmore and Walter Craig (John Boles) have always been the best and closest of friends.

Mrs. Harold and a maid are gossiping about what a long-suffering husband Walter Craig is when Mrs. Harold's worst fears are realized: Mrs. Craig suddenly returns home, bringing her niece, Ethel Landreth (Dorothy Wilson), with her. Mrs. Craig has arranged things in Albany so that her sister and her sister's doctor have advised her to go home and take Ethel with her. Ethel, nineteen years old, is distressed, for she has not had a chance to tell her mother that she has virtually promised Professor Gene Fredericks (Robert Allen) to marry him, and it might comfort her mother, who likes Professor Fredericks, to know that her daughter is in good hands. Mrs. Craig is not so sure about that; a college professor does not make very much money. Mrs. Craig has no romantic illusions; she has seen to it that her marriage is an emancipation for her. She has not been exactly dishonest in her marriage, but she has cleverly connived a kind of independence and authority over the man she married, which has made her actually independent of everybody. It is evident that Mrs. Craig values her home more than she does her husband; in fact, she is obsessed by her home. She had seen her own mother dispossessed of her house when her husband, Mrs. Craig's father, abandoned her for another woman; and Mrs. Craig has long ago determined that such a thing will never happen to her.

After sending Ethel upstairs to rest, Mrs. Craig inspects her house and finds fresh scratches on the polished stairs. Also, there are fresh roses in the room, and fresh flowers have shed their petals on the carpets. It is even more irksome for her to know that at this very moment Miss Austen (Alma Kruger), Mr. Craig's aunt who lives in the house, is upstairs in her room entertaining the neighbor, Mrs. Frazier (Billie Burke), who had brought the roses from her own garden. Mrs. Craig is certain that Mrs. Frazier is a busybody who has used the roses as an excuse to get inside the house, which she has been dying to see. Because of these circumstances, Mrs. Craig's homecoming is not a particularly happy one. The scene is set, and the remainder of the action takes place in a single night and the following morning. In less than sixteen hours, the destiny of Mrs. Craig is plotted and resolved.

Insecure and overly cautious, Mrs. Craig has made it clear that she wishes to live to herself, and, as Miss Austen notes, "People who live to themselves are generally left to themselves." One by one, the people close to Mrs. Craig see her clearly for what she is and abandon her. Unwittingly, she involves her husband as a suspect in the murder of Fergus Passmore and his wife; and, had Passmore not left a letter taking blame for his own suicide and the murder of his wife because she had betrayed him, Walter Craig could have been looked upon by the police as a suspect. She has called her husband "a romantic fool," and Walter Craig, his eyes opened to her dishonesties, prepares to desert her. Then, Professor Gene Fredericks arrives, disconcerted, and persuades Ethel to return to Albany with him. Miss Austen announces that she has long wanted to travel extensively, and packs her bags, taking not only her personal possessions but Mrs. Harold, the housekeeper, with her.

Alone at last in the house, Mrs. Craig receives a telegram: her sister in Albany has died. Stunned, she cannot give way to grief. When Mrs. Frazier, the kindly neighbor, comes by with more roses, Mrs. Craig accepts them numbly and confides, because she must tell somebody, that she has just received word that her sister has died. Mrs. Frazier is sympathetic, but withdraws. Mrs. Craig stands alone on the stairs, her arms laden with fresh roses, unmindful that their petals are falling softly onto her beloved carpet.

The brilliance of this 1936 version comes from the star, Rosalind Russell, who was borrowed for the picture from M-G-M, and from the director, Dorothy Arzner. Russell always had a talent for bringing warmth to the many cold and calculating characters she portrayed in films. *Craig's Wife* made her a star in her own right and opened producers' eyes to that rare gift she had for making unsympathetic parts acceptable to audiences; afterwards she made a career of playing hard-headed business women. For her part, director Dorothy Arzner was ideal. At that time she was the only woman in Hollywood working as a director. This smart, mannish-looking woman had worked her way up from the editing department to the position of director through hard work and a no-nonsense attitude. *Craig's Wife* is certainly the best film Arzner ever directed. She brought to it an awareness and sympathy for the plight of women. Her own personal experiences in her career gave Arzner insight into the character of Harriet Craig; whereas the establishment saw Harriet as a bad woman, Arzner saw her as a victim of society.

Craig's Wife was very well received by critics. *Photoplay* magazine named it one of the best of the month, and it is generally acknowledged to be the picture that opened up Russell's career.

Larry Lee Holland

CRIME WITHOUT PASSION

Released: 1934
Production: Ben Hecht and Charles MacArthur; released by Paramount
Direction: Ben Hecht and Charles MacArthur
Screenplay: Ben Hecht and Charles MacArthur; based on the story *The Caballero of the Law* by Ben Hecht and Charles MacArthur
Cinematography: Lee Garmes
Editing: no listing
Running time: 70 minutes

Principal characters:

Lee Gentry	Claude Rains
Carmen Brown	Margo
Katy Costello	Whitney Bourne
Eddie White	Stanley Ridges
Buster Malloy	Paula Trueman
O'Brien	Leslie Adams
Della	Greta Granstedt
Miss Keeley	Esther Dale
Lieutenant Norton	Charles Kennedy
Judge	Fuller Mellish

Ben Hecht and Charles MacArthur were two of this century's leading playwrights and screenplay writers, responsible for *The Front Page* (1931) and *Twentieth Century* (1934) among many others, who had the happy knack of writing works which appealed both to the masses and to the intelligentsia. Like most writers, they found Hollywood's manner of film production distasteful, but unlike most writers, they decided to do something about it. In 1934, they created their own company, which would combine the best techniques of Broadway and Hollywood. Hecht and MacArthur gathered around them a small staff and made their headquarters not in Hollywood but at the former Paramount Astoria Studios on New York's Long Island. They jointly directed their own productions, with noted cameraman Lee Garmes joining them as associate director; it was an astonishing move to have the cameraman as director, but one certainly not without merit, since a cameraman could best understand lighting set-ups, camera angles, and the basic look of each scene. In all, Garmes photographed eleven films scripted by Ben Hecht, who once wrote, "Nothing I ever encountered in the movies was as uniquely talented as the eyes of Lee Garmes." The production team of Hecht and MacArthur turned out only four features: *Crime Without Passion* (1934), *The Scoundrel* (1935), *Soak the Rich* (1935), and *Once in a Blue Moon* (1936). Although only the first two were moderately successful, the team's effort was a noble experiment in independent production belonging more to the present than to the 1930's.

In their first production, *Crime Without Passion*, Hecht and MacArthur give strong indication of what type of filmmaking they planned. The sets are stark and simple, reminiscent of the stage rather than the screen. For their leading man, they chose Claude Rains, who had just made a big hit in *The Invisible Man* (1933), but who in that film had hardly given the impression he was capable of playing the complex hero of *Crime Without Passion*. The two leading ladies were both unknown. Margo was a dancer, chosen because she photographed well and because the character she was portraying was a dancer. Whitney Bourne was a New York socialite with no previous film experience. As *Photoplay* (October, 1934) explained, "For Hollywood's star system, they have supreme contempt. In choosing a cast for their pictures they use Broadway technique. In other words, they search for players who will fit parts, not for people who are known as favorites."

Crime Without Passion probably has one of the most stunning openings ever conceived, an impressive pseudo-Freudian montage of an eye, the vague image of a man firing a gun, a drop of blood, and then three women, in white, soaring from the blood up through the skyscrapers of New York. With maniacal laughter, they smash windows behind which lustful men and women make love, until the falling, broken glass spells out *Crime Without Passion*. As the first title explains, the three women are the Furies, the three sisters of evil who lurk behind men's dreams. The antihero of *Crime Without Passion* senses their presence as the plot unfolds and comments that they are looking in through the windows at his crime. The opening montage sequence, plus a shorter, less impressive one later in the film, was the work of Slavko Vorkapich, a Yugoslav immigrant who came to Hollywood in the 1920's and soon became recognized as the screen's expert at montage.

The film's leading figure—he is not a hero since he is a damnable character without ethics and totally egotistical, rather like the Noel Coward character in *The Scoundrel*—is a lawyer named Lee Gentry (Claude Rains). He is called "The Champion of the Damned" because his eloquent speeches in the courtroom have helped acquit many a guilty murderer. He is seen in action in the opening scenes, ridiculing the district attorney and the police officer investigating the murder. Later, after a not-guilty verdict is returned by the jury, he will admit unconcernedly that a miscarriage of justice has taken place. When the press—and one of the reporters here bears more than a coincidental resemblance to Hecht—question him about a Grand Jury investigation of his courtroom behavior and his tampering with evidence, Gentry makes a statement that "the only crime punishable by death is stupidity." It is a statement which he himself will prove to be true later. Of all Gentry's friends and colleagues, the only one that seems to have a genuine affection for him is his middle-aged secretary, Miss Keeley (Esther Dale).

Lee Gentry has fallen in love with wealthy and elegant Katy Costello (Whitney Bourne), but rather than simply admit to his former girl friend, nightclub dancer Carmen Brown (Margo), that he no longer loves her Gentry must devise a complex scheme to end the affair. When Carmen's former boyfriend Eddie White (Stanley Ridges) visits her, Gentry contrives to arrive immediately afterwards and feign jealousy in order to end the affair. All appears to have worked out as he planned, except that a fellow nightclub performer reveals to Carmen that Gentry knew more than he pretended.

Carmen sends a telegram to Gentry indicating that she will take her own life and, in a telephone call, hysterically says she cannot live without him. Gentry goes over to Carmen's apartment and, in a struggle, accidentally shoots her. Good—if not particularly honest—criminal lawyer that he is, Gentry quickly moves to cover up his crime. He fakes an alibi, pretending to have been at the movies all afternoon. He even tells Katy of his crime, knowing that by revealing the truth to her she will not give him away. Here his plan backfires, however, for although Katy will not expose him, neither will she have anything more to do with him. When the police officer and the district attorney come to escort him to a Grand Jury hearing, Gentry even tricks them into going via Carmen's apartment building so that he may retrieve an incriminating telegram that he had accidentally dropped there.

The Grand Jury, of course, exonerates the wily Gentry, and that evening he goes to Carmen's nightclub—all part of his elaborate cover-up scheme—only to meet a female acquaintance who had accidentally seen him that afternoon and reveals she knows he was not at the movies at the time he claims. Gentry gets hysterical with her, just as her companion, Eddie White, returns to her table. The two men get into a ridiculous, unnecessary fight, and Gentry kills White. Turning from the body to the dance floor, Gentry is horrified to see Carmen appear—he had not killed her at all; the bullet had merely grazed her head. As Gentry has so succinctly put it at the beginning of the film, "the only crime punishable by death is stupidity."

Press and public alike are delighted to see Lee Gentry a broken man about to face trial for murder. He is being tried for murder in the first degree because in his elaborate plan to rid himself of Carmen Brown, he had threatened Eddie White, thus explaining the motive for the shooting in the nightclub. Gentry's alter ego, which appears frequently in double exposure during the second half of the film, helping him to cover up the supposed murder of Carmen Brown, now urges Gentry to take the murder weapon and shoot himself. Gentry cannot, and his alter-ego calls him a coward while the three furies laugh hysterically. In perhaps an unprecedented move for a film from this era, the technical credits appear on screen after the film is over, something which did not become commonplace until the 1960's.

Crime Without Passion was received with considerable enthusiasm by the critics. Mordaunt Hall in *The New York Times* (September 1, 1934) wrote, "It is a drama blessed with marked originality and photographed with consummate artistry." *Photoplay* (November, 1934) described it as "A picture you can never forget." *Variety* (September 4, 1934) considered it "An exciting seventy minutes of entertainment." The public, unfortunately, was less enthusiastic, and *Crime Without Passion* basically played only at art houses, such as the Filmarte in Los Angeles. Viewed today, it is a taut, tightly constructed, psychological melodrama, well photographed and conceived. The dialogue sounds stilted, however, not perhaps because of the writing but rather because of the delivery of inexperienced players.

Anthony Slide

THE CRIMSON PIRATE

Released: 1952
Production: Harold Hecht for Warner Bros.
Direction: Robert Siodmak
Screenplay: Roland Kibbee
Cinematography: Otto Heller
Editing: Jack Harris
Running time: 104 minutes

> *Principal characters:*
> Captain Vallo, The Crimson Pirate ... Burt Lancaster
> Ojo .... Nick Cravat
> Consuelo .... Eva Bartok
> Baron Gruda .... Leslie Bradley
> Humble Bellows .... Torin Thatcher
> Professor Prudence .... James Hayter
> Sebastian, El Libre .... Frederick Leister

There is a joy found in *The Crimson Pirate* that exists in few other films. Whether it is through Burt Lancaster's smiling asides to the audience or through the near-slapstick distortions of scientific principle and historical facts that this feeling of impish amusement is conveyed is of little significance. What is crucial is that everyone from director Robert Siodmak on down was able to appreciate the limitations of a project of this nature, shot on location without the facilities of a modern Hollywood studio, and abandon themselves to the fun inherent in the script. If it did nothing else, *The Crimson Pirate* can certainly be remembered as one film which focused almost entirely on thrills and the exhilaration of exciting action.

As the film opens the Crimson Pirate (Burt Lancaster) overtakes a king's ship bound for the isle of Cobra. It is discovered that the cargo of the captured ship is a large cache of munitions and the sole passenger is Baron Gruda (Leslie Bradley), an emissary from the king sent to crush an impending rebellion on the island headed by a lover of democracy called "el Libre." In true pirate fashion the captain of this band of cutthroats plans to sell this booty of captured munitions to the rebels while at the same time informing the king's men where the rebels are based. In order to do this he must first rescue el Libre from prison where he awaits execution. This beautiful double-cross is complicated when the captain falls in love with Consuelo (Eva Bartok), el Libre's daughter.

Realizing that the Crimson Pirate's new plan to turn the guns over to the rebels without payment violates the "pirate code," the crew decides to mutiny. The newly elected skipper, Humble Bellows (Torin Thatcher), cannot kill his captain so he sets the Crimson Pirate, his first mate Ojo (Nick Cravat), and

Professor Prudence (James Hayter), an associate of el Libre, adrift shackled to a small dingy without food or water. By a clever bit of deductive reasoning Professor Prudence manages to capsize their dingy and eventually walk to shore using air trapped in the overturned boat to breathe. It soon becomes apparent that the Crimson Pirate must join the rebels if he is to rescue his crew, who have themselves been double-crossed by the treacherous Baron Gruda, save el Libre, whose real name is Sebastian (Frederick Leister), from his planned execution, and snatch Consuelo from the greedy hands of the governor of Cobra, who intends to marry her in the hopes of stopping the rebellion. At the back of his mind, however, is the overriding desire to destroy Gruda.

A wild battle takes place on the day of the governor's planned wedding with all sorts of crazy, anachronistic weapons, high-explosives, hot-air balloons, and flame throwers designed by Professor Prudence. With this exotic arsenal and the element of surprise it is hoped that the rebels can overcome the king's troops. The inevitable final showdown takes place onboard the Baron's ship. The Crimson Pirate and his repatriated crew engage the king's marines in savagely funny hand-to-hand combat. The outcome of this free-for-all puts Consuelo in the arms of the Crimson Pirate and the mute Ojo into a comic mime forecasting the perils of wedlock.

"Remember, in a pirate ship, in pirate waters, in a pirate world ask *no* questions; believe only what you see. . . . No! believe half of what you see!" From these few well-chosen words from Lancaster before the credits of the film, Siodmak manages to create the perfect aesthetic climate for one of Hollywood's purest examples of high-camp entertainment. Shot on location in Europe, this remarkable swashbuckler features Lancaster and his former circus partner Cravat as a pair of devil-may-care pirates. The film is nonstop action from start to finish. Throughout the twisting plot, Lancaster as the Crimson Pirate, seems to embody the reincarnated spirit of Douglas Fairbanks. There are sequences in which Lancaster and Cravat elude two squads of guards through acrobatic feats that can only be described as sheer escapism.

A review of Siodmak's career as a director reveals some interesting facts. One is his association with Lancaster from his debut in the stunning *film noir* *The Killers* (1946) and the equally celebrated *Criss Cross* (1948). Another fact is his peripheral treatment of escapist genre films such as *The Son of Dracula* (1943) and *The Cobra Woman* (1944). In *The Crimson Pirate* Siodmak is able to combine both of these strengths to create one of Hollywood's most popular swashbucklers. Although this film does not have the element of studio-based control which is so apparent in the films Siodmak made at Universal and for David O. Selznick during the mid-1940's, there is a certain charm in the exploits of the Crimson Pirate that allows it to transcend its modest budget. The stunts performed by Lancaster and Cravat are nothing less than incredible, as they bounce from building to building, run toward a three-story-tall grain silo that is splitting at the seams, and hang from ropes attached to a hot-air balloon in order to transfer onto the rigging of a ship anchored in a secluded harbor.

Warner Bros. had a great tradition of swashbucklers with films such as *Captain Blood* (1935), *The Sea Hawk* (1943), and *The Adventures of Robin Hood* (1938), starring Errol Flynn. With *The Crimson Pirate* and *The Flame and the Arrow* (1950) Lancaster almost singlehandedly rejuvenated Warner Bros.' role as the prime producer of swashbuckling films. By the early 1950's, however, audiences were not as eager to suspend disbelief and give in to a dashing hero, and the genre soon died.

There is a certain panache that Flynn possessed that was able to permit him to transcend the banality of the scripts of the later swashbucklers such as *The Master of Ballantrae* (1953) and *The Adventures of Captain Fabian* (1951). Lancaster, on the other hand, was more at home in the broad lampoon of the swashbuckling tradition found in *The Crimson Pirate* than in the earlier, more serious *The Flame and the Arrow*. This comic sense has rarely been displayed by Lancaster on screen, however; his acrobatics were displayed well in *Trapeze* (1956), but few of his later films deviated from the serious, almost melodramatic roles with which he has become associated. While *The Rainmaker* (1956) and *Elmer Gantry* (1962), the latter for which he won an Oscar, contain many light, playful moments, it is the Lancaster of *The Sweet Smell of Success* (1957) and *Seven Days in May* (1964) that most filmgoers remember. It is unfortunate that in recent years he has confined himself (or has been confined) to brooding characterizations.

Carl F. Macek

CROSSFIRE

Released: 1947
Production: Adrian Scott for RKO/Radio
Direction: Edward Dmytryk
Screenplay: John Paxton; based on the novel *The Brick Foxhole* by Richard Brooks
Cinematography: J. Roy Hunt
Editing: Harry Gerstad
Running time: 86 minutes

Principal characters:
Captain Finlay	Robert Young
Sergeant Peter Keeley	Robert Mitchum
Montgomery	Robert Ryan
Ginny Tremaine	Gloria Grahame
The Man	Paul Kelly
Joseph Samuels	Sam Levene
Mary Mitchell	Jacqueline White
Floyd Bowers	Steve Brodie
Mitchell	George Cooper
Leroy	William Phipps

Post-World War II film releases from Hollywood often turned to less appealing aspects of American life such as racial bigotry, religious animosity, and crime for thematic story lines. In the case of the 1947 film *Crossfire*, racial hatred manifested by the vicious anti-Semitic soldier, Montgomery (Robert Ryan), leads to a tragic conclusion: the murder of a Jew in a senseless and brutal fashion. Although 1947 would also witness the release of another major American film dealing with the existence of anti-Semitism in America, the Oscar-winning *Gentleman's Agreement*, *Crossfire* had the added distinction of treating a sociological problem within the context of a suspenseful narrative, carefully designed by director Edward Dmytryk to draw the audience into the inner world of a bigot.

In the story, Montgomery harbors an irrational hatred for foreigners and Jews. He is a soldier on active duty who conveys his seething hatreds to anyone who will listen. He is obsessed and fearful of the "contamination" he believes will be the natural result of contact with Jews. As the character is artfully developed by Ryan, we see a man with the mind and temperament of a bully, often caught up in the midst of a racial diatribe. In a bar one night with two of his soldier friends, Montgomery finds himself seated next to a mild-mannered man named Joseph Samuels (Sam Levene) whom Montgomery discovers is a Jew. As he becomes drunker, Montgomery's rage increases toward the Jew; he sees himself confronted with his absolute enemy and, in a spasm of brutality passively watched by his army friends, Montgomery pursues the man outside and beats him to death. The murder scene stuns the audience, for the crime itself is so wrapped up in the taunting, irrational anti-Semitism of Montgomery. There is a motive for the crime: a man is dead because of what he is pictured to be within the paranoid mind of a disturbed human being.

Now that the narrative has been firmly established and a motive for a crime, however senseless, planted in the audience's mind, it remains for the director to shift the focus of the film to the major theme: the discovery by men of good will—in this case the civilian police inspector Captain Finlay (Robert Young)—that hatred can inspire murder. Finley begins to understand the crime. Through careful reconstruction of the facts of the crime itself based on the recollections of one of the soldiers who has known Montgomery and who watched him murder Samuels, Finlay sees a motive. Through careful crosscutting, director Dmytryk shows how Finlay makes a case against Montgomery, slowly, with great care for details. Montgomery himself knows that he must cover up and protect himself. Realizing that he will soon be directly accused by the soldier, Montgomery kills him. The investigation, continues, however, and, aided by army Sergeant Peter Keeley (Robert Mitchum), a trap is constructed.

Together with the police, Keeley has amassed evidence directly implicating Montgomery in Samuels' murder. Through careful cross-examinations in Finlay's office, Keeley confronts those who knew Montgomery well, and, as the camera focuses tightly on the faces of Montgomery's acquaintances, the depth of the man's racial sickness is made plain: each person who knew Montgomery was aware of the incredible hatred the soldier felt. Once Montgomery himself is brought to face his accusers, his shifting glances and strained voice articulate what Finlay and Keeley have long since discovered. Montgomery is placed under arrest, attempts to escape from jail, and is shot and killed.

It is the suspense involved in the investigation of the personality and life of Montgomery that carries the entire film. Although it is not easy to understand the basis of Montgomery's attitudes (his blind hatred of anything he considers to be different is never actually explained; the actual causes are, one is led to believe, part of an aura of religious and racial animosity that simply exists within society), it does become clear that tragedy will result from such feelings. Dmytryk's direction carefully pulls together the subtle nuances of the very real personality changes occurring within the minds of the major characters. Finlay is appalled by what he sees in Montgomery's life; the camera closes in on his face as he begins to unravel for himself the motive for the crime. In a startling moment of brilliant cinematography, the audience can note the disgust Finlay feels as he stares at the accused soldier. Here is a man of good will who, for the first time in his life, discovers hatred in the face of another man.

Crossfire avoids a simplistic presentation of a highly charged theme. The nature of the story—a man obsessed by a furious bigotry causing him to respond and act—might have been, in the hands of less skilled filmmakers, turned into a moralistic and didactic work. Instead, one is introduced, through the superb acting of Ryan, to a character whose feelings and reactions are imbued with a realistic fervor; Montgomery hates openly, and all of his overt mannerisms are carefully crafted. There are, for example, several scenes in which Montgomery, confronted by his accusers, dramatically changes—his face begins to reveal the psychopathic nature of his illness. Dmytryk has established a tempo for the film—sharply defined crosscuts illustrating the reactions of Finlay to the emotional diatribes of Montgomery—that manage to convey a sense of the depth of the man that the policeman has encountered. The same is also true of the scenes involving Montgomery and Keeley, a man who, like Finlay, discovers a hatred he has never experienced before. *Crossfire* deserves attention as a psychological portrait that focuses on men under great pressure of discovery, and also as a social message film.

At the same time that one becomes involved with the discovery and changes taking place in the minds of the major characters, there is always a sense of the tragedy inherent in the film's theme: an innocent man has been murdered. The gentleness of the victim's expressions are in marked contrast with those of his murderer. Once again, the camera captures the sense of discovery felt by the victim who, although he is unaware of his ultimate fate, still feels through the malicious tension conveyed by Montgomery that the man he has met, through accident, is evil.

By juxtaposing several simply photographed scenes (much of the film's action occurs within the confines of simply staged sets), Dmytryk and his players have accomplished a great deal. The viewer is presented with a case study of a perverted crime. Despite the occasional lengthy dialogue between the central characters, *Crossfire* succeeds as a dramatic rendering of what was, in the postwar world of American society, a seriously neglected problem. Film critics were quick to notice that the film was setting a pattern for an improved, although uncomfortable, thematic emphasis; the darker side of human motives had, it seemed, finally arrived in Hollywood.

The film, which was shot entirely at night, has held its dramatic impact over the years. Although *Gentlemen's Agreement* won an Oscar that same year as Best Picture, contemporary critics feel that *Crossfire* is by far a better film.

Larry S. Rudner

CRY THE BELOVED COUNTRY

Released: 1951
Production: Zoltan Korda for Lopert Films
Direction: Zoltan Korda
Screenplay: Alan Paton; based on his novel of the same name
Cinematography: Robert Krasker
Editing: David Eady
Running time: 105 minutes

Principal characters:

Stephen Kumalo	Canada Lee
James Jarvis	Charles Carson
Reverend Msimangu	Sidney Poitier
Father Vincent	Geoffrey Keen
Margaret Jarvis	Joyce Carey
Martens	Michael Goodlife
Absalom	Lionel Ngakane
John Kumalo	Edric Connor
Gertrude	Ribbon Dhlamini
Mary	Vivien Clinton
Mrs. Kumalo	Albertina Temba

Cry the Beloved Country is the soit of film generally praised for its good intentions and noble characters rather than for the successful dramatic realization of its themes. It is a bit too plodding to be particularly revelatory and too self-conscious to be electric. It is well-meaning, however, and it does get its anti-apartheid message across.

The film opens in the country with parallel stories of two men who have left their village to go to Johannesburg: black Absalom Kumalo (Lionel Ngakane), the son of Stephen Kumalo (Canada Lee), the local umfundisi, or priest; and white Arthur Jarvis (who is not seen on screen), the son of a wealthy farmer, James Jarvis (Charles Carson), who has devoted his life to bettering relations between black and white men. Absalom murders Arthur while robbing his home. Hearing that his son is in trouble, the umfundisi journeys to Johannesburg, where, with the help of priests from a poor mission, especially Father Msimangu (Sidney Poitier), Kumalo begins to search for Absalom and for his daughter, Gertrude (Ribbon Dhlamini), who has become a prostitute. He discovers that Absalom had been in a reformatory, and then had left to marry a girl whom he had made pregnant, and then, turning to robbery, had shot Arthur. Kumalo finds his son, but it is too late; the boy stands trial and is found guilty and sentenced to hang. Kumalo returns to his church believing that his son's shame dictates that he must leave it. Margaret Jarvis (Joyce Carey), Arthur's mother, dies, Kumalo sends flowers, and James tells him that it was her last wish that he build a new church for the village and that Kumalo must stay to be its umfundisi. If Kumalo leaves the countryside, it will mean that their suffering will have taught them nothing.

Cry the Beloved Country is a well-rounded film, carefully worked out so that each event has its parallel, each beginning its end; every negative act has its positive counterpart. It opens with a narrator praising the rich South African soil and saying that although some is fertile and well irrigated, nearby there is other land that cannot support its people. The young men have left their villages to seek work elsewhere. The film closes with Kumalo striding across the hills, looking at the glory of his "beloved country" and kneeling to pray. The film tells the stories of two men who go to Johannesburg and die there, one covering himself with honor and praise, the other becoming a criminal and dying a murderer's death. In both cases their fathers come after them and, in the city, learn to understand why their sons behaved as they did. James Jarvis does not approve of Arthur's mixing with blacks; he feels that even shaking hands with a black man is shameful. At Arthur's funeral, however, a black who worked with him offers to shake his hand and Jarvis takes it. He has been reading Arthur's thoughts on apartheid and prejudice and has begun to see how meaningful his son's life was. Kumalo, frustrated at every turn by the poverty and meanness of his people's lives and unable to find Absalom, becomes bitter and nearly loses his faith, but is restored by the kindness of Father Vincent (Geoffrey Keen), the head of the mission, and Reverend Msimangu. Even this sequence has its double. Martens (Michael Goodlife), the kind-hearted warden at the reformatory, temporarily loses his conviction that he can help people like Absalom who have been entrusted to him. Absalom's reversion to criminal behavior shakes his faith. In the last scene, Jarvis and Kumalo meet and shake hands. Both have turned away from resentment toward comprehension and peace.

The film has a tendency to become preachy, as in the rather static sequences in which Jarvis reads Arthur's ideas. The action simply stops, and director Zoltan Korda plasters Arthur's notes, full of compassion and do-goodism, up on the screen. Kumalo trudges around Johannesburg confronted by waste and destitution. In his somber way he tries to instill those he meets with some notion of "the right thing." He is like a black saint (and the film has a white one in the memory of Arthur) who has taken vows of poverty to move among the poor bringing the light. He is more human and believable at the beginning when, arriving in the city, he is taken in by a black sharpie who steals his bus fare, or when he confesses his dismay at everything that has happened and begins to feel sorry for himself.

The most meaningful statement *Cry the Beloved Country* makes is about the disruption of men's lives. The white man's greed has pushed ugly hills up out of the earth on the outskirts of Johannesburg. The black man's need for work has caused a social dislocation in his home village and in the city. There is not enough labor to work the farms; the towns are inhabited by the very old and the very young; and in the cities there is a lack of adequate housing for the people who flock there looking for work.

Over and over the film stresses the damage apartheid causes and the importance of the efforts men like Arthur are making to mend the wounds caused by separatism. When Kumalo rides through the suburbs of the city in a wooden third-class train compartment, he sees the luxurious apartments the whites inhabit. Then he finds his daughter living in Sophiatown, a collection of shacks slanting together on unpaved streets. For further contrast there is Arthur's home, a large airy house on a residential street. There is the difference in opportunities for white and black. Arthur has received an education and uses it to better the lives of men less fortunate than himself; Absalom Kumalo has none and is forced into a life of petty crime.

In spite of being filmed on location, *Cry the Beloved Country* has almost no visual style. The sharp black and white of the sun against the shanty towns and the gloomy interiors lit by naked light bulbs are presented without refinement. The white hills formed by the gold digging, the industrial area around Johannesburg, make a nighttime hell out of Kumalo's first look at the city. There is no stress on any of these aspects, however; the emphasis is entirely verbal, as the characters explain, sometimes repetitively, how they feel.

The acting is generally first-rate. Lee, grizzled and sorrowful, is a bit ponderous, but he is also moving and dignified. Not yet a star, Poitier has third billing in this, his second film; he is dynamic and brings energy to his role. The individuals in the film are, after all, spokesmen for a point of view; they are emblems as much as they are human beings, and as a result the film has an overall air of piety that becomes annoying at times.

Still, *Cry the Beloved Country* is a commendable effort, a film that actually has something worthwhile to say and delivers its message in a straightforward manner without bothering to make it more palatable by cloaking it in Hollywood prettiness. *Lost in the Stars*, the Kurt Weill/Maxwell Anderson musical based on Alan Paton's novel, opened on Broadway in 1949. The lyrics of "Train to Johannesburg" contain the theme of the film reduced to its most essential terms: "White man go to Johannesburg. He come back. Black man go to Johannesburg. Never come back." It is this dichotomy, indicative of inequality and injustice, which is the heart of the film.

Judith M. Kass

CYRANO DE BERGERAC

Released: 1950
Production: Stanley Kramer for the Stanley Kramer Company; released by
United Artists
Direction: Michael Gordon
Screenplay: Carl Foreman; based on the play of the same name by Edmond
Rostand
Cinematography: Franz Planer
Editing: Harry Gerstad
Running time: 112 minutes

Principal characters:
Cyrano de Bergerac .... José Ferrer (AA)
Roxane .... Mala Powers
Christian de Neuvillette .... William Prince
Le Bret .... Morris Carnovsky
Comte de Guiche .... Ralph Clanton
Ragueneau .... Lloyd Corrigan

Cyrano-Savinien-Hercule de Bergerac (José Ferrer) is a seventeenth century French soldier and poet as much feared for his ready wit and satires in
the press as he is for his skilled sword arm. He has also written a play; but
he rejects an offer from Cardinal Richelieu to have it produced under his
sponsorship because the Cardinal insists on changing a few lines.

Cyrano is secretly in love with his cousin, the beautiful Roxane (Mala
Powers); but Roxane loves the Baron Christian de Neuvillette (William
Prince), a handsome new member of Cyrano's regiment, the elite Cadets of
Gascoyne. Cyrano, whose nose is overly large, is miserably aware of his ugly
countenance and goes out of his way to become friends with de Neuvillette,
as his cousin has asked. Christian confesses that he loves Roxane in return,
but is much too shy to speak the things that are in his heart. Cyrano eagerly
proposes that he write Christian's love letters to Roxane for him. She is
thrilled by the letters, and by the pretty speeches that Cyrano puts into
Christian's mouth; but the ardent young Baron grows uneasy when he suspects
that it is Cyrano's words Roxane loves, and not himself. He attempts to woo
her in his own words, but can manage no more than a stammered "I love
you . . . very much" before retreating to beg Cyrano to come to his rescue.

The night is dark; Roxane is waiting on her balcony; and from the shadows
Cyrano can at last pour out in his own voice the words of love he would never
dare speak for himself. With Cyrano's help, Christian and Roxane are secretly
married that same night, just before the Comte de Guiche (Ralph Clanton)
arrives with news that their regiment has been posted to the front and that
they march at once. Even during the worst of the subsequent fighting (France

is at war with Spain), Cyrano manages to slip through the lines every night with a fresh love letter ostensibly written by Christian. His eloquence has never burned higher; and Roxane makes her way to where the Cadets are besieged before Arras to tell her husband that whereas she married him for his outward good looks, his letters have made her love him for his soul.

Christian finally realizes that Cyrano has loved Roxane too, and confronts Cyrano to demand that he tell Roxane everything and make her choose between them. But, before Cyrano can comply, Christian is mortally wounded on a scouting mission behind the enemy lines. He is carried back to the French camp, where Cyrano, in Roxane's presence, tells Christian that he alone has been the man she loved. After Christian's death, Roxane withdraws to a convent, where for fourteen years she cherishes his memory and what she believes to have been his last letter to her. Her only contacts with the outside world are the occasional visits she receives from a few old friends, including Cyrano, who comes every Saturday to amuse her with the latest gossip from the Court and to please her by talking about Christian.

One Friday night, as Cyrano is leaving the pastry shop owned by his friend Ragueneau (Lloyd Corrigan), an amateur poet as well as a cook, Cyrano is set upon and wounded by a gang of assassins hired by a nobleman he has angered with his published satires. Although the doctor warns him that to leave his bed means death, Cyrano painfully makes his way to the convent the next afternoon for his weekly visit with Roxane. He asks to be allowed to see Christian's last letter ("Farewell, Roxane, because today I die"); and his impassioned reading reminds her of the voice that had spoken to her out of the darkness beneath her balcony on her wedding night. She tells Cyrano that now she realizes he has been the man whose soul she loved, but it is too late: Cyrano dies of his wounds, proclaiming that when he meets God he will salute Him with the emblem of the Cadets of Gascoyne and the symbol of his own proudly maintained independence, "my white plume!"

Such is the story of Stanley Kramer's film and the play by Edmond Rostand (1868-1918) on which it was based. One would hardly guess from Rostand's melodramatic plot that Cyrano was a real person, whose dates were 1619-1655. He was, indeed, well-known in his own time as a soldier, poet, satirist, and playwright; and he was reputed to have had a long nose (although it could not have been as long as the magnificent proboscis makeup artists Gustaf and Josef Norin created for José Ferrer in the film). Cyrano's accomplishments, when one looks them up, are quite impressive: he was a pioneer in the field of science fiction (his series of proposals to Guiche, at one point in the play, for breaking free of the earth's gravity were taken from Cyrano's *Histoire comique des états et empires de la lune*); and his plays *Le Pédant joué* and *La Mort d'Agrippine* are still highly regarded in France. He undoubtedly deserved better than Rostand's portrait of him as a self-loathing masochist and, by virtue of his fourteen years' deference to Roxane's mistaken memory of Christian, one of the greatest chumps in dramatic literature.

The reason that *Cyrano de Bergerac*, for all its shameless hokum, has held the boards since it was first performed by the great French actor Coquelin in 1897 is that Rostand disguised the banality of his dramatic conception in verse of a rich sonorousness that is as satisfying for actors to speak as it is for audiences to hear. The play was performed in English by Richard Mansfield as early as 1899; but the translation by Brian Hooker that American and British audiences are familiar with today (and on which Carl Foreman's screenplay was based) was commissioned by Walter Hampden and first performed in 1923. As Brooks Atkinson has written, "the Brian Hooker translation is not only so distinguished but also so familiar that we have almost forgotten that Rostand did not write it himself." Hooker was a Broadway lyricist whose only other notable work was the libretto he cowrote with William H. Post for *The Vagabond King*. There would seem to be no explanation other than clairvoyance for the skill with which he found equivalents for Rostand's Alexandrines in the iambic pentameter of English dramatic verse. Had Hampden, when he decided to revive the play, stuck with the translation used by Mansfield (in which the familiar line that Hooker rendered "And then as I end the refrain, thrust home!" had emerged as "And then at the envoi's end, *touché!*"), *Cyrano de Bergerac* in English might long ago have entered the same limbo as such once-popular works by Rostand as *La Princesse Lointaine*, *La Samaritaine*, and *L'Aiglon*.

In recent years, the more ridiculous aspects of the story (such as Roxane's arrival at Arras with Ragueneau in a coach and four just as the beleaguered Cadets are bracing themselves for a ferocious Spanish assault) have usually been played for their value as comedy, without detracting from the seriousness of such moments as Cyrano's great speech rejecting Guiche's offer of patronage or Guiche's avowal of dissatisfaction in the last act.

Michael Gordon, the director of the film version, later demonstrated a flair for comedy in *Pillow Talk* (1959)—one of the first and best of the Doris Day vehicles of the late 1950's and early 1960's—and in such subsequent trifles as *Boys' Night Out* (1962) and *Move Over Darling* (1963). His treatment of *Cyrano de Bergerac* is squarely (in both senses of the word, as Dwight Macdonald once said) in the solemn tradition of the typical Hollywood "prestige" picture, however. The few notes of levity that creep in—such as the sudden disappearance of the actor Montfleury when Cyrano orders him off the stage in midperformance and all that is left is his handkerchief floating in the air, or Cyrano's impatience when he is coaching Christian in his speeches to Roxane—are obvious bits of comedy relief inserted into a story that needs none. Most of the principal actors—Mala Powers, William Prince, Ralph Clanton, and Morris Carnovsky (who plays Le Bret, the captain of Cyrano's regiment)—intone their lines as if Rostand and Hooker were Shakespeare and they were afraid they might not measure up. Only José Ferrer, who had already played Cyrano on the stage, seems to have been in on the joke of the story: Cyrano's masochism and self-pity are fascinating because of the delight he himself takes in the spectacle of his own suffering. Ferrer is not a "great" actor in the sense that Olivier or John Gielgud is great, but then great acting in a superior potboiler like *Cyrano de Bergerac* is not what is required for the film's success. Ferrer's witty performance, which makes watching the film pleasurable in spite of the generally mediocre acting of the supporting cast and Rudolph Sternad's *papier-mâché* sets, was recognized by the members of the Academy of Motion Picture Arts and Sciences when they voted him the film's only Oscar nomination and he won the Award for Best Actor of 1950.

Cyrano de Bergerac on the screen has an interesting history as a vehicle for testing technical innovations: Coquelin himself performed the first-act duel scene for the camera and phonograph in one of the earliest experiments with talking pictures; and an Italian production of 1925 was photographed throughout in a primitive color process. Kramer in 1950 was not willing to go to the expense of Technicolor (a mistake, for the story cries out for color and it might have diverted the eye a little from the overall cheapness of the production); but his black-and-white film was photographed with the new Garutso Balanced Lens, which allowed a greater depth of focus than was possible with most camera lenses of the day. This meant that the spectators in the duel scene, for instance, could now be photographed as clearly as Cyrano and his opponent. The result was an illusion of seeing in three dimensions what was otherwise difficult to achieve in the days of the narrow screen.

Charles Hopkins

D.O.A.

Released: 1949
Production: Leo C. Popkin for United Artists/Cardinal
Direction: Rudolph Maté
Screenplay: Russell Rouse and Clarence Green
Cinematography: Ernest Laszlo
Editing: Arthur H. Nadel
Music: Dmitri Tiomkin
Running time: 83 minutes

> *Principal characters:*
> Frank Bigelow .... Edmond O'Brien
> Paula Gibson .... Pamela Britton
> Majak ....Luther Adler
> Miss Foster .... Beverly Campbell
> Mrs. Phillips .... Lynn Baggett
> Halliday .... William Ching
> Chester ....Neville Brand
> Marla Rakubian .... Laurette Luez
> Bell Hop .... Jerry Paris

An elementary thematic concern of literally every *film noir* involves the intrusion of a nightmarish criminal underworld into the orderly stream of everyday life, provoking an irreversible transition from a stable existence toward one filled with painful insecurity, rampant cynicism, and violent, unforeseen death. The heart of Rudolph Maté's *D.O.A.* lies well within this basic premise, and while it is by no means the perfect example of *film noir*, it does contain a great many specific elements normally associated with the classics of the genre. Both its underlying cinematic structure and its moral tone fall well within the confines of *film noir* sensibility, and its demonstration of the tendency for ordinary people to become enmeshed in a chain of events beyond their control places *D.O.A.* firmly inside the *film noir* tradition.

The primary inspiration for *D.O.A.* was a little-known German film entitled, *Der Mann, Der Seinen Mörder Sucht* (1931, The Man Who Seeks His Murderer). Directed by Robert Siodmak, the film dealt with a dying man's frantic attempts to uncover the cause of his impending unnatural demise. *D.O.A.* maintains this basic plot premise in which a murder victim functions as his own detective, and by doing so, brings to the film a refreshingly unique point of view.

As the opening credits roll, we follow a man walking unsteadily along a dark street into a police station and through its winding corridors which inevitably lead to a door marked "Homicide Division." He is Frank Bigelow (Edmond O'Brien), an accountant who lives "in a little town called Banning out in the desert on the way to Palm Springs," a sedate little community lying just beyond the bright lights, wealth, and corruption of a more glittering metropolis. Bigelow informs a group of detectives that he wishes to report a murder, and when questioned as to just who has been killed, he blankly replies, "I was." Thus the stage has been set for a lengthy flashback in which Bigelow relates the unfortunate circumstances surrounding his "death." A superimposed whirlpool effect draws both viewer and participant into Bigelow's tormented brain as the story unfolds through his own narration.

We enter Bigelow's life just prior to his immersion into the dark world of vice, uncertainty, and death that is the realm of *film noir*. He is depicted here as a modestly successful accountant with a small yet comfortable office and practice. He has an attractive secretary named Paula Gibson (Pamela Britton) who happens also to be his fiancée, and a vague, undefined troubling of the spirit. As Bigelow prepares to leave for a short vacation in San Francisco, Paula outlines his dilemma as she sees it. "You're just like any other man only a little more so," she explains. "You have a feeling of being trapped, hemmed in, and you don't know whether or not you like it." Bigelow, then, is the archtypal *film noir* hero: an ordinary man leading an ordinary life, who has a stable income, the respect of his peers, and a woman's love, but who still yearns for the excitement and passion that the American dream has forever promised, but rarely delivers.

These initial scenes are shot in what has become known as the "American style," utilizing flat, straight-on medium shots and unadventurous, regularized lighting strategies, all of which are beacons to Bigelow's normal, stable life-style and environment. As Bigelow descends deeper and deeper into the horrors of the underworld, however, this style disappears and the more common *film noir* elements of odd angles, darkness illuminated by blazing spots of light, and irregular cutting begin to dominate.

On his first night in San Francisco, Bigelow goes to a nightclub with a group of people he met at his hotel. A jumping black jazz band pours hot music into the room. Musicians and patrons alike become caught up and swept away with the ecstasy of the crazy jive. Sexual tension and unbridled sensuality fill the club as Bigelow, also captivated by the atmosphere, approaches a beautiful blond seated at the bar. As he arranges a liaison for later in the evening, a sinister-looking man, seen only from the rear, switches drinks on Bigelow, who, concentrating on the woman , notices nothing. When he finally returns to his drink, he senses that it tastes peculiar, and promptly orders a replacement.

Returning to his hotel room, Bigelow is clearly caught between his feelings for the simple, loving Paula and the excitement generated by the big city and its sensual pleasures. He decides in favor of his stable relationship when he tears up the phone number given him by the blond at the bar, but his momentary deviation from the straight and narrow will not go unpunished.

Later in the evening he wakes up feeling quite ill, a condition he naturally attributes to too much alcohol and the nightclub atmosphere. When he still feels poorly in the morning, however, he undergoes a medical examination in a local hospital. The doctors inform him that he has suffered "luminous" (radiation) poisoning and will die within just a few days. To demonstrate, a doctor brings out a vial of radioactive liquid, turns out the lights, and shows Bigelow the fluid's luminosity. When he utters the words, "and then death!," he turns the lights back on. Clearly Bigelow has been murdered, but his lights have not yet gone out.

While preparations are being made to admit him to the hospital, Bigelow escapes in a panic. He races through the city streets, and everywhere he turns, he is reminded that as he is dying and that life continues all around him. He rests by a newsstand where displayed copies of *Life* magazine form a solid line around his head. He sees a lovely little girl playing ball and a beautiful young couple in love. People everywhere are enjoying life, but Bigelow is already "dead."

Determined to unmask his killers (the thought of going to the police or of spending his last hours with Paula never enter his mind), Bigelow begins a frantic and initially fruitless search. Finally, Paula tells him that a man named Phillips, for whom Bigelow had notarized a bill of sale for a shipment of iridium, has been desperately trying to locate him. Bigelow flies down to Phillips' Los Angeles-based firm and discovers to his horror that the man committed suicide just the day before. The iridium, he learns, was stolen and Phillips had been arrested for selling it. Bigelow reasons that Phillips had wanted to find him, as the notarized bill of sale would clear Phillips with the law. He also concludes that Phillips has been murdered and that his killers are also responsible for his own impending death. Both conclusions turn out to be true as Bigelow discovers that Phillips' wife (Lynn Baggett) and her lover Halliday (William Ching), who is now the company's new president, killed Phillips. After this first murder, they had poisoned Bigelow, fearing he knew everything. After a lengthy chase through the streets of Los Angeles, Bigelow kills Halliday and explains his story to the police. "All I did was notarize one little paper, one little paper out of hundreds," he tells the police. Those prove to be his last words, and he dies as the police silently look on.

D.O.A. is filled with *film noir* elements that lie firmly within its convoluted narrative. It is a film caught between the documentary and the surreal, for its plot content is entirely factual (a technical adviser is credited at the end) while its visual style constantly and ironically undercuts these facts. Darkness, crazy shadows, eerie music, odd camera placements, interior voices, flashbacks, wipes, dissolves, and ironic juxtapositions abound. Criminal types range from seemingly respectable businessmen to effete, cultured foreigners to childish, psychotic killers. The fact that Bigelow becomes an obsessed, revenge-motivated killer himself reveals the *film noir* assumption that any man can be as tough as the most vicious murderer when pushed far enough.

Above all, *D.O.A.* demonstrates that the criminal world always lurks just under the surface of, and often poses as, middle-class normality, pointing to a rather radical dichotomy between the seamy and safe sides of life, never letting go of the implication that the former will someday usurp the latter. All of these factors show the world as being a state of nature rather than an aberration, as it was in the gangster films of the 1930's. Chaos and confusion have become the new social norms. No one is safe; no one can control his life to any great degree; and no one can escape once the wheels begin to turn. Along with every other *film noir* from 1945 to the present day, *D.O.A.* reveals that while American society may appear calm on the surface, dark currents run just beneath our rain-slicked city streets.

Daniel Einstein

DADDY LONG LEGS

Released: 1955
Production: Samuel G. Engel for Twentieth Century-Fox
Direction: Jean Negulesco
Screenplay: Phoebe Ephron and Henry Ephron; based on the novel and play
 of the same name by Jean Webster
Cinematography: Leon Shamroy
Editing: William Reynolds
Music: Johnny Mercer and Alex North
Running time: 126 minutes

> *Principal characters:*
> Jervis Pendleton III .... Fred Astaire
> Julie André .... Leslie Caron
> Linda Pendleton .... Terry Moore
> Miss Prichard .... Thelma Ritter
> Griggs ....Fred Clark
> Sally McBride .... Charlotte Austin
> Ambassador Alexander Williamson .... Larry Keating
> Gertrude Pendleton .... Kathryn Givney
> Jimmy McBride .... Kelly Brown
> Madame Sevanne .... Ann Codee

According to Stanley Green and Burt Goldblatt's book *Starring Fred As-taire,* Twentieth Century-Fox studio chief Darryl Zanuck had originally conceived a musical version of *Daddy Long Legs,* Jean Webster's sentimental 1912 novel, as a vehicle for Mitzi Gaynor in 1951. The story had a longer history as a movie property than that, however: Mary Pickford had starred in the first screen *Daddy Long Legs* in 1919; and there had also been an early talkie version with Janet Gaynor and Warner Baxter in 1931. When Zanuck revived the project early in 1954, it was as a showcase for the young French star Leslie Caron, who had been well received by American audiences in the M-G-M musicals *An American in Paris* (1951) and *Lili* (1953). Miss Caron's training had been in ballet; and it was planned that the film would include two lengthy dream sequences in the manner of the elaborate ballet Gene Kelly had devised for *An American in Paris.*

Fox had not been in the forefront of the postwar development of the big Hollywood musical. Instead, M-G-M had that honor, with producers Arthur Freed and Joe Pasternak, directors Vincente Minnelli, Gene Kelly, and Stanley Donen, and such stars as Kelly, Judy Garland, Frank Sinatra, Fred Astaire, Jane Powell, Ann Miller, and Howard Keel all under contract. Fox's biggest musical star during those years was the pretty but not notably talented Betty Grable, followed closely by the "South American bombshell," Carmen Miranda. Zanuck's decision to commit his studio's resources to so costly a project as an original musical at a time when even M-G-M was curtailing production of these expensive entertainments may seem paradoxical; but it should be remembered that Fox was then in the process of introducing CinemaScope and stereophonic sound, and that the musical form was ideally suited to show off these new developments in screen technology.

Jean Webster's original story described the May-December romance of a vivacious, intelligent orphan girl and the wealthy bachelor who has been anonymously sponsoring her education at an exclusive women's college. Caron's partner in the musical version would obviously have to be a dancer. Zanuck offered the role to a man who, as it happened, had never worked for Fox before but who had long since become the twentieth century's leading exponent of the traditional art of the song and dance man. Fred Astaire was fifty-four years old when *Daddy Long Legs* went into rehearsal. His contract with M-G-M had expired after the release of *The Band Wagon* (1953); and he had been contemplating retirement when Fox unexpectedly sent him the script he later described as "one of the best ever to come my way."

Screenwriters Phoebe and Henry Ephron used only the bare outline of Webster's story as a frame on which to hang the different elements that would have to be integrated into Zanuck's musical. To begin with, a way had to be found to reconcile Caron's French origin and accent with the character of Judy Abbot, the very American heroine of the original novel. The solution was simple enough: Judy Abbot became Julie André, an eighteen-year-old foundling who has lived since infancy in an orphanage outside Paris. Astaire plays Jervis Pendleton III (the same name as the character in the novel), a breezy American industrialist who goes to France on an economic mission for the State Department. When the limousine in which he and his fellow "experts" are traveling gets stuck in the mud of a French country lane, Jervis hikes over to the orphanage to see if they have a car he can borrow.

While waiting to speak to the woman in charge, Madame Sevanne (Ann Codee), he catches sight of Julie through a window as she guides the younger children through an English lesson in song. Jervis is captivated by her intelligence and joyful spirit; and, when he reaches Paris, he asks the American ambassador how he can adopt her. The ambassador (played to stuffy perfection by Larry Keating) is horrified at the thought of helping Jervis adopt an eighteen-year-old girl. "Do you have any idea how easy it is to lose a job in the State Department these days?," he asks, in what for a light entertainment is a pretty straightforward reference to the McCarthy-inspired paranoia of the early 1950's. Jervis agrees merely to sponsor Julie anonymously at a United States women's college; and, when the arrangements have been completed, he motors back to the orphanage to tell the good news to Madame Sevanne. Julie is overjoyed at her good fortune, but disappointed that her only contact with her benefactor, whom she has been told to address as "John Smith," is to be through the monthly letter she must write reporting her progress in school. When she returns to her dormitory, the children tell her that they have seen the long-legged shadow (like a *faucheux*, or daddy long legs) of an American visitor leaving Madame Sevanne's office. Jervis had hidden himself during Julie's interview with Madame Sevanne, and Julie had not seen him during his previous visit to the orphanage; so the children's meager description is all the information she has about the physical appearance of "John Smith."

In America, Julie easily adjusts to the routine of college life. She gets along well with her roommates, Sally McBride (Charlotte Austin) and Linda Pendleton, Jervis' niece (Terry Moore), who knows nothing about her uncle's connection with this mysterious French girl. Soon, Julie even has a beau, Sally's brother Jimmy (Kelly Brown); but she is lonely for someone she can think of as family, and pours her heart out in her monthly letter to "John Smith," whom she fondly addresses as "Daddy Long Legs." Jervis, meanwhile, has forgotten all about Miss André.

The only people who have read Julie's letters are Jervis' associate, Griggs (Fred Clark), and his warm-hearted secretary Miss Prichard (Thelma Ritter). As time passes, Julie writes of her growing despondency at the failure of "John Smith" to reply to anything she asks or tells him, until finally Griggs, at Miss Prichard's urging, marches into Jervis' office and lays the whole voluminous file of Julie's correspondence in his lap. Jervis is at first taken aback at the amount of stationery Julie has gone through in just two years; but, as he reads, he finds himself becoming captivated by her all over again. (The form of the novel *Daddy Long Legs* is epistolary: except for a brief opening chapter, the whole of the story is told in Judy Abbot's letters to Jervis—whose identity as her secret benefactor is not revealed until the end.)

Jervis phones his sister-in-law Gertrude (Kathryn Givney) to suggest that the two of them drive up to the college to visit his niece Linda, whom Jervis has not seen since she was a baby. Mrs. Pendleton is puzzled by Jervis' sudden rush of family feeling, but tells him that he can be her escort when she chaperones the spring dance, if he wishes. At the dance, as Jervis had hoped, Linda introduces him to her roommate, Miss André. In spite of the difference in their ages, Jervis and Julie are attracted to each other at once, and even distinguish themselves among the other couples with their stylish footwork in a novelty dance step, the Sluefoot.

Jervis invites Linda and Julie to be his guests for a weekend in New York. When Linda catches a cold at the last minute and is unable to come, Julie decides to go anyway. Jervis is at first embarrassed to take Julie to the hotel suite he has booked without Linda; but that evening, after dinner, he finally confesses to Julie that he has fallen in love with her. The song Astaire sings at this point, "Something's Gotta Give," was the film's one big hit. It was nominated for the Academy Award for Best Song of 1955, but lost to "Love Is a Many Splendored Thing." Jervis chastely deposits Julie back at the door of her suite after a romantic night out on the town; and the next morning, he arrives for breakfast with an engagement ring in his pocket.

While they are talking out on the terrace, their words of love are overheard by Jervis' friend the American ambassador (Larry Keating), who has come back to the States on official business and has spent the night in the adjoining suite before going on to Washington. The ambassador telephones Julie's suite and tells Jervis to come next door at once. When they are sitting together, Jervis protests that, whatever his friend may think, he has kept his guardianship of Julie a secret from her. Jervis finally agrees that even if Julie does not know exactly how much she owes him, her apparent love may be only a young girl's natural gratitude for the attention shown her by an older, obviously sophisticated man; and that she would probably be happier with Jimmy McBride, who is at least her own age. Without going back to her suite, Jervis telephones Julie and tells her that he has been suddenly called out of the country on a mysterious government mission, from which he will not return for some time.

Julie brokenheartedly follows Jervis' progress from one world capital to the next in the gossip columns, which link him with a succession of beautiful women. When, on the eve of her graduation, Julie writes "John Smith" a letter pleading for his advice, Miss Prichard takes matters into her own hands and sends Jervis a cablegram telling him that Griggs is not expected to live and that he has to return to New York at once. Jervis is furious when he arrives and discovers the trick that has been played on him. He is about to make Griggs impersonate "John Smith" for Julie's benefit when Linda bursts in with news that she and Jimmy McBride are in love with each other and to ask his help in persuading her mother to give them a big wedding. Jervis, his conscience now clear, is waiting when Julie drives up with Miss Prichard to confess that he has been "John Smith"—alias Daddy Long Legs—and to ask her to marry him. As Jervis and Julie waltz happily together, Griggs and Miss Prichard slip back into the office for a well-deserved drink.

Daddy Long Legs opened to good reviews and received Academy Award nominations in two other categories—Color Art Direction and Best Scoring of a Musical Picture—in addition to Best Song. Arthur Knight spoke for many reviewers when he wrote in the *Saturday Review* that the film "gives Fred Astaire one of his best opportunities in ages to display both his peculiar charm and his dancing skill." Why then, if the film was generally well received when it opened, is it so little seen today? It is revived much less often than such Astaire musicals as *The Band Wagon, Easter Parade* (1948), or almost any of the films he made with Ginger Rogers. Johnny Mercer's original score (a rarity in an era when film musicals were increasingly based on works that had been popular on the stage) included no other new songs on the level of "Something's Gotta Give"; but "History of the Beat," "C-A-T Spells Cat," and "Sluefoot" were nicely calculated to display the "peculiar charm and

. . . dancing skill" of both Caron and Astaire. At Astaire's suggestion, an eleven-year-old Mercer ballad, "Dream," was used as a motif for Julie's musings about the identity of her mysterious benefactor. The film's chief distinction, in fact, may lie in its quality as a late specimen of the musical conceived as a vehicle for the talents of a few star performers.

Every objection the audience could make to the improbable romantic pairing of the two leads and to the contrived story was anticipated in the script of *Daddy Long Legs*. Is Astaire obviously at least thirty years older than Caron? Jervis' sister-in-law is on hand at the occasion of his first meeting with Julie to remind him that he is "a well-traveled piece of luggage." Is it patently incredible that the American ambassador should be right next door on the morning Jervis intends to propose to Julie? As Jervis storms out after their interview, he yells over his shoulder: "Do you have any idea how many hotel rooms there are in New York?" "But, Jervis," the ambassador pleads, "I *always* stop at this hotel."

Even the circumstance that the film includes *two* dream ballets is explained when one sees them and realizes that the first—in which Jervis imagines himself as Julie had described him in three favorite daydreams: as a Texas oil millionaire, as an international playboy, and, literally, as her guardian angel—is tailored to show off Astaire's ballroom-*cum*-tap style of dancing; and that the second—in which Julie imagines herself vainly pursuing Jervis after their breakup to Paris, Hong Kong, and Rio at carnival time—has been designed to show off Caron's training in ballet. The music for this second sequence was composed by Alex North, and includes the score for an original ballet, *Le Papilon*, which Caron dances while imagining herself as a member of the corps de ballet of the Paris Opera. That the filmmakers were unable to devise a sequence that would showcase the talents of both performers at the same time points up the fundamental weakness in *Daddy Long Legs* that has kept it from being considered one of the great movie musicals. That elusive quality that makes us care about the protagonists of a musical drama has sometimes been called chemistry, sometimes heart; and it is just this quality that *Daddy Long Legs* painfully lacks. Both Astaire and Caron are likable performers; but we never for a minute believe that they are two people in love. Astaire not only looks like Caron's uncle, but seems to have an uncle's affection for her; that special warmth that animated his scenes with Ginger Rogers is missing from his scenes with Caron. In the final dream ballet, when Julie is dancing her heart out in *Le Papilon*, Jervis is shown coldly observing her performance from a stage box. Not only is this a long way from the closeness of "Cheek to Cheek," it is even further removed from the performing philosophy of the man who, asked to sum up his career, replied, "I just dance."

Charles Hopkins

DANGEROUS

Released: 1935
Production: Harry Joe Brown for Warner Bros.
Direction: Alfred E. Green
Screenplay: Laird Doyle; based on his original screen story
Cinematography: Ernest Haller
Editing: Thomas Richards
Running time: 80 minutes

> *Principal characters:*
> Joyce Heath .... Bette Davis (AA)
> Don Bellows .... Franchot Tone
> Gail Armitage .... Margaret Lindsay
> Mrs. Williams .... Alison Skipworth
> Gordon Heath .... John Eldredge

If Bette Davis had not won the Best Actress Academy Award in 1935, *Dangerous* might long ago have been forgotten. She gives a stunning performance as Joyce Heath, an alcoholic stage star with a self-destructive complex, although she herself described her condition as "punch drunk" by the time she started filming the story, because she had made four features in a row during 1934 and four more in 1935 when she was assigned to *Dangerous*. In 1934 Davis had played opposite Leslie Howard in *Of Human Bondage*, as the selfish, cruel waitress who persecutes the crippled hero who is hopelessly in love with her, and finally dies a wretched, lonely death. Despite the critical praise given to Davis for that film, she failed to win even an Academy Award nomination for her role. This caused considerable notoriety at the time, even creating a faction of Academy of Motion Picture Arts and Sciences members who wanted to start an unprecedented "write-in" campaign for the final voting. This did not happen, however, and Claudette Colbert won the Oscar for Best Actress for her role in Frank Capra's multi-Oscar-winning comedy, *It Happened One Night*.

When nominations for Best Actress were made the following year, Davis was among the women so honored, perhaps in response to her snub of the previous year. Although Davis has said that she thought that Katharine Hepburn in *Alice Adams* gave the best performance of 1935, Davis won the award, her first of two. Many people today agree with Davis' estimation of the film that it was "maudlin and mawkish, with a pretense at quality," but reviewers at the time praised it for its "colorful, punchy dialogue." They also applauded director Alfred E. Greene's treatment of the story as well as Ernest Haller's cinematography.

In the film, Joyce Heath (Bette Davis), a "vitally tempestuous creature," has ruined her reputation as an actress and has come to be regarded in her profession as something of a jinx. She not only has calamities happen to her, but also seems to invite them to happen with her outrageous, willfully unprofessional conduct, which includes excessive drinking. Joyce, however, not only has a record for self-destruction; she has also destroyed the men in her life, ruining or bankrupting anyone who has shown her the slightest affection or loyalty.

At the time when the story begins, no producer will hire her. Theatrically blacklisted, she has become an alcoholic in the depths of her own self-destruction. One night while she is in this state, a talented and wealthy architect named Don Bellows (Franchot Tone) recognizes her in a seedy bar. She is alone, downing straight gin at ten cents a glass (cheap even in 1935). She has been Bellows' idol ever since his adolescence when he saw her give a classic performance as the young Juliet in William Shakespeare's *Romeo and Juliet*. Fascinated again in spite of her bedraggled alcoholic condition, he takes her home with him. He lives in the country in the kind of perfect house that one would associate with a rich architect, but his housekeeper, Mrs. Williams (Alison Skipworth), is not very happy at the prospect of having a drunken woman in her house.

Joyce does not reform immediately while staying with Bellows. She delights in warning him to have nothing to do with her, and is alternately vicious, coy, hysterical, and full of self-pity. He is attentive and kind to her, however, and she eventually falls as much in love with him as he is with her. He breaks his engagement to wed Gail Armitage (Margaret Lindsay), a society girl, and puts up money for a play to star Joyce. He hopes that this will reestablish her as Broadway's leading actress. He also asks Joyce to marry him, but as it turns out, she is trapped in a secret marriage that she made long ago to Gordon Heath (John Eldredge), a failure whose worst crime was that he loved her to excess. She asks Heath for a divorce, but he, still in love with Joyce, refuses. Frustrated and furious, Joyce plans to destroy both Heath and herself in an accident. As she drives her car at top speed, she hits a tree, causing serious injury to herself and permanent damage to Gordon. By this time, Bellows, disillusioned and finally completely aware of Joyce's innate destructive nature, backs out of his association with her and goes back to Gail. Joyce finally recognizes the fact that she is her own worst enemy and by hard work reestablishes herself triumphantly on Broadway. She also devotes her private life to the disabled Gordon, the loving husband she almost totally destroyed.

The character of Joyce Heath gave Davis an opportunity to convey all of the most intense emotions of which she was capable, from anxiety to zealousness, including liberal amounts of her famous screen "bitchiness." The character of Mildred in *Of Human Bondage* had prepared her well for such a characterization. The happiness that Joyce finds at the finale of *Dangerous* is made believable only by the actress' convincing switch to selflessness. Davis is surrounded by professionals in *Dangerous* who were not as fortunate as she, however; Tone, Lindsay, Skipworth, and Eldridge are unable to do much with their one-dimensional supporting roles. The weak script creates pasteboard characters, and only the hardest work by the actors gives their characters even the slightest believability. The film is almost totally carried by the character of Joyce Heath, and Davis uses all of her well-known acting tricks to make the role credible.

Dangerous was successful at the box office, particularly as a "woman's picture," although men also responded to it. It turned out to be one of Warner Bros.' biggest financial successes of 1935. It might seem that after Davis won the Oscar for *Dangerous*, her home studio would have given her a succession of brilliant starring roles, but that was not the case. In the following year, Davis had only one role (with Howard and Humphrey Bogart in *The Petrified Forest*) that had any quality. After a subsequent film, *Satan Met a Lady* (1936), a zany version of *The Maltese Falcon* by Dashiell Hammett, she refused her next assignment and was suspended by Warner Bros. She promptly went to England to make a film, but was sued by her studio, who won the suit, forcing her to return to her contract work. Ironically, however, Warner Bros. treated her much better after that, gave her many roles well-suited to her screen *persona*, and even paid her legal costs for the lawsuit. Three years after *Dangerous* she earned her second Oscar for *Jezebel*, a film thought by many critics to be her best effort.

Davis was nominated for Oscars eight more times: for *Dark Victory* (1939), *The Letter* (1940), *The Little Foxes* (1941), *Now, Voyager* (1942), *Mr. Skeffington* (1944), *All About Eve* (1950), and *What Ever Happened to Baby Jane?* (1962). She is also the only woman ever to win the Life Achievement Award given by the American Film Institute.

Davis has stated that "Everything in my career dates B. B. (Before *Bondage*) and A. B. (After *Bondage*)." Actually it was *Dangerous* that officially turned the tide in her favor, although she still had to fight after that to get good starring roles at her studio. *Dangerous* is better than its script because Davis gives it "class"; she makes it an important film through her multidimensional, realistic, and flamboyant portrayal of Joyce Heath. *Dangerous* proved that Davis was a star in her own right and eased the way for her to demand and get star treatment from her studio. Grudgingly they came around, and somehow, even today, one thinks of Davis as a Warner Bros. star. She gave that studio prestige, and she was the only female star that they had who was a lasting box-office draw as well as a critic's delight.

Larry Lee Holland

THE DARK MIRROR

Released: 1946
Production: Nunnally Johnson for Universal-International
Direction: Robert Siodmak
Screenplay: Nunnally Johnson; based on an original story by Vladimir Pozner
Cinematography: Milton Krasner
Editing: Ernest Nims
Special effects: J. Devereaux Jennings and Paul Lerpae
Running time: 85 minutes

Principal characters:
Terry Collins/Ruth Collins .... Olivia de Havilland
Dr. Scott Elliott .... Lew Ayres
Lieutenant Stevenson .... Thomas Mitchell
District Attorney .... Charles Evans
Dr. Peralta's secretary .... Marta Mitrovich

The Dark Mirror is an intriguing murder mystery in which most of the detective work is done by a psychologist because the police lieutenant is baffled and seems to be blocked by a legal loophole. Identical twins are involved in the crime and become the focus of the film, but the carefully crafted script by Nunnally Johnson makes the device more than a clever gimmick. The audience remains just as perplexed as is the lieutenant because of an intricate series of events that lead bit by bit to a conclusion that seems consistent with what has gone before rather than being a surprise ending in which the least likely person is found to be the murderer.

Robert Siodmak was an ideal choice to direct the film, having directed *The Spiral Staircase* (1946), a quite successful thriller that also combined psychology and atmosphere. His opening is characteristic of the *film noir* works that were so prominent in the 1940's. We see a dark, shadowy room lighted only by a knocked-over lamp, then we see a broken mirror, and finally a man's body with a knife in it.

The film then shifts to the police detective investigating the crime, Lieutenant Stevenson (Thomas Mitchell). He finds that the murdered man was a Dr. Frank Peralta, and in interviews with people who knew him or lived near his apartment he finds that two people saw a young woman leave the apartment house at about the time the murder probably occurred. Based on information from Dr. Peralta's secretary (Marta Mitrovich), they suspect Terry Collins (Olivia de Havilland), who works at a newsstand in the medical building where the doctor had his office. When both witnesses positively identify her as the woman who left the scene of the murder, Lieutenant Stevenson is sure he has a strong suspect, but the young woman has a perfect alibi for the whole evening and three people support that alibi. In exasperation

Stevenson exclaims that the whole situation makes no more sense to him "than Chinese music."

When the lieutenant visits Miss Collins at her apartment he finds the solution to the puzzle, but he also finds himself in an even more difficult and frustrating predicament. Terry Collins has a twin sister, Ruth (also played by de Havilland), although no one at the medical building knows it, and the two alternate in the job at the magazine stand. Stevenson is now certain that he has in front of him one woman who may very well have killed Dr. Peralta and one who was four miles away at the time. His only problem is which is which. The sisters refuse to tell, and the law will not allow him to arrest both. They are taken to the office of the District Attorney (Charles Evans), but all he can do is lecture them on the immorality of what they are doing and set them free.

Lieutenant Stevenson is, however, unwilling to drop the case. He has learned that another doctor in the building, Scott Elliott (Lew Ayres), is a psychologist who has studied twins for much of his professional career. He asks Dr. Elliott if he can find out which sister is the guilty one, but Elliott balks at the idea because he believes that as a scientist he should not be doing undercover work for the police. He does, however, decide to study the two if they will agree, simply as a research project. The sisters, surprisingly, agree to be studied, partly because they need the money, and thus begins a long series of sessions at Elliott's office in which he examines each individually, using such devices as ink blots, word association tests, and a lie detector.

Meanwhile we have seen the sisters alone together and have found out that it was Terry who was in Dr. Peralta's apartment that night, but she does not admit killing him. In fact, she bitterly accuses Ruth of unfairly suspecting her.

After Elliott has studied them for a while, he tells the lieutenant that "one of the young ladies is insane," and two elements of the plot begin to interact. Dr. Elliott is falling in love with Ruth, and Terry—whom Elliott has described as "a paranoiac, capable of doing anything"—has begun to threaten Ruth and to try to drive her insane. Terry is motivated partly by fear of being found out and partly by jealousy, since she wants Elliott's romantic attention. "If you ever suspected me," Terry says to Ruth, "I don't know what I'd do." Later she tells Ruth that she (Ruth) has been waking in the night and sobbing, and she acts surprised that Ruth does not remember this; when she says to Ruth, "Just remember, I'll always be with you," it is chilling rather than comforting to the audience and to Ruth.

After Lieutenant Stevenson convinces Dr. Elliott that he must warn Ruth that her sister is dangerously mentally ill, Elliott calls Ruth and makes an appointment to see her that night at eleven o'clock. It is Terry, however, pretending to be Ruth, who talks to him on the telephone, setting up what could be a dangerous situation for both Ruth and Elliott. Ruth, however, happens to stop by to see the doctor earlier in the evening; so when Terry arrives at eleven we are fairly sure that the doctor recognizes her even though she continues the pretense that she is Ruth and Elliott talks to her as if she were Ruth. He tells her that her sister Terry is sick and abnormal and should receive professional treatment. He attributes Terry's illness to the agonies of jealousy she has felt because men have always preferred Ruth to her. When "Ruth" resists the idea of treatment for Terry, Elliott turns to her and says, "If *you* refuse, *Terry*, I'm afraid I'll have to tell who killed Frank Peralta and why." Elliott has deduced that Terry had come to realize that Peralta, who was dating Terry but frequently saw Ruth at the magazine stand (without knowing she was a different person), was actually in love with Ruth and that Terry killed Peralta in a jealous rage.

Then Lieutenant Stevenson calls with the news that Ruth has killed herself, and Terry and Elliott rush to the apartment, although Terry is unmoved by the news. At the apartment however, Terry becomes upset, claims to be Ruth, and "confesses" that it was her dead sister Terry who murdered Peralta. Then Ruth comes into the room alive and all the pretense and mystery are over. The film ends with Elliott asking Ruth, "Why are you so much more beautiful than your sister?"

Thus the case has been solved by a combination of the police detective's expertise and the psychologist's intellectual approach, with each gaining a new appreciation of the other's work. Indeed, even before the final events, the lieutenant has remarked to one of his associates that Elliott is "a very smart guy for a college man."

Although he gets only third billing, Mitchell as Lieutenant Stevenson gives what is in many ways the most engaging and convincing performance in the film. He conveys a common-sense professionalism as well as a conviction that no one should "beat a square rap." His performance is quite different from those of the usual "Irish drunk" parts which characterized much of his career. The excellent low-key portrayal of the psychologist by Ayres avoids the common Hollywood stereotype of the intellectual as too stuffy to know anything about real life.

It is, of course, de Havilland playing twin sisters (with some help from the special effects department) who is at the center of *The Dark Mirror*. She accomplishes the difficult task of constructing two separate characterizations that must many times overcome the confusion of the audience. The fact that she does so with subtle distinctions rather than exaggerated effect is a great credit to her talent and that of the director, Robert Siodmak. Ironically, de Havilland won the Oscar in 1946 for another film, *To Each His Own*; it was the first of her two Academy Awards for Best Actress. It is a tribute to her abilities as an actress that she gave her brilliant performance in *The Dark Mirror* in the same year as an Oscar-winning one.

Marilynn Wilson

DARK VICTORY

Released: 1939
Production: Hal B. Wallis for Warner Bros.
Direction: Edmund Goulding
Screenplay: Casey Robinson; based on the play of the same name by George
  Emerson Brewer, Jr., and Bertram Bloch
Cinematography: Ernest Haller
Editing: William Holmes
Running time: 106 minutes

Principal characters:
Judith Traherne .... Bette Davis
Dr. Frederick Steele .... George Brent
Ann King .... Geraldine Fitzgerald
Michael O'Leary .... Humphrey Bogart
Alec Hamin .... Ronald Reagan

One of the most famous films of the 1930's, *Dark Victory* features a memorable Bette Davis performance. As Judith Traherne, a rich young socialite dying of a brain tumor, Davis proves through the integrity of her acting that it is not necessary to be sentimental or banal in this kind of role and lifts the film above mere melodrama. So sincere and compelling is her performance that it is difficult to imagine any other interpretation of the role, though two versions of the story were filmed later.

Before they meet, the film's two main characters are complete opposites. Judith Traherne is rich, young, and attractive—the center of attention wherever she goes. She plays bridge, trains and shows her horses, sails, fishes, and travels. She feels that she is so young and strong that nothing can touch her. Dr. Frederick Steele (George Brent), on the other hand, is a mature and skillful brain surgeon, respected by his colleagues and completely dedicated to his work. He has little time or inclination to engage in the pursuit of pleasure. He is more interested in discovering the causes of brain tumors and is giving up his practice to spend all of his time on research.

When the two first meet, therefore, they are contemptuous and hostile. Judith comes to Steele's office as he is moving out of it, because her doctor thinks she needs to see a specialist. She has been having severe headaches and occasional attacks of double vision. We have already seen her fail to take her horse over a jump because she saw two of them. She wants to ignore her illness and is very antagonistic to the surgeon. Steele wants to finish moving out and at first thinks she is just a "Long Island nitwit" with a silly complaint.

The scene in the doctor's office is one of the best-written, acted, and directed in the entire film. Scarcely a word is wasted as the dialogue reveals the characters of Judith and Steele while it advances the story. Through her nervous movements and rapid delivery of her lines, Bette Davis conveys how frightened and vulnerable Judith is beneath her surface bravado. When she tries to light her cigarette, Steele must guide her hand. Instead of the conventional static shots of two people talking, director Edmund Goulding uses Judith's nervous movements to show the two characters from every angle. In this cinematic way, Goulding shows Judith and Steele literally, as well as figuratively, circling around each other. Steele probes, trying by means of exploratory questions and simple tests to discover the nature and extent of Judith's illness. Judith tries desperately to keep her poise and prevent her fear from surfacing. By the end of the scene Steele recognizes the seriousness of her illness and postpones his plans to abandon his practice for research. He decides, instead, to operate on Judith.

He performs the operation but finds the tumor inoperable. According to his own diagnosis and that of all the doctors he consults, Judith will live normally for a few months and then die quickly. Her only warning will be a loss of vision shortly before she dies. Steele decides to keep this information from Judith and let her think that the operation has cured her.

Since their first meeting, Judith and Steele have changed their opinions of each other. Steele's contempt turns to curiosity and then to liking. Judith begins to respect Steele, then to trust him, and finally to love him. She has begun to feel that her life is empty and self-centered, and she tells Steele that it must be good to believe in what one is doing. She finds that her love for him gives her, for the first time, something to think of besides "horses and hats and food." On his part, Steele, who has never before been interested in women, realizes that he too has fallen in love. They plan to marry, and Judith is eager to share his life and help with his research, visualizing herself as the wife of a famous scientist—a Mrs. Louis Pasteur. Although the conventions of the romantic melodrama dictate that Judith fall in love with her doctor and he with her, it is perfectly believable that she should fall in love with the man who has apparently saved her life, and that he would be attracted to such a vibrantly alive woman as Judith.

When Judith accidentally discovers the truth about her illness, her dream world is shattered. She is enraged and overwhelmed by the knowledge and by Steele's deception, and she refuses to see him again. Beginning a frenzied, unceasing round of partying and drinking, she refuses to rest or sleep because it is a "waste of time; time doesn't sleep." At the horse show she takes enormous risks to win first prize because she knows it is her last chance. All the time she presents a bitter, cynical front to the world. At last, however, she realizes that she must seek her peace with Steele; she calls him to apologize, saying that she does not know what to do. "It's the waiting, day and night," she tells him, asking for his help. They decide to marry and go to Vermont as they originally had planned.

The poignance of the final sequence is a result of Goulding's sensitive direction and the restraint and sincerity of Davis' performance. Steele and Judith are planning a trip to New York where he is to present a paper on the progress of his research. But as Judith's sight begins to fail, she realizes that death is only a few hours away. Because his research is so important, she conceals this fact from Steele and sends him off to New York. After his departure, she reveals the truth to her best friend, Ann King (Geraldine Fitzgerald), who is visiting them, before also sending her away, saying that she must show Steele that she can face death alone. Judith's victory is that she is able to face death with dignity—"beautifully, finely, peacefully"—as Steele had wished her to.

In the final scene the camera follows Judith as she haltingly climbs the stairs to her room, saying good-bye to her dogs on the way. She lies down on the bed, telling her maid Martha that she does not want to be disturbed. Martha pulls down the blinds, covers Judith with a quilt, and leaves the room, carefully closing the door. The final shot shows Judith blindly gazing into space as the camera slowly goes out of focus. No description of the scene can avoid making it sound too melodramatic, but because of Davis' compelling performance it is completely believable and touching.

Indeed, the acting in the entire film is outstanding except for that of Humphrey Bogart, who is miscast in the minor role of Judith's horse trainer. Geraldine Fitzgerald gives an excellent performance as Judith's secretary-companion and best friend, and George Brent is equally deserving of praise. As Frederick Steele, he gives a quiet performance entirely appropriate to his role, investing the character of the doctor with the charm to make believable Judith's attraction to him, and the strength to justify her trust. However, in the final analysis *Dark Victory* is Bette Davis' film, and it is her performance that dominates it and makes it truly memorable.

Julia Johnson

DAVID AND LISA

Released: 1962
Production: Paul M. Heller for Continental
Direction: Frank Perry
Screenplay: Eleanor Perry; based on the book of the same name by Theodore
  Isaac Rubin
Cinematography: Leonard Hirschfield
Editing: Irving Oshman
Running time: 94 minutes

Principal characters:
David Clemens	Keir Dullea
Lisa	Janet Margolin
Doctor Alan Swinford	Howard da Silva
Mrs. Clemens	Neva Patterson
John	Clifton James
Mr. Clemens	Richard McMurray
Simon	Matthew Arden
Carlos	Jaime Sanchez

David and Lisa, based on an actual case history written by Dr. Theodore
Isaac Rubin, is a brilliant, sensitive film which explores the need that human
beings have for one another; the strength and healing power of love; and the
discomfort that the outside world experiences in confronting the fact of mental
illness.

David (Keir Dullea) is a seventeen-year-old boy who has a high I.Q. and
suffers from an obsessive neurosis. He lives in morbid fear of dirt and has an
insane desire to stop time in order to cheat death. He avoids being touched
because "a touch can kill." He hates his mother, distrusts his father, and is
antagonistic toward the head of the school for the mentally disturbed which
he attends. He avoids the other patients except for a girl named Lisa (Janet
Margolin), a fifteen-year-old girl with brown eyes who suffers from schizophrenia. In the guise of Lisa, she is a silly little four-year-old who talks
constantly in gibberish seasoned with rhyme; as Muriel, she is a demure,
reticent adolescent who communicates in writing because she cannot talk.
Unwittingly, David and Lisa help each other by caring; Lisa's trouble (the
film never explains its roots) is somewhat ameliorated by David's feelings for
her. Since the characters' psychological states are not very clearly defined,
the audience must accept the situation primarily at face value; but the visual
and verbal aspects of mental illness are strongly conveyed by Dullea and
Margolin. They poignantly present their characters' increasing curiosity and
ultimate attachment to each other in the environment of a cheerless institution; their performances are the core of the film. The change in the two

patients as they become more friendly and as David learns to accept the psychiatrist fully is recounted in good cinematic style and with sound psychology.

As the film opens, David Clemens is brought to the school for the mentally disturbed by his mother (Neva Patterson). As he waits in the hall, he is silently observed by another patient, Lisa (Janet Margolin), who is hiding behind the balustrade. When another student, Simon (Matthew Arden) comes downstairs to welcome David and accidentally touches him, David's reaction verges on hysteria; he says that touch can kill. Later, after David is shown to his room, Dr. Swinford (Howard da Silva) talks with his mother, who is defensive and contends that David's phobia about being touched did not result from anything that she or her husband did.

The next day, David explores the school, and in a day room, he sees Lisa with her teacher, John (Clifton James). He is fascinated as he watches Lisa stomping around and speaking in rhymes. In subsequent scenes, David's antisocial attitude is established. He arrives late for dinner and does not respond to his tablemates. He ignores their suggestions concerning activities and refuses to join any clubs, because he despises clubs, bowling, and exercise, claiming that they are for idiots. At other times, he walks out of his classroom, keeps to himself, and refuses to let Dr. Swinford in to see him.

The only one that David seems drawn to is Lisa. Oddly enough, he is interested in psychiatry, and he first views Lisa only as a fascinating case. He watches her as she leaps up and down saying "I'm a lump and I like to jump." When John says, "You're a girl, Lisa," she abruptly stops jumping and begins to draw. Later, as David is seated alone at a table, Lisa sits down and watches him and then shows him something she wrote. He corrects her spelling and then asks her why she does not comb her hair. He tells her that he will play with her, but she feels rejected by his criticism and walks away.

Another time, David observes Lisa drawing. Her hand goes off the pad of paper, however, and she begins to write on the walls. When John immediately takes the crayon away from her, she shouts angry rhymes at him. Later, a concerned David asks John if he might speak with him about Lisa's case. He says that he has been studying Lisa and thinks that she has adolescent schizophrenia and has a difficult time with authority figures. He suggests that John must be permissive with her. When John tells him that he appreciates his ideas and touches him on the shoulder as he speaks, David responds with fury. After he calms down, he has another confrontation with Lisa and asks her why she rhymes. She expresses her anger with him, however, by advancing toward him with her finger pointed at his chest. He begins to panic and warns her not to touch him. Although she stops short of actual physical contact and walks away, the audience realizes that now she is capable of exercising some control in her relationship with David despite her lack of elaborate verbalization.

At a subsequent meeting between David and his own doctor, the boy brings up one of the themes of the film—love between people. David talks to Dr. Swinford about clocks and time pieces, expressing disgust that most of them are inaccurate. He advances a plan to construct an electronic clock which would always keep the exact time. David believes that time is important and cannot be stopped. He tells Dr. Swinford that he (the doctor) is going to die and asks him if he is afraid. He says that if they could stop time, they would be safe. The psychiatrist tells David that they cannot add to the time allotted them; they can only be alive. He adds that one takes a chance whenever he or she loves another person. In another brief scene which is equally important to the beginning of Lisa's recovery, David meets her outdoors. She asks him: "David, David, look at me. Who do you see? Who do you see?" He responds: "I see a girl who looks like a pearl." She smiles broadly and runs to tell John that she is a pearl of a girl. Later, in bed, Lisa strokes her own face and body; she is becoming aware of herself as a young woman in a positive sense.

In the following sequence, David's mother comes to visit and becomes upset by one of the students, Carlos (Jaime Sanchez), who starts to flirt with her and speaks of his own mother, who, he claims, is a prostitute. This unfortunate visit causes David's parents to remove him from the school against his will. He becomes angry with Dr. Swinford since he believes the doctor does not care for him, although the psychiatrist assures him that he tried to fight the parents' decision. At home, Mrs. Clemens deludes herself that there is nothing wrong with her son and expresses her wish that David go to an Ivy League school. David's responses are icy; his cold fury very obvious. He runs away from home and returns to the school, asking Dr. Swinford to take him in since he has no place else to go. Later, he tells Dr. Swinford that when he left home he saw a black woman at the train station. She had her arm around her little boy, and David pretended he was her son because she really liked her child. When the doctor informs David that he talked with his parents and they consented to his remaining at the school, David says that he hates his parents.

On a subsequent student outing to an art museum, Lisa begins to act strangely when she, David, and Simon look at a sculpture of a family group. After the boys leave, Lisa climbs onto the work and embraces the figure of the mother and child. It takes David and one of the teachers to persuade her finally to come down, which she does reluctantly. Although Lisa's background is neither discussed nor depicted in the film, this scene serves to give the viewer a tiny clue as to Lisa's needs and offers a small piece in the puzzle of what may have caused her illness.

One evening as she is drawing, Lisa makes an important breakthrough. When she signs her name, she writes "Muriel X Lisa," circles the two names, and then adds "Me." John says that that is right, that she is Lisa, not Muriel. She dashes off happily to find David, who is listening to Simon play the piano.

Simon resents her intrusion and becomes upset when she turns on the metronome and begins to move her head in rhythm with its ticking. David sides with Simon and tells the girl to get out. She hollers back in rhyme and runs away from school, taking a train to the city.

The film then cuts back and forth between the school and Lisa's bewildered wanderings in the city. Her adventure frightens her, and she returns to the art museum seeking comfort from the statue she remembers embracing. She peers through the locked door, but cannot get to the sculpture. Back at the school, David expresses to Dr. Swinford the thought that one does not run away from something, but goes to something just as he did the night he returned to the school. David's intuition leads him to believe that Lisa may have gone back to the museum to find solace from the mother figure she liked.

David and the psychiatrist drive to the museum. In the early morning light, David rushes up the steps of the building and finds Lisa asleep in the doorway. He calls to her and she answers him, but not in rhyme. She complains that he was nice to Simon but mean to her. David apologizes. He points out to her that she did not talk in rhyme, therefore she is Muriel. She responds: "Lisa-Muriel, the same. I am me." David begins to weep. The film ends with the young people walking down the museum steps hand in hand. The conclusion does not leave the viewer with the feeling that David and Lisa are completely cured, yet one does perceive that their journey toward recovery has begun.

David and Lisa was the first feature film made by Frank and Eleanor Perry; he directed it, and she wrote the script. Since it was a low-budget film, they used location shots in Philadelphia, which enhances the realistic feeling of the production. Also, since they could not afford to employ well-known stars, two unknowns were cast in the principal roles. Both Dullea and Margolin turn in impeccable, sensitive performances as disturbed adolescents who find the road to recovery via their love for each other. In fact, they received Best Actor and Best Actress awards at the 1962 San Francisco Film Festival for their parts in this film. Dullea in particular works with a subtlety, accuracy, and intensity of feeling that indicates significant talent. Silva is believable and low-keyed in his part as the psychiatrist. The entire cast gives fine performances and provides good backup for the principals.

Director Perry, previously an associate producer of Broadway plays, apparently found his forte in cinema; his first film won the Best Picture by a New Director award at the 1962 Venice Film Festival. In his use of the camera and in the pace of his cutting, he displays a rare film sense. Yet in his inspiration and direction of his performers, he reveals a more profound gift: a psychological sensitivity toward the humanity in his characters and an appreciation for the strength of the human heart.

Fern L. Gagné

DAVID COPPERFIELD

Released: 1935
Production: David O. Selznick for Metro-Goldwyn-Mayer
Direction: George Cukor
Screenplay: Howard Estabrook; based on Hugh Walpole's adaptation of the novel of the same name by Charles Dickens
Cinematography: Oliver T. Marsh
Editing: Robert J. Kern
Running time: 133 minutes

Principal characters:
Micawber .... W. C. Fields
David Copperfield (younger) .. Freddie Bartholomew
David Copperfield (older) .... Frank Lawton
Mrs. Copperfield .... Elizabeth Allan
Nurse Peggoty .... Jessie Ralph
Dan Peggoty .... Lionel Barrymore
Mr. Murdstone .... Basil Rathbone
Betsey Trotwood .... Edna May Oliver
Mr. Dick .... Lennox Pawle
Dora .... Maureen O'Sullivan
Agnes (younger) .... Marilyn Knowlden
Agnes (older) .... Madge Evans
Little Em'ly (younger) .... Fay Chaldecott
Little Em'ly (older) .... Florine McKinney
Ham .... John Buckler
Steerforth .... Hugh Williams
Uriah Heep .... Roland Young
Mr. Wickfield .... Lewis Stone

In *David Copperfield*, director George Cukor brought to the screen one of the most beloved works in English literature. Cukor's film is a fairly literal adaptation of Dickens' novel, and like the original, the film has its flaws. Both are episodic and overly sentimental; however, also like Dickens' novel, Cukor's *David Copperfield* has strengths that far outweigh its weaknesses. Dickens had no peer when it came to creating and bringing to life a gallery of marvelously engaging (or in the case of his villains, repulsive) characters; and it is on this aspect of the novel that Cukor has chosen to concentrate. Cukor and producer David O. Selznick gathered a star-studded cast, and, given the large number of important roles in the film (some of which had to be filled twice, as the characters moved from childhood to adulthood), the two men managed to match the actors and the parts remarkably well.

The ups and downs of young Master David Copperfield are, of course, familiar to all. His story, and thus the film, divides fairly neatly into two parts: that of David the boy (Freddie Bartholomew) and David the young man

(Frank Lawton). David's father dies six months before he is born. David and his mother (Elizabeth Allan) are inseparable until, when David is about six, Mrs. Copperfield is courted by, and eventually marries, Mr. Murdstone (Basil Rathbone), a cold, self-righteous man who comes to dominate his young wife and her son. David's principal ally through this strife is his nurse, Peggoty (Jessie Ralph), a large, cheerful woman who is eventually dismissed by Murdstone. Before that happens, however, David spends a few idyllic weeks with Peggoty at the home of her brother Dan (Lionel Barrymore), a sailor. At Dan's home in Yarmouth, David meets two children who will play important roles in his adult life: Peggoty's niece, Little Em'ly (Fay Chaldecott), and his nephew, Ham (John Buckler).

When David's mother dies in childbirth, Murdstone abandons all pretense of caring for David, and the young lad is packed off to London "to work, to work, to work." Thus begins David's involvement with one of the novel's and the film's most memorable characters, Wilkins Micawber (W. C. Fields), with whom Murdstone has chosen to board David. Micawber is a fraud, but he is such a genial fraud that David, as well as the audience, loves him from the start. He makes his initial entrance climbing gingerly over the rooftops of London in an effort to elude the creditors that perpetually dog his trail. As he drops through the skylight into the midst of his startled family and their new lodger, he announces grandly "I have thwarted the malevolent machinations of our enemies. In short, I have arrived." Although he admits to being temporarily short of funds (a chronic condition, as David soon discovers), Micawber is always "confidently expecting something to turn up." David is separated from his new friend when Micawber and his family are arrested and sent to debtors' prison. "Copperfield," says the dejected Micawber, "you perceive before you the shattered fragment of a temple once called man."

David's last stop in his boyhood is Dover, where he seeks shelter from his father's sister, Betsey Trotwood (Edna May Oliver), who lives with her eccentric cousin, Mr. Dick (Lennox Pawle). One of the most engaging characters in the film, Mr. Dick is quite mad, but friendly and entirely harmless. He and David take to each other immediately, and once again David is happy. In Dover, he is sent to live with the Wickfield family, which includes old Mr. Wickfield (Lewis Stone), a prosperous but alcoholic businessman; his daughter Agnes (Marilyn Knowlden), who is David's age; and Wickfield's clerk, Uriah Heep (Roland Young), an obsequious toady who is forever proclaiming what an "'umble person" he is, all the while worming his way into his employer's confidence.

Several years pass. By the time David graduates from school, many important things have transpired. It is clear to the audience (although not to David) that Agnes (Madge Evans) is in love with young Copperfield; Mr. Wickfield has fallen completely under Uriah Heep's influence; and Heep has employed Mr. Micawber. David, meanwhile, returns to London to seek his fortune as a writer. In London, David meets Steerforth (Hugh Williams), an old school chum, and the two become inseparable. They attend an opera, where David meets the beautiful but childlike Dora (Maureen O'Sullivan), whom he will soon marry.

In a fateful turn of events, he takes Steerforth to meet the Peggotys. This meeting, although cordial, turns out to be disastrous for everyone concerned. Although Em'ly (Florine McKinney), by now grown up, is engaged to marry Ham, she falls in love with Steerforth, who takes her away and later abandons her in Italy. In a bit of overly neat irony, Steerforth and Ham die together shortly thereafter, as Steerforth's yacht capsizes in a storm near Yarmouth, and Ham, not knowing its owner, dies in an attempt to save the ship.

Meanwhile, David marries Dora, hurting loyal Agnes deeply. The Copperfields' happiness is shortlived, however, when David's child-bride withers and dies of a mysterious ailment soon after their marriage. Agnes is threatened by Uriah Heep, who has by now taken over Wickfield's business and is demanding the hand of his former employer's daughter. Heep's chicanery is unmasked by his trusted clerk, Micawber, who, surrounded by David, the Wickfields, Betsey Trotwood, and Mr. Dick, calls Heep "the most consummate villain that ever existed. Heep of infamy, I defy you," he declaims. Confronted by evidence of forgery and other duplicity, Heep reverts to his 'umble self, and the day is saved. Beaming, Micawber asserts that "What I have done, I have done for England, home, and beauty."

After all this melodrama, everything ends on a happy note. As Betsey Trotwood and Mr. Dick look on, David confesses his love to Agnes. " High time, too, eh, Mr. Dick?" asks Aunt Betsey. Mr. Dick replies with a broad wink, which ends the film.

The successful cinematic adaptation of *David Copperfield* hinged on two points—the audience's familiarity with and love for Dickens' novel, and the cast of characters assembled by Cukor and Selznick that bring it to life. Clearly, far too much goes on in Dickens' sprawling novel to bring it all to the screen in a film of manageable length. Instead, Cukor and his writers, Howard Estabrook and Hugh Walpole, have selected the most important episodes from the novel and have woven them together in a coherent series of vignettes which (thanks to the English novelist Walpole's marvelous ear for language) convey a genuine sense of the novel's unique joys.

The casting was, in many instances, genuinely felicitous. The challenge here, as Cukor himself has noted, was to find actors who could preserve the eccentricities of the Dickens characters without turning them into caricatures. Indeed, the only character with no quirks or peculiarities is David Copperfield himself, which tends to render him, as many critics of the novel have pointed out, the least interesting character in his own story. Young David, as played by Bartholomew, gives an all-out assault on the tear ducts of the audience which would have been disastrous in a less sentimental story; here, his performance is just right. Lawton is agreeably earnest as David Copperfield the man, although somewhat bland in comparison to the rich assembly of Hollywood's finest character actors.

Rathbone and Young make suitably loathsome villains. Rathbone's Murdstone is cold and soulless, showing no emotion except hostility. Young's Uriah Heep, on the other hand, fairly oozes with sleazy, sycophantic greed. Oliver is wonderful as the horsey but loving Aunt Betsey Trotwood, and Pawle is even better as the mad Mr. Dick. Pawle's sweet gentleness lights up the screen during his brief appearances in the film. Fields, who got top billing in the film for his portrayal of Mr. Micawber, inevitably brought much of himself to Micawber; his penchant for placing his hat on his upturned cane is only the most obvious example. There is a good deal of Dickens in the larcenous but good hearted screen *persona* that Fields created for himself. Wilkins Micawber was Fields's only straight dramatic part (if Micawber can be said to be a straight dramatic part), and he performed beautifully.

Cukor's *David Copperfield* rates high marks for an honest and satisfying effort at what must be conceded was an impossible task. The film ranks with David Lean's *Great Expectations* (1947) and *Oliver Twist* (1948) and with Carol Reed's 1968 musical *Oliver!* as the most successful of the numerous cinematic adaptations of Dickens' novels.

Robert Mitchell

DAWN PATROL

Released: 1938
Production: Hal B. Wallis for Warner Bros.
Direction: Edmund Goulding
Screenplay: Seton I. Miller and Dan Totheroh; based on the story "Flight Commander" by John Monk Saunders and Howard Hawks
Cinematography: Tony Gaudio
Editing: Ralph Dawson
Running time: 107 minutes

> *Principal characters:*
> Captain Courtney ....Errol Flynn
> Lieutenant Scott ....David Niven
> Major Brand .... Basil Rathbone
> Phipps .... Donald Crisp

War is "a great big stupid game," an insane fact of life; but perhaps a man may find meaning in his life by the way in which he faces death. This is the view expressed in the 1930 Howard Hawks film *The Dawn Patrol*. When Warner Bros. decided to remake this cinema classic in 1938, the philosophical slant remained the same, and, although dialogue was revised and an all-British cast was selected, the original was faithfully repeated in all other respects; even the spectacular flying footage of the earlier film was used in the remake. Both versions are excellent films, but the 1938 production has the advantage that Errol Flynn and David Niven play the doomed comrades.

The 59th Squadron of the British Royal Flying Corps is in France in 1915. With obsolete equipment, this undermanned squadron confronts a superior force of German flyers led by ace pilot, Richter. Captain Courtney (Errol Flynn) is the flamboyant and courageous leader of "A" Flight, supported by his friend, Lieutenant Scott (David Niven). We see their great affection for each other when Scott is shot down while attempting to aid another pilot in trouble. As Courtney grieves for his friend, Scott appears, drunk and waving champagne bottles, to turn his wake into a victory celebration. Sophomoric pranks and joyful drinking bouts add to the lighthearted tone which dominates the early scenes.

Flynn and Niven are very effective as the dashing comrades Courtney and Scott. They exhibit a sincere friendship and regard for each other that is impossible to doubt, and Niven displays a particular charm as the tipsy, irreverent Scott. However, the warmth and humor of these scenes is played against a menacing backdrop. Brandy and soda are liberally dispensed in the officers' club bar, and the flyers drink while the names of their dead comrades are struck from the roster and a phonograph plays "Poor Butterfly."

While this sense of doom begins to shadow every scene on the ground, the air battles continue as exhausted men risk their lives in patched-up aircraft. The flying sequences in the *Dawn Patrol* remain breathtaking even today. Diving and spinning, the vintage fighters engage in dogfights above a peaceful countryside. Close-ups of Niven and Flynn were intergrated into the original footage, and the result is a beautiful, flawless piece of filmmaking.

Basil Rathbone plays the unsympathetic role of Major Brand, Squadron Commander. It is he who must send young men up to die, unable to furnish them with sufficient training or adequate equipment. We first view Brand as a rather stern headmaster trying to curb the undergraduate antics of Courtney and Scott. When they disobey orders and fly off in a daring raid on the German command post, he upbraids them with a vehemence that seems unnecessary. But Brand is a man on the verge of cracking. His voice breaks as he agonizes to Phipps, his *aide-de-camp*, "It's a slaughterhouse, that's what it is, and I'm the executioner." The edge of hysteria in Rathbone's performance prepares us for what happens to Courtney when he assumes command of the squadron. Brand takes an insane delight in turning over command to Courtney. The captain has called him a butcher for sending untried pilots to their deaths, and now Brand fairly gloats over the prospect of Courtney having that responsibility.

The captain is a commander now. No longer Scott's devil-may-care drinking companion, he drinks alone as his nerve buckles under the weight of his responsibilities. Donald Crisp as Phipps watches the change, displaying a marvelous sympathy as the older man who has seen it all before.

Faced with the chronic shortage of manpower, Courtney must order Scott's inexperienced younger brother into action. The boy is killed and the friends argue bitterly. The shift in mood from gallant gaiety to agonized despair brings the futility of war, especially this war, into sharp relief. Scott next volunteers for what amounts to a suicide mission, a lone attack on a German munitions dump; but before he leaves, the two old friends are reconciled over drinks. Courtney gets Scott thoroughly drunk and flies the mission himself. In a spectacular action sequence he blows up the munitions dump but is shot down and killed by Richter. It is left to Scott to assume the burdens of command.

The futility expressed in the *Dawn Patrol* is matched only by its fatalism. The flyers sing as they stand in the bar:

> So stand by your glasses steady.
> This world is a world of lies.
> Here's to the dead already—
> Hurrah for the next man who dies!

Cheryl Karnes

THE DAWN PATROL

Released: 1930
Production: Robert North for First National/Warner Bros.
Direction: Howard Hawks
Screenplay: Howard Hawks, Dan Totheroh, and Seton I. Miller; based on
  the short story "The Flight Commander" by John Monk Saunders (AA)
Cinematography: Ernest Haller
Editing: Ray Curtiss
Running time: 95 minutes

> *Principal characters:*
> Courtney .... Richard Barthelmess
> Scott .... Douglas Fairbanks, Jr.
> Major Brand .... Neil Hamilton
> Gordon Scott (younger brother) .... William Janney
> Hollister .... Gardner James

This classic saga of British flyers in World War I is one of a group of films spanning the transition from silents to sound which skillfully reenacted that war. Although a late example of its type, *The Dawn Patrol* was well-received and won an Academy Award in the original story category. Its success ultimately prompted a remake in 1938 which cleverly incorporated the stunning aerial sequences of the original. Formally, its story would be adaptable to any wartime setting. Rather than an episode, it relates a pattern of action and reaction, perceived by the film to be so unchanging and unresolvable that it becomes a cycle which can only be endlessly repeated. War never ends in *The Dawn Patrol*.

At the center of the drama is the friendship between Courtney (Richard Barthelmess) and Scott (Douglas Fairbanks, Jr.), two young men whose relationship precedes their service as flyers. At the outset of the story, "Court" and "Scotto" (as they call each other) are veterans, flying each mission together and coming through alive as younger and greener men die. It is the job of the flight commander, Major Brand (Neil Hamilton), to send into the air the unseasoned replacements as needed and to expect death to be a routine part of each mission. The job has taken a toll on his nerves; he drinks too much and sleeps little. Sustained by camaraderie, Courtney, Scott, and the other men know only that they must follow orders and be prepared to die. The psychological pressures of command are beyond their understanding, and Brand must remain aloof from their circle. A leader among the flyers, Courtney is openly scornful of Brand, but ironically, it is he who must take Brand's place when the major is promoted. Like his predecessor, he begins to go without sleep and to drink compulsively. His relationship with Scott is strained as his friend assumes his own former role as leader among the group of flyers. Finally, a rupture occurs. Scott's younger brother Gordon (William Janney) arrives with a group of replacements, and Scott unreasonably implores Courtney not to send him on a mission the next day. Courtney's duty is clear. All the flyers are needed, and he cannot make an exception for the sake of friendship. The young man dies on his first mission, and Scott blames Courtney. When a single flyer is needed for a daring suicide mission over Germany, Scott volunteers; but Courtney, remembering the other's low tolerance for alcohol, cleverly gets him drunk and takes his place. Succeeding in bombing his targets, Courtney is then shot down by ace German flyer von Richter. He dies knowing that Scott's feelings toward him have never really changed. The grief-stricken Scott takes command; in the final scene, he emerges calmly from his office to give orders to the group from which he is himself now isolated.

The behavior of the characters in *The Dawn Patrol* has been described as stoical and existential. They never appear to be motivated by patriotism or even a keen sense of duty, and they demonstrate professional respect rather than hatred for their enemy counterparts. Their willingness to keep flying missions until they die is understood to be the manifestation of an acceptance that this defines their existence and that it is a situation which must be honored out of self-respect. As a result, while they complain that the war is rotten and tragically absurd, they invariably respond to orders with the words "Right" and "It'll be done." The narrative is a bleak one, but the values it unsentimentally celebrates stand against its chilling background with a steadfast warmth. The film finds a place for individual feeling and action, even if they must ultimately be absorbed into the cycle. For example, at the outset of the story, one of the flyers, Hollister (Gardner James), returns from a mission on which his best friend has died. Overwhelmed by the loss, he appears to suffer a breakdown, alienating himself from his comrades and bitterly resenting the surface gaiety with which they carry on. Later in the film, we learn that Hollister has himself died, and that he has perished bravely, helping save another flyer. Expressions of extreme emotion are constantly permitted in the film, but they never rupture the fundamental sense of professionalism which prohibits the flyers from abandoning their roles.

The most telling instance of an individual altering an event without betraying the nature of his world is Courtney's decision to fly in Scott's place. Easily understood as a gesture of friendship, the action is even more meaningful if it is perceived as a gesture of the will. Knowing that either he or Scott will die, Courtney makes a choice; and this choice exists independently of his position as flight commander, affirming his individuality without being an act of rebellion. It is not incidental that on an earlier mission, Scott's plane had been shot down and he had been presumed dead. Courtney's response to the apparent fact of Scott's death has already registered, and it is something which he does not wish to suffer twice. The tone of the reunion between the two men when Scott turns up alive and that of Courtney's tender farewell later as Scott passes out after having apologized are very similar. Scott has also shown that he knows how to die, but Courtney's decision is more thoughtful. He knows that Scott has volunteered in the aftermath of his brother's death, for which Scott was not responsible. Replacing him, Courtney is able to restore the sense of things as they were, not as his command dictates they will be.

As war and flying tended to connote masculinity in this period, *The Dawn Patrol* is presented with an opportunity which it daringly engages. The characters of Courtney and Scott possess a softness and vulnerability which could be described as feminine. Classically gallant in manner and bearing in responding to orders and doing their jobs, the two male protagonists are soft-spoken and gentle in their more personal moments, especially with each other. Scott wears a loud polka-dot shirt, and the song he listens to endlessly on a worn record during the evenings is the bittersweet "Poor Butterfly." He relies on Courtney to put him to bed when he has had too much to drink, and the other always obliges with a smile. Both men weep openly and unashamedly during the course of the film, and as Courtney leaves Scott for the last time, he tenderly caresses the other's hair. Clearly, the two men openly love each other, but in a way that no one could find objectionable or questionable. Necessarily lacking the company of women, they do not suppress the emotions which are part of male-female relationships, even if the sexual fulfillment that normally accompanies such emotions is not available and not desired with another male. Secure in their masculinity, they are finding a way to express themselves as integrated human beings. These two characters and the presentation of their relationship make recent attempts in the cinema to break down "macho" stereotypes seem timid.

The adventurous treatment of characterization and narrative structure in the film extends to other aspects of its presentation. This was the first sound film of director Howard Hawks, and although his silent films (most notably, *A Girl in Every Port* in 1928) are not negligible works, it was with *The Dawn Patrol* that he hit his stride. One of the unfortunate myths of cinema is that the first years of sound were aesthetically dull—that the sound was primitive and that the camera never moved. In fact, while there have been technological advances in sound recording, aesthetic approaches to it were most interesting in this early period, as demonstrated in films directed by Josef von Sternberg, Jean Renoir, Alfred Hitchcock, and others. At the same time, these films possess considerable fluidity of camera movement often enhanced by image-sound tensions. *The Dawn Patrol* addresses the challenges posed by sound with resourcefulness and subtlety. The aerial sequences were photographed in the same manner as in a silent film, with the accompanying sound imaginatively invented afterward. The interior dialogue scenes were generally recorded directly, and Hawks's predilection for direct and concise (but not static) images registers the terse dialogue exchanges effectively. At other times, a sophisticated sound mix softens the effect of these unadorned readings.

Sequences such as those in the recreation room where the men drink, listen to records, and join in communal song combine dialogue, music, and sounds of offscreen action, providing a rich complexity of direct and indirect sound which does not inhibit the camera. In the middle of one of these sequences, the camera might abruptly track in to a close-up of Hollister's anguished face or concentrate on a doorway while the men continue their conversations offscreen.

It is sometimes claimed that actors trained in the silent cinema were unsure of themselves when asked to deliver dialogue. This is unfortunately true in the case of Hamilton, who is a bit stiff and theatrical as Brand. On the other hand, the performances of both Barthelmess and Fairbanks are carefully judged and very moving. In the more intimate scenes, they lower their voices and register a disarming genuineness, seemingly oblivious of camera and microphones.

The thoughtfulness with which Hawks was approaching formal problems as he defined his artistic personality is as exciting in this film as in the superficially more dazzling *Scarface* (1932). He was moving toward a deceivingly informal style, defined by a camera which would feign unobtrusiveness and by playing which would seem spontaneous and free of self-consciousness. These stylistic qualities are present but not pronounced in *The Dawn Patrol*. The intermittent melodramatic titles, describing stages of the action like those of a silent film, underline the artificial presentation of the story in the same way as the film's technically ostentatious and visually expressionistic moments. At the same time, artifice consistently yields to understatement in the most dramatic moments. The subject of *The Dawn Patrol* was clearly one for which Hawks had great feeling—a fact confirmed by the recurrence of similar situations, characters, and narrative structures in such later films as *The Road to Glory* and *Ceiling Zero* (both 1936) and *Only Angels Have Wings* (1939). Compatible material and the challenge of sound combined to hasten his maturity as an artist. Both the screenplay, which he adapted with two others from John Monk Saunders' admirably spare story, and the direction reveal his distinctive artistic voice at this relatively early stage.

The 1938 remake of *The Dawn Patrol*, a respectable work in its own right, compares intriguingly with the original. Although it follows the screenplay of the Hawks film with considerable fidelity, it has a different tone, the causes of which are several. The remake seeks a conventional dramatic vividness in the most emotional moments. For example, when Scott returns after being thought dead, the writing is unaltered. Director Edmund Goulding, however, displays large close-ups of both Courtney and Scott and has them welcome each other heartily, while Hawks keeps the two men in two-shot and affectingly underplays their evident responses to each other. The 1930 version is essentially a pacifist work, consistent in this respect with other war films of its time. The 1938 version was made at a time when America's involvement in World War II was becoming imminent, and while it superficially retains the feeling of tragic waste embedded in the narrative, it views the flyers' actions less abstractly. Courtney's speech to Scott's brother is one scene that is subtly transformed. In the original, Courtney simply tells the other that although death is virtually inevitable for each of the flyers, the important thing is for each man to die knowing that he has done his best. The Courtney of the remake (played by a well-cast Errol Flynn) again delivers the speech quietly but says more, seeking through his words to find a larger purpose for the required deaths.

Interestingly, Hawks himself subsequently made a film, *Air Force* (1943), in which patriotic sentiment was not only desirable but also required. A very typical Hawks film in its emphasis on devotion among the members of a group, it makes no effort to undermine the attitudes which understandably prevailed in almost every film made during World War II. Free of such attitudes, his version of *The Dawn Patrol* possesses a perspective on men in war which remains comprehensible and stimulating to the contemporary mind. Both aesthetically and philosophically, it is a film which has aged exceptionally well.

                                                                                                    Blake Lucas

A DAY AT THE RACES

Released: 1937
Production: Max Siegal for Metro-Goldwyn-Mayer
Direction: Sam Wood
Screenplay: Robert Pirosh, George Seaton, and George Oppenheimer; based
   on a story by Robert Pirosh and George Seaton
Cinematography: Joseph Ruttenberg
Editing: Frank E. Hull
Running time: 109 minutes

> *Principal characters:*
> Doctor Hugo Z. Hackenbush .... Groucho Marx
> Tony .... Chico Marx
> Stuffy .... Harpo Marx
> Gil Stewart .... Allan Jones
> Judy Standish .... Maureen O'Sullivan
> Emily Upjohn .... Margaret Dumont
> Flo Marlowe .... Esther Muir

Nothing about a Marx Brothers film is either off-the-wall or spontaneous, although many people believe this to be the case; and everything about a Marx Brothers film is zany, inspired, and riotous. The true aficionado of the Marx Brothers catalogue could probably discuss at length the reason why *A Day at the Races* (1937) is not as good as (or is better than) *A Night at the Opera* (1935), which is not as good as (or is better than) *Duck Soup* (1933) or *Horse Feathers* (1932). The average viewer and relisher of comedic anarchy, however, would be hard put to say anything about any one of those films until he was able to stop laughing. No Marx Brothers film is capable of garnering awards for plots rife with probing, sensitive dialogue, but no one seems to care. The wonderful thing about their films is that they make us laugh, and *A Day at the Races* is no exception.

In this film, Groucho is Dr. Hugo Z. Hackenbush, a horse doctor who takes charge of a sanatorium owned by Judy Standish (Maureen O'Sullivan). The sanatorium is in trouble. A deep-eyed villain named Morgan (Douglas Dumbrille), is going to foreclose on the sanatorium's mortgage unless Judy can come up with the funds to save it. One of her rich patients, Emily Upjohn, played by the unbeatable and underrated Margaret Dumont, will make up the deficit only if her "dear Dr. Hackenbush" is put in charge. She is an admirer of the doctor because he has told her that she has double-blood pressure, which confirms her worst suspicions. Hackenbush's true professional status is doubted by Stuffy (Harpo Marx), a jockey, and Tony (Chico Marx), a racing tipster, who are friends of Judy. He is also under suspicion by the villainous bankers who are scheming to get control of the sanatorium. Only when Stuffy and Tony have proof that Hackenbash is indeed a fraud do they have confidence in him. In a wonderful salute to loyalty they both follow suit when, Hackenbush, with his leg shot full of novocaine, exits with that leg wrapped around his other one, and his two new supporters walk out the door the same way.

Gil Stewart (Allan Jones) is a struggling singer who owns a race horse (hence the connection with the title) and, because of his beautiful singing voice, good looks, and winning ways, is Judy's suitor. Their road to true love is not without mishap, however, which the Marx Brothers try to ease for them. There is a subplot involving Flo Marlowe (Esther Muir), a slinky seductress hoping to catch Hackenbush, but she gets caught by Stuffy and Tony, who in order to save their friend, wallpaper her to the wall. It is one of the funniest scenes in the film, but even it is topped by a gem of a scene in which Stuffy tries to pantomine for Tony that Hackenbush is in trouble. Harpo's mime as Stuffy is perfect, but outmatched by Chico as Tony's misinterpretation. First, Harpo outlines a large mustache to indicate who the message is about. Chico understands—it is about Buffalo Bill. Harpo tries again, now adding the famous Groucho crouching walk. Buffalo Bill ice skating? In frustration Harpo leaps into a furious attack on a nearby hedge. "Oh," Chico says with immediate recognition, "Hack-a-bush."

Of course, in the end, all is well. Stewart's horse wins the race, which saves the day, the sanatorium, and his love, Judy. Before the predictable conclusion, however, comes much madness and a spectacular production sequence at a water carnival with bathing beauties smiling, although water is running into their eyes and an audience precariously seated on floating rafts. Another similarly zany scene is an embarrassing number (at least by today's standards) in which Stuffy leads a cavalcade of stereotypical blacks in a silly pied-piper number to "All God's Children Got Rhythm." Neither sequence has anything to do with the progression of the fragile plot, which is of almost no consequence in this, or any, Marx Brothers film.

Two classic routines are placed, seemingly regardless of the sequence of events, between the main titles and the end credits. First, there is a code-book bit. As a tipster, Tony sells Hackenbush a tip on a horse; then, in order to interpret the tip, he sells him a code book, and finally a Breeder's Guide. The scene is fast, short, and furiously funny. The other hilarious routine is the examining-room sequence. In order to appreciate the scene's precise choreography, one should see it repeatedly, however, so much happens so fast. Dumont as Emily Upjohn is strapped into the examining chair, and the medical profession's most infamous examination gets under way. The patient is given a shave by Tony, has her shoes shined by Hackenbush, and is manicured by Stuffy. Back to business, Groucho calls for "X-ray! X-ray!," and in comes Stuffy with an armload of evening newspapers. A nurse's uniform is whisked off her, the fire sprinklers are turned on, and a horse gallops in, then out, with the Marx Brothers on its back. If this makes no sense, it does not matter at all, because it is not supposed to.

What went into the making of *A Day at the Races*, however, was not as funny or madcap or spontaneous as one would like to believe. It may seem like fun to imagine a trip to the set where "Minny's boys" (a well-known nickname given to the brothers because their mother's name was Minny) frolicked on the set and threw the crew into convulsions of laughter as they clowned their way into box-office successes. Such was not the case, however; from its inception, *A Day at the Races* took two years and eighteen scripts before it received final approval. When that approval was given, it then went on the stage before live audiences across the country as *Scenes from a Day at the Races*. Farmers, car salesmen, housewives, and insurance salesman all were given the opportunity, by means of preview cards, to voice their likes and dislikes; and each voice was listened to and seriously considered.

Irving Thalberg, a true "Hollywood mogul" in every sense of the word, was in command of the film as head of production at M-G-M, and it was at his insistence that story-line after story-line be revised. Because the writers and the Marx Brothers so respected him, they complied. Unfortunately during the writing phase, at the age of thirty-seven and with a serious heart condition, Thalberg died of pneumonia. Eventually Thalberg's brother-in-law, Laurence Weingarten, was placed in charge, and a completely new regime began, which meant more story conferences, more production meetings, and more revisions. Once the script got final approval, the incredible saga of the screenplay credit hassles began with Al Boasberg, the dissident writer, eventually coming away with no credit at all.

The reception of *A Day at the Races* was varied. It won many new fans, but lost many others. Many thought the movie was a film of stolen gags, as the joke went, because someone must have stolen the gags since they were not in the film. In the Republic of Latvia the film even was banned on the grounds that it was "worthless."

The relationship between the stars and the director was at best testy. There is a popular story that one day in a fit of frustration, the director, Sam Wood, noted more for such films as *King's Row* (1942), directed the following tirade at his stars: "You can't make an actor out of clay," to which, Groucho responded, "And you can't make a director out of Wood." The anecdote may not be true, but, as with a vast majority of *bona fide* and specious Marxisms, nobody seems to mind. As in all of the Marx Brothers films, the gags in *A Day at the Races* are the most important things, not the believability of the plot.

Juliette Friedgen

THE DAY OF THE LOCUST

Released: 1975
Production: Jerome Hellman for Paramount
Direction: John Schlesinger
Screenplay: Waldo Salt; based on the novel of the same name by Nathanael West
Cinematography: Conrad Hall
Editing: Jim Clark
Music: John Barry
Running time: 144 minutes

> *Principal characters:*
> Homer Simpson .... Donald Sutherland
> Faye Greener .... Karen Black
> Harry .... Burgess Meredith
> Tod Hackett .... William Atherton

Nathanael West, more a prophet than a monitor of contemporary issues, wrote about many timely themes during his short life. In *The Day of the Locust*, he gave a thorough treatment of an insidious but familiar process in American life: how the dreams we are taught to nurture die, and what can become of human nature as it helplessly watches the slow death. British director John Schlesinger's film of this short novel came at an especially poignant time. Americans, no longer involved in war or other burning social issues, began to turn back upon themselves and their history as a source of entertainment. This phenomenon resembled in many ways the vanity of the 1930's that prompted so many to drop everything and head for Southern California in search of the "big break" into motion pictures, hoping it would bring them the security and happiness they could not find elsewhere. Accordingly, both the subject matter and the sheer appearance of Schlesinger's film of West's story are significant in contemporary American cultural history.

In the film, Tod Hackett (William Atherton), a set designer, has come to Hollywood in an attempt to make a name for himself. He lives in a court where Faye Greener (Karen Black) also rents a bungalow as she, too, waits for her opportunity to achieve fame as an actress. Tod becomes quite taken by Faye, and although she is able to mete out occasional evidence of affection and caring for those who demand it of her, her life is clearly governed by her own egoistic search for stardom. Tod becomes wrapped up first in his shared enthusiasm for the progress Faye sees taking place in her career, then by his helpless and pitying interest in how she strives to reach her goals. The woman displays her true self to Tod long before she admits to herself what she is doing. She decides to live with an older man, Homer Simpson (Donald Sutherland), who is willing to give her all his money, thereby providing her with the accoutrements she feels she needs to make herself more available for "discovery." All he asks in return is that she stay with him. His intention is that he will likewise be more available for her affection, should she grow to love him.

As this film progresses, however, it becomes obvious that the essence of life in this success-crazed industry lies in the striving and longing for goals, rather than in attainment of the desired end. In the film, no one ever reaches those goals. The film luminaries are treated as superhuman, if not inhuman, individuals. On the other hand, individuals who still strive to attain one status or another show various ways of molding themselves to the contorted values and standards of a culture lying in wait for instantaneous stardom, wealth, and happiness.

Faye attempts to achieve her desired status by manipulating her outward appearance to coincide with what she wants to become, hoping that her goal will be realized all in good time. Black's interpretation of this character makes it clear that Faye has been able to last as long as she has through sheer persistence and a willingness to see herself as nothing more than her character on the screen. In this she is similar to those who only know her from her brief moments on film. She has a definite underlying penchant toward violence and mercilessness, and this is a necessary and pivotal quality in both West's novella and screenwriter Waldo Salt's script. In both the film and the novella from which the screenplay was derived, the traits of mercilessness and violence pervade a large segment of this culture that allows itself to be duped into thriving on brief glimpses of fictitious characters and holding those images up as models for the rest of life. In Faye's case, these traits are not only necessary for the development of her career, but they also allow her to take advantage of Homer and his offers with very little, if any, regret at all.

Homer, on the other hand, appears to be the direct opposite of Faye. Willing to relinquish all his money for Faye's happiness, he houses her, feeds her, clothes her, and allows himself to be abused by her to the point that Faye eventually despises him for his very spinelessness. In actuality, however, both he and Faye are leeches. Each of them is convinced that what he needs and wants exists in his distorted version of society, and each is convinced that all he needs to do to accomplish his goals is to wait and persist.

Although Tod does not come any closer to true success than either Faye or Homer, he has one capacity that neither of the others possesses, the ability to evaluate and reject. Whereas both Faye and Homer are consumed by their goals, Tod is able to recognize that his efforts have led him to circumstances incompatible with human life. Although his ambition is strong, his desire to survive is even stronger.

In addition to this primary plot, *The Day of the Locust* contains episodic events for the major and minor characters that afford Schlesinger the opportunity for many spectacular sets. Each is increasingly larger than life. The first such set is an actual one, the huge Hollywood sign which symbolizes for many the grand-scale fame and success they crave. It is at this site that Faye first tells Tod, in a provocative and coquettish manner usually reserved only for the screen, of her aspirations and minor successes so far. Yet in the background of this scene, there is a group of tourists who have just disembarked from their tour bus and are listening to their guide. By listening with them to this scenario in the background, we learn a bit of the sign's history, including the fact that a Broadway actress who had hoped to find stardom in motion pictures, but did not, hanged herself in desperation from one of the letters of the sign. As Faye and Tod talk, the wind blows, and we see that the sign, too, is fragile and blows in the wind.

Schlesinger's scenes help to underscore the increasing violence found in West's novella and Salt's screenplay. One of the first explicitly violent scenes concerns a bloody cockfight to which Tod and Faye go in search of diversion. The building in which the cockfight is held is large and airy, yet the men attending are crowded together in the center hovering over the bloody, fighting cocks, talking and laughing loudly, waving their money for bets above their heads and encouraging still more bloodshed.

The final scene of *The Day of the Locust* is a chaotic synthesis of all the dehumanizing and violent themes inherent in the body of the film. A major event, a Hollywood movie premiere, is scheduled, and many of the characters are drawn into the crowd to worship the filmstars in a bizarre rendition of what appears to be some ancient and sacred tribal ritual. For no ascertainable reason, the event turns into a riot, and fighting and bloodshed are rampant, not merely within the ranks of the spectators, but also against the film luminaries they have come to worship. In this scene, a major theme of West's work comes to the fore. The crowd not only wants to adore its gods and goddesses, but, parallel to ancient legends of many cultures, it also wants virtually to consume them, and this is a succinct example of the film's view of the whole of American society. The people are hungry for violence; they need it to survive. As they hover on the brink of World War II (Schlesinger inserts newspaper headlines forboding this fact throughout the film), if they cannot find a suitable target for their aggressions and bloodthirstiness, they will turn on themselves, even on their heroes. For in order to survive they must destroy, and their will to survive is strong.

Although not particularly successful at the box office, the film did well critically and in retrospect is a fine example of Schlesinger's work. Like West's original work, it is not enjoyable, but it has something to show society, and particularly the film industry, about itself.

Bonnie Fraser

THE DAY THE EARTH STOOD STILL

Released: 1951
Production: Julian C. Blaustein for Twentieth Century-Fox
Direction: Robert Wise
Screenplay: Edmond H. North; based on the novel *Farewell to the Master* by
  Harry Bates
Cinematography: Leo Tover
Editing: William Reynolds
Music: Bernard Herrmann
Running time: 93 minutes

> *Principal characters:*
> Klaatu .... Michael Rennie
> Helen Benson .... Patricia Neal
> Tom Stevens .... Hugh Marlowe
> Dr. Barnhardt .... Sam Jaffe
> Bobby Benson .... Billy Gray

The anxieties felt at the dawning of the atomic age, combined with the rise
of UFO sightings in the late 1940's, set the stage for this literate science-fiction
thriller concerning a flying saucer which lands in Washington, D.C. As the
film opens, Klaatu (Michael Rennie), an envoy from a highly advanced gal-
actic federation, emerges from his star ship accompanied by a nine-foot-tall
robot. His initial reception is misread as hostile by a complement of troops
who have surrounded the flying saucer. After an interrogation in which
Klaatu's warnings are not conveyed to the authorities, the alien escapes from
his detention and becomes a fugitive while hoping to find someone willing to
listen to his crucial message. Disguised as a human, Klaatu eventually turns
to the scientific community, represented by Dr. Barnhardt (Sam Jaffe), with
his warning. He explains that the earth has been monitored for years by a
federation of advanced beings dedicated to universal peace. Klaatu goes on
to explain that the aggressive nature of humanity, enhanced by the potential
for destruction inherent in nuclear weapons, endangers not only the earth but
also in many ways the entire universe. His mission is to convince the major
world powers to rechannel their aggressive tendencies and concentrate on
humanitarian goals or face total annihilation.

To illustrate that what he is saying is not merely an idle threat, Klaatu
completely shuts down all forms of man-made power (except in essential areas
such as hospitals) for a period of twenty-four hours. Realizing that he might
not be able to convince the world leaders to react in time and also anticipating
that he could be killed before he has completed his mission, Klaatu entrusts
to a sympathetic widow. Helen Benson (Patricia Neal), with whom he lives
in a boarding house and who is aware of his secret, a particular phrase which

must be repeated to Gort, his cybernetic bodyguard, in the event of his death. The alien's suspicions are borne out when he is discovered and killed. Later, making her way through a security area, the widow reaches the robot and repeats the phrase, "Gort, Klaatu berrada nikto." At these words, the once immobile guardian stalks the streets of the nation's capital in search of the corpse of his companion.

After returning the lifeless body of Klaatu to the star ship, Gort proceeds to resurrect him for a brief period of time. It is at this point that Klaatu reminds the assembly of scientists of the threat of nuclear destruction. Before he leaves, Klaatu entrusts Gort with the task of remaining behind to make sure that the new course of peace and human rights is rigidly adhered to by the people of the earth.

The Day the Earth Stood Still is an unusually effective science-fiction film. One reason for this is the semidocumentary style in which director Robert Wise chose to present his film. There is a sense of immediacy inherent in this particular style of filmmaking which gives the fantastic subject matter a more convincing environment. Wise's direction is crisp and straightforward. His earlier work as editor of Orson Welles's *Citizen Kane* (1941) and his directorial assignments of *film noir* subjects such as *Born To Kill* (1947) and *The Set-Up* (1949) contribute to make *The Day the Earth Stood Still* a film of powerful, uncomplicated images.

The period of the Cold War and the UFO hysteria in which *The Day the Earth Stood Still* was produced also added to the effectiveness of the film. There were a great many anxieties about atomic secrets and the possibility of a third world war, so when a film dealing with a powerful liberal philosophy was presented, it was received with mixed emotions. There is an overriding social allegory which is woven into the very fabric of this thriller, and which allows the film to transcend its fantastic premise and concentrate on a fundamental faith in the goodness of humanity. It is easy to construe Klaatu as a Christ figure who sacrifices his life in order to preserve civilization. Simple situations such as his resurrection or his choice of "Carpenter" as his surname when he passes for human underline the overt Christian philosophy of this so-called federation of advanced beings. It was a refreshing point of view which gave an optimistic energy to *The Day the Earth Stood Still*, a point of view which relieved some of the tensions of the world condition. Additionally, the importance of a faithful child, Helen's son Bobby (Billy Gray), as Klaatu's ally and helper was a look toward a future of hope.

Beyond this philosophical prediliction *The Day the Earth Stood Still* is a masterful piece of entertainment. Rennie as Klaatu is perfectly restrained and noble. Neal as the widow is believable, and the supporting cast is excellent. The implications of atomic abuses also must have struck a cord with many filmmakers at the time, since this film heralded a series of science-fiction thrillers overflowing with monsters formed out of the ashes of atomic bombs and nuclear waste. Few were as restrained as *The Day the Earth Stood Still.* Yet Rennie remained the model of the benevolent visitor from the stars for years to come.

The music by Bernard Herrmann is also an important factor in the success of *The Day the Earth Stood Still.* There is a feeling of otherworldliness that is uncanny in Herrmann's music; he creates a proper atmosphere of tension and fear through electronic manipulation and eerie tonal effects. It is not often that the music can serve as a correlative for the action of a film, and yet in this particular assignment Herrmann was able to instill into his music an alien beauty and force which completely complements the film.

Although *The Day the Earth Stood Still* has its roots in a short story by Harry Bates published in a science-fiction magazine more than a decade earlier, this film was able to capture the fear and anxieties of both the UFO craze and the fears of an impending nuclear holocaust. There was very little in the way of exotic special effects (as in later science-fiction films such as *Close Encounters of the Third Kind*, 1977). The film concentrated on the implications of dealing with a race of beings more powerful and technologically advanced than humans, rather than becoming overwhelmed at the fact that "we are not alone."

It is not inconceivable to draw a comparison between this film and Steven Speilberg's *Close Encounters of the Third Kind.* In a sense, both films deal with the discovery that life exists outside this planet. While *Close Encounters of the Third Kind* deals introspectively with the problems of an average man trying to come to grips with the fact of his close encounter, *The Day the Earth Stood Still* eliminates the sense of wonder, replacing it with anxiety and mistrust. The conclusion of both films is optimistic, although *The Day the Earth Stood Still* betrays the cynicism of the cultural climate during the 1950's.

The message found in *The Day the Earth Stood Still* might seem banal by contemporary standards. In a period of ultraconservatism, however, this altruistic ambience was a very different and perhaps even courageous statement.

Carl Macek

DAYS OF WINE AND ROSES

Released: 1962
Production: Martin Manulis for Warner Bros.
Direction: Blake Edwards
Screenplay: J P Miller; based on his teleplay of the same name
Cinematography: Philip H. Lathrop
Editing: Patrick McCormack
Art direction: Joseph Wright; set decoration, George James Hopkins
Song: Henry Mancini and Johnny Mercer, "Days of Wine and Roses" (AA)
Running time: 117 minutes

> *Principal characters:*
> Joe Clay ....Jack Lemmon
> Kirsten Arnesen Clay .... Lee Remick
> Ellis Arnesen ....Charles Bickford
> Debbie Clay ....Debbie Megowan
> Jim Hungerford .... Jack Klugman

Days of Wine and Roses, a Martin Manulis production for Warner Bros., is the most graphic and sensitive film treatment of the subject of alcoholism since the inspired performances given by Ray Milland in *The Lost Weekend* (1945), and by Burt Lancaster and Shirley Booth in *Come Back Little Sheba* (1952). Manulis, well-known for his production of the outstanding television shows *Climax* and *Playhouse 90*, hired Blake Edwards to direct the film version of J P Miller's highly acclaimed television drama. Edwards, a top television and motion picture director, was responsible for the creation of the *Peter Gunn* and *Mr. Lucky* series for television, and his film credits include *Operation Petticoat* (1959) and *Breakfast at Tiffany's* (1961). Miller's powerful drama tells the story of Joe Clay (Jack Lemmon) and Kirsten Arnesen (Lee Remick), who, while very much in love, also share an irresistible attraction to alcohol. Under Edwards' sensitive and taut direction, the film compassionately yet honestly follows the couple's gradual decline into alcoholism, and it is with mounting anxiety and increased involvement that the audience watches the pair struggle to work out their problem.

The story is set in San Francisco, which is captured in all its diverse beauty through Philip H. Lathrop's cinematography. The opening scene of the film takes place in a San Francisco bar where Joe Clay, a hard-drinking public relations man, is busy plying his trade. A very important friend of Joe's client, Prince Aben el Sud, is holding a party aboard the Prince's yacht, and, as the Prince's public relations man, it is Joe's job to stock the party with beautiful girls. Lemmon is entirely believable as the fast-talking, hard-drinking, slightly cynical Joe; he brings the character alive as a competitive individual suffering from the unhealthy stress brought to bear on him by society's complex business structure. Joe meets Kirsten Arnesen at the party aboard the Prince's yacht. This first encounter is a disaster for Joe, who, muddled by too much alcohol, mistakes Kirsten, who is actually the client's secretary, for one of the party girls he has invited. Lee Remick plays Kirsten as a wholesome, assertive woman who is tinged with a certain sadness that makes her both appealing and memorable. In an effort to atone for his blunder, Joe visits Kirsten at her office and begs to make amends by taking her to dinner. The couple's future is foreshadowed during their first date, when Joe induces Kirsten, a chocolate addict, to try her first drink, a chocolate Brandy Alexander. It is not long before Kirsten loses her initial distaste for alcohol and learns to appreciate the feeling of well-being that it instills.

We first meet Kirsten's father, Ellis Arnesen (Charles Bickford), when the exuberant young couple arrive at his home late one night to break the news that they were married that evening. Bickford, who is a fine actor, is given a rather ambiguous role in this film. His initially impassive reaction to Joe and Kirsten's marriage seems to be more a device to advance the plot than anything else. Later he helps them, but again he is not important *per se*, but merely because he causes them to act.

Joe and Kirsten's slide into alcoholism is barely perceptible at first, since the couple has a fashionable apartment on Pacific Street, a beautiful baby daughter, and a mutual love and concern for each other. After eight years have passed, however, Joe and Kirsten have become totally dependent on alcohol, and their world is disintegrating rapidly. Joe's career is floundering after having lost half a dozen jobs because of his drinking; and Kirsten has embraced alcohol with the same zeal she had previously shown for life. The story has the mood of relentless inevitability as Joe and Kirsten's marriage begins to fall apart, their child becomes neglected and withdrawn, and they are reduced to living in the slums. Particularly in this portion of the film, Lemmon (as did Burt Lancaster in 1952's *Come Back Little Sheba*) displays a depth and range of emotion unequaled in his previous acting experience; he is at all times entirely believable, and compels a profound involvement on the part of the audience. Remick, likewise, shows how Kirsten can sink to the depths of despair and degradation while still maintaining some last vestige of misplaced pride and integrity, thus making her condition all the more heartbreaking. Edwards' direction is at times brilliant, for he develops the full potential of Miller's story without preaching or resorting to clichés.

In a desperate attempt to save themselves, the couple moves in with Kirsten's father at his nursery, and, after a few weeks of abstinence and hard work, they appear healthy once again. Joe, however, convincing himself that he has gained back his self-control, sneaks two pints of whiskey into his and Kirsten's room. After the two bottles are finished, Joe goes in search of a bottle he had hidden in the greenhouse. His brain fogged by alcohol, he is unable to remember its exact location, and growing more distraught and violent by the minute, he practically destroys the greenhouse in his search. Following his total collapse, Joe is placed in the violent ward of a hospital where, through his befuddled brain and physical agony, he begins to realize the depths to which he has fallen. In this hospital scene, Lemmon gives one of the most demanding performances of his acting career; his intensity is almost terrifying. After his physical torment subsides, Joe meets Jim Hungerford (Jack Klugman), who offers him help through Alcoholics Anonymous. Having finally faced the reality of his condition, Joe attends one of the group's meetings. Kirsten, however, refuses to accompany him, adamantly denying that she is an alcoholic. When Joe returns from the meeting, Kirsten is gone.

Through Jim's continued support and encouragement, Joe begins a tenuous journey to recovery; and, while holding down a full-time job, he also takes on the responsibility of his daughter Debbie (Debbie Megowan), giving her the care and love she has lacked for so long. Almost a year later, Kirsten appears at Joe's apartment, pleading to be taken back. Much to his dismay, however, she still refuses to admit she is an alcoholic and informs him that she could never stop drinking entirely. He knows he can never take her back under her conditions, although for one moment as she turns to leave, his love for her nearly destroys his resolve. The final scene of the film shows Joe looking at Kirsten through his window after telling their daughter that someday perhaps she will return.

The Days of Wine and Roses, while presenting a poignant love story with great emotional impact, also makes an enlightened and compelling statement about alcoholism. The film received six Academy Award nominations: for Best Actor, Best Actress, Best Art Direction, Best Set Decoration, Best Costume Design, and Best Song. Henry Mancini and Johnny Mercer went on to receive the Academy Award for Best Song. In addition to being a great film, *Days of Wine and Roses* had an accelerating effect on the careers of its principal characters. Jack Lemmon went on to star in such diverse films as *Save the Tiger* (1973), for which he received an Academy Award, *The Front Page* (1974), and, more recently, *The China Syndrome* (1979). Lee Remick has given fine performances in a number of films including *Hallelujah Trail* (1965) and *The Europeans* (1979). Jack Klugman gravitated to television and earned an Emmy award in 1971 and 1973 for his costarring role in *The Odd Couple*. Charles Bickford, whose film career spanned nearly forty years, acted in only one more film, *A Big Hand for the Little Lady* (1966), before his death in 1967.

D. Gail Huskins

DEAD END

Released: 1937
Production: Samuel Goldwyn for Goldwyn Studios
Direction: William Wyler
Screenplay: Lillian Hellman; based on the play of the same name by Sidney Kingslcy
Cinematography: Gregg Toland
Editing: Daniel Mandell
Art direction: Richard Day
Running time: 93 minutes

Principal characters:
Baby Face Martin .... Humphrey Bogart
Drina .... Sylvia Sidney
Dave .... Joel McCrea
Kay .... Wendy Barrie
Francie .... Claire Trevor
Tommy .... Billy Halop
Dippy .... Huntz Hall
Angel .... Bobby Jordan
Spit .... Leo Gorcey
T. B. .... Gabriel Dell
Philip .... Charles Peck
Mrs. Martin .... Marjorie Main

In 1937, Warner Bros. seemed to have a monopoly on films dealing with social problems and injustice in America. *Dead End*, adapted from Sidney Kingsley's long-running Broadway hit play of the same name, was Samuel Goldwyn's version of this type of Warner Bros. film, for its theme was poverty and corruption in New York's lower East Side. The play was about slum children who lived in close proximity to both the rich penthouse dwellers and the criminals spawned in the city streets. Still feeling the effects of the depression, Americans could easily identify with this subject. In spite of its many overtheatrical moments, there is enough of a documentary flavor in *Dead End* to have convinced audiences of the 1930's that what they were seeing on the screen was the genuine human condition.

Goldwyn wisely chose William Wyler to direct the film. Although they had developed a rapport while working together on *Dodsworth* (1936) and *These Three* (1936) for Goldwyn Pictures, Goldwyn still did not trust Wyler completely and vetoed the director's request to shoot the film on location on the East side of Manhattan. Goldwyn thought he could retain more control by building sets and keeping the production tied to his back lot. The set that was finally built was the talk of Hollywood. Designer Richard Day, who had just won an Oscar for *Dodsworth*, created a magnificent complex of seedy apartment buildings, shops, a luxury hotel complete with penthouse, and a model of the filthy East River in which the Dead End Kids could swim. Goldwyn hired Lillian Hellman, whose hit play *The Children's Hour* had been the basis for *These Three*, to write the screenplay. As for casting, Humphrey Bogart was borrowed from Warner Bros. to play Baby Face Martin, the criminal antihero who is one of the role models for the youthful slum dwellers. Bogart was still relatively new to films, and in *Dead End* he was able to build his first complete character since his role as the psychopath Duke Mantee in *The Petrified Forest* (1936) at Warner Bros.

As the film opens, cinematographer Gregg Toland beautifully swings his camera around to show a group of adolescent boys, obviously very poor, swimming in the East River, while around them life of all sorts is teeming. In the penthouse of the hotel apartment off the river, an expensively dressed young boy is having breakfast with his father. Women from the tenements are hanging out clothes and men are loitering on street corners. Tommy (Billy Halop), the leader of the gang of boys, has been reared by his sister Drina (Sylvia Sidney), a sensitive girl waging a losing battle to get herself and her brother away from their pitiful surroundings. Drina is in love with Dave (Joel McCrea), an unemployed architect who is also anxious to escape the neighborhood. In melodramatic fashion, however, Dave is infatuated with Kay (Wendy Barrie), a woman kept very luxuriously by a New York businessman in an apartment on the river.

As the horseplay between the gang of boys goes on, including beating up Philip (Charles Peck), the "rich kid," into the neighborhood comes Baby Face Martin (Humphrey Bogart), a known killer who has returned to his childhood home to see his mother and his ex-sweetheart. Martin has a price on his head and has had his face changed by plastic surgery. His confrontations with the neighborhood form the rest of the story. For the boys he is a hero who enjoys an easy life of crime, full of excitement and money; for Dave, Martin represents what he could have become if he had given in to the despair he so often felt. Martin's mother (Marjorie Main) completely rejects her son. In one of the most memorable scenes in the film, the work-weathered old woman tells her son that he has never brought her anything but trouble, then slaps him and slams the door in his face. Francie (Claire Trevor), Martin's girl, did not wait for him and is now out on the streets.

Events culminate when Martin, in an effort to "get back" at the neighborhood, decides to kidnap Philip. When Dave tries to interfere, he is superficially stabbed by Martin, but he still manages to overpower one of Martin's henchmen, take his gun, and kill Martin. The police come, and Dave learns that he will receive a reward for turning in Martin. He sees this as his chance to go away with Kay, but decides she is really not for him. The police look for Tommy, who has stolen Philip's watch and who nearly kills Spit (Leo Gorcey), the gang member who reported him to the police. Drina and Dave find Tommy in time to save Spit and talk Tommy into giving himself up to the police. The officers take Tommy away as Drina finds comfort in Dave's arms. The film ends on a hopeful note with Dave planning to use his reward money to hire a lawyer who will save Tommy from reform school and enable them to leave the dead end street forever.

Dead End seems a bit dated now, especially since its protagonists are portrayed as such glaring examples of good and evil; it contains so many outstanding moments, however, that it is still fascinating. When Sidney pushes back her hair to show the bruise on her forehead that resulted from a blow received on the picket line, she represents the working girl of the 1930's fighting with her union to give her a break. Just as moving are the Dead End Kids—Billy Halop, Huntz Hall, Bobby Jordan, Leo Gorcey, and Gabriel Dell. They were also in the stage production and seemed to come from the very tenements in which the story took place. When they are on screen, the forced histrionics of the film fade away and *Dead End* becomes a social document. The film launched the careers of the Dead End Kids, who were to appear together in numerous other films of a similar, although less socially significant, vein.

Dead End pleased both critics and audiences, and *The New York Post* devoted an editorial to it stating that the best thing that could have been done at the last session of Congress would have been to show the film to the committee that crippled the Wagner Housing Act. The film received four Oscar nominations, for Best Picture, Best Supporting Actress, Best Direction, and Best Art Direction, but lost in a year which boasted *Lost Horizon*, *The Life of Émile Zola*, *The Good Earth*, and the original *A Star Is Born*. The combination of Goldwyn, Wyler, and Hellman was to surface again, however, four year's later when they collaborated on another unforgettable film, *The Little Foxes* (1941).

Joan Cohen

DEATH OF A SALESMAN

Released: 1952
Production: Stanley Kramer for Columbia
Direction: Laslo Benedek
Screenplay: Stanley Roberts; based on the play of the same name by Arthur Miller
Cinematography: Franz Planer
Editing: William A. Lyon
Running time: 115 minutes

> *Principal characters:*
> Willy Loman .... Fredric March
> Linda Loman .... Mildred Dunnock
> Biff .... Kevin McCarthy
> Happy .... Cameron Mitchell
> Charley .... Howard Smith
> Ben .... Royal Beal

Arthur Miller's *Death of a Salesman* is frequently regarded as the best modern American tragedy, although it is not a Classical tragedy because its hero does not suffer a fall from grace. In fact, its protagonist is no hero in the usual sense of the word, nor is he a man who has ever achieved greatness or a state of grace in any aspect of his life.

Willy Loman (Fredric March) is a pathetic traveling salesman who has spent his life worshiping success and popularity, a man living a life of delusion and never really facing up to reality. But the key to Willy is that he is a human being to whom we respond with compassion because the fate he suffers touches us all. *Death of a Salesman* is an indictment of the American economic system which rates the individual only by what he has achieved, or how much money he has made, and then tosses him aside just like any other dispensable commodity when he can no longer produce at peak level.

Miller's play opened at the Morosco Theatre in New York City on February 10, 1949, starred Lee J. Cobb, and ran for 742 performances. It became one of the most praised and honored of American plays, winning almost every award available: the Pulitzer Prize, the New York Drama Circle Critics Award, the Theatre Club's Gold Medal, the Newspaper Guild's Front Page Award, the Donaldson Award, and the Antoinette Perry (Tony) Award as best drama of the year.

In translating the play to the screen, producer Stanley Kramer, director Laslo Benedek, and screenwriter Stanley Roberts made every effort to remain faithful to the original. Those changes that were necessary were achieved without cinematic tricks. For many, the screen version is regarded as better than the stage play, largely because of the strong sense of intuition and humanity brought to the role of Willy Loman by Fredric March.

Willy Loman is a man in his early sixties who has spent his life as a traveling salesman covering the New England territory. Selling has been the all-consuming passion of his life, and success and popularity are his gods. What Willy cannot admit is that he has never been very good at his job, and time and life have passed him by. He has never faced up to the reality of life; in fact, his "tragedy" is that his life has been wasted on delusions of success. He has always been a braggart who was determined to be well-liked. His philosophy of selling was based on false hopes and appearances: "It's not what you say, it's how you say it—personality always wins the day. Start big and you'll end up big. It's important not only to be liked, but to be well-liked."

In his prime, a good week in New England meant one hundred dollars but there are no more good weeks and Willy's world is closing in on him. Miller has constructed the play as if Willy is trapped in the prison he has built around himself. This same sense of claustrophobia is maintained brilliantly in the film. He is now sixty-three and at the end of his tether. He is a mentally tired and physically exhausted man with thirty years of frustration behind him and nothing to which he can look forward. He is often confused, and his mind frequently wanders back to the "good old days." He is unable to drive his car, and not to drive is not to sell. When he seeks a transfer to his company's New York office, Willy is fired. He is no longer useful in the competitive business world and is as dispensable as the wares he has sold for thirty years.

Miller wrote the play using a series of flashbacks in Willy's memory to illustrate his past life. As his past unravels before us through his reveries, we see that Willy's ambitions have eroded all of his personal relationships. He has one good friend, Charley (Howard Smith), who now looks at him with pity. His life of deceit and mediocrity has undermined his relationship with his two grown sons, who are disappointments to their father.

The older son, Biff (Kevin McCarthy), has become a worthless drifter since he discovered his father in a hotel room with another woman years before. Though Biff has lost respect for his father, he does make an effort to force Willy to abandon the false pretenses of his life and face reality, but to no avail. The younger son, Happy (Cameron Mitchell), while fairly successful in business, is a chauvinistic womanizer who likewise fails to face reality. Willy's loyal and long-suffering wife, Linda (Mildred Dunnock), realizes that her husband's fate is sealed, but she is steadfast in her efforts to be supportive. She knows that he is only a shell of the man he once was, and that he has given up hope and wants to die.

Willy refuses an offer of a job made by his friend Charley. In one of his mental "wanderings," he listens to the advice of his dead brother, Ben (Royal Beal), and realizes that once dead, because of his twenty-thousand-dollar insurance policy, he will be worth more to his family than he is alive. Resolute that this is what fate has dealt him, Willy drives away in his car to commit suicide. Willy had bragged that his funeral would be attended by all his business colleagues and clients, attesting to his success and popularity, but the only mourner besides his family is his friend Charley, who says, "Nobody ought to blame him. A salesman has got to dream. It comes with the territory."

Death of a Salesman is a devastating portrait of the frustrations of the little man in a society that worships success. Willy is neither an attractive nor a likable man, and onstage his character was criticized for being removed from the audience, too cold to elicit sympathy. Most critics agree that in the film version, Fredric March's inner resources as an actor reveal an understanding of Willy far beyond that delineated by the script.

March is regarded by many as America's finest screen actor. Romano Tozzi wrote in *Films in Review* in 1958: "The essence of March's excellence is his integrity. He is a skilled craftsman, is blessed with an exceptionally fine speaking voice, and is a well-informed and intelligent man. But beyond these priceless assets is the more valuable one of sincerity." Many admirers consider March's portrayal of Willy Loman as the crowning achievement of his re-markable career, although his performance failed to capture an Academy Award.

In addition to March's performance in *Death of a Salesman*, the other performances were also first-rate. Cameron Mitchell as Happy and Howard Smith as Charley had come from the Broadway version, and Kevin McCarthy as Biff gives an impressive performance as the older son. The wonderful Mildred Dunnock, also from the stage version, gives as luminous and subtle a performance as any on the screen that year. She is an actress of merit whose talent has rarely been utilized to the fullest on film.

In bringing the play to the screen, Laslo Benedek took Willy's "wanderings" and turned them into internal monologues. These transitions in time and place suited the film medium perfectly, and the film is strengthened by pre-senting these as realistic rather than dream sequences. Though not often seen on television or in revival houses, this screen version of *Death of a Salesman* remains one of the best film adaptations of an American stage play, and Fredric March's acting ranks with the best.

Ronald Bowers

DEATH TAKES A HOLIDAY

Released: 1934
Production: E. Lloyd Sheldon for Paramount
Direction: Mitchell Leisen
Screenplay: Maxwell Anderson, Gladys Lehman, and Walter Ferris; based
on the play of the same name by Alberto Casella, adapted from the Italian
by Walter Ferris
Cinematography: Charles Lang
Editing: no listing
Art direction: Ernst Fegte
Costume design: Travis Banton and Edith Head
Running time: 78 minutes

     Principal characters:
     Prince Sirki .... Fredric March
     Grazia .... Evelyn Venable
     Duke Lambert .... Sir Guy Standing
     Alda .... Katherine Alexander
     Rhoda .... Gail Patrick

Speculations about death and the prospects of the hereafter had already
been popular subjects for the theater by the time motion pictures came into
being at the beginning of the twentieth century. Some of the earliest films
made in the United States and Europe continued this line of thought, utilizing
crude double exposure techniques to create ghosts. By the mid-1930's, when
horror movies such as *Dracula* (1931) had presented a terrifying view of the
afterlife, Mitchell Leisen's film *Death Takes a Holiday* was unique in that it
presented a view of death which was reasonable and ultimately comforting.

The script by Maxwell Anderson, Gladys Lehman, and Walter Ferris closely
followed the story line of Anderson's popular play of the same title, which
in turn had been derived from an old play by Alberto Casella. The story
begins as Duke Lambert (Sir Guy Standing) and his various house guests
return to Lambert's palazzo after a happy afternoon's drive to await the arrival
of another guest, Prince Sirki (Fredric March). One member of the party,
the Princess Grazia (Evelyn Venable), seems oblivious to the merriment of
the others. Walking out into the garden, she feels an indescribable sensation
pass over her and she faints. The others take her inside, and when she is
revived, she cannot explain what happened. "An icy wind seemed to touch
me, only it wasn't a wind," she says.

Late that night as he is putting out the lights, Duke Lambert is confronted
with a black apparition. The apparition gradually becomes more opaque until
it assumes the human form of the long-awaited Prince Sirki, who has actually
just died. The Duke attempts to shoot the apparition with his gun but without

effect. It reveals that it is Death, come to earth in the guise of the handsome Prince Sirki to try to discover why humanity fears him so and to learn what earthly pleasures could be so great as to cause a desire to prolong life. Hearing the shots, the alarmed guests come downstairs and are introduced to the strange Prince Sirki. Only the radiant Grazia is unafraid of him.

For the next three days, as Death takes his "holiday," no person, animal, or plant on earth dies. Death enjoys all earthly pleasures: the life of luxury in the Duke's palazzo, constant winnings at the race track and in the casino, and the attentions of two seductive women (Gail Patrick and Katherine Alexander). Despite all this, he fails to find any quality in human life as profound as death.

At the end of the third day, the Duke throws a lavish party. As his time on earth draws to a close, Death lets his true identity become more and more obvious, and the two seductive women run in terror as they begin to perceive it. Only Grazia remains unafraid of Sirki, and quietly they slip into the garden where their love is consummated.

Returning, they console Grazia's terrified mother and the other party guests. As the clock strikes twelve, Death relinquishes his human form and once again becomes the black apparition. He tells Grazia, "Now you see me as I really am," and she replies, "I've always seen you that way. I love you." His final statement is, "Now I know that Love is stronger than Death," and Grazia joins him. As they disappear, a breeze scatters newly fallen leaves across their path. Death's holiday is over.

A mood piece depending on a careful mixture of sentimentality, sophistication, and complex visual imagery as a background for the intricate drama, *Death Takes a Holiday* was an assignment tailor-made for Mitchell Leisen. Having risen through the ranks as costume designer and art director for many Cecil B. De Mille productions, and later serving as associate director on *The Sign of the Cross* (1932), *Tonight Is Ours* (1933), and *The Eagle and the Hawk* (1933), all of which starred Fredric March, Leisen had a broad background in many phases of the motion picture business. His first solo directorial effort, a religious story entitled *Cradle Song* (1933), proved to Paramount that he could handle serious story material with taste and sensitivity. When *Cradle Song* was released while *Death Takes a Holiday* was in production, its success with the critics and at the box office confirmed the faith the studio had in its new director.

Leisen had already undergone eight years of psychoanalysis when he started the film, and this experience helped him when Maxwell Anderson said he worried that he had never found a motivation for Grazia's inexplicable behavior in following Death. Leisen later recalled, "I said to Max, 'She simply does not want to live; just take the attitude that she has gone out into the garden and caught pneumonia and does not have the will to live.' "

Leisen and the writers agreed to retain the existentialistic viewpoint of the play. Although it takes place in Spain, there is no mention of Catholicism except for a brief moment in the opening sequence when Grazia is seen praying in a cathedral. The hereafter to which she goes is not that of the traditional Christian heaven, but rather a simple state of peace and quiet.

The casting of all the leading roles was very fortunate. Fredric March's theatrical style of delivery undermined some of his roles, but is perfectly appropriate for Death, whose inexperience in behaving like a human causes him to overact somewhat. Evelyn Venable's interpretation of the difficult role of Grazia is sublime. It was only her second screen part (the first had been *Cradle Song*). In person she was vivacious, robust, and almost as large as March, but Leisen was able to elicit from her a dreamy, ethereal quality which made Grazia believable. *Death Takes a Holiday*'s first preview was held in Pasadena while Venable was working on *David Harum*, and she invited the whole *David Harum* company to attend the preview with her. Hal Mohr, the cinematographer on *David Harum*, would later remember, "I thought she was a cute kid, but I never paid much attention to her until I saw her coming down the stairs to meet Grazia for the first time and that was it, I really fell." Venable and Mohr were married, and she retired from the screen. Leisen decided to cast Kent Taylor as Grazia's fiancé, Corrado, because he resembled Fredric March.

Paramount executives were afraid of releasing a film with the word "death" in the title, so they arranged for a one-week test run in Fresno, California, under the alternative title, *Strange Holiday*. Then they ran it in Sacramento for a week under the original title, and did much greater business, so that the title *Death Takes a Holiday* was retained. The film opened in March, 1934, to excellent reviews and box-office success. *Photoplay* wrote, ". . . this picture is an experience no intelligent person should miss. "We were right behind Mae West," Mitchell Leisen would later recall proudly.

David Chierichetti

DEATH WISH

Released: 1974
Production: Hal Landers, Bobby Roberts, and Michael Winner for Dino de
  Laurentiis; released by Paramount
Direction: Michael Winner
Screenplay: Wendell Mayes; based on the novel of the same name by Brian
  Garfield
Cinematography: Arthur J. Ornitz
Editing: Bernard Gribble
Running time: 93 minutes

Principal characters:
Paul Kersey .... Charles Bronson
Joanna Kersey .... Hope Lange
Inspector Frank Ochoa .... Vincent Gardenia
Carol Kersey Toby .... Kathleen Tolan
Jack Toby .... Steven Keats

1974 saw the release of what normally would have been just another routine
if slickly directed and photographed action film. *Death Wish*'s theme, however,
that an ordinary citizen seeking revenge and becoming a violent, one-man
vigilante squad, hit a raw spot with the American public at a time when crime
in the streets was steadily intensifying while police efforts to quell it seemed
largely ineffectual.

In the film, Paul Kersey (Charles Bronson) is a successful Manhattan
architect who espouses all the "accepted" liberal views. We first see him
beneath the credits frolicking with his wife Joanna (Hope Lange) on an idyllic
sunny vacation in Hawaii. Back in New York, three young thugs posing as
delivery boys assault and kill his wife and rape his married daughter Carol
(Kathleen Tolan), which leaves her in a state of catatonia. Attempting to live
and cope with the horrendous deed, Kersey's liberal beliefs of leniency toward
delinquents and street crime disintegrate. When the police are unable to solve
the crime, Kersey feels a slowly overriding need for revenge. Soon after, on
business and recuperating in Arizona, Kersey is taken by a client to a pistol
range where he demonstrates his long unpracticed but expert skill with a gun.
As a parting gift, the client gives him a pearl-handled .32 caliber revolver.

Returning to New York, and further upset when his son-in-law Jack (Steven
Keats) tells him that Carol is no better, Kersey begins to haunt dark parks,
alleys, and subways, inviting attack, then killing his assailants. He soon
becomes a media hero (although his identity is unknown) called the "N.Y.
Vigilante." The police, with the investigation led by Inspector Frank Ochoa
(Vincent Gardenia), slowly begin to track him down. Meanwhile, with
Kersey's continuing activities, muggings in the city are cut nearly in half, and

city authorities, who do not want Kersey to become a martyr, order Ochoa to act discreetly. Kersey is wounded on one of his forays and captured by the police, although Ochoa denies to the press that he has Kersey in custody. Instead of booking him for his killings, he suggests to Kersey that he seek a business transfer to another city and leave town quietly. The final scene of the film, suggesting the sequel that was eventually made in 1981, has Kersey arriving in Chicago. While at the airport, suitcase in hand, he notices some deadbeat youths disturbing a woman. Silently, he raises his thumb and forefinger like a gun, takes aim, and "fires." (In the sequel, Kersey lives in Los Angeles, where his Mexican maid and teenaged daughter are both raped and killed.)

While restricted to adult attendance by its MPAA rating of R, *Death Wish* set off controversy among all factions of citizenry, no matter what age, race, sex, economic level, or profession, who lined up in droves to see it. It also aroused much ire from the leaders in society, politics, law enforcement, and medicine. Concerning the latter, press inquiries to doctors found only one psychiatrist who felt the film was dangerous, capable of causing imitative behavior, with the rest believing that it functioned as healthy fantasy release for its audience. Characteristic of the establishment "nay"-saying was the United States Catholic Conference, which slapped the picture with its "C" (Condemned) rating as a "pernicious appeal to the dark side of the American character."

Because of such furor, the film was an immediate hit and came to the forefront of a group of other films, beginning in 1971 with *Dirty Harry* and continuing with its sequel *Magnum Force* (1973) and *Walking Tall* and *The Longest Yard* (both 1974), that were denounced for their neo-Fascist philosophy. By 1979, *Variety* showed a distributor rental figure of $8.8 million for the film. It had the quick effect of spawning many imitative, often cheaply made versions of the same revenge/vigilante story, their production not limited to America but worldwide.

Death Wish was popular with audiences for another reason: it was a simple, extremely well-paced and violent melodrama featuring a strong, sympathetic central figure. (The plot is nearly that of a Western.) The film is quite canny in its emotional manipulation of the audience; the opening murder and rape scenes are protracted and ugly, so that viewers immediately side with Kersey in his anger and frustration. The film is also cleverly made to avoid the charge of racism; despite the crime statistics, *Death Wish*'s muggers are a fully integrated lot, and the three responsible for the initial violence are out-and-out inhuman crazies.

Critically, among the professional reviewers, the motion picture had more defenders than attackers. Naturally, in a film as seemingly volatile as *Death Wish*, there was little middle ground of opinion. Several writers did feel that the film presented an unrealistically harsh view of New York, with the film, of course, being made by out-of-towners (director Michael Winner was from London, and screenwriter Wendell Mayes from Los Angeles.) The film originated when Winner took the novel to Dino de Laurentiis, who saw its commercial possibilities. The producer claims that Bronson shared their enthusiasm and signed immediately. Mayes, who had previously written the screenplays for *The Poseidon Adventure* (1972), *Advise and Consent* (1962), and *Anatomy of a Murder* (1957), wrote the script. Production began in Hawaii on January 17, 1974, and continued in Tucson before moving to New York. Principal photography ended in March, and the film was released later that year.

Much of the credit for the film's effectiveness goes to Winner, an ebullient, fast-working English director (snidely described in a film source as "his own best publicist") who took University degrees in law and economics while working as a reporter. He began making short films in the mid-1950's. His early English features, made in the mid-1960's, most notably *I'll Never Forget Whatshisname* (1967), were lively, efficient, intelligent films. Since then, he has prolifically specialized in internationally casted action films in all genres, shot entirely on location with steadily increasing budgets, with varying degrees of success and excess. Several were made with Bronson: *Chato's Land* (1971), *The Mechanic* (1972), and *The Stone Killer* (1973), with the latter uniting the pair with Laurentiis.

By the time of the production of *Death Wish*, Laurentiis had been involved in some six hundred films, and a year earlier had moved his production headquarters to New York (*Death Wish* was his fourth film there) from Rome, where he had built Cinecittà, a huge studio complex. His early films (*Bitter Rice*, 1950; *La Strada*, 1956; and *Cabiria*, 1957) closely associated him with the Italian Neo-Realist movement. From that point on, however, he turned increasingly to more commercial enterprises, from epics such as *The Bible* (1966) and *Waterloo* (1969), to genre items such as *Barbarella* (1968), *Mafioso* (1964), *Anzio* (1968), and the lamentable *King Kong* (1976) remake. On occasion, one of his films, such as *Serpico* (1972), proves distinguished.

Bronson's career has paralleled that of Clint Eastwood to a certain extent. He appeared in routine 1950's films in the United States before going to Europe, where he became a huge star largely with *The Magnificent Seven* (1960), *The Great Escape* (1963), and *The Dirty Dozen* (1967). At one point, Bronson was the world's most "bankable" star, at a time when only buffs with good memories knew who he was. Finally, with *Death Wish*, he became a box-office superstar and has continued to be a much sought-after actor. Many critics found his work in *Death Wish* admirable, forging a convincing portrait of a man slowly and fearfully turning to violence, which he previously abhorred, and ultimately becoming trapped by it.

Almost the only participant unhappy with the film was Brian Garfield, author of the source novel, who felt that the filmmakers unconscionably converted his evil, psychotic killer into a film knight in shining armor. When

CBS, in 1976, announced their intention to telecast the picture, albeit in a heavily edited version, Garfield went to the press to complain, calling the film "dangerous" and sure to "incite kooks." The film, however, was aired without incident. Interestingly, Garfield, partly to atone for the film's sins, wrote a follow-up novel to *Death Wish* called *Death Sentence*, in which he offered alternative solutions to crime other than the vigilantism which the film seemed to advocate. Thus far, it has never been optioned for filming, with Laurentiis one of the first to pass it up.

David Bartholomew

THE DEER HUNTER

Released: 1978
Production: John Peverall for EMI Films; released by Universal (AA)
Direction: Michael Cimino (AA)
Screenplay: Deric Washburn; based on a story by Michael Cimino, Deric Washburn, Louis Garfinkle, and Quinn K. Redeker
Cinematography: Vilmos Zsigmond
Editing: Peter Zinner (AA)
Sound: Richard Portman, William McCaughey, Aaron Rochin, and Darin Knight (AA)
Running time: 180 minutes

Principal characters:
Michael .... Robert De Niro
Nick .... Christopher Walken (AA)
Steven .... John Savage
Stan .... John Cazale
Linda .... Meryl Streep
Axel .... Chuck Aspegren

In a year that was in many ways dominated by quality cinematic reflections of the war in Vietnam such as *Coming Home* and *Go Tell the Spartans*, *The Deer Hunter* won two of the most prestigious and coveted awards of 1978: the New York Film Critics' Circle Award for best English-language film of the year and the Academy Award for the Best Picture of the Year. Among the film's four other Academy Awards was one given to Michael Cimino for Best Director.

The film is epic in scope. Unlike *Coming Home*, in which the war takes place offscreen, and in which we are shown relatively little of the protagonists' lives before they begin to be affected by Vietnam, Cimino in *The Deer Hunter* provides the audience with a substantial amount of detail about his characters' lives both before they go to war and during combat, as well as about their lives in the aftermath of the war. The result is a long film that occasionally seems to lose its way, particularly during the first third, in which Cimino concentrates on character development at the expense of furthering the plot. Once the action moves to Vietnam, however, *The Deer Hunter* becomes a taut, compelling narrative in which Cimino is able to reveal the purgative as well as the destructive effects of war at its worst.

The Deer Hunter is a film of metaphors and images, and opens with an image that is to recur frequently—an awesome blast of fire. In the film's Vietnam sequences, fire signifies destruction and terror; at the beginning, however, the image is less malignant. The flames come from a blast furnace in the Pennsylvania steel mill in which the film's Ukrainian-American protagonists work. This is the last day on the job for Michael (Robert De Niro), Nick (Christopher Walken), and Steven (John Savage). Steven is to be married, and all three are soon to be sent to Vietnam.

As they leave work, the three men, accompanied by their friends Stan (John Cazale) and Axel, head for their neighborhood bar. Cimino demonstrates the camaraderie and affection the men have for one another as they sing along with Frankie Valli on the jukebox, engage in boisterous banter, shoot pool, and down endless bottles of beer. For the most part these are simple, uncomplicated men who clearly revel in one another's company. The only hint of discomfort is provided, not by the imminent departure of three of them, but by Steven's impending marriage, which threatens to interfere with a farewell deer hunt that Michael has suggested.

As they dress for the wedding, Michael and Nick discuss deer hunting. Nick enjoys the aesthetic aspects of the hunt—the mountains and the trees. Michael, on the other hand, is the complete hunter and takes pains to impart his philosophy to Nick: the deer must be killed "with one shot," he emphasizes, "one shot."

Michael, the eldest of his group and its natural leader, is, however, painfully shy and inarticulate around women. Cimino first reveals this side of Michael's personality at Steven's wedding reception. All of his companions are paired off with their girl friends, but Michael stands alone at the bar drinking beer. He is clearly infatuated with Nick's girl friend Linda (Meryl Streep), but cannot bring himself to do more than offer her beer and lurch hesitantly in her direction.

The wedding reception and its aftermath, which are depicted in seemingly endless scenes that could have been shortened without damaging the film in the least, bring out complicated emotions in the three friends. Steven is confused and unhappy because Angela, his bride, is pregnant by another man. The normally inhibited Michael, affected by both the emotion of the occasion and the vast quantity of beer he has consumed, responds by shedding his clothes and running alongside the wedding party. Nick is forced to acknowledge that he loves his hometown, and makes Michael promise that he will bring his body back to Pennsylvania should he die in Vietnam.

Michael leads his friends on a deer hunt before going overseas. Although the hunt is successful, Michael is unhappy because the others refuse to take the endeavor seriously. To Michael, deer hunting is almost a religious rite, and he appears to respect his quarry more than he does his friends. At this point in the film, however, he does not respect the deer enough to spare its life. As evidenced by its title, the film's central metaphor is the deer hunt, and Michael is "the Deer Hunter." He soon learns, however, what it is like to be the game rather than the hunter.

In another blaze of fire, this time rockets, grenades, and flame throwers, the scene shifts to Vietnam. An American unit, including Michael, Nick, and Steven, has been captured by the Viet Cong, who use their prisoners in a bizarre and deadly form of entertainment. The captives are forced to play Russian roulette while their brutal captors wager on who will be the first to die. Cimino directs the scene with a sure hand, and the effect is riveting. The terror and the tension snap something inside both Steven, who eventually recovers, and Nick, who never does; but they bring out the best in Michael, who persuades his captors to put not one but three bullets in the gun, which he then uses on them. The scene is graphic without being sensational. The real violence is that of the spirit—the look on the faces of the sadistically portrayed Viet Cong is far more horrifying than the sight of spurting blood.

The three men escape, but are soon separated. Nick is taken to a hospital in Saigon where he begins to put himself together after his ordeal. He roams the streets in search of his friends, and, hearing the sound of gunfire, discovers that he has stumbled onto a civilian version of the Russian roulette game he endured as a POW. Willing contestants play against one another for a share of the gambling proceeds. Ironically, one of the spectators at the game is Michael, although Nick does not see him. As all of the horror of his own captivity floods back into his mind, Nick snatches a revolver, puts it to his head, and pulls the trigger. The chamber is empty, but something within Nick snaps again, this time for good. He staggers from the room and is taken in tow by the game's proprietor, who promises to make him rich by entering him as a contestant in the suicidal "sport." Michael pursues, but is unable to overtake the pair.

The film follows Michael back to Pennsylvania. He is clearly a changed man. He avoids a welcome home party arranged by his friends, choosing instead to visit Linda, whose picture he has carried throughout the war. She is glad to see him, but the thought of Nick, coupled with Michael's natural reticence, makes communication awkward. They continue seeing each other, however, and Linda finally suggests that they go to bed to "comfort each other." Michael does not want to lose Linda, but he cannot bring himself to respond to her. In addition, he learns that Steven is somewhere in town, although his exact whereabouts is unknown. Michael cannot bring himself to seek out his friend. Cimino thus paints a picture of a man tied in knots by his own suppressed emotions.

That knot is untied during the film's second symbolic deer hunt. While his friends carouse, Michael stalks a magnificent buck. When he gets the animal in his sights, however, he deliberately aims high and fires. "OK?" he shouts, "OK?" It is both a question and an affirmation. Having been both the hunter and the hunted, he discovers within himself the strength *not* to kill. This discovery unlocks a number of doors for Michael. He is able to make love to Linda, and he contacts Steven, who is in a local veteran's hospital, having lost an arm and both legs to the war. He persuades the reluctant Steven to rejoin his family, and, remembering his promise, returns to Vietnam to reclaim his friend Nick.

The next sequences, set in Vietnam, are the most effective and the most harrowing of the film. It is mid-1975, and Vietnam is about to fall to the Communists. Michael arrives in Saigon amid the desperate eleventh-hour attempts of most to flee the country. Overloaded helicopters buck and crash to the ground, and terrified would-be refugees stage full-scale riots as they attempt to board anything moving out of the city. Fires burn out of control, and the river itself seems to be aflame.

Michael locates Nick at the gambling house where the Russian roulette game still flourishes even as the city disintegrates. He attempts to persuade Nick to leave with him, but Nick's eyes are blank; he has spent two years staring death in the face, and he no longer recognizes his best friend. Desperate, Michael buys his way into the game. He will risk suicide to shock Nick back to his senses. As the wrenching tension mounts, both men raise the gun to their heads and pull the trigger. Both survive the first round. As an extra bullet is added to the gun before Nick's next turn, Michael asks Nick to remember their deer hunts in the mountains. Nick smiles in recognition. "One shot," he recalls. He puts the gun to his temple and kills himself.

The film concludes back in Pennsylvania after Nick's funeral. His friends gather in their favorite bar. Though Nick's death grieves them, it seems to signal the end of their ordeal. Steven is reconciled with Angela, and Michael and Linda are together. After an awkward silence, someone begins to hum "God Bless America," and everyone joins in, bringing the film to a close. By ending the film in this way, Cimino reaffirms the sense of community that has pervaded the entire story. Together, they have survived.

Cimino draws first-rate performances from virtually every member of the cast. Christopher Walken won an Academy Award as Best Supporting Actor for his portrayal of Nick, and the performances of John Savage and John Cazale are on a par with Walken's. Walken's transformation of Nick from a bright, sensitive young man into a compulsively suicidal zombie is as convincing as it is horrifying. Savage brings a mixture of nervous energy and sweetness to the character of Steven; and Cazale plays Stan much as he did the part of Fredo Corleone in *The Godfather, Part II* (1974)—as a basically weak man given to macho posturing as compensation. Meryl Streep is likewise excellent as Linda, the film's only major female character. Linda is an island of sanity amidst the physical and psychic chaos of the film.

The Deer Hunter, however, is anchored by the performance of Robert De Niro. His portrayal of Michael is a masterpiece of subtlety and understatement. The dialogue he is given is spare; even more than the rest of the characters in the film, Michael is inarticulate. De Niro compensates by acting with his face—he has never been as expressive. From his explosive rage at his Vietnamese captors to the tenderness he exhibits towards Linda and Nick,

De Niro's performance is flawless.

The film itself, however, is not without flaws, primarily in the first third, which tends to drag. Cimino seems to enjoy the macho camaraderie and the Ukrainian wedding so much that he forgets to keep the plot moving. In addition, some critics have charged Cimino with racism, claiming that he has portrayed all Vietnamese as venal, sadistic killers, and that *The Deer Hunter* represents the Pentagon's version of the war. This is surely a misreading of the film. It was clearly never Cimino's intention to present a balanced, politically "correct" analysis of the war in Vietnam. The director has been quoted as saying that his protagonists are simply "trying to support each other. They are not endorsing anything except their common humanity— their common frailty, their need for each other." While liberals or conservatives who are in search of propaganda are bound to be disappointed in *The Deer Hunter*, viewers who are willing to settle for a gripping story directed with verve and vision and acted with skill and passion will find *The Deer Hunter* a richly rewarding cinematic experience.

Robert Mitchell

THE DEFIANT ONES

Released: 1958
Production: Stanley Kramer for United Artists
Direction: Stanley Kramer
Screenplay: Nathan E. Douglas and Harold Jacob Smith
Cinematography: Sam Leavitt (AA)
Editing: Frederic Knudtson
Running time: 97 minutes

Principal characters:
Joker Jackson	Tony Curtis
Noah Cullen	Sidney Poitier
Sheriff Max Muller	Theodore Bikel
Big Sam	Lon Chaney, Jr.
The Woman	Cara Williams
Billy	Kevin Coughlin

Throughout his career as a producer and director, Stanley Kramer has stood in diametric opposition to an old Hollywood adage often attributed to Sam Goldwyn, that "if you want to send a message, use Western Union." Many of Kramer's films are overtly concerned with social issues, and his position is always that of a political liberal. If, with the passage of time, some of his theses—in the case of *The Defiant Ones*, the idea of the brotherhood of man and the desirability of racial harmony—have come to seem self-evident, they were by no means self-evident when the films were originally released.

When *The Defiant Ones* was released in 1958, the nation had only tentatively begun to commit itself to the goal of racial equality. The Supreme Court outlawed segregated schools, but the process of integration was resulting in massive resistance in the South, and the passage of the landmark Civil Rights Act of 1964 was still in the future. If, in 1958, it seemed to some observers that many whites would never willingly associate with blacks, Kramer had an answer. He produced *The Defiant Ones*, a film showing how two men filled with violent racial antipathy came to respect each other as human beings when forced by circumstances to do so. Kramer's protagonists are literally chained together. This chain symbolizes the inextricable connection between blacks and whites in American society; the experience of living and working together—even if this cooperation is imposed by law and is initially involuntary—should ultimately produce a greater understanding and harmony between the races. This is the implicit message in *The Defiant Ones*.

As the film opens, a group of convicts on a chain gang is being transported by truck back to prison. One of them, a black man named Noah Cullen (Sidney Poitier), is defiantly singing and chanting a song called "Long Gone from Bowling Green." Joker Jackson (Tony Curtis), the white prisoner to whom he is chained, tells him to shut up and calls him a nigger when he refuses. Racial epithets fill the air, and the two men come to blows. The conflict becomes so violent that the truck driver loses control of his vehicle and it plunges off the road. In the ensuing confusion, Noah and Joker escape, still chained together.

The two men are pursued by Sheriff Max Muller (Theodore Bikel) and a motley crew of white townspeople that Muller is forced to deputize for assistance. This group includes the owner of the bloodhounds and dobermans being used to track the escapees, as well as a dim-witted young man who carries a portable radio that blares rock-and-roll music at top volume, much to the disgust of the rest of the posse. Kramer uses this radio as the only comic relief from the intensity of the rest of the film. In addition, he uses the radio in two other ways. The meaninglessness of the music it plays is contrasted with the poignant and deeply felt blues that Noah Cullen sings at the beginning and end of the film. Almost every time the scene shifts from Joker and Noah to the Sheriff and his posse, the transition is heralded by the appearance of music from this radio on the soundtrack.

The efforts of Noah and Joker to break the chain joining them together are unsuccessful. Kramer uses a series of short scenes alternating between the escapees and the posse to establish the basic predicament of each group. The convicts' problem is how to elude the posse while bound together at the wrist by three feet of chain. The physical problems imposed by the chain are considerable, but these problems are insignificant compared to the problems caused by the fact that the two men hate each other.

Sheriff Muller has problems of his own. He is a humane man and wants to recapture the two escapees without harming them. His posse, however, has no such compunctions; they would gladly see Noah and Joker dead. Kramer thus underlines his point with irony: just as Noah and Joker are slowed by mutual antipathy in their attempt to escape, so is the Sheriff's efforts to apprehend the two men hindered by dissension in his ranks.

With the film's basic themes thus foreshadowed, Kramer begins to concentrate on the subtly changing relationship between Noah and Joker. Of the two men, Joker Jackson, the white, is the more bigoted. His racisim is cultural, something, as Noah says, that he breathed in when he was born and that he has been spitting back out ever since. Noah, on the other hand, has been given a better reason to resent whites: a lifetime of racist oppression which culminated in the eviction of his family from their farm by a white man. When Noah resisted this eviction, he was sent to prison for assault.

The hostility between the two men flares constantly, usually as a result of one of Joker's racist insults. Gradually, however, these incidents grow less frequent. Midway through the film, Noah and Joker have their first real conversation (all previous dialogue between the two having been argument or insult). They have stumbled upon a small village which contains a general store where they hope to find tools to break the chain that binds them together. While they await the cover of darkness, they discuss their personal histories— their childhoods, their families, their hopes and fears. They do not become fast friends as a result, but the fact that they converse at all without fighting is significant.

Up to this point, the two fugitives had kept away from people; then, in two long sequences, they interact with other men and women. The first encounter comes as a result of the two men's abortive raid on the general store. Attempting to enter the store through a skylight, Joker slips and injures his wrist, pulling Noah down on top of him and crashing into loaded shelves in the process. The noise rouses the villagers, and the two men are captured.

The mob of townspeople are eager to lynch the convicts. Protesting that no one ever lynched a white man in the South, Joker is stunned to discover that the chain that links him to Noah physically has also linked the two of them spiritually, at least in the minds of the villagers. Only the intervention of Big Sam (Lon Chaney, Jr.), who later reveals to Noah and Joker that he is an ex-convict himself, saves them from the mob. Sam first dissuades the mob from lynching the escapees, and later that night he sneaks into the barn in which they are being held and sets them free.

After making good their escape, Noah and Joker quarrel once more. Their recent brush with death has pushed both men past the breaking point, and this time words cannot settle the argument. In an impressively staged scene, the two men begin to fight savagely. Kramer enhances the effect by placing the camera close to the ground and shooting up at an angle, thus outlining the action against the sky. With no background to provide a distraction, the ferocity of the battle is enhanced.

Just as it appears that the only way the fight will end is with the death of one of the participants, the two men are stopped by a young boy (Kevin Coughlin) with a rifle. Joker knocks the boy down, and he strikes his head on a rock, rendering him momentarily unconscious. Joker wants to run, but Noah insists that they stay and help the boy. When the boy regains consciousness, he is terrified by the sight of a black man and instinctively runs to Joker for shelter. Kramer here underlines Noah's earlier statement that prejudice is something that is breathed in at birth.

The two men learn the boy's name—Billy—and that he and his mother (Cara Williams) live alone in an isolated farmhouse. Assuming that Noah is Joker's prisoner, Billy leads the men to his home, where they force his mother to fix them a meal. Oddly enough, she is more intrigued than frightened by the situation, although she offers Noah food only after Joker insists. This is the first indication that Joker's attitude toward Noah has changed, and as soon as this psychological link is revealed, their physical link is finally broken. With a hammer and chisel, they sever the chain that has bound them together.

Thus Kramer sets the stage for a genuine test of their new relationship.

The question that must be answered is whether or not the two men respect each other enough to stay together now that cooperation is no longer mandatory. Noah is tested first, and he proves loyal to Joker. No sooner are the two men freed from their chain than Joker collapses; his injured wrist has become badly infected. Noah, who might have taken this opportunity to flee, chooses to stay until his partner recovers.

That night, Billy's mother—never given a name in the film—comes to Joker's bedside. When he awakens, they talk and discover that they have much in common—including a deep sense of loneliness. They sleep together that night. Convinced that Joker is her ticket out of her lonely life and that Noah is a threat to her plans, Billy's mother schemes to separate the two men. She asks Joker to leave with her and suggests that Noah could escape easily on his own by hopping one of the trains that passes on the nearby tracks. Joker is uneasy about splitting up with Noah, but is ultimately persuaded to do so.

After Noah has left, however, the woman reveals that the path between her house and the railroad tracks is an impenatrable swamp, and that Noah has virtually no chance of surviving his run for freedom. Joker is furious; what he thought was only a separation from Noah has become a betrayal. He strikes the woman, and Billy shoots him in the shoulder. Finally, he staggers off in pursuit of Noah. As it turns out, he leaves just ahead of the Sheriff, who has tracked the men down. There is one last confrontation between the Sheriff and his posse over whether to use the vicious dogs to hunt the convicts down. The Sheriff wins the argument, but it is clear that if his humanitarian methods fail, he will lose his job.

Joker catches up with Noah, and the two men race through the swamp pursued by the Sheriff and his posse. They reach the train, and Noah jumps aboard, but Joker, weakened by the loss of blood from his wound, cannot make it. Noah extends his hand and Joker grabs for it, but by now he is dead weight, and Noah is pulled from the train. As they sit, exhausted, Noah cradles the wounded Joker in his arms. "We gave 'em a hell of a run for it, didn't we?," Joker asks. As the Sheriff approaches, Noah begins to sing "Long Gone from Bowling Green;" while the screen fades to black, he chuckles.

Thus Kramer resolves the film's two conflicts in a positive way. The conflict between Sheriff Muller and his posse indicates that the issue of race is not the sole source of disharmony in the world; and the fact that the Sheriff's humane tactics resulted in the recapture of the escapees shows that the humanitarian approach need not be ineffectual. The more important conflict, of course, is the racial antagonism between Joker Jackson and Noah Cullen. The hardwon resolution of this conflict reflects Kramer's basic optimism about the prospect for racial harmony in society at large.

At the time of its release, *The Defiant Ones* was controversial, at least among the general populace. Critics were less divided. The film received eight Academy Award nominations, including Best Picture and Best Director. Bikel as the stolid, oddly pacifistic Sherrif Muller and Williams as the lonely, conniving woman who tries to separate Joker and Noah turn in solid performances that won them justified nominations for Best Supporting Actor and Actress. Chaney is memorable in the smaller role of Big Sam, the ex-convict who helped Noah and Joker escape from the lynch mob. Poitier and Curtis turn in truly memorable performances in extremely demanding roles. Poitier's performance is perhaps the superior of the two, since Noah Cullen's character is a good deal more complex than that of Joker Jackson, and thus requires more subtlety to put across. Joker is all rage and desperation. Noah is angry and desperate too, but he has an instinctive compassion as well, which is something that Joker is only beginning to learn as the film ends. Both men received Academy Award nominations as Best Actor for their performances.

As good as the acting is, however, the primary focus of *The Defiant Ones* is its message, an affirmation of the brotherhood of man. Ironically, the original strength of the film has been diluted somewhat by the passage of time; the sentiments are less radical, more commonplace. If the message of brotherhood seems a bit obvious now, however, it is surely no less valid. *The Defiant Ones* is not merely a social document; it is an important and powerful cinematic landmark.

Robert Mitchell

DELIVERANCE

Released: 1972
Production: John Boorman and Elmer Enterprises Films for Warner Bros.
Direction: John Boorman
Screenplay: James Dickey; based on his novel of the same name
Cinematography: Vilmos Zsigmond
Editing: Tom Priestley
Running time: 109 minutes

> *Principal characters:*
> Ed Gentry .... Jon Voight
> Lewis Medlock .... Burt Reynolds
> Bobby Trippe .... Ned Beatty
> Drew Ballinger .... Ronny Cox
> Sheriff Bullard .... James Dickey

Deliverance is, at first glance, an exciting but obvious mix of fairly standard themes: the rape of nature by "progress," the city men who find their own "heart of darkness" in the dangerous rapids, the horrifying degeneracy of backwoods folk, and the breakdown of civilized morality under survival conditions. Along with these literary themes, biblical allusions, primarily to the flood which will cleanse a sinful world, add to the first-glance impression of obvious allegory; but this impression is deceptive.

In-depth critical articles demonstrate this deceptiveness in their contradictory interpretations of the film. Some call it a "boyish adventure turned sour," others bemoan the *macho* cliches which Lewis Medlock (Burt Reynolds) both voices and stands for, while still others see a rejection of these values in Lewis' fate. Jon Voight's performance as Ed Gentry, the timid but curious city-dweller who eventually is thrust into a leadership role, elicited particularly diverse comment. Some praised his convincing transformation, others found his mild-mannered personality hard to believe. Actually, this early part of his performance is compromised by too-obvious symbols: he clutches a pipe in his teeth in awkward moments and is given ridiculous lines which ring hollow even when he is supposed to be drunk. Worst of all, he continues to treat the brutally sadistic mountain men who torment him and Bobby Trippe (Ned Beatty) like fellow board members, repeating "Gentlemen, there must be some misunderstanding" long after it is an appropriate response. The very diversity of serious reactions to *Deliverance* indicates its strongest quality: it remains a richly ambiguous film from viewing to viewing.

Deliverance won five major prizes at the Fifth Annual Atlanta Film Festival and was nominated for three Academy Awards: Best Picture, Best Direction, and Best Editing. Adapted by James Dickey from his critically successful novel, the story concerns four city men who decide to canoe down the Cahulawassee River, which is about to be flooded in a "progressive" measure to dam the river and put the entire area at the bottom of a lake. Lewis is the *machismo*-driven leader of the group who wants the "machines and the system to break down," leaving only "survival." Bobby is an overweight salesman, and Drew Ballinger (Ronnie Cox) is a gentle, decent, guitar-playing soul who is least able to cope with the events of their odyssey.

The four men first have to deal with the mountain folk to hire someone to drive their cars down to their landing point, and their different reactions are clues to their characters. Bobby finds the people repulsive in their genetic inbreeding; Drew makes musical contact with a seemingly retarded boy in the film's famous "dueling banjoes" sequence; Lewis bargains with the men; and Ed looks on, curious but uninvolved.

Once on the river, the men experience the exuberant thrill of the wild rapids, and camp at night in boozy comradeship. The next day Ed and Bobby stop in the thick wilderness and are attacked by two degenerate mountain men. Ed is tied while one rapes Bobby, then just as the other prepares to force Ed to perform fellatio on him, Lewis shoots an arrow through the first man with his powerful bow. The four argue over what they should do next: Lewis urges that they bury the body, while Drew thinks they should take it with them and report the incident to the police. Lewis wins out, and they bury the man, whose outstretched arm will not willingly stay underground.

They leave in a near panic, and a shaken Drew fails to put his lifejacket on. Just before they reach the dangerous rapids, Drew falls (or jumps) over-board, and in the ensuing confusion, both canoes capsize and the men are swept down the rocky rapids. Lewis' leg is badly broken, and Drew, the audience learns later, is killed. Thinking that Drew was shot by the murdered rapist's companion, Ed scales the difficult cliff and kills the man he finds there. Similar to the question of whether Drew was actually shot, the certainty of the second man's identity is not clear. The three men continue on to town, where Sheriff Bullard (James Dickey) does not quite believe their story but lets them go, telling them never to do anything like this again, and not to return. At home in bed with his wife, Ed wakes in fear at his dream of a stiff hand breaking through the smooth surface of the lake.

Ambiguities abound. Is man raping the river by damming it, as Lewis claims in his voice-over at the beginning of the film, or is the flood represented by the lake cleansing the evil of the town? Is the virgin river and dense wilderness surrounding it pure and ennobling or evil? Are the backwoods people an affront to nature in their genetic deficiencies, or do they only appear horrible from the city men's point of view? Who is innocent? Some reviewers called the poverty-stricken natives "simpletons," but we have to agree with the man who tells the four, "you don't know nothin'" in response to their plan to canoe down the river. When asked why they are doing it, Lewis answers, "Because it's there," and a mountain man sensibly replies:

"It's there alright. You get in there and can't get out, you gonna wish it wasn't."

The teasing homosexual quality of Ed and Lewis' relationship is restricted almost entirely to visual elements in the film (it is more extensive in the book), although Lewis does pointedly ask Ed why he comes on these trips with him. Lewis is photographed sensuously, especially from Ed's point of view. The homosexual element is another flirtation for Ed and Lewis, just as is the danger of the river. The men seem titillated by the possibilities, until both sexual and danger attractions turn ugly as they become real during the rape and the later injuries and death. Special mention must be made of the rape scene, which is one of the most honest rape sequences ever filmed. Neither character involved is attractive, so that perverse erotic appeal does not exist. Instead of being sexy, the rape is violent, repulsive, humiliating, and ugly. No attempt is made to glamorize it; actors and filmmakers are to be congratulated for showing the true nature of this violent act that so much fiction makes attractive.

During Ed's transformation from a passive observer to a man of action, his voyeurism, a central element of his character, is destroyed. He is forced to watch Bobby's rape, then to see his hero Lewis nearly helpless after his leg is injured. Ed, who earlier could not shoot a deer, kills a man. The change in him is a key to the title of the film; but here too is fertile ambiguity. Is Ed "delivered," and if so, from what state and to what state? He has become a killer, a leader, a man of responsibility and of guilt. His deliverance is from naïveté, security, and innocence to liberating yet incriminating responsibility. Never again will any of the men see "civilization" and "nature" as simple dichotomies. They came looking for momentary deliverance from boredom, tame technology, and security, but found the necessary correlative to what they were seeking: deliverance from comfort and from innocence into complexity. The mountain men who daily face the "survival" conditions Lewis romantically longs for are not ennobled, but rather become sadistic brutes. The river is not a symbol for virgin purity or for degeneracy; it is a potent force which can push men farther in the direction in which they are already headed.

The visual style of *Deliverance* is a major factor in the rich ambiguity the film poses. Under extremely difficult conditions, the film was shot in sequence (an unusual and expensive method), using U.S. Navy Underwater Demolition team rafts outfitted with cameras. Director of cinematography Vilmos Zsigmond used long lenses to keep characters in close-up, abstracting them from their environment. There are extremely long takes throughout the film, unusual for such fast action, which create an impression of a sensuous, dreamy flow. The intimacy of close-ups and tight frame also gives the film an impressive immediacy, seeming to draw the viewer right into the river.

Deliverance is an excellent example of Hollywood's "new wave" of location shooting. The mix of literary themes and realistic visual style is particularly fruitful when easy answers are refused, and the complex tangle of causes and effects are left up to the viewer to unravel.

Janey Place

DESIGN FOR LIVING

Released: 1933
Production: Ernst Lubitsch for Paramount
Direction: Ernst Lubitsch
Screenplay: Ben Hecht; based on the play of the same name by Noel Coward
Cinematography: Victor Milner
Editing: Francis Marsh
Interior decoration: Hans Dreier
Running time: 90 minutes

> *Principal characters:*
> Tom .... Fredric March
> George .... Gary Cooper
> Gilda .... Miriam Hopkins
> Max Plunkett .... Edward Everett Horton

Although *Design for Living* is adapted from a play by Noel Coward which featured Alfred Lunt, Lynn Fontanne, and Coward himself, the film is a free adaptation owing not much more to the play than the basic premise of a *menage-a-trois*. In place of three sophisticated theater types, the film has down-to-earth Gary Cooper, Fredric March, and Miriam Hopkins; and Ben Hecht, who wrote the screenplay, has boasted of keeping only one line of dialogue originally written by Coward. Ernst Lubitsch could be counted on to invest this material with his own personality, as he invariably did in all of his films, and the result is an affecting comedy that is one of his finest works. Although Lubitsch is sometimes accused of squandering his talent on frivolous trifles, it is to his credit that there is no false solemnity in his films, that he could keep them light and sparkling while unfailingly revealing touching depths of emotion in his characters in the midst of so much laughter.

Lubitsch's heroine is Gilda (Miriam Hopkins), who combines the best qualities of mother, lover, partner, and good luck charm in encouraging the artistic endeavors of Tom (Fredric March) and George (Gary Cooper), two friends who both fall in love with her at the same time. Believing themselves capable of an unconventional arrangement to solve their romantic problems, the three guileless Americans agree that they will live together without sex and that Gilda will be the inspiration for the two unsuccessful men to become famous as playwright and painter, respectively. When Tom's play becomes a hit, however, he must travel to London alone, leaving George and Gilda together on the Continent. The arrangement fails, and Tom returns to find George, now a successful painter, living happily with Gilda. As Gilda still loves Tom as well as George, she becomes Tom's lover in George's absence, and soon the threesome is back where it began, with the result that Gilda resolves to marry the prissy Max Plunkett (Edward Everett Horton). The two buddies manage to steal her away before the wedding, and Gilda, Tom, and George find themselves together in the back of a taxi vowing, perhaps more knowingly, to return to the terms of the original agreement.

The most startling aspect of this situation, which is at once comic and morally challenging, is that the heroine never conceals the fact that she is in love with both men and is unwilling to lose either one. This places Tom and George in a position of having to be liberated men long before such a concept even existed. Gilda may be embraced as a glorious role model who personifies much that is meaningful in an emerging feminist spirit, but Tom and George, although sometimes bewildered and melancholy on her account, deserve our affection for much the same reason. Throughout the film, they strive with Gilda to find a new world, free of jealousy and inappropriate values, without ever failing to be humanly vulnerable. Although the film does not explicitly endorse a life-style which would permit Gilda to be the lover of both men, its images affirm that this is the true solution to the problem, and there is a subtle implication that the threesome is ready to accept this solution after the fadeout.

The film's inherited title cleverly offers a clue to a conflict between reason and instinct. The characters *design* a relationship which excludes physical love, but *living* is not possible within such a design. Whenever Gilda, George, and Tom are shown together in a single image, a feeling of balance and harmony is achieved. The separation of one of these characters from the group creates tension. The two men complement each other in every way, and their friendship is completed by their adoration of Gilda. It makes perfect sense that she is never able to choose between them. The complexity of affection shared by all three of these people makes the situation entrancingly romantic.

Lubitsch has a great deal of fun with this romanticism. In a lovingly designed garrett shared by the two starving artists, Gilda shows up for a date and attractively falls back on a couch which immediately reveals that it is covered with dust. The dust rises, causing the *femme fatale* to cough at the exact moment she is most determined to show her composure. Later in the story, when she has put the room into a more orderly fashion, Gilda is left alone with George. They speak of their gentleman's agreement with Tom, and Gilda, unable to resist the temptation of pleasure, once more relaxes on the couch, seductively admitting, "I'm no gentleman."

While all of the scenes involving the threesome are captivating, as are those involving any two of the three characters, the best moment is reserved for Tom alone. Estranged from George and Gilda, Tom is leading the life of a successful playwright without pleasure. He goes to the theater where his inane comedy, *Goodnight, Bassington*, is playing. As he solemnly walks down the aisle with an irresistibly melancholy expression, the audience which fills the theater laughs unreservedly at every ridiculous line of dialogue coming from the stage. The climax of the scene is reached when the curtain line—which finds the hapless Bassington admonished with insipid words of wisdom once spoken by Max Plunkett and remembered by the discerning Tom—is greeted with the loudest laughter yet and thunderous applause. Tom reacts with all the emotional expressiveness of a zombie.

Without forgetting that the 1930's abounded in memorable comedies, it is appropriate to single out *Design for Living* as one of the most sophisticated, provocative, and funny films of that decade. Hecht, a writer supremely adaptable to the differing personalities of an impressive number of great directors, provides a Lubitsch script which rivals those of Samson Raphaelson in romantic richness and sparkling wit. The offbeat casting of March and Cooper is extremely effective, the touch of naïveté which these two actors possess making the characters of Tom and George endearingly sweet and lovable. It must be admitted, however, that March is considerably more convincing than Cooper in a drunk scene. Hopkins had previously appeared in several Lubitsch films, but even her beguiling performance opposite the supremely elegant Herbert Marshall in *Trouble in Paradise* (1932) is less lustrous than her incarnation of the bewitching Gilda, a woman in whom boldness and innocence coexist so appealingly that it is absolutely credible that the two men do not seek relationships with less complex women. The film is also enhanced by the lovely visual design and lighting expected in Lubitsch's work and, above all, by the limpidity and discretion of the director's style, which, at its most assured, is one of the most graceful to be found in cinema.

Blake Lucas

DESIGNING WOMAN

Released: 1957
Production: Dore Schary for Metro-Goldwyn-Mayer
Direction: Vincente Minnelli
Screenplay: George Wells (AA); based on a suggestion by Helen Rose
Cinematography: John Alton
Editing: Adrienne Fazan
Art direction: William A. Horning and Preston Ames; set decoration, Edwin
    B. Willis and Henry Grace
Costume design: Helen Rose
Choreography: Jack Cole and Barrie Chase
Running time: 118 minutes

Principal characters:
Mike Hagen	Gregory Peck
Marilla Hagen	Lauren Bacall
Lori Shannon	Dolores Gray
Ned Hammerstein	Sam Levene
Zachary Wilde	Tom Helmore
Maxie Stultz	Mickey Shaughnessy
Randy Owens	Jack Cole

Designing Woman is reminiscent of films starring the much-loved team of Katharine Hepburn and Spencer Tracy, especially *Woman of the Year* (1942), which had united that couple on screen for the first time. The film grew out of a suggestion, for which costume designer Helen Rose was credited, to have a sports writer and a fashion designer marry. This was a clever and imaginative idea, and it is easy to imagine Tracy and Hepburn in the respective roles, even as late as 1957, with their superb comic timing and the special romantic chemistry between them undiminished by time. Moreover, both had worked very effectively under the direction of Vincente Minnelli, Hepburn in *Undercurrent* (1946) and Tracy in *Father of the Bride* (1950) and *Father's Little Dividend* (1951). For whatever reason, however, it appears they were never involved in the project. James Stewart and Grace Kelly were tentatively set to star in the film, having already demonstrated a pleasing rapport in *Rear Window* (1954), a dissimilar work but one in which the two characters, a rugged journalist and a sophisticated model, are roughly equivalent. According to Stewart, he did not want to do the film without Kelly, who unexpectedly retired as the result of her marriage to Prince Ranier of Monaco.

Warm thoughts of Stewart and Kelly, let alone Tracy and Hepburn, should not obscure the fact that Gregory Peck and Lauren Bacall are more than acceptable in the film. In one sense, their unfamiliarity with each other is an advantage, as the story concerns a man and woman who know almost nothing about each other before their marriage and the adjustments each must make to bring stability and permanence to the relationship. The rare opportunity to play comedy was one which greatly pleased Peck, and both he and Bacall are surprisingly amusing. Inevitable comparisons with Tracy and Hepburn are mildly ungracious, and they do not serve to illuminate the particular charm of *Designing Woman*. For all its affinities with earlier romantic and screwball comedies, the film has a distinctive character of its own. Imagination, wit, and a pleasing unpredictability easily lift it to the level of the best Tracy-Hepburn films.

Marilla (Lauren Bacall) and Mike Hagen (Gregory Peck) are both from New York, but they meet in Southern California; and their brief romantic courtship is not intruded upon by the disparate realities of their respective worlds at home. Once they arrive back in New York as man and wife, however, she is dismayed by his prosaic apartment and he is intimidated by the elegance and spaciousness of hers. Bowing to practicality, Mike moves in with Marilla. The two are then introduced to each other's friends and milieus. Marilla is sickened by the sight of blood at a prize fight, and Mike is contemptuous of the ceremonious gentility of a fashion show. Complicating matters further, both Mike and Marilla must resolve their past romantic involvements. Mike is unreasonably resentful of Broadway producer Zachary Wilde (Tom Helmore), although Marilla had refused Wilde's proposals of marriage. At the same time, frightened by Marilla's potential jealousy, Mike unwisely attempts to conceal his former relationship with musical star Lori Shannon (Dolores Gray). Conflict between the couple accelerates when Mike attempts to hold his weekly poker game at their apartment on the same night that Marilla is hosting a production meeting for a Broadway show on which she is working. Both Mike and Marilla single out one of the other's associates for scorn. Marilla is appalled by punchdrunk ex-fighter Maxie Stultz (Mickey Shaughnessy), while Mike is embarrassed by the effusive choreographer Randy Owens (Jack Cole). Neither is being fair. Maxie, both humorously and pitiably uncomprehending of the realities of life, was once a champion. Randy, although ridiculously posturing, is an artist. Overhearing Mike's brutal and thoughtless insinuation that he is a homosexual, Randy confronts the other with dignity, brandishing photos of his wife and children and expressing his willingness to defend his honor physically.

Resolution of the differences between Mike and Marilla is made more difficult by ensuing events. Both Wilde and Lori are involved in the same Broadway show as Marilla. Mike is sent into hiding by his editor Ned Hammerstein (Sam Levene) in order to complete an exposé of the involvement of mobsters in the fight game. With Maxie assigned as a bodyguard, Mike holes up in a hotel but fools Marilla into believing he is traveling around the country to report on the New York Yankees baseball team. Ultimately, Mike jeopardizes his safety to reconcile with Marilla, and surprisingly, it is the agile

Owens who subdues the gangsters with his balletic kicks and jumps. In the end, Wilde and Lori become romantic partners, Mike and Marilla are reunited, accepting each other with a new maturity, and Maxie continues to train, confident that a comeback awaits him.

Two related motifs, one serious and one fanciful, provide the fabric which serves the work's design. The serious motif is the difficulty of adjustment in marriage. Differing attitudes, experiences, and ways of life must somehow be accepted by even the most ardent lovers if marriage is to succeed. Mike and Marilla both look at life subjectively. Confronted by the other's world, each regards it as bizarre and threatening. The jealousy and petulance evinced in the responses of Mike and Marilla to Zachary Wilde and Lori Shannon may seem childish and quaint, but as a symptom of the mutual insecurity with which they confront their differences, this emotional immaturity is very meaningful.

The second and more fanciful motif is the convergence of four separate worlds: fashion, news reporting, the theater, and the underworld. It is this convergence which aggravates the problems of the central couple and makes the situations presented so funny. A highlight is the sharing of the apartment by the two groups respectively associated with Mike and Marilla. Initially, a dividing screen separates the groups, but as the sequence progresses, people from each group begin to wander throughout the space of the apartment. The screen is opened and the ritual poker players must observe the creative enthusiasm of Randy, who begins to dance about the apartment with abandon. Director Minnelli, enamored of the visual humor and disarming mood implicit in the juxtaposition of milieus, composes much of the sequence so that the groups share the space within a shot. This disharmony between foreground and background is engagingly reckless. It also visually provokes an unsought complicity between the groups which amusingly undermines the accepted patterns of behavior particular to each milieu. The sequence is at once magical and credible, and as a consequence, the individual perceptions of reality to which Mike and Marilla cling are accorded a strange respect at the same time that they are revealed to be tenuous.

These motifs are not at all surprising in a work by Minnelli, and their latent presence in the premise of *Designing Woman* explains his attraction to the project. From *Father of the Bride* to *The Courtship of Eddie's Father* (1963), all of his comedies have involved courtship and marriage. These subjects are not unusual in American comedy, but Minnelli's predilection for finding a whimsical or nightmarish weirdness in character and situation and the humor he derives from this predilection are idiosyncrasies of his art. Minnelli was generally brought into projects at an early stage, and *Designing Woman* was no exception, so it is natural that the director's personality is evident in George Wells's Academy Award-winning screenplay as well as in the realized film.

Both men deserve credit for the delightful character touches and incidental inventiveness which enliven the work. The moment in which Lori, informed by Mike of his sudden marriage, calmly pushes a plate of ravioli onto his lap is a high point, well-placed in the script and hilariously underplayed by Peck and Gray. The use of a multiple point of view to tell the story contributes immeasurably to the playful mood so well-sustained throughout the film. The device of a narrated flashback had been favored by Minnelli in two earlier comedies, *Father of the Bride* and *The Long, Long Trailer* (1954), but in those instances there was only one narrator. In *Designing Woman*, five voices—those of Mike, Marilla, Lori Shannon, Zachary Wilde, and Maxie Stultz—alternate. The resulting contradictory accounts of the events presented in the narrative enriches the audience's perspective as well as enhances the film's comic intentions.

The attention to decor and color characteristic of Minnelli's films is wonderfully manifested in the varying visual moods of *Designing Woman*'s contrasting worlds. Tasteful and lovely, Marilla's apartment is the opposite of the sleazy hotel room in which Mike is isolated with Maxie. The theater, the boxing arena, the fashion salon—each has a distinctive look, sometimes pretty, sometimes gaudy, always evocative. John Alton's lighting also contributes expressively to the film's fanciful nature. One example of this is the distorting glow on Maxie's face whenever his mind is most unhinged. This touch of artificiality is appropriate to Maxie, next to Randy Owens the film's most surprising character. Minnelli's characters often seem to be dreaming while awake, and Maxie provides a nice twist to this predisposition. He sleeps with his eyes open.

Blake Lucas

DESK SET

Released: 1957
Production: Henry Ephron for Twentieth Century-Fox
Direction: Walter Lang
Screenplay: Henry Ephron and Phoebe Ephron; based on the play of the same name by William Marchant
Cinematography: Daniel L. Fapp
Editing: Robert Simpson
Running time: 103 minutes

Principal characters:

Richard Sumner	Spencer Tracy
Barbara "Bunny" Watson	Katharine Hepburn
Mike Cutler	Gig Young
Peg Costello	Joan Blondell
Sylvia	Dina Merrill
Ruthie	Sue Randall
Miss Warriner	Neva Patterson
Smithers	Harry Ellerbe
Mr. Azae	Nicholas Joy

Motion pictures about career women usually focus on an assumed conflict between a woman's career and her femininity. Some of these films, such as *His Girl Friday* (1940), *Woman of the Year* (1942), and *Adam's Rib* (1949), use comedy to illustrate this conflict. *Desk Set* differs from these films because the problem of its career-woman protagonist, Bunny Watson (Katharine Hepburn), is not preserving her womanliness but preserving her job. Bunny's job is one which has been long dominated by women—the reference librarian—but an executive decision has been made to replace her with a machine. Ironically, the machine itself is "female." It has been titled "Miss Emmy," a nickname composed by humanizing its official title of "Emmarac," but it is actually an inside joke against the television media. ("Emmy," of course, refers to the yearly awards presented by the National Academy of Television Arts and Sciences.) "Miss Emmy" is a machine designed to replace "the girls" of the Federal Broadcasting Company's research department. The girls must prove that their job skills cannot be usurped by a machine.

No one questions their femininity. In fact, in Bunny's first scene she waltzes into her office and shows her staff the new dress she has purchased to dazzle Mike Cutler (Gig Young) in hopes that he will ask her to the company's yearly dinner dance. The staff responds with appropriate girlishness. Only Peg Costello (Joan Blondell) throws a bit of cold water onto the gay plans by indicating that Bunny's seven-year romance with Mike Cutler has all the charm of an "old coat."

After the character of Bunny and the office staff is established, Richard Sumner (Spencer Tracy) walks quietly in to visit the department prior to installing the Emmarac computer that he designed. Sumner meets Bunny, and the two wage mental warfare over lunch. This scene takes full advantage of the famous Tracy-Hepburn tradition. She is once again the quick-witted, incisive feminist while he is a seemingly conventional and complacent male with a curious mind but stubborn attitudes. The Tracy-Hepburn tradition informs the audience immediately that these two will fall in love with each other albeit against their wills. Bunny is determined not to allow her staff to be replaced with a machine, and Sumner is determined that his machine shall be installed.

Love emerging out of competition with a man is a familiar theme in films about career women. In the films previously mentioned, *Woman of the Year*, *Adam's Rib*, and others, the woman relinquishes ideals of independence to receive love. The woman is usually pictured as insolently aggressive while the man is tolerantly confident of his point-of-view. This basic premise is especially true in the Tracy-Hepburn films. Tracy's characters usually give Hepburn's just enough rope with which to hang themselves. When Hepburn sneaks into her estranged husband's apartment in George Stevens's *Woman of the Year*, she attempts to prepare a complete breakfast even though she does not even know how to use a toaster successfully. Her cooking is an attempt to win acclaim from him by being more womanly. The idea is offensive to feminists, but the scene is uproariously funny.

Competition in *Desk Set* is of a different sort. Here, the inventor of the computer is not perceived as the competition. Instead, the machine itself is the threat. In fact, Bunny must ultimately compete with "Miss Emmy" in order to win Richard Sumner's love. She orders Richard to prove his love by allowing "Miss Emmy" to go full tilt and break down. When the inevitable destruction has ocurred, Bunny provides the hairpin with which Richard is allowed to repair the machine. Ultimately Bunny and Richard establish a trade-off in which Bunny proves that a human brain is needed in the research department while Richard shows that Emmarac can liberate the research staff from repetitious routine. Thus, this motion picture has at least one fully realized modern idea of the computer age as well as presenting a career woman who does not have to give up her job for love.

Besides the unusual triangle of Bunny, Sumner, and "Miss Emmy," there is also the triangle of Bunny, Sumner, and Mike Cutler, the promising network executive who has courted Bunny for seven years. It is obvious from the beginning that Cutler will be the loser in this contest for Bunny's affections, principally because of our expectations of a Tracy-Hepburn film. Beyond that, however, Cutler's eager-beaver "man in the gray-flannel suit" personality is ill-suited to Hepburn's frizzy hair and independent demeanor. Hepburn looks just as jubilantly nonconformist in *Desk Set* as she did as Jo in *Little Women* some twenty-four years earlier. Cutler, played with banal aplomb by Young, frets constantly about feasibility studies and his imminent promotion. He drops everything, including a marriage proposal, in midsentence if the boss rings for him.

The film's fast-paced narrative and the capable performances of all the actors make *Desk Set* enjoyable entertainment. The dialogue is witty, and Hepburn's barbed jibes are answered with appropriately dry humor by Tracy. Blondell plays Peg, a wise-cracking contrast to the otherwise sophomoric reference staff. Also, her cynicism counters Young's perennial zealousness. The milieu of the television network is not emphasized, and the film could take place within any corporate structure. The film thus misses an opportunity to comment upon the cultural phenomenon of the still-infant electronic media during its first decade of national preeminence.

The original Broadway play was produced by Robert Fryer and Lawrence Carr from the play by William Marchant and starred Shirley Booth. Henry and Phoebe Ephron, who adapted the play for the screen, change the ending considerably: it was their idea for the computer expert and Bunny to fall in love. Indeed, the Ephrons built their careers upon translating Broadway plays to the Technicolor screen. Among their often shared credits are *Carousel* (1956), *Daddy Long Legs* (1955), and *The Best Things in Life are Free* (1956). Director Walter Lang also specialized in transforming plays into motion pictures; his credits include *The King and I* (1956), and *Can-Can* (1960).

Elizabeth Ward

THE DESPERATE HOURS

Released: 1955
Production: William Wyler for Paramount
Direction: William Wyler
Screenplay: Joseph Hayes; based on his novel and play of the same name
Cinematography: Lee Garmes
Editing: Robert Swink
Running time: 112 minutes

Principal characters:
Glenn Griffin	Humphrey Bogart
Dan Hilliard	Fredric March
Jesse Bard	Arthur Kennedy
Eleanor Hilliard	Martha Scott
Hal Griffin	Dewey Martin
Chuck (Cindy's boyfriend)	Gig Young
Cindy Hilliard	Mary Murphy
Ralphie Hilliard	Richard Eyer
Kobish	Robert Middleton

When *The Desperate Hours* opened in October, 1955, the reviews were good, although not ecstatic. Although director William Wyler received critical praise for his fine craftsmanship, and the stars, Humphrey Bogart and Fredric March, were mentioned as having given their usual excellent performances, the film did not receive well-deserved plaudits—perhaps because all of the elements were predictable.

Wyler had, by this point in his career, directed some fifty feature films, received eleven Academy Award nominations and two Academy Awards, plus two New York Film Critics Awards and numerous foreign honors. One of his most successful and best-loved films, *Roman Holiday* (1953), was still fresh in the mind of the public. In short, no one expected him to do less than a fine job.

The same is true of Bogart's performance. In his role as Glenn Griffin, he is the leader of three escaped convicts who take over a typical house in an average American city and hold the family hostage. Outlaws, ex-cons, gangsters, social deviates: Bogart had played them all at one time or another, and he played them to perfection. This was a role he could walk through with his eyes closed; yet a close study of his performance reveals that he gave the part much more than just a walk-through.

His squint-eyed, dry-mouthed portrait of a criminal awaiting his chance for revenge is blood-chilling. There is a ferocity about his being that is just below the surface, always on the verge of exploding, and this is what creates the tension between him and the March character, Dan Hilliard. As Hilliard tells his wife Eleanor (Martha Scott) at one point, "Griffin hates me. He hated me before he even saw me. I can't explain it. Every hour some new black hole appears in him. . . . God knows what a mind like that will turn to. . . ." Bogart makes us believe the truth of that statement in every scene.

As Dan Hilliard, March was also re-creating a familiar role. He had played solid, upright, perfectly average citizens most of his career. In *The Desperate Hours*, if Bogart is believably unstable, March is believably average. He is the unheroic hero, forced into the role and not sure of his ability to change anything. As the "desperate hours" pass (the Hilliard home is occupied by the Griffin gang for about thirty-six hours in all), March counsels and comforts his wife, his ten-year-old son Ralphie (Richard Eyer), and his teenage daughter Cindy (Mary Murphy), but he derives his strength as much from them as they do from him. When he does act, it is because his family, little by little, has made him aware of his options and his choices. March's performance creates as complete a characterization as does Bogart's. Quiet despair counterpointing tense courage is present in his eyes, in the set of his jaw and of his shoulders. It is a thoroughly believable portrait of an average family man under siege.

Dan Hilliard works in a department store. We see him going to work one morning, kissing his wife good-bye. We see his daughter Cindy leave for work and his son Ralphie leave for school. When the doorbell rings, Mrs. Hilliard opens the door unsuspectingly and admits the three hoodlums who take over her home. Glenn Griffin, his younger brother Hal (Dewey Martin), and the big, hulking Sam Kobish (Robert Middleton) have just escaped from the state penitentiary. Glenn Griffin has a score to settle with Jesse Bard (Arthur Kennedy), a cop who not only sent him to prison, but also broke his jaw so it had to be wired in place for months. Griffin spent those months in the penitentiary plotting his revenge.

The Griffin gang holes up in the Hilliard home to wait for Glenn's girl friend to deliver some money; then they intend to hire a killer to go after Bard. The plan is simple, but problems start to crop up. Glenn receives word that his girl friend has been arrested for running a red light; she will not be able to arrive by midnight as they had planned. He instructs her to put the money in the mail special delivery to Dan Hilliard's office; the gang will have to remain in the Hilliard home for at least another day.

On day number two, Mr. Patterson, the man who collects the trash, becomes inquisitive. He spots the gang's getaway car hidden in the garage and makes the connection between it, some coffee cups and cigarettes on the Hilliard kitchen table, and a stack of newspapers with headlines telling of the Griffin gang's escape from prison. He makes a note of the car's license number but it is the last note he ever writes. Kobish takes him for a ride in his own trash truck and kills him.

This is the gang's first mistake. Jesse Bard has been at the stationhouse directing the search for the twenty-four hours since the breakout occurred.

Bard has a hunch that Griffin and his gang will show up locally to settle their old score. When Patterson's body is found and the license number on a scrap in his pocket links him to the Griffin gang, Bard has all he needs. Also in the pocket are the checks he had collected on his morning rounds, and it becomes a simple exercise for Bard to find the neighborhood Patterson had been working. Before he can set to work combing the neighborhood, however, he receives an anonymous note (sent by Dan Hilliard) advising him that innocent people's lives are at stake. Reluctantly, Bard calls off a door-to-door search of the area.

Up until now, the basic point of tension has been the duel of nerves between Dan Hilliard and Glenn Griffin. Now the pace quickens. The duel is amplified; conflicts erupt on all levels. There is one between Bard and a hard-line cop who believes the law should close in, without regard to the anonymous citizen's plea. There is one between Glenn Griffin and his younger brother Hal, who, angered by the long, senseless wait, takes off into the night and is shot and killed by police. There is one between Hilliard and his wife, and another between Cindy and her boyfriend Chuck (Gig Young).

Each conflict, besides demonstrating heightened tension, advances the plot by leading inevitably to the climax. When Cindy and her boyfriend quarrel, he finds himself with her house keys after she slams the door in his face. He is later able to sneak inside the house to make his own inept attempt at heroics. When Hal is shot down, a gun registered to Daniel Hilliard is found in his possession: now Bard knows not only the neighborhood but also the house that is his target. Hal's death also serves to advance Glenn's breakdown and to shift the relationship between Glenn and Hilliard. Instead of the swaggering brute who calls all the shots, Glenn is diminished to an emotional, irrational man with a gun.

The last few minutes of the film are tense and masterfully plotted. Wyler has drawn some criticism for shooting the film using his usual deep focus technique rather than relying on rapid cutting to build suspense. In these last few minutes, that criticism may be justified, yet Wyler's deep focus technique has its advantages. The technique, developed by Wyler and the famous cinematographer Gregg Toland many years before, allowed Wyler to show both action and reaction in one shot, and it eliminated numerous cuts from one character's face to another's. One of Wyler's most famous scenes was one of the earliest he shot in deep focus. In *The Little Foxes* (1941), Bette Davis stands in the foreground in close focus while in deep focus, her invalid husband (Herbert Marshall) struggles to climb the stairs. Davis has been abusing her husband to the point that he becomes short of breath, and he begs her to fetch his medication. Then, out of desperation, he tries to make it upstairs on his own. Wyler holds the focus on Davis' face as we watch Marshall die of a coronary in the background. The effect could not have been more chilling.

Thrillers and melodramas, in particular, generally employ rapid cutting to build suspense. Wyler's technique is less manipulative. It allows the viewer to take in several factors at once and to make his own judgments. In this sense, the technique is an excellent match for cinematographer Lee Garmes' stark, documentary style. Garmes was a veteran cameraman who had worked with Wyler only once before, on *Detective Story* (1951). During that collaboration, he had introduced Wyler to a new invention: with his camera mounted on a crab dolly, it could be moved anywhere without tracks. In both *Detective Story* and *The Desperate Hours*, this technique combines beautifully with the material.

In *The Desperate Hours*, shot in stark black-and-white, the camera seems to stalk through the house and focus on the muzzle of a gun or the menacing snarl of a thug. It picks out the threatening elements, then broadens its view to give us a sense of the hopelessly closed-in setting. The conflict emerges as clearly from the blocking of scenes, the lighting, and the camera angles as it does from the script and plotting. We feel the Hilliards' suffocation, their sense of helplessness, isolated as they are from the outside world, living with the constant threat that if one makes a foolish move, the others will die; and with the equally present threat that one of the hoodlums—or for that matter the police—may become trigger-happy and they will die anyway.

When a film "works," it is because the combination of elements is greater than the sum of the parts. Each of its elements—the casting, the acting, the plotting, the writing, the directing, the lighting, the camera angles and techniques—combines with the others to heighten the effects of the individual components. Wyler, as many critics have noted, is a difficult director to characterize. There is no Wyler "touch"; no signature element. He moves easily from light comedy to searing drama, from Westerns to war movies. He is responsible both for *Funny Girl* (1968) and for *The Collector* (1965). What Wyler does do almost unerringly is to match his material with the right actors and the right technicians to create films that "work."

Julie Barker

DESTINATION MOON

Released: 1950
Production: George Pal for Universal
Direction: Irving Pichel
Screenplay: Rip Van Ronkel, Robert Heinlein, and James O'Hanlon; based
    on the novel *Rocket Ship Galileo* by Robert Heinlein
Cinematography: Lionel Lindon
Editing: Duke Goldstone
Art direction: Ernest Fegte
Set decoration: George Sawley
Special effects: George Pal and Eagle-Lion Classics (AA)
Running time: 90 minutes

> *Principal characters:*
> Barnes ....John Archer
> Cargreaves .... Warner Anderson
> General Thayer .... Tom Powers
> Sweeney .... Dick Wesson

In an era of pseudodocumentary melodramas fostered by postwar neo-realism, George Pal managed to create, independently, the ultimate fictional "documentary" in *Destination Moon*. The race for space is the focus of this serious attempt to show how man could go where he had never gone before. *Destination Moon* follows a group of scientists as they convince the government to undergo a project that would send a manned rocket to the moon. The scientists detail, in very specific terms, the various stresses and hazards that may be encountered on a voyage through space. There are endless tests: determinations to be made in regard to the number of crew members, how to deal with weightlessness, how to walk on the surface of the moon, and others which are based on actual considerations of space scientists. Every detail is given a great deal of scrutiny prior to the rocket launching. The schedule proceeds according to plan, and the four select scientists go into space like intrepid Cub Scouts out for their first taste of camping in the wilds.

There are minor crises which are encountered on the way to the moon, none of which prove to be too much for the able-bodied crew. Once on the moon, however, the scientists realize that they have insufficient fuel to make the trip back to earth. After serious soul-searching and heroic attempts at volunteering to stay behind, an ingenious method of discarding empty space suits and canisters is proposed. They blast back into space and prove that man is indeed able to conquer the stars.

Destination Moon was praised for its realistic approach to an extremely fantastic plot. The special effects by George Pal Productions are simple and effective. The producer, Pal himself, is quite comfortable with the concept of the fantastic; he produced and directed a large number of stop-motion animated short subjects, called *Puppetoons*, during the early 1940's. He was drawn to this area again and again in such films as *When Worlds Collide* (1951), *War of the Worlds* (1953), *The Conquest of Space* (1955), and the brilliant fantasy film *The Time Machine* (1960). Pal's work has been consistently praised for its elaborate detail and effectiveness, and *Destination Moon* itself received a special citation from the Academy of Motion Picture Arts and Sciences for its "realism." *When Worlds Collide* won an Academy Award the next year for special photographic effects. Other Pal films have become standards of the science-fiction genre, gaining a large cult as well as critical following.

If there is a factor which tends to isolate Pal's films from contemporary science-fiction films, it is their overt piousness. There is a religious presence felt in so many aspects of Pal's films that the introduction of divine providence becomes cloying and at times embarrassing. The most preposterous situation occurs in *Conquest in Space*, which characterizes religious fanaticism to the extreme. *War of the Worlds'* use of the church as sanctuary against the invading Martians and the sermonizing done by the minister also point strongly to this bias. This simplistic view of the universe seen in Pal's films may have been overlooked during the time of their initial release, but on repeated viewings, the message comes through far too loudly.

Of all of Pal's films, *Destination Moon* suffers the least from this piety. The script, adapted by famed science-fiction author Robert Heinlein from his own novel, is rooted in fact. The drama deals with man's conquest of the unknown, and there is a sense of joy laced throughout the technological sophistication of *Destination Moon* that is unmistakable. The actors express this joy on an emotional level that is rather unusual, and their freedom in communicating their triumphs and anxieties is the real pleasure of *Destination Moon*. In an era in which man has actually walked on the moon, the implications of this scientific novel have long since worn off. What remains is the pioneering spirit of Pal and Heinlein as conveyed through the film. Both the physical beauty of a trip through outer space and the emotional response by the actors as they voyage through space contribute to the success of the film.

Pal's later films have generated mixed reactions. His 1975 film *Doc Savage*, which was his last, was received with limited success. What is surprising, however, is that the naïve quality criticized in *Doc Savage* is consistent with Pal's other films. He was an uncomplicated filmmaker who focused on the fantastic element inherent in the medium. From *Destination Moon* through *Doc Savage*, Pal managed to produce a series of imaginative films which bear the stamp of honest innocence and everlasting wonder.

Carl F. Macek

DESTINATION TOKYO

Released: 1943
Production: Jerry Wald for Warner Bros.
Direction: Delmer Daves
Screenplay: Delmer Daves and Albert Maltz; based on an original story by
  Steve Fisher
Cinematography: Bert Glennon
Editing: Christian Nyby
Running time: 135 minutes

Principal characters:

Captain Cassidy	Cary Grant
Wolf	John Garfield
Cookie	Alan Hale
Raymond	John Ridgely
Tin Can	Dane Clark
Pills	William Prince
Tommy Adams	Robert Hutton
Mike	Tom Tully
Sparks	John Forsythe

When *Destination Tokyo* was released at the end of 1943, the United States was in the midst of World War II. Hollywood joined the rest of the country in promoting the war effort. This film, which deals with the *U. S. S. Copperfin*, a submarine on a secret mission to get into Tokyo Bay and send back meteorological information necessary for the first American bombing of the Japanese capital, was part of Hollywood's patriotic contribution. It is also an excellent example of the type of war propaganda film which was popular at the time.

The film portrays the enemy as accepting values alien to American culture. Tin Can (Dane Clark), a Greek-American crewman aboard the *Copperfin*, articulates all the crew's perception of a vast "difference between them and us." The submarine's skipper, Captain Cassidy (Cary Grant), depicts the Japanese way of life as "a system that puts daggers in the hands of five-year-old children." He hopes that American military might will allow those children to have roller skates instead of weapons of war. Japanese life is also criticized for its economic imbalance; there are no labor unions, and the average worker's salary is only seven dollars per week. Moreover, the Japanese have no conception of love for women and children as Americans do. Their language, in fact, has no terminology for familial love, according to the film. Despite these criticisms of Japan, however, the submariners realize that it is the despotic government of the country that is the real enemy, not the Japanese people.

Not only is the cultural chasm between Japan and the United States apparent in the negative comments about the enemy's way of life, but the film also affords a positive albeit idealized portrayal of American values as represented by the *Copperfin*'s crew. Special emphasis is placed on family values. Captain Cassidy is a good family man who reminisces about taking his son for his first haircut. Mike (Tom Tully), an Irish-American crewman, also loves his family and frequently retires into the ship's recreation office to listen to a recording of his wife's voice on the phonograph. Another seaman, Tommy Adams (Robert Hutton), is a youth away from home for the first time, who preserves family contact by displaying a picture of his sister while other men do the same for their wives and sweethearts. Tin Can's ties extend beyond the nuclear family to include an honored uncle, executed in his native Greece by the Nazis. Tin Can perceives his role in the war as avenger for his kinsman's death.

While the crew members are devoted to their families back home, they also create a family atmosphere aboard the submarine. Despite their diversity in personality, they cooperate effectively both to accomplish their military objective and to accommodate the personal needs of one another. The first stop on the way to Tokyo is the Aleutian Islands, where they pick up Raymond (John Ridgely), the meteorologist whose analysis of conditions in Japan is required for the success of the bombing of Tokyo. He immediately becomes part of the crew. Two of them, the inveterate ladies' man Wolf (John Garfield) and communications specialist Sparks (John Forsythe), readily agree to join Raymond on his dangerous assignment. This involves their being landed on the shore of Tokyo Bay and remaining there to gather weather data. These men willingly risk their lives for their country as, in fact, do all members of the *Copperfin*'s crew in the perilous mission into mine-infested Tokyo Bay.

The cooperative spirit manifest in the way the crew handles their mission is also evident in their treatment of one another. They are especially concerned with the welfare of young Tommy Adams. For example, when Tommy first assumes his watch, he thinks he sees an enemy plane. The submarine dives and anxiously awaits the explosions of bombs, but a careful search of the sky through the periscope reveals the plane to be an albatross. The captain exhibits a paternal understanding of the inexperienced crewman's error, saying that he would rather dive for innumerable false alarms than to ignore a real danger. Tommy also experiences his first battle death when Mike, who has befriended the young man and has reaffirmed his religious convictions, dies. The pilot of a downed Japanese fighter plane, whom Mike is trying to pull aboard the *Copperfin*, stabs the sailor in the back. The crew share the sense of loss of their beloved compatriot. Tommy proves himself a worthy member of the submarine's family when he defuses a bomb that has lodged in the ship's bulkheads.

Perhaps the most important personal crisis during the film occurs when Tommy contracts an appendicitis while the ship is hiding on the floor of Tokyo

Bay. Since no doctor is available, Pills (William Prince), the pharmacist's mate, must perform surgery. Assisted by Captain Cassidy who administers ether, by the encouraging philosophy of Cookie (Alan Hale), and by Tin Can's reading of the instructions from a medical textbook, Pills successfully removes the inflamed appendix. Not only does Tommy Adams recover, but also Pills, who had not believed in God, finds faith.

As if a dangerous spying mission and a serious operation under difficult conditions were not enough action, *Destination Tokyo* also depicts the *Copperfin* in battle with a Japanese warship. As the submarine leaves Tokyo Bay, having successfully completed its mission, the captain and crew cannot resist sinking an enemy aircraft carrier. This action, while sàtisfying the bellicose tendencies of the men, reveals the submarine's whereabouts to the Japanese navy. A destroyer bombards them with depth charges until the *Copperfin* turns on its adversary, sending well-aimed torpedoes into its hull.

Destination Tokyo suffers the limitations of any topical film in that it lacks sufficient perspective on its subject, in this case the Pacific theater during World War II. For example, the sentiments of the crew, which represent the film's own point of view, reflect patriotic posturing more than a clear appreciation of the issues being contested in the war. The film is also overly long and contains too many characters who are little more than stock figures even though the acting is well done. Furthermore, as most contemporary critics pointed out, the plot lacks credibility. The film is filled with action, however, and several of the performances are capable. The film's chief interest, however, lies in the attitudes it reveals. A period piece, *Destination Tokyo* both captures and projects the spirit of wartime America.

Frances M. Malpezzi
William M. Clements

DESTRY RIDES AGAIN

Released: 1939
Production: Joe Pasternak for Universal
Direction: George Marshall
Screenplay: Felix Jackson, Gertrude Purcell, and Henry Myers; based on Felix Jackson's screen story, adapted from the novel of the same name by Max Brand
Cinematography: Hal Mohr
Editing: Milton Carruth
Running time: 94 minutes

Principal characters:
Frenchy .... Marlene Dietrich
Tom Destry, Jr. .... James Stewart
Washington Dimsdale .... Charles Winninger
Boris Callahan .... Mischa Auer
Kent .... Brian Donlevy
Lily Belle Callahan .... Una Merkel
Judge Slade .... Samuel S. Hinds

A brisk comedy-Western, *Destry Rides Again* successfully combines laughter and action, and, because of several key decisions, the film transcends its genre. Marlene Dietrich, who usually played elegant and glamorous roles, was cast as a tawdry hostess in a saloon, and James Stewart, who had never appeared in a Western, was cast as a young lawman. The unexpected pairing of the two in a genre unfamiliar to both proved to be inspired. Dietrich and Stewart work well together, and the script, which treats the conventional Western situation with affectionate humor, allows them to display their considerable comedic abilities.

In the opening scene, the camera, moving smoothly and continuously from one part of the saloon to another, introduces all the important characters. By the time the scene ends, the situation which will confront Tom Destry (James Stewart) is completely understood. A typical brawling and lawless Western town, Bottleneck is dominated by Kent (Brian Donlevy), the owner of the Last Chance Saloon. Aided by Frenchy (Marlene Dietrich), the hostess for his saloon, he cheats at card games in order to gain control of a strip of land that will prevent ranchers from driving their herds to market unless they pay him a handsome toll for the privilege. The town's corrupt, tobacco-chewing Mayor, Judge Slade (Samuel S. Hinds), is also part of Kent's gang, but Bottleneck's sheriff is not. When he confronts Kent with evidence of his land-grab schemes, the sheriff is killed, and the venal Mayor appoints the town drunk, Washington Dimsdale (Charles Winninger), to the now-vacant office.

Wash takes his job seriously, however, and sends for Tom Destry, son of the famous but now deceased Marshall Destry under whom Wash once served as a deputy. Having prepared the townspeople for a tough lawman, Wash is embarrassed by the mild-mannered, unarmed man whom they first see holding a frilly parasol and a birdcage for a lady alighting from the stagecoach. Although Wash tells him that everyone is laughing at him, Destry shrugs and says first impressions are foolish anyway. Wash then introduces Destry to Frenchy, "the real boss of Bottleneck," but Destry barely has time to murmur politely that he "always likes to know who's boss," before Kent approaches, determined to establish his domination of Destry. He demands Destry's gun, but finds he cannot provoke a fight because Destry does not carry a gun. The crowd laughs uproariously at this lanky buffoon who does not seem to have enough spirit to stand up to Kent. Mockingly, Frenchy hands him a mop and a pail of water so that he can clean up the town.

A comic set-piece is the fight which follows between Frenchy and an angry townswoman, Lily Belle Callahan (Una Merkel), while the crowd and Kent are still laughing at Destry. Mrs. Callahan is angry because Frenchy has won the pants of her husband, Boris (Mischa Auer), in a poker game. They engage in a kicking, scratching, wrestling fight that Destry stops by pouring a pail of water over them. Furious, Frenchy begins punching, kicking, and clawing Destry, then works up to throwing glasses at him, and finally grabs a six-gun and starts shooting at him. Escaping, Destry tells her she has a "knack for making a stranger feel right at home."

Destry persuades a now-dubious Wash to swear him in as a deputy by explaining that, although his father did things the old way, he is going to do them the new way: "If you shoot it out with 'em it makes 'em heroes. Put 'em behind bars and they look little and cheap." He does not carry a gun because his father had one when he was shot in the back, which is why he believes in "law and order—without guns."

It becomes quickly apparent that Destry also believes in the educational value of storytelling. He starts each story with the words, "I once had a friend," and is seldom without an appropriate anecdote to illustrate a principle or point out a moral. His slow, sometimes exasperating drawl and his fondness for storytelling also give hot tempers time to cool and Destry time to think. Although his chief weapon in taming Bottleneck is his cool temper and sense of humor, he knows there is a time for action and does not hesitate to demonstrate his skill with a six-gun to overawe some rowdy troublemakers.

He uses his brains to trick Kent and his gang into leading Wash and Boris, whose dream has always been to become a cowboy, to the body of the murdered sheriff. He then arrests one of the gang members and sends for a federal judge to keep the crooked Mayor from trying the case. Kent's men, however, raid the jail, kill Wash, and rescue the prisoner, but Destry is saved by Frenchy, who lures him away from the jail because she does not want him killed.

Under her tough façade, Frenchy has the proverbial heart of gold, at least where Destry is concerned. She gives him her lucky rabbit's foot to carry and tries to smooth over any friction between him and Kent. Frenchy also attempts to persuade Destry to come to New Orleans to see her, but after Destry learns what has happened at the jail, he is interested only in bringing Wash's murderers to justice.

As Destry and the townsmen attack Kent and his men, who have barricaded themselves in the saloon, Frenchy desperately tries to rally the respectable women of the town to his aid. At first hostile and resentful, at her suggestion, they eventually form themselves into a band armed with pitchforks and gardening implements. Forcing themselves between the two opposing sides, they march into the saloon where they engage in hand-to-hand combat with the gang.

Destry, meanwhile, has forced his way into the saloon's second story and begins searching for Kent in the wild melee below him. As Destry descends into the surging crowd, Kent stalks him from behind. At the last moment, Frenchy sees Kent and forces her way to Destry's side, throwing her arms around him in time to take Kent's bullet in the back. Destry immediately shoots Kent, and Frenchy dies in his arms.

In the film's last sequence, Destry strolls down the street whittling industriously, accompanied by an admiring youngster who copies his drawl and other mannerisms. Our last glimpse of Destry is similar to our first; he is telling a story about marriage to an admiring young woman.

Exceptionally well-paced and well-written, *Destry Rides Again* shows director George Marshall's talent for both comedy and action, and the performances of James Stewart and Marlene Dietrich add the final polish to an almost perfect Western spoof. James Stewart as Destry is pleasant, likable, easygoing, and humorous. But underneath this mild-mannered façade is the soul of a true town-tamer, which emerges when the action requires it. His sure, deft characterization adds immeasurably to the likableness and depth of Destry.

Destry Rides Again revived Marlene Dietrich's faded film career. As Frenchy, the tough, brazen saloon singer who seems impervious to everything but Destry's charm and has a sense of humor to match his own, she has a role similar to her famous screen debut in *The Blue Angel* (1930). She sings two songs, "Little Joe" and "See What the Boys in the Back Room Will Have," with robust vitality and a twinkle in her eye in the inimitable, throaty Dietrich manner. Uncertain about the role, Dietrich took it only after being advised to do so by her mentor, director Josef von Sternberg. After *Destry Rides Again* she frequently was cast in roles that were variations on the part of Frenchy just as she had previously been cast in variations of her Sternberg-directed roles.

The achievement of *Destry Rides Again* is that it nicely balances the serious elements of the Max Brand novel from which it was adapted against the comic elements of the script to produce a film which is funny but not a burlesque. The 1954 remake, *Destry*, with Audie Murphy, is merely ordinary.

Julia Johnson

DETECTIVE STORY

Released: 1951
Production: William Wyler for Paramount
Direction: William Wyler
Screenplay: Philip Yordon; based on the play of the same name by Sidney Kingsley
Cinematography: Lee Garmes
Editing: Robert Swink
Running time: 103 minutes

Principal characters:
Detective James McLeod .... Kirk Douglas
Mary McLeod .... Eleanor Parker
Detective Lou Brody .... William Bendix
Shoplifter .... Lee Grant
Arthur Kindred .... Craig Hill
Susan Carmichael .... Cathy O'Donnell
Lieutenant Monahan .... Horace McMahon
Endicott Sims .... Warner Anderson
Karl Schneider .... George Macready
Charley Gennini, first burglar .... Joseph Wiseman
Lewis Abbott, second burglar .... Michael Strong

Detective Story tells of one eventful day in a New York City Police Precinct Station. In a change of theme, however, the villain of the piece is *not* one of the criminals brought into the station, although they all are unsavory enough. Giving an outstanding performance, Kirk Douglas plays Detective James McLeod, a man with his own personal code of justice. So certain is McLeod of the difference between right and wrong that he will resort to anything, even violence, to get a judgment that he thinks is deserved. Under the capable hands of director William Wyler, *Detective Story* became a modern morality play acted out in one room. What emerges is an exciting, taut film with unforgettable performances from all involved.

Detective Story was first a long-running Broadway play written by Sidney Kingsley, starring Ralph Bellamy. When Wyler decided to adapt it for the screen, he cast five members of the original Broadway cast—Horace McMahon, Lee Grant, Joseph Wiseman, Michael Strong, and James Maloney. Of these actors, only McMahon had had previous screen experience. Wyler also chose to reproduce almost exactly the Broadway stage set and confine the action to the Police Station—a wise choice that gives the film great strength as the tension builds to an almost unbearable level. Within the contained walls of the Precinct Station, all kinds of characters wander in and out, some giving the film comic relief. There is the wisecracking but scared shoplifter, beautifully executed by Grant; Wiseman's maniacal burglar; and the inquisitive police reporter. It is Detective McLeod, however, who is the film's pivot. Because of his criminal father, who drove his mother insane, McLeod developed a vicious hatred for all law-breakers and lost the distinction between revenge and justice. As Douglas plays him, McLeod sees all men as guilty until proven innocent, and even then there is doubt.

The cast rehearsed with Wyler for two weeks on the set before shooting began, and the resulting film has the poise and the polish of a Broadway repertory company working together. There are no false notes either in the structure of the film or in the performances. Everything is timed perfectly, and the events are presented with vivid honesty; *Detective Story* pulls no punches. In the quiescent 1950's when words such as abortion could not be mentioned on film, the motion picture gets its message across without having to resort to rough language or unnecessary brutality. It is all there, however; McLeod is a man on strings, and when at last he begins to show signs of cracking by beating up a suspect, the scene is highly effective. Yet McLeod is not entirely an unsympathetic character. Although he is warped in judgment, sufficient reason is given for his behavior for the audience to understand, if not to condone his actions. Also, another side of McLeod is shown by his genuine affection for his wife, Mary (Eleanor Parker). When this relationship begins to turn sour on him, it is more than he can bear.

Detective Story was well researched by both Wyler and Douglas. Prior to production, both men saw the New York play and also spent many hours at the 16th precinct on West 47th Street talking with the detectives there. Douglas even helped the policemen interrogate and fingerprint prisoners. He then played the part of McLeod on stage at the Sombrero Theater in Phoenix, Arizona. All of this scrupulous background work, plus the extensive rehearsal time, made the cast and creators of *Detective Story* unusually well prepared. Cinematographer Lee Garmes worked the cameras and light movements simultaneously with the actors' rehearsals, so that by the time the film was ready to be shot, it was a simple matter. This was Wyler's second adaptation of a Kingsley play; he had directed *Dead End* for Samuel Goldwyn in 1937, using a similar one-set approach. Since *Detective Story*, in contrast to *Dead End*, is all interior, its action is more claustrophobic and intense. Furthermore, the film somehow seems less dated than *Dead End* because it is primarily a look into the mind of a disturbed man rather than a probe into social conditions in a particular time period.

The film starts on a busier than usual afternoon at the 21st Police Station in Manhattan. A frightened little shoplifter (Lee Grant) is brought in by one of the detectives, but since the last van leaves before her fingerprints are taken, she must remain at the police station until she is taken to court. Detective Jim McLeod arrives with a young man, Arthur Kindred (Craig Hill), accused of embezzling some of his employer's money. Kindred tries to call his girl friend, Joy Carmichael, but she is not at home, and her sister Susan (Cathy O'Donnell) comes down to the station. McLeod is told by Lieutenant Monahan (Horace McMahon), head of the precinct, that Dr. Schneider (George Macready), the suspected abortionist for whom McLeod has a warrant out, will surrender himself if his lawyer can guarantee that McLeod will not assault him. McLeod reluctantly agrees—he has a reputation for toughness and loathes the disbarred doctor. Out in the squad room, two burglars are brought in who give their names as Charley Gennini (Joseph Wiseman) and Lewis Abbott (Michael Strong). They were caught in the act of stealing, but Charley hysterically denies everything. McLeod has promised his wife Mary that he will be home in an hour, so he quickly tries to get rid of all the business at hand. Mary is the only person about whom he cares.

When Arthur Kindred's employer comes and offers to drop charges if Arthur will replace the money, McLeod refuses to show any leniency, even though it is the boy's first offense. Arthur had stolen money to satisfy the greed of his girl friend Joy, but he is truly repentant. McLeod, however, will not budge, and his partner Detective Brody (William Bendix) feels that he is not human. Dr. Schneider comes into the station with his lawyer Sims (Warner Anderson), but McLeod's case against him fades when it is learned that his star witness has died. In frustrated rage, McLeod beats up Schneider, who has to be taken away in an ambulance. Sims, furious at McLeod, hints at a personal reason for McLeod's hatred of Schneider, and Monahan investigates immediately.

That evening the Lieutenant uncovers something hidden in Mary McLeod's past. Before she met her husband, she had made a youthful mistake with a married man and had gone to Schneider to seek his help in finding someone to adopt her baby. The child died, however, and Mary was unable to have any more children. When McLeod learns of this, he is stunned and overcome with grief. His wife comes to the station, where they have a bitter quarrel. Brody talks to McLeod and convinces him to try to forget what Mary did and to ask her forgiveness. The two have a brief reconciliation, but McLeod cannot stop bitterly referring to Mary's past. Mary realizes that her husband will never let her forget her one big mistake, and she decides to leave him. McLeod is defeated: he has lost the one person who means something to him and is more like his father than he can ever admit.

Out in the squad room, Charley the burglar suddenly overpowers his guards and draws a gun on the assembled detectives. McLeod tries to disarm him, but is mortally wounded. Dying, he makes his first compromise and gasps out to Brody to drop the charge against Arthur Kindred and to free him. As McLeod's colleagues do what they can for him, Susan and Arthur, having fallen in love at the station, walk out into the night hand in hand.

Detective Story was hailed by the critics, with Douglas especially praised. One critic said that "by shifting violence on to the side of the law, Hollywood has neatly sidestepped the censor without sacrificing the box office." This is what so many reviewers found interesting about the film. The quiet men were usually the criminals and the angry, harsh ones the detectives. *Detective Story* was also part of a revival of a genre that had gone out of fashion in the 1950's. Partly in the tradition of Warner Bros.' cops-and-robbers movies such as *Little Caesar* (1931) or *Scarface* (1932), it also resembled *film noir* with such antecedents as *Double Indemnity* (1944) and *Call Northside 777* (1948). It proved that Hollywood could still turn out the tense, exciting crime films for which it was famous. *Detective Story* is certainly at the top of that class of filmmaking. Wyler's adroit handling of his actors and Garmes's expert cinematography help to make it a memorable film. As one writer put it: "*Detective Story* turned melodrama into poetry."

Joan Cohen

THE DEVIL AND DANIEL WEBSTER
(ALL THAT MONEY CAN BUY)

Released: 1941
Production: William Dieterle for William Dieterle and RKO/Radio
Direction: William Dieterle
Screenplay: Dan Totheroh and Stephen Vincent Benét; based on the story
"The Devil and Daniel Webster" by Stephen Vincent Benét
Cinematography: Joseph H. August
Editing: Robert Wise
Music: Bernard Herrmann (AA)
Running time: 109 minutes

Principal characters:

Daniel Webster	Edward Arnold
Mr. Scratch	Walter Huston
Ma Stone	Jane Darwell
Belle	Simone Simon
Mary Stone	Anne Shirley
Jabez Stone	James Craig
Squire Slossum	Gene Lockhart
Miser Stevens	John Qualen

Stephen Vincent Benét's short story "The Devil and Daniel Webster" was published in the *Saturday Evening Post* in 1937. A reworking of the Faust legend in the guise of an American folktale, it tells the story of a New England farmer, Jabez Stone, who in 1840 agrees to sell his soul to the devil in return for seven years of prosperity. When the devil (who, in deference to local custom, calls himself Mr. Scratch) comes to collect, however, Jabez claims his right as an American citizen to a trial before a judge and jury—an *American* judge and an *American* jury, he emphasizes. Mr. Scratch chuckles and agrees; but he insists that the trial, which will take place in Jabez's barn, has to be conducted before a judge and jury of his choosing. So up they come, out of the floor of Jabez's barn, the ghosts of Judge Hawthorne of the Salem Witch Trials, and of Captain Kidd, Simon Girty, Benedict Arnold, and nine other cutthroats, knaves, and traitors: American all. Jabez would have been lost at this point, except that he has for his lawyer the greatest American of his time: Daniel Webster, United States Senator from Massachusetts, statesman, patriot, and outspoken champion of "Liberty *and* Union, now and forever, one and inseparable!" Webster looks over Scratch's jury and realizes that what these poor damned souls had in common with Jabez was that they, too, had once had an opportunity to participate in the building of a free, new land. He develops this theme with all the eloquence that has made him the foremost speaker in a Senate renowned for its oratory; and when he is done, Jabez is acquitted. Scratch accepts the jury's verdict; but he also promises

Webster that he will see that he never becomes President—which, of course, Webster never did.

Scratch's court sitting in Jabez's barn was a picture to tempt any dramatist, and within a year Benét's story had become the basis for an opera, with music by Douglas Moore, and a play. The fantastic element in the story also made it ideal for presentation as a motion picture, except for one thing: the Hollywood studios of the day were not interested in stories, however "cinematic," that did not provide opportunities for glamour and spectacle and that lacked good parts for star actors. (Daniel and the devil were both good parts; but they could only be played by experienced character actors, not handsome leading men.) Had it not been for director William Dieterle, who had formed his own production company under the aegis of RKO, *The Devil and Daniel Webster* might never have reached the screen. Fortunately, because he was his own producer, Dieterle was allowed to complete the film without any of the usual Hollywood compromises. Benét himself was hired to write the script, in collaboration with Dan Totheroh. To play Daniel and Mr. Scratch, Dieterle was able to hire two of Hollywood's best character actors, who turned in ideal performances in roles for which they were ideally suited. As Daniel Webster, Edward Arnold was the same genial, shrewd political boss he had played for director Frank Capra in *Mr. Smith Goes to Washington* (1939) and *Meet John Doe* (1941), but this time his guile was squarely on the side of right. Walter Huston, in his first good screen role since his stage success in *Knickerbocker Holiday* (1938), played Mr. Scratch as a typical Yankee peddlar, shrewd as Webster, humorous, a ready flatterer, always willing to listen to a proposition but inflexible once a bargain has been struck. The film's most memorable image is of Huston at the end of the picture, after he has stolen and finished eating the pie that Ma Stone (Jane Darwell) baked for Daniel's breakfast. He wipes off his mouth and begins looking around for his next victim. He spies the audience sitting in the theater, and moves closer to the camera. After looking left and right around the auditorium, he suddenly catches sight of the ideal prospect and, with a broad grin on his face, points his finger unmistakably at Y-O-U. This scene does not appear in the text of the screenplay that John Gassner and Dudley Nichols published in *Twenty Best Film Plays* in 1943; and it is possible that it was worked out between Huston and Dieterle on the set during shooting. For his performance, Huston was nominated for the Academy Award for Best Actor of 1941, but lost to Gary Cooper for *Sergeant York*.

In keeping with the story's quality as a folktale, all of the characters were conceived as types rather than as individuals—with the important exceptions of Jabez Stone (James Craig) and his wife, who thus became the audience's "link" with the fantastic happenings on screen. Craig gave what was probably the best performance of his undistinguished career. He had not yet grown the mustache that made him look like a second-string Clark Gable (which seemed to be his function during his later years at M-G-M); and he projected to the full Jabez's boyishness, warm-heartedness, and impetuosity. As Mary, Jabez's wife, Anne Shirley was given little to do for most of the picture except to fret over her husband's growing hardness and estrangement from her once he has made his pact with the devil. Mary is the one who finally goes to Daniel Webster when the seven years are up; but, until then, it is easy to sympathize with Jabez and his impatience at her continual "But Jabez, you said we'd *never* change!" The strange, childlike French actress Simone Simon found in the part of Belle, Scratch's friend from "over the mountain" who comes to tempt Jabez, one of her few good American roles. Her only other effective performance in an American movie was as the obsessed heroine of Val Lewton and Jacques Tourneur's *Cat People* (1942). Gene Lockhart's Squire Slossum was an ordinary small-town hypocrite of the type he played so well; but John Qualen's Miser Stevens, another of Scratch's victims whose soul, when the devil claims it, is no larger than a moth, may just be, after Daniel and Scratch, the best-realized character in the film. Qualen will probably always be identified with his role as the stubborn tenant farmer who refuses to leave his land in *The Grapes of Wrath* (1940); but as Miser Stevens he created an unforgettable portrait of a man whose soul has shrunk to the dimensions of his pocket-book. The presence of Darwell in the cast also calls up memories of *The Grapes of Wrath*, but only because her performance as Ma Stone is indistinguishable from her performance as Ma Joad. This was not Darwell's fault; she had just won the Academy Award for Ma Joad, and, reading the published screenplay for *The Devil and Daniel Webster*, it is impossible to believe that the part of Jabez's mother was written with anyone but Darwell again playing Ma Joad in mind. Ma Stone is supposed to be a type, of course, just as Squire Slossum, Miser Stevens, Mr. Scratch, and even Daniel Webster are types; but one wishes that in this instance Dieterle had selected an actress whose performance might have been a little less predictable, such as Marjorie Main.

In the 1920's when he was a screen actor in Germany, Dieterle had played Valentin in F. W. Murnau's monumental silent production of *Faust* (1926). Not surprisingly, when he came to direct his gentler American version of the story, Dieterle tried to give it a little of the same visual style. With his cinematographer, the great Joseph August, he worked out a lighting scheme that emphasized the supernatural elements in the script (in sequences shot on stylized studio sets) by contrasting them with scenes of everyday life shot as naturalistically as possible (on location, or at least out of doors, in full sunlight). Somehow the mixture works; and even Scratch (who is in his glory, moving through the shadows of Jabez's barn) is no less believable when he suddenly turns up banging a drum among a crowd of townspeople who have assembled to hear Daniel give a speech in the open air.

As a film, *The Devil and Daniel Webster* was just one product of the self-conscious mythologizing of the American past that was a characteristic activity of many artists and writers in the period before and during World War II. When Daniel pleads with Scratch's jury to "give Jabez Stone another chance to walk upon the earth among the trees, the growing corn, the smell of grass in spring," he was speaking for men who had every reason to fear that the "common, small, good" things in life might soon be taken away from them. Bernard Herrmann's Academy Award-winning score, which was based on folk motifs expressed in a sophisticated symphonic idiom, represented a musical affirmation of traditional American values. Along with this affirmation often went a Depression-bred commitment to social activism: the political message of *The Devil and Daniel Webster* seems to be that Jabez Stone should not have sold his soul to the devil when he found himself unable to pay his debts, but should have accepted his neighbors' invitation to join the Grange instead.

It is unhappily still true of Hollywood studios like RKO that, while they are sometimes willing to finance an unconventional production such as *The Devil and Daniel Webster*, they often become frightened and begin tinkering with the completed film before it can find an audience in the form its maker intended. In the case of Dieterle's film, it was pointed out in the first trade reviews that the logical, "pre-sold" title was *The Devil and Daniel Webster*, the title of Benét's well-known original story. There was an old Hollywood superstition, however, that pictures with *Devil* in the title never did well, for example *The Devil Is a Woman* (1935). The film version of "The Devil and Daniel Webster" was therefore previewed as *Here Is a Man* before someone thought of calling it *All That Money Can Buy* (from Scratch's offer of "money—and all that money can buy" in return for Jabez's soul). When the film did poorly in its first engagements, it was withdrawn and reissued at intervals in different parts of the country as *Daniel and the Devil* and, finally, *The Devil and Daniel Webster*, the title under which it is usually shown today. The film is indexed in the 1941 issues of the *Reader's Guide to Periodical Literature* as *All That Money Can Buy*; however, references in publications are evenly divided between *All That Money Can Buy* and *The Devil and Daniel Webster*. To complicate matters further, RKO kept re-editing the film, so that what was trade-shown as *Here Is a Man* at 106 minutes may have run as long as 112 minutes when it opened as *All That Money Can Buy* in New York. At one point in the 1940's, the film may actually have been distributed in versions running less than ninety minutes; but the version of *The Devil and Daniel Webster* that is distributed most widely today, on the nontheatrical circuit and to television, runs 109 minutes.

Charles Hopkins

THE DEVIL AND MISS JONES

Released: 1941
Production: Frank Ross and Norman Krasna for RKO/Radio
Direction: Sam Wood
Screenplay: Norman Krasna
Cinematography: Harry Stradling
Editing: Sheman Todd
Production design: William Cameron Menzies
Running time: 92 minutes

Principal characters:
Mary Jones .... Jean Arthur
J. P. Merrick .... Charles Coburn
Joe O'Brien .... Robert Cummings
Hooper .... Edmond Gwenn
Elizabeth Ellis .... Spring Byington

The Devil and Miss Jones is an unusual comedy—unusual both in its social-minded message, which forms the backbone of the plot, and also in its out-landish production design. The story involves the struggle of workers in Neeley's department store in New York to form a union and negotiate for wages and benefits. J. P. Merrick (Charles Coburn), the richest man in the world (who also happens to own Neeley's), decides to impersonate a humble clerk and uncover the people responsible for the unrest in his store. While working undercover as a slipper salesman, Merrick is befriended by Mary Jones (Jean Arthur), a likable fellow clerk whose altruistic nature begins to affect the snobbish old fogey. He double-dates with Mary and Joe O'Brien (Robert Cummings), one of the union organizers who has been fired. That afternoon at the beach is the turning point in Merrick's life. He is literally surrounded by flesh. Hundreds of people squirm and fight for a small patch of sand and a place in the sun on Coney Island. He discusses economics with Joe and flirts with his date, a delightful middle-aged woman named Elizabeth (Spring Byington).

Eventually, Merrick is separated from his group. Feeling uncomfortable in his rented swimming suit, he tries to find his clothes. He is quite a novice at dealing with people firsthand, and after wandering around tired and hungry for hours, he decides to take matters in his own hands. He tries to swap his expensive gold watch for a dime for the telephone at the drugstore and is arrested. Later at the police station, Mary, Joe, and Elizabeth find him arguing with the desk sergeant. Joe intervenes, and after mouthing all sorts of political rhetoric, he manages to get Merrick out of the grip of the police. This minor triumph is quickly changed when Mary discovers a card which has fallen out of Merrick's wallet stating that he is a private investigator (his cover to the store executives). She panics and during the next working day plans to knock him out to retrieve a list of names given to him by Joe which details all of the workers sympathetic to the unionization of the store.

She never gets a chance to hit him, although a pair of shoes falls on his head. They are hauled into the manager's office, and a minor riot ensues when Mary gets on the loud-speaker and asks the workers to stage a walkout. Everything comes to a head when the leaders of the workers are asked to bring their grievances to Mr. Merrick himself at his mansion. The shock makes Mary scream when she realizes that this humble slipper salesman-cum-private-detective is in reality the richest man in the world; Joe merely faints. Everything ends for the best when Mary and Joe and Merrick and Elizabeth have a double wedding and take the entire work force of the department store with them on an ocean voyage honeymoon to Hawaii.

Throughout this interwoven plot the basic relationship between labor and management is emphasized. The ivory tower environment of Merrick is contrasted vividly with the stark life-style of the middle-class workers. Joe cannot wed Mary because he has no job, and he has no job because of his activities as a union organizer. Merrick, as a lowly shoe salesman, enjoys a brown-bag lunch of tuna puffs prepared by Elizabeth in the park rather than the crumbled graham crackers in milk which he is served day after tedious day in the sanctity of his dark and brooding mansion. The contrasts are strong and basic. Real people enjoy life to the fullest; as Merrick becomes a real person, his carefully constructed world begins to dissolve around him, and he is happier for it. Coburn is excellent in showing the gradual yet inevitable change that takes place in J. P. Merrick. He suits the role of a plutocrat to perfection, yet he has the ability to transform himself into a warm and lovable character. His sympathetic nature is reinforced by Mary's enthusiasm; Arthur plays her character to the fullest. She typifies the free spirit of American woman, and her screen presence is unmistakable.

Sam Wood's direction is perfect during the transitional beach scene. He packs people into the frame of the scene as if they were sardines. His use of low-angle set-ups enhances the sense of alienation felt by Merrick. The true genius of the strong visual quality found in *The Devil and Miss Jones*, however, is the production design provided by William Cameron Menzies.

The attention to detail is quite remarkable. Menzies, who is credited with the beauty of *Gone with the Wind* (1939), is able to give depth and definition to the sets. He suggests personality through different architectural styles. At times this attention to detail seems out of place for a screwball comedy, yet the effect of this highly visual backdrop manages to convey the desired attitudes without wasting time with dialogue.

The Devil and Miss Jones is a comedy that presents a serious economic dilemma. It is quite different from Frank Capra's similar comedies, such as *Mr. Deeds Goes to Town* (1936) or *You Can't Take It with You* (1938), which revolve around the "little man." The difference in *The Devil and Miss Jones*, written by Norman Krasna, is that the major area of concentration is the transition of the plutocrat rather than the confirmation of the average man.

Carl F. Macek

DIAL M FOR MURDER

Released: 1954
Production: Alfred Hitchcock for Warner Bros.
Direction: Alfred Hitchcock
Screenplay: Frederick Knott; based on his play of the same name
Cinematography: Robert Burks
Editing: Rudi Fehr
Running time: 105 minutes

> *Principal characters:*
> Tony Wendice .... Ray Milland
> Margot Wendice .... Grace Kelly
> Mark Halliday .... Robert Cummings
> Inspector Hubbard .... John Williams
> Captain Lesgate .... Anthony Dawson

Alfred Hitchcock, the undisputed master of suspense, retains the theatrical origins of this lovely melodrama by confining most of the action to one room. The result is an intellectual chase scene for the mind rather than the body, as the audience watches the police inspector unravel the puzzle of the keys. The success of the film rests with the sound plotting of the script, the fine pacing, and the cinematography. Since there is only one action scene, a stabbing which occurs halfway through the movie, most of the tension is derived from the way Hitchcock first involves the audience in the murder scheme, and then in the efforts to entrap the murderer.

From the beginning it is clear that charming tennis pro Tony Wendice (Ray Milland), is planning to have his beautiful but unfaithful wife, Margot (Grace Kelly), murdered. Tony, who is nothing if not thorough, has been planning her demise for more than a year, ever since he discovered that she was having an affair with Mark Halliday (Robert Cummings), an American television mystery writer. Having married Margot for her money, Tony is now afraid that she will seek a divorce, thereby depriving him of his luxurious life style.

In the first scenes, Margot, seeing Mark for the first time in a year, explains that she had stopped their correspondence after the one love letter she had saved had been stolen from her purse at Victoria Station six months before. After that she had received two extortion letters, but the money she had sent in payment had never been collected by the blackmailer. She is convinced that Tony knows nothing of their affair.

The audience soon learns that Tony not only knows about the liaison, but that he is also her extortionist. Furthermore, Margot is not the only person he is going to blackmail. Pleading a heavy workload, Tony backs out of the theater engagement he and Margot have planned with Mark. Playing the role of the congenial, unsuspecting husband, he invites Mark to join him at a banquet being held at his club the following night. After Margot and Mark leave, Tony lures Captain Lesgate (Anthony Dawson), a disreputable rogue, over to the apartment. Lesgate, whose real name is Swann, was at Cambridge at the same time as Tony, who even then recognized a soul as unscrupulous as his own. Having followed Lesgate's activities for several months, Tony has now amassed a portfolio of crimes sufficient to convince Lesgate that he must carry out Tony's well-conceived plan, or he will go to jail.

Throughout the film Hitchcock uses a ground-level camera to capture the interaction between the players. As Tony outlines the perfect murder, however, the camera shifts overhead to give the audience a godlike perspective. Lesgate is to arrive at 10:37 the following night, take the key from under the carpet of the fifth step of the stairway just outside the apartment door, enter the flat, and hide behind the draperies behind the desk. Tony will excuse himself from the dinner at 10:40 to call his boss, but first will call home. When the phone rings, Margot will get out of bed and come to the desk, where Lesgate will strangle her. He will then whistle into the phone, at which point Tony will hang up and call his boss to support his alibi. When the deed is done, Tony will pay Lesgate a thousand pounds, which he has unobtrusively been saving at the rate of twenty pounds per week.

The next night the camera is returned to the human, fallible level to watch the drama unfold. Much of Hitchcock's brilliance is revealed in the way he manipulates the audience's involvement. When Margot suddenly announces her intention to go to a movie, thereby ruining all of Tony's masterful planning, the audience roots for him as he persuades her to stay home. Ironically, his vain suggestion that she clip articles for his scrapbook results in the ultimate failure of his plan, by providing her with the weapon she needs for her own defense. Tony unobtrusively removes her latchkey from her purse and places it under the carpet in the stairway before he and Mark leave for dinner.

When Lesgate enters the apartment that night, Hitchcock uses the technique of "film time" to stretch out action which normally would take only a few seconds. The result is an increase in the level of tension as the importance of the events is emphasized. In one of the few cuts outside the apartment, the audience sees that Tony's watch is slow and that Lesgate is about to leave. To the audience's relief, the call comes through just in time, and as Margot answers the phone, Lesgate slips a knotted stocking around her neck and begins violently choking her. The dim lighting creates an ominous atmosphere which emphasizes her agony as she struggles against his superior strength. Suddenly, however, she is able to grasp the scissors on the desk and plunge them into her assailant. In the one truly gruesome shot, Lesgate falls on his back, driving the scissors in deeper.

Tony, realizing that the plan has gone awry, now comes on the line to tell Margot not to call the police until he gets home. Panic-stricken and grateful to hear his voice, Margot follows his instructions. Clever as well as diabolical, Tony quickly alters the plan to make it appear that Lesgate had been blackmailing Margot, who in turn killed him. Tony plants Mark's love letter on Lesgate, removes the latchkey from the victim's pocket and places it in Margot's purse, and hides a knotted silk stocking in the wastebasket before calling the police.

From here on the tension is derived from a cat-and-mouse game between Tony and Inspector Hubbard (John Williams), an investigator who is the epitome of the British detective. The audience now begins to identify with the inquisitive, perceptive Inspector.

The bewildered Margot is amazed to find that all the evidence is suddenly distorted against her. Tony, as her loyal husband, staunchly defends her on the surface, while subtly providing all the evidence needed to convict her of first-degree murder. He informs the Inspector that he is sure that Margot does not know Lesgate (that is, Swann), but that he had known him briefly in college; he had only seen Swann once since, and that was at Victoria Station six months before. This, together with the love letter found in Lesgate's pocket, makes the blackmail motive for murder very plausible. When the silk stocking is found in the wastebasket, it appears likely that Margot's neck bruises were self-inflicted. The most damning piece of evidence, however, is the fact that the carpet and the condition of Lesgate's shoes prove that he must have come in through the front door, and that she must have let him in.

For the trial, Hitchcock maintains a claustrophobic intensity by using an effective series of close-ups of Margot's face illuminated with colored lights against a neutral backdrop. She is convicted of first-degree murder and sentenced to death. Wiley Inspector Hubbard, however, is bothered by the fact that Lesgate carried no latchkey, so the day before the sentence is to be carried out, he devises a scheme to unearth new evidence. Hubbard goes to the apartment purportedly to question Tony about the large sums of money he has been spending lately, but during the course of the interview the Inspector manages to switch raincoats with Tony. He suggests Tony drop by the station to pick up some of Margot's possessions. After Tony goes out, Hubbard uses the key inside Tony's raincoat to enter the apartment. Upon returning, he finds that Mark has broken in hoping to find evidence to save Margot.

Inspector Hubbard then initiates step one. Margot is driven to the front door and told to go inside the apartment. The Inspector and Mark wait quietly inside the darkened flat and listen as she enters the building, walks down the hallway, and tries to open the door with the key from her purse. When she is unable to open the door, she walks back outside. Hitchcock heightens the effectiveness of this scene with the use of real tiles in the hallway which emphasize the drama as the footsteps echo and recede.

The police then rush Margot's purse back to the station where Tony soon picks it up. Inspector Hubbard explains to Mark and Margot that the key in her purse was Lesgate's own latchkey and that he has Tony's key. The Inspector has located Margot's key under the carpet on the fifth step of the stairway; she has proven that she did not know it was there; her fate now rests on proving that Tony does know. The tension mounts as Tony's footsteps are heard in the hallway. He tries the key from Margot's purse; it does not work; he starts out, then stops. Suddenly, he realizes that Lesgate must have returned the key to the step before entering the apartment. He retrieves it, unlocks the door, and turns on the light, illuminating the scene.

Though Hitchcock maintains the theatricality of the production by confining the action to one room, he uses close-ups to capture the terror on the actors' faces which would be missed on stage. Changes in lighting, from the dimly lit attack scene to the symbolic illumination of the villain at the end, add to the atmosphere. Hitchcock's use of color also helps set the mood. Margot is first dressed in lovely colors, she is wearing white when attacked, and as her plight becomes desperate she wears black.

Though most audiences saw *Dial M for Murder* in the traditional format, it was filmed in Naturalvision, Warner Bros.' version of 3-D. The 3-D format was useful in this case, not for special effects, but for giving the film additional depth and intimacy within the confining set.

Hitchcock, always noted for his inconspicuous appearances in his films, has cleverly worked himself into a reunion picture which Tony shows to Lesgate during their interview.

The performances are generally good. John Williams and Anthony Dawson reenacted their Broadway roles. Williams is well cast as the Scotland Yard-type detective who enjoys unraveling clues. Dawson has made a career out of playing snakelike villain roles. Ray Milland is convincingly pathological as the venal Tony, and Grace Kelly is good at conveying bewilderment and terror. All in all, Hitchcock's talent for creating suspense blends with Frederick Knott's well-crafted plot to provide an interesting and diverting mystery.

Anne Louise Lynch

DIARY OF A MAD HOUSEWIFE

Released: 1970
Production: Frank Perry for Universal
Direction: Frank Perry
Screenplay: Eleanor Perry; based on the novel of the same name by Sue Kaufman
Cinematography: Ellis W. Carter
Editing: Grant Whytock
Running time: 100 minutes

Principal characters:
Jonathan Balser	Richard Benjamin
George Prager	Frank Langella
Tina Balser	Carrie Snodgress
Sylvie Balser	Lorraine Cullen
Liz Balser	Frannie Michel
Man in Group Therapy Session	Peter Boyle

In the mid-1960's, increasing numbers of women were becoming aware of the limitations of their role as females. Society dictated that a young girl stayed home and helped her mother wash dishes while her brothers climbed trees and scraped their knees. While "boys would be boys," the thought of girls gashing their elbows was most unladylike. Generally, as a girl got older, she passively waited for Mr. Right to sweep her into heaven. If he did not appear with an engagement ring by the time she was twenty-one, she was sure to be an old maid. Once married, she tended house and managed the babies while her husband earned the money and made the decisions. She had no choices. Later, young women who had been weaned on television, civil rights marches, and Vietnam War protests began to ponder their lives and question the premise that their existences must be based on a traditional dependence on men. *Diary of a Mad Housewife*, released in 1970, is one of the earliest films to chronicle the emerging conflict between the old order and the new woman who must learn to accept responsibility for her own life.

Tina Balser (Carrie Snodgress), has, outwardly, an ideal life for a woman. She is married to Jonathan (Richard Benjamin), a successful lawyer, and has two young daughters. She is not content with her existence, however; her status-seeking husband oppressively nags her, and her children are spoiled and constantly complain. She is propositioned by George Prager (Frank Langella), an egotistical writer, at an art gallery opening. Fed up with her mundane life, she accepts and becomes his mistress, but Prager is no less tyrannical than her husband, and the affair deteriorates. A party Jonathan has been planning fizzles, and he admits to his wife that he has not been a "good" husband—he has had an affair, he has mismanaged their money, and his job with his law firm is in jeopardy. Tina soon ends her relationship with Prager and joins a therapy group in an attempt to sort out her life.

Tina is no robust, dynamic wonder woman, and certainly no icon for feminists. She is awkward and defensive as she ponders her existence and takes action against her negative condition. Her attempt at group therapy is no radical solution. Tina is a pampered housewife who is bored by her drab surroundings and stifled by the unreasonable demands of her husband and children, yet she realizes that she, and she alone, is the only person who can take charge of herself. The act of attending group therapy is a courageous decision for a woman who has been molded and shaped into a set, narrow life-style since birth and who has no peer support for her actions. Tina is a realistic character with conflicts and contradictions who is searching for a life-style in which she can thrive.

As Tina is a fully defined character attempting to gain insights into her life, both her husband and her lover are presented as one-dimensional, chauvinistic villains. Jonathan Balser is a neurotic, bullying lout who is interested only in materialism. He has no mind of his own, his tastes and opinions being dictated by what is acceptable and fashionable to the society of chic, Upper East Side New York. He is obsessed with upward mobility: he spews off brand names of products and high-class clothing as if he were a walking advertisement for posh Fifth Avenue specialty shops. He cheats on his wife—a macho endeavor—but is ultimately depicted as not worthy of manhood. He is unable to manage money and endangers his position in his law firm. George Prager is no less one-dimensional: he is deluded in the belief that he is perfect, that the lady of his choice will be enslaved by his masculinity, and that he can ridicule his women at will. He, too, is less than the man he pretends to be— Tina accuses him of being latently homosexual, and the impression is that he is indeed hiding something. Tina is the only sane person of the three, and screenwriter Eleanor Perry would have done well to humanize Jonathan and George. Both are narrow creations, stereotyped visions of men who, despite their delusions, are not really men and are less human than women.

Nevertheless, the late Perry and her husband Frank, the director of *Diary of a Mad Housewife*, shrewdly capture the essence of a certain New York life-style—plush, chic, upper-middle-class, and "in," but ultimately predatory and phony. Most of the film is shot in interior, enclosed settings, such as art galleries laden with paintings and cluttered apartments, which help to convey Tina's inward confusion. The film is most relevant, however, for its portrayal of a woman who realizes she must take action. Some of the Perrys' other films deal with characters in crisis who also must undergo change or question the values imposed on them by others. In *David and Lisa* (1963), for example, two mentally retarded teenagers realize that they are capable of happiness. In *The Swimmer* (1968), a middle-aged suburban man must come to terms with the affluent existence he despises.

Diary of a Mad Housewife is the forerunner of a genre of films which portray women rebelling against a stultifying life style and environment and searching for their own identities. Among them are *Alice Doesn't Live Here Anymore* (1974), *A Woman Under the Influence* (1974), *Coming Home* (1978), and *An Unmarried Woman* (1978). Snodgress, in her first starring role, received glowing notices for her work. She is appropriately vulnerable as she awkwardly takes action and attempts to resolve the uncertainties in her mind. One critic even suggested that she "evokes . . . the talent of the late Margaret Sullivan." The film did moderately well, taking in $6,100,000 at the box office.

Snodgress was nominated for an Academy Award, losing out (with Jane Alexander in *The Great White Hope*, Ali MacGraw for *Love Story*, and Sarah Miles for *Ryan's Daughter*) to Glenda Jackson in *Women in Love*, but she was a double Golden Globe winner, for Best Actress and Most Promising Newcomer. The actress temporarily chose not to pursue a film career, and left acting to live with rock star Neil Young. She later returned to her profession, and has been cast in uninspired roles in such average-to-mediocre entertainments as Brian de Palma's *The Fury* (1980) and the television movies *Love's Dark Ride* and *Fast Friends*.

Benjamin is appropriately snide and condescending as Jonathan, but Langella is a revelation as Prager. He is menacingly sensual and authoritarian, and was named Best Supporting Actor by the National Board of Review for his performance here and in Mel Brooks's *The Twelve Chairs* (1970). Some of the qualities of George Prager are in his stage and screen portrayal of *Dracula* (1979). In a bit at the end of *Diary of a Mad Housewife*, a pre-*Joe* (1970) Peter Boyle appears as a harassed participant in Tina's therapy session.

Diary of a Mad Housewife is dated when one compares Tina Balser's manner of dealing with her problems and relating to men and to herself with that of the heroines played by Ellen Burstyn, Jane Fonda, Jill Clayburgh, and Gena Rowlands, yet the character of Tina is a definite cinematic step in the direction of the depiction of women as other than happy housewives and hookers.

Rob Edelman

THE DIARY OF ANNE FRANK

Released: 1959
Production: George Stevens for Twentieth Century-Fox
Direction: George Stevens
Screenplay: Frances Goodrich and Albert Hackett; based on their play of the same name and adapted from the novel *Anne Frank: The Diary of a Young Girl*
Cinematography: William C. Mellor (AA)
Editing: David Bretherton, Robert Swink, and William Mace
Art direction: Lyle R. Wheeler and George W. Davis (AA); set decoration, Walter M. Scott and Stuart A. Reiss (AA)
Running time: 170 minutes

> *Principal characters:*
> Anne Frank .... Millie Perkins
> Otto Frank .... Joseph Schildkraut
> Mrs. Van Daan .... Shelley Winters (AA)
> Mr. Dussell ....Ed Wynn
> Peter Van Daan .... Richard Beymer
> Mrs. Frank ....Gusti Huber
> Mr. Van Daan ....Lou Jacobi
> Margot Frank .... Diane Baker

When *Anne Frank: The Diary of a Young Girl* was published in English in 1952, it almost immediately became a best-seller. Its immense appeal was based partly on the personality of the real Anne Frank as revealed in her diary and partly on the specific and personal view it presented of a horror nearly too large to comprehend—the killing of millions of Jews by the Nazis. The smallest personal details in the narrative are set against a huge and impersonal evil. The book has remained in print since 1952 and is still a moving story, especially considering the tender age of its authoress. Frances Goodrich and Albert Hackett transformed the book into a play, *The Diary of Anne Frank*, that began a successful run on Broadway in 1955 and won three major awards, including a Pulitzer Prize. Thus it was a moving, significant, and already popular work that director George Stevens presented on the screen in 1959.

The story is, in essence, a simple one. In order to escape from the Nazis in Amsterdam during World War II, two Jewish families and one other Jewish man hide for more than two years in a loft above a spice factory where their only contact with the outside world is through the two people who hide them and a radio. They never leave the loft until very near the end of the war, when they are discovered and sent to concentration camps. The story is told by Anne Frank, who is thirteen when they enter the hiding place and whose diary is found three years later by her father, the only member of the entire group to survive the camps.

The film interweaves three dominant themes: the fear of discovery by the Nazis, which is ever-present, the frictions caused by a group of people having to live in such close quarters for so long, and a young girl's normal adolescent development taking place in such abnormal surroundings.

The film begins with an old man getting out of a truck and going into a building. It is Otto Frank (Joseph Schildkraut), the sole survivor, who is returning for the first time to the loft where the eight had stayed in hiding for so long. He finds little but his daughter's diary. At the end of this long, nearly wordless sequence he begins reading the diary as a dissolve takes us back to three years before.

The two Jewish families, the Franks and the Van Daans, have just arrived in their attic hiding place, and Mr. Frank is explaining the restrictions under which they must live for as long as they stay. Since they are above a factory, they must be absolutely silent during the day so that the workers below will never suspect anyone is there. Because their protectors have only three forged ration cards with which to buy them food, they will have a very limited supply. Frank's explanation is interrupted by the siren of the "green police," a sound which will be a continual reminder throughout the film of the menace from which they all are hiding.

The Frank family consists of the father, mother (Gusti Huber), and two daughters, Margot (Diane Baker) and her younger sister Anne (Millie Perkins). The Van Daans (Lou Jacobi and Shelley Winters) have a son, Peter (Richard Beymer). After some time they accept one more person into their hiding place, Dussell (Ed Wynn), a dentist who had always considered himself just a Dutch citizen until the authorities discovered his Jewish heritage. He brings with him grim news of the persecution of the Jews in the city, including many that the two families knew personally. The somewhat sour dentist is frequently an irritation to the others, even though he is often correct in his concerns and worries, such as his belief that allowing Peter to keep a cat is an unnecessary risk.

One of Van Daan's chief concerns is food. Before, he was used to indulging his appetite, and in the hiding place he is never able to get used to the sparse rations. Near the end he is caught stealing food from the common supply and breaks down in shame for what he has done. His wife, on the other hand, is inordinately fond of her fur coat, which is her only reminder of her previous style of living. When Anne spills some milk on the coat, Mrs. Van Daan treats the accident as a major catastrophe, and later her husband's desire to have the coat sold precipitates a bitter fight between the two.

Anne has many of an adolescent's usual problems with adults, but they are magnified by the unusual situation. She must share a room with Dussell, and their incompatibility produces a good deal of bickering. Anne gets along quite well with her father, but she is convinced that her mother can never understand her. When she realizes how much she has hurt her mother, she tries to make amends by giving her a gift of a piece of paper saying that she (Anne) will do whatever she is told for ten hours. Dussell's immediate response is, "You wouldn't want to sell that?"

Anne's chief concern, besides the ones they all share, becomes her romance with Peter Van Daan. It is not approved by Mrs. Van Daan and is, of course, quite circumscribed by the confined circumstances. A curious ritual develops in which Anne goes to her own room to get ready to see Peter (while the ousted Dussell fumes outside the door); then she walks through the main room full of adults to Peter's room where they have a prescribed time of privacy. Their first kiss is presented in a dramatic—perhaps too dramatic—fashion. The two figures are seen in silhouette to a silent sound track; then they kiss and the music begins and swells.

There is naturally much tension in the film, particularly in a few scenes in which the group is in danger of being discovered. In one scene a Nazi patrol searches the building below the attic while we watch Peter's cat almost knock a metal funnel off a shelf. In another scene a burglar breaks into the building below but is scared away by noise caused by the animal. There are also moments of comedy. When the group gets the news over the radio that the Allies have landed in Europe, Van Daan is moaning about his shame for stealing the food. Dussell interrupts him: "Stop it. You're spoiling the whole invasion."

The comedy and the tension and the boredom end, however, when finally they are discovered by the "green police." Anne has written in her diary, "I still believe—in spite of everything—that people are really good at heart." After a kiss between Anne and Peter and shots of the anxious group listening to the sound below them there is a freeze frame as Frank says, "We have lived in fear; now we can live in hope."

To capture the confined setting of the film, director George Stevens had an exact replica of the loft, which is still in existence, constructed with only one side removed. Ordinary film sets have movable walls and no ceilings so that the lighting and camera equipment may be put wherever the director desires, but Stevens thought the self-imposed limitation would force him and cinematographer William C. Mellor to keep the audience aware of the claustrophobic quality of the living quarters. The technique is largely successful, although Stevens sometimes defeats his purpose by showing us shots of things going on outside that the group in the loft could never see. He also dissipates some of the force of the film by the length of individual scenes and the length of the whole film (three hours including an intermission); a shorter, more tightly paced film might have better sustained the audience's emotion. Mellor received a well-deserved Oscar for his camerawork, as did four others—Lyle R. Wheeler, George W. Davis, Walter M. Scott, and Stuart A. Reiss—for the art direction and set decoration.

Although only Winters won an Oscar for the acting in *The Diary of Anne Frank*, the three actors who re-created their Broadway roles are also excellent. Schildkraut, who makes the almost too saintly figure of Otto Frank believable, Huger as Mrs. Frank, and Jacobi as Van Daan all expose the human foibles of their characters. Wynn's performance as Dussell is good although he was still a relative novice as a serious actor, having given his first noncomic performance in the 1956 *Playhouse 90* production of *Requiem for a Heavyweight* on television. To play the central role of Anne, Perkins, a young model, was chosen. She looks right for the role and does a good job overall, although her inexperience as an actress occasionally shows.

One of the chief virtues of *The Diary of Anne Frank* is the audience's knowledge that the film presents a true story about one of the greatest evils of our century. Stevens only needed to do justice to his subject, and he has done so.

Timothy W. Johnson

DINNER AT EIGHT

Released: 1933
Production: David O. Selznick for Metro-Goldwyn-Mayer
Direction: George Cukor
Screenplay: Frances Marion and Herman J. Mankiewicz, with additional dialogue by Donald Ogden Stewart; based on the play of the same name by George S. Kaufman and Edna Ferber
Cinematography: William Daniels
Editing: Ben Lewis
Running time: 110 minutes

Principal characters:

Carlotta Vance	Marie Dressler
Larry Renault	John Barrymore
Dan Packard	Wallace Beery
Kitty Packard	Jean Harlow
Oliver Jordan	Lionel Barrymore
Max Kane	Lee Tracy
Dr. Wayne Talbot	Edmund Lowe
Mrs. Talbot	Karen Morley
Mrs. Oliver Jordan	Billie Burke
Paula Jordan	Madge Evans
Jo Stengel	Jean Hersholt

When *Dinner at Eight* opened on Broadway in October of 1932, it was an instant success. It ran for 232 performances at the Music Box Theatre, and the rights to film it were acquired by M-G-M, where Irving Thalberg, who never received screen credit on any picture he personally supervised, planned it as one of his own productions for 1933. Thalberg, however, fell seriously ill and was forced to take a vacation from filmmaking. Louis B. Mayer turned over production to his son-in-law, David O. Selznick, who gave *Dinner at Eight* preferential treatment, bringing over his friend, George Cukor, from RKO.

The two men established the film as an all-star feature presenting ten stars in the leading roles. M-G-M had done very well during the 1930's with a series of productions that were truly all-star, starting in 1932 with *Grand Hotel*. Now, with ten players featured in *Dinner at Eight*, all of whom rated top billing, even the subsidiary roles were filled by performers who were known at the box office, such as Karen Morley, Louise Closser Hale, Phillips Holmes, and May Robson. The film proved to be one of M-G-M's biggest moneymakers, although it did not earn a single Academy Award nomination, perhaps because it was slick, glamorous, sophisticated, and had almost no real heart. Selznick gave the production his own touch of glitter, and Cukor, with the help of a very smartly written screenplay, made the story move smoothly, with all episodes leading up to the final scene in the Jordan drawing-room.

Dinner at Eight is basically the story of a fashionable dinner party given by a socialite wife, Mrs. Oliver Jordan (Billie Burke). Unknown to her, not only is the Jordan Steamship Line on the verge of financial disaster, but her husband (Lionel Barrymore) is on the brink of a physical breakdown. A week before the dinner party, Mrs. Jordan has acquired Lord and Lady Ferncliffe as honored guests, and she is building her guest list around them. She is having Dr. Wayne Talbot (Edmund Lowe) and his wife (Karen Morley), and Carlotta Vance (Marie Dressler), who had once been a great star in the theater. Oliver asks her also to invite Dan Packard (Wallace Beery) and his wife Kitty (Jean Harlow). Packard, who lives somewhere out West and owns freight lines, might be able to do Jordan some good. What Jordan does not know is that Packard plans to acquire the ailing Jordan line for as small a sum as possible.

When Kitty tells her husband that they have been invited to dinner at the Jordans on the coming Friday, he says they are not going. When he learns that Lord and Lady Ferncliffe will be there, however, he admits that he has been trying for years to meet the Ferncliffes and changes his mind. He leaves his wife's boudoir before Dr. Talbot arrives. Almost at once the relationship between Kitty and Dr. Talbot is established. He is a Park Avenue doctor with a "bedside manner," and already Kitty is becoming one of his most demanding patients.

Millicent Jordan has all her guests' acceptances, but she needs an extra man because Carlotta Vance is coming by herself. She decides to invite Larry Renault (John Barrymore), a stage star who had gone into the movies and made a big hit, until he began drinking. As a result of liquor and his advancing years, he can no longer get film roles. Now he is in New York seeking a play that will put him back in circulation. What Millicent does not know is that her daughter Paula (Madge Evans), engaged to marry the socially prominent Ernest DeGraff within a month, has caught the fancy of Renault, and Paula and Renault are enjoying a secret, if somewhat indiscreet, love affair. Larry tries to talk Paula out of the crush she has developed on him, pointing out that she is nineteen, while he is in his forties and burned out; but Paula is determined that nothing shall hurt their lovely affair.

On the day of his wife's dinner party, Oliver Jordan suffers an acute heart attack and is taken to Dr. Talbot's office. The doctor recognizes that Jordan will not live more than a few months, and mildly suggests that he skip his wife's dinner party that night and get a little rest. Jordan is not fooled by the doctor's demeanor, but he also will not disappoint Millicent; he will be the host as usual.

It does not take long for Jordan to learn the worst about his failing steamship line. Although he has asked Carlotta to hold onto her stock, she has sold it that afternoon, because of her own financial problems, to a man named James K. Baldridge. Jordan learns that another block of stock has been sold by other friends to the same man. He knows that Baldridge is a front name to cover the identity of the real buyer, who is Dan Packard.

The Packards have an argument as they are dressing for the Jordans' dinner, and Dan accuses Kitty of cheating on him. Kitty denies it; she has seen no other man except the doctor, and her maid verifies that. When she threatens him with her knowledge of his crooked deals, the argument is stalemated, with Kitty forcing Dan to make good on the Jordan stock in exchange for her silence.

Larry Renault's fate is more tragic. He has insulted the one Broadway producer who might have given him a choice supporting role, insisting that he will accept nothing but the lead; this causes his hitherto faithful agent to turn on him. Alone and half-drunk, Larry realizes that he is going nowhere; he is financially broke and virtually friendless. He locks the door, stuffs pillows and clothing at the door and window cracks, turns on the gas, and sits in front of the heater in his dinner clothes, waiting.

The guests begin to arrive at the Jordans' home for dinner. At the last minute, the secretary to Lord and Lady Ferncliffe, who were the *raison d'être* for the dinner, has called to say that they are sorry, but they are in Florida and unable to attend the party. Millicent, who is distraught over the preparations for the party, has gotten her cousins to substitute at the last moment. Because Millicent is so caught up in her own petty little world, she fails to realize how ill her husband is and chastizes him for wishing to go to bed early. She also refuses to listen to her daughter as Paula tries to tell her mother of her love for Renault.

The stories are neatly wrapped up before the guests sit down to dinner. Oliver is told by Packard that his company has been saved, shortly after Millicent tearfully tells her husband that their life will be "happier than ever" when she learns of his financial and physical worries. She admits to her frivolousness and promises to change. The Jordans' daughter decides to marry her fiancé after all when Carlotta informs her that Renault has killed himself; Paula realizes the hopelessness of that love and she walks into dinner on Ernest DeGraff's arm.

Thus, all the plots and subplots of the story are resolved just before the guests sit down to their dinner. The final lines of the film are a classically funny interchange between Carlotta and Kitty. Kitty observes brightly, "I was reading a book the other day," an admission that brings an incredulous look to Carlotta's face, but Kitty goes on blithely: "It's about civilization or something. Do you know, the guy said machinery is going to take the place of every profession." Carlotta grunts to herself with a meaningful look at the sensuous Kitty, "Oh, my dear. That's something you'll never have to worry about."

Top billing went to Marie Dressler, who played her part as legitimately as she could; Cukor somehow managed to get her to soft pedal her usual mugging. Carlotta Vance, the actress played by Dressler, was supposed to have been an intimate of Somerset Maugham, Michael Arlen, and Charlie Chaplin. There are elements of famous socialite and actress Maxine Elliott in the background of Carlotta as written by Kaufman and Ferber, but there is never anything of the upper crust society woman in Dressler's characterization.

John Barrymore and Wallace Beery got second and third billing. Barrymore brings elegance to his role of Larry Renault, and Beery, who had been co-starring in several films with Dressler, manages some mugging of his own as the uncouth Westerner, Dan Packard. Fourth billing went to Jean Harlow, who positively blooms under Cukor's experienced direction. The role of Kitty Packard is so well-written as to be almost actress-proof, and Harlow plays it with the innocent but nonetheless malevolent joyousness that she first displayed in *Red-Headed Woman* (1932).

Lionel Barrymore is sympathetic as the dying Oliver, underplaying the part effectively; Lee Tracy gives one of his best performances as the faithful actor's agent, Max Kane. Edmund Lowe has just the right virility and polish for the society doctor, Wayne Talbot; and Billie Burke, who had been annoyingly saccharine in her first talking roles, is perfect as a fluttering matron unaware that her fine house is tumbling down. Madge Evans brings youthful beauty and sincerity to her role as the daughter, Paula Jordan, and Jean Hersholt is perfect as Jo Stengel, the producer willing to give the fading Larry Renault a second chance.

The play had boasted a series of subplots devoted to the servants who prepared and served the dinner, but the downstairs part of the play was cut and the upstairs emphasized in the movie version. *Dinner at Eight* marked David O. Selznick's debut as a producer at M-G-M (he followed it with another 1933 all-star production that is forgotten today: *Night Flight*, with both John and Lionel Barrymore, Helen Hayes, Clark Gable, Robert Montgomery, Myrna Loy, and William Gargan). *Dinner at Eight* remains a top favorite and is certain to be included in every retrospective of the best from M-G-M in the 1930's.

DeWitt Bodeen

THE DIRTY DOZEN

Released: 1967
Production: Kenneth Hyman for Metro-Goldwyn-Mayer
Direction: Robert Aldrich
Screenplay: Nunnally Johnson and Lukas Heller; based on the novel of the same name by E. M. Nathanson
Cinematography: Edward Scaife
Editing: Michael Luciano
Sound effects: John Poyner (AA)
Running time: 149 minutes

> *Principal characters:*
> Major Reisman .... Lee Marvin
> General Worden .... Ernest Borgnine
> Joseph Wladislaw .... Charles Bronson
> Robert Jefferson .... Jim Brown
> Victor Franko .... John Cassavetes
> Sergeant Bowren .... Richard Jaeckel
> Major Max Armbruster .... George Kennedy
> Colonel Everett Dasher Breed .... Robert Ryan
> Archer Maggott .... Telly Savalas
> Vernon Pinkley .... Donald Sutherland
> Samson Posey .... Clint Walker

In *The Dirty Dozen*, a box-office sensation in 1967, Lee Marvin led a band of murderers, psychopaths, and sex maniacs on a violent suicide mission during which the misfits acquitted themselves as military heroes. Released at a time when the United States antiwar movement was nearing its most passionate level, it fascinated "dove" moviegoers who were totally ready to accept the delineation of top soldiers as manic slaughterers, as well as "hawk-ish" audiences who applauded the Dozen's brutal combat. *The Dirty Dozen* became one of the greatest box-office successes in M-G-M's history.

Based on E. M. Nathanson's novel and directed by Robert Aldrich, *The Dirty Dozen* tells the story of Major Reisman (Lee Marvin), who is assigned by General Worden (Ernest Borgnine) to train twelve convicted G. I.'s for a suicide mission. The task: parachute into Nazi-infested France, attack a chateau retreat for top Nazi officers, and completely destroy it. Reisman thinks the plan "stinks" but reluctantly accepts, and soon meets his troops: Chicago hoodlum and psychopath Victor Franko (John Cassavetes); murderer Joseph Wladislaw (Charles Bronson); white-hating black Robert Jefferson (Jim Brown); moronic Vernon Pinkley (Donald Sutherland); and Southern bigot, religious fanatic, and sex fiend Archer Maggott (Telly Savalas) among them. The odd group accepts the proposal, hoping they may win pardons if they survive. At first they all resent Reisman, but he, with the aid of Sergeant

Bowren (Richard Jaeckel), eventually wins their respect by controlling them with browbeating, bullying, and leadership.

Reisman's greatest aid in producing a fighting unit comes when pompous Colonel Everett Dasher Breed (Robert Ryan), of West Point distinction, pits his highly disciplined troops against the Dozen in war games. The Dirty Dozen, who ironically earn that nickname not because of their morals but because they are at one point deprived of soap, triumph in the contest, capturing the entire staff of the abashed Breed and winning the go-ahead for their mission. Here the theme of the film is pungently conveyed, as Breed's men, full of discipline, training, and military logic, prove no match for the Dozen and their crafty, underhanded tactics.

The plane carrying Reisman, Bowren, and the Dozen is soon over France, and they parachute to the site of their mission. Wladislaw, who speaks fluent German, and Reisman, who speaks not a word of it, disguise themselves as German officers and penetrate the chalet as the soldiers take their various stations outside. Director Aldrich ingeniously presents the very proper, well-groomed, aristocratic German officers, their lovely concubines, and the beautiful accoutrements of the retreat, creating a marvelous contrast to the grimy conspirators who lurk outside, waiting to destroy such representations of impeccable civilization.

The mission is proceeding well when Maggott cracks. The deranged maniac crawls into a posh bedroom, snares the young lover of an officer, sadistically taunts her with knife play, and slays her. Then, seemingly enjoying a perverted sexual release, the madly grinning Maggott begins shooting off his machine gun, betraying the plot. He is killed by Jefferson, and in the ensuing horror of grenade explosions and machine gun bursts, the Allies corral the officers and girls into the cellars, pour gasoline-soaked grenades down the ventilator shafts, and totally destroy the chateau.

The final scene takes place in a hospital; only Reisman, Wladislaw, and Bowren are still alive. The survivors hear General Worden's news that the dead criminals will be listed in the annals as gallant soldiers who honorably gave their lives for love of country.

Predominately rave reviews greeted *The Dirty Dozen* when it was released in the summer of 1967: *Variety* called it "An exciting, well-mounted, and grimly realistic World War II drama. . . ." Judith Crist of NBC's "Today Show" said it was ". . . one of the best and least compromising he-man adventure films. . . ." There was, however, a very vocal minority who despised the film, such as Bosley Crowther of the *New York Times*, who found the film ", . . . astonishingly wanton . . . downright preposterous." Decrying the violence and the grim moral, such critics did, however, affect the movie's reception at the box office. *The Dirty Dozen* soared into the top ten money-makers of M-G-M's forty-year history, grossing $20,170,000. It did not succeed, however, in persuading the Motion Picture Academy of its merits at awards time. *The Dirty Dozen* won only one Oscar; John Poyner for his Sound effects; and reaped only one major nomination, John Cassavetes for Best Supporting Actor. He lost, ironically, to *Cool Hand Luke*'s George Kennedy, who appeared in *The Dirty Dozen* as sympathetic Major Armbruster, Worden's cohort. The film placed fifth in the *Film Daily* 1967 "Ten Best" roster.

The Dirty Dozen remains a riveting, exciting film; it scored powerful ratings when first shown on television, although it was considerably edited, and it continues to fascinate not only because of its plot, but also because of the several small parts played by future "superstars," such as Charles Bronson, Donald Sutherland, and Telly Savalas. Marvin is superbly taut as Reisman, and all of the Dozen, with the exception of singer Trini Lopez as Pedro Jiminez, obviously revel in their grotesquely picaresque roles. Topping the lot for the acting honors are Cassavetes, who plays his part of the psychotic Franko with morsels of sardonic humor, and Telly Savalas, whose bug-eycd, Dixie-drawling, maniacal Maggott appears a very distant relation to his more familiar role as television's lollipop-sucking Kojack.

Many antiwar pictures followed *The Dirty Dozen*. In most however, the military denizens were caricatured as bloodthirsty buffoons, as in *M*A*S*H* (1970) and *Alice's Restaurant* (1969). None, however, took the compelling slant of *The Dirty Dozen*: that war, a horrible event, can only be truly ended by horrible means, most effectively concocted and executed by horrible men.

Gregory William Mank

DIRTY HARRY

Released: 1971
Production: Don Siegel for Malpaso Company Productions; released by
  Warner Bros.
Direction: Don Siegel
Screenplay: Harry Julian Fink, R. M. Fink, and Dean Riesner; based on a
  story by Harry Julian Fink and R. M. Fink
Cinematography: Bruce Surtees
Editing: Carl Pingitore
Running time: 103 minutes

Principal characters:
Harry Callahan .... Clint Eastwood
Bressler .... Harry Guardino
Chico .... Reni Santoni
Killer (Scorpio) .... Andy Robinson
Chief .... John Larch
Mayor .... John Vernon

Dirty Harry is the first in a series of three movies (including *Magnum
Force*, 1973; and *The Enforcer*, 1976) about the adventures of Detective Harry
Callahan of the San Francisco Police Department. All three films star Clint
Eastwood as Harry, all are controversial, and all were very successful, each
one earning more at the box office than its predecessor. They all depend on
intense action and graphic violence to lure the audiences. The appeal of the
Eastwood *persona* also draws people to the theater, as does the more dubious
attraction of the Callahan character. While the two sequels are not without
merit, *Dirty Harry* is the most successful in terms of cinematic artistry and
deserves a close examination.

The film opens with a sniper on a rooftop in San Francisco shooting a girl
in a nearby swimming pool. The killer leaves a note demanding money and
threatening to kill a priest or a black person next. The note is signed
"Scorpio." Detective Harry Callahan is called in to investigate and apprehend
the murderer.

Harry (Clint Eastwood), both coolly professional and rudely contemptuous
of authority, is assigned a partner by the Police Chief (John Larch). Harry
is dismayed to discover that the partner is a rookie, a Mexican-American,
and college-educated, all serious liabilities. Chico (Reni Santoni) is eager to
learn and to prove himself to the man widely known in the department as
Dirty Harry. As they begin their investigation, they accidentally interrupt a
bank robbery in progress. In a spectacular sequence, Harry quickly and
violently captures the robbers. His methods are brutal and extralegal and
clearly explain his nickname.

Scorpio (Andy Robinson) is spotted on another rooftop, and Harry and Chico attempt to capture him, but he escapes. After a young black man is killed, Harry sets a trap using a policeman disguised as a priest. Scorpio takes the bait, but once again escapes before Harry can capture him. Scorpio next sends the police a note informing them that he has buried a young girl alive with only a little oxygen to sustain her. He will tell the police where she is if they give him $200,000. The Mayor (John Vernon) assigns Harry to deliver the ransom and instructs him not to attempt to capture the killer. Chico shadows Harry as Scorpio leads him on a chase across the city, ending finally in a park, where Harry and Chico are shot in their attempt to capture Scorpio, although Harry manages to stab Scorpio in the leg.

After being treated for his gunshot wound, Harry learns from a doctor in the hospital emergency room that the groundskeeper at Kezar Stadium has just been treated for a stab wound in the leg. Harry goes to the stadium, kicks in the door of the room where Scorpio lives, and wounds him in the ensuing struggle. He tortures the killer into revealing the location of the kidnaped girl, but it is too late—the girl is dead.

Harry next discovers that the District Attorney has released Scorpio. Because Harry used illegal means to capture and coerce a confession from the killer, the case against Scorpio would be defeated in court. Harry is incensed, and, disobeying orders, determines to capture Scorpio again. He begins to follow and harass the killer all over the city. Scorpio then pays a black man to beat him, and complains to the Police Chief that Harry had done the beating. Harry is called off the case.

Next Scorpio robs a liquor store, hijacks a school bus with a woman driver and six children as passengers, and calls the police demanding money and an escape plane. Harry is told to deliver the ransom to the airport, but instead, he leaps on the bus as it passes under a railway trestle. The driver faints, and the bus veers into a quarry yard. Harry chases Scorpio to the edge of a pond where he is cornered. Scorpio grabs a boy as a shield. Harry shoots Scorpio, narrowly missing the boy, and Scorpio falls into the muddy water. Harry tosses his police badge into the water, turns and walks down the road away from the approaching police cars as the film ends.

American society is based on a system of laws, but there is something in the American character that admires the anarchic hero who functions successfully regardless of the law. Whether frontiersman or soldier, America relied upon men willing to go beyond the law to protect society from the savages and outlaws encountered in the wilderness. Competence and success were more important than observance of the law, even though the advance of the law was a measure of the advance of civilization. Dirty Harry is a direct descendant of those mythological heroes of our past. Confronted with the savage, he is prepared to use extralegal means to eliminate the pathological threat to society. While the film audience may deplore the illegality of Harry's methods, they applaud his success in eliminating the threat. Harry, like the heroes of the past, functions primarily as a mythological hero. The real world of the San Francisco Police Department is much more complex than the world depicted in the film. The audience admires Harry precisely because he provides simple solutions to problems that are very complex in reality. It is easy to believe that Harry has the answers to society's ills; it is very satisfying, even cathartic, to cheer him on to the ultimate elimination of the villain. Through Harry, the audience can experience vicariously his coping with a frustrating and difficult existence.

The controversy surrounding the film centered on Harry's use of extralegal methods to capture the killer, and the film's criticism of the Supreme Court's criminal rights decisions. Harry certainly does not like the decisions. But it is less clear that the director, Don Siegel, and the writers share Harry's beliefs. The film asks how society should respond to the monster in its midst, but provides no answers. Harry's response is characteristic, but society cannot allow him simply to dispose of a badge and walk away from the problem.

Siegel maintains suspense and swift action throughout the film. He works against the San Francisco image as a pretty, picturesque city to convey a more sinister urban aspect. In his first film role, Andy Robinson as the killer is extremely effective. He displays the cunning and the pathology of the character without becoming a grotesque caricature. Clint Eastwood goes beyond his usual screen image to portray a character whose obsession matches his quarry's pathology. Harry becomes more like Scorpio as the film progresses. When he realizes what is happening to him, he despises Scorpio for pushing him to the brink.

Dirty Harry is a superb example of the police genre; it is also one of the best films Don Siegel has directed, and Clint Eastwood gives one of his best performances. It is one of a trio of highly popular films which speak to conditions in America in the early 1970's. Finally, *Dirty Harry* raises serious questions about law enforcement in America. Its audience can choose to be satisfied with the solution Harry provides, but the filmmakers suggest that their hero may be wrong.

Don K Thompson

DR. EHRLICH'S MAGIC BULLET

Released: 1940
Production: Hal B. Wallis for Warner Bros.
Direction: William Dieterle
Screenplay: John Huston, Heinz Herald, and Norman Burnside; based on an
   idea by Norman Burnside and biographical material in the possession of
   Dr. Ehrlich's family
Cinematography: James Wong Howe
Editing: Warren Low
Running time: 103 minutes

> *Principal characters:*
> Dr. Paul Ehrlich .... Edward G. Robinson
> Dr. Emil Von Behring .... Otto Kruger
> Mrs. Ehrlich .... Ruth Gordon

The quest for knowledge is a difficult subject to present effectively on film. It is usually romanticized or oversimplified to make it palatable to filmgoers. *Dr. Ehrlich's Magic Bullet* is one of the few Hollywood films that treats such a theme with dignity and power while remaining absorbing and entertaining. It is the story of Paul Ehrlich, the turn-of-the-century German scientist who searched for what he called "magic bullets" to cure disease.

As the film opens the viewer sees Ehrlich (Edward G. Robinson) as a young doctor frustrated that he must prescribe meaningless treatments for diseases that medical science does not understand. When a young patient whom Ehrlich is treating for syphilis realizes that there is no cure for his disease and kills himself, Ehrlich wants to quit his position at the hospital and devote all his time to research in an attempt to understand and cure disease. Because he has a family to support, however, he compromises by keeping his post at the hospital and doing research at night.

One night he goes to a medical meeting when he is supposed to be on duty at the hospital. He is fired and must continue his research at home. His success in staining the tubercle bacillus then earns him an appointment to the prestigious Koch Institute, where he is allowed to study whatever he wishes. His work at the Institute, however, is delayed because he has contracted tuberculosis in his earlier research. Forced to spend nearly a year in Egypt recuperating, he becomes frustrated by the enforced idleness. He tells his wife that rest, sunshine, and milk are the three things he hates most. Upon returning to Germany he begins work on immunization, based on an idea he developed after an experience with a snake-bite victim in Egypt. He combines his knowledge with that of his colleague and friend Dr. Emil Von Behring (Otto Kruger) to produce a serum which cures diphtheria. Later, he conducts a long series of experiments which finally lead to a cure for syphilis.

When the cure is used before being fully tested, thousands of others are cured, although a few people die; the medical establishment accuses Ehrlich of neglectfully causing the deaths of these people. Ehrlich charges his opponents with libel, and the issue is brought to trial. At the climax of the trial, Behring, with whom Ehrlich has had a falling-out, is brought in to testify against him. Unexpectedly, he testifies in Ehrlich's favor, saying that Ehrlich has caused the death of syphilis itself. This statement brings tears to Ehrlich's eyes and assures his victory in the trial, but the physical strain has been too much and he dies soon afterward.

Dr. Ehrlich's Magic Bullet does a good job of conveying on film the process and method of scientific research. It makes the principles involved clear to the average viewer without undue simplification or overdramatization. There are no discoveries made by a lucky guess or a dramatic development at midnight. The scriptwriters do perhaps stretch things a bit when they have Ehrlich berate his wife for ruining an experiment by lighting his stove, only to find the heat was exactly what was needed for success. However, that is the only serious concession to the usual tendency of Hollywood to sentimentalize or romanticize scientific endeavor. Particularly effective is the use of color in the otherwise black-and-white film to show the microscope slides. The artistry of the filmmakers is also exhibited in the sequence showing a cure for syphilis from the patient's point of view. Blind before the treatment begins, the patient is visited daily by Ehrlich. We see the doctor through the patient's eyes, as each day he appears less blurry.

Ehrlich's scientific research, as presented by the film, is in three stages. First he works on dyes that will stain one microscopic substance but no other. His first practical application of this work is to find a way to stain the bacillus of tuberculosis so that it can be easily seen and identified, thus making diagnosis of tuberculosis a simple matter. Then, while in Egypt recuperating from the tuberculosis he contracted during the research, he is called to treat a man and a boy who have been bitten by a poisonous snake. The boy dies, but the man, who has been bitten four times before, is scarcely affected. Ehrlich finds that each time the man is bitten he suffers less, and when he returns to Germany he decides to pursue this phenomenon of immunity. This work, too, soon has a practical use as he combines his work with that of his friend and colleague Behring to produce a serum to treat diphtheria. His third major project is finding a cure for syphilis by developing a substance which combines arsenic with the spirochaete of syphilis to cure the illness without the arsenic injuring the cells of the body. He expects that it may require nearly one hundred experiments to find just the right substance, but it is not until the 606th that success is reached.

While Ehrlich was working on his cure for syphilis early in this century, there was great opposition to his work. Many people considered the disease a punishment for sin and thought it should not be cured, a fact which is touched upon in the film. Since the disease was still seldom discussed publicly in 1940, the filmmakers were required by the censorship board to use the word "syphilis" as few times as possible and to avoid any sensationalism. Also barely mentioned in the film is the fact that some of the opposition to Ehrlich was anti-Semitic.

The conflict between research and healing is a serious theme of the film. When Ehrlich wants to quit practicing medicine in order to do research, it is not because he is insensitive to people but because he sees that helping patients requires more knowledge than medical science possesses, and he cannot be content with prescribing useless remedies. After he starts working on the theory of immunity, however, he becomes more removed from people. Behring comes to him for help in developing a serum for diphtheria while an epidemic of the disease is ravaging the country, but Ehrlich is not interested in helping him. Only after an emotional outburst by Behring does Ehrlich begin to help Behring with the work on the diphtheria cure. Once they have developed the serum and are given permission to test it on a group of sick children, Ehrlich comes into contact with patients again and his scientific objectivity disappears. When he sees the mothers of the children, he cannot withhold the medicine from the control group no matter how experimentally sound that procedure might be for testing the effectiveness of the serum. Despite protests from the hospital administration, he injects all the children. Later, the issue arises again when he develops the cure for syphilis but wants to do extensive testing for a year before the medicine is released for use. Again he is persuaded that people suffering from the disease should be helped as soon as possible. As a result a few people die after being treated, but balanced against the thousands who are cured the few are, as Behring says at the trial, "martyrs to the public good." In addition, Ehrlich does not hesitate to take personal risks in his research. Once the syphilis cure is perfected in animal studies, he plans to inoculate himself in order to be the first human on which it is tested.

Though the script is not a perfectly accurate picture of Ehrlich's life, it skillfully condenses and engrossingly presents the essence of his career. It is the outstanding achievement of Edward G. Robinson and director William Dieterle that they make Ehrlich a believable figure. Indeed, domestic scenes are interwoven with the scientific to show that though he is dedicated to his research, he is still human in his emotions and feelings. Tired of playing the two-dimensional gangster roles for which he is best known, Robinson fought for the role of Ehrlich; and once he got the role, he proved his acting skill and range in a fine performance which makes us remember Dr. Ehrlich and forget who is playing him. *Dr. Ehrlich's Magic Bullet* is serious Hollywood screen biography at its best.

Timothy W. Johnson

DR. JEKYLL AND MR. HYDE

Released: 1932
Production: Rouben Mamoulian for Paramount
Direction: Rouben Mamoulian
Screenplay: Samuel Hoffenstein and Percy Heath; based on the novel of the same name by Robert Louis Stevenson
Cinematography: Karl Struss
Editing: William Shea
Running time: 90 minutes

Principal characters:
Dr. Henry Jekyll/Mr. Hyde .... Fredric March (AA)
Ivy Pearson .... Miriam Hopkins
Muriel Carew .... Rose Hobart
Brigadier General Carew .... Halliwell Hobbes
Dr. Lanyan .... Holmes Herbert
Poole .... Edgar Norton

Very few characters have struck the chord of man's imagination with more resonance than Robert Louis Stevenson's Dr. Jekyll, for in his duality he represents the struggle of good and evil within the individual. It is a struggle that has always intrigued, puzzled, and preoccupied men. As early as 1908, Hollywood's fledgling filmmakers recognized the potential box-office appeal of Stevenson's spine-chilling classic. It was a story that possessed all the winning ingredients: horror, suspense, romance, and morality. Only three of the Jekyll and Hyde films have done justice to Stevenson's literary master-piece—the inspired performance given by John Barrymore in 1920, the 1932 version starring Fredric March as the infamous doctor, and the Victor Fleming 1941 production starring Spencer Tracy. The 1932 film was produced and directed by Rouben Mamoulian, who was acknowledged and esteemed as one of the most inspired and innovative Broadway directors during the 1930's. Although *Dr. Jekyll and Mr. Hyde* was only Mamoulian's third film, he infused this stunning melodrama with a theatrical virtuosity which perfectly expressed the brooding, bizarre quality of Stevenson's character.

Dr. Jekyll (Fredric March), is a man unshackled by the taboos of conven-tion. As Karl Struss's camera pans a filled-to-capacity auditorium of students and distinguished medical men, Dr. Jekyll leans on his dais and elaborates on his theory of the dualistic nature of the human psyche. "I have found," he explains, "that certain agents, certain chemicals have the power to disturb the trembling immateriality of the seemingly solid body in which we walk." The reaction to this heretical proclamation is immediate and sharply divided, some believing the doctor to be a savior, others convinced that he is in league with the devil.

In addition to his research and lectures, Jekyll unselfishly devotes long hours of his time to a free medical clinic, causing him, on this particular evening, to arrive late at a dinner party held at the home of Brigadier General Carew (Halliwell Hobbes), Jekyll's future father-in-law. However, Muriel Carew (Rose Hobart), Jekyll's fiancée, forgives the good doctor for his tardiness, and as they stroll in the garden, they discuss their impending marriage on which the general has imposed an eight-month waiting period. Jekyll leaves the Carew home in the company of his good friend, Dr. Lanyan (Holmes Herbert). Suddenly their reverie is broken by a noisy scuffle between a man and a woman in the dimly lit street ahead. Rushing forward, Jekyll drives off the assailant and helps the manhandled young woman upstairs to her rooms. Encouraged by his solicitous ministrations, the cockney woman, Ivy Pearson (Miriam Hopkins), becomes coquettish and attempts to seduce him. However, she fails, and with the scene rather abrubtly ended, the audience realizes that Ivy will reappear later in the film.

Following this is a scene which takes place in Jekyll's laboratory where, after three days of unflagging experimentation, Jekyll has produced a bubbling elixir which awaits its final test. The doctor hesitates for one long moment, then raises the flask and drinks the foaming potion. Suddenly, a spasm convulses his body, and he writhes in pain, his face horribly contorted. This scene portraying the initial transformation from Dr. Jekyll to Mr. Hyde is a cinemagraphic masterpiece since it was done without the usual series of dissolves to accommodate makeup changes. The use of a number of colored gelatin filters caused March's makeup to appear to change and, as Struss's camera relentlessly focuses on Jekyll's face, the audience watches in horror as the evil in his soul permeates and contorts his features into a dark and loathsome mask of wickedness and malice before their very eyes. Moving with an animal's quick grace, Hyde grins savagely in the mirror and then, throwing a cape around his shoulders, leaves the lab by the back door.

In a later scene, the doctor restlessly paces his lab, his life in limbo. General Carew, concerned over Jekyll's refusal to give up his research, has taken his daughter to Bath on an extended holiday. A telegram from Bath informing the doctor that Muriel will not be returning for at least another month incites Jekyll to action. Downing a draft of the potion, he changes quickly to Hyde and slinks off into the foggy London streets. After making inquiries at Ivy Pearson's boarding house about her whereabouts, Hyde proceeds to the Blue Boar dance hall where, amidst the bacchanalian revelry, he observes Ivy flitting about with debauched abandon. Hyde snatches up a broken glass and with a savage, threatening gesture, chases away Ivy's escort. Then, with a wolfish, terrifying intensity, he turns to Ivy and says, "You'll come with me, eh?"

From this point on, the pace of the movie quickens dramatically; time lapses are effected through a series of dissolves and slow fades as Jekyll catapults, through the character of Mr. Hyde, toward an abyss from which there is no escape. The sound effects, including the use of quickening heart-beats, builds suspense throughout the ensuing scenes to a raw, nerve-jangling level of intensity. Having been informed of the recent return to London of General Carew and his daughter, Jekyll is deeply disturbed and full of remorse over his recent indulgences. Deciding to end his double life, he sends his butler, Poole (Edgar Norton), with a fifty-pound note and a message to be delivered to Ivy. In addition, he gives his butler the key to the rear door of his lab, stating that he will no longer have need of it.

Later, Ivy arrives at the doctor's home to return his money and beg his assistance in freeing herself from Hyde's sadistic attentions. Jekyll, remorseful over the anguish which he has caused her, promises that she will never see Hyde again. However, Jekyll has unleashed the licentious Mr. Hyde once too often. The fragile chain of conscious control has been irrevocably broken and the beast lurks ever-present, unshackled, and ready to claw its way into the upper consciousness of Jekyll's mind. Totally unaware of this irreversible change that has occurred within himself, Jekyll strolls happily through the park on his way to the Carew home. Following their return from Bath, the General has undergone a change of heart and agreed to an early marriage between Dr. Jekyll and his daughter, and this is the night the formal wedding announcement is to be made. Suddenly, with dynamic primitive force, Hyde takes over Jekyll's body and walks towards Ivy's flat. Here, he informs the terrified Ivy that he is the wonderful Dr. Jekyll in which she has believed; then, with a pagan enjoyment, he wantonly takes her life. Smashing his way through the curious onlookers who have heard Ivy's screams and gathered on the stairs, Hyde escapes into the safety of the darkness.

Unable to return to his laboratory and no longer being in possession of the rear door key, Hyde sends a message by porter to his friend Lanyan, instructing him to retrieve certain chemicals from his lab and give them to a messenger whom Jekyll will send to Lanyan's home at midnight. Lanyan, however, refuses to release the package to the suspicious-looking Mr. Hyde. Having no choice, Hyde mixes and drinks the potion, reverting to Dr. Jekyll before the disbelieving, horrified eyes of his friend. Jekyll swears Lanyan to secrecy, promising that in return for his trust, he will give up Muriel and never again take the potion.

With a heavy heart, Jekyll arrives at the Carew home and informs Muriel that he is releasing her from her marriage commitment. However, as he leaves the house, Hyde again takes possession of Jekyll's mind and body. Reentering the house, he pursues Muriel, who screams at the sight of this horrifying stranger. General Carew comes to his daughter's rescue, but Hyde savagely beats the old man with his cane and escapes into the night. Two constables, alerted by the General's cries for help, take up the chase, tracking their suspect to the home of Dr. Jekyll. Frantically Hyde mixes his potion with the constables pounding on the door. At the last second, as the door finally succumbs to their persistent barrage, Hyde changes back to Jekyll and convinces the officers who have burst into the room that the murderer, Hyde, has been there but has escaped by the back door. At this moment, Lanyan appears and reveals to the constables that Jekyll himself is the ruthless, cold-blooded killer whom they seek. Shock and anger at Lanyan's betrayal brings the ever-present Hyde back to the surface. He attacks Lanyan and then the police until his frenzy of unbridled hatred is finally halted by a bullet; and, as the formless evil power slowly dissipates, Jekyll emerges to claim his dying and desecrated body.

Mamoulian's finely etched, visual interpretation of *Dr. Jekyll and Mr. Hyde* possesses the timeless elegance of the Stevenson classic. Each scene is a hand-carved cameo, perfect in lighting and composition. The characters of Jekyll and Hyde allowed Mamoulian to draw upon the full range of his theatrical genius, to portray the elemental struggle of man's emotions against a background of rich symbolic imagery. In one scene, violence is juxtaposed against a lyric view of romantic statuary, and in another, a bubbling cauldron flickers in the flames of a fireplace, providing a fleeting symbolic glimpse of the hell lurking in man's soul. March is stunning in his portrayal of Jekyll and Hyde, a role which earned him an Academy Award for Best Actor. His interpretation of Hyde's unsheathed wickedness pares Jekyll's civilized veneer in one clean, devastating stroke, stupefying audiences with its raw and savage intensity, and making the Mamoulian production of *Dr. Jekyll and Mr. Hyde* a classic of the horror film genre.

D. Gail Huskins

DR. JEKYLL AND MR. HYDE

Released: 1941
Production: Victor Saville for Metro-Goldwyn-Mayer
Direction: Victor Fleming
Screenplay: John Lee Mahin; based on the novel of the same name by Robert Louis Stevenson
Cinematography: Joseph Ruttenberg
Editing: Harold F. Kress
Special effects: Warren Newcombe
Montage effects: Peter Ballbusch
Music: Franz Waxman
Running time: 127 minutes

Principal characters:
Dr. Henry Jekyll/Mr. Hyde .... Spencer Tracy
Ivy Peterson .... Ingrid Bergman
Beatrix Emery .... Lana Turner
Sir Charles Emery .... Donald Crisp
Dr. John Lanyon .... Ian Hunter
Sam Higgins .... Barton MacLane
The Bishop .... C. Aubrey Smith
Poole .... Peter Godfrey

In 1885, Robert Louis Stevenson, the celebrated Scottish novelist, had a strange nightmare in which he envisioned man's personality as being split into two diametrically opposed aspects; this strange dream provided the inspiration for his immortal novel, *Dr. Jekyll and Mr. Hyde.* The dual nature of mankind was a chilling but intriguing premise, one that was to engage the creative imaginations of numerous film producers. Of the many films which handle this theme, only the three versions of Stevenson's classic story are worthy of note: the 1920 production starring John Barrymore; the 1932 version with Fredric March; and the 1941 Victor Saville production. Saville's film starred Spencer Tracy, who had won Oscars for Best Actor two years in a row: for *Captains Courageous* in 1937 and *Boys' Town* in 1938. Saville spared no expense in this production; Victor Fleming, acclaimed for *The Wizard of Oz* (1939) and *Gone with the Wind* (1939), was named as director.

The film opens on a quiet Sunday morning in London as the camera, under Joseph Ruttenberg's expert direction, pans a church steeple while bells toll melodiously in the background. Inside one of London's most prestigious churches, the bishop is delivering a eulogy in honor of Queen Victoria's Golden Jubilee. Suddenly the derisive voice of a distraught parishioner, Sam Higgins (Barton MacLane), pierces the tranquillity of the service. As he is being subdued, the noted mental health specialist Dr. Henry Jekyll (Spencer

Tracy) intervenes and orders the man taken to Camden Hospital for observation and treatment. Here, Jekyll importunes the heads of the hospital to
allow him to test his theory that the evil in a man's soul can be separated
and, consequently, eliminated or expelled. However, the distinguished doctors
frown on his request, believing that his proposal trespasses into the domain
of religion.

In the scene that follows, Dr. Jekyll arrives late at a dinner party and takes
his seat beside his fiancée, Beatrix Emery (Lana Turner). Close-ups focus on
individual guests or groups of guests, painting intimate portraits and establishing the relationships between the members of the dinner party. Jekyll,
stung by his rejection at the hospital, elaborates on his theory of man's dual
nature, seeking a glimmer of understanding and support from the distinguished medical men attending the dinner. His discourse, however, is met
with both fear and rejection.

On the way home from the party, Jekyll, accompanied by his friend Dr.
John Lanyon (Ian Hunter), comes upon a young woman in distress. The two
men scare off her assailant and escort her to her lodgings. Feigning a sprained
ankle, the woman, an amoral barmaid named Ivy Peterson (Ingrid Bergman),
tricks Jekyll into carrying her up to her flat, where she openly flirts with him.
Jekyll, both mesmerized and shocked by her behavior, forgets himself for a
moment and kisses her. Bergman manages to infuse an air of realism into the
essentially stereotyped and poorly written role of Ivy.

The scene shifts to Jekyll's laboratory, where, posed against a backdrop of
test tube racks and bubbling flasks, he drinks a foaming potion. The change
is immediate and horrifying to behold, as Jekyll's features become coarse and
primitive, his eyebrows shaggy, his hair disheveled, and his voice low and
guttural. In addition to these outward changes, a montage of dreamlike sequences by technical expert Peter Ballbusch visually indicates the inward,
mental changes as Jekyll's inhibitions slip silently beneath the surface of his
conscious mind and evil bubbles up out of the depths to claim precedence.
This physical personification of Jekyll's baser nature gives himself the name
of Mr. Hyde.

Much later, after the drug has lost its effect, Jekyll is treated to an unexpected visit by Beatrix, who is in a state of distress because she has dreamed
that he is slipping away from her. As the lovers embrace, Beatrix's father, Sir
Charles Emery (Donald Crisp), arrives. Angered at finding his unchaperoned
daughter in Jekyll's company and upset by Jekyll's previous refusal to give
up his unorthodox research, he announces his intention of taking his daughter
to the Continent, far away from Jekyll's influence.

During a subsequent transformation, Hyde goes in search of Ivy until he
finds her, singing and laughing, serving drinks in a sleazy music hall. After
paying the bar manager to fire her, he gives her money and sends her home
in a cab. Without her job, she is now completely dependent on him for her

survival. Fleming uses a number of imaginative techniques to magnify the ongoing struggle between good and evil in the story. For example, he uses the concept of light and dark to mirror the difference between the two women in Jekyll's life. Beatrix, symbolizing good, has blond hair, wears light, airy clothing, and is usually presented in brightly lit surroundings; Ivy, by contrast, has dark hair and generally wears dark, somber clothing. She is a nocturnal creature who frequents dark alleys and dimly lit rooms. Franz Waxman's musical score accentuates further the differences between the two women: the light, airy waltz is repeatedly associated with Beatrix, and the earthy rhythm of the dance hall polka with Ivy.

Jekyll returns home from one of his clandestine visits to find a telegram informing him that his fiancée is returning home. Resolving to give up his indulgences, Jekyll sends Ivy fifty pounds to enable her to leave London for good. The meeting between Jekyll and Beatrix following their long, enforced separation is a most happy affair, for Sir Charles has relented and agreed to an early marriage. However, upon his return home from the joyful reunion, the doctor is stunned to find Ivy waiting in his consulting room. Remembering his previous kindness to her, the distraught Ivy, bewildered by Hyde's cruel treatment of her and believing the fifty pounds to be merely a ploy to trap her into trying to escape, has sought the assistance of Dr. Jekyll in a last effort to retain her sanity.

The night that follows begins on a light note with Jekyll on his way to a reception where his forthcoming marriage will be announced. However, the night soon turns sinister as Jekyll finds himself uncontrollably reverting to Hyde. He arrives at Ivy's flat, where he sadistically discloses that he is the kind doctor whose help she had sought. Horrified, Ivy becomes hysterical and attempts to escape; Hyde kills her and flees into the dark, fog-shrouded streets.

Unable to enter his home because he is no longer in possession of the back door key to his laboratory, Hyde leaves a note for his friend, Dr. Lanyon, asking him to obtain the crucial vials from his laboratory and give them to a messenger whom Jekyll says he will send. However, Lanyon is suspicious and refuses to give the vials to the bogus messenger, Hyde, without some assurance that Dr. Jekyll is safe. Having no recourse, Jekyll drinks the potion, and after reverting to his normal state, he confides to his friend that he can no longer control his transformations. Knowing there is no chance now that he can marry Beatrix, Jekyll goes to her and tells her that he can never see her again. However, as he turns to leave, he reverts again to the monstrous Hyde, the sight of which causes Beatrix to swoon. Sir Charles hurries to her rescue but Hyde strikes him a killing blow and rushes off. His cape billowing and flapping like great black wings, he flees through the murky London streets. Breaking into his house, he knocks down his servant and locks himself in the laboratory.

Meanwhile, Dr. Lanyon, who has joined the police at the scene of the crime, recognizes the cane lying by Sir Charles' lifeless body as belonging to Dr. Jekyll. They arrive at Jekyll's house, where Jekyll attempts to deny the accusations of his friend, but the horrifying transformation begins again. Hyde goes beserk and attacks Lanyon, leaving his friend no option but to shoot him. With death approaching, Jekyll's soul returns to him and Hyde gives up the body he has abused and destroyed. As in the opening scene, the camera pans the church steeple and bells toll, signifying tranquillity and the return of normalcy.

Fleming's *Dr. Jekyll and Mr. Hyde* is a superlative example of what Hollywood's technology can accomplish; this 1941 version of Stevenson's classic has a polish and flow unmatched in March's 1932 version. The film received three Academy Award nominations, for the black-and-white cinematography by Joseph Ruttenberg; the film editing by Harold F. Kress; and the music score by Franz Waxman. In addition, Ingrid Bergman won the critics' acclaim for her laudable performance as the tormented Ivy Peterson; the actress has gone on to win three Academy Awards during her career: two for Best Actress (*Gaslight*, 1944; *Anastasia*, 1956) and one for Best Supporting Actress (*Murder on the Orient Express*, 1974).

D. Gail Huskins

DR. KILDARE'S STRANGE CASE

Released: 1940
Production: Metro-Goldwyn-Mayer
Direction: Harold S. Bucquet
Screenplay: Harry Ruskin and Willis Goldbeck; based on the characters created by Max Brand
Cinematography: John F. Seitz
Editing: Gene Ruggiero
Running time: 76 minutes

Principal characters:

Dr. James Kildare	Lew Ayres
Dr. Leonard Gillespie	Lionel Barrymore
Mary Lamont	Laraine Day
Dr. Stephen Kildare	Samuel S. Hinds
Joe Wayman	Nat Pendleton
Dr. Carewe	Walter Kingsford
Sally	Marie Blake
Dr. Gregory Lane	Shepperd Strudwick
Nurse Molly Byrd	Alma Kruger

Throughout the history of cinema, a wide variety of characters have proven popular enough in a single to spawn a series of sequels. From singing cowboys to talking mules, if the first film was a hit, successors very often followed. By the late 1930's, studios began to look for properties that would yield not one but several hits. M-G-M was tremendously successful in 1938 with the first of its Andy Hardy series, and later that same year, the studio came back with a pair of characters that were equally as popular—Dr. James Kildare, a brilliant young diagnostician, and his crusty mentor, Dr. Leonard Gillespie. The characters were taken from a group of popular stories by Max Brand, who was better known as a writer of Western novels. Together, through various actors and directors, Kildare and Gillespie worked their homespun medical miracles for more than ten years.

The first of these films, *Interns Can't Make Money* (1937), was directed by Alfred Santell and featured Joel McCrea as Kildare. Later, when Metro matched director Harold S. Bucquet with actors Lew Ayres and Lionel Barrymore (the best of the Kildares and the only Gillespie, respectively), they hit upon a chemistry that was truly memorable. The first of the Bucquet-Ayres-Barrymore Kildares was *Young Doctor Kildare*, released in 1938. Metro had come out with a jaundiced look at the medical profession in King Vidor's *The Citadel* earlier that year, but *Young Doctor Kildare* took an entirely different approach. The physicians in Kildare's world had the same reverence for medicine that Judge Hardy had for the law in the Andy Hardy series.

This dedication to their calling, along with the affection and mutual respect among the series' principal characters, was the key to the Kildare films' enduring popularity.

The series, which has a definite sequence, begins when Dr. James Kildare (Lew Ayres) returns to his parents' home, having just completed medical school in the footsteps of his father. The younger Kildare has decided to forgo a career as a country doctor; he wants, instead, to broaden his horizons in New York City. Although his father, Dr. Stephen Kildare (Samuel S. Hinds), is disappointed, he accedes to his son's wishes and offers him some homespun advice: "Whenever you are in doubt as to what ails a patient, give him bicarbonate of soda and see how he looks in the morning." Thus armed, Kildare sets off for New York, winding up at Blair General Hospital, under the tutelage of Dr. Leonard Gillespie (Lionel Barrymore), a delightful old curmudgeon who is the wisecracking urban equivalent of the elder Kildare. With the introduction of these two main characters, the film, and, indeed, the whole series begins.

The two men complement each other perfectly. Kildare is every mother's ideal son. He is earnest without being sanctimonious, confident without being brash—in short, a Boy Scout with a medical degree. Gillespie is roguish and rambunctious, despite being confined to a wheelchair (in the Kildare films, the wheelchair is somehow linked to the fact that Gillespie is dying slowly of cancer; in fact, it was a plot device concocted to accommodate Barrymnore's arthritis and hip joint problems). The fact that the whole effect gave Gillespie the appearance of then-President Franklin D. Roosevelt probably did not hurt either. A brilliant diagnostician, Gillespie drives both himself and Kildare mercilessly; nevertheless, his affection for the younger man is evident. He sees Kildare as a worthy successor, and continues, throughout the series, to groom him for that position.

That the two men clicked onscreen was evident to Metro even before the film was released. Thus the studio shot an unusual closing scene for *Young Doctor Kildare*. In what amounted to an epilogue, Ayres and Barrymore appeared on a stage and announced that they would be returning in a series of Kildare sequels. In addition to Ayres and Barrymore, a number of other actors also appeared regularly as characters in the series. Head Nurse Molly Byrd (Alma Kruger) is Gillespie's personal assistant, and fully his match in their verbal jousts. She is as intent on keeping him alive and healthy as he seems to be at working himself to death. Joe Wayman (Nat Pendleton) is the rough but good-natured ambulance driver who figures in many moments of comic relief; Sally (Marie Blake), the hospital switchboard operator, is his girl friend. Dr. Carewe (Walter Kingsford), as the head of Blair General Hospital, is often Kildare's and Gillespie's nemesis, with his insistence on following the rules to the letter. Kildare's romantic interest is most often nurse Mary Lamont (Laraine Day), to whom he becomes engaged, but who dies in one of the last films of the Ayres/Kildare series, *Dr. Kildare's Wedding Day* (1941). Kildare's impoverished status as an intern—and his highminded reluctance to ask any woman to play second fiddle to his career—keeps his pursuit of Mary low-key, but she always winds up with him rather than any rival suitor by the last reel.

Dr. Kildare's Strange Case, perhaps the best of the Kildare films, contains all of the elements that made the series so successful. There were numerous plots, all going on at once, and many intertwined with the others. Typically, Kildare risks disgrace to follow his conscience, encountering opposition from everyone—even, temporarily, from Dr. Gillespie. By the end of the film, however, Kildare's insight and courage triumph over conventional wisdom, and he is vindicated. As the film opens, the overworked and penurious Kildare is in danger of losing Mary Lamont to a successful brain surgeon at Blair General Hospital. The surgeon, Dr. Gregory Lane (Shepperd Strudwick), however, is having a run of bad luck: all of his recent patients have died. Kildare and Gillespie believe in Lane's surgical skills, and Kildare is put in the awkward position of defending his romantic rival. He handles the situation with dignity and aplomb, as usual, professing sincerely to want only what is best for Mary.

When one of Lane's patients lapses into insanity after a particularly delicate operation, it is the last straw for Dr. Carewe, who is on the verge of suspending Lane. Kildare risks his career to help save Lane's reputation—and his patient's life. With Mary Lamont's help, he administers a hazardous and controversial treatment known as the "insulin shock cure." In the face of the disapproval of both Carewe and Gillespie, Kildare's therapy is nevertheless successful. The patient's sanity is restored, and when he reveals that he has had a history of mental troubles predating the operation, Dr. Lane is vindicated as well.

Meanwhile, Kildare mulls over a lucrative job offer from the prestigious Messinger Institute. He would command five hundred dollars a month (versus his twenty dollars a month salary at Blair General Hospital) and the free use of a house. Gillespie urges him to accept the offer, noting that this would enable him to compete with Gregory Lane financially for Mary Lamont's affections. Kildare is tempted, but ultimately decides to stay an intern, much to Gillespie's—and the audience's—relief. To do otherwise would be to abandon his dream of succeeding Gillespie as Blair's chief diagnostician. Fortunately, all of this prompts Kildare to be honest with Mary about his feelings for her. He asks her to wait for him—five years is the time they agree upon—and she gladly accepts. The film ends with Kildare sneaking away from a lecture by Gillespie to have dinner with Mary.

Dr. Kildare's Strange Case has all of the qualities that made the Kildare series popular—tension, romance, camaraderie, humor, nobility, and dedication. Ayres continued in the series until 1942. At that time, during the early part of World War II, he declared himself a conscientious objector, and

M-G-M dropped him from the series because of the unpopularity of his position. After Ayres's departure, the emphasis of the stories switched to Gillespie and a series of young Metro stars, notably Van Johnson, took the role of the young assistant, now under different names in each film. When the series ended in 1947, after no less than fifteen films, the Kildare character was dormant for awhile. The films were resurrected on television late shows around the country in the 1950's, however; and in 1961, a television series called *Dr. Kildare*, starring Richard Chamberlain as Kildare and Raymond Massey as Gillespie, started up the Kildare vogue anew. The television series lasted for seven years. Metro's instincts in 1938 were sound. Dr. Kildare is truly one of the most enduring characters in the history of popular entertainment, and is still seen frequently on late-night television.

Robert Mitchell

DR. ZHIVAGO

Released: 1965
Production: Carlo Ponti for Metro-Goldwyn-Mayer
Direction: David Lean
Screenplay: Robert Bolt (AA); based on the novel of the same name by
  Boris Pasternak
Cinematography: Freddie A. Young (AA)
Editing: Norman Savage
Music: Maurice Jarre (AA)
Art direction: John Box and Terry March (AA); set decoration, Dario Simon
  (AA)
Costume design: Phyllis Dalton (AA)
Running time: 197 minutes

> *Principal characters:*
> Yuri .... Omar Sharif
> Tonya .... Geraldine Chaplin
> Lara .... Julie Christie
> Pasha .... Tom Courtenay
> Yevgraf .... Alec Guinness
> Anna .... Siobhan McKenna
> Alexander .... Ralph Richardson
> Komarovsky .... Rod Steiger
> The Girl .... Rita Tushingham

Dr. Zhivago is a radiant film, combining deep passion, art, and social commentary with stunning cinematography and an electrifying musical score. These and other qualities make *Dr. Zhivago* excellent cinema as all elements are skillfully incorporated into an epic historical saga. One of the most powerfully engrossing films ever made, *Dr. Zhivago* could very well have been successful solely on the original Boris Pasternak story, skillfully adapted to the screen by Robert Bolt. Set in Russia during the tumultuous years between 1905 and 1935, *Dr. Zhivago* chronicles the intense, rich, always heroic, but often tragic life of Yuri Zhivago (Omar Sharif). Zhivago, the orphaned son of an impoverished Russian nobleman, is reared by a gentle, aristocratic family wealthy enough to divide its days between living in St. Petersburg, the capital city of tsarist Russia, and in a lavish family estate in the provinces. Nurtured in this caring environment, Zhivago matures into a sensitive poet and physician; and, as his emotions ripen, he turns his affections toward the family's daughter Tonya (Geraldine Chaplin), whom he ultimately marries. Their lives, sheltered by love, cultural refinement, and professional stability, insulate the Zhivagos from the seamier side of life which was the lot of most Russians living before 1917.

The film is not about harmonious domesticity, however. Rather, it deals with human reactions to cataclysmic events which disrupt this insulated domesticity. The Russian Revolution of 1905, the horrors of World War I, the Bolshevik Revolution of 1917, and the subsequent civil war of 1918-1920 snare the Zhivagos into a social disruption perhaps unequaled in the twentieth century.

As a physician, Zhivago is pressed into service during World War I, and his life is never the same afterwards. There he meets the selfless chief nurse Lara (Julie Christie) whom Zhivago grows to respect for her gentle strength and capacity to nurture unbendingly in the middle of extraordinary suffering. Respect turns to love, yet Zhivago returns at the end of the war to Tonya and his family, adjusting to the dramatic new social milieu created by the new Bolshevik government. While stripped of most of their prewar riches, Zhivago's family still retains the habits of refinement, if not the actual substance. At their now commandeered country estate, Zhivago again meets Lara. Their love based on respect now spawns into a full-fledged romance; but events disrupt their passionate relationship.

On one visit to the estate, Zhivago is kidnaped by a band of Bolshevik soldiers, now entrenched in a tragic civil war; he never sees his family again since they are forced to flee to Paris because of their previous aristocratic connections. After traveling with the Bolshevik forces for the winter, Zhivago escapes, wandering half-crazed back to Lara. They live briefly together, and it is a time during which Zhivago produces his best and most intense poetry. This brief emotional and aesthetic coupling, however, does not last. Lara is forced to leave Russia because her husband, Pasha (Tom Courtenay), from whom she has been long estranged, is now deemed dangerous to the new state because he had once been a leader of the revolution. Now all of Pasha's contacts are in danger as well, and after he is found dead near Lara's house, she decides to leave Russia with the help of the unscrupulous Boris Komarovsky (Rod Steiger) with whom she had an affair as a girl. Komarovsky slithers his way through the film as an amoral, self-serving, lecherous survivor with many contacts. He is the antithesis of Zhivago, as detestable as Zhivago is admirable; still, his connections save Lara from a certain death. Escape means that Lara will never see Zhivago again, but should she stay, Zhivago also might die because of her relationship to Pasha.

Dr. Zhivago is Boris Pasternak's most passionate work. Elaborate and intricate, the novel commands intense emotional responses from the audience. Robert Bolt takes some liberties with the novel without harming the essential story. One such change is the manner in which the tale is related. In the novel, an absent third person relates the story; in the film, however, the story is told by Yevgraf (Alec Guinness), Yuri's brother, who relates Zhivago's story to a girl (Rita Tushingham) whom we suspect may be the daughter of Lara and Zhivago, who had been lost since childhood.

The success of the film rests largely with the story line; *Dr. Zhivago* is an excellent example of a writer's film. The acting is also of a universally high caliber. Omar Sharif offers one of his strongest performances; he is thoroughly convincing as the intensely passionate, sensitive, and generous Zhivago. He is boldly committed to his profession, his family, his lover, and his poetry; these commitments, pursued without reservation, complicate his life and create both his strengths and weaknesses. Geraldine Chaplin as Tonya, the gentle, accepting, always loving wife, is equally convincing. Rod Steiger and Tom Courtenay convey perfectly the qualities of their respective characters. The film is further enhanced by an unforgettable Oscar-winning score by Maurice Jarre—who had previously earned an Academy Award for his orchestration of *Lawrence of Arabia* (1962)—and by the breathtaking cinematography. The landscape photographs are meticulously composed and emphasize the enormous majesty of the Russian environment, an environment which, similar to the social forces at work in the film, reiterate the broader, uncontrollable elements in life which shape and often overwhelm the main characters.

Dr. Zhivago is a lavish, expansive film, and one which, although produced in America, captures the Russian tradition of epic works of art, whether they be historic films or novels. It is rich in strong characters who act forcefully, at times heroically, yet who are always subject to the upheavals of society. Repeatedly in and out of harmony with society but never estranged from it, the characters' lives are complexly interwoven with those of the individuals around them. This is the stuff from which great films are made, and *Dr. Zhivago* is a film that will not be quickly forgotten.

The film fared extremely well at the box office both initially and in later re-releases. It also had one of the largest viewing audiences to date when it appeared on television. The film ultimately won five Academy Awards: for Jarre's musical score, Freddie A. Young's cinematography, Robert Bolt's screenplay, Phyllis Dalton's costumes, the art direction of John Box and Terry March, and set decorations of Dario Simon. Additional nominations were earned in other categories; however, the big Oscar-winner that year was *The Sound of Music*, an all-time audience favorite. *Dr. Zhivago*'s only nomination in an acting category went to Tom Courtenay for Best Supporting Actor; he lost to Martin Balsam for *A Thousand Clowns*. Julie Christie won the Oscar that year for Best Actress, but it was for her work in *Darling* rather than *Dr. Zhivago*.

John G. Tomlinson, Jr.

DODSWORTH

Released: 1936
Production: Samuel Goldwyn for United Artists
Direction: William Wyler
Screenplay: Sidney Howard; based on the novel and play of the same name
by Sinclair Lewis
Cinematography: Rudolph Maté
Editing: Daniel Mandell
Art direction: Richard Day (AA)
Running time: 90 minutes

Principal characters:
Sam Dodsworth	Walter Huston
Fran Dodsworth	Ruth Chatterton
Edith Cortright	Mary Astor
Arnold Iselin	Paul Lukas
Major Clyde Lockert	David Niven
Baroness Von Obersdorf	Mme. Maria Ouspenskaya

It is fortunate for filmgoing audiences that Sam Goldwyn was a stubborn man, for without his obstinacy, *Dodsworth* might never have been made. Even though his studio turned out many entertaining products year after year, Goldwyn wanted very much to do movies of importance, and the highly successful Broadway play of Sinclair Lewis' novel was one in which he was particularly interested. Against the recommendations of his advisers, who told him that *Dodsworth* would not have any appeal because it was about middle-aged people, Goldwyn proceeded to pay $160,000 for the film rights and brought Walter Huston, who had played Dodsworth on the New York stage, to Hollywood to star in the film.

Part of the appeal of *Dodsworth* lies in its uncomplicated story. Sam Dodsworth (Walter Huston) is an automobile industry magnate who has retired. At the urging of his wife Fran (Ruth Chatterton), he takes his first trip to Europe aboard the Queen Mary because she wants him to see the world. He is not particularly enthusiastic, and goes more to please her than anything else. The trip, however, becomes a psychologically fatal voyage: after much pain, anguish, revelations of true character, and selfish upheaval, their marriage is ruined. Fran Dodsworth is caught up with the desire to experience "life" before life leaves her behind. She wants the party to go on forever, without her getting old. Because of this, her husband becomes a constantly distasteful reminder that the years are passing; so she turns to younger men, first on the ship and then in cities throughout Europe.

Sam Dodsworth is an uncultured but devoted husband who is ready to stand almost anything once, even adultery, and who cannot rid himself of the deep sense of responsibility he has accumulated in twenty years of marriage. However, he is also human, and while his wife is pursuing various younger men with exotic accents, he meets a genteel, understanding widow, Edith Cortright (Mary Astor), who is capable and willing to give him the affection and company his wife will not. Their relationship is based on living life for the day without expectations on the future, but their idyll is shattered by a phone call from Fran. Rejected by her last suitor and his baroness mother, Fran says that she is ready to go home and settle down. Sam's sense of loyalty and honor leave him no alternative but to go with her; she is his wife, representing the life he has known. As their ship prepares to leave port, however, Fran's shallow repentence for what she has done quickly evaporates and her mean self-centeredness surfaces. It takes only moments for Sam to realize that his wife and the life back home are no longer what he wants. As Edith Cortright stands watching the luxury ship pull out to sea, a small dinghy ties up at the dock with a beaming Sam aboard, returning to the new life he has chosen.

Dodsworth is an extremely well-made and well-acted film. Sam Dodsworth is a man we understand and respect, if not altogether believe for there is a basic improbability inherent in the story, and therefore, in Sam's character; how could he and Fran have been married for twenty years before he realized what a priggish, selfish, vain woman she was? Perhaps all his years spent building his automobile business kept him from really knowing his wife; or perhaps he simply cannot believe that she is the woman he married.

Dodsworth is a very personal story which gives the impression of a film of large scope, mainly because of Walter Huston's portrayal. Since he commanded the role on Broadway for two years prior to the movie, it was a role in which he was as comfortable as any actor could be, and yet the acting is entirely fresh. Huston's Dodsworth is a man of sympathy, humor, irony, and delicacy, and it is sometimes impossible to tell what in Dodsworth is Huston and what is Sinclair Lewis, since the actor fits the character perfectly.

As Fran Dodsworth, Ruth Chatterton creates one of film's most despicable women; her dialogue spews forth venomously and she is consummate in displaying the character's embittered egotism through the way she holds her body, tight and self-conscious, like someone always on display. The character of Edith Cortright is as far removed as possible from the usual "other woman," and Mary Astor plays her with remarkable grace and intelligence. Also adding to the character of the film is the casting of a young man named David Niven as Major Clive Lockert in his first role for Goldwyn, although he had had a contract with the studio for some time.

Although *Dodsworth* is essentially a static and talky film, William Wyler has directed it skillfully in cinematic terms. It easily could have been a visually confining piece, but it is not; the pace flows evenly and is dramatically balanced to sustain the impact of important scenes, then eases naturally back into the expository. The look of the film is grand, expensive, and very Continental, although most of the major shooting took place at the Goldwyn studios in Hollywood. Only a small second-unit was sent to Europe to film the exteriors which give the film such a colorful background.

Goldwyn's insistence that *Dodsworth* was important and thus had to be perfect almost kept *Dodsworth* from ultimately being filmed. Sidney Howard's dramatization of the novel was submitted; according to those involved, it was well-constructed and, in fact, expertly concealed some of the story's basic flaws. Goldwyn, however, brought in another writer, who was then embarrassed because he could find no way to improve upon Howard's adaptation. Over the next two years, Goldwyn hired and fired five more writers and accepted, then rejected, eight different drafts before he finally realized that he could not improve on Howard's version, and that adaptation at last became the official screenplay.

Juliette Freidgen

DOG DAY AFTERNOON

Released: 1975
Production: Martin Bregman and Martin Elfand for Warner Bros.
Direction: Sidney Lumet
Screenplay: Frank Pierson (AA); based on a *Life* magazine article "The Boys in the Bank" by P. F. Kluge and Thomas Moore
Cinematography: Victor J. Kemper
Editing: Dede Allen
Running time: 130 minutes

Principal characters:
Sonny .... Al Pacino
Sal .... John Cazale
Leon .... Chris Sarandon
Sheldon .... James Broderick
Moretti .... Charles Durning
Mulvaney .... Sully Boyar
Angie .... Susan Peretz
Sylvia .... Penny Allen
Jenny .... Carol Kane
Miriam .... Marcia Jean Kurtz
Bobby .... Gary Springer

In August, 1972, two gunmen attempted to rob a Chase Manhattan Bank branch office in Brooklyn, New York. Caught in the act, the pair held nine bank employees hostage for a period of fourteen hours, turning the robbery into an event worthy of live television coverage. One of the perpetrators, an admitted bisexual and former bank teller named John Wojtowicz, claimed he needed money to finance a sex change operation for his "girl friend." This bizarre scenario ended in disaster: while attempting to board a jet at Kennedy Airport to fly out of the country, Wojtowicz was captured and his cohort killed. These events are re-created in *Dog Day Afternoon*, a perceptive blend of comedy and pathos.

Although the robbers and their caper are fictionalized for the film, the events remain just as bizarre as they were in reality. The robbery begins in the manner of a comedy routine as Sonny (Al Pacino), the homosexual desperado, hops around and issues orders to those in the bank as if he is directing a three-ring circus. After their initial shock, the bank hostages become part of the show. They watch themselves on television and take a pizza break; women vainly primp their hair in anticipation of their appearance on the nightly news. Sonny even shows one of the young girls drill and ceremony techniques with his rifle.

Sal (John Cazale), Sonny's partner in crime, says little and appears to be in a constant fog; thus, most of the action centers around Sonny, who is portrayed as an outcast, a man who has been pushed and tormented from birth. His mother has refused to acknowledge that he is an adult and manages his life in spite of his wishes. In the midst of his troubles, all she can murmur is, "How beautiful you were as a baby." Angie (Susan Peretz), his overweight wife, carries on about her problems and refuses to let him complete a sentence when she talks to him over the telephone. She has grown to resemble a pig, and defensively explains that she is not at the bank site because she is unable to hire a babysitter.

It is no wonder, then, that Sonny has turned to Leon (Chris Sarandon), a woman trapped in a man's body. In an extremely well-played telephone scene between the two—which compares favorably with the Luise Rainer soliloquy in *The Great Ziegfeld* (1936)—it is revealed that Leon is the only person who has ever made an honest effort to listen to what is on Sonny's mind. Despite the rather shallow reference that Sonny's homosexuality is the result of the emasculating women in his life, it is to the filmmakers' credit that homosexuals are portrayed as human beings with complex lives and emotions. Although Sonny and Leon are not typical, everyday citizens, neither are they one-dimensional limp-wristed stereotypes. Before filming commenced, the script was carefully scrutinized by the National Gay Task Force, an image-conscious homosexual organization.

Certainly, while Sonny is unemployed and anonymous, a mere speck in the sea of eight million New York faces, he is also an individual, a man desperately trying to define himself. He is compassionate and evinces a genuine sympathy for the inconvenience he is causing the hostages. In a scene in which he dictates his will, he expresses his love for both his wife and mother in spite of their personalities. It is clear that his motive for robbing the bank is not merely monetary; the act is his way of lashing out at a society which has dehumanized him. It is his moment in the spotlight as he struts out in front of the bank, performs for the crowd to win their support, and, in an ultimate irony, throws a bundle of paper bills at his audience.

However, after his capture, with the gun of an FBI agent pointed at his head, Sonny is the portrait of the consummate loser. He appears bewildered as he is read his rights, with the thunder of jet planes taking off and landing in the background. His day of glory has ended, and he knows that all he has left is the anonymity of a jail cell.

Whether comically hopping around the bank and waving his rifle or stoically reading his will, Al Pacino is perfectly cast as Sonny and gives a bravura performance. His voice rises when he is nervous; his tongue lashes out, he shrugs his shoulders, twitches his eyes, and his fingers nervously crumple a paper ball. From his screen debut as a junkie in *The Panic in Needle Park* (1971) through his roles as the honest cop bucking the corrupt system in *Serpico* (1973) and as Michael Corleone in *The Godfather* (1971) and *The*

Godfather, Part II (1974), Pacino has proved to be one of the more durable ethnic antiheroes of the 1970's.

Pacino is ably assisted by a hand-picked cast of character types, notably Chris Sarandon as Leon and Penny Allen as a bold bank teller. Sarandon brings a special humanity to a character who could easily have been played as a caricature; Allen is appropriately mouthy as a hostage who will not sit back and accept her fate. Charles Durning and James Broderick are cast as police officers (Durning was inexplicably selected over Sarandon as the year's Best Supporting Actor by the National Board of Review), while a pre-*Hester Street* (1975) Carol Kane may be seen as one of the prisoners. John Cazale is adequate as Sal, rivaling his best film role as the wormy Fredo Corleone in *The Godfather* and *The Godfather, Part II*.

Frank Pierson's screenplay is both funny and touching, and the film is crisply directed by Sidney Lumet. Over the past two decades, Lumet has consistently utilized New York City exteriors more creatively than any other director. The streets and neighborhoods of the city are the on-location sets of *The Pawnbroker* (1965), *A View from the Bridge* (1961), *The Anderson Tapes* (1971), *Bye Bye Braverman* (1968), and *Serpico*, among others. In *The Pawnbroker* and *Serpico*, he most successfully captures the grit and soul of the city; in *The Wiz* (1978), he transforms locations from the Brooklyn Bridge to the subways, the ghetto streets to the World Trade Center, into a majestic fairyland. *Dog Day Afternoon* was shot outside a warehouse in the Park Slope section of Brooklyn since Lumet was unable to film on the site of the actual robbery, several miles away, on Avenue P in Midwood.

Dog Day Afternoon's one glaring weakness is that it is too much of a comedy with dramatic touches in the first half, then a drama with comic bits in the second. While Sonny's personality is completely explored, very little is revealed about his partner. Overall, though, *Dog Day Afternoon* is an entertaining and insightful re-creation of reality. The film, which cost $3,500,000 to produce, was a box-office smash. It has earned $22,500,000 since its release, and was the seventh-highest grossing film of 1975. *Dog Day Afternoon* was Oscar-nominated for Best Picture, Best Actor (Al Pacino), Best Supporting Actor (Chris Sarandon, in his screen debut), Best Director, and Best Screenplay. All were losers: only Frank Pierson was honored for his script, as he also was by the Writers Guild of America. However, the Union of Film Critics in Athens voted the film the best to be released in Greece for the year, the National Board of Review named it to its Ten Best List, and Pacino was cited as Best Actor at the San Sebastian Film Festival and by the British Academy, the latter for both *Dog Day Afternoon* and *The Godfather, Part II*.

John Wojtowicz, the actual lead robber, was sentenced to a twenty-year prison term for his part in the robbery. He received $7,500 and a percentage of the net profit for his permission to be depicted in the film. Under a New

York State law passed in 1977, the state Crime Victims Compensation Board made available to the original hostages monies from *Dog Day Afternoon*'s earnings owed to Wojtowicz. After its release, Wojtowicz called *Dog Day Afternoon* "only thirty percent true." The filmmakers, however, claimed from the outset that it was only "based on a true incident." Wojtowicz was paroled in November, 1978.

In 1975, Wojtowicz's wife Carmen filed a lawsuit in New York State Supreme Court against Warner Bros., the film's distributor, and Dell Publishing and Delacorte Press, publishers of the follow-up novel. Mrs. Wojtowicz claimed the depiction of her character in the film constituted an invasion of her privacy. In turn, the Authors League of America, fearing costly legal actions if "unidentified" persons could sue filmmakers or novelists whose works were based on fact (Mrs. Wojtowicz was not actually named or pictured in the film), filed an Amicus Curiae brief in favor of the defendants. The case was dismissed in 1978.

Rob Edelman

DOUBLE INDEMNITY

Released: 1944
Production: Joseph Sistrom for Paramount
Direction: Billy Wilder
Screenplay: Billy Wilder and Raymond Chandler; based on the novel *Three of a Kind* by James M. Cain
Cinematography: John F. Seitz
Editing: Doane Harrison
Costume design: Edith Head
Music: Miklos Rozsa
Running time: 107 minutes

Principal characters:
Walter Neff .... Fred MacMurray
Phyllis Dietrichson .... Barbara Stanwyck
Barton Keyes .... Edward G. Robinson
Mr. Jackson .... Porter Hall
Lola Dietrichson .... Jean Heather

It is difficult to believe that such a brilliant film as *Double Indemnity* was only Billy Wilder's third directorial assignment. An immensely talented and volatile Austrian who left Europe in the 1930's to escape from Hitler, Wilder had a long and successful career as a screenwriter, both in Europe and the United States, but often made studio producers uneasy because of his ability to expose human weakness on the screen. Wilder has a sardonic wit and the ability to turn bad taste into good box office, as demonstrated in his first film directed in the United States—*The Major and the Minor* (1942), a pre-Lolita comedy in which Ray Milland is attracted to Ginger Rogers disguised as a twelve-year-old child.

In spite of the fact that *Double Indemnity* is now firmly established as a classic, it was a difficult project for Wilder. Paramount producer Joe Sistrom discovered James M. Cain's novella "Double Indemnity," which had appeared as a serial in Liberty magazine in 1936. The plot appealed immediately to Wilder but Charles Brackett, his long-time collaborator, hated the story so much that he refused either to work on the screenplay or to produce the film. This refusal terminated a working relationship that had lasted for seven years, and another writer had to be found. James M. Cain was the obvious choice to help adapt the story, but he was at that time working at Twentieth Century-Fox on *Western Union* (1941). Sistrom then suggested Raymond Chandler, since he thought that his writing style was rather similar to Cain's—a comparison that never failed to annoy Chandler.

Sistrom was partly right: although Chandler was a better writer than Cain, both men were particularly responsive to the ambience of California. Chandler's style was quite unique, however; and after reading a copy of *The Big Sleep* at one sitting, Wilder realized that its author was an ideal partner for this film. Unfortunately, Chandler had a severe drinking problem and no experience at writing screenplays (it was his first assignment); he did not seem much interested in moviemaking, had never collaborated with another writer, and hated Wilder on sight (the feeling was mutual). Chandler had hoped to finish the screenplay quickly, and he produced his version in five weeks. Wilder was not satisfied, and they worked together on the script for six months; Chandler was also forced to stay around the studio during filming.

Then came the problem of casting, although in retrospect it seems strange that any problems arose at all. The screenplay was touted around Hollywood, and not one of the leading actors of the day wanted to play the part of Walter Neff; *Double Indemnity* was considered to be a distasteful and immoral film. Wilder wanted Fred MacMurray to play the role—a strange choice, since the role of Neff required him to play a likable insurance agent who commits a brutal murder. The murder was not a crime of passion which the audience could understand, nor an accidental murder, but a calculated crime for lust and gain. Until then, MacMurray's career had been in light comedy, but Wilder finally persuaded him to accept the part; MacMurray thought it would end his career, but instead it was the best role he ever had in films.

Double Indemnity has an unusual plot in that the killer is identified in the opening scenes, a technique used repeatedly since then but uncommon at the time. Walter Neff (Fred MacMurray) is dictating an office memo to his boss. Neff is clearly dying from gunshot wounds but has returned late at night to the offices of the large insurance company for which he works. The dictation allows Neff's voice to change subtly from that of confessor to narrator and leads us into the flashback. This device is almost always effective but works exceptionally well in this case for it allows Chandler's descriptive linking passages to be spoken by a narrator, using language which would have been too literary as spoken dialogue.

The events related in the flashback begin as Walter Neff makes a seemingly routine call on a customer about auto insurance. The house he visits is a Spanish-style and slightly run down house in Glendale, California; the customer is out but Neff asks to see the man's wife instead. It would be difficult to forget Barbara Stanwyck's first appearance as Phyllis Dietrichson: she has been taking a sunbath and appears at the top of the staircase wearing only a bathtowel and a look of cool appraisal. Stanwyck is a gifted and intelligent actress, not strictly beautiful in the Hollywood style of Lana Turner or Heddy Lamarr, and her career has been that of an actress rather than a sex symbol. In this role, however, she conveys superbly a kind of sluttish sexuality. It is clear that there is a mutual attraction between Neff and Phyllis. His is a purely physical one, but she has a strangely calculating look. Neff is invited back to the house, Dietrichson is again out, and this time the maid is significantly absent as well.

Phyllis is wearing a dress this time, sexy but not blatantly so, and as she descends the staircase, the camera tracks along focusing on her chain anklet. She is, of course, unhappily married to an older man (his second wife), and is desperate to escape the boredom of life with a husband she hates, a resentful stepdaughter, and an allowance that does not begin to buy all the things she wants. She married for a kind of security and now finds herself a prisoner; but she does not intend to walk out empty-handed. She is obviously an experienced predator, and after conveying her interest in Neff, she warily outlines her plan to take out a large insurance policy on her husband's life. She wishes to have the policy signed as though it were for auto insurance, and she wishes her husband to know nothing about the arrangement. The conversation is like a chess game. Neff is responsive to her, but too astute to be fooled by an insurance deal which is obviously a prologue to murder. He rejects the whole idea and leaves, but the attraction is too strong; they meet again and he is drawn into her plan. Perhaps he also feels that as an insurance agent he is in an ideal position to plan and execute a fool-proof insurance fraud.

Like all murders planned so that two people can be together, the planning and aftermath of the crime inevitably mean that from the beginning, the parties concerned cannot meet without arousing suspicion. Most of their meetings take place in the very mundane atmosphere of a supermarket (Chandler used Jerry's Market on Melrose Avenue in Los Angeles for the locale), and these scenes are stunningly effective. Phyllis methodically selects groceries and at the same time coolly outlines the murder plan. It is in these scenes particularly that Stanwyck's acting is so strong, as she convinces us not only that Phyllis is capable of getting rid of her husband, but also that she is capable of persuading her lover not only to be an accomplice but also actually to commit the crime. The murder is carried out, while the camera rests on Phyllis Dietrichson's face as she remains virtually unmoved by the brutal killing taking place beside her. After the body has been carefully placed near the railway tracks (the policy now includes a double indemnity clause to include a rail accident), they must now wait for the insurance company to pay. The authorities seem to accept a verdict of accidental death, but the insurance company is more suspicious and throws out the claim.

Neff's boss at the insurance company is Burton Keyes (Edward G. Robinson), and he and Neff are friends as well as colleagues. Keyes loves the insurance business and seemingly has no private life at all. It is significant that at one time he was engaged, but this was abruptly terminated after he had the insurance company investigate his prospective wife. Keyes looks upon the insurance company business not as a collection of files and claims but as an endlessly fascinating series of case histories, constantly challenging him. When Keyes gets a phony claim, his dyspepsia gives him no peace; and the

Dietrichson claim gives his digestion a very hard time indeed.

The role of Burton Keyes could have been a rather colorless one had it not been for the magnetic presence of Edward G. Robinson. In one scene he reels off a long list of insurance company statistics on different types of death, with subdivisions for each section, to illustrate the improbability of the Dietrichson claim. Very few actors could have brought that kind of dialogue to life, but Robinson succeeds.

As the story draws to a close, the lovers continue to meet only in the supermarket, but now Neff is very nervous and wants to get out. Phyllis takes off her dark glasses, and, over a display of canned goods, informs him with chilling calm that people who commit murders cannot get off the trolley car when they choose but must stay together "all the way down the line." Neff finally kills Phyllis, and the film ends as he painfully makes his way to Keyes's office and, while dying of gunshot wounds himself, confesses his crime to his boss. The ending of *Double Indemnity* was changed after filming the original ending showing Neff in the gas chamber at Folsom. Wilder, against all advice, insisted on scrapping the footage and writing and filming a different ending. His decision was a fortunate one: the final scene between Keyes and Neff is beautifully done and manages to convince the audience that Walter Neff, although a murderer, does deserve some sympathy.

Elizabeth Leese

A DOUBLE LIFE

Released: 1947
Production: Michael Kanin for Universal
Direction: George Cukor
Screenplay: Ruth Gordon and Garson Kanin
Cinematography: Milton Krasner
Editing: Robert Parrish
Music: Miklos Rozsa (AA)
Running time: 103 minutes

> *Principal characters:*
> Anthony John .... Ronald Colman (AA)
> Brita .... Signe Hasso
> Bill Friend .... Edmond O'Brien
> Pat Kroll ....Shelley Winters
> Max Lasker .... Philip Loeb
> Victor Donlan .... Ray Collins

The story of *A Double Life* concerns an actor who becomes so immersed in his roles that his identification with the characters he plays overwhelms his private life. While the situation in this compelling film is so extreme that it leads Anthony John (Ronald Colman) to unreasoning jealousy and murder, the essential problem of an artist's need for detachment from his creative power is moving even without the melodrama of the plot. The character reflects on his difficulties very early in the film, demonstrating a consciousness of his mysterious impulse to live his roles and winning considerable audience sympathy by virtue of his earnestness. Tony is from the beginning a lonely and endearing figure, perhaps too idealistic about himself and too fragile in his emotions. He is estranged from his wife, Brita (Signe Hasso), although they still love each other and still work together. He yearns for a stability which seems remote.

The actor's loss of balance occurs when he takes on the role of Othello in a production of the Shakespearean drama. Before this, we see him playing in a light and witty comedy, *A Gentleman's Gentleman*. The play has been successful and Tony has been playing his role for a long time. As a result, he is as charming and sophisticated offstage as he is on. A reconciliation with Brita seems possible, but Tony yields to the temptation of playing the tragic role which he knows may consume him. Gloomily, he wanders at night through the city, perhaps believing that this nocturnal solitude will unlock the key to the demanding characterization. He meets a waitress, Pat Kroll (Shelley Winters). Vulgar and unrefined, she is the opposite of Brita, but her openness attracts Tony. He sleeps with her, then forgets her.

Later, when *Othello* has become a smash hit and Tony's brilliant performance as the jealous Moor is starting to take its toll as a result of nightly performances, he seeks out Pat once more. He has already made Othello's jealousy a part of himself, suspecting his wife and an innocent press agent, Bill Friend (Edmond O'Brien), of an affair. As in the case of Shakespeare's protagonist, his suspicions are unwarranted. The difference is that his actor's imagination is the villain, poisoning his thoughts as the character Iago poisoned those of Othello in the play. In a demented state, he projects his jealousy onto Pat, who, with amusing guilelessness, asks if she should "put out the light." The Shakespearean phrase and the visually striking darkness which follows as Tony, repeating the line, does turn out the light, results in the death of the poor waitress. Ultimately, it is Friend who has the insight to suspect that Tony is the murderer, although there is nothing to link him to Pat other than the *Othello* style of the killing. Mortally wounding himself on stage after almost strangling Brita, he dies finishing his role.

In realizing this material, director George Cukor and writers Ruth Gordon and Garson Kanin demonstrate not only a sympathetic understanding of the character but also their love of theater. The rehearsal sequences which precede the major part of the narrative are no less fascinating than the melodrama which follows, although they are completely devoid of melodrama. What we see are actors tirelessly practicing and the details of work on the play's physical presentation, but these moments perfectly capture the process of creating an individual production from a text which exists only in words. The imagination of Cukor's own staging and Milton Krasner's lighting conveys the excitement of theater in a positive way, in contrast to the negative effect this same excitement has on the film's protagonist.

Further, there are lengthy excerpts from the play itself. Fortunately, Colman is a superb actor, and he is a credible Othello, as convincing playing Anthony John acting the role as he is playing Tony as a tragically disturbed individual. The climactic scenes of Shakespeare's tragedy are presented twice. In the second rendition, which is also the climax of the film, Tony gives a more deeply felt reading of his lines, and it is appropriate to call attention to Cukor's discernment and Colman's ability in making the earlier reading not unworthy of comparison to the second. That first reading is dramatically persuasive, convincing as the performance of a celebrated actor, and lacking only the touching self-knowledge of the dying Tony which makes the second reading singularly poignant.

Colman is well-cast as an actor but no less impressive as an individual struggling to make his life as successful as his career. Tony's beautiful voice and gentlemanly bearing do not desert him offstage, but he never appears to be an affected man. On the contrary, he comes across as a man of deep feeling and sensitivity, and he is unfailingly sympathetic, even after he has murdered Pat. Colman's past performances in such films as *Lost Horizon* (1937) and *A Tale Of Two Cities* (1935) were undoubtedly a factor in the Academy Award he won for *A Double Life*, but that does not change the fact that the award is well-deserved. His performance confirms Cukor's richly merited reputation as an actor's director, as do the less central performances. The only other striking role is that of Pat, and Winters perfectly expresses Pat's sexual sophistication and her lack of psychological awareness, but the director commendably balances the playing of Colman and Winters by making the other characterizations restrained but not dull. Hasso's Brita and O'Brien's Friend register as human beings of considerable dimension, whose feelings toward Tony have a rich complexity. Similarly, Ray Collins' insightful director Donlon and Philip Loeb's cultured producer Lasker are not the expected theatrical types.

This was the first of seven films on which Kanin and Gordon collaborated with Cukor. Most of the others are comedies, in some cases featuring the celebrated team of Katharine Hepburn and Spencer Tracy and in others the irrepressible Judy Holliday, although *The Actress* (1953), starring Jean Simmons, is an affectionate reminiscence of Gordon's early years. *A Double Life*, the only straight drama by the Cukor-Kanin-Gordon team, is less highly regarded than the other films, in spite of the awards won by Colman and Miklos Rozsa, who composed a typically evocative score. The film deserves a better reputation. It is generally agreed that the performances are excellent and the theater sequences brilliantly realized, but the story has been spoken of as excessively melodramatic. It is this melodrama, however, which brings out the best in Cukor. The material forces him into a more dazzling visual realization than called for by his previous films. The *film noir* atmosphere and the hallucinations of the possessed Anthony John, as well as the visual commentary on Tony's emotional state which the story requires even when he is performing, are brought off by the director with remarkable flair. It would be unjust to criticize the less visually assertive films which Cukor has made, notably in the 1930's, as many of those films are superb and perhaps more subtle than *A Double Life*. It is impossible not to notice, however, that in most of the films that follow this one, the director shows a greater consciousness with regard to stylistic interpretation. The captivating visual boldness of *A Star Is Born* (1954) and *Bhowani Junction* (1956) can be directly traced to *A Double Life*. If for no other reason, it is a key film.

Blake Lucas

DOWNHILL RACER

Released: 1969
Production: Richard Gregson for Wildwood; released by Paramount
Direction: Michael Ritchie
Screenplay: James Salter
Cinematography: Brian Probyn
Editing: Richard Harris
Running time: 101 minutes

> *Principal characters:*
> David Chappellet .... Robert Redford
> Eugene Claire .... Gene Hackman
> Carole Stahl ....Camilla Sparv
> D. K. Bryan .... Kenneth Kirk
> Johnny Creech .... Jim McMullan
> Mr. Chappellet ....Walter Stroud
> Lena .... Carole Carle
> Machet .... Michael Vogler

Downhill Racer grew out of Robert Redford's desire to make a different kind of sports film. He regarded the typical portrayal of athletes by Hollywood as too idealized and reportedly wished to present an athlete who was a "creep." The problem, of course, in presenting the idea that athletics does not necessarily build character and that a person can be a winner in sports and still be a shallow and limited human being is that the audience may not be interested in such a character. *Downhill Racer* effectively solves this creative problem by portraying not only the personality of the protagonist but also his relations with his coach and team members, the physical excitement of the sport, and its coverage by the media. Although Redford's name appears in the film's credits only for his acting, it was produced by his own production company, Wildwood, and Redford exercised a good deal of creative control over the project, including selecting Michael Ritchie as director even though Ritchie's experience at the time was only in television and he had never before directed a feature film.

Downhill Racer has a definite plot, but that plot is developed in a series of nearly self-contained episodes, essentially long vignettes. Each episode presents another facet of the character of the protagonist or his world of competitive sports. *Downhill Racer* is the story of David Chappellet (Robert Redford), a skier from Idaho Springs, Colorado. We do not, however, see him in the film's first episode. Instead, a montage of shots of ski competition with frequent freeze-frames under the credits builds up to the downhill run of an unidentified American skier who is injured and has to be taken to the hospital. It is not until a few minutes later that we realize that this event has made it necessary for the American ski coach, Eugene Claire (Gene Hackman), to send for Chappellet and D. K. Bryan (Kenneth Kirk) as replacements for the remainder of his team's European skiing season.

When we do see Chappellet, we immediately notice that he is very provincial, unfamiliar with and unsympathetic to foreign lands and foreign customs. We also soon find that he is not inclined to be cooperative with his teammates or his coach. When he is assigned the eighty-eighth position for the first race, he refuses to ski because he believes that he deserves a better position. He does ski, however, in the next race, and almost the entire run is seen from his viewpoint in a sequence which visually stresses the excitement, danger, and beauty of the sport of downhill skiing. He does quite well in the competition, finishing ahead of the star of the American team, Johnny Creech (Jim McMullan). "Maybe next time I'll get to start in the top fifty," Chappellet remarks sarcastically.

Even though he remains essentially callous, boorish, self-centered, and inarticulate, Chappellet's success makes him a focus of attention for the media covering the events as well as for an important ski manufacturer, Machet (Michael Vogler), who wants the winner of the Olympics to use his skis. Chappellet begins an affair with Machet's assistant, Carole Stahl (Camilla Sparv), which continues over two seasons, but he is unable to give her much real attention. In one of the two scenes in which he is most happy with her he listens delightedly as she translates his press notices for him. On the other hand, when they are sitting in her car and she is talking to him about her Christmas vacation, he blows the car horn to stop her.

Between the two seasons we get a glimpse of Chappellet's home life when he returns to Idaho Falls, where he fits in little better than he did in the foreign cities. His father (Walter Stroud) greets him perfunctorily: "Hello. I got your postcard. Your cousin said to thank you for the stamps." He neither gets nor gives much more from his hometown girl friend, Lena (Carole Carle).

The essential thread of the film is David as athlete, although we see that the rest of his life is shaped by the fact that he is an athlete. Rather than teaching him anything, the athletic life of David Chappellet has isolated him so much from "ordinary" life that he seems unable to handle either success or failure. Much of this theme is brought out in the scenes between Chappellet and Claire, his coach. It is Claire's opinion that Chappellet has a certain ability, skill, and dedication to the sport, but that his dedication is only enough to cut him off from the rest of life, not enough to make him a really first-rate skier. The coach tells Chappellet at one point that he has neither consistency nor desire to learn.

Another of Chappellet's deficiencies seen by both the coach and the other members of the team is his lack of consideration for the team. Even though one skier does remark that skiing is "not exactly a team sport," Chappellet ignores his responsibility to the others by challenging Creech to an informal race at the end of a workout. This endangers both skiers and causes Creech to take a spill. Chappellet's only response to criticism of this action is that Creech did not have to race him. In what is obviously (perhaps too obviously) meant to be the statement of the film's theme, Claire says to Chappellet, "You never had any real education did you? All you ever had was your skis, and that's not enough."

Later, Creech breaks his leg and Chappellet is left as the only hope of the American team in the Olympics. He proves equal to the occasion athletically, winning the gold medal in the downhill event, but we see that emotionally and mentally he has still not found his way. Before the event a sportscaster asks him about his plans for after the Olympics and Chappellet can only respond, "This is it." After his victory he is again asked about his plans and he replies, "I don't know" three times. This ending, incidentally, prefigures the ending of a later Redford film, *The Candidate* (1972), in which the Redford character wins the election and then asks what he should do next.

In addition to the episodic nature of the narrative, the most notable element of the style of the film is its semidocumentary photography. A portion of the film is footage of actual skiing events, and much of the scripted portions are photographed as if they were simply being caught by a documentary cinematographer on the scene. this technique both integrates the two types of footage and also adds verisimilitude to the story, especially since modern audiences are familiar with documentaries on sports and sports figures. The keys to the success of *Downhill Racer* are the excellent performances of Redford as the skier and Hackman as the coach. Redford performs the difficult feat of keeping us interested in a character who is neither sympathetic nor expressive, and Hackman nicely keeps his character from being excessively platitudinous or excessively sentimental.

Critical response to *Downhill Racer* was quite favorable, but the box-office response was not as good, perhaps because too many people thought of it as just another sports film.

Timothy W. Johnson

DRACULA

Released: 1931
Production: Universal
Direction: Tod Browning
Screenplay: Garrett Fort; based on Hamilton Deane's and John L. Balder-
   ston's stage adaptation of the novel of the same name by Bram Stoker
Cinematography: Karl Freund
Editing: Milton Carruth
Running time: 84 minutes

Principal characters:
Count Dracula .... Bela Lugosi
Mina .... Helen Chandler
Jonathan Harker .... David Manners
Renfield .... Dwight Frye
Professor Van Helsing .... Edward Van Sloan

Bram Stoker's *Dracula*, published in 1897, is an outstanding gothic novel.
It is a long tale, replete with the conventions of its day—sentimental subplots,
the letter format of the opening chapters, lengthy reported conversations—
yet it remains eminently readable even in an age of novelettes and journalistic
prose. It has been subjected to Freudian analysis, interpreted as a metaphor
for the repression of female sexuality, and dismissed as a hack writer's "penny
dreadful." Yet *Dracula* has never been out of print, and since the early days
of the cinema the tale of an aristocratic vampire who travels from Eastern
Europe to Victorian London in pursuit of human blood has fascinated filmmakers throughout the world. The United States, Great Britain, France,
Germany, Japan, and Mexico have all produced distinctive Draculas of their
own.
   The first film version, produced independently of any of the stage versions
circulating in the early years of this century, was a German silent film released
in 1922. Directed by F. W. Murnau, *Nosferatu: A Symphony in Terror* features
the extraordinary character actor, Max Schreck (whose name means "Terror"
in German), as the undead count. Though Murnau, who was unwilling to pay
for the rights to Stoker's novel, gave his film a different title, he drew heavily
on the original work for his screenplay. The transition from novel to film is
most assured. Of all the screen versions, *Nosferatu* is perhaps the truest to
the spirit of the book. It is a masterpiece of narrative in its own right, weeding
out the longer, less exotic sections and stretching the boundaries of the medium with unsettling use of negative images and fast-motion. A court action
brought by Stoker's widow resulted in the destruction of many prints of
Murnau's film (though *Nosferatu* survives in a variety of versions), and it was

not until almost ten years later that an "official" *Dracula* film was undertaken. The director was Tod Browning, veteran of macabre silent films such as *The Unknown* (1927) and *London after Midnight* (1927), and the production company was Carl Laemmle's Universal Pictures.

Renfield (Dwight Frye), an English businessman, is on the last stage of his coach journey to the castle of Count Dracula (Bela Lugosi), a Transylvanian nobleman who plans to purchase property in London. The locals, a sullen and suspicious crew, mysteriously cross themselves at the mention of the Count's name, and urge Renfield to abandon his trip. He presses on, only to be abandoned by his driver at a bleak crossroads. Here he is met by a mute coachman and conducted at a frantic pace into the Count's abode. Dracula, who appears only between sunset and sunrise, proves a refined, almost congenial host; but as the days pass, Renfield realizes that he is being kept a prisoner, and worse, that he is in danger of losing his immortal soul. For Dracula is a vampire—a reanimated corpse who feeds off the blood of the living, turning his victims into vampires in the process. A cunning fiend, the Count plans to take up residence in a land where the prevailing skepticism will enable him to pursue his career undetected.

Once he decides that he has learned enough about England from his unwilling guest, Dracula sets sail for the White Cliffs ensconsed within a casket containing his native earth. Ever-hungry, he decimates the cargo vessel's crew en route. For a while after arriving in England he finds his strange need for blood satisfied, until he encounters Professor Van Helsing (Edward Van Sloan), a middle-European doctor who has dedicated his life to battling the undead. Van Helsing recognizes Dracula as a vampire as he does not cast a shadow nor a reflection, and henceforth the battlelines are drawn. The Count pits his creatures, among them Renfield, now the dessicated inmate of a lunatic asylum, against Van Helsing and his allies. Their prize is the soul of his latest victim, Mina (Helen Chandler). After a savage struggle the forces of light triumph, and Van Helsing destroys the vampire in time-honored fashion, with a wooden stake through the heart.

The most obvious problem with Universal's *Dracula* is its script: even a first-rate cast and high production values cannot compensate for the mediocre screenplay, adapted not from Stoker's novel but from a hacked-out melodrama in which the most interesting occurrences take place offstage. Dracula's skill at metamorphosis; his control over bats, rats, and wolves; his phenomenal strength; and the scene in which he crawls head-first down the castle wall are dropped in favor of Garrett Fort's trite dialogue. Even the Count's demise is depicted by an offscreen groan—a tragically insipid end for evil incarnate. And despite his distinguished career in silent pictures, Tod Browning's *mise-en-scene* is rather tedious. The fact that *Dracula* was an early talking picture, constrained by cumbrous equipment, does not excuse sloppy pace and poor staging. In contrast, *Frankenstein*, directed the same year by James

Whale, is visually innovative and cohesive. Unlike Browning's film it stands the test of time remarkably well.

What saves *Dracula* from mediocrity is its cast. Some of the supporting players, particularly Edward Van Sloan and Dwight Frye (who also played the sadistic dwarf in *Frankenstein*), are excellent; while in the title role Bela Lugosi established himself as the definitive screen vampire. Born in Hungary, Lugosi had worked with Murnau (*Der Januskopf*, 1920) before emigrating to the United States. After a diverse stage and film career, he played Dracula on Broadway and was invited to portray the Count in pictures following the death of Browning's first choice, silent horror-star Lon Chaney. Aquiline and perhaps too exotic to be cast as a "straight" leading man, Lugosi was instantly identified with Stoker's character. Without a doubt, he is at his best when saying Stoker's lines: "I never drink . . . wine," or "Wolves . . . children of the night . . . what music they make." Such dialogue, immaculately delivered, stands many stories above the vapid verbalizing of playwrights Deane and Balderston. And today, with subsequent competition from powerful presences such as Christopher Lee, John Carradine, and Klaus Kinski, Lugosi's performance has not been bettered.

Without Lugosi's unique contribution, the history of Universal Pictures might have been quite different. *Dracula*, released on Valentine's Day of 1931, was the company's largest grossing film in years. It launched the most celebrated of all the horror-picture cycles, a series which included the individual adventures of Dracula, Frankenstein's monster, the Mummy, the Wolf Man, and the Invisible Man, and which, in its declining years, incorporated them all into such formula potboilers as *Abbott and Costello Meet Frankenstein* (1948). Despite its less inventive latter days, the Universal cycle boasted a distinguished repertory of actors and distinctive cinematography and production design, the art direction being fashioned after the dusty vaults and dark interiors created by Charles Hall for *Dracula*.

Lugosi himself auditioned for the monster's role in *Frankenstein*, but decided not to take the part (which, unlike the simple makeup job on *Dracula*, demanded four hours of preparation daily). Instead, the role went to an English actor named William Henry Pratt, better known as Boris Karloff. Between them, the two men cornered the market on the best horror roles for almost twenty years, and both men went on acting up until their deaths. Despite sequels and imitations, Lugosi and Karloff remain in the popular imagination and critical esteem alike the definitive Dracula and Frankenstein, and their portrayals kept the candle of supernatural unease burning well into the all-too-real twentieth century.

V. I. Huxner

DRUMS ALONG THE MOHAWK

Released: 1939
Production: Raymond Griffith for Twentieth Century-Fox
Direction: John Ford
Screenplay: Lamar Trotti and Sonya Levien; based on the novel of the same
    name by Walter D. Edmonds
Cinematography: Bert Glennon
Editing: Robert Simpson
Running time: 130 minutes

> *Principal characters:*
> Gilbert Martin ....Henry Fonda
> Lana (Magdelana) Martin .... Claudette Colbert
> Mrs. McKlennar .... Edna May Oliver
> Caldwell ....John Carradine
> Reverend Rosenkrantz ....Arthur Shields
> General Nicholas Herkimer .... Roger Imhof
> Adam Helmer .... Ward Bond
> Blue Back ....Chief Big Tree

In the twelve-month period from March 2, 1939, through March 15, 1940, John Ford released four films: *Stagecoach* (1939), *Young Mr. Lincoln* (1939), *Drums Along the Mohawk*, and *The Grapes of Wrath* (1940). There is general agreement among film scholars that *Stagecoach*, *Young Mr. Lincoln*, and *The Grapes of Wrath* are major achievements in Ford's fifty-year film career. It is generally conceded that *Drums Along the Mohawk*, does not quite match the astonishing creativity of the other three films of this highly productive period; this is not to suggest, however, that the film is not without significant merit. It is an exciting and vivid film—Ford's first in color—and is directly concerned with a theme which Ford would examine many times in the next thirty-five years—that of Americans settling the frontier.

The film begins in Albany, New York, just before the Revolutionary War at the wedding of Lana Borst (Claudette Colbert) to Gilbert Martin (Henry Fonda). Lana, the daughter of a wealthy Dutch burgher, is accustomed to the comforts and pleasures of a settled town; her husband, a yeoman farmer, will take her to his frontier homestead in the Mohawk Valley. After the wedding, they leave her father's home in a wagon leading a cow and proceed west into the wilderness. They spend their wedding night at an inn, where they have a troubling encounter with a sinister man named Caldwell (John Carradine) who is most interested in Gil's political views on the crisis between the colonies and England.

The next evening they arrive at the cabin Gil has constructed for his bride. It is a small, stark hovel compared to her father's brick mansion in Albany, and Lana is shocked, thoroughly frightened, and drenched by the fierce thunderstorm through which they have driven; but when an Indian invades the cabin, she collapses in total hysteria. Gil slaps her back to sensibility, and when Lana calms down, he introduces the Indian as Blue Back (Chief Big Tree), a friend and "a better Christian than you or I."

In a series of short scenes, Lana is shown slowly adjusting to the life of a farm wife. Gil takes her to the fort, which is the center of community life; here she meets the other farm wives and watches the men drill as militia in order to defend themselves against a possible attack by the English and the Indians. That attack comes swiftly, and Lana and Gil are forced to abandon the farm and flee to the fort. The Indians are driven back by the militia at the fort, but in the process, the Martins have lost everything including the baby Lana was carrying.

Without either home or money, Gil hires himself out to work the farm of Mrs. McKlennar (Edna May Oliver), a robust and willful woman who is steadfast in her love for her late husband, Barney. She is also kind and motherly and soon looks upon Gil and Lana as her children. She waits with Lana when Gil is called to go off to fight with the militia, and when the soldiers finally return, she sets up a hospital in her kitchen. Gil, however, does not return with the militia, and Lana sets out to search for him, finding him ultimately in a ditch, unable to walk. Lana manages to bring him back to the house to tend to his wounds. As Gil awakens after a recuperative period, Lana tells him that she is expecting another child. Meanwhile, downstairs in the kitchen, General Nicholas Herkimer (Roger Imhof), the leader of the successful campaign, dies of his wounds.

In the spring, amid much drunken celebration by the father's friends, Gil and Lana's baby is born. Just as life seems to be improving for the Martins, the Indians attack once more, led by Caldwell, the Tory agent whom the Martins had met on their wedding night. During this attack, the Indians invade Mrs. McKlennar's bedroom, and in a comic battle of wills, she forces them to carry her bed out of the house which they have set on fire. Although the Martins manage to escape to the fort with the feisty widow, Mrs. McKlennar is killed in the ensuing attack on the fort.

With the fort in grave danger and the women helping the men defend it, a farmer volunteers to go for help by night. When he is quickly captured and tied to a burning haywagon by the Indians, Reverend Rosenkrantz (Arthur Shields), a militant minister, shoots him to save him from the more painful death by fire. Gil, volunteering to run for help, gets away from the fort, but is soon discovered by three Indians who start pursuing him in an epic foot race that lasts past daybreak. Gil finally is victorious in outdistancing his pursuers and returns with the soldiers, who break the siege and enter the fort to raise the new American flag—a symbol which seems to promise the settlers a new era of peace in which they can raise their families in the fertile valley.

John Ford would never again be quite so positive about the settling of the American continent; in his very next film, *The Grapes of Wrath*, he would deal with the failure of America to care for all her people, and World War II would further challenge his belief in the morality of America's past. But in 1939, he was convinced that taking the land from the Indians was both necessary and proper, and the Indians in the film are portrayed as truly savage, with no evidence of humanity. They are more like demons than men, with the only good Indian being a Christian, an emasculated comic figure who has no real function in the community.

The white settlers are portrayed as decent, moral people who yearn only for peace in order to farm their rich valley and to rear their families; they are the people who will make America great, and there is no sense that they have committed any wrong in driving the Indians from the land. Ford here presents good and evil only in shades of black and white whereas in his later films, the grays would predominate. *Drums Along the Mohawk* was Ford's last film in which everything was simple and clear-cut.

Ford was always to prefer the look of black-and-white cinematography to color, but he worked easily with color from the beginning, and his sense of color composition in *Drums Along the Mohawk* is superb. He uses color to enhance the mood of the story; the Indians, for example, are associated with fire, like demons from hell. In the foot race sequence, while the Indians seem strongest at night, Gil grows stronger as day breaks, and the arrival of a glorious Technicolor dawn signals his triumph.

Henry Fonda starred in three of the four films Ford directed during this period, but there is very little similarity in the three characters Fonda plays: Abraham Lincoln in *Young Mr. Lincoln*, Tom Joad in *The Grapes of Wrath*, and Gil Martin in *Drums Along the Mohawk*. Fonda demonstrates the depth and power of his skill and talent in all three roles, and his Gil Martin characterization portrays a stalwart young farmer sure of himself and his young country as he and his wife begin their life together. The scene in which Gil holds his newborn child for the first time is a model of acting as Fonda conveys excitement, awe, pride, embarrassment, and the burden of responsibility, in a charmingly comic manner. Edna May Oliver was nominated for Best Supporting Actress in her role as Mrs. McKlennar; her superb performance is full of nuance as well as the bolder strokes of an endearing and broadly comic character. Arthur Shields is memorable in his small role as the fighting parson, a character Ford would return to again in *The Searchers* (1956). Although Ford would return to the theme of settlers confronting the wilderness many times during his career, he never again would view their efforts with quite the same equanimity as he does in *Drums Along the Mohawk*.

Don K Thompson

DUCK SOUP

Released: 1933
Production: Paramount
Direction: Leo McCarey
Screenplay: Bert Kalmar and Harry Ruby, with additional dialogue by Arthur
  Sheekman and Nat Perrin
Cinematography: Henry Sharp
Editing: Leroy Stone
Music: Bert Kalmar and Harry Ruby
Running time: 70 minutes

> *Principal characters:*
> Rufus T. Firefly ....Groucho Marx
> Chicolini ....Chico Marx
> Brownie ....Harpo Marx
> Bob Rolland ....Zeppo Marx
> Mrs. Teasdale .... Margaret Dumont
> Ambassador Trentino .... Louis Calhern
> Vera Marcal .... Raquel Torres
> Lemonade Dealer .... Edgar Kennedy

The zany, surreal humor of the Marx Brothers is at once irrational, irreverent, and irrepressible. Each of the four is an individual. Groucho is the consummate phony, with his greasepaint moustache, oversized clothes, and doubletalk. Harpo, the silent one, is touchingly human in his elemental responses to his siblings and to everyone and everything else. Chico is as thick in his Italian accent as he is in intelligence, yet he always manages to outsmart the obtuse Groucho. Zeppo, the least interesting of the quartet, is something of a nice-looking straight man, similar in *Duck Soup* to actor/singer Alan Jones in *A Night at the Opera* (1935), and is easily the closest of the four to approach rationality. Yet as the Marx Brothers collectively assault the pomposity and hypocrisy of a "sane" world in the thick of the Depression and on the brink of a World War, these differences blend into a unified, hilarious whole.

It is hopeless to cite the funniest Marx Brothers film; *A Night at the Opera*, *A Day at the Races* (1937), *Horsefeathers* (1932), *The Cocoanuts* (1929), *Animal Crackers* (1930), and *Monkey Business* (1952) all have their ardent supporters, but *Duck Soup* is undeniably their most striking and most bitingly satiric film. Released during the nadir of the Depression, *Duck Soup* is a lampoon of war and Fascism. Groucho is Rufus T. Firefly, the dictator of a mythical kingdom called Freedonia. Firefly is no mature head of state: even though he is ostensibly the most powerful man in Freedonia, his irresponsibility and pride in his own stupidity continuously mock the concept of authority. Chico is Chicolini, a peanut vender who becomes Freedonia's Minister of War, and Harpo is Brownie, Firefly's chauffeur; the pair are spies for Trentino (Louis Calhern), the Ambassador of neighboring Sylvania, and they comically stand up to both their employers. Zeppo, in his last Marx Brothers film, appears as Firefly's secretary.

Trentino desires to take control of Freedonia by a *coup d'etat*. Armed conflict between the countries is inevitable, however, when Firefly slaps Trentino's face once too often—a trivial reason for a declaration of war. The actual combat is pointless, a slapstick struggle, with no attempt made by Firefly to defeat the enemy. Margaret Dumont, a veteran of several Marx Brothers films, is also in the cast as Mrs. Teasdale, the richest widow in Freedonia and Firefly's most ardent supporter.

Duck Soup is packed with an ample quota of Marx Brothers mayhem. Most of the bits are in the same comic vein as their earlier films, and *Duck Soup* is certainly no departure in style for the team. Yet the film is funny whether or not one is cognizant of their brand of humor. The outbreak of war is celebrated, as the quartet leads the production number "The Country's Going to War" replete with barn dance and opera, hillbilly and blues songs, including "All God's Chillun Got Guns" (although throughout the film, Harpo and Chico do not play their characteristic instruments, harp and piano). Harpo hands various personages his leg, which promptly goes limp. He produces a blow torch from his trousers and cuts cigars, ties, coattails and sausages with a pair of scissors. Calhern asks Harpo to inquire about Groucho's record as president; Harpo immediately produces a gramophone record; when Calhern throws it in the air, Harpo shoots it with a rifle and Chico rings a bell on Calhern's desk, hands Harpo a cigar as a prize, and slams a cigar box on Calhern's fingers. Harpo and Chico harass a lemonade dealer (Edgar Kennedy) with a rapid-fire series of physical assaults. Harpo impersonates Paul Revere and seduces a beautiful blonde whom he sees undressing in her bedroom; her husband, the lemonade seller, returns and eventually settles down in his bath—on top of a submerged Harpo.

Groucho's initial appearance is heralded by trumpets blasting, guards raising their swords, and girls tossing flowers; he fails to materialize, and the singing of the Freedonia National Anthem is repeated; he finally arrives by sliding down a firepole from his upstairs bedroom, lining up with his own honor guard and asking, "Who are we waiting for?" Groucho is transported about in a motorcycle and sidecar driven by Harpo; first, the cycle alone is operable, then only the car. Groucho keeps his cabinet waiting while he plays a game of jacks. He and Chico continuously spar in bizarre bits of conversation, with Groucho usually the foil for his brother. For example, questioner Groucho is convinced by Chico that he must respond to the ridiculous query he has put to Groucho: "What is it that has four pairs of pants, lives in Philadelphia and it never rains but pours?" Groucho informs Chico that the latter will not be commissioned to the position of Minister of War as originally planned; when Groucho tells Chico what the job is, Chico responds: "Good, I'll take it"; Groucho replies: "Sold."

Shells zoom through a window during the climactic battle sequence, until Groucho pulls down the blinds. Groucho asks assistance from the world: the response is a menagerie of athletes (a runner, rowers, swimmers) and animals (elephants, gorillas, giraffes). Groucho, dressed in a white nightgown and cap, peers into a false mirror; the reflection is first one, then two Grouchos, impersonated by a similarly garbed Harpo and Chico. Last, of course, Dumont is constantly and mercilessly chided and insulted by Groucho: Groucho asks her for a lock of her hair, but quickly amends the request by adding: "I'm letting you off lightly—I was going to ask for the whole wig." At the film's conclusion, when Dumont patriotically sings the Freedonia National Anthem at the victory over Sylvania, she is pelted with cooking apples by the Marx Brothers.

Duck Soup is short, only 70 minutes, and it has been crisply directed by Leo McCarey. McCarey is the only top comedy director ever to helm a Marx Brothers opus: among his other early films are *The Kid from Spain* (1932), with Eddie Cantor, Busby Berkeley musical numbers, and Betty Grable and Paulette Goddard in the chorus; *Six of a Kind* (1934), with Burns and Allen, W. C. Fields, Mary Boland, Charles Ruggles, and Alison Skipworth; *Belle of the Nineties* (1934), with Mae West; *Ruggles of Red Gap* (1935), with Charles Laughton, Zazu Pitts, Charles Ruggles, and Mary Boland; and the classic screwball comedy, *The Awful Truth* (1937), with Cary Grant and Irene Dunne.

Curiously, the critical reception to *Duck Soup* was mixed. Some reviewers heralded it for its humor, but just as many felt that it was not amusing in comparison to the Marx Brothers' previous films. The nonparticipation of S. J. Perelman, George S. Kaufman, and Morris Ryskind in the writing of the screenplay and music was cited as the major culprit. More recently, however, *Duck Soup* has come to be regarded as a spirited, timeless burlesque of the pomposity of politicians and the absurdity of war.

Rob Edelman

DUEL IN THE SUN

Released: 1946
Production: David O. Selznick for Selznick Studios
Direction: King Vidor
Screenplay: David O. Selznick and Oliver H. P. Garrett; based on the novel
of the same name by Niven Busch
Cinematography: Lee Garmes
Editing: William Ziegler and John Saure
Running time: 138 minutes

Principal characters:
Pearl Chavez	Jennifer Jones
Lewt McCanles	Gregory Peck
Jesse McCanles	Joseph Cotton
McCanles	Lionel Barrymore
Laura Belle McCanles	Lillian Gish
Preacher	Walter Huston
Chavez	Herbert Marshall
Sam Pierce	Charles Bickford
Chavez's wife	Tilly Losch

Duel in the Sun is one of the most expensive, controversial, and financially profitable Westerns ever made. At a cost of more than five million dollars, it was an attempt by producer David O. Selznick to duplicate the success of his own *Gone with the Wind* (1939) in a new setting. The history of the production of *Duel in the Sun* parallels that of *Gone with the Wind*, with Selznick's ever-changing vision and compulsive perfectionism leading to an almost constant flux in personnel (there were no less than six directors and three cinematographers involved in the project) as well as a ballooning budget. As screenwriter, Selznick revised the script weekly; as producer, he agonized over rushes daily, eventually causing King Vidor, the director credited on the film and who contributed most to the finished product, to throw up his hands in despair and walk off the set. The story of *Duel in the Sun*'s making can be traced in a seemingly unending series of memos from Selznick to the director, the cinematographer, and the stars. No detail was too petty for Selznick's supervision, from lighting to the sweat on Jennifer Jones's face. This extremism did not cease with the film's completion. An advertising blitz, costing more than three million dollars alone, was initiated for the film in major cities throughout the United States, resulting in saturation booking.

The reception of *Duel in the Sun* by the press and the industry was disappointing. Hoping for a repeat of the critical acclaim which greeted *Gone with the Wind*, Selznick was confronted instead with vilification and hostility from all quarters, particularly from the religious community. Over a period of months Selznick became embroiled in negotiations with the Catholic

Church's censorship arm, the Legion of Decency. Each line and each shot of the movie was examined by the Legion, and those considered too explicit were marked for deletion. Ultimately Selznick had no choice but to bow to their wishes, since the Legion's power over American Catholics was, at that time, something to be reckoned with. The film was pulled for editing, and an approved version was released.

What so frightened the Legion of Decency and its coguardians of morality in the religious community was the blatant eroticism of the film. *Duel in the Sun* is a film *par excellence* about what the French call *amour fou*, or mad love. It is the kind of love in which the lovers disregard all conventions of society and morality to pursue their often self-destructive passion for each other, self-destructive because their love is inextricably intermeshed with hate. In the opening scene of the film the heroine's parents are introduced, initiating the cycle of mad love which characterizes the rest of the film. Chavez (Herbert Marshall), a dignified aristocrat who in marrying an unfaithful Indian woman (Tilly Losch) has descended to the depths of border-town life, finds his wife with another man and murders them. The child of this stormy union, Pearl, is sent by her father, before his execution, to live with his ex-fiancée Laura Belle (Lillian Gish), now married to a cattle baron named McCanles (Lionel Barrymore). The marriage between this delicate woman and her greedy, cantankerous husband is a cold and unhappy one with none of the passion which we are led to believe marked Laura Belle's affair with Chavez. The only hint of what might have been a former tenderness in this marriage is revealed during Laura Belle's deathbed scene, when a distraught McCanles collapses in his wheelchair.

The center of the film and the peak of the cycle is Pearl (Jennifer Jones). *Duel in the Sun* is her story, the story of a battle between convention and savagery, respectability and lasciviousness, between a dignity inherited from her father and a sensuality passed on by her mother. As Chavez and his wife symbolize this contradiction in Pearl, so do the McCanles sons, Lewt (Gregory Peck) and Jesse (Joseph Cotton). Jesse is the quiet, genteel, conventional Abel while Lewt is the vicious, sensual, passionate Cain. For Pearl they represent the paths she may choose to follow, and in true schizophrenic fashion she chooses both. Jesse supplies her with stability and educates and protects her, but this is not enough; she needs the intensity of Lewt's passion as well. It is a passion caught up in violence. They make love against the backdrop of a storm after threatening each other with physical harm. While Jesse is associated with warm interiors, docile cattle, and benevolent, progressive builders of railroads, Lewt is tied to guns (he tries to kill his own brother, extending the Cain-Abel analogy even further), dynamite (he blows up a railroad train), stallions, and the barren outdoors. Pearl and Lewt's affair is of highly destructive proportions. Recognizing this, she retreats back into respectability periodically, first with Jesse, but when rejected by him, with an older man, Sam Pierce (Charles Bickford), whom Lewt challenges and kills, forcing Pearl back into his arms.

The final scene takes place in the mountains. Pearl now acts as defender of convention and propriety by stopping Lewt from harming the offspring of Jesse and the genteel Easterner who has taken Pearl's place. Her shoot-out with Lewt is the apotheosis of *amour fou*. In defending convention Pearl commits an act of outrageous savagery as the lovers fatally wound each other and then crawl across rock and sand to rest in each other's arms.

Duel in the Sun has been called a "horse opera" and is one of the few Westerns which deserves that epithet. It takes most of the conventions of the Western and expands them, weighs them down, and elaborates on them in a manner which combines elements of grand opera and Baroque art. A gun-fight in a saloon is composed like a Caravaggio painting with a single light cutting the darkness, two figures at opposite sides of the frame in focus, and a blast of gunfire. A dance and barbecue opens up with an incredibly complex tracking shot over the entire crowd. Characters are exaggerated as well. The down-and-out gambler Chavez becomes a tragic Shakespearean figure (especially as played by Marshall); a traveling minister (Walter Huston) becomes a hypocritical, lecherous Bible-thumper who has designs on Pearl. Emotions are also on a grand scale. Love, hate, revenge, and greed rock each character, creating trauma after trauma. Even the plot is overblown, with a simple battle between the railroad (protecting the homesteaders) and the cattle barons over territory (something that often occurred during the opening of the West) becoming, in typical Selznick fashion, an epic allegory of the small individual versus big business, progress versus the old order, and liberty versus authoritarianism. In short, the film is a highly dramatic rendering of American myths.

The eroticism of *Duel in the Sun* is created by a manipulation of the elements of setting, cinematography, acting, and costuming. Pearl is darkened through makeup to give her an earthy look. She wears scoop-necked, tight-fitting blouses which outline her breasts, Indian blankets which reveal soft shoulders, and full, loose skirts which expose shapely legs. Jones breathes a real passion into the role of Pearl, and it is ultimately her sensual savvy which brings the character to life.

The financial success of *Duel in the Sun* was not immediate; it took several re-releases for the film to realize a profit. The lesson Selznick learned from this experience was a bitter one. It taught him that the genre he had worked so hard to perfect—the dramatic epic—would have to be abandoned, at least on his part. A producer with tastes like his would have to learn to control his flamboyance or get out of the business. The day of the creative independent producer striving to mold films in his own grand style was virtually to disappear. Epics would be produced again, but never with a personal touch like Selznick's. After this disappointment, Selznick produced a few more pictures, but none with the scope of *Duel in the Sun* or *Gone with the Wind*. In 1958, after *A Farewell to Arms* (1957), he ceased production activities altogether, and he died in 1965.

James Ursini

DYNAMITE

Released: 1929
Production: Cecil B. De Mille for Metro-Goldwyn-Mayer
Direction: Cecil B. De Mille
Screenplay: Jeanie Macpherson, with additional dialogue by John Howard Lawson and Gladys Unger
Cinematography: Peverell Marley
Editing: Anne Bauchens
Running time: 129 minutes

Principal characters:
Cynthia Crothers .... Kay Johnson
Hagon Derk .... Charles Bickford
Roger Towne .... Conrad Nagel
Marcia Towne .... Julia Faye
Katie Derk .... Muriel McCormack
Marco, the "Sheik" .... Joel McCrea

The addition of dialogue and sound to a motion picture was a device that was certain to intrigue Cecil B. De Mille. He had come from the theater originally, where he had acted in and written plays, and subsequently turned to the silent picture medium, where as a director and producer he presented fifty-two features between 1914 and 1929, most of them big moneymakers for Paramount. During the silent era, he and D. W. Griffith were the only directors whose names were the principal box-office attraction of their films. De Mille could not wait to try dialogue in a feature. In that 1928-1929 season many filmmakers experimented with talking sequences, giving birth to the part-talkie, which was nothing more than a bastard form doomed to fade into oblivion.

After his big religious film, the story of Christ called *The King of Kings* (1927), De Mille wanted something modern and completely different. A wave of atheism was sweeping the country, and De Mille decided to try his luck with a story about those who defy God, called *The Godless Girl* (1929). By the time the picture was made and he had previewed it, he was disappointed. There was little shock value in the film; it had become nothing more than an old-fashioned pictorial sermon. The talking film was what was drawing in the dollars, and De Mille decided to jump on the bandwagon. He held up release on *The Godless Girl*, reshot the last two scenes in dialogue written by Beulah Marie Dix and Jeanie Macpherson, and added sound, which built up the fight scenes and added drama to the burning reformatory sequence. The picture was released as a part-talkie by Pathé, but by that time there were so many of those around that *The Godless Girl* scarcely made a ripple in the current.

De Mille and his wife took a trip abroad, where he reevaluated his career. He made a new releasing deal with M-G-M, and decided that his first full-length talking feature would be the kind of fashionable melodrama that had made him surefire at Paramount. The new picture would have an original story by Jeanie Macpherson, and while she would write some of the dialogue, most of it was designed by two up-to-date playwrights, John Howard Lawson and Gladys Unger. It would have its full quota of sex and sin, and it would be climaxed by the kind of smashing denouement that had made him famous. It would be a lavish society picture about life as it was never lived among the millionaires, and it would build to a wild, melodramatic finale in which the three principals are caught in a mine cave-in deep in the bowels of the earth. It would become the noisiest talkie to date, and, fittingly, it would be called *Dynamite*.

The gimmick that starts the plot was not new; in fact, it went back several centuries to a time in England when, if a bachelor were awaiting the executioner's axe, he might very well be visited by a heavily veiled lady with a priest in attendance. If the man who was to die would agree to marry the heavily veiled lady, those he left behind would be blessed with secret riches, while he would take on the heavy debts his lady had accrued, and his subsequent execution would automatically cancel those debts, freeing her from possibly going to debtor's prison. This device had been used to good effect in an early all-color (Prizma) feature by J. Stuart Blackton, *The Glorious Adventure*, in which Lady Diana Manners became the bride of a criminal (Victor McLaglen) just before the great London fire swept through the city.

De Mille's story tells about Cynthia Crothers (Kay Johnson), rich and very social, who is in love with Roger Towne (Conrad Nagel), a playboy who loves her but unfortunately has a wife, Marcia (Julia Faye) whose every hour is taken up with a handsome gigolo called Marco, the "Sheik" (Joel McCrea). By the terms of her grandfather's will, Cynthia must be married by a certain date or forfeit the extravagant fortune left in waiting for her. Cynthia, however, wants only to marry Roger, who is not available, although his wife Marcia hints that were Cynthia to give her enough money, she might consider a quick divorce from Roger, which would leave her able to afford Marco.

Meanwhile, in the jail of a nearby mining town, Hagon Derk (Charles Bickford) is incarcerated, having been found guilty of murder, although he maintains his innocence. Hagon will be executed at midnight of a certain day, unable to leave his young sister, Katie (Muriel McCormack), anything but tears and a grim future as ward of the court. An attorney makes the deal with Hagon, who consents to marry Cynthia Crothers, and she, in turn, being his widow, will see to it that his sister is well educated and provided for. Cynthia weds Hagon in his cell and returns to her mansion to await word that she is now a widow soon to inherit her grandfather's sizable fortune. On the very eve of Hagon's exection, however, the real murderer is apprehended and confesses to the crime. Hagon finds himself a free man and goes to see the wife he now claims.

Cynthia is appalled by the turn of events, and when Hagon comes to her, she is repelled by him. Likewise, Hagon is disgusted by her and her sybaritic way of life. He returns to the mining town and the job he had once held there. Meanwhile, Cynthia finds that in order to inherit her grandfather's fortune, she must be able to prove that she is lawfully Mrs. Hagon Derk living with her husband in his newly found freedom.

She returns to the mining town with Roger, and they go down inside the mine to seek out Hagon, hoping to finalize a new deal with him. Now comes the big scene, De Mille's long-awaited climax. As the three meet deep in the earth, the ground trembles with an explosion that shakes and wrecks the mine. The three—Cynthia, Hagon, and Roger—are trapped, and in the hours that intervene while their lives are at stake, Cynthia finds that Hagon is a husband worth having and he changes his mind about her being wanton. Roger realizes that only he can open a way of life for the two of them. With a stick of dynamite he clears the shaft so they can escape, although in so doing, he traps himself and is killed. Hagon then leads his wife back to the light and freedom.

Audiences were well aware that the plot was corny, even in 1929, but they relished it just the same. With *Dynamite* De Mille once more proved that he had the public firmly in hand. He knew what they wanted, and he gave it to them. The scenes of high life, with adultery, champagne, and sin, were something in which to revel, and the dramatic disaster in the mine climaxing the action was horrifying, strikingly realistic, and certainly boasted the loudest series of explosions yet recorded on film. *Dynamite* played in Los Angeles at the Carthay Circle Theater, and every night at the same hour for blocks around, residents in the Circle area knew that the cacophony shattering the peaceful quiet of their neighborhood was Mr. De Mille's nightly mineshattering finale.

As players in *Dynamite*, De Mille used in the principal roles three actors who had had vast stage experience and could handle their dialogue like professionals. He chose red-headed Charles Bickford, an actor from Broadway who had made ruffians his specialty, to play Hagon Derk. It was Bickford's first film for De Mille, his first indeed before any camera, and one of the few heroic romantic roles he ever got to play. Cynthia Crothers, the social butterfly who finds that there is more to life than a vast amount of money, is played by Kay Johnson. New to films, she had enjoyed a rich career on the stage as the heroine of such plays as *Beggar on Horseback* (1924), *Crime* (1927), and *A Free Soul* (1928). She was also the wife of the noted director/actor, John Cromwell. Conrad Nagel as Roger Towne was a popular hero in De Mille's silent films who, before he entered pictures, had enjoyed a genuinely successful career onstage as a William A. Brady star. Julia Faye, whose name appears in almost every De Mille cast since 1918, played her first speaking role for De Mille as Marcia Towne. There is also a very distinguished debut in the film: playing Marco, the "Sheik," is Joel McCrea, who was to become a film star for decades and would play the hero for De Mille years later in *Union Pacific* (1939).

Dynamite broke the ice in talking pictures for De Mille and made a great deal of money at the box office. His two subsequent features at M-G-M were hardly of the same caliber. He then signed again at the newly reorganized Paramount Studios, and beginning in 1932 with *The Sign of the Cross* made a long series of extravagant specials that did nothing but make money; there were fifteen extraordinary extravaganzas, ending in 1956 with his extravagant production of *The Ten Commandments*.

DeWitt Bodeen

EAST OF EDEN

Released: 1955
Production: Elia Kazan for Warner Bros.
Direction: Elia Kazan
Screenplay: Paul Osborn; based on the novel of the same name by John Steinbeck
Cinematography: Ted McCord
Editing: Owen Marks
Running time: 115 minutes

> *Principal characters:*
> Cal Trask .... James Dean
> Abra .... Julie Harris
> Adam Trask .... Raymond Massey
> Aron Trask .... Richard Davalos
> Kate .... Jo Van Fleet (AA)

The film *East of Eden* is a period piece, an attempt to reconstruct faithfully Monterey and Salinas, California, in 1917. The title and basic story are both taken from the 1952 novel by John Steinbeck, an American author who was born in Salinas in 1902 and who devoted much of his writing to stories set in this same locale. Popular at the time of the film's casting, the novel proved a superb vehicle to begin the all too brief, dazzling career of James Dean, whose performance dominates the film and provides a large degree of its power and critical interest.

While the film's director, Elia Kazan, remains an accomplished *auteur*, Dean's three extant films—*East of Eden*, *Rebel Without a Cause* (1955), and the less successful *Giant* (1956)—all under different directors, are united more by the young star's acting style and skill than by any *auteur* considerations. His accidental death on September 30, 1955 (at age twenty-four, while driving his Porsche sportscar to the Salinas road races), began a posthumous, cultlike recognition, perhaps matched only by the death of Valentino in 1926. To this day, his moody, introspective, sometimes mumbled, often method performances capture audience interest; and he is as well known in Tokyo or London as he is in Indiana, where he grew up. His acting style has been judged imitative, especially in comparison to early Marlon Brando performances. Still, his unique charisma makes otherwise modest films such as *East of Eden* and *Rebel Without a Cause* very special artifacts.

Steinbeck's novel was in part intended to modernize the Biblical myth of Cain and Abel. Spanning two generations, it concentrates on the figures of Adam Trask (the favorite son) and his Cainlike brother Charles. Further, Adam's twin sons, the adored Aron and the misunderstood Caleb, are parallel Abel-Cain figures. Steinbeck's vision of Caleb as more misunderstood than malevolent, more neurotic than evil, seems today an uncanny match for the very *persona* Dean was developing in early television and theatrical performances. And while Dean's national and international fame came primarily from the later *Rebel Without a Cause*, released close to the time of his death, his dominance as Cal Trask in *East of Eden* was assurance of stardom.

Appropriately, the screenplay focuses more on the second generation, especially on the character of Cal and on his clumsy search both to give and to receive love. The film, in fact, begins with a love triangle. The respected and conservative Aron (Richard Davalos) is close to marriage with the girl Abra (Julie Harris); the rejected and moody Cal is puzzled by his (to his own mind evil) attraction to the same girl. Throughout the film, the mutual love between Cal and Abra progresses at extraordinary expense to Cal's brother and father (Raymond Massey). But, ironically, that same growing love provides index to Cal's psychological metamorphosis. The hurt, halting incompetence of Cal's early emotions are replaced by rich, mature relationships at the film's end.

Such progress is not without cost. Beyond Cal's reluctant courting of Abra are two actions, one springing from kindness, the other from hate, that together result in much evil for Cal's family. First, Cal's father is an idealistic man who exhausts his small funds in an attempt to develop a method for shipping ice-packed produce. Although he cares for his son, he neither understands him nor expresses his love for him. In the hope of gaining that love, Cal secretly borrows five thousand dollars to take advantage of a coming wartime market for beans. When the profits from this successful venture are presented to the father, the money is rejected; the ensuing heated dialogue causes the father to become paralyzed by an apparent stroke. Second, Aron naïvely believes his mother is dead, while in fact she is Kate (Jo Van Fleet), the madam of a nearby brothel. Cal, in contrast, knows this (in fact, he borrows his capital from her). Feeling guilty as a result of his father's stroke, Cal brings Aron to the brothel, destroying his brother's illusions and, apparently, his sanity as well.

The slender credibility of these strange situations is mitigated only by Dean's credible performance. His shy, sly, and very brave meeting with his mother to borrow a then vast sum is successful in part because we are made to believe the genetic bond of similar personalities; but more important is Dean's amalgam of boyish charm and an uncanny understanding of the world's ways. And Dean's *persona* always seems barely to contain, barely to hide a capability for anger and violence that allows the terrible argument with his father or the devilish vengeance that has him bring together harlot mother with angelic son. The film's rather abrupt ending makes the eventual reconciliations and Cal's transformed characterization ring untrue.

Beyond Dean's legendary acting, as well as good supporting performances by Julie Harris, Raymond Massey, and Jo Van Fleet, the film is also interesting from two separate perspectives. First, a classic concern for film theory and criticism has been the comparison between novels and their cinematic translations. A number of Steinbeck's works (for example, *Grapes of Wrath*, 1940) have enjoyed such translation, and *East of Eden* is an interesting example. Second, the film remains true to Steinbeck's fine attention to local color, offering enough historical accuracy to provide a fictionalized yet valuable insight into an America of decades past.

Perhaps future generations will come to view Dean's acting in a comparable manner: of historical interest, as an example of a fashion that differs from contemporary taste. For the present, however, his art has survived a quarter century of cinematic change and evolution, continuing to please diverse, ever more sophisticated audiences.

Edward S. Small

EASTER PARADE

Released: 1948
Production: Arthur Freed for Metro-Goldwyn-Mayer
Direction: Charles Walters
Screenplay: Sidney Sheldon, Frances Goodrich, and Albert Hackett; based
   on a screen story by Frances Goodrich and Albert Hackett
Cinematography: Harry Stradling
Editing: Albert Akst
Music: Johnny Green and Roger Edens (AA)
Song: Irving Berlin
Running time: 103 minutes

> *Principal characters:*
> Hannah Brown .... Judy Garland
> Don Hewes .... Fred Astaire
> Nadine Hale .... Ann Miller
> Jonathan Harrow III (Johnny) .... Peter Lawford

If *Easter Parade* were not one of the brightest and most enjoyable musicals of the 1940's, it would still be memorable as the only film in which Judy Garland and Fred Astaire performed together. However, in addition to the happy pairing of two of the screen's finest entertainers, the film offers the music of Irving Berlin and the contributions of the talented members of M-G-M's top musical production unit. The result is a film of great style, energy, and humor which offers a wide variety of musical numbers and performing styles.

The plot of *Easter Parade* consists essentially of a backstage romance set in the days of vaudeville. Don Hewes (Fred Astaire) learns that his dancing partner, Nadine Hale (Ann Miller), intends to leave their act to star in a Broadway musical. He attempts to change her mind by singing the romantic ballad "It Only Happens When I Dance with You," but Nadine is adamant. Don leaves angrily and has dinner with his friend Jonathan Harrow III (Peter Lawford) at a small cafe where a floorshow is in progress. Hurt by Nadine's rejection, Don tells Johnny he could take any girl out of the show's chorus line and make her as successful as Nadine. The girl he chooses is Hannah Brown (Judy Garland), who at first takes Don's offer of a job as his dancing partner as a joke. Upon learning who he is, however, Hannah quits her job and reports to Don's rehearsal hall the next morning.

Don soon realizes that Hannah is ill-equipped to fill Nadine's shoes, but he persists in his attempts to pattern her style and personality after his former partner's. The resulting act is a fiasco. Stung by his failure and by Nadine's accusation that Hannah is only an unsuccessful copy of her, Don at last understands the mistake he has made. He changes their act to suit Hannah's talents and the two become a great success. By this time, however, romantic complications have arisen: Johnny has fallen in love with Hannah, and Hannah with Don. Don continues to regard her as no more than a dancing partner, however, and she interprets his rivalry with Nadine as love.

Don turns down an offer from the Ziegfeld Follies when he learns that Nadine is the show's star, but he and Hannah are soon offered a show of their own. Hannah finally confronts Don with her feelings for him. They kiss and Don realizes that he has been in love with Hannah all along. Their show opens and is a tremendous hit. Don performs a snappy, stylish dance solo, "Steppin' Out with My Baby," while Hannah watches with delight from the wings. The two then join forces, dressed in tramp costumes, for "A Couple of Swells," and the audience cheers its approval. Now that their personal and professional lives are in harmony, it seems that nothing can stand in their way.

Nothing, that is, except Nadine. To celebrate their opening, Don takes Hannah to see Nadine's show, and the applause which greets their entrance angers Nadine. She invites Don onstage to dance with her, and Hannah leaves in tears, convinced that he still loves Nadine. She returns to the café where they first met and tells her troubles to the bartender in the song "Better Luck Next Time." The next morning, Easter Sunday, Johnny, who realizes his own love for Hannah is hopeless, persuades her that she must go after Don if she loves him. So Hannah arrives at Don's apartment with flowers, candy, and an "Easter Bonnet" for him—a top hat with a rabbit inside. She sings "Easter Parade" to him and he presents her with an Easter Bonnet of her own. The two link arms and, with Don now singing to Hannah, they join the splendid Easter Parade on Fifth Avenue.

The central attraction in *Easter Parade* is certainly the performances of its two stars. The pairing of Astaire and Garland was the result of a fortunate accident rather than the foresight of studio executives. The film had originally been planned as a vehicle for Judy Garland and Gene Kelly, but Kelly broke an ankle during rehearsals and Astaire came out of a brief period of retirement to take his place. He and Garland had both appeared in *Ziegfeld Follies of 1946* (the same film in which Astaire and Kelly did their memorable "Babbitt and the Bromide" dance together), but they had not performed in any of the same scenes. With her lively manner and nervous intensity, Garland had always seemed a more natural match for Kelly, while Astaire's partners had generally been cool, graceful, and somewhat restrained.

In *Easter Parade*, however, the differences in their styles are perfectly suited to the conflict between Don and Hannah. Don's efforts to transform the warm, down-to-earth Hannah into an aloof, ethereal dancing partner meet with dismal failure. It is only when he recognizes Hannah's (and Garland's) natural humor and vibrancy that the act begins to work. The merging of Astaire's elegance and Garland's buoyancy results in the film's best-remembered number, the classic "We're a Couple of Swells." Dressed in tattered tramp costumes, the two indulge in a high-spirited romp while singing a comical, mocking song about the life of the very rich. This humorous spoof of refinement and social graces presents a perfect blending of the equally remarkable, though widely different, talents of these two legendary performers.

Easter Parade is one of the most truly "musical" of all musical films. From its opening song "Happy Easter" to the final choruses of "Easter Parade," the film is filled with songs and dances which serve to illustrate and enhance both its story line and the emotions of its characters. Songs such as "Drum Crazy" and "Steppin' Out with My Baby" provide Astaire with opportunities to display his graceful, innovative dance techniques, while "Better Luck Next Time" presents a showcase for Garland's touching, emotional vocal style. Ann Miller is also given a spectacular solo, the rousing "Shakin' the Blues Away," and even Peter Lawford has a chance to display his musical abilities in a duet with Garland, "A Fella with an Umbrella." Many of the songs in the film were written by Berlin during the period in which the story is set, lending a very genuine feeling to the film's atmosphere.

Easter Parade is a product of the musical unit at M-G-M which was headed by producer Arthur Freed. The Freed unit was composed of a number of the top Hollywood musical talents of the 1940's and 1950's and was responsible for such films as *Meet Me in St. Louis* (1944), *An American in Paris* (1951), and *The Band Wagon* (1953). *Easter Parade*'s credits include Cedric Gibbons as art director, Johnny Green as musical director, and Roger Edens as associate producer. The film had originally been planned for Vincente Minnelli, the unit's principal director, but marital problems between Minnelli and Judy Garland resulted in the film's reassignment to Charles Walters. Although Walters' direction lacks the precision and delicacy of touch which Minnelli might have brought to the film, his presence lends it an exuberance which makes *Easter Parade* an enduring favorite among Hollywood musicals.

Janet E. Lorenz

EASY LIVING

Released: 1937
Production: Arthur Hornblow, Jr., for Paramount
Direction: Mitchell Leisen
Screenplay: Preston Sturges; based on the novel of the same name by Vera
  Caspary
Cinematography: Ted Tetzlaff
Editing: Doane Harrison
Running time: 87 minutes

> *Principal characters:*
> Mary Smith .... Jean Arthur
> J. B. Ball .... Edward Arnold
> John Ball, Jr. .... Ray Milland
> Mrs. J. B. Ball .... Mary Nash
> Mr. Louis Louis .... Luis Alberni
> Van Buren .... Franklin Pangborn

During the 1930's, the "screwball" comedy thrived in Hollywood to an
almost manic degree. In a sense, this era of the slapstick comedy was only
natural, for it came during the Depression, and by the end of the decade one
did not have to be a sage to know that another world war was just over the
horizon. The only antidote for the troubled times was laughter, and as the
threat of disaster deepened, the comedies turned more hysterical. Most
depression comedies were about the very rich, for it is easier to laugh when
one knows that even those with money do not have it easy. *Easy Living* was
made by a group of experts: novelist Vera Caspary was an expert in the light
romantic story; nobody wrote funnier screenplays than Preston Sturges; and
there was no director who was so much a master of the elegant soufflé as
Mitchell Leisen. With a cast headed by one of the outstanding comediennes
in show business, Jean Arthur, *Easy Living* is constructed with one laugh
topping the other, the most pleasant hour and twenty-seven minutes then to
be seen.

It all begins with J. B. Ball (Edward Arnold), a steel magnate, living in a
handsome penthouse on Fifth Avenue, New York. He starts his day quarreling
with his extravagant wife (Mary Nash), who has just bought a very expensive
fur coat. In a fit of rage, he seizes the coat, marches onto the terrace, and
throws the coat out over Fifth Avenue. It plummets downward, landing on
the head of a working girl named Mary Smith (Jean Arthur), who is riding
to work atop a double-decker bus. She gets off the bus and tries to return the
coat, but J. B. Ball not only insists on her keeping it, but also takes her to
a milliner's shop, where he buys her a fur hat to match. Then, because she
is already late for work, he insists that he drive her in his cab to her office.

Complications immediately snarl the normal life of Mary Smith. She is not only late for work, but she is also boldly wearing a coat and hat she could never afford on her salary as a stenographer for a magazine called *Boy's Constant Companion*. She is fired from her job.

Meanwhile, because she has been seen in the company of J. B. Ball, and he has been billed for the coat and hat, word gets around that he is keeping a mistress named Mary Smith. She, in fact, is counting her change, wondering how she is going to afford lunch. The manager of the Louis Hotel, Mr. Louis Louis (Luis Alberni), thinks it would be very good for business if she were a resident there. Almost before she realizes it, Mary is living in the fanciest suite in the Louis, with unlimited credit and a limousine at her disposal. She finds that she can have anything her heart desires. The one thing she wants most at that moment is a good hot cup of coffee, so she goes to a nearby Automat for it.

At the Automat she meets Johnny Ball (Ray Milland), J. B.'s independent son, who has had an argument with his father and is working behind the counter at the Automat. One of the most hilarious sequences ever staged in a comedy feature follows. Accidentally, the little windows over the commodities offered for sale go out of commission, one row after another flipping open, shooting plates of food out among the startled customers. Word gets onto the street, and in a moment the Automat is jammed with hungry customers snatching at the free food being spewed forth. Through it all, Mary Smith sits calmly by herself at an end table, delicately eating her chicken pie as she sips her coffee. She naturally gets together with Johnny Ball.

Buyers of stock, believing Mary to be the mistress of J. B. and therefore privy to inside information, query her as to the actual state of the market. Knowing nothing, she gives facetious answers with a straight face and finds herself first causing a panic of buying and then one of selling. She also gets involved with the so-called common man and makes friends with a select handful, portrayed by such experts of comedy as Alberni, Franklin Pangborn, William Demarest, Barlowe Borland, and Andrew Tombes. Mary Smith is a nice, sensible girl who is no fool, accepting everything she is offered; and, like many another nice, sensible girl, she ends up marrying the millionaire's son. Both the millionaire and his eccentric wife are proud to have her as their daughter-in-law. She has brains, and there is a deficiency of that commodity among the Balls.

Easy Living was quickly recognized as one of the freshest comedies on the market, and although some critics dissented, taking a dim view of its wacky goings-on, the public loved it, and everybody had a good time. Paramount did well with a series of zany comedies during that decade. They not only had Leisen and Sturges under contract, but they also had commitments with the best of the stylish comediennes of the era, such as Arthur, Carole Lombard, Claudette Colbert, and Barbara Stanwyck. Paramount also had such leading men as Milland, Fred MacMurray, and Henry Fonda, to say nothing of "gentlemen" comic stars such as Bing Crosby, Bob Hope, and W. C. Fields. A Paramount motion picture might be not only the best show in town, but it might also be the funniest.

Arthur was one of the brightest of all screen comediennes; she remains a favorite in the public memory because she looks and talks as ordinary people do. Actually, she is an unusually pretty girl who can be glamourous if the part requires it. She also possesses one of the most individual voices in the business—low-pitched, husky, with a charming little crack or break in it. She received her first contract at Paramount during the silent era, but, unable to crash through to more important roles, she went to New York and became a hit in a few plays. She then returned to Hollywood, where her services were divided mostly on a commitment basis between Paramount and Columbia. She is the best example of the old adage that if an actress can play comedy, she can play anything. Arthur not only shone in farces such as *Easy Living*, stylish black humor comedies such as *A Foreign Affair* (1948), Frank Capra comedies such as *Mr. Deeds Goes to Town* (1936), *You Can't Take It with You* (1938), and *Mr. Smith Goes to Washington* (1939), and George Stevens comedies such as *The More the Merrier* (1943) and *The Talk of the Town* (1942), but she also proved to be an effective dramatic actress in *Diamond Jim* (1935) and *History Is Made at Night* (1937). She also handled Western roles capably in a variety of films, such as *Arizona* (1941) and *Shane* (1953). She was excellent as Calamity Jane, with Gary Cooper in Cecil B. De Mille's *The Plainsman* (1936). She has always been one of the most versatile actresses on stage or screen, and it is regrettable that since *Shane*, she has chosen to stay away from the screen, preferring to lecture in the Drama Department of Vassar and at Stephens College. Like Barbara Stanwyck and Irene Dunne, however, she has never really officially retired, so there is always the possibility that if the right property and the right director came along, she might take another turn before the cameras. Her timing has always been the best; she is a film editor's delight. *Easy Living*, is a perfect example of how effortless and how varied her style of playing can be.

Leisen, who directed *Easy Living* and many other smart comedies for Paramount, was trained as an architect and went originally into interior design and costuming in his early Hollywood career. From 1919 to 1933 he worked as a costumer for De Mille and Douglas Fairbanks; when De Mille set up his own company, Leisen went with him as an art director. Back at Paramount in 1933, he worked briefly as an assistant director, and in that year directed his first feature film, *Cradle Songs*, a delicate drama of nuns in a convent who rear a baby orphan to womanhood. Neither it nor *Death Takes a Holiday*, a fantasy he directed in 1934, gave any indication that he could direct a series of bright farces, culminating in *Easy Living*.

Sturges, during his youth, flitted around Europe, his mother being a close

friend and confidante of dancer Isadora Duncan. He was always a nonconformist who secretly wanted to be a successful stockbroker. He first wrote a
most engaging Broadway comedy, *Strictly Dishonorable*, and then, because
he had a way with words, he had no trouble getting work as a screenplay
writer in Hollywood, where he worked behind a typewriter from 1930 to 1938.
Paramount gave him his first chance to direct the scripts he wrote, and a
brilliant series of extraordinary comedies followed from 1940 through 1944,
giving sparkle to the war years. He then left Paramount, but his subsequent
work showed little evidence of the fresh comic touch that had blessed his
Paramount films. In *Easy Living* he was at his zany best. He had in Leisen
a director who understood him and knew exactly how to interpret his script;
and in Arthur he had a real artist, a woman who could play comedy or drama
with equal ease. *Easy Living* represents the only time the three of them
worked together. That is unfortunate, because they were a trio of professionals
who seemed to bring out the best in one another.

DeWitt Bodeen

EASY RIDER

Released: 1969
Production: Peter Fonda for Columbia
Direction: Dennis Hopper
Screenplay: Peter Fonda, Dennis Hopper, and Terry Southern
Cinematography: Laszlo Kovacs
Editing: Donn Cambern
Running time: 94 minutes

> *Principal characters:*
> Wyatt (Captain America) .... Peter Fonda
> Billy .... Dennis Hopper
> George Hanson .... Jack Nicholson

Easy Rider was, in 1969, both a propaganda film and a phenomenon of popular culture. It was the first time that what had come to be called the "counterculture" was featured in a major motion picture, and the men who made the film were well aware of the fact. The viewpoint of *Easy Rider* is not, however, wholehearted endorsement of its two counterculture "heroes," as too many people supposed; its outlook is more subtle than that and makes the film more than a period piece.

Easy Rider is basically the creation of two men: Peter Fonda and Dennis Hopper. Together with Terry Southern, they wrote the screenplay; Fonda produced the film, Hopper directed it, and both played leading roles. The story is essentially that of a journey. Two men, Billy (Dennis Hopper) and Wyatt (Peter Fonda), who is also called Captain America, smuggle cocaine from Mexico to California. Then, with the huge amount of money they have made, they head east on their motorcycles, bound for New Orleans and the Mardi Gras.

On their journey they encounter a variety of people. At a small ranch where they stop to fix one of their motorcycles, they stay to eat a meal, and Wyatt proclaims that the rancher should be proud because "You do your own thing in your own time." At a commune they find some of the members bickering and others sowing seed on unplowed, sandy ground, but Wyatt says, as if pronouncing a benediction, "They're gonna make it." In a small town where they join a parade on their motorcycles and are jailed for parading without a permit, their scruffy appearance does not endear them to the police—Billy has especially long hair and a moustache.

Also in jail is George Hanson (Jack Nicholson), a liberal young lawyer whose alcoholic binges frequently land him there. Dissatisfied with his restricted life, George decides to go to New Orleans with Wyatt and Billy. The next day when the three go into a cafe, all the customers make ill-natured comments and the waitress refuses to wait on them. That night around a campfire (hotels and motels will not take them), George tells Wyatt and Billy that people are certain to resent anyone who is free. After they all go to sleep, they are attacked by some of the men from the cafe, and George is killed.

Wyatt and Billy next go on to New Orleans, where they pick up two prostitutes in a brothel and wander through the Mardi Gras celebration. Then, in a cemetery, all four take a hallucinogenic drug. We see their drug experience, represented in a long, purposely chaotic sequence of brief and often distorted glimpses of the characters and the cemetery. After they leave New Orleans and continue east, Wyatt says to Billy, "We blew it." Billy does not understand, and Wyatt does not explain. The next day on the highway, two men in a pickup truck pull alongside Billy and point a shotgun at him; when he replies with an obscene gesture, they shoot him. Wyatt goes for help, but the men shoot him also, and the last thing we see is his burning motocycle beside the road.

Not only in its story but also in its style, *Easy Rider* broke with many Hollywood conventions. Little time is spent giving the background of the characters or explanations of their actions. In addition, two devices are used alternately to speed up and slow down the pace of the film. Rather than using a dissolve between scenes (having one scene slowly disappear as the next slowly appears), the makers of *Easy Rider* show a few quick glimpses of the next scene just before the previous scene ends. For example, a night scene will be interrupted by a few momentary views of daylight shortly before a morning scene begins. In an extension of this device, there is one flashforward in the film. While they are in the brothel in New Orleans, Wyatt is looking at the pictures on the wall, and he suddenly sees, for only a moment, an image of his motorcycle burning beside the road. At that time neither he nor the audience knows what it means. The flash shots quicken the pace of the film, but at other times the pace is deliberately relaxed by sequences of the men riding their motorcycles to a background of rock music. Besides varying the pace, these interludes serve to break up the story into stanzas and to emphasize the continuity of the journey. In addition, the fact that the words of the songs frequently reinforce or comment on the action can be suggested by some of their titles: "The Pusher," "Born To Be Wild," and "It's Alright Ma (I'm Only Bleeding)."

Easy Rider is too often seen as a blatant attack on middle-class mores, but its depiction of values is neither so simple nor so onesided as that. The generation gap and the counterculture are perhaps overemphasized and over-discussed, but the fact remains that, especially in 1969, the hair, clothes, and motorcycles of the protagonists were certain to provoke a strong reaction in any viewer. The feelings expressed in the cafe scene were the feelings of many in the audience; many others uncritically admired Wyatt and Billy. The film itself tries to change the uncritical reaction of both groups. It tries, usually successfully, to make a viewer who at first automatically rejects Wyatt and Billy feel sympathy for them ninety minutes later, enough to be moved by their deaths and by the film as a whole. The film also tries, although less successfully, to make the uncritical admirer of the two "heroes" see that behind their rebellion is little but emptiness and greed.

After smuggling the cocaine, for example, the two men begin their journey with a flourish of freedom—Wyatt throws away his wristwatch—but on the sound track is "The Pusher," a song that is strongly and quite overtly against the pushers of such drugs. They stop at a gas station and take gas without paying, even though they have thousands of dollars. The last shot of the station shows a poor child looking out the window. At the commune, Billy and Wyatt find a group of people who are barely surviving, yet they give them nothing more than a short ride on their motorcycles. Finally, in a moment of introspection, Wyatt recognizes that they "blew it." Though the statement seems out of character and Billy does not understand it, we can see that they certainly did blow it, both by choosing to sell hard drugs and by what they did with their lives and money afterwards. Indeed, in this way *Easy Rider* is like a gangster film, in which the audience is expected to feel some sympathy or identification with the gangster without admiring him.

Easy Rider is a film of contrasts. The interludes of motorcycling to rock songs contrast with the episodes between; the way of life of Wyatt and Billy contrasts with that of all the people they meet; and the low-key and rather flat characterizations of Wyatt and Billy sets off the fully realized characterization of George Hanson. As a counterbalance to the emptiness of Peter Fonda's Wyatt and the vague restlessness and paranoia of Dennis Hopper's Billy, Jack Nicholson's portrayal of George is crucial to the film, and Nicholson more than meets the challenge. First seen in a jail cell as he awakens from an alcoholic binge, he immediately animates the screen. He then proceeds to create a memorable and moving portrayal of the young lawyer, the son of a powerful man, who finds himself stuck in a small town until the chance encounter with Wyatt and Billy pushes him into trying to escape. Whether explaining freedom or expounding on UFO's, he is articulate and engrossing.

The other actors are not so exceptional. Fonda and Hopper satisfactorily fill the emotionally limited roles they wrote for themselves, but some of the people in the cafe and jail scenes were chosen because they were "real" people rather than actors and looked "right." Unfortunately, they sound more like bad actors than like real people.

Though much of *Easy Rider*'s immense popularity when it was first released was due to its contemporary subject matter and music, it is much more than a topical film. It remains remarkable for its artful stanzaic structure, for the performance of Jack Nicholson, and for its theme of the use and abuse of freedom.

Timothy W. Johnson

EDGE OF THE CITY

Released: 1957
Production: David Susskind for Metro-Goldwyn-Mayer
Direction: Martin Ritt
Screenplay: Robert Alan Aurthur; based on his television play *A Man Is Ten Feet Tall*
Cinematography: Joseph Brun
Editing: Sidney Meyers
Running time: 86 minutes

Principal characters:
Axel North	John Cassavetes
Tommy Tyler	Sidney Poitier
Charles Malik	Jack Warden
Ellen Wilson	Kathleen Maguire
Lucy Tyler	Ruby Dee
Mr. Nordmann	Robert Simon
Mrs. Nordmann	Ruth White

Sidney Poitier was the dominant black actor of the 1950's, the first of his race consistently to win starring roles in films. While Poitier was no carbon copy of Clarence Muse or Stepin' Fetchit, however, his films still show him as a black in a white society who willingly sacrifices his cultural heritage and blackness to be accepted by whites and on white terms. To gain this approval, he had to be no less than perfect. The cinematic Poitier was intelligent, refined, and sexually neutral; he remained calm when harassed; any complaining came from reason rather than rage. His characterizations fostered a new stereotype, and he became the "Good Negro" to white audiences. To black audiences, who were still attempting to meet white middle-class standards, the neat, deghettoized actor was an acceptable if unreal role model. *Edge of the City*, one of his best films of the decade, offers a representative Poitier characterization.

Edge of the City was adapted from *A Man Is Ten Feet Tall*, a drama written by Robert Alan Aurthur which had previously been produced for television. Poitier also had starred in that version, and won a Sylvania Award as best television actor during the 1955-1956 season. The plot, a sort of integrated *On the Waterfront* (1954), centers on two men: Tommy Tyler (Sidney Poitier), a noble, happy-go-lucky railway yard worker on New York City's West Side; and Axel North (John Cassavetes), a rebellious, bewildered army deserter who is befriended by Tyler. Tyler secures a job for North alongside him and soon invites him home to meet his family. He becomes North's mentor, protector, and friend. Charlie Malik (Jack Warden), a bullying boss, persistently insults both men because North always prefers working with the black man.

When North refuses to fight Malik, Tyler must take his place. Although he is winning, Tyler begs his adversary to stop. As he turns his back, Malik stabs him with a baling hook, and the Christ-like Tyler dies in North's arms. Predictably the white man avenges his black friend's death, and by this heroic act, he finds himself acknowledging his responsibility as a human being.

The relationship between Poitier's Tyler and Cassavetes' North in *Edge of the City* is intriguing. Despite the liberation of Poitier from shuffling feet, a pullman porter profession, and a "dees/dems/does" dialect, Cassavetes' character remains the master to Poitier's servant. Tyler, good, clean, and perfect, is still an idealized black as envisioned by his white "brother." The footloose North rebelliously confronts and rejects the hypocrisy he perceives in white society. He is more at home with the outcast Tyler, on the outside simply because of the color of his skin, than with those of his own race. Tyler is sympathetic to North and serves as ego support for his rebellion, but he never dares to compete with the white man for attention. Eventually, he dies out of loyalty to his friend, and the white man must avenge his demise. Tyler is merely an instrument in the catharsis of North from rootlessness to responsibility.

Despite these shortcomings, Tommy Tyler is one of Poitier's finest, most humanistic roles of the decade. Although he remains subservient to North, it is Tyler, the black man, who extends his hand to lift the white man out of his troubles. He is a three-dimensional character, strong, sensitive, and humane, a man of conscience. He is no caricatured black, but a symbol of brotherly love.

Edge of the City is also noteworthy as the directorial debut of Martin Ritt. Ritt is an *auteur* of social consciousness. From *Edge of the City* through *Paris Blues* (1961), in which jazz musicians Poitier and Paul Newman romance tourists Diahann Carroll and Joanne Woodward on the Left Bank; *Conrack* (1974), which tells the story of white educator Jon Voight who teaches at a rural black school; and more recently, *Norma Rae* (1979), about a Southern cotton mill worker, Sally Field, and a New York Jewish labor organizer, Ron Leibman, who unionize a factory, Ritt's characters clasp hands in friendship and trust despite their ethnic or cultural differences. His themes and denouements may be seen by some as overly idealized, but they are certainly not without merit.

Edge of the City is a well-acted film; two decades after its release, the performances remain fresh and poignant. Of particular note in the cast is Ruby Dee, who renders a fine supporting performance as Poitier's loyal wife, Lucy. She is especially moving when she breaks down after learning from North of her husband's death, telling him to get away from her with his "white money" when he offers to help her. Poitier and Dee appeared together as husband and wife in no less than five features: *No Way Out* (1950), *Go, Man, Go* (1954), *Virgin Island* (1959), and *A Raisin in the Sun* (1961), as well as

Edge of the City. The film was favorably reviewed by the critics; consistently cited were the scenes between Tyler and North as their friendship flourishes.

Edge of the City (along with *The Defiant Ones*, 1958, in which Tony Curtis costars as an escaped convict shackled to fellow prisoner Poitier, who sacrifices his freedom to come to the rescue of his newly found white "brother," and for which Poitier earned his first Oscar nomination) helped to affirm the actor's status as a talented performer and Hollywood star. During the next decade, he reached his zenith, winning an Academy Award in 1963 for *Lilies of the Field*. In 1967 he starred in no less than three blockbusters: he was the Nobel Prize candidate/fiancé of white Katharine Houghton in Stanley Kramer's *Guess Who's Coming to Dinner*; a schoolteacher who tames a brood of rebellious British teenagers in the entertaining *To Sir with Love* and a police officer from the North who solves a murder case and wins the respect of a bigoted Southern sheriff played by Rod Steiger in the Academy Award-winning *In the Heat of the Night*.

Black films of the following decade were made expressly for black audiences. Such motion pictures as *Super Fly* (1972), *Black Caesar* (1973), *The Spook Who Sat by the Door* (1973), and *Mandingo* (1975) are violence-oriented, reverse racist diatribes in which all blacks are "supercool" studs hustling to survive in a white world of oppression. Far more positive are films such as *Shaft* (1971), *Sounder* (1972), *Cooley High* (1975), and *A Hero Ain't Nothin' But a Sandwich* (1978). These features either attempt to deal with the black experience and the problems of black survival in a serious, humanistic manner or depict blacks as real, identifiable heroes/heroines in nonmessage stories meant to be pure entertainment.

The Poitier screen *persona* may be as unreal as it is outdated, but he nevertheless filled a role that was necessary in the break from the traditional, shuffling stereotyped Uncle Tom. His early portrayals marked a major step toward insightful characterizations and away from the blatant racism which dates back to *The Birth of a Nation*, (1915), and his later roles have shown him to be one of the major acting talents of the 1960's and 1970's.

Rob Edelman

THE EGG AND I

Released: 1947
Production: Chester Erskine and Fred F. Finklehoffe for Universal-International
Direction: Chester Erskine
Screenplay: Chester Erskine and Fred F. Finklehoffe; based on the novel of the same name by Betty MacDonald
Cinematography: Milton Krasner
Editing. Russell Schoengarth
Running time: 108 minutes

Principal characters:

Betty	Claudette Colbert
Bob	Fred MacMurray
Ma Kettle	Marjorie Main
Harriett Putnam	Louise Allbritton
Pa Kettle	Percy Kilbride
Tom Kettle	Richard Long
Birdie Hicks	Esther Dale

Betty MacDonald's humorous memoir of life with her first husband, Robert Heskett, on an egg ranch in the Pacific Northwest in the late 1920's was serialized in *Atlantic Monthly* in 1945. When *The Egg and I* came out as a book later that year, the publisher, J. P. Lippincott, ordered five printings totalling sixty-one thousand copies within the first ten days. A year later, sales had passed the one million mark; the book seemed permanently installed at the top of every best-seller list; and MacDonald and her second husband, Donald, had received that ultimate accolade of mid-twentieth century celebrity, a "visit" from *Life* magazine, which was duly recorded in the issue of March 18, 1946.

A movie sale for *The Egg and I* was inevitable. What may have surprised some people, however, was that the book was sold, not to Warner Bros., M-G-M, or one of the other "major" studios, but to Universal-International, the newly formed amalgamation of Universal Pictures, one of the oldest studios in Hollywood, and William Goetz's International Pictures, an independent production company that had been responsible for such highly regarded films of the preceding few years as *The Woman in the Window* (1944) and *Scarlet Street* (1945), both directed by Fritz Lang, *The Dark Mirror* (1946), directed by Robert Siodmak, and *The Stranger* (1946), directed by Orson Welles. Under its founder, Carl Laemmle, and his brilliant young assistant, Irving Thalberg, Universal had once been an industry leader, with stars such as Eric von Stroheim and Lon Chaney under contract, and such films as *Foolish Wives* (1922), *The Hunchback of Notre Dame* (1923), *The Phantom of the Opera* (1925), and *All Quiet on the Western Front* (1930) to its credit. By the 1940's, however, after many reorganizations and years of mismanagement by Laemmle's son, Carl, Jr., the studio was known chiefly for Bud Abbott and Lou Costello comedies, the Basil Rathbone-Nigel Bruce Sherlock Holmes mysteries, desert spectaculars starring Maria Montez and Jon Hall, and the increasingly ludicrous sequels to its classic horror films of the early 1930's, *Frankenstein* (1931), *Dracula* (1931), and *The Mummy* (1932).

The merger with International, and the new company's purchase of a bestseller such as *The Egg and I*, were signs that Universal was determined to recapture some of its former glory. Two stars with established reputations in the field of light comedy, Claudette Colbert and Fred MacMurray, were signed for the parts of Betty and Bob. Betty and Bob Heskett were divorced in 1931. Some early reviewers of *The Egg and I* had described the "MacDonalds' " struggle on their ranch—a natural mistake, since Betty had not written of her divorce or called her husband anything except Bob. Possibly out of a desire to protect Robert Heskett's privacy, this mistake was perpetuated in the movie. Another case of popular misinformation was occasioned by the circumstance that Colbert and MacMurray had both just ended long-term associations with Paramount. As a result, many people today think that *The Egg and I* was a Paramount picture. The screenplay was written by Chester Erskine, a former playwright with many years of theatrical experience, and Fred F. Finklehoffe, a seasoned screenwriter whose previous films included the successful *Brother Rat* (1940), *Babes on Broadway* (1941), and *Meet Me in St. Louis* (1944). The two men were allowed to produce their own screenplay, and Erskine, who had directed plays for Charles Frohman, the Schuberts, and the Theatre Guild, made *The Egg and I* the vehicle for his debut as a motion picture director.

The result was justly condemned by Bosley Crowther in his *New York Times* review of April 25, 1947, as a "watered-down rewrite" that failed completely to capture the "earthy tang" of the book. (Some of MacDonald's experiences had been "earthy" indeed, such as her encounter with a neighbor who, at their first meeting, had offered to perform an abortion on her, for a small fee, whenever she asked him to. Given the restrictions of the Production Code that was still in effect in 1947, there was no way Erskine and Finklehoffe could have worked that incident into their script.) Instead of the ruggedly beautiful Olympic Peninsula scenery that MacDonald had described so evocatively, the film offered only a few prop pine trees standing in front of a cyclorama to suggest a vaguely Northwestern locale. The period was updated to 1946, to emphasize the similarity of Heskett's dream of owning his own farm with the dreams of many returning servicemen after World War II

The book's "plot" had consisted of episodes from young Betty's continual struggle with such unpleasant facts of rural life as the absence of electricity and modern plumbing, and her difficulty in adjusting to the ways of her mountain neighbors. Betty was a precocious eighteen-year-old when Heskett married her out of college in 1927, and, one suspects, a terrific snob. A few of these incidents (chiefly Betty's difficulty in learning to cook on an antiquated cast-iron stove) formed the basis for situation comedy-style "gag" sequences in the film; but Erskine and Finklehoffe relied on a character of their own invention to provide them with material for a conventional dramatic crisis.

In the film, one of Betty and Bob's first callers at the ranch is a glamorous divorcée, Harriett Putnam (Louise Allbritton), who arouses Betty's jealousy because she owns a ranch equipped with all the latest conveniences, and because she is obviously attracted to Bob. Near the end of the story, Bob meets with Harriett to discuss buying her ranch, but without telling Betty because he wants to surprise her. Betty, who has just discovered that she is pregnant, learns of the meeting, and furiously comes to the conclusion that Bob and Harriett are having an affair behind her back. She goes home to her mother without giving Bob a chance to explain, and somewhat implausibly goes through the full term of her pregnancy and gives birth to a baby girl without reading any of Bob's frantic letters or having any communication with him at all. Finally, at her mother's urging, she returns with the baby intending to surprise him. Betty is the surprised one, however, when her cab driver stops at the Putnam ranch (which Bob had bought after all), and she sees Bob's old car parked next to Harriett's sleek station wagon. Betty is furious all over again, and only calms down long enough to learn that Harriett is gone in time for the inevitable happy ending.

As Crowther said, the general tone was of "a quaint and cozy cut-up for the reliable women's trade"; and perhaps the most surprising thing about the film was that it not only repeated the book's success, but was also reissued profitably in 1955. Profitability alone would not justify an article about *The Egg and I* in this reference work, however; many films are released every year to equally great success that are forgotten a few years later by everyone except specialists in film history. What gave *The Egg and I*, as a book and as a film, a special place in cultural history was its introduction of two memorable characters—in fact, a whole family—into the gallery of American folklore.

In the book, MacDonald had described how she looked with dismay at her first batch of home-baked bread, which was "pale yellow" in color and tasted like "something we had cleaned out of the cooler," and, at Bob's suggestion, had taken a sample loaf to a neighbor, Mrs. Kettle, for her diagnosis. As it happened, Mrs. Kettle, a mountainous woman from whose "pretty head cascaded a series of breasts and stomachs which made her look like a cookie jar shaped like a woman," was just taking out of the oven "fourteen of the biggest, crustiest, lightest loaves of bread" that Betty had ever seen. Mrs. Kettle amiably wiped her hands on her dirty housedress, tasted Betty's bread, and pronounced her verdict: "Goddamn stuff stinks."

Mrs. Kettle, her shiftless husband, and their brood of fifteen children were easily the most memorable of the many memorable characters that Betty and Bob Heskett encountered during the two years they lived on their ranch. (Betty's neighbors as described in her book were undoubtedly all fictionalized composites, but the general accuracy of her recollection may be judged from the circumstance that she was later sued by members of two separate families who claimed that she had libeled them as the "Kettles.") In the film, Mrs.— or Ma—Kettle was played by the veteran character actress Marjorie Main, who had already created a long screen gallery of motherly landladies and bad-tempered domestics. Her physical appearance was not as grotesque as MacDonald's description of Ma, but she fully conveyed the good-heartedness that won Betty over in spite of Mrs. Kettle's slatternly appearance and earthy ways. (Needless to say, Mrs. Kettle's profanity and gossip about her neighbors' sex lives did not make it to the screen, nor did her comfortable habit of receiving visitors while seated in her doorless privy.) In the book, Betty described Pa Kettle as a close cousin to Erskine Caldwell's Jeeter Lester (in *Tobacco Road*, 1932): a dirty, lazy Northwestern hillbilly who spoke with a pronounced lisp through a thick black mustache. Someone like Henry Hull— who created the part of Jeeter on the stage—would probably have made a screen Pa Kettle who closely matched Betty's conception; but the role instead went to Percy Kilbride, a gentle, soft-spoken New Englander who created an indelible image of low-keyed guile that brought him his first real public notice after years in small parts (including a role as a handyman in *George Washington Slept Here*, 1942, that was like a sketch for his performance as Pa Kettle).

As played by Main and Kilbride, Ma and Pa Kettle stole the movie of *The Egg and I* as easily as they had stolen the book. (Main, in fact, received the film's only Academy Award nomination, although she lost in the Best Supporting Actress category to Celeste Holm in *Gentleman's Agreement*.) The Kettles were naturals for their own series of second-feature comedies, a fact that was not lost on the management team at Universal-International, which never entirely abandoned the old Universal's commitment to dependably profitable "bread and butter" filmmaking. (One could argue, in fact, that Universal's present eminence as a leading producer of motion pictures and filmed series for television is a continuation of this policy.) In 1949 the studio released *Ma and Pa Kettle*, the first of nine sequels to *The Egg and I*. Bob and Betty MacDonald did not appear as characters in this or any of the subsequent Kettle films, which instead relied on such devices as having Pa Kettle win a modern, fully equipped "dream house" in a contest to engineer the city versus country confrontations that lay at the heart of their comedy. The Kettle series was produced by Leonard Goldstein and, after his death, by Richard Wilson and Howard Christie. The directors included Charles

Lamont, Edward Sedgwick, Charles Barton, Lee Sholem, and Virgil Vogel, who kept the Kettles in motion at an increasingly farcical pace without disappointing their fans or, it must be said, stamping any film in the series with something that could be recognized as a personal point of view.

An important subplot in *The Egg and I* had concerned the oldest Kettle son, Tom (Richard Long), a bright boy who was encouraged by Betty to fulfill his dream of going to college. In *Ma and Pa Kettle*, Long returned with a magazine-writer girl friend (Meg Randall), whom he subsequently married (in *Ma and Pa Kettle Go to Town*, 1950). Long and Randall dropped out of the series after *Ma and Pa Kettle Back on the Farm* (1951), but their place as the "normal" members of the Kettle family was taken by Lori Nelson, who played the oldest Kettle daughter in *Ma and Pa Kettle at the Fair* (1952) and in *Ma and Pa Kettle at Waikiki* (which was filmed in 1953 but not released until 1955). Other recurring characters included a pathologically tidy farm woman named Birdie Hicks (Esther Dale), who had been Ma's natural rival as early as *The Egg and I* (like the Kettles, Mrs. Hicks had also been a character in MacDonald's book), and Meg Randall's stuffy parents, played by Ray Collins and Barbara Brown. Collins and Brown were perfect foils for Main and Kilbride in *Ma and Pa Kettle Go to Town* and *Ma and Pa Kettle on Vacation* (1953). (In this last film, the two ill-matched sets of in-laws wound up in Paris together.)

Percy Kilbride decided to retire after *Ma and Pa Kettle at Home* (1954), but the producers announced that the series would continue without him. In *The Kettles in the Ozarks* (1956), Main journeyed south without Pa to cross swords with his equally shiftless hillbilly cousin, played by Arthur Hunnicutt. By this time, even the usually friendly trade press was reporting (in the words of *Daily Variety*), that the " 'Kettles' series [was] beginning to wear thin"; but the studio released one more film, *Ma and Pa Kettle on Old MacDonald's Farm*, to end the series in 1957. Parker Fennelly, who had played "Titus Moody," another rural con man with a New England twang, on Fred Allen's radio show, took the part of Pa, but he was unable to erase the image created by Kilbride in the role. In a sense, the last film took the series full circle by having the Kettles return, not to their own ramshackle farm, but to Bob and Betty MacDonald's old ranch, where Ma promoted a match between a lumberjack (John Smith) and a spoiled rich girl (Gloria Talbott), whom she undertook to instruct in the duties of a proper farm wife, just as she had coached MacDonald ten years before.

It was suggested as a reason for the series' demise that movie audiences of the late 1950's were too sophisticated for the Kettles' brand of rural humor; but it seems fairer to say that Ma and Pa Kettle—along with Francis the Talking Mule, the Bowery Boys, Blondie, and all the other once popular second-feature characters—were victims of television, which had captured the regular movie audience in small towns where the "B"-picture series had always been strongest. That the basic appeal of rural comedy had not diminished was indicated by the success a few years later of such television series as *The Beverly Hillbillies*, *Petticoat Junction*, and *Green Acres*. This last show, in fact, with its theme of a city couple (played by Eddie Albert and Eva Gabor) who were constantly being outwitted by a country bumpkin (Pat Butram), was nothing more than a reworking of the basic situation that audiences had laughed at in *The Egg and I*.

Charles Hopkins

THE ELECTRIC HORSEMAN

Released: 1979
Production: Ray Stark for Ray Stark-Wildwood; released by Columbia and Universal
Direction: Sydney Pollack
Screenplay: Robert Garland; based on Robert Garland and Paul Gaer's adaptation of an original story by Shelly Burton
Cinematography: Owen Roizman
Editing: Sheldon Kahn
Running time: 120 minutes

Principal characters:
Sonny Steele	Robert Redford
Hallie Martin	Jane Fonda
Wendell	Willie Nelson
Hunt Sears	John Saxon
Charlotta	Valerie Perrine
Fitzgerald	Nicolas Coster
Gus Atwater	Will Hare
Leroy	Timothy Scott
Danny Miles	Allan Arbus

The Electric Horseman, a likable and well-made romantic comedy with a minor antiestablishment theme, is in the tradition of Frank Capra's Oscar-winning *It Happened One Night* (1934). As in the Capra film, the chief virtues are the superb but easy acting of the stars and the witty dialogue of the script. *The Electric Horseman*, however, introduces some modern variations on the conventions of the romantic comedies of the 1930's and 1940's.

With great artistry and economy, the shots under the credits portray the career of five-time world champion cowboy Sonny Steele (Robert Redford). He wins his rodeo championships, suffers a few broken bones along the way, and is signed by Ampco Corporation to promote its Ranch Breakfast cereal. The beginning of his career with Ampco is shown through a shot of a commercial artist adding a moustache to Sonny's picture, a photography session with Sonny now wearing a moustache, and a series of posters advertising Sonny's appearances as the Ranch Breakfast Cowboy. There is not a word of dialogue during this sequence, only the voice of country singer Willie Nelson singing "My Heroes Have Always Been Cowboys."

As the credits end, we find out what the job of Ranch Breakfast Cowboy has become. Sonny is intoxicated and late for an appearance as his sidekicks, Wendell (Willie Nelson) and Leroy (Timothy Scott), struggle to dress him in his special costume. Once he is dressed and mounted on a horse, he rides onto a darkened football field as part of a half-time show. His flashy cowboy costume is electrified so that he is outlined in lights (hence the title), and he holds up a giant box of Ranch Breakfast as he rides around the field, but this time he is too drunk to stay on the horse and he falls off. Now we hear Willie Nelson singing again, but this time the song is "Mama, Don't Let Your Babies Grow Up to Be Cowboys."

The central action of the plot begins in Las Vegas, where the Ampco conglomerate is holding a convention and media event at Caesar's Palace. The Ampco people are trying to buy a bank and want everything to go smoothly. Hallie Martin (Jane Fonda) is a television reporter looking for a story, and when the Ampco public relations man, Fitzgerald (Nicolas Coster), suggests that she not interview Sonny, Hallie decides that there is something to hide and that Sonny will be her story. Sonny meanwhile has found that Ampco has bought a twelve-million-dollar thoroughbred horse, Rising Star, to be another of its "corporate symbols." He is upset when he sees the animal on display in the Caesar's Palace parking lot and even more upset when he finds that various drugs have been administered to keep the horse tranquil enough to take part in a stage show but that its inflamed tendon has not been properly treated because Ampco does not want the horse to appear with a bandage on its leg.

Sonny confronts the head of Ampco, Hunt Sears (John Saxon), with his complaints about how the horse is being treated, but Sears tells him that he is not to interfere in corporate policy. "Sir, I used to rodeo," Sonny says. "I was good at it." Sears merely replies, "That's irrelevant."

Sonny is therefore forced to take matters into his own hands. During the "Disco Magic" portion of the Ampco stage show, he mounts Rising Star, turns on his electrified costume, and rides the horse across the stage, through the casino, and off down the street. In his electric cowboy suit riding down the garish Las Vegas strip, Sonny is an impressive sight, but the director of the show, Danny Miles (Allan Arbus), is upset because he has ruined the "whole concept" of the show, and Sears is afraid the publicity will ruin his three-hundred-million-dollar merger with the bank. "One drunken cowboy," he mutters.

The emphasis of *The Electric Horseman* then shifts from the "liberation" of both Sonny and the horse to the relationship between Sonny and Hallie. It begins as romances always do in the old-fashioned romantic comedies, with two people of different backgrounds battling each other. In the 1930's the battling would have lasted until the final part of the film when the two would have recognized their love, gotten married, and presumably lived happily ever after. In *The Electric Horseman* the romance comes sooner and the two separate at the end, but the attention to characterization and subtlety of feelings is the same as in the older films.

Hallie had already confronted Sonny at a press conference with questions about why he was late for the conference and whether he actually ate Ranch

Breakfast cereal, and—referring to the fact that he had been a cowboy and was now a cereal salesman—had asked the universal television reporter's question: "How do you feel about that?" Now she finds that Sonny is a bigger story than she could have imagined. In an effort to find Sonny she interviews Leroy and replays a tape recording of her earlier interview with Wendell. Through these interviews she finds Gus Atwater (Will Hare), a somewhat demented friend of Sonny who lives in the desert, and through Gus she finds Sonny.

When Hallie finds Sonny, he attacks her both physically and verbally. He is startled by her sudden appearance in the dark, afraid that she has told others where he is, and angry at her desire for a story, "any story." Sonny finally persuades her to leave, but the next day as he buys some supplies at a small store he sees her on television reporting what she learned from a "wide-ranging conversation" lasting "many hours." Sonny then decides that if he is going to be on television he wants to tell his story himself; so he telephones Hallie and tells her to bring a camera and to meet him alone at a remote location. There he explains on camera that the stallion has earned a better life, tells Hallie that he is going to set the horse loose, and sends Hallie away with the videotape. He has not gotten rid of her, however, because she soon returns to warn him that the police are waiting for him and that she must go with him or she will be legally forced to tell all she knows. She has already told her network to meet her at Rim Rock Canyon, where she has deduced Sonny is taking the horse, but she of course does not tell Sonny that. She still sees him merely as a big and exclusive story for herself.

Gradually their hostility toward each other changes to more tender feelings. As they finally embrace, a slow dissolve takes us to the next morning. Their romance is based on a mutual respect as Hallie begins to understand what Sonny is doing and why he is doing it and Sonny appreciates that Hallie is good at her job. Now Hallie regrets telling the network to have a camera crew waiting at Rim Rock Canyon, and she tries unsuccessfully to get word to her boss to cancel that plan. That night she tells Sonny what she has done and that she lied about having to stay with him or face legal troubles. The news does not change his plans, however; the next day when they reach a quiet secluded valley, he releases Rising Star, telling him, "make something out of yourself now." Hallie is amazed that the network crew is not there, but Sonny is not because they are in Silver Reef. He had never intended to go to Rim Rock Canyon; that was Hallie's mistaken assumption.

The film cuts from Rising Star running free to a small coffee shop and bus station. Hallie is taking a bus and going back to her job; Sonny is going to look for something simple to do. As he sees her off, Sonny says, "I keep wanting to thank you—but then I keep wondering what for." The film ends with Hallie reporting on television from New York while Sonny walks along a road halfheartedly trying to hitch a ride.

Credit for the success of *The Electric Horseman* belongs primarily to the script and the acting. The script, by Robert Garland from a screen story by Garland and Paul Gaer that is based on a story by Shelly Burton, is both unhurried and packed with information that reveals both plot and character. These details of both plot and characterization are continually revealed, but they are never overemphasized. The result is a coherent narrative that gives the audience credit for the intelligence to follow it without having every point underlined. The dialogue is also witty but unforced. The Ampco personnel are characterized less subtly than the others, however; in addition, some pertinent points about the media in our society are made even if they are not deeply explored. The main points concern the all-too-frequent desire of reporters to find a story rather than the truth and the fact that a person may become more famous and rich as a "corporate symbol" than for what he does well that made him celebrated in the first place. An example of this is the fact that Joe DiMaggio may be known to more people today as a spokesman for a coffee machine than as a star baseball player. The only bad sequence in the film is a chase in which Sonny, who is riding Rising Star, incredibly escapes from several police cars and motorcycles.

The acting is superb. Both Redford and Fonda play their roles with an ease that makes them credible but with perfect timing so that nothing in the script is lost and much is added. Redford and Fonda may be major stars, but they are also excellent actors. They are well supported by virtually every member of the cast, with country singer Nelson as Wendell and Valerie Perrine as Sonny's ex-wife deserving special notice. *The Electric Horseman* is skillfully made and enjoyable enough to reward repeated viewings, but some reviewers faulted the film for not being what they expected. Other reviewers, however, recognized its virtues, as did the public, which made it one of the ten most popular films of the year.

Timothy W. Johnson

ELMER GANTRY

Released: 1960
Production: Bernard Smith for United Artists
Direction: Richard Brooks
Screenplay: Richard Brooks (AA); based on the novel of the same name by
  Sinclair Lewis
Cinematography: John Alton
Editing: Marge Fowler
Art direction: Ed Carrere
Costume design: Dorothy Jeakins
Music: André Previn
Running time: 146 minutes

Principal characters:
Elmer Gantry	Burt Lancaster (AA)
Sister Sharon Falconer	Jean Simmons
Jim Lefferts	Arthur Kennedy
Lulu Bains	Shirley Jones (AA)
William L. Morgan	Dean Jagger
Sister Rachel	Patti Page
George Babbitt	Edward Andrews

Who is Elmer Gantry? Is he a savior or a scoundrel, a charlatan or a saint? This grinning, likable man at times appears to be the incarnation of insincerity and deviousness, but in a conversation with the atheistic newspaperman, Jim Lefferts (Arthur Kennedy), Gantry (Burt Lancaster) confesses that he does believe in the Lord, and it follows that he sees goodness in his questionable preaching. Gantry tells Lefferts that it is good for people to get down on their knees and pray. Throughout his story, he is fond of wistfully exclaiming, "Love is the morning and the evening star." Is this poetic declaration merely a clever phrase the rogue uses to gain the affections of women, or is it something the man believes in even though the tone of his voice mocks the words? Although he treats revivalism as theater and is forever giving a performance as God's messenger, Gantry is in his way both theologian and spiritual seeker. Having been expelled from a religious seminary for yielding to the temptations of the flesh, he is a man finding his own way to express the struggles of the soul, a way which requires that he be both angel and devil.

As Gantry exists both to question and to validate divine will, the film of which he is the protagonist exists in light and shadow, its figures traveling in and out of darkness with a vibrancy accentuated by the gaudy colors utilized solely for expressive purposes. In the first scene, when Gantry, drunk on Christmas Eve, convinces the apathetic customers that they should give their money to charity, he is a figure emerging from a literal blackness and becoming charismatic not only through movement but because a glaring light illuminates him. Later, the hard light associated with Gantry dominates all of his scenes as an evangelist, while in other scenes he moves in and out of the deep black shadows which daringly fill many of the images. Sister Sharon (Jean Simmons) is characterized by the dazzling white of her costume in the revival scenes, identifying her as an innocent sent from heaven. The hell on earth, of which the house of prostitution in which Lulu Baines (Shirley Jones) lives is only the most direct manifestation, is often visualized in artificial blues, reds, and yellows which fill the walls of interiors when there is no realistic justification for them. *Elmer Gantry* is a film in which the period detail beautifully evokes the Midwest of the 1920's, but in which at the same time a visual abstractness deliriously separates the story from naturalistic representation, revealing its true subject to be the contradictions within the soul.

The feverishness with which the film portrays the struggle between heaven and hell is never more evident than in the climax of the burning tent, in which Sister Sharon perishes. Having been led into the sin of her relationship with Gantry, she now believes that she is redeemed, and she is reaffirmed in her faith that she carries a divine message. As if God has intervened to punish her for her pride, calling upon the fires of hell to consume her, an image is imposed in which the orange flames overwhelm the spiritual white of her garments.

Gantry is powerless to save Sharon. Throughout the story, his ambivalent intentions have reaped a whirlwind. He is perceived as being right in chastising Jim Lefferts, with whom he maintains a friendly relationship; but the logic which Lefferts represents, while that of a devil's advocate, at least has the merit of temporarily exposing the sham of Sister Sharon's righteousness, which may be self-delusion on her part but is cynically used by Gantry. In his relationship with women, Gantry is never an unjust seducer. His love for Sharon is genuine, and her response to him is natural and should not provoke in her a feeling of shame. Gantry's mistake is in leaving her trapped between her spiritual aspirations and her worldly desires.

Similarly, Gantry is unjust to Lulu Baines. However, he is not blamed for having seduced an innocent girl and driven her into prostitution, since it is implied that Lulu's background as the daughter of a minister is responsible for the course her life takes. Rather, Gantry's mistake in his treatment of Lulu, for which he suffers, is his failure to understand that her love for him is strong enough to demand renewed expression, even if this must take the negative form of blackmail. Gantry has a certain perceptiveness about life, and he makes clever use of it in his relationships with the other characters; but he is blind to his own power as a catalyst in bringing about a tragedy which the film ambiguously suggests might be the result either of social and historical forces or of the will of God.

Elmer Gantry is a film which has enjoyed popularity and critical success for both good and bad reasons. As an adaptation of a controversial novel, it was bound to receive attention, and the skillfulness of Richard Brooks's adaptation has won deserved praise. The explicit subject of the story is the hold revivalism has over a great section of America, but the naïveté of the followers of Gantry and Sister Sharon is not enough to arouse a sense of self-importance in a film. While the film may have won some merited awards because Brooks was considered courageous to have undertaken it, its style found an appreciative following among the more adventurous European critics, whose perceptions of American films have always shown enviable insight.

It is appropriate that Brooks would realize this film with a fervor not always found in his work. The unbridled religious hysteria which Gantry uses like an artist cries out for a visual excitement which Brooks has provided with the skill of a conjurer. The color photography of *Elmer Gantry* owes a great deal to John Alton, an artist in his own right, whose lighting reminds us that he had made a reputation in black and white and showed a similar feeling for color with his first opportunity in that medium (the ballet in *An American in Paris*, 1951); but Brooks shares the credit for having chosen Alton and for having inspired the cameraman by composing vivid images.

Brooks also is responsible for the cast, and the actors make a notable contribution not only in the vividness of their physical presences but in the intensity with which they play their roles. A nice balance is achieved in the casting. The men are all expected choices, but the casting of the female roles is rather startling. Burt Lancaster is no surprise as a dynamic and colorful Gantry, just as Arthur Kennedy is ideal to convey the skepticism of Lefferts. Similarly, Dean Jagger has had many roles of weak men similar to Sharon's pathetic manager, Bill Morgan, and Edward Andrews might have been born to play the hypocritical businessman, George Babbitt. On the other hand, Jean Simmons might have been thought too refined to play the fiery Sister Sharon, but the impression of breeding and intelligence which are part of her image contribute to making this performance one of her most striking. The lovely Patti Page, a stranger to cinema, was picked to play a singer in the revival troupe whom Gantry seduces, and she is effective because her naturalness and reticence provide contrast to the prevailing mood. Especially offbeat is the casting of Shirley Jones, who revels in her role as a prostitute. Previously, sweet and wholesome girls had been her specialty, and the characterization cleverly comments on this, as Lulu was once sweet and wholesome herself.

The film was Brooks's first independent venture after ten years as a contract director at M-G-M, and he flaunted the opportunity by insisting that the film be shot in the unfashionable aspect ratio of 1.33, demonstrating scorn for the 1.85 and CinemaScope ratios which had been insisted upon in his M-G-M films. Brooks has often spoken of the ludicrousness of many of his M-G-M projects, although he wrote the scripts for most of them; and superficially, *Elmer Gantry*, which represents his blossoming into an artist, would seem to justify his view that a studio director is a slave. In retrospect, however, interesting themes and stylistic beauties may be found in many of his M-G-M films, of which one, *The Last Hunt* (1956), is as fascinating as *Elmer Gantry*. On the other hand, none of his later films is realized in quite so striking a manner as this one, although his gifts have been intermittently evident in all of them. In the context of Brooks's career, *Elmer Gantry* does not demonstrate the virtues of greater freedom; it only shows the level of artistry of which Brooks is capable but which has so often mysteriously eluded him.

Blake Lucas

THE EMPEROR JONES

Released: 1933
Production: John Krimsky and Gifford Cochran; released by United Artists
Direction: Dudley Murphy
Screenplay: DuBose Heyward; based on the play of the same name by Eugene
    O'Neill
Cinematography: Ernest Haller
Editing: Grant Whytock
Running time: 72 minutes

Principal characters:
Brutus Jones	Paul Robeson
Smithers	Dudley Digges
Jeff	Frank Wilson
Undine	Fredi Washington
Dolly	Ruby Elzy
Lem	George Haymid Stamper

Based on Eugene O'Neill's 1920 stage *tour de force*, the film version of *The Emperor Jones* opens up the play, principally by picking up the bits of Jones's earlier life from the flashes given in his jungle flight and restructuring the first half of the film upon an expanded version of these events. Thus, O'Neill's play begins with Jones's exodus from his palace, while the film begins with his foray into the white man's world as a Pullman porter. Particularly fascinating is the film's addition of the mirror motif: it is through this image in a series of mirrors that we see the gradual transformation of Brutus Jones (Paul Robeson) from self-satisfaction as a porter to his eventual personal belief in himself as "Emperor."

Robeson's portrayal of Jones is masterful, whether he is singing, "travellin,' " or playing the penny-ante island ruler. After graduating from Princeton, Robeson played the Brutus Jones role on the stage, went on to do a series of musical plays in New York and in Britain, and finally agreed to do the film version of the play, his first sound film, in 1932. *The Emperor Jones* was one of the few films of which he was proud. Independently produced, the film was a reasonable financial success, although it did bear the period stigmata of being an "art film." The director, Dudley Murphy (assisted by William C. De Mille, who apparently finished the film), had collaborated with Fernand Leger on the classic experimental film *Ballet Mecanique* in 1924, then went on to direct Bessie Smith in *St. Louis Blues* (1929).

The credits of *The Emperor Jones* are superimposed over a group of dancing natives; this shot slowly dissolves into a marvelous down-home gospel meeting alive with dancing and hand-clapping. As the minister intones a benediction for brother Brutus Jones, who is about to leave for the big world, the film cuts to Brutus admiring himself in front of the mirror in his new Pullman porter uniform. The film then cuts back and forth between the church and Brutus' departure from his home and wife Dolly (Ruby Elzy). The couple stop by the church to receive farewell congratulations, allowing Brutus the opportunity to sing "Now Let Me Fly." Suddenly, he is on his way, and fellow porter and friend Jeff (Frank Wilson) gives Brutus his first lecture on "high finance"—how to get the biggest tips by analyzing passengers' shoes while polishing them.

To the background of "The St. Louis Blues" Jeff introduces Brutus to his first Harlem club and also to his girl friend Undine (Fredi Washington), whom Brutus proceeds to steal. There follows a montage of the totally unprincipled Brutus' climb up through the Pullman heirarchy. Always humming and singing snatches of "I'm Travellin'," he is transferred to "The President's" private car, where he tries his hand at a little financial blackmail. Over his head in the white man's world of high finance, Brutus is promptly demoted, but when the more sensible Undine points out this fact, he drops her. Later, in another Harlem club, Brutus and his new date Belle meet Jeff and Undine. Still in love with him, Undine attacks Belle in the middle of the dance floor and Brutus walks out again, "travellin' light."

Another train montage takes Brutus to a Savannah poolroom where heavy betting between himself and Jeff turns up loaded dice. Jeff pulls a knife but is killed by Brutus in the ensuing fight, and Brutus takes flight. The film cuts to Brutus on a chain gang, breaking rocks between breathtaking renditions of "John Henry" and "Water Boy." When a guard tries to harass him into beating a fellow convict, Brutus escapes, to return briefly to his wife for aid.

Always moving, Brutus ends up shoveling coal in a freighter's boiler room, jumps ship, and heads for an inhospitable island (based on Haiti) where he is quickly captured, condemned to jail by the dissolute black leader, and saved by being sold to the sly white trader Smithers (Dudley Digges). Teaching the natives to play dice, Brutus quickly gambles his way up to a partnership with Smithers.

On a routine trip to the island palace to further bilk the ruling "General," Brutus purposely provokes the palace guard into shooting him. Since the bullets prove harmless to him (he had filled all the guns with blanks), he is able to promote the myth that he is invincible except to a silver bullet. Thus, cowing the superstitious guards, Brutus pulls off a bloodless *coup*, and, admiring himself in a palace mirror, dubs himself "The Emperor Jones."

Brutus is next seen after a two-and-a-half-year period during which he has decorated the palace in mirrors, dressed himself and his attendants in eighteenth century finery, and bled the natives dry and to the edge of revolt. One day, after perpetrating a particularly vicious bit of punishment on the natives, Brutus is awakened by Smithers to find an empty palace, his court and guards having fled during the night. Brutus instantly "resigns the job of Emperor" and takes off to the hills in an attempt to escape to the sea before the native revolutionaries capture him. Dressed in his imperial uniform and carrying only a revolver loaded with six bullets—five lead, and one silver, the latter his charm—Brutus enters the jungle to the steady background beat of the natives' drum.

A masterful monologue by Brutus during his tortuous flight through the jungle keeps the second half of the film very much alive with excitement. As the darkness descends and Brutus cannot find his food stash, the drum beat begins to effect him, and his composure disintegrates. Vignettes from his past life appear to haunt him, and he begins to shoot at his fears: "wild pigs," a crap-shooting Jeff, and the chain gang guard. Hallucinating a service in his old Baptist church, Brutus sings "Daniel in the Lion's Den" and prays for forgiveness. Finally, he imagines he sees a witch doctor who conjures up a crocodile, at which Brutus shoots his last bullet—the silver one. Maddened and shorn of his fine clothes, Brutus is finally driven by the drums into a native ambush. Only when he is killed by a series of silver bullets does the drum stop beating. After expiring in the natives' camp in the presence of their leader, Lem (George Haymid Stamper), and the white trader, Smithers takes his hat off to Brutus, commenting that "yer died in the 'eighth o' style."

Although *The Emperor Jones* may be somewhat dated in its presentation of a black man, it is still tremendously effective as a view of everyman meeting his primal fears and trying to deal with them. It is really a one-man show, however, and Robeson's bravura performance holds the film together and makes it ageless.

The Emperor Jones is acknowledged to be Robeson's finest American film. Because Robeson wanted to break away from the stereotyped roles which he was offered in American films, he began making films in Europe in the 1930's, most notably *Sanders of the River* (1935), produced by British impressario Zoltan Korda. Because even these films turned out to be, in essence, the same type of exploitive films which were made in the United States, Robeson became disenchanted with them as well. His well-publicized affiliation with the Communist Party beginning in the 1930's and other problems created a furor around him which badly hurt his career. His last film was *Tales of Manhattan* (1942), and he died in relative obscurity in 1976 in Philadelphia.

Kathleen Karr

THE ENCHANTED COTTAGE

Released: 1945
Production: Harriet Parsons for RKO/Radio
Direction: John Cromwell
Screenplay: DeWitt Bodeen and Herman J. Mankiewicz; based on the play
   of the same name by Sir Arthur Wing Pinero
Cinematography: Ted Tetzlaff
Editing: Joseph Noriega
Music: Roy Webb
Running time: 92 minutes

   Principal characters:
   Laura Pennington .... Dorothy McGuire
   Oliver Bradford .... Robert Young
   Major John Hillgrove .... Herbert Marshall
   Mrs. Minnett .... Mildred Natwick
   Beatrice Alexander .... Hillary Brooke
   Violet Price .... Spring Byington
   Frederick Price .... Richard Gaines

   When Sir Arthur Wing Pinero wrote the play *The Enchanted Cottage* it was
with the idea of trying to raise the morale of the men who came out of World
War I as human derelicts, scarred and maimed for the rest of their lives. It
was first produced with success on the London stage in 1922, and the following
year William A. Brady presented it on Broadway with Katharine Cornell as
its ugly duckling heroine. In 1924, it was filmed by First National as a silent
motion picture costarring Richard Barthelmess and May McAvoy as the
lovers. In the first years of the talking film, RKO/Radio acquired the rights
to the play, and first there was talk about Helen Twelvetrees making a new
version, then Helen Mack, and later Ginger Rogers. Nothing came of remake
plans, however, until World War II, when Harriet Parsons, one of Hollywood's
few female producers, was placed under contract by RKO. As is customary
with new producers searching for a suitable story, she went through the
catalogue of properties that the studio owned. She was attracted by *The
Enchanted Cottage* and believed that with the world at war, the time was right
to refilm the story, bringing it up to date and setting it in New England rather
than in the English countryside, the setting of the original drama.
   Parsons asked that DeWitt Bodeen, also under contract to RKO, be assigned to work with her on the project as screenwriter, and the film finally
went into production in 1944 under the direction of John Cromwell, who
brought in Herman J. Mankiewicz for a rewrite. David O. Selznick took a
personal interest in the project, lending his contract star, Dorothy McGuire,
to play the heroine. Cromwell very correctly knew that the only way to

present a fantasy romance was realistically. The people in *The Enchanted Cottage* are very human and real, and the audience is led to believe that a "miracle" could take place.

The cottage of the title is on the New England seacoast and consists of only one wing of an estate built by an Englishman. The rest of the house was destroyed by fire, but the wing survives, inhabited by a widow, Mrs. Minnett (Mildred Natwick), who once lived there with her husband, and now acts as a housekeeper, renting out the cottage to honeymooners as the original owner had been accustomed to do. The lovers who lived in the cottage were always supremely happy, for they realized their love in an atmosphere of sublime harmony and contentment.

In the nearby village lives a lonely girl, an ugly duckling named Laura Pennington (Dorothy McGuire), and when Mrs. Minnett engages her services as a helper, Laura welcomes the opportunity of living in an environment that harbors warmth and care. Oliver Bradford (Robert Young) has heard about the enchantment the cottage weaves for lovers, and he brings his bride-to-be, Beatrice Alexander (Hillary Brooke), to look over the dwelling as an ideal honeymoon site for them. Before they can marry, however, the country goes to war, and Oliver, who is in the Air Corps, is immediately called to duty.

He comes back to the cottage alone, sooner than expected, for he has been seriously injured in a plane crash. The seventh nerve on one side of his face has been severed, and there is no hope for his recovery or help for the unsightly twist that distorts his facial expression. He has sought the cottage as a retreat from the world. Laura, in her severe plainness and lack of any prettiness, is the only person to whom he can talk. A neighbor, Major John Hillgrove (Herbert Marshall), who is blind, visits them, and he senses what is quietly happening; they are falling in love. They get married; later, they come to Hillgrove one night to confess that they have stayed away from the world, even avoiding the sight of Mrs. Minnett, ever since they became man and wife. For on their honeymoon night, a "miracle" took place. Oliver looked upon Laura and found her lovely and desirable; she saw him as she had first seen him, handsome, straight, and unmarred.

Hillgrove tries to persuade them that the "miracle" is true. He tells them to treasure it, believe in it, and continue to remain apart from others. And so they do, until the world intrudes. Oliver's superficial parents, mother and stepfather, come to see them. Their new world falls in ruins when they realize that they are the same as they have always been; there is no "miracle," even though every time they look at each other they continue to see each other as desirable. It is only those who are unsighted, like the Major, who can see them as they see themselves. Mrs. Minnett explains the "miracle" by telling them that they have fallen in love, that a man and a woman in love have a gift of sight that is not granted to other people. She has watched them from the beginning, and on the day of their wedding she saw their love blaze up like kindling wood. She tells them to keep that love burning and they will never be anything to each other but fair and handsome. That is the charm; that is the only enchantment that the cottage holds, and it is of their own making.

Audiences were themselves caught up in the enchantment. Although scorned by some critics, *The Enchanted Cottage* became one of the best-liked films of 1945, and its popularity has never dwindled; it is still a favorite on retrospective programs and is consistently screened on television. It became one of the few romances mingling fact with fancy that were popular during the war, and grateful servicemen who had been wounded and scarred in conflict took time to write the studio, the producer, the stars, and even the writers, telling them how much they appreciated the film and how they hoped that the people at home would also see it and so understand its theme, a philosophy they themselves knew to be true.

Dorothy McGuire, who had been introduced to the movie world through her stage success *Claudia*, played the homely spinster, Laura, with remarkable delicacy and warmth. In all other productions of *The Enchanted Cottage*, for the stage and the silent screen, Laura had been misshapen, cursed with a crooked nose, buck teeth, and near-sighted vision. One shoulder was higher than the other, and she walked with a limp. McGuire was adamant about not playing Laura with those encumbrances. She insisted on playing the part with no makeup, her hair drab and lifeless, her clothes homemade, and badly fitted. She maintained that the real job of the production department was to make her ravishingly beautiful. It became the task of Eddie Stevenson, costume designer, to make two of everything she wore: one that fitted her perfectly and another that did not fit at all. The makeup department and hairdressers, often the bane of the director and cinematographer, were not to touch her. McGuire had her way, and she made Laura believably drab, a Cinderella who never deserted the hearth. Only in her eyes was there any sign of beauty; she thought herself plain, and so she became plain. The role of Oliver was Robert Young's own favorite of all the parts he played; in later years he even named the home he built in Southern California "The Enchanted Cottage." Mrs. Minnett was one of Mildred Natwick's first screen roles, and she was absolutely right for the part. The audience believed in her proudly defiant confession at the climax of the film when she says that were the man she once loved to rise from his grave and walk in at the moment, she would be fair to him, for they too had loved, and the enchantment held fast.

Herbert Marshall's cultivated tones and calm acceptance of a "miracle" in which he can believe because he is sightless, make that "miracle" all the more believable. It is Marshall, as Major Hillgrove, who provides the frame for the story. Being a musician, he has composed a tone poem for the piano called "The Enchanted Cottage," and his friends have gathered in his house to hear him play it. As he starts to play an introductory passage featuring the major theme, he narrates the story, and there is a flashback to its natural beginnings, with necessary exposition backgrounded by him over the piano tones.

The Enchanted Cottage is a delicate piece of work. It weaves a spell of enchantment over the audience so that they believe, they sympathize, and they hope that Laura and Oliver will know a love and happiness unmarred by ugliness. It dispenses with the moments of fantasy indulged in by the play and the silent film. There are no wraiths, no shadows of other lovers from other times crowding the scene. Words, pictures, and a score that enhances them make the charm come real. The remarkable thing is that audiences today, seeing the picture for the first time, are caught up in its spell. It simply provokes imagination by making its audience believe in it as possible—and it becomes real.

DeWitt Bodeen

THE ENEMY BELOW

Released: 1957
Production: Dick Powell for Twentieth Century-Fox
Direction: Dick Powell
Screenplay: Wendell Mayes; based on the novel of the same name by D. A. Rayner
Cinematography: Harold Rosson
Editing: Stuart Gilmore
Special effects: Walter Rossi (AA)
Running time: 98 minutes

Principal characters:

Captain Murrell	Robert Mitchum
Von Stolberg	Curt Jurgens
Lieutenant Ware	Al (David) Hedison
Schwaffer	Theodore Bikel
Doctor	Russell Collins
Von Holem	Kurt Kreuger
Ensign Merry	Doug McClure

Films featuring men in war most often focus on the direct, face-to-face confrontation aspect of combat, rifles, machine guns, and grenades. Shots of soldiers blowing each other to oblivion make for visually exciting cinema. Often, however, real war can be a game of nerves, of wait-and-see or think-and-outthink-your-adversary strategy. *The Enemy Below*, released in 1957, is not a standard war film since the scenario stresses the strategical, chess-game aspect of war. Outwait the enemy, anticipate his moves, plan a strategy, try to outwit him, and, then, hopefully, checkmate him.

The film is not devoid of violence, as an American destroyer and German U-boat do fire torpedoes and depth charges at each other. Still, it is closer in content to Jean Renoir's *Grand Illusion* (1937), considered by some the greatest film ever made. *The Enemy Below* stresses the respect that two dedicated soldiers can have for each other, even though they are on opposite sides of the battle lines.

Robert Mitchum stars in the film as Murrell, the calm, cool, but haggard captain of the United States destroyer *Haines*. Murrell's nemesis is Von Stolberg (Curt Jurgens, in his American film debut), the war-weary commander of the U-boat. While on patrol in the South Atlantic, the *Haines* makes radar contact with the U-boat, headed for a rendezvous with a Nazi surface raider. Von Stolberg becomes aware of the contact and sets his ship on a zig-zag course in order to evade the *Haines*'s pursuit. Murrell, anticipating Von Stolberg's strategy, holds a steady course. The German thinks he has escaped, but the *Haines* has stayed with the U-boat. Murrell baits Von Stolberg into firing two torpedoes that miss. In response, depth charges are dropped from the *Haines*, but they do not hit their target either. The U-boat sets its course, but the destroyer follows and overtakes it. Von Stolberg lowers his ship to a dangerous depth of 310 meters after more depth charges are dropped. Murrell in turn stops the *Haines*. Both skippers wait out each other in silence.

Finally, Von Stolberg moves. His submarine is followed by the *Haines*, which drops additional depth charges at intervals. The German anticipates the destroyer's position and fires its four remaining torpedoes. One torpedo hits the *Haines*. Murrell orders his crew to set fake fires, assuming correctly, that Von Stolberg will be tricked into surfacing. According to Murrell, this is the "first foolish thing he's done." Now, both ships shoot at each other; both are hit hard and are doomed. The *Haines* finally rams the U-boat, and both Americans and Germans end up sharing the same life boats. Murrell and Von Stolberg face each other from the decks of their respective ships and salute. Murrell helps his adversary escape his sinking boat by throwing him a rope, but Von Stolberg fails to save his mortally wounded second-in-command, Schwaffer (Theodore Bikel). The life boats are picked up by another American destroyer and, at the finale, the two skippers share a cigarette as they gaze out at the sea.

The Enemy Below is based on an actual incident which occurred during World War II. As a suspense drama it is first-rate, with director Dick Powell and screenwriter Wendell Mayes keeping the viewer fully engrossed in the proceedings. The film is primarily noteworthy for its depiction of the German, Von Stolberg, who is not merely the "enemy," an anonymous Nazi submarine commander. As conceived by Mayes and portrayed by Jurgens, he is a fully three-dimensional character, a career soldier trying to do his job to the best of his abilities. Because of this interpretation, *The Enemy Below* could never have been made during the war years when Germany had not yet been defeated. At that time, to keep up morale, Hollywood's war films were propaganda, with patriotic scenarios depicting the Germans and Japanese as dirty "Krauts" and "Nips," vicious sadists killing and maiming eighteen-year-old American draftees who, six months before, had been playing high-school football and who had never set foot east of Kentucky or west of Kansas. By 1957, twelve years after the war had ended, enough time had passed for a German soldier to be presented in an American film as a human being, not a caricature who stomps around yelling "Heil Hitler." Incidentally, the Germans, and Von Stolberg in particular, are no Nazis; the commander is simply a navy man and even spouts some anti-Nazi rhetoric about "the new Germany, a machine." The manner in which the sailors from each ship assist one another in abandoning their respective vessels to the safety of the lifeboats—despite the fact that they are at war and should be killing one another—is touching. Whether by choice or by chance, *The Enemy Below* is an effective commentary on the stupidity and wastefulness of war.

Powell, star of musicals during the 1930's and of mysteries during the mid-1940's, began his career as a director in 1953 with *Split Second*. His other films are *The Conquerer* (1956), *The Hunters* (1958), and *The Enemy Below*. Powell's work is adequate (with the exception of the laughable *The Conquerer*), and *The Enemy Below* is easily his best effort. In particular, he intercuts easily between scenes juxtaposing the commanders of both ships.

Jurgens, Mitchum, and the other members of the all-male cast offer fine performances. Mitchum is a vastly underrated actor who has managed to remain a top star for more than thirty-five years. This film is the first of two he made with Powell. In the other film, *The Hunters*, he plays an ace fighter pilot in the Korean War. Jurgens, originally a journalist in his native Germany, first gained recognition in America playing a Nazi officer who rebels against his party in *The Devil's General* (1955), a role that is not dissimilar to his Von Stolberg. He is a star of the European stage and has become a star and supporting actor in international films.

The Enemy Below was unfortunately a box-office failure, not even ranking among the top ninety-seven grossing films of 1957, according to *Variety*, and earned less than one million dollars. The reviews were good, however; the National Board of Review even named the film to its ten-best list, and *Time* magazine selected it as one of the twelve best films of the year. Also, Walter Rossi's excellent special effects earned him an Academy Award.

Rob Edelman

ENTER THE DRAGON

Released: 1973
Production: Fred Weintraub and Paul Heller; released by Warner Bros.
Direction: Robert Clouse
Screenplay: Michael Allin
Cinematography: Gilbert Hubbs
Editing: Kurt Hirschler and George Watters
Running time: 98 minutes

Principal characters:
Lee .... Bruce Lee
Roper .... John Saxon
Williams ....Jim Kelly
Han .... Shih Kien
Oharra ....Bob Wall
Tania ....Ahna Capri
Su-Lin .... Angela Mao-Ying

Legendary Oriental superstar Bruce Lee made his final screen appearance in *Enter the Dragon*, the first United States-produced martial arts film. Because of Lee's untimely death at the age of thirty-three and the film's status as the most lavishly produced film of its genre (and the first one to be filmed in English), *Enter the Dragon* has come to be regarded by critics and audiences alike as the definitive martial arts film. Its fame has been compounded by the fact that it has attained both cult status and phenomenal box-office success, with worldwide earnings reportedly in excess of one hundred million dollars. Its story line is slim, with an accent on action, notably battles involving the Oriental arts of self defense; the film is also marked by surprisingly strong production values and a capable cast, led by the indomitable Lee.

Appropriately, the film opens with a look at Lee in action, as he displays his pantherlike grace, coupled with deadly skill, during an exhibition. Cast simply as "Lee," a member of an Oriental temple, he is visited by a representative of an agency that "functions as gatherers of information—evidence upon which interested governments can act." Lee, who has been sought out because of his command of the martial arts, is asked to enter an upcoming tournament which will be held on an island fortress. The event's sponsor is Han (Shih Kien), who is suspected of dealing in white slavery and opium, and Lee is asked to locate evidence against him.

For Lee, the assignment is a vendetta. At one time, Han was a member of Lee's temple. By leaving it, Lee feels Han has insulted both the temple and its teachings. Most important, however, is the fact that Han's henchmen were responsible for the death of Su-Lin (Angela Mao Ying), Lee's sister.

En route to the island, which is located near Hong Kong, Lee comes in contact with fellow tournament hopefuls. Through a series of flashbacks delivered in lapse dissolve effects, the audience sees why the principal characters have chosen to participate. Roper (John Saxon), an American with a penchant for gambling, left the United States because of gambling debts totaling $175,000—and a bank account of only $64.43. Williams (Jim Kelly), an American black, had been involved in a fracas with bigoted police officers. For both Roper and Williams, therefore, the tournament provides temporary escape, with the added possibility of financial reward, should they win their bouts. Lee's flashback involves the beautiful Su-Lin, herself a martial arts expert, as she bravely battles to the death. Leading the horde of attackers against the diminutive young woman is Oharra (Bob Wall), Han's right-hand man. Before she dies, Su-Lin is able to scar Oharra's cheek.

Once at the island fortress, tournament participants are feted at an opulent, colorful banquet, complete with Sumo wrestlers. The event is brought to a dramatic, virtual standstill when Han, accompanied by a group of attractive women, makes his entrance. At Han's command, the women display remarkable and deadly dart-throwing skills. Lee recognizes one of the women as an operative for the agency that has hired him.

He is able to talk with the girl personally later that night, after Tania (Ahna Capri), Han's hostess, visits the guests to make sure they are comfortable. Among the pleasures she offers is women. Williams matter-of-factly chooses four women as companions for the night; Roper requests that Tania stay with him, and she is happy to oblige. Lee asks to see the young woman who threw the darts. His interest is strictly professional, and after being summoned to his room, the girl confesses that she has been unable to compile evidence against Han.

It remains for Lee to do the investigating, despite the fact that Han has issued orders that strictly forbid the guests from moving freely about the grounds. Lee's nighttime discoveries lead to a shaft which enters an underground chamber. After lowering himself inside, he locates opium-making facilities. His search is interrupted by the arrival of several guards, but they are overcome by the deft Lee.

Han retaliates the following day during tournament activities. At this point, the viewer has witnessed the considerable skills of Roper and Williams (Williams' style is labeled "unorthodox but effective"), but Lee's talents and reputation remain a mystery to the tournament contenders and Han's soldiers. Lee's skills fairly burst into view when he is paired in deadly battle against Oharra, who bears the ugly scar inflicted by Su-Lin. Although the menacing Oharra dwarfs Lee, Lee moves swiftly, with deadly aim. He culminates the battle by stomping Oharra to death in front of a startled crowd, satisfying his own vengeance. The gory scene, with its combined acrobatics, balletlike beauty, and undeniable violence, gives credence to Lee's statement about his fighting style, "you can call it the art of fighting without fighting."

Following the day's startling competition, Williams is summoned to Han's office. There Han reveals that his tournaments are actually fronts to find salesmen to peddle his illegal wares. "Man, you come right out of a comic book," says a disbelieving Williams. Unwilling to work for Han, Williams then comes up against Han's martial arts prowess. Caught off-guard by a blow from the steel hand worn by Han, Williams is killed. Han next introduces Roper to his illegal operations. On a tour of the underground facilities, Roper is witness to the manufacture of opium, as well as the enslavement of young women who are being forced into drug addiction. Han also escorts Roper through a bizarre, museumlike hall which showcases various vicious murder implements, including a number of "attachments" for Han's hand. Roper shows little emotion during the tour, but he shows his basic goodness when he rescues a cat from death by a guillotine in the museum. After seeing the mutilated body of Williams, he turns against Han, insisting he will never align himself with him.

Through Roper, Lee learns of the workings of Han's organization. Convinced he has the evidence he needs, he decides to send word to the agency, which has promised retaliatory troops. To get a message through, Lee must get into Han's "control room." He accomplishes the mission by slipping a cobra into the room. After the frightened attendants flee, Lee sends word.

Afterward, he is confronted by Han's men—literally dozens of them—all of whom Lee successfully and incredulously battles. The entire island then becomes a battleground after Lee sets free legions of men who have been unjustly imprisoned by Han (they are described as "the refuse found in waterfront bars"). Han's prisoners, clad in black, battle his soldiers, who ironically wear white. Roper is among those battling Han's soldiers.

The inevitable battle between Lee and Han follows. It is a grueling, drawn-out affair during which Han (unfairly) replaces his steel hand with a "claw." After a flurry of lightning-fast moves, the claw leaves its mark across Lee's face and bare chest. Prior to a last angry assault, Lee runs his fingers across his wounds. After bringing them to his mouth and dramatically tasting his own blood, he lashes out against Han. The fight, which has taken place in Han's unsettling exhibit hall, comes to an end as Han is impaled on one of his own spears. At film's end, Lee and Roper are the only principals to have survived the bloody melee. The final seconds are devoted to a lingering close-up of the insidious claw worn by Han.

With its liberal dose of blood and gore, along with its rather tawdry qualities, including the white slavery subplot, *Enter the Dragon* is a decidedly exploitative work; however, under the taut direction of Robert Clouse, who has wisely chosen to emphasize action and Lee's role, the film emerges as a polished work. For fans of its genre, it is highly diverting, and the martial arts encounters which form the basis of the film are carried out with imaginative flair. One of the film's most intriguing scenes takes place in a hall of mirrors, during the battle between Lee and Han, which has the antagonist as well as the viewer confused by the multi-image effect. This stunningly-photographed sequence was obviously copied from the mirror funhouse scene of Orson Welles's *Lady from Shanghai*, (1948), but with a clever twist. *Enter the Dragon* also blatantly borrows from other films, including the James Bond series, for in addition to Lee's super-agent status, Han carries a white persian cat, imitative of Bond's archvillain, Ernst Stavro Blofeld. Since directing *Darker than Amber* in 1970, Clouse has come to be known for his fast-paced action films, and in fact has called himself "the poor man's [Sam] Peckinpah." In *Enter the Dragon*, he proves himself particularly adept at showcasing martial arts battles.

Although the film's characterizations are meager, performances are adequate. Saxon, who portrays Roper, has long been underrated, despite his convincing portrayals (often as the heavy, because of his dark, rather sinister good looks), which have been relegated mostly to "B"-pictures. Kelly, in his acting debut as Williams, also proves suitable, coming to the role after establishing himself as a martial arts expert (he was International Middleweight Karate Champion of 1971).

The indisputable highlight of the film, however, is Lee. Hardly an imposing figure in terms of size, with no commanding ability in dialogue delivery (in fact, he speaks with a slight lisp), Lee nevertheless possesses a charismatic screen presence. Audience response to a Lee performance is probably highest when he lets loose one of his famed shrieks (signifying impending attack), and soars across the screen, displaying his prowess with karate, judo, hapkido, tai-chih, or kung fu.

Lee's death of an edema (swelling) of the brain came at the height of his career, thus assuring his cult status, as well as enduring rumors regarding the cause of his death. Ironically, the man who by his very name defined the martial-arts genre was an American by birth, a one-time waiter in a Chinese restaurant and a 4-F army reject.

Lee's credits include a string of Hong Kong-produced films, often made for famed Oriental producer Raymond Chow, including *Fists of Fury* (1972) and *The Chinese Connection* (1973). He also appeared as Kato in the 1966 ABC-television series, *The Green Hornet*. Lee, who staged the impressive fight sequences for *Enter the Dragon*, also supervised stunts and karate sequences in American feature films, including *Marlowe* and *The Wrecking Crew* (both in 1969).

Years after his death, the Lee legend persists. Numerous martial arts films have attempted to summon up the Lee presence, including *The Black Dragon Revenges the Death of Bruce Lee* (released in London in 1979). Perhaps the most peculiar "Bruce Lee film" is *Game of Death*. Released six years after Lee's death, the film contains fight footage of the actual Lee, but story line sequences utilize two Lee look-alikes. Films such as this one give impetus to the various Lee myths, especially the one that proclaims that Lee still lives. For the uninitiated, the proliferation of martial arts films which boast actors whose names are similar to Lee's and whose faces and actions are almost identical to the original causes confusion and furthers the myth that the actor Bruce Lee and the character performing his type of part are one and the same.

Pat H. Broeske

EXECUTIVE SUITE

Released: 1954
Production: John Houseman for Metro-Goldwyn-Mayer
Direction: Robert Wise
Screenplay: Ernest Lehman; based on the novel of the same name by Cameron Hawley
Cinematography: George J. Folsey
Editing: Ralph E. Winters
Running time: 104 minutes

Principal characters:
McDonald Walling .... William Holden
Mary Blemond Walling .... June Allyson
Julia O. Treadway .... Barbara Stanwyck
Loren Phineas Shaw .... Fredric March
Frederick Y. Alderson .... Walter Pidgeon
Eva Bardeman .... Shelley Winters
Josiah Walter Dudley .... Paul Douglas
George Nyle Caswell .... Louis Calhern
Jesse Q. Grimm .... Dean Jagger
Erica Martin .... Nina Foch

The film *Executive Suite* introduced a new direction in post-Depression era success or corruption stories. American audiences had grown familiar with the stories of individuals born into families ravaged by economic chaos who, with intelligence and hard work, rose to success. Unlike the cynical examination of one man's rise to success and power such as Orson Welles's *Citizen Kane* (1941), *Executive Suite* concerns a team of men. This new theme was consistent with the shape of big business two decades after the Depression. Seldom before had there been a motion picture that had exploited the rivalries and the jockeying for position among the highest executives of American corporate business as in this film.

Ernest Lehman wrote the screenplay, based on a Cameron Hawley novel. Hawley had been the advertising director of the Armstrong Cork Company in Pennsylvania until he left his job, apparently, to write the book. The novel offered the reader an inside look at the workings of big business. After Metro-Goldwyn-Mayer acquired the screen rights, producer John Houseman enlisted the directional talents of Robert Wise and amassed a crowded billing of big-name stars. Houseman's previous hits, *The Bad and the Beautiful* (1952) and *Julius Caesar* (1953), were also made with large star casts, and it was all part of a relatively new Hollywood trend designed to increase box-office potential in the new television age.

In the opening scenes, the president of Treadway Corporation, Avery Bullard, having sent a telegram calling for a 6:00 P.M. Executive Board meeting, walks out of the office and promptly falls down dead. Although Treadway is a fifty-year-old company and America's third largest manufacturer of fine furniture, Bullard had been running a one-man operation and had never appointed an Executive Vice President. Suddenly, the one-man company is left without its one man, and the situation sets off a competitive search for a successor among the Board of Directors. The ensuing drama brings together seven diverse personalities, and virtually all of the action occurs within a twenty-four-hour period between two 6:00 P.M. meetings.

The audience is introduced to the directors at the meeting originally called for by the deceased president. George Caswell (Louis Calhern) is the cynical member. He had witnessed Bullard's death and immediately ordered his broker to sell the bulk of his Treadway stock short before the market closed; he thinks that he will make a huge profit when he buys it back after the price drops. Fred Alderson (Walter Pidgeon) is an old, seasoned Vice President. He was around from the beginning and helped to build the company as Bullard's right-arm man. Another old-timer, Production Manager Jesse Grimm (Dean Jagger), originally built the factory. He is now disheartened, and, had Bullard been present, he would have resigned at the meeting. Walter Dudley (Paul Douglas) is Chief of Sales, and a rather ineffectual person who is threatened by his position. He is having an affair with his secretary, Eva (Shelley Winters). Julia Treadway (Barbara Stanwyck), whose father founded the company, is the major stockholder. Threatening to dispose of her holdings has been the only way she could capture the attention of Bullard, with whom she had been in love for many years, although they never married. Loren Shaw (Fredric March) and Don Walling (William Holden) are the two most fully-developed characters. Shaw is the champion efficiency expert who devotes himself to convenience and improved earnings. The young Chief of Design and Development, Don Walling, is the spokesman for corporate morality. He wants to rebuild the earliest dreams of the company: to make the best product.

The plot proceeds rapidly. It is revealed to the viewer that Loren Shaw is fighting the most aggressively for the top position. Shaw is mechanical and conniving; he understands each man's weaknesses and he plays on them. Because of his unsympathetic yet efficient actions, Treadway lost no money after Bullard's death. George Caswell, therefore, lost a great deal by selling his stock. Shaw knows this and buys Caswell's vote with a promise of a large stock gift. He knows about Walt Dudley's affair with Eva, and, with an unstated threat of exposure, secures Dudley's vote as well. In another display of conniving, he gives fatherly sympathy to the distraught Julia Treadway and obtains her proxy. The others are vehemently opposed to his obvious aspiration, but cannot find another nomination.

It becomes understood that Fred Alderson is a perennial second man. He has always been number two, and is by his nature of that caste; he knows that Avery Bullard never considered him as a candidate. Don Walling maintains ideological contentions that are similar to Alderson's, and the two men band together. They fail to make a candidate of Jesse Grimm when they learn of his intention to resign, and they soon discover that Shaw has manipulated their second choice, Walter Dudley. Don Walling, the obvious choice from the start, is the only man left. Grimm, who does not like Walling, supports him to prevent the election of Loren Shaw. Walling has an argument with the indifferent Miss Treadway, and, for the first time ever, she appears at the six o'clock meeting. Without her proxy, Shaw's three votes are not enough to elect. In the end, Don Walling's passionate, idealistic oration wins Julia's approval, and her vote elects him, while causing the corporate demise of Mr. Shaw.

The fast-paced, highly involved plot is emblematic of the production's overall slickness. George Folsey's cinematography is unobtrusive, merely recording each portrait of a conversation, and it was nominated for an Oscar. There is neither a musical score nor any vigorous action, making the production rely almost entirely on the dialogue and the actors' abilities to pull it off. Dramatically, the film is fairly successful. March's portrayal of Loren Shaw, subtle and unnerving, commands attention throughout the film. Calhern also offers a notable performance. Nina Foch, Stanwyck, Holden, and Pidgeon give very adequate performances as well, but, like many star-studded films, the script does not live up to the actor's dramatic capabilities. In this way, the film is shallow. Don Walling's less-than-believable speech on quality and employee self-respect is anticlimactic, as the viewer had heard it all through the film. The female characters typify embarrassingly empty personalities, and the part of Walling's wife, as played by June Allyson, seems an unnecessary addition to the film. The only acting nomination by the Motion Picture Academy, however, did come to one of the women, Foch, in a supporting role.

As predicted by the studio and the producer, the film was a relative hit at the box office. More important, it set the stage for a growing interest in group, or team, dramas. It also prepared the way for a number of mid-1950's "corporate" dramas of a similar ilk such as *A Woman's World* (1954) and *Patterns* (1956), which further explored power struggles, business scruples, and the American executive. In 1976, an unsuccessful television series based on *Executive Suite* was produced by Stanley Rubin and Norman Felton.

Ralph Angel

THE EXORCIST

Released: 1973
Production: William Peter Blatty for Warner Bros.
Direction: William Friedkin
Screenplay: William Peter Blatty (AA); based on his novel of the same name
Cinematography: Owen Roizman and Billy Williams
Editing: Jordan Leondopoulos, Bud Smith, Evan Lottman, and Norman Gay
Sound: Robert Knudson and Chris Newman (AA)
Running time: 121 minutes

 Principal characters:
  Chris MacNeil .... Ellen Burstyn
  Regan MacNeil .... Linda Blair
  Father Damien Karras .... Jason Miller
  Father Merrin .... Max von Sydow
  Lieutenant Kinderman .... Lee J. Cobb
  Burke Dennings .... Jack MacGowran

The 1970's was the decade of the blockbuster, as movies from *The Godfather* (1972) to *Star Wars* (1977) completely rewrote the definition of a financially successful film. Grosses of over $100,000,000 became, if not exactly commonplace, at least no longer unheard of. *The Exorcist*, released late in 1973, was one of the first cinematic blockbusters. However, whereas *The Godfather* attracted its audiences on the strength of the acting of Marlon Brando and Al Pacino and a richly textured plot involving organized crime—a traditional source of fascination for American moviegoers—and whereas *Star Wars* took advantage of its dazzling special effects and a resurgence of interest in science fiction, *The Exorcist* captured its audience's imagination with a bit of orthodox (albeit esoteric) Christian theology and a lot of pure horror. It concerned the exorcism of demonic spirits from the body of a possessed child.

Based on the hugely successful novel of the same name by William Peter Blatty, *The Exorcist* was in many ways presold; by the time the movie was released, five million copies of the novel had been sold. Blatty produced the film and wrote the screenplay, which followed the outline of his novel closely, and his friend William Friedkin directed. Aided by some gruesome special effects, these men, together with young actress Linda Blair, put together a horrific masterpiece. The film's fans may have been badly frightened or even physically nauseated by *The Exorcist*, but they certainly were not disappointed.

The film opens innocently enough at an archaeological dig in Iraq, supervised by Father Merrin (Max von Sydow), a scholarly Jesuit. The first hint that something unusual is afoot occurs with the discovery of a small, gargoylelike statuette. Suddenly, an eerie wind begins to blow, and dogs begin fighting among themselves. Although it will be a while before the precise nature of the ancient evil manifests itself, Blatty and Friedkin have made it clear in the film that a demonic force has been loosed upon the world.

The scene shifts to Washington, D.C., and the lives of actress Chris MacNeil (Ellen Burstyn) and her twelve-year-old daughter Regan (Linda Blair). A divorcée, Chris leads a relatively unglamorous life despite her acting profession, and Regan is a bright, attractive young girl. Chris's closest friend is her director, Burke Dennings (Jack MacGowran), and both are casually acquainted with a number of Jesuit priests from nearby Georgetown University, one of whom is Father Damien Karras (Jason Miller), a psychologist whose job it is to counsel his fellow priests who feel that they are losing their vocation. Ironically, Father Karras is himself in the midst of a crisis of faith. Exhausted from sharing the burdens of others, Karras will soon face an even more strenuous test: he will be called upon to confront the incarnation of the devil himself.

The demon enters the MacNeils' lives subtly at first. Soon, however, the mysterious noises in the attic and the inexplicable open windows give way to a more disturbing phenomenon. Regan begins to act strangely. At one of Chris's dinner parties, Regan enters in bedclothes, urinates on the floor in front of the guests, and tells Burke that he is going to die. Horrified, Chris confronts her daughter in her bedroom after everyone has left only to discover that Regan is as puzzled and terrified by her behavior as is Chris. The filmmakers also introduce in this scene the first of their special effects for horror: as Chris attempts to comfort Regan, the bed upon which they are lying is racked with violent convulsions.

Regan's spells and seizures grow more uncontrollable, and Chris seeks medical assistance. A variety of doctors offer a variety of diagnoses, but none is able to help, and Chris despairs of convincing the doctors of the extraordinary nature of Regan's affliction. The once-pretty girl is growing more physically repulsive every day, and spends much of the time tossing violently in her bed, screaming gutteral obscenities.

Finally, however, a group of physicians at a psychiatric clinic begin to grope towards an accurate assessment of Regan's problem. Her symptoms, they say, match those of persons in primitive cultures who are believed to have been possessed by demons, and they suggest that an exorcism be performed on Regan. Furious, Chris declines to involve "witch doctors" in her search for a cure for her daughter. Meanwhile, Regan's prediction about Burke comes true; he is found dead outside the MacNeil's house. The police say that he was thrown from an upstairs window by a person of great strength. The only one in the house, however, has been the bedridden Regan.

Although Blatty and Friedkin have constructed a film that has been, up to this point, nerve-racking, they now turn the screws even tighter. The manifestation of Regan's possession becomes so grotesque that the film is almost painful to watch. One of *The Exorcist*'s most horrifying scenes occurs immediately after the psychiatric diagnosis of demonic possession. A crucifix has mysteriously appeared under Regan's pillow, and the by now horribly disfigured child begins to masturbate violently with it. The scene concludes with Regan spinning her head around a full 360 degrees several times in rapid succession, grinning hellishly all the while. That part of the audience which has not long since shut its eyes or simply left the theater is invariably left gasping for breath.

The incident causes Chris to abandon her initial skepticism about the diagnosis of demonic possession, and she takes her problem to Father Karras, who, though inclined to doubt Regan's possession, nevertheless agrees to see the child-monster. His interest intensifies when he is approached by Lieutenant Kinderman (Lee J. Cobb), who has been placed in charge of the Burke Dennings homicide investigation. Stating that the murder had ritualistic overtones, Kinderman asks the priest to watch for any of his flock who might be capable, physically and psychologically, of committing the murder. It soon becomes clear, first to Chris, then to Father Karras, and finally to Lieutenant Kinderman, that it was indeed Regan who killed the director.

Visits to Regan's bedside gradually convince the skeptical Karras that the girl is inhabited by a genuine demon. He is unimpressed by the physical manifestations of the possession, although these are both remarkable and revolting: the Regan-demon can reduce the room temperature at will, and spews bilious green vomit all over Karras. What is left of the real Regan writes "HELP ME" in angry red welts on the child-monster's abdomen. Instead, he is persuaded by the extensive knowledge of Catholic theology displayed by the demon that is using Regan as its mouthpiece. Karras requests permission from his superiors to conduct an exorcism. They agree and bring in an older priest, their most experienced exorcist, to assist him. Of course, this turns out to be Father Merrin, the archaeologist who had inadvertently released the demon in the first place.

Ironically, the exorcism itself turns out to be almost an anticlimax. Blatty and Friedkin merely offer a reprise of the grisly special effects that they have displayed throughout the film. Temperatures drop, bodies levitate, and vomit and curses spew forth as the demon fights with the holy men for possession of Regan's body and soul. The demon ultimately loses, but he exacts a price— both priests die during the exorcism. Regan, however, is made whole again, and, mercifully, remembers nothing of her ordeal.

The Exorcist must surely be the only R-rated film in history to have been made with the full cooperation of the Roman Catholic Church. Blatty and Friedkin assure us that, at least regarding the exorcism sequences, everything in the film is based on fact. The theological authenticity of the film, however, is largely beside the point. The impact of *The Exorcist* lies in its hideously realistic special effects and in the acting of the principals in the cast.

Ellen Burstyn, Jason Miller, and Linda Blair all garnered Academy Award nominations for their work on the film. Burstyn's Chris MacNeil is more the worried mother than the glamorous movie queen; she grows convincingly haggard as her daughter's ordeal is prolonged. Miller's Father Karras is a study in craggy intensity; driven at first by his loss of faith, and then, once his faith in God is restored, by the undeniable reality of the existence of the Devil and by the necessity of destroying this evil, Karras never has a moment's peace until he gives his life to save Regan's at the film's climax.

The most remarkable of the film's performances, however, is that of Linda Blair as Regan. A hitherto unknown twelve-year-old girl whose appearance in *The Exorcist* marked her acting debut, Blair was not asked to do much real acting. With the exception of the beginning and end of the film, when Regan appears as a normal child, the makeup men and special effects people take over the development of the character. Still, Blair deserves a good deal of credit for having survived the acting experience intact.

William Friedkin took Blatty's novel-turned-screenplay, which won an Academy Award, and transferred it to the screen virtually intact; and the impact of the film is undeniable. Friedkin melded the story, the actors, and the special effects into what must be described as a disgusting masterpiece. This seeming contradiction may account for the film's mixed reception by the critics; newspaper accounts at the time of *The Exorcist*'s release invariably mentioned that people in the audience literally became physically ill during some scenes, although curiously, this seemed only to add to the film's mystique. Some critics were outraged and said so emphatically. Others liked the film, and Hollywood gave *The Exorcist* its stamp of approval with ten Academy Award nominations and two awards (Best Screenplay and Best Sound). The ultimate judgment regarding *The Exorcist*, however, was rendered by its audiences who flocked to see it by the millions. Controversial though it may have been, it remains one of the cinema's all-time box-office moneymakers. The film spawned a host of imitators, including a disastrous sequel, and lifted horror films out of the realm of the B-movie and into big-budget respectability; but none of *The Exorcist*'s successors equalled the original, either in popularity or quality.

Robert Mitchell

A FACE IN THE CROWD

Released: 1957
Production: Elia Kazan for Warner Bros.
Direction: Elia Kazan
Screenplay: Budd Schulberg; based on his short story "Your Arkansas Traveler"
Cinematography: Harry Stradling and Gayne Rescher
Editing: Gene Milford
Running time: 125 minutes

> *Principal characters:*
> Lonesome Rhodes .... Andy Griffith
> Marcia Jeffries .... Patricia Neal
> Joey Kiely .... Anthony Franciosa
> Mel Miller .... Walter Matthau
> Betty Lou Fleckum .... Lee Remick
> J. B. Jeffries .... Howard Smith

Since the release of *A Face in the Crowd* in 1957, public events have continued to bear witness to the prescience of Elia Kazan and Budd Schulberg. The film is an exploration of the function of television in American society and was, as director Kazan has observed, "ahead of its time." At the time of its release, reception and reviews of the film ranged from positive to mixed to negative. Both its style and content were criticized as exaggerated. In terms of style, the film is in fact an uneasy combination of satire and melodrama. Its treatment of television, however, has proved to be far from exaggerated. Payola, TV quiz scandals, the book *The Selling of the President*, and a brief glance at the Top Ten shows in the Neilsen ratings attest to, if anything, the film's restraint in exploring television as a powerful and inevitably corrupt medium.

A Face in the Crowd portrays the birth, rise, and fall of a media "hero." During the hero's rise to fame, television as a vehicle for advertising and selling products and the manipulation of the medium for political purposes are dealt with; during his decline (which is abrupt) it is the power and intelligence of the American people which are affirmed. From the film, it is obvious that Kazan and Schulberg were convinced of the power of advertising and hopeful about the intelligence of the American viewing public when subjected to ad agencies' tactics.

This film was the second successful collaboration of writer Schulberg and director Kazan following the highly effective and Academy Award-winning *On the Waterfront* (1954). Kazan, as a veteran theater director, was an actor's director and comfortable with eliciting performances from actors; moreover, as he moved away from Hollywood studio productions, he was developing a fluid, highly realistic visual style. Schulberg had an eye for satire and had written about another fictional monster/victim of the world of entertainment; Sammy Glick in *What Makes Sammy Run?* Their combined skills in directing actors and creating characterizations, as well as shared attitudes toward their work (which caused them to spend months researching the domain of advertising), contribute to the impact of *A Face in the Crowd*. The film's satire is grounded firmly in reality, both visually and verbally.

The film was shot on location in Arkansas, Memphis, and New York City, following the trail of Lonesome Rhodes (Andy Griffith), the folksy media hero. The talents of "real" people in all the locales is utilized, including current television personalities. For the principal characters, Kazan looked mainly to Broadway for talent, and the film marked the successful screen debuts of Griffith, Lee Remick, and Anthony Franciosa. Patricia Neal returned to the screen for one of her best roles after a four-year absence from Hollywood.

The film is extremely well-structured and, in fact, in the first half hour contains all of the elements which will later be explored and amplified. We see flashes of the corruption and corruptibility of the unknown Lonesome Rhodes and the relationship among business, politics, and the media in a very small town. The structure of Piggott, Arkansas, and New York City are exactly the same; only their sizes are different.

Lonesome Rhodes is discovered in Piggott, Arkansas, by Marcia Jeffries (Patricia Neal), an Eastern college-educated woman who works for the radio station owned by her uncle, J. B. Jeffries (Howard Smith). Her businessman uncle not only owns the town radio station, but also the newspaper and the printing press. Larry Rhodes is in jail for drifting. Marcia puts him on her interview program on which he proves to be a seductive (in more ways than one) natural talent, playing the guitar, spouting folk tales and wisdom, and showing his identification with the lives of the "little" people. He rises to the top at KGRK; housewives are charmed into sending him cookies, while sponsors are charmed into buying time on his program. After Lonesome ridicules a candidate out of office on the air, he gets the glimmer of potential power in his eye. He is delighted to leave the small town for Memphis television with Marcia in tow, and she, who has been charmed by his "down-to-earth" qualities, gets her first clue that his raunchy ingenuousness might be but another aspect of his performing talent.

As the performing domain of Rhodes widens, so does the frenzy of the film increase. The pace quickens in Memphis as he perfects his "little people lost in the big city" act, derides his sponsors, and watches sales climb. He is sold to New York's highest bidder by a kindred spirit, an opportunist named Joey Kiely (Anthony Franciosa). Once in New York, on national television, Lonesome's powers as a shrewd manipulator of the medium come to full flower. He sells himself to the viewers, and he sells products. In several chilling montages we see the creation of Lonesome Rhodes as an institution: public relations tours, telethons, dedications, political events, and a marriage made in media heaven to a drum majorette. As Lonesome becomes increasingly attracted to the arena of right-wing politics, the contradictions inherent in his character and his position emerge. While masquerading as the folksy friend of the people, he drops a lot of bodies along the way, including an unmentioned first wife; a gullible young second wife; Marcia, the woman who gave him his start and organized his television programs; and various ulcer-prone television writers and ad executives.

Lonesome links up with the right-wing purveyors of a product which is an empty package: a political candidate with only a good profile who is looking for an image to attract the constituency which Lonesome describes as "rednecks, housewives, shut-ins, peapickers . . . everybody who's got to jump when somebody else blows the whistle." Marcia Jeffries blows the whistle on Lonesome by not pulling the plug while he is engaging in his usual post-broadcast derision of his loyal fans, the "trained seals who watch his program and listen to his advice." From that point on, he quickly falls to the bottom, ending at a political rally with no one in attendance except a few "little" people—the black waiters who are paid to be there.

If *A Face in the Crowd* ends in melodrama, it is nevertheless highly effective satire, exposing the actual workings of an industry which has continued to demand attention for sparse entertainment and high levels of abuse.

Connie McFeeley

FACES

Released: 1968
Production: Maurice McEndree for Continental
Direction: John Cassavetes
Screenplay: John Cassavetes
Cinematography: Al Ruban
Editing: Maurice McEndree
Running time: 130 minutes

Principal characters:
Richard Forst ....John Marley
Jeannie Rapp .... Gena Rowlands
Maria Forst .... Lynn Carlin
Chet .... Seymour Cassel
Stella ....,. Elizabeth Deering
Freddie ....Fred Draper

John Cassavetes is an American writer-director who is difficult to pigeon-hole into a specific style, theme, or influence. A very personal filmmaker, he has been described as the father of the American New Wave and variously as a maverick, renegade, and iconoclast. His intuitive, improvisational approach to film does not fit into the "system" of the motion picture industry; in fact, the industry avoids Cassavetes as much as Cassavetes avoids the industry. His films have been glowingly praised and voraciously panned, but it is impossible to come away from a Cassavetes film without feeling the emotional impact of what he puts on the screen. The ability to capture on screen the raw, exposed nerve endings of daily life and the uncanny facility for making actors come "alive" are Cassavetes' greatest attributes as a direc-tor. Cassavetes insists that he is "basically not a director," but adds that "I'm a man who believes in the validity of a person's inner desires," and goes on to explain that his purpose as a writer-director is to get on the screen those varied human emotions no matter how "ugly or beautiful" and to have audiences respond to them for the reality they possess.

Cassavetes was born in New York City on December 9, 1929, and is of Greek heritage. He attended Colgate University, where the plays of Robert E. Sherwood inspired him to study acting at the American Academy of Dra-matic Art in New York City. After graduating from the AADA in 1953 (where he met his wife, actress Gena Rowlands), he acted in television and in films. His screen credits as an actor have included *Edge of the City* (1957), *The Killers* (1964), *The Dirty Dozen* (1967), *Rosemary's Baby* (1968), *Brass Target* (1979), and roles in such productions of his own as *Husbands* (1970), *Minnie and Moskowitz* (1971), and *Opening Night* (1978).

Cassavetes' writing-directing debut occurred in 1960 with *Shadows*, and in the years since, he has directed only eight more films. *Shadows*, which remains his favorite film, and which received the Critics Award at the Venice Film Festival, is a *cinéma vérité* rites of passage depiction of three orphaned blacks. *Too Late Blues* (1961), a commercial spin-off of *Shadows* produced for Paramount and starring Bobby Darin and Stella Stevens, Cassavetes regards as a failure. His third film was *A Child Is Waiting* (1962) starring Burt Lancaster and Judy Garland, a semidocumentary about retarded children, which Stanley Kramer produced for United Artists from a script which Abby Mann wrote, based upon Cassavetes story idea. Cassavetes regards this film as a failure because of Kramer's sentimentalizing it via the editing.

Faces (1968) was Cassavetes' fourth film, and was followed by *Husbands*, the story of three married buddies who set out on a binge following the funeral of one of their good friends. The film starred Cassavetes' close friends Ben Gazarra and Peter Falk and is considered one of his best films. *Minnie and Moskowitz*, which Cassavetes calls his "entertainment" outing, chronicles an unconventional romance between a blonde WASP (Gena Rowlands) and a long-haired hippie who parks cars for a living (Seymour Cassel).

A Woman Under the Influence (1974) is probably Cassavetes' best film and contains one of the screen's most extraordinary female performances—that of Rowlands as a lower-middle-class housewife who has a mental breakdown. For this wonderful, inventive portrayal Rowlands received the National Board of Review of Motion Pictures Award and the Golden Globe as Best Actress of 1974. Cassavetes' next film was *Opening Night*, a compelling depiction of the disintegration of an alcoholic actress with another marvelous performance by Rowlands. The film, which could use some editing despite Cassavetes' reluctance to do so, earned praise at the Berlin Film Festival but failed to gain a wide release in the United States. His 1980 film *Gloria*, again starring Rowlands, is probably his most financially successful film.

All of Cassavetes' films deal with emotional alienation in modern society and a (often subconscious) desire to change one's life, break out of the emptiness of life and gain emotional freedom. This search is the crux of *Faces*— which, simplified, is the story of two middle-class, middle-aged marrieds who endeavor to overcome the hollowness of their marital existence through infidelity. It is Cassavetes' rejection of the dull, phony convention of modern life and not without its own sense of prescience in that this film was made several years before it became fashionable to participate in "open marriage."

Faces is a two-hour-and-ten-minute film which took eight months to make and nearly four years to edit, after Cassavetes' first cut ran six hours. The film cost an incredibly meager $200,000 and was shot mostly in the Cassavetes' own home. Its leading characters, Richard Forst (John Marley) and his wife Maria (Lynn Carlin), are veterans of a childless, fourteen-year marriage. Both are fed up with the superficial pretense of their lives and yet see little they can do to change it constructively. Forst is a successful television producer, and he and his wife live in middle-class luxury bored with the emptiness and banality of their existence.

Forst leaves work one evening and goes to a bar with a male companion where they pick up a call-girl named Jeannie Rapp (Gena Rowlands) and there begins a thirty-six-hour disintegration of a marriage. Forst and his friend Freddie accompany Jeannie to her apartment where they obscure their sexual desire behind silly jokes and sillier songs ("I Dream of Jeannie") until Freddie snidely refers to Jeannie as a cheap pick-up and leaves.

While the attraction between Forst and Jeannie is mutual, he also leaves and goes home to his wife. Their confrontation over dinner and an aborted attempt at lovemaking is likewise veiled in endless jokes, neither of them saying what they mean until finally Forst exclaims, "I want a divorce," and returns to the bar where he had picked up Jeannie. From the bar he telephones Jeannie who is by now entertaining several friends of both sexes. Forst joins them and ends up spending the night with Jeannie.

In the meantime Maria has joined several of her friends for a night of dancing, during which they pick up a congenial, aging surfer-gigolo named Chet (Seymour Cassel), who, like the middle-aged women, is searching for an emotional haven. They all make fools of themselves vying for his sexual favors, and Maria invites them all back to her home. One of the most poignant scenes occurs when Stella (Elizabeth Deering), an overweight "Jewish mother" type of woman, embraces Chet and begs him to take her home. He does so but returns to spend the night with Maria.

Throughout these obviously clichéd happenings, Cassavetes reveals the pain and anxiety of each of his characters by focusing his hand-held camera endlessly on his actors—their faces—in focus and then distorted. He focuses on their hands and legs, capturing all of their embarrassing and pathetically vulnerable body language, groping with his lens on them as they grope for their lives. All the while the camera is peeling off their façades, layer by layer, to expose their real faces underneath. One of Cassavetes' directorial credos is that while his scripts are written, the "acting" is not. He instructs his actors by saying, "Listen, we've got to go further and we've got to go underneath." It is this probing camera which lifts Cassavetes' rather ordinary situations into emotionally moving theatrical experiences. Just when we think the camera has stayed too long on one shot or one actor, something marvelous and spontaneous occurs which makes the wait worthwhile.

The film ends the next morning after both husband and wife have committed adultery. Chet is trying to revive an almost catatonic Maria, who in guilt over her indiscretion has taken an overdose of sleeping pills. Chet manages to revive her, then hears Forst returning home, and with the comic flourish of a swashbuckler, jumps out the window of the one-story house and races across the lawn—but not before Forst sees his departure. The final scene shows both husband and wife sitting on the staircase in embarrassed silence. Cassavetes seems to indicate that somehow there is communication between the two because somehow they are survivors.

The hallmark of *Faces* is the excellent ensemble acting. Marley as Forst received the Best Actor Award at the Venice Film Festival, and Rowlands gives another of her wonderfully vulnerable performances as Jeannie the prostitute. Carlin, here making her acting debut, is exquisite—a cross between the graceful beauty of Loretta Young and the sensuousness of Ava Gardner.

The film provides no answers regarding marriage. In fact, Cassavetes said it best in an interview: "I don't know anything about marriage at all. I've been married a long time. But I don't know anything about marriage. I don't know anyone who does."

Ronald Bowers

A FAMILY AFFAIR

Released: 1937
Production: Lucien Hubbard and Samuel Marx for Metro-Goldwyn-Mayer
Direction: George B. Seitz
Screenplay: Kay Van Riper; based on the play *Skidding* by Aurania Rouverol
Cinematography: Lester White
Editing: George Boemler
Running time: 69 minutes

Principal characters:
Judge James Hardy	Lionel Barrymore
Andy Hardy	Mickey Rooney
Mrs. Hardy	Spring Byington
Marion Hardy	Cecilia Parker
Joan Hardy	Julie Haydon
Bill Martin	Allen Vincent
Wayne Trant	Eric Linden
Polly Benedict	Margaret Marquis

A Family Affair was the first of the Andy Hardy films, which were popular in the 1930's and 1940's. They portrayed that era's ideal America: small-town life, a close-knit family, the virtues of honesty and perserverance, and, most importantly, justice triumphant in the end. Plots varied throughout the series as Andy grew up and went away to college, but the films always featured the light comedy of Andy's romantic misadventures set against a story of Judge Hardy's integrity in the face of political expediency.

A Family Affair opens in Carvel, California, whose population is twenty-five thousand. Three of the town's most powerful men (the head of a local engineering firm, the editor of the town newspaper, and Judge Hardy's campaign manager) confront Judge James Hardy (Lionel Barrymore) in his chambers. They are angry because he has granted a restraining order against the new thirty-million-dollar aqueduct that is about to be built near Carvel. The three argue that the aqueduct will be a tremendous boon to the area's economy in this, the Depression, and that the Judge is hurting Carvel by not letting the construction proceed. Judge Hardy listens patiently and then calmly explains that, according to the law, he had no choice about signing the restraining order, since legitimate litigation is pending. Not satisfied by his explanation, the three men threaten the Judge with a challenge to his reelection in the next primary, but he remains unperturbed. Judge Hardy is the film's anchor, and director George B. Seitz wastes no time in establishing his character. In the opening scene we learn of his professional integrity and of the powerful sense of self-confidence that enables him to retain his serenity in the face of adversity, something that will be tested throughout the film.

At the Hardy home, the news is that daughter Marion Hardy (Cecilia Parker) is coming home after a year at college, and the family will be reunited again. Teenage son Andy (Mickey Rooney) still lives at home, and another daughter, Joan (Julie Haydon), is married to Bill Martin (Allen Vincent). As we soon learn, however, all is not well between Bill and Joan. Outside the Hardy home, Bill tells Joan that their marriage is finished, and Joan must go to the Hardy reunion dinner alone. Andy has a problem too, albeit a considerably less serious one. His mother insists that he attend a party, whereby he complains, "Holy jumpin' Jerusalem, a party with girls?" Marion, meanwhile, has met a young man named Wayne Trant (Eric Linden) on the train to Carvel, and the two are quite smitten with each other. Marion agrees to see Wayne after the dinner, although she is a bit nervous about introducing to her parents a man with whom she has spent an unchaperoned train ride.

The dinner commences, with Joan making an excuse for Bill's absence. Marion introduces Wayne to the family, and although Mrs. Hardy (Spring Byington) is a bit uneasy over the story of their train ride, Judge Hardy calms her fears, and the young man makes a good impression. He has come to Carvel, it develops, to work on the new aqueduct. Thus the filmmakers place additional moral pressure on the Judge, since his decision to delay construction on the aqueduct will now have a direct effect on a member of his own family. He keeps this knowledge to himself for the time being, however, to avoid spoiling his family's evening.

Andy's troubles appear to deepen when his mother volunteers him as an escort for Polly Benedict (Margaret Marquis), a girl whom he has not seen since grade school, to the party he is already attending with great reluctance. Andy is a well-meaning but overexuberant young man in his early teens. Although his problems are real enough to him, they are absurdly trivial compared to the difficulties faced by the other Hardys. Director Seitz uses his overreactions to provide comic relief from the film's more serious moments. It is a dispirited Andy Hardy who arrives at Polly Benedict's doorstep. His spirits lift, however, when she answers his knock. During her years away from Carvel, she has grown into a lovely young lady, and Andy is quite taken with her.

Meanwhile, at the Hardy home, Joan breaks down, announcing that she and Bill are separating. He had been neglecting her, she explains, and she went with a male friend to a dive called the Blue Rabbit Inn, where, after drinking too much champagne, the pair began necking. It was just a harmless flirtation, she swears, and it went no further, but Bill found out about the incident and is insisting on a divorce. Although Joan apologizes to her parents for bringing this trouble upon them, the Hardys are very supportive. "What's a mother and father for if they can't stand by in times of trouble," asks the Judge. Although his own problems are escalating, Judge Hardy is still able to offer comfort to his family.

Just how serious his political problems are is revealed by the headline on the next morning's newspaper, which reveals a move by outraged citizens to have the Judge impeached. Hardy remains calm, preferring to tease Andy about the lipstick on his collar, but the situation is clearly deteriorating. By the end of the day, he has been offered a bribe to withdraw his restraining order against the aqueduct (he angrily throws the man out of his office), and the only ones in town left on his side are his family and his campaign manager, who has decided to stick with the Judge even though his instinct tells him that the Judge's stubborn integrity may mean political suicide for both of them.

Support for the Judge's position begins to erode even within his own family, as illustrated in the next few scenes. Marion and Wayne, parked on a country road, argue about her father's role in blocking construction on the aqueduct. Although Marion at first takes her father's side, she realizes how much Wayne means to her and vows to persuade the Judge to relent. Meanwhile, Polly Benedict's father has refused to let his daughter see Andy on account of the Judge's controversial decision, and the Hardys' neighbors will not speak to the Judge as he walks down the street. Andy and Marion both confront their father, who insists that he is only doing his duty, which is to carry out the law. Marion calls him an old fogey and leaves the room in tears, but Andy, although younger, is more reasonable. He agrees to read the Judge's oath of office and consider the matter. After mulling over the implications of the oath, Andy is persuaded that his father is right.

The sternest test of the Judge's willingness to stand behind his convictions comes when the editor of the town newspaper finds out about Joan's marital difficulties. He threatens to print the story of Joan's escapades at the Blue Rabbit Inn unless Judge Hardy lifts his restraining order against the aqueduct. Once again, however, the Judge stands firm. Despite all of the adversity besetting him and his family, including Joan's discovery that she is pregnant with her estranged husband's child, the Judge remains relentlessly good-humored and optimistic, assuring everyone concerned that all will work out for the best.

The film's denouement begins later that night when Judge Hardy receives a mysterious phone call. He leaves a note ordering his wife and Joan to appear at the political convention being held the next day (at which the Judge's renomination for office is being contested), but offering no explanation for his disappearance. He then visits Joan's husband Bill. Again offering no explanation, he asks Bill to accompany him on an urgent mission relating to the aqueduct, and Bill reluctantly agrees to come.

At the convention the next day, his opponent's nomination is cheered wildly, but when the Judge's campaign manager attempts to defend the Hardy record, his efforts are met with boos and catcalls—both about the aqueduct and about the incident at the Blue Rabbit Inn, which has been published in the newspaper in a thoroughly distorted manner. Joan and Mrs. Hardy sit cringing through the whole process.

Suddenly Judge Hardy strides through the crowd, takes the floor, and forces the crowd to listen. He exposes the newspaper's blackmail attempt, and, in a dramatic moment, produces Joan's husband Bill, who embraces his wife and denies that they are about to get a divorce. Then the Judge turns to the matter of the aqueduct. It turns out that the previous night's mysterious phone call was from a respected firm of geologists in Denver. Their intensive study of the plans for the aqueduct reveal it to be nothing more than an elaborate attempt to divert all of Carvel's water to a large California city, leaving Carvel and its sister towns literally high and dry and bringing economic ruin to the entire area. Amid cheers, Judge Hardy makes the restraining order against the aqueduct permanent, and he is renominated to the judgeship by acclamation as his political enemies stand by helplessly.

In the final scene, the entire family crowds around the Judge, their problems solved. Joan and Bill are reunited; Polly Benedict rushes up to apologize to Andy; and the Judge assures Wayne Trant that the state legislature will soon pass a law authorizing the construction of a legitimate aqueduct program on which Wayne will be able to work. By doing his duty and standing up for what he believes in, Judge Hardy has brought about a happy ending.

A Family Affair is undeniably simplistic in many respects, but its obvious sincerity allows it to rise above the level of cliché. Many of the characters are stock types which function more as symbols than as real people, but two of them stand out. Barrymore is outstanding as Judge James Hardy. He constantly projects an image of warmth, serenity, and optimism and is eminently believable as the film's pillar of strength. It is Andy Hardy, however, who caught the audience's imagination; and, although Rooney's part in *A Family Affair* is a relatively small one, he plays it for all it is worth. His "gee-whiz," slightly off-center portrayal of the almost All-American Boy became the prototype for many comic adolescent heroes, from Henry Aldrich to Beaver Cleaver.

As the Andy Hardy series developed, Lewis Stone replaced Barrymore as the stern but loving Judge Hardy, and Andy's misadventures came to dominate the films. The basic theme, however, remained the same: the American family pulling together and winning. Ultimately, *A Family Affair* is the cinematic equivalent of Norman Rockwell's *Saturday Evening Post* covers—an idealized reflection of an era when the virtues of hearth and home were defended unquestioningly. The Academy of Motion Picture Arts and Sciences, recognizing the strengths that the Andy Hardy series embodied, gave the series a special Academy Award in 1942 "for its achievement in representing the American way of life."

Robert Mitchell

FANNY

Released: 1961
Production: Joshua Logan for Warner Bros.
Direction: Joshua Logan
Screenplay: Julius J. Epstein; based on the play of the same name by Joshua
  Logan and the French trilogy *Marius, Fanny,* and *César* by Marcel Pagnol
Cinematography: Jack Cardiff
Editing: William Reynolds
Music: Harold Rome
Running time: 133 minutes

Principal characters:
Fanny .... Leslie Caron
Panisse .... Maurice Chevalier
César .... Charles Boyer
Marius .... Horst Buchholz
Honorine .... Georgette Anys

The 1961 *Fanny* was the third filmed version of the same story. French novelist and director Marcel Pagnol first introduced the character of Fanny to the screen, along with her charming family and friends, in his classic trilogy about Marseilles made between 1931 and 1936: *Fanny, Marius,* and *César*. These films, adapted from Pagnol's plays of the same names, became very successful in France and were also highly acclaimed in the United States, where they continued to be shown in "art" film houses for more than two decades. In 1938, American director James Whale made yet another version, *Port of Seven Seas*; but the story was greatly changed and was almost unrecognizable as Pagnol's.

In 1954 Joshua Logan and S. N. Behrman wrote a Broadway musical of the story, with music and lyrics by Harold Rome. The play *Fanny* was a smash hit and inspired Logan to attempt another screen version of the Marseilles melodrama. Logan and screenwriter Julius Epstein went back to Pagnol's film for the new project, combining all three stories from thc trilogy into one film, *Fanny*. The new picture was not a musical, although Harold Rome's music was used as background. What finally emerged was something between Gallic sophistication and Hollywood romanticism. The cast was appropriately European, mostly French, with Maurice Chevalier and Charles Boyer as the two older gentlemen who are close to Fanny, and Leslie Caron and Horst Buchholz as the young couple, Fanny and Marius.

The story turns on the pathetic predicament of Fanny, the daughter of fishmonger Honorinc (Georgette Anys). She has been in love since childhood with Marius, the son of César. Marius is a handsome youth who helps his father in his small waterside café, but longs to go to sea and has made secret

arrangements to sail on a schooner bound for "the isles beneath the sea."
The sea is everywhere in the film: it is the setting for all of the characters'
lives; it is the enemy for Fanny and, ultimately, for Marius; and it provides
a livelihood for the residents of Marseilles. Fanny and Marius are deeply in
love as the film opens, but Marius is torn between his love for her and his
terrible aching for a life at sea. Counterpoised with the two lovers are their
parents and their friends of the waterfront, who offer them support and
advice. The night before Marius is to depart, he and Fanny confess their love
to each other and spend the night together. When morning comes, Marius
offers to stay behind and let his ship leave without him; but Fanny, knowing
he will never be happy on land, sends him away.

Marius' departure marks the end of the first "act" of the film. The second
part begins with Fanny's realization that she is going to have Marius' child.
César and Honorine do their best to console her, but Fanny is desolate.
Hearing of their plight, Panisse, a wealthy sail merchant and good friend of
both families, offers a way out. A lonely widower, he has always admired
Fanny and offers her marriage with the understanding that the child, if a son,
would bear his name and some day take over his business. At first César is
against the idea of his grandson having such an old father, but he reconsiders
when Honorine points out that the child may stand to inherit a very large
fortune some day. Fanny also reluctantly agrees to the plan. She respects
Panisse and knows that he is aware that she does not love him. The marriage
takes place, and several months later a son, Cesario, is born.

In the third and final part of the film, Fanny is confronted with her past.
A year goes by. Fanny is reasonably happy and has learned to care for Panisse,
for he is generous to her and the boy, making sure they want for nothing.
César acts as godfather and Uncle to Cesario, but is as close to him as a
grandfather would be. Then the inevitable happens and Marius returns home.
Completely disillusioned by his experiences at sea (his beloved isles turned
out to be volcanic ash), he seeks out his father who tells him of Fanny's new
life and warns him not to make trouble for the family of Panisse. When Marius
confronts Fanny while Panisse is away, she considers running off with him,
but soon realizes that they could never be happy that way. Embittered, Marius
leaves and finds a job as a garage mechanic in a nearby town.

Nine years pass. Cesario grows up fascinated by the sea, causing Fanny to
worry that he is his father all over again. A friend takes the boy to see Marius,
and they become great friends. When Fanny learns of this, she is furious and
confronts Marius. They find they still love each other, but Fanny will not
leave Panisse. After much persuasion by Cesario, Fanny invites Marius to the
boy's ninth birthday party. At the party, Panisse sees the affection that the
boy has for his natural father and also sees in Fanny's eyes that she still cares
for Marius. Panisse becomes very ill, and Fanny is truly worried that she will
lose him. He becomes worse and calls all of his friends, including Marius, to

his bedside. From his deathbed, the old man dictates a letter to César in which he asks Marius to marry Fanny when he is gone, and the film ends on this bittersweet note.

Fanny manifests great spirit and reverence for life. Although it is an American film, it has a distinct European flavor. There is overemphasis on broad comedy in some of the scenes and some rather stiff staging, but the truth of the characters that Pagnol created some thirty years ago still asserts itself, and the honesty of their emotions comes through. The acting is uniformly excellent, but does not always mesh well. Both Boyer and Chevalier, suave charmers in films for years, seem a bit out of place in Marseilles, especially Boyer as a saloon keeper. Chevalier is his own delightful self, and when pitted against the sullen behavior of Bucholz's Marius, it is a bit hard to understand Fanny's dilemma. Caron is radiant as Fanny. She had been exhibiting her gamin charm in American films since *An American in Paris* (1951), and brought a naturalness and warmth to the role of Fanny that made it her best performance since the 1958 Academy Award-winning *Gigi*. The film was well received by critics and brought Boyer an Oscar nomination for supporting actor. Although the familiar songs were missed by fans of the Broadway musical, the sound track of the original score at least evokes the atmosphere of Logan's play, and the beautiful cinematography of Jack Cardiff evokes the Marseilles waterfront to perfection. The one unfortunate result of the film was that the original Pagnol trilogy was withdrawn from circulation in America for many years, and only recently has it been possible to see it again in revival houses.

Joan Cohen

FAREWELL, MY LOVELY

Released: 1975
Production: George Pappas and Jerry Bruckheimer for Avco Embassy
Direction: Dick Richards
Screenplay: David Zelag Goodman; based on the novel of the same name by
   Raymond Chandler
Cinematography: John A. Alonzo
Editing: Walter Thompson and Joel Cox
Music: David Shire
Running time: 95 minutes

Principal characters:
Philip Marlowe .... Robert Mitchum
Helen Grayle/Velma .... Charlotte Rampling
Lieutenant Nulty .... John Ireland
Mrs. Florian .... Sylvia Miles
Moose Malloy .... Jack O'Halloran
Mr. Grayle ....Jim Thompson
Marriott .... John O'Leary
Amthor ....Kate Murtagh

In *Farewell, My Lovely*, director Dick Richards has successfully captured
the ambience of both the hard-boiled school of literature and the traditional
film noir. This 1975 film is the third adaptation of Raymond Chandler's famous
suspense novel. Coming after a B-budget adaptation with the series hero
"The Falcon" substituting for Philip Marlowe in Edward Dymytrk's brilliant
Murder, My Sweet (1944) thirty years earlier, *Farewell, My Lovely* might be
considered a remake. Fortunately, Dick Richards and screenwriter David
Zelag Goodman went to the original source material to develop their version.
What emerges is a successful interpretation of Chandler and a studied homage
to the era which produced this unique style of literature. In the film, Philip
Marlowe (Robert Mitchum), an aging Los Angeles private investigator, is
sought in connection with several murders. Meeting with the police, Marlowe
begins to tell the complex story of Moose Malloy and Velma. Answers to all
the police's questions are wound up in that story.

As soon as Malloy (Jack O'Halloran) gets out of prison, he stumbles upon
Marlowe and hires the private eye to find his ex-girl friend, Velma. The search
then leads Marlowe from the murder of a black nightclub owner to the widow
of Velma's ex-boss. The trail dries up at Camarillo State Hospital with a
woman Marlowe believes to be Velma. She is not. Marlowe then gets another
unusual job: accompanying Marriott (John O'Leary), an effeminate patsy,
on a wild-goose chase to recover a stolen jade necklace. This assignment
seems much simpler, but it is not; Marriott is murdered and Marlowe is
framed for the crime. He talks his way out of the charge and tries to find

Marriott's killer on his own. Marlowe looks up Mr. Grayle (Jim Thompson), a collector of jade, hoping to get a lead. Escalating coincidences link Marriott with Mrs. Grayle (Charlotte Rampling). After flirting with Marlowe, Mrs. Grayle also employs him, this time to find out who killed her friend Marriott. As if the story were not complex enough, Amthor (Kate Murtagh), a big-time Los Angeles madame, kidnaps Marlowe. It seems that she, like the police, is looking for Moose Malloy; but her methods are much less genteel than theirs. She resorts to drugs, and Marlowe is left in a room with a corpse to sleep off the effects.

Marlowe is eventually propositioned by nearly every influential character in the film in order to find Moose. He eventually does, and he sets up a meeting with the real Velma through the widow of her ex-boss. The whole meeting smells of double-cross and Marlowe begins to put the pieces together. Through the course of his unconventional investigation, Marlowe begins to suspect that Malloy and Marriott have something in common. That something turns out to be Velma, now known as Mrs. Grayle. She has moved up the social ladder and has been trying to put Malloy out of the way in order to keep her past hidden. The death of several incidental characters is of little consequence to Velma as long as her past is not exposed. In a final shoot-out onboard an offshore gambling ship, Velma kills Malloy and Marlowe shoots her in the stomach. Nearly every element of the novel is incorporated into this film. The weak romantic interplay between Marlowe and Mrs. Grayle's stepdaughter which gave John Paxton's screenplay of *Murder, My Sweet* a positive reinforcement (a romance which was not in the original novel) is not present in this recent version. Marlowe is presented as a middle-aged investigator who, although not perfect, is able to make a living by going through other people's trash.

The use of prostitution, vice, and corruption which was only hinted at in the earlier films is developed with a vengeance in *Farewell, My Lovely*; much of this atmosphere can be credited to an interest in simulating the aura of the *film noir*. A strong feeling of homage is present not only in the period settings but also in the situations and relationships developed in *Farewell, My Lovely*. One of the key elements which contributes to this *film noir*-type attitude was the selection of Robert Mitchum to portray Philip Marlowe. Placed in context, it is easy to link Mitchum with the *film noir*, in that many of his early successes came in such films as *Out of the Past* (1947) and *Macao* (1952). However, by the time of *Farewell, My Lovely*, Mitchum had replaced his boyish charisma and hulking physique for a "hound-dogged" expression and world-weariness which more aptly suits the character of the *film noir*. There is also a sense of *déjà vu* present in John Ireland's portrayal of Lieu-tenant Nulty, whose early career consisted mostly of roles in B-budget *films noir*.

Although she does not give the same sense of having been there before,

Charlotte Rampling plays the *femme fatale* to the hilt. Her screen presence is reminiscent of both Lauren Bacall and Lizabeth Scott. The characterization of the fatal woman is central to the development of the *film noir*. There is a certain decadence which follows a situation in which a woman is able to offer sexual identity which transcends middle-class restrictions. Rampling as Velma/Helen Grayle oozes with a sexual magnetism, so that it is not difficult to see how she could so thoroughly captivate a character like Moose Malloy. This ability to manipulate people, to make them respond without a sense of control, is also central to the *film noir* attitude.

Seen after *Chinatown* (1974) and *The Long Goodbye* (1973), *Farewell, My Lovely* is easier to place in line with the more traditional *film noir* moods and tone. In Robert Altman's *The Long Goodbye*, one of the more complex Chandler novels was brought to the screen. The setting, however, was contemporary and the milieu was typically Altman. The characterizations and situations did little to point out the basic existentialism of the novel; rather, the entire film maintained a dreamlike quality which overemphasized the negativism of the plot. Roman Polanski's *Chinatown* was cosmetically a homage to the *film noir* in its period setting, stiff dialogue, and grotesque characters; yet for all its association with the past, the tone of *Chinatown* is basically modern, the situations elliptical, and the logic of the characters not so much chaotic as decadently perverse. Gittes, the private eye hero, has the sense of emotional control that somehow never took root in classic *films noir*. *Farewell, My Lovely* falls somewhere in between these two films. A definite homage to the *film noir* era, the film does not flaunt its period settings. Whatever flashiness was found in *Chinatown* or whatever esoteric narrative structure was used in *The Long Goodbye*, neither approaches the mood of the *film noir* as successfully as *Farewell, My Lovely*. In this film, the characters and drama do not seem contrived; and no matter how unlikely the events of the plot might become, a suspension of disbelief is maintained.

Carl F. Macek

A FAREWELL TO ARMS

Released: 1932
Production: Paramount
Direction: Frank Borzage
Screenplay: Benjamin Glazer and Oliver H. P. Garrett; based on the novel
  of the same name by Ernest Hemingway
Cinematography: Charles Lang (AA)
Editing: Otho Lovering
Sound: Harold C. Lewis (AA)
Running time: 78 minutes

> *Principal characters:*
> Frederic Henry .... Gary Cooper
> Catherine Barkley .... Helen Hayes
> Major Rinaldi .... Adolphe Menjou
> Helen Ferguson .... Mary Philips
> The Priest .... Jack La Rue

Romance amid the chaos of World War I is the major theme of Frank
Borzage's screen version of Ernest Hemingway's novel *A Farewell to Arms*.
Unlike the original novel, which was a powerful indictment of war and its
effects upon the participants, the film is highly idealized and chooses to make
a statement through its dramatization of a touching love story. Yet some of
Hemingway's hardboiled realism of detail and the ultimate tragedy of the
characters' love temper the film's idealism and create a powerful picture of
love and war.

The behind-the-lines romance of Frederic Henry (Gary Cooper) and Catherine Barkley (Helen Hayes) begins as a casual meeting during an air raid.
This encounter does little to preface the romantic involvement they soon
share. Frederic's friend Rinaldi (Adolphe Menjou) is also attracted to Catherine and experiences some jealousy when Frederic begins to get serious
about her. Later, as an ambulance driver, Frederic is wounded and sent to
recuperate in a hospital in which Catherine is working. Rinaldi becomes
aware that Frederic's fascination with the nurse is more than a mere wartime
romance of little consequence. Rinaldi is also quick to realize that something
tragic may come of their love affair. This sentiment is also echoed by Catherine's friend, Helen Ferguson (Mary Philips), who tells Catharine and Frederic that they will never marry. To her, love is merely an illusion; fighting and
dying are the only realities.

After Frederic returns to the front, Catherine leaves her post at the hospital
and sets up residence in a Swiss village near the Italian border. She is pregnant
and feels it is best to live alone in a small flat rather than face the authorities
and expose Frederic to almost certain punishment. The lovers write letters

which, for one reason or another, are never delivered. Worried that something may have happened to Catherine, Frederic deserts his post and returns to the hospital in an attempt to be reunited with her. Catherine is not there and his search for her is hampered by Ferguson, who hates Frederic for making her friend pregnant. His continued absence without leave causes Frederic to face charges of desertion if he is ever captured.

Rinaldi, meanwhile, finds his old friend and tells him that Catherine is in Switzerland. Frederic makes his way without delay to Switzerland by boat from Italy. There he finds that Catherine, because of complications of her pregnancy, is dying. He arrives too late to help either her or their child; the baby is stillborn and Catherine is beyond help. Her death comes almost at the moment of armistice. Frederic is heartbroken; the pain of this loss is too great to bear. He speaks to her as she dies, hoping against hope that she will live. He proclaims his love for her, a love that will transcend her death, and she dies in his arms.

As the first Hemingway novel to be turned into a film, *A Farewell to Arms* is distinguished on several levels. The most obvious element of this sentimental film is the ensemble acting of Gary Cooper, Helen Hayes, and Adolphe Menjou. Helen Hayes brings her incredible screen presence to her portrayal of Catherine. As one of the most respected actresses of the Broadway stage, Hayes was much sought after by motion picture studios. It is a testament to her personal stature as an actress that she chose to make so few films. Her ability to convey a convincing romance between herself and the lanky Gary Cooper is remarkable; another actress of her diminutive size might have made the entire affair seem ludicrous. Menjou adds the perfect blend of sophistication and humor necessary to carry this unhappy tale of ill-fated lovers. Gary Cooper is the perfect Hemingway hero. Having spent a great deal of his early career portraying World War I soldiers, it was only a short step to the more pessimistic characters of Hemingway's writings.

Frank Borzage made a career out of directing some of the most romantic films of Hollywood. In addition to *A Farewell to Arms*, he made such memorable romantic films as *History Is Made at Night* (1937), *Man's Castle* (1934), and the bittersweet *Moonrise* (1948). In the manner of such directors as Douglas Sirk and John M. Stahl, Borzage is able to present touching romantic films without the cloying quality that so often accompanies such stories. He was a straightforward director whose early experience as a silent film director of B-budget Westerns and genre films taught him the techniques of filmmaking.

In addition to Borzage, *A Farewell to Arms* also boasts the talents of cinematographer Charles Lang, who received an Academy Award for his work in this film. The montage sequence of Frederic trying to return to Catherine is breathtaking. Likewise, Lang's prolonged take which begins, from Frederic's point of view, rolling into the hospital, going through winding corridors, and eventually ending with Catherine's face filling the lens as she and Frederic meet in a loving embrace, is magnificent. The images of destruction and horror brought about by the war are enhanced by subtle superimpositions and religious icons which lend an overriding sense of morality to the sequences.

A Farewell to Arms was a bold film which presented the situation of clandestine love with candor and simplicity. It was not exactly as vivid a description of war and its aftermath as was Hemingway's original novel, and yet the film was able to capture the irony of Hemingway's chaotic world. It is only because of the perseverance of Borzage that Catherine was allowed to die at the end of the film; an alternative version was shot in which she recovers and supposedly lives happily ever after with her adoring Frederic. The fact that Hemingway's ending was finally decided upon—something that was frowned upon by certain studio advisers as being unacceptable to a large portion of the viewing public—is the key which allows the unabashed romanticism of *A Farewell to Arms* to survive the pitfalls of most unrequited love stories.

Carl F. Macek

THE FARMER'S DAUGHTER

Released: 1947
Production: Dore Schary for RKO/Radio
Direction: H. C. Potter
Screenplay: Allen Rivkin and Laura Kerr; based on the play *Hulda, Daughter of Parliament* by Juhri Trevataa
Cinematography: Milton Krasner
Editing: Harry Marker
Costume design: Edith Head
Running time: 97 minutes

Principal characters:
Katrin Holstrom .... Loretta Young (AA)
Glenn Morley .... Joseph Cotton
Clancy .... Charles Bickford
Mrs. Morley .... Ethel Barrymore
Adolph Petree .... Rhys Williams
Mrs. Holstrom .... Anna Q. Nilsson
Anders Finley .... Art Baker

Based on the Scandinavian play *Hulda, Daughter of Parliament* by Juhri Trevataa and originally entitled *Katie for Congress*, *The Farmer's Daughter* stars Loretta Young as Katrin Holstrom a beautiful Swedish girl from a Minnesota farm who goes to the big city and eventually finds herself running for Congress. Katrin leaves her home and the comfortable security of her loving family, which includes several brawny brothers, and heads to "Capital City" to begin her study of nursing. To save bus fare, she accepts a ride with itinerant worker Adolph Petree (Rhys Williams), who has just painted her father's barn, but the man soon tricks her when an accident forces them to spend the night in a tourist camp. After he borrows all of Katrin's money for repairs, Adolph claims he is unable to repay her, and she must find her way to the city herself.

Without any money, Katrin is forced to take a job as a maid. She finds employment with Glenn Morley (Joseph Cotton), a young, handsome Minnesota congressman, and Mrs. Morley (Ethel Barrymore), his rich and politically influential mother, who is the widow of a famous United States senator. Intelligent and efficient, Katrin soon becomes indispensable to the Morley household, and at one point when the skating congressman falls through the ice, Katrin even gives him a rub-down with her Swedish massage technique. At the same time, the housemaid surprises her employees with her interest in politics; for the public-speaking class in which she has enrolled, Katrin practices elocution with Woodrow Wilson's comments on democratic principles. Soon, without invitation, she enters the family's political discussions, and for Glenn, she becomes an amusing, then annoying problem, when she expresses political opinions contrary to his own. Katrin, however, thinks, clearly and independently and Glenn finds his irritation turning into interest and infatuation.

When a congressman from a neighboring district dies, a meeting of party leaders is held at the Morley house in order to select new candidates to fill the vacated seat. Anders Finley (Art Baker), whom the Morley's reluctantly accept, is chosen, but the outspoken Katrin vehemently disapproves and airs her protesting convictions at a political rally. After these verbal attacks and objections, the favorably impressed opposition persuades Katrin to accept their Congressional nomination against Finley. She agrees, quits her job as housekeeper, and says good-bye to the angry Glenn Morley and his more sympathetic mother. Following a smear campaign by Adolph Petree against Katrin which almost ruins her, the Morleys uncover the tourist camp facts and discover that Finley paid Petree to defame Katrin, and the scandal is published. With Glenn Morley now on her side, Katrin easily wins the election by a landslide. Glenn and Katrin decide to get married, and the two congresspeople go off together to Washington, D.C. A socially conscious comedy-drama, *The Farmer's Daughter* is an entertaining exposé of political shenanigans. It not only provides funny commentary about the peculiar voting habits of many American citizens, but it also presents, with good humor, the view that truth is above politics. Indeed, the film is a positive statement about United States democracy and patriotism.

Young plays the fiery reformer with intelligence and charm and convinces us with her character's rare political honesty. As the blunt-questioning political Cinderella, Young's peasant Swedish accent is also believable. Interestingly, *The Farmer's Daughter* was originally intended as a starring vehicle for Swedish actress Ingrid Bergman, but Bergman turned the part down following a falling-out with independent producer David O. Selznick. Later Dore Schary took over as producer, and Young won the Academy Award for Best Actress for the part, in competition with Joan Crawford in *Possessed*, Susan Hayward in *Smash Up*, Dorothy McGuire in *Gentleman's Agreement*, and Rosalind Russell in *Mourning Becomes Electra*.

At the age of thirty-six when she made *The Farmer's Daughter*, Young had been in films for almost twenty years. She was featured as a young teenager in several silent films, most notably *Laugh Clown Laugh* (1928) with Lon Chaney, and had gradually become a major star by the mid-1930's when she began contract work for Twentieth Century-Fox. From that time until she retired from films to begin her long-running television anthology, *The Loretta Young Show*, she was a successful film star. Usually playing up her beautiful features and elegant mannerisms, she starred in a number of successful films with other Fox stars such as Don Ameche and Tyrone Power. Interestingly, the three films in which she gives perhaps her best performances, *The Farmer's*

Daughter, Rachel and the Stranger (1948), and *Come to the Stable* (1949), gave her the opportunity for parts which went against her usual screen image.

Cotton is also excellent as Congressman Morley. An actor who has moved among starring and character parts throughout his long career, Cotton has always given competent performances in a wide variety of roles. His light comedic touch here is as pleasing as was his penetrating performance as the psychotic killer in Alfred Hitchcock's *Shadow of a Doubt* (1943). Barrymore, as the dry and witty matriarch of a political family, is also enjoyable to watch as she masterfully delivers some of the best lines in the film, next to Young's. Charles Bickford as the hard-nosed yet devoted Clancy, who becomes Katrin's mentor and strongest supporter, won an Oscar nomination for his role, losing to Edmund Gwenn for *Miracle on 34th Street*. The rest of the cast, which consisted of many well-known character actors such as Williams, Baker, and former silent screen star Anna Q. Nilsson as Katrin's mother, is equally good in small roles. As a historical footnote, three of Katrin's strapping brothers are played by actors who would later become famous: Lex Barker, Keith Andes, and James Arness, using his real name, James Aurness.

Although there are some rather implausible moments in the film—especially when the politically powerful Morleys switch allegiances during the middle of Congressional campaign—the film still presents a solid case for the future of democracy and is a highly enjoyable film as well.

Janet St. Clair

FAT CITY

Released: 1972
Production: Ray Stark for Columbia
Direction: John Huston
Screenplay: Leonard Gardner; based on his novel of the same name
Cinematography: Conrad Hall
Editing: Margaret Booth
Running time: 100 minutes

Principal characters:
    Billy Tully .... Stacy Keach
    Ernie Munger .... Jeff Bridges
    Oma .... Susan Tyrell
    Faye .... Candy Clark
    Ruben .... Nicholas Colasanto
    Earl .... Curtis Cokes
    Lucero .... Sixto Rodriguez

After a ten-year self-imposed exile filled with flawed and abandoned projects, John Huston was to direct *Fat City* as a labor of love. *Night of the Iguana*, released in 1964, proved to the Hollywood film industry that the "Monster," as he was affectionately called by his late pal Humphrey Bogart, had not lost his touch. That had been eight years earlier, however, and by 1972, Huston's "bankability" was again in question. When he discovered Leonard Gardner's lean, gritty novel chronicling the lives of would-be and has-been fighters drinking and killing time in Stockton, California, Huston knew that he wanted to film it. The down-and-outer has always been a prominent figure in Huston's work; at seventeen, he had himself been a fair welterweight and had traveled the tanktown circuit in California which included towns like Watsonville and Stockton.

Taking along cinematographer Conrad Hall (*Cool Hand Luke*, 1967, and *In Cold Blood*, 1967), he set about re-creating the feel and smell of the place. Anyone who has seen *Fat City* can bear witness to how well the pair succeeded. Originally Huston had wanted Marlon Brando for the role of Billy Tully (the two men had gotten along and Brando had delivered a brilliant performance in Huston's adaptation of Carson McCullers' *Reflections in a Golden Eye*, 1967); but he had proved to be unavailable, and Stacy Keach was engaged to portray Billy Tully, a man who has seen his dreams dashed and, at twenty-nine, considers his life to be over. Much less well-known to the public than Brando, it would be difficult to think of an actor who could have handled the role better than did Keach.

Billy Tully is a fighter who has taken one punch too many. One of the walking wounded, a form of entropy has taken over his life. Partially, this is because of his wife's decision to walk away from the dead end of their life together; partially it is because, outside of boxing, there are few places Billy can go. At the beginning of the film he is dividing his time between halfhearted workouts at the YMCA with the dim notion of a comeback in mind, and the fields of the San Joaquin Valley where he earns enough money picking fruit to pay for wine and a cheap room.

One day at the YMCA he begins sparring with a young man named Ernie Munger (Jeff Bridges). Billy is surprised at Munger's prowess and suggests that he look up Ruben Luna (Nicholas Colasanto), a promoter who had once managed his own career. Billy sees in Ernie the cocky kid that he used to be. The youth is both an inspiration and a threat: an inspiration because he is the catalyst that causes Billy to begin training in earnest and a threat because he is a reminder to the older man of how much his reflexes have deteriorated during his absence from the ring. Billy trains, but cannot help wondering whether his best days are not gone forever and his dream of a comeback sheer folly. Ruben Luna also sees in Ernie the potential Billy had had before his marriage went on the rocks; yet he also retains enough faith in Billy as a fighter to want to manage him again if he is genuinely serious about training.

The lives of Billy and Ernie also intersect romantically. Ernie is trapped into marriage with Faye (Candy Clark), and Billy meets Oma (Susan Tyrell) in a Stockton dive. When Billy and Oma first see each other, she is involved in a stormy affair with a black man named Earl (Curtis Cokes). She bends Billy's ear with diatribes about the decline of the white race, at the same time berating Earl, who impassively absorbs her verbal abuse. When Earl is arrested on some minor charge, Oma continues arguing and drinking in the same bar, and eventually mutual loneliness brings Oma and Billy together after one of the most off-center, pugnacious courtships in film history. In order to prove his inarticulate need for her, Billy smashes his head against the glass-topped jukebox. Suddenly, in Oma's eyes, he is transformed into a battered Romeo ("the only sonofabitch worth a shit in this place"). The pair exit like drunken lovebirds. Yet all the while they are together, the cardboard carton containing Earl's possessions sits in Oma's closet as a reminder of the transience of her relationship with Billy. Billy realizes that the relationship is an impossible one, but his desperate loneliness compels him to try to make it work. He suffers her abuse as Earl did, attempts to get her to cut down on the drinking which is destroying her, and even cajoles her into eating. His reward is almost always a curse.

Ruben sets up a match for Billy, who has been training in earnest for his reentry into the ring against a fighter named Lucero (Sixto Rodriguez) in the Stockton Memorial Stadium. Lucero travels by bus from Mexico, arriving in town alone. He is a calm, taciturn man more reminiscent of a gunfighter or a matador than of a prizefighter. Perhaps because he is not good enough any more, or because his life has turned into an endless series of losses, Billy is no match for Lucero.

His ultimate defeat, however, does not take place in the ring. Upon Earl's release from jail, he is taken back by Oma, and Billy is once again shut out from what is most probably his last chance for a measure of happiness. He sees Ernie off to travel the same punchy circuit that he himself has traveled.

Fat City is the dark side of *Rocky* (1976). It is a story of the "bottom dogs" that Edward Dahlberg and Nelson Algren once wrote about. The expression itself is a metaphor for whatever a man's dream might be. The film opened late in 1972 to excellent notices and poor box office. The same, however, was true of what is possibly Huston's greatest work, *The Treasure of the Sierra Madre* (1947); and, like the earlier film, *Fat City* is gradually being recognized as the important work that it is. Bridges as Ernie plays well opposite Keach. Tyrell was nominated for an Academy Award for Best Supporting Actress for her portrayal of Oma, and, although she has not become a major star, she remains in demand and often dominates the usually high-quality projects in which she appears. As with all Huston films, even the casting of minor characters was meticulous. Rodriguez, a professional boxer, brought total authenticity to the role of Lucero, and the assemblage of battered pugs made it clear that the fight game breaks far more men than it elevates.

If there is a recurring theme running through the fabric of Huston's work, it is that dreams are elusive and that man is, often unwittingly, his own opponent. The broken, uncomprehending face of Billy lingers long in the mind of anyone fortunate enough to see this remarkable film.

Michael Shepler

FATHER GOOSE

Released: 1964
Production: Robert Arthur for Universal
Direction: Ralph Nelson
Screenplay: Peter Stone and Frank Tarloff (AA); based on the short story
 "A Place of Dragons" by S. H. Barnett (AA)
Cinematography: Charles Lang
Editing: Ted Kent
Song: Cy Coleman and Caroline Leigh
Running time: 115 minutes

Principal characters:
<pre>
Walter Eckland .... Cary Grant
Catherine Freneau .... Leslie Caron
Commander Frank Houghton .... Trevor Howard
Stebbings .... Jack Good
Elizabeth .... Stephanie Berrington
Harriet .... Jennifer Berrington
Kristina .... Verina Greenlaw
Angelique .... Laurelle Felsette
Dominique .... Nicole Felsette
Anne ....Pip Sparke
Jenny .... Sharyl Locke
</pre>

If *Father Goose* qualifies as a classic for any one reason, it would have to be the presence of Cary Grant. It was primarily through his interest in the original property that the film was made; it represented a new departure for him in terms of characterization, and it ended up being his penultimate film. He made *Walk, Don't Run* the next year, and then retired to pursue business interests and rear his daughter.

The title *Father Goose* is figurative and indirect but also quite appropriate. Walter Eckland (Cary Grant), a late 1930's dropout bumming around the South Pacific, is commandeered by his friend in the British Navy, Frank Houghton (Trevor Howard), to perform the job of "coast watcher," which consists of observing enemy sea and air movements from a remote island just after the beginning of World War II. His code name is "Mother Goose." He is not at his job very long before his solitary life becomes interrupted by a gaggle of tiny schoolgirls and their headmistress, Catherine Freneau (Leslie Caron), who are escaping from the approaching Japanese. Since the British are occupied with the war effort, Catherine and the girls are left in Walter's care indefinitely, a prospect that chills her and mortifies him. She hides his liquor, since it sets a bad example for the children, and criticizes his loutish behavior and unshaven appearance. He calls her a hypocrite, exactly the type of falsely proper, preachy moralist that caused him to drop out of the rat race.

Circumstances, however, dictate that they stay together. The islands are now swarming with Japanese troops, and there are any number of close calls in which both Walter and Catherine have to act calmly in order to protect the children. She proves more adaptable to the primitive living conditions than expected, and, for his part, he demonstrates a knack for communicating with the little girls. In one instance he is able to get one who had been traumatized into muteness to speak. By the time of the film's climax, Walter and Catherine have confessed their love for each other. They court very briefly, marry by radio from headquarters, and are attacked by the Japanese from the air in the middle of the cermony, so everyone must dash back and forth from cover to the microphone. The ceremony ends just as the Japanese infantry lands on their beach. Catherine takes the small motorboat, escaping with the girls, and Walter pulls out as a decoy in the cruiser. There is a tense climax as he encounters and lures a Japanese ship out into the open sea, where he knows an American submarinc is waiting. He nearly gets killed in the torpedo fire, but survives and joins the girls and his new bride. At the end, they are all rescued together.

Universal Studio's promotional material touted *Father Goose* as a radical break from Grant's traditional *persona*, stating: "Gone is the clean-shaven face; gone the impeccable tailoring that has distinguished Cary Grant throughout his long career." The part of Walter Eckland, however, was not a departure in the deepest sense. The Grant screen *persona* always resents the intrusion of anyone, whether they are crooks, liars, unimaginative cops, flighty and/or mysterious women, wealthy people of both sexes or plain ordinary citizens. His surliness forms the cornerstone of his charm. No one else has ever made his distaste seem quite so personal, or likable, except perhps W. C. Fields. Yet, whereas Fields was puffy and vaudevillean, often seeking to cheat first rather than be cheated, Grant is debonair, handsome, and very much the lady's man who merely does not want to be cheated at all. The winning aspect of his misanthropy in *Father Goose* is that he manages to be so honorable about it at the same time. These qualities are simply externalized for the first time here and to a maximum degree. As a result, even though he looks grubby clad in his oily jeans, his dapper magnetism comes across.

Caron is the film's other great asset. French, lithe, and very beautiful, she has a unique presence that is striking, but not altogether unprecedented in the gallery of Grant heroines. Caron's almond eyes and high cheekbones offset his soft, clefted features in much the same way Katharine Hepburn's did in her early films with Grant. Her performance invites comparison with the best leading ladies. There is a scene, the crucial one in bringing the lovers' feelings about each other into the open, in which Caron's particular brilliance is made very clear. Catherine believes, mistakenly, that she has been bitten by a snake. Because the only breeds in the islands are deadly poisonous,

Walter thinks he is helping her to die as he gets her drunk and tucks her in. The drunkenness is a first for Catherine. Caron's slinky, balletic movements as her limbs wind in and out of each other in the lotus position, simply to bring a cup to her lips, tell far more about her character than the dialogue does.

The script, based on a story by S. H. Barnett and constructed originally by Frank Tarloff, was taken through its last draft by Peter Stone, who had earlier worked with Grant on *Charade* (1963). *Father Goose* is no less believable for being a star vehicle, although much of its comic tone—Walter Eckland trading popeyed looks with everyone from pelicans to children—simply would not have been effective with anyone other than Grant. Even the dialogue seems made to order. A good example is Walter's reply when Frank tells him he needs a "volunteer" for the coast-watching service. He says, "Oh, I'd love to, Frank, but I've already volunteered for another watching service—the 'Watch Out for Walter Eckland Service'—it's damned important work, too."

The storytelling itself is well structured. From the opening scene, in which Walter sails his boat along idly, ignoring the explosive air attack taking place on a nearby island and switching the channel on his radio from war reports to the film's musical theme, "Pass Me By," no detail is superfluous. Everything is constructed with a purpose that pays off somewhere, either in the film's dramatic climax or in delineation of the central themes. There is also a system of confidantes and foil figures employed in various scenes. Frank has an assistant, Stebbings (Jack Good), to whom he has to explain everything; the little girls, playing with the radio, confide their troubles (which include progress reports of Walter and Catherine's relationship) to Frank, who in turn, needing Walter's help, but unable to relieve his bitterness at having so many demanding women on his hands, is forced to confide in Catherine; Catherine, at one point, drunk and thinking she has been snake bitten (it turned out to be a two-pronged branch instead) confides in Walter, who, thinking she is about to die, also confides in her. Like all of the best Cary Grant films, the story moves, sometimes meanders, but is never boring.

Ralph Nelson, who also directed *Lilies of the Field* (1963) and *Charley* (1968), is equal to the script. The supporting cast—Howard, Jack Good, and the little girls, Verina Greenlaw, Pip Sparke, Sharyl Locke, Stephanie and Jennifer Berrington, Nicole and Laurelle Felsette—are all excellent. The special effects—matte work, miniatures and opticals (to turn large Bahaman islands into small South Pacific ones, and render a realistic cameo of the Japanese Navy)—are extremely well done.

Father Goose opened as the Christmas show at Radio City Music Hall and went on to become a worldwide hit, gaining an Oscar for Best Screenplay. The critical reaction, on the other hand, was either condescending or negative. Arthur Knight of the *Saturday Review* saw it as suited "for the smaller fry," but "far removed from great comedy, which needs a good pinch of vulgarity."

Brendan Gill of *The New Yorker* similarly lamented the bygone era of *Bringing Up Baby* (1938) and its like. Although it is clear that these critics have, to some extent, a valid point (the most substantial being tht the film lacks spontaneity and draws heavily on the basic premise of *The African Queen*, 1951), one must bear in mind that 1964-1965 was a curious time. It was a watershed year in both American history and Hollywood filmmaking. Readiness among viewers and critics for more candid treatments of human (particularly sexual) relationships was in conflict with the traditional box-office ideal of "the film for the whole family." Thus, *Father Goose* was particularly appropriate as it was a sophisticated family comedy, and, as such, probably the last really successful film of its kind. *Father Goose* is a small gem that will endure.

F. X. Feeney

FATHER OF THE BRIDE

Released: 1950
Production: Pandro S. Berman for Metro-Goldwyn-Mayer
Direction: Vincente Minnelli
Screenplay: Frances Goodrich and Albert Hackett; based on the novel of the
  same name by Edward Streeter
Cinematography: John Alton
Editing: Ferris Webster
Running time: 93 minutes

Principal characters:
Stanley T. Banks .... Spencer Tracy
Ellie Banks .... Joan Bennett
Kay Banks .... Elizabeth Taylor
Buckley Dunstan .... Don Taylor
Doris Dunstan .... Billie Burke
Herbert Dunstan .... Moroni Olsen

In 1950 Vincente Minnelli directed a quick comedy while he waited to begin
production on *An American in Paris* (1951). That quickly made comedy
became a classic film in its own right and a large financial success for
M-G-M. *Father of the Bride* scrutinized all the little courtesies, frustrations,
and complex displays of good manners required in putting on a wedding. The
bride, Kay Banks, is played by Elizabeth Taylor, but as the title of the film
indicates, this is not really her story. Her character is fairly sketchy, delineated
only enough to let us know that she is a typical idealized American girl from
a steady family in a small town in the late 1940's. She is in love and wants to
get married. This story is about the effects of the wedding on her family,
particularly Spencer Tracy as Stanley Banks, the father of the bride.

If the goal of every young girl is to be married, as this film implies, then
what is the goal of every young girl's husband? To be the father of the bride,
suggests this film. There is no one prouder than Stanley from the moment
that his daughter announces her intentions at the dinner table to the moment
that she and her new husband drive down the road on their honeymoon.
There is also no one more confused or more surprised and unlucky than the
man who is about to lose his "baby girl" to a strange boy. At best, Stanley
is filled with extremely mixed emotions, all of them funny and quite touching.
After all, Stanley is digging into his own pocket to finance the loss of his
daughter, a girl for whom nothing is good enough.

The opening image of the film offers a very broad clue to its general intent.
The camera slowly moves past the debris which remains of the wedding
reception, pausing when it comes across a pair of feet belonging to Stanley.
Sunk in his chair with weary satisfaction, he turns directly to the camera to

inform the viewer that he is in his current privileged position because he is the father of the bride. Stanley knows exactly what that means and is determined to share his knowledge. It means having a quiet family dinner shattered one night with your daughter's announcement of her marriage plans. Stanley does not even know the boy, whose name is Buckley Dunstan (Don Taylor), so he waits nonchalantly by the window the next time the boy comes to call and peeks through the pane to give him the once-over. He is not good enough; Stanley winces to look at him. Every time Stanley tries to worry about Kay's decision with his wife Ellie (Joan Bennett), however, she tells him to calm down and go to bed.

The father of the bride carries a heavy burden, at least in his own mind. He has to check the boy out. A painful interview ensues. Minnelli conveys the slow passage of time with the detail of a close-up of the ashtray placed near Stanley's chair. As Stanley nervously drones on, the ashtray fills with matches. Finally Minnelli pulls his camera back to reveal Buckley's bored face. That interview with the intended is followed by Stanley's next determined effort to do the right thing when Buckley's parents get the once-over. This interview, at least, is reassuring for Stanley. As he and his wife drive up to the house, which is quite large, Stanley observes that these people are all right; they have money. Herbie (Moroni Olsen) and Doris Dunstan (Billie Burke) are gracious hosts with thoughtful decanters of liquor on the coffee table. Ellie is also gracious, but Stanley first warms to the task of drinking the host's liquor, becoming quite talkative with his captive audience, and then falls asleep. Another interview has not quite gone according to plan. This same pattern of confident expectation and humorous realization follows Stanley from the party he throws to celebrate the engagement announcement, to meetings with the caterer, to church rehearsals for the wedding. At one point Stanley gets a little desperate with the weight of his ceremonial duties and offers his daughter some money to elope. His family quickly brings him back to the realization of his duties, however, and he is back with the caterer's bills and his good suit.

By the night before the wedding, Stanley is quite nervous, and his anxiety provides Minnelli an opportunity for a surreal dream sequence in which a distorted Stanley bounces down the aisle, his shoes sticking to the floor. Grotesque, horrified faces look on, overlapping in close-up. The organist is a goblin reminiscent of the terrors of old horror films. The bride screams in fear at her father's *faux pas*. Stanley awakens from the nightmare and heads for the kitchen. There he finds his daughter, also unable to sleep. Father and daughter touchingly reassure each other about the day to come, eating sandwiches and milk.

Because Stanley has already faced the worst in his nightmare and worked through his nervousness over sandwiches and milk in the kitchen, the actual wedding day finds him relatively calm. He is a rock of Gibraltar in the midst of pandemonium at home and confidently plays his part in a beautiful church ceremony. Only during the reception does he finally realize the terrible fact of his daughter's departure. He tries to find her to say good-bye, but cannot make his way through the press of the reception crowd. As he watches from a distance, the newlyweds' car pulls away.

All these events bring the story back to a disconsolate Stanley, surveying the mess of the reception's aftermath. As he ponders the wreckage, the phone rings. It is Kay, calling to thank her father and mother before she leaves on her honeymoon. After talking with her, Stanley turns to his wife, feeling much better. "My daughter's my daughter all of her life—our life," he tells her. Then the two of them have a sentimental dance in the midst of the party debris. The last shot of the film pulls away from the two in the dark, through a doorway which frames them dancing. In that silhouetted tableau it's possible to see the husband of the bride become the father of the bride.

Clearly, *Father of the Bride* is not the story of the romance of bride and groom. It is the comedy of manners, a courtship of social flagbearers. Along with conveying the humor of wedding preparations, however, from in-laws to decorators, involving church, home, and painful finances, the film depicts the poignant position of those involved in the ceremony. Stanley is funny but also quite touching, a man who is in a very real sense about to lose his daughter. What the father of the bride learns is to place his relationship to his daughter in a new framework. Now he is not simply daddy, but the father of the bride. All of the comedy and the lovely sentimental quality of the film derives from the title Stanley assumes and the education he acquires from his new status. The sympathy that the audience feels for Stanley is in no small part due to Tracy's delightful performance. Although the others in the cast are good, his at times wise, at times befuddled, Stanley is the highlight of the film.

The success of *Father of the Bride* led to a sequel, *Father's Little Dividend* (1951), which picks up where the first film ended. The sequel relies much more on the relationship between Kay and Buckley as they endure a first year of marriage and a first child. By this time Taylor was becoming a more popular star, and it was perhaps for this reason that the relationship between the newlyweds became the central focus of the plot. This was unfortunate, however, as the sequel did not stand up at all well to the original film either as a comedy or box-office moneymaker. Eventually the story led to a short television series in the early 1960's, but despite the appearance of M-G-M stock player Leon Ames as the father, it had little of the sparkle of Minnelli's original film.

Leslie Donaldson

FEAR STRIKES OUT

Released: 1957
Production: Alan Pakula for Paramount
Direction: Robert Mulligan
Screenplay: Ted Berkman and Raphael Blau; based on the autobiography of
  the same name by Jimmy Piersall and Al Hirshberg
Cinematography: Haskell Boggs
Editing: Aaron Stell
Running time: 100 minutes

Principal characters:

Jimmy Piersall (older)	Anthony Perkins
John Piersall	Karl Malden
Mary Piersall	Norma Moore
Mrs. John Piersall	Perry Wilson
Doctor Brown	Adam Williams
Joe Cronin	Bart Burns
Jimmy (younger)	Peter J. Votrian

Real-life sports figures have often inspired good cinema—*The Pride of the Yankees* (1942, about baseball's Lou Gehrig) and *Knute Rockne—All American* (1940, about Notre Dame's famous football coach) are two obvious examples. In almost every such film that comes to mind, the subject is someone whose skills had taken him to the top of his sport. This is not the case with Robert Mulligan's *Fear Strikes Out*, however, a film based on Jimmy Piersall's autobiography.

The Baseball Encyclopedia reveals that Jimmy Piersall spent seventeen years in major league baseball, most of them with the Boston Red Sox. His lifetime batting average of .272 is well under the magic .300 mark that separates the potential Hall of Famers from the journeymen. Nevertheless, Piersall had a remarkable career—one that fully warranted an autobiography and film biography of a mediocre athlete still in his twenties. For Piersall in his heyday (the early 1950's) was one of the best-known and most controversial figures in baseball. He was an inveterate clown, umpire baiter, and brawler. Indeed, Billy Martin's fight with Piersall in 1952 was the first in a long line of that celebrated player-manager's celebrated bouts of fisticuffs. Midway into the 1952 season, Piersall was clearly losing control. At twenty-three, he suffered a complete, and very public, mental breakdown. *Fear Strikes Out* is the story of this breakdown and of Piersall's recovery from it.

Mulligan establishes the root causes of Piersall's anxieties early. In the film's first scene, John Piersall (Karl Malden) arrives home from work early because he has lost his job in a quarrel with his foreman. He quickly shrugs this off as a minor irritant, however, and turns his attention to his twelve-year-old son (Peter J. Votrian), who is practicing hook slides in the yard. The elder Piersall had been a semiprofessional ballplayer in his younger days, and he is obsessed with the idea that his son will someday star in the big leagues. Young Jimmy is desperate for his father's approval, but John Piersall offers only criticism. Jimmy can never do well enough to please him.

The first scene ends with a game of catch between Jimmy and his father. The elder Piersall is throwing the ball much too hard, and the boy begins to weep silently in pain, although he never stops returning the throws. The camera follows the flight of the ball, and suddenly the scene changes. The ball hurtles over a real baseball diamond, cutting down a runner sliding towards home plate. Mulligan has neatly moved the action into Jimmy's late adolescence.

The scene shifts to five years later, as Jimmy (Anthony Perkins), a high school junior, has just helped his team win the state championship with a great throw. Elated, he runs to share the moment with his father, only to be rebuffed. Every word of praise John Piersall utters is countered by two of criticism; he recites a litany of every slight mistake Jimmy made during the game. Obviously, nothing has changed between Jimmy and his father in the past five years. The poisonous nature of their relationship is gradually driving the younger man close to insanity. He slouches into the dressing room, gulps a handful of aspirin, and lurches, fully dressed, into the shower.

The Boston Red Sox hold Jimmy in higher esteem than does his father; they scout him extensively during his senior year. Although Piersall spends most of that season a nervous wreck—his attention is more on his father in the stands than on the game—he plays well enough to earn a contract with the Red Sox, who send him down to their minor league farm club in Scranton, Pennsylvania.

In Scranton, Jimmy does well. He is third in the league in batting average (his father carps that he should have been first), and, more importantly, his social life blossoms away from the influence of John Piersall. He meets Mary (Norma Moore), a pretty nurse, and the two fall in love. Jimmy's sense of humor, something that has not been revealed up to this point, asserts itself. Piersall seems on his way to becoming a well-rounded human being; but then the season ends, and it is time to return home. By this time, he and Mary have wed, and they move in with Jimmy's parents.

The next year is mixed for the young Piersalls. They have a baby daughter, and Jimmy does well the next season in Louisville (the Red Sox's highest minor league team), but his father fumes continually because Jimmy is "rotting" in the minor leagues. The decision of whether or not to buy a house sends Jimmy into hysterics; clearly he is losing his grip on reality. His deterioration continues during spring training, when he is given a slot on the major league club as a shortstop. Jimmy is stunned: all of his training, all of the programming by his father, has been for the outfield. He becomes literally paranoid about the switch, convinced that the Red Sox want him to fail and disgrace himself in front of his father.

John Piersall finds his son crying under the bleachers at his old high school. Blind to his son's distress, he lashes out: "You want them to call you yellow? If that's what you want, then you're no son of mine." His father's taunts pull Jimmy out of hysterics, but not back into any semblance of normality. Instead, he becomes an automaton, mumbling under his breath and raging at his teammates, whom he considers slackers. Finally, he picks a fight with one of them and is suspended from the team by his manager, Joe Cronin (Bart Burns). Mulligan makes it clear that Piersall is unconsciously hoping to get thrown out so that he will not have to risk failure at shortstop.

After his father intercedes, Cronin reinstates Jimmy as an outfielder. This time, he has no excuse for failure. The game in which Jimmy returns to the team is one of the most shocking and effective scenes in the whole film. It is a night game. Jimmy stands, alone and intent, in the outfield, his isolation intensified by the darkness surrounding him. The press had labeled him a "problem boy," and the crowd is unsympathetic. The soundtrack pulses with noise as the tension mounts.

Finally it is Jimmy's turn at bat. His father is in the stands, and the pitcher stalls, feeding his anxiety. Jimmy swings futilely at the first two pitches, but on the third, he hits a home run. The audience relaxes momentarily, thinking that the tension has lifted. As Jimmy crosses home plate, however, he continues to run. Charging towards his father's seat in the stands, he screams "I showed 'em," over and over again, and attempts to climb over the screen and into the grandstand. Dragged into the dugout by his teammates, he grabs a bat and begins swinging wildly. He has finally snapped under the pressure that has been building for more than a decade. This scene is the dramatic highlight of the film. Shocking and yet utterly convincing, it is the logical culmination of all that came before it in the film. *Fear Strikes Out* is only half over, however, with the story of Jimmy Piersall's recovery yet to be told.

The next scene takes place in a hospital. A Dr. Brown (Adam Williams) is explaining Jimmy's mental breakdown to the Piersalls. "You'll handle Jimmy easy, won't you," his father pleads—an ironic touch on the part of screenwriters Ted Berkman and Raphael Blau, since John Piersall never handled his son gently in his entire life. It is only after electroshock therapy that Jimmy begins to struggle back from his illness. Under Dr. Brown's careful tutelage, he begins to examine the corrosive relationship with his father that led to his problems. Initially, he resists blaming his father: "Why, if it hadn't been for him pushing me, I wouldn't be where I am today," he exclaims. Realizing the irony of those words—they are, of course, quite literally true—he bolts from the psychiatrist's office. When he returns moments later, he is on the road to recovery.

The elder Piersall also comes to understand his failure as a father through the course of Jimmy's illness. When his son finally confronts him with the words "All my life I've been splitting my gut to please you, and I never could. You're killing me," John Piersall goes home and cries. The two are reconciled later; Mulligan establishes this reconciliation neatly. Father and son, after a bit of nervous small talk, begin playing catch. In contrast to the similar scene early in the film, however, there is no tension or pain involved; this time, it is just a pleasant game.

The film ends as Jimmy is about to make his comeback with the Red Sox. Once more, his family is in the stands; for once, however, they are more nervous than he is. He embraces his wife and assures her that, although he is a bit frightened, he is ready to play ball for himself, not for his father. "I want to. I wanna play," he grins. The final shot is of a relaxed and confident Jimmy Piersall walking towards the field.

Mulligan's decision to end the film before his protagonist returns to the fray is both significant and sound, for Mulligan is aware that his film, and Piersall's biography, were only incidentally about baseball. The real story was that of a mind in torment, how it got that way, and how it recovered. Piersall's recovery is complete when he makes the decision to play because *he* wants to. His success or failure, while obviously not a trivial matter, is secondary to the fact that he decides to try.

Since *Fear Strikes Out* is centered on the relationship between Jimmy Piersall and his father, Perkins and Malden carry the bulk of the acting load, and they do so commendably. Malden has been a distinguished character actor for years, winning an Academy Award as Best Supporting Actor in Elia Kazan's *A Streetcar Named Desire* in 1951. The character of John Piersall is fairly one-dimensional as written; his main function in the film (perhaps, to be fair to the screenwriters, simply mirroring his role in Jimmy's life) is to intimidate his son. Even Malden's acting skills could not have turned the elder Piersall into a well-rounded human being, but by the end of the film, Malden is able to inject into his character a certain amount of sympathy. An occasional moment of tenderness surfaces before the gruffness takes over. These moments pave the way for John Piersall's reconciliation with his son at the end of the film.

Perkins, on the other hand, was a relative newcomer to the screen, and *Fear Strikes Out* marked the first full flowering of the acting skills that would characterize his career from then on. He excelled at playing troubled young men (with his role as Norman Bates in Alfred Hitchcock's *Psycho* in 1960 representing the apex of his career), and his portrayal of Jimmy Piersall gave him ample opportunity to convey his character's mental anguish. His angular, expressive face clearly reflects the torment in his character's soul. Among the other actors, Williams was fairly wooden as Dr. Brown, Jimmy's psychiatrist; but Moore was appealing in her role as Mary Piersall, Jimmy's understanding wife.

Fear Strikes Out marked the directorial debut of Mulligan. Mulligan went on to direct a wide variety of films—such a wide variety, in fact, that he has been criticized for lacking any distinguishing point of view. There has been, however, at least one recurring theme in many of Mulligan's films, such as *To Kill a Mockingbird* (1962), *Summer of '42* (1971), and *The Other* (1972): that of youth under stress. *Fear Strikes Out* was perhaps atypical of the best of these films, for it was based on fact.

There are two primary criticisms to be made of *Fear Strikes Out*. First, the film offers only a hint—mostly in his courtship of Mary—of Piersall's renowned sense of humor. His antics on the field made him a great crowd favorite, and his colorful personality paved the way for his career in broadcasting after his playing days were over. Mulligan evidently decided that an examination of this aspect of Piersall's life would have distracted from the seriousness of the film. He may have been correct, but *Fear Strikes Out* might have benefited from an occasional comic moment to relieve the tension. Second, and perhaps inevitably, the portion of the film dealing with Piersall's recovery is less interesting than that dealing with his breakdown. The slow, steady process of healing is always difficult to dramatize.

Despite these cavils, however, *Fear Strikes Out* remains an interesting and worthwhile film. It showcases the acting talents of Perkins and Malden and presents a sympathetic view of mental illness to a portion of filmdom's audience—the sports fans—to whom such a view may have been unfamiliar. Indeed, *Fear Strikes Out* is noteworthy primarily because it presents a view of a sports figure as a real person, not simply as an on-the-field hero.

Robert Mitchell

FIDDLER ON THE ROOF

Released: 1971
Production: Norman Jewison for United Artists
Direction: Norman Jewison
Screenplay: Joseph Stein; based on his stage adaptation of the writings of Sholom Aleichem
Cinematography: Oswald Morris (AA)
Editing: Antony Gibbs and Robert Lawrence
Choreography: Tom Abbott; based on the stage choreography of Jerome Robbins
Sound: Gordon K. McCallum and David Hildyard (AA)
Music: John Williams (AA)
Song: Sheldon Harnick and Jerry Bock
Running time: 180 minutes

Principal characters:
Tevye	Topol
Golde	Norma Crane
Yente	Molly Picon
Motel	Leonard Frey
Tzeitel	Rosalind Harris
Hodel	Michele Marsh
Chava	Neva Small
Perchik	Michael Glaser
Lazar Wolf	Paul Mann

In 1971, at the time of filming *Fiddler on the Roof*, the movie musical was experiencing a major decline. Recent attempts to re-create the successful musical comedies of the 1940's and 1950's, as in the cases of *Star!* (1968) and *Paint Your Wagon* (1969), had failed miserably. Yet *Fiddler on the Roof* was such an internationally successful stage show with an excellent script and libretto that a film version was perhaps inevitable.

The adaptation of a Broadway musical to the screen was a rather awesome task. In the case of *Fiddler on the Roof* it was necessary to integrate the theatricality of the play with the ingrained realism of the screen. Norman Jewison was the director chosen by Walter Mirisch and United Artists to translate the play into film. At that time, Jewison was known largely for his work in television on eight Judy Garland shows, and in film on two Doris Day comedies and a Tony Curtis vehicle. Just prior to being approached by Mirisch for *Fiddler on the Roof*, however, Jewison had received acclaim for his films *The Russians Are Coming, The Russians Are Coming* (1966) and *In the Heat of the Night*, the latter winning an Oscar for the year 1967. Jewison, perhaps inspired by the success of *Fiddler on the Roof*, would go on to do *Jesus Christ, Superstar* (1973).

Fiddler on the Roof deals with the life of Russian Jews at the time of the 1905 pogroms carried out by the Tsar. On a smaller scale, it is the story of the dairyman Tevye, struggling for survival and adapting to a new, often bewildering world. This irrevocable move towards change is exemplified in the manner of the courtships and subsequent marriages of Tevye's three oldest daughters, as they break from the tradition of matchmakers and prearranged marriages.

The movie opens with Tevye (Topol) contemplating the way of life in Anatevka. He speaks to God and directs many of his musings to the audience. This device, used continually throughout the film, allows the audience a closer identification with the character of Tevye, and was an ingenious way of adapting Tevye's numerous monologues to the screen. Next, Tevye introduces us to the villagers, all at work, who break into the song "Tradition." Tom Abbott, the film's choreographer, was faced with the challenge of making the dance sequences derive naturally from the action, and of allowing for a seemingly smooth-flowing return to that action. The dance sequences would need to contribute to and be a necessary, rather than a superfluous, part of the movie. This effect is successful with "Tradition," as the dance derives from the work each villager is doing and contributes to the feeling of a village celebration, of a hard-working people still able to appreciate life.

Tevye continues on his way to his home, where he is confronted by his practical, long-suffering wife Golde (Norma Crane) and by his five daughters, three of whom are at a marriageable age. Why all daughters, asks Tevye, with a glance towards heaven and a shrug of the shoulders. The family gathers for dinner and a Sabbath prayer. The happiness, stability, and devotion to tradition depicted thus far are soon, however, to be threatened.

The oldest daughter, Tzeitel (Rosalind Harris), has become secretly engaged to Motel (Leonard Frey), the poor tailor, and rebels against a prearranged marriage with the wealthy old butcher, Lazar Wolf (Paul Mann). Tzeitzel and Motel confront Tevye, who is, after all, a good man and a loving father. He tries to think his way out of the dilemma. As the audience is included in Tevye's ponderings, the camera draws away from the other characters, who remain frozen. This repeated device is another acknowledgment of the film's legitimate stage source.

Deciding in favor of his daughter's happiness, Tevye is faced with the problem of explaining matters to Golde. He does so with the marvelous abstract dream sequence, which is the film's only lapse into fantasy and theatricality. In it, Golde's long-dead grandmother advises marriage between Tzeitel and Motel, since the fact that Lazar Wolf had previously been married would bring bad luck to the couple.

Tevye is a man beset by troubles; and no sooner is this first problem solved than the next storm cloud appears in the form of the film's revolutionary element, Perchik (Michael Glaser). Brought into the family as a tutor for the girls, he soon becomes involved with Tevye's second daughter, Hodel (Michele Marsh). As they approach Tevye merely for his blessing, rather than for permission to marry, he becomes more and more angry and frustrated at this defiance of tradition. Not being narrow-minded, however, Tevye himself begins to wonder whether this new practice of marrying for love is perhaps not better than the old tradition of marrying a selected stranger whom one might learn to love. Returning home, he asks Golde, "Do You Love Me?" in one of the movie's most touching scenes.

Eventually, however, Tevye is unable to reconcile himself entirely to the new way of doing things. As the pogroms continue and the residents of Anatevka are faced with eviction by the Russians, another of Tevye's daughters, Chava (Neva Small), becomes involved with a Russian officer. Tevye cannot condone this break not only with tradition but with religion as well, and he turns his back on his daughter.

The film closes with a mass exodus of Jews from Anatevka, which the film was more successful in depicting than the stage version had been. The final song, "Anatevka," sung as the villagers all file out along the road, expresses nostalgia for times past as well as a determination to face the future.

In keeping with the world of Sholom Aleichem, upon whose writings *Fiddler on the Roof* is based, Jewison strove for authentic detail. To achieve this, filming was done in Yugoslavia rather than on a Hollywood set. Jewison took great care with every aspect of the production. In his search for a location, he wanted a place far removed from the twentieth century with a warm, earthy quality and real peasants in the background. Elements of three different towns were incorporated in order to get the feel of the different sides of Anatevka. Jewison was so concerned with authenticity that Tevye's house, barn, and cheese hut were constructed with materials dating from the turn of the century.

The title *Fiddler on the Roof* was originally inspired by a painting by Marc Chagall, and Jewison wanted the overall production to aspire to the particular quality reflected in Chagall's art. The village of Lekenik, which served as residential Anatevka, conveyed that quality, as did the work of the film's cinematographer, Oswald Morris, who was awarded an Oscar for his cinematography. The dream sequence, much expanded for the screen, reflected the special Chagall quality in its style, design, and color. All other scenes were filmed through a silk stocking, resulting in the muted colors of the landscapes and the warm brown earth tones so evident in the overall production. Other members of the production staff whose excellent work earned them Academy Awards were John Williams for his adaptation and treatment of the music, and Gordon K. McCallum and David Hildyard for sound.

The acting in *Fiddler on the Roof* was uniformly excellent, with a fine cast headed by the Israeli actor Topol in the monumental role of Tevye. Chosen over Zero Mostel, who had headed the Broadway cast and set the type for every Tevye that followed, Topol, who had starred in the London production, was considered potentially a better movie actor, possessing more warmth and dignity, together with a sensual quality no previous Tevye had possessed. It was a fine enough performance, endowed with wisdom, humor, and vigor, to earn Topol an Academy Award nomination for Best Actor, although he lost to Gene Hackman for *The French Connection*. Other outstanding performances were Norma Crane's exasperated but warm Golde; Leonard Frey's enormously endearing Motel, possessed of an inner strength unknown possibly even to him; Rosalind Harris' equally appealing Tzeitel; and the delightful Yente of the veteran actress Molly Picon.

An enormous popular success, *Fiddler on the Roof* was acclaimed, for the most part, by the critics, and was nominated for an Academy Award for Best Picture of 1971, losing to *The French Connection*. What adverse criticism the film did receive derived from problems directly related to the medium of film: complaints that the movie was more ethnic, detailed, and realistic, and larger and less stylized than the Broadway musical. These problems could not effectively be avoided, however, given the nature of the screen. They are, instead, assets. *Fiddler on the Roof* remains one of the strongest movie musicals of recent years.

Grace Anne Morsberger

FILM

Released: 1966
Production: Evergreen Theatre, Inc.
Direction: Alan Schneider
Screenplay: Samuel Beckett
Cinematography: Boris Kaufman
Editing: Sidney Meyers
Running time: 22 minutes

> *Principal characters:*
> The man .... Buster Keaton

The work of all dramatists is divided between journalism and poetry. Samuel Beckett has always approached drama the way he has approached his novels and stories, as poetic exercise. His genius has been one of condensation and suggestion, evoking haunting responses from the simplest materials, like a man in a furnished room listening to a voice (*Eh, Joe?*) or to a tape recorder (*Krapp's Last Tape*). A few vaudeville turns are strung together in *Waiting for Godot* to become a harrowing cosmic joke. Often his stage pictures are still-lifes that take on ineffable overtones as a single element begins to move. In the plays, and even more so in the novels, he has passed from settings as recognizable as Ireland to no-man's-land and then to a void that may simply be a map of our collective consciousness. His dramas make metaphors of minimal elements—whispers, broken phrases, pratfalls, ashcans, mounds of earth, strings of memories. There may be less of the journalist and more of the poet in Beckett than in any major dramatist to date. In his own classic phrase, he does not write about something; he writes something.

In *Film*, his only produced screenplay to date, he and his director, Alan Schneider, the man most often associated with staging Beckett in the United States, have created a film whose power lies precisely in this: it does not mean what it says. In a literal sense, it says nothing at all; but, like any great poem, it means what it is.

A man (Buster Keaton) is in flight from the eyes of the world and from the camera, which pursues him while keeping to an angle that avoids showing his face. People on the street are annoyed when he jostles them. A woman in a vestibule does not see him at all. But when these characters look into the pursuing camera—look at "us"—they are horrified, their mouths agape.

In the sanctuary of his room the man curtains his window, covers his mirror, shades his bird and goldfish, puts out his cat and dog, tears up his photos, and finally dozes off in his rocker, apparently safe from scrutiny. But then the camera tracks slowly around to face him at last and wake him by the very intensity of its gaze. The man looks up—into his own face, staring down at him with a terrible, haunting impassivity, neither angry nor bitter, just there.

The man in the rocking chair covers his eyes and slumps in despair. The standing figure continues relentlessly staring.

Discovering Beckett for the first time, it is often easiest to explain what he is by what he is not. *Film* is only twenty-two minutes long, with one main character played by Keaton at the age of sixty-nine. There is no dialogue, no color, no music, no titles, no sound of any kind, and no glimpse of Keaton's face until those final, shattering seconds.

What we are offered is two states of perception. The first is Keaton's as he runs, loping through the street in a long cumbersome overcoat with a kerchief over his face, clambering up the stairs, sneaking up on a mirror from underneath it to cover it lest he glimpse himself; putting out the cat only to have the dog come in; putting out the dog only to have the cat reenter. He is clumsy, precise, obsessive, funny, and, in the end, agonized in horror and defeat, covering his eyes, knowing that he cannot avoid his own self-perception.

The second mode of seeing, of course, is the camera's as it pursues. It is unlikely that any major American film since *Lady in the Lake* (1946) has so pointedly and repeatedly called attention to itself as a photographed object. The looks of the people in the street and the old woman in the vestibule remind us of their pursuing presence—and prepare us for the terror that is coming. When Keaton stands staring down at himself in the rocking chair, the geography of the film is revealed. For then we see how the two kinds of perception make up the contours of a single consciousness—one mind—the halves of a psyche, looking out on the world and in on itself. By sundering the eye (camera) and the object (Keaton), Beckett has made *Film* into a model of consciousness.

Beckett is clear about his intentions. In the preface to the published version (Grove Press, 1969), he gives as his text Berkeley's theory that to be is to be perceived; to be alive is to suffer self-perception. There is no escape. *Film* is the picture of a mind, including that part of consciousness we may fear but never evade. It has the deeply disturbing impact of a horror film, almost a horror film for philosophers. The real horror is never monsters or outlandish creatures, not mutants or bogeymen to frighten children. The true horror is continuing to see ourselves clearly, without escape, as long as we live.

The production serves Beckett beautifully in every way. Boris Kaufman's lighting washes the man's room in a neutral white, a soft, limbo light that brings the grainy plaster of the walls slightly into relief, as if to emphasize their emptiness. It picks up the sparkle in every eye—fish's, parrot's, passerby's, and finally even Keaton's—so as to increase the intensity of its observation.

Each move is orchestrated by Alan Schneider with a lunatic precision and craftiness. Keaton is diabolically clever about avoiding being seen. And Keaton himself, viewed from behind, shambling with a mixture of grace and awkwardness, or viewed from in front with a face of monumental, stoic sadness, is beyond acting. He is the embodiment of Beckett's *Film*, the perfect expression of that mind we have entered, that mesh which holds us.

The winner of a Nobel Prize, Beckett is recognized today as one of the most important writers of the century and possibly the most enduring, influential dramatist of our time. In all his work, the questions of perception and consciousness are central. Indeed, that work can be seen as a continuing examination and re-creation of modern consciousness. It is all of a piece with this small, simple, twenty-two-minute film that is just what meets the eye, and just what cannot bear the scrutiny of that eye.

Ted Gershuny

A FINE MADNESS

Released: 1966
Production: Jerome Hellman for Pan Arts; released by Warner Bros.
Direction: Irvin Kershner
Screenplay: Elliott Baker; based on his novel of the same name
Cinematography: Ted McCord
Editing: William Ziegler
Running time: 104 minutes

Principal characters:

Samson Shillito	Sean Connery
Rhoda Shillito	Joanne Woodward
Lydia West	Jean Seberg
Dr. West	Patrick O'Neal
Dr. Kropotkin	Colleen Dewhurst
Dr. Menken	Clive Revill
Dr. Vorbeck	Werner Peters
Daniel Papp	John Fiedler
Secretary	Sue Ann Langdon

The screenplay for *A Fine Madness* was written by Elliott Baker, adapted from his novel of the same name. The film is a satirical comedy about a bullheaded Bohemian poet named Samson Shillito and his nonconformist lifestyle. Feeling battered and bruised by a heartless, uncaring society, he clings tenaciously to his dream of writing the greatest poem of his career. Although his creative juices have dried up some five years earlier, he never wavers in his belief that they will flow again, given time, inspiration, and the proper working conditions. The poem becomes his obsession, a goal to be defended against all odds. He is the talented intellectual down on his luck, fighting against impossible odds.

As the film begins, Samson Shillito (Sean Connery) is seen moodily hunched over a kitchen table in his seedy Manhattan apartment. His wife, Rhoda (Joanne Woodward), is fixing a hasty breakfast before rushing off to work. Almost immediately the audience is interested in how these two people with conflicting personalities ever got together in the first place. They are a classic example of the old adage of opposites attracting, for good-hearted Rhoda is an uneducated, gum-chewing, hard-working waitress and Samson is, by contrast, a brooding, frustrated intellectual. About all they have in common are their impetuous, violent tempers and their shared goal of Samson's creating a masterpiece.

Producer Jerome Hellman has chosen his settings well, shooting the entire film on location in New York amid grubby brownstone tenements and swank Park Avenue high-rises that provide the perfect background and atmosphere for the struggling poet. Indeed, the colorful, bustling New York backdrop compensates for some unevenness in the film, injecting a note of reality into the rather bizarre symphony of events that is being acted out.

As the story progresses, Samson, wearing the uniform of the "Athena Carpet Cleaning Company," wends his way toward a posh office building in downtown Manhattan. En route, he is beset by two zealous alimony process servers who threaten him with legal action if he continues to ignore his financial obligation to his former wife. This is the first of many such encounters; Samson is plagued by these dogged zealots throughout the film. Subsequent episodes lose some of their freshness and pointed humor but serve the important function of bringing home to the audience a keen sense of Samson's helplessness and frustration. While busily shampooing carpets, Samson's eye is caught by a blonde secretary (Sue Ann Langdon). In the hilarious debacle that follows, he proceeds, amid a torrent of bubbles and aghast onlookers, to demolish the reputation of both the "Athena Carpet Cleaning Company" and the blonde secretary.

Losing his job with the cleaning company, Samson intensifies his search for three hundred dollars with which to pay his back alimony. He enlists the aid of a friend who reluctantly arranges for Samson to give a poetry reading for a women's league composed of stuffy, rich, middle-aged "patrons of the arts." His railings against motherhood and practically every other subject sacred to the hearts of these pillars of society provide one of the funniest sequences in the movie. When he describes them as red roses who should open their corsets and bloom, it is more than they can bear. Shedding their veneer of civility and sophistication, they attack him with gusto. The ever-faithful Rhoda arrives barely in time to rescue him from the vengeance of this enraged mob of solid citizens. A most enterprising woman, she not only secures Samson's safety, but also extracts payment for the ill-fated poetry reading.

Rather than using the money to pacify the alimony servers, however, Rhoda engages the services of a polished Park Avenue psychiatrist, Dr. Oliver West (Patrick O'Neal), whose specialty is rejuvenating dried-up geniuses. O'Neal is perfect in his tongue-in-cheek portrayal. The psychiatrist is smooth-talking, nattily dressed at all times, and blessed with all the trappings of success. He has a home on Long Island with a kidney-shaped swimming pool, two late-model cars, two spoiled children, and a bored, unhappy wife, Lydia (Jean Seberg), who tries to fill her empty days with harp, ballet, and macrame lessons.

Director Irvin Kershner keeps the action going at top speed, rushing from one sequence to another, barely giving us time to grasp the impact of what is happening before he bowls us over again. Indeed, as the main characters scurry madly in and out of tenements, office buildings, training gyms, and sanatoriums, one has the peculiar feeling that the entire film is really a series of isolated incidents glimpsed through the window of a runaway train. Yet they represent exactly the type of life that Samson is living. We realize that his own misguided energy is precisely the reason for his failure as a poet.

Eventually, Samson is convinced by Dr. West to commit himself to a private sanatorium where he will be treated and also will have the peace and quiet to work on his poem, while out of the reach of the alimony servers. All goes well until he is discovered by Dr. West frolicking in the hydrobath with the doctor's wife, who is visiting the sanatorium. As a result, Samson is given a lobotomy to curb his antisocial behavior, a solution which the enraged Dr. West had previously opposed, along with Dr. Kropotkin (Colleen Dewhurst), another of Samson's romantic conquests and ardent admirers.

Clive Revill as Dr. Menken and Werner Peters as Dr. Vorbeck add a sinister, "mad-scientist" air to the hospital scene. These overzealous doctors are in the habit of performing unorthodox experimental operations on their patients in the name of scientific research. They provide the perfect excuse for Baker to poke a satirical finger at the so-called "experts" in the field of mental health care. Having performed the lobotomy, meant to curb the violent side of human nature and thus return its recipient to an active, useful role in society, they are confronted with a patient in the person of Samson Shillito who comes out of the anesthesia in a fit of rage and promptly proceeds to demolish everything and everybody blocking his exit from the sanatorium.

All is not lost, however; Lydia, feeling guilty over the part she has unwittingly played in precipitating the ill-fated operation, writes Samson a check that brings his alimony payments up to date. In the final scene, we find Rhoda timorously confessing that she is four months pregnant and begging Samson not to be angry. He blusters; but one is left with the impression that he is not, perhaps, too furious.

Connery runs rampant through *A Fine Madness*. As James Bond, a role closely associated with his name, Connery had already shown a flair for light comedy and a capacity for depicting violence. In *A Fine Madness*, he reveals a previously unsuspected talent for both slapstick comedy and raw emotionalism, evoking a range of emotions from poignant and sad to utterly hilarious. Woodward, his long-suffering albeit loving wife, manages to add a certain credence and dimension to the character of Rhoda despite the confines of a relatively unimportant and stereotyped role. All in all, *A Fine Madness* is a fine film.

D. Gail Huskins

FIVE EASY PIECES

Released: 1970
Production: Bob Rafelson and Richard Wechsler for Columbia
Direction: Bob Rafelson
Screenplay: Adrien Joyce; based on a story by Bob Rafelson and Adrien Joyce
Cinematography: Laszlo Kovacs
Editing: Christopher Holmes and Gerald Sheppard
Running time: 98 minutes

Principal characters:
Robert Eroica Dupea .... Jack Nicholson
Rayette Dipesto ....Karen Black
Partita Dupea .... Lois Smith
Catherine Van Ost .... Susan Anspach
Elton .... Billy "Green" Bush
Stoney .... Fannie Flagg
Betty .... Sally Ann Struthers
Nicholas Dupea .... William Challee

On the surface, it may not seem that a feature such as *Five Easy Pieces* would have had a wide public appeal; it was both thoughtful and intelligent and had nothing to do with the youth problems of the 1960's. Instead, it was a comedy-drama of a mature man's search for his own identity, and the fact that it elicited a positive response from moviegoers is indicative of its realistic treatment of a psychological problem that many have faced, particularly during the troubled decade in which the film is set.

Five Easy Pieces tells the story of Robert Eroica Dupea (Jack Nicholson), formerly a brilliant concert pianist, who has now abandoned his old life-style, adopted a fake Southern accent, and taken a job as an oil-rigger in the Southern California oil fields. He has completely turned away from classical music and from his old friends and is living with a featherbrained woman named Rayette Dipesto (Karen Black); their best friends are his fellow worker, Elton (Billy "Green" Bush), and his wife Stoney (Fannie Flagg). Why Dupea is masquerading like this and seeking the company of people so far removed from his intellectual background remains something of a mystery. When he learns that Rayette is pregnant, he quits his job and abandons her, realizing that she is trying to trap him into marriage.

Dupea goes into Los Angeles and attends a recording session of his sister, Partita (Lois Smith), who, like him, is an accomplished pianist. It is evident now that he is no common oil laborer; he is the music-oriented and very brilliant son of a family of wealthy and eccentric musicians who has been unable to run from what he calls his "auspicious beginnings." Partita, however, informs him that their father has had a stroke which has paralyzed his vocal chords, and is now confined to his home in the state of Washington.

Dupea, meanwhile, cannot shake Rayette, so he takes her with him when he drives north to Washington to visit his dying father. On the way there is a brilliant interlude when they pick up a couple of female hitch-hikers, one of them a brassy lesbian who is thumbing her way to Alaska with her girl friend because they are obsessed with cleanliness and have heard that Alaska is ecologically clean. They go to a roadside restaurant, and, in the most memorable sequence of the film, Dupea deliberately quarrels with the waitress and the owner. This whole sequence is brilliantly executed, and although it is admittedly a deviation from the main story line, it, more than anything else, explains Dupea's psyche and sets the stage for his subsequent behavior when he reaches his father's home.

He realizes that Rayette is too offbeat to present to his family, so he deposits her in a nearby motel and goes on to his father's home by himself. He dines there with his father, who has been painfully stricken dumb, his sister, and Catherine Van Ost (Susan Anspach), a charming piano student who is visiting the family with her boyfriend. Dupea immediately recognizes in Catherine the kind of girl who is in every way right for him. He boldly woos her, and although she resists his advances at first, she is attracted, and they make love.

Rayette rebels at being installed in a motel, and appears on the scene as Dupea's sweetheart. The family is coolly amused by her brashness, and they invite her to stay with them. Dupea is furious with her, but helpless to control her behavior. Furthermore, he has a disappointing confrontation with his father, and when he asks Catherine to go away with him, she turns him down because he lacks stability. Dupea leaves, and Rayette, who sticks to him like a leech, accompanies him on the way back to Los Angeles. He realizes that she is the most exasperating female he has ever encountered, and at a truck stop he manages to ditch her and get a ride back to somewhere else with a compatible truck driver. He has left his car for her, but wants nothing more to do with her, for he is off on a new journey to find himself in a new way. The title *Five Easy Pieces* does not refer to the sexual conquests of the main character as many filmgoers believe, but to the name of an elementary book of music which all piano students know; once they have learned that quintet of "easy" pieces, they are ready to learn advanced compositions. In other words, once they have mastered the basics, they are ready for the real compositions. Likewise, Dupea, once he has found himself, may be ready to face life.

More than one critic has commented that, in style, the film is more French than it is Hollywood, more like Truffaut's *Shoot the Piano Player* (1960) or Eric Rohmer's *My Night at Maud's* (1969). Its screenplay by Adrien Joyce (from a story by Bob Rafelson and Adrien Joyce) is immaculately constructed, and although it won an Academy Award nomination, the Oscar went to the writers of *Patton* (1970). The film is neatly directed by Bob Rafelson, who had previously worked with Nicholson in a film the latter wrote, entitled *Head* (1968).

Jack Nicholson has acted in a series of "B" pictures from 1957 to 1969, and had a devoted following by the time he played the lawyer who takes to the road with Peter Fonda and Dennis Hopper in *Easy Rider* (1969). Nicholson has a kind of wry, provocative amusement in his eyes that makes him ideal for the casually inconoclastic characters he plays so well. His success has continued in all his subsequent films, including *Carnal Knowledge* (1971), *The Last Detail* (1973), *Chinatown* (1974), and, finally, the picture that brought him an Academy Award in 1975, *One Flew Over the Cuckoo's Nest*.

DeWitt Bodeen

FIVE FINGERS

Released: 1952
Production: Otto Lang for Twentieth Century-Fox
Direction: Joseph L. Mankiewicz
Screenplay: Michael Wilson and Joseph L. Mankiewicz (uncredited); based
    on the novel *Operation Cicero* by L. C. Moyzisch
Cinematography: Norbert Brodine
Editing: James B. Clark
Music: Bernard Herrmann
Running time: 108 minutes

> *Principal characters:*
> Ulysses Diello ("Cicero") .... James Mason
> Countess Anna Staviska ....Danielle Darrieux
> George Travers .... Michael Rennie
> Sir Frederic .... Walter Hampden
> L. C. Moyzisch .... Oscar Karlweis
> Colonel Von Richter .... Herbert Berghof
> Count Von Papen ....John Wengraf

When *All About Eve* won the Academy Award for Best Picture of 1950, the Oscar, as was customary, was accepted by the producer of the film, Darryl F. Zanuck of Twentieth Century-Fox. Zanuck was only too aware, however, that the real winner that evening was Joseph L. Mankiewicz, who for the second year in a row had won Academy Awards for Best Original Screenplay and Best Direction. Mankiewicz's 1949 Oscars were for *A Letter to Three Wives*, although the picture itself was passed over by the Academy voters in favor of *All the King's Men*. Shortly after *All About Eve* was released, and while Mankiewicz was still preparing *People Will Talk* (1951), his next project, Zanuck wrote Mankiewicz a confidential memo informing him that his films for the studio would no longer be released as Zanuck productions. Zanuck later relented and accepted credit as the producer of *People Will Talk*, but Mankiewicz had already reached the conclusion that it was time he left Twentieth Century-Fox, where he had been under contract since 1943 after years of experience as a writer and producer at Paramount and M-G-M.

While casting about for a project that would enable him to work out his contract without the sort of major creative effort called for by *All About Eve*, Mankiewicz came across a completed screenplay by Michael Wilson which was just about to go into production. Wilson's script, which at that point was still called *Operation Cicero* after the title of the book by L. C. Moyzisch on which it was based, was a fictionalized account of the means whereby the valet to the British Ambassador to Turkey during World War II was able to photograph and sell to German intelligence copies of most of the Allies' top secret documents, including the final plans for the Normandy invasion of 1944. Moyzisch had been an attaché with the German embassy in Turkey, and Cicero was the code name given the valet by German intelligence. In Mankiewicz's revised screenplay for *Five Fingers*, the cynical German Ambassador, Von Papen, remarks that what has surprised him about his superior's choice of the name of the famous Roman orator and statesman was that they had even heard of him. Mankiewicz enthusiastically wrote Zanuck that he thought the script had "more than just potentialities—it is *on the verge* of being superb." The picture had already been assigned to Henry Hathaway, but Zanuck gave *Operation Cicero* to Mankiewicz with the stipulation that he not take a writer's credit for his script revisions, and that he accept Zanuck's friend, Otto Lang, as nominal producer. According to Mankiewicz's biographer Kenneth L. Geist, Lang was a former ski instructor who was learning the picture business from Zanuck in return for his tutelage on the slopes. Mankiewicz began by going through Wilson's script and, without changing his outline of the action, replacing most of the original dialogue with new lines of his own invention. Wilson has since contended that "no more than twenty-five to thirty lines" were rewritten by Mankiewicz, although textual comparisons of the Wilson and Mankiewicz screenplays prove otherwise.

Operation Cicero had been planned as a late entry in the well-received series of semidocumentary films Fox had produced since the war. At Zanuck's insistence, the title was changed to the meaningless *Five Fingers* because three of the studio's biggest hits in the genre had also had numerals in their titles: *The House on 92nd Street* (1945), *13 Rue Madeleine* (1946), and *Call Northside 777* (1948). A Fox-produced television series called *5 Fingers* also ran for a short time on NBC in 1959; but except that it was concerned with espionage, it bore no other resemblance to Mankiewicz's film. Most of the semidocumentaries carried full-frame titles proudly announcing that they were based on fact and had been filmed in the locales where the events depicted had originally taken place. Mankiewicz and a camera crew spent seven weeks in Ankara and Istanbul shooting exterior scenes with doubles for the actors who would appear in the interiors to be shot after they returned to Hollywood. While Mankiewicz was in Turkey, he arranged a series of meetings with Eliaza Bazna, the real-life "Cicero" of the story. Bazna offered to sell Mankiewicz some additional information that Moyzisch had not included in his book. Mankiewicz refused Bazna's offer "on principle," according to Geist, but he arranged to have their meetings photographed by a man with a hidden camera. The pictures thus obtained provided useful publicity when they were featured in an article in *Life* magazine.

Mankiewicz later described Bazna as "the most obvious-looking villain I've ever met. He was almost bald with wisps of hair across his head, gold teeth, and two different-color eyes." In the film, Bazna, called Diello, is played by the darkly handsome James Mason, who nevertheless conveys the moral ugliness of a man who is willing to sell the Nazis information which could help them win the war. With the utmost self-confidence, Diello arrogantly stops Moyzisch (Oscar Karlweis) outside his quarters in the German embassy in Ankara and demands to speak to him alone. He tells Moyzisch that, in exchange for £20,000 the first week and £15,000 a week thereafter, he will supply him with rolls of film containing photographs of every top secret document that crosses the British Ambassador's desk. Moyzisch reports Diello's offer to Von Papen (John Wengraf), who in turn informs his superiors in Berlin. German intelligence agrees to pay Diello the sums he has asked, but they are too mistrustful to make proper use of the information he gives them.

Diello's motive in asking for so much money is revealed in his scenes with the Countess Staviska (Danielle Darrieux), the beautiful but impoverished widow of his previous employer, a Polish count. Since the start of the war, the Countess has been living in exile in Turkey, where Diello had met her again after his arrival with the British Ambassador. On the night that he receives his first payment from Moyzisch, Diello stops by her squalid apartment with a proposition: he will give her £5,000 and extra money to set up a decent establishment if she will occasionally allow him to use her house as a place in which to conduct the mysterious "business" that provides him with his handsome income. He tells her that when he has accumulated £200,000 he plans to escape to Rio de Janeiro where, at last, he can live as the gentleman he has always dreamed of becoming. He suggests that she might like to continue sharing his wealth, at which point she slaps his face "because, in the manner of an inferior, you tried to buy something you didn't think you merited on your own." The character of the Countess had no counterpart in Bazna's life, but was invented by Wilson in his original screenplay. The dialogue for Diello's scenes with her was the most heavily reworked by Mankiewicz of any part of Wilson's script. The interaction of Diello's snobbery and the Countess' need for money crackles with an energy and tension far stronger than any motive of physical desire.

British intelligence soon gets wind of the security leak in the Turkish embassy, and special agent George Travers (Michael Rennie) flies to Ankara to alert Diello's employer (Walter Hampden). Travers has the embassy safe wired so that a loud alarm will sound if anyone tries to unlock it without letting him know first. In the meantime, Colonel Von Richter (Herbert Berghof), a Gestapo agent who has taken over from Moyzisch as the Nazis' contact with Diello, has become curious about repeated references he finds in Cicero's documents to a mysterious Operation Overlord. He suspects, correctly, that Overlord is the Allies' code word for their inevitable invasion of Nazi-occupied Western Europe, the so-called Second Front. He asks Diello to bring him copies of every document he can find containing references to Overlord. Diello agrees, but when he realizes that Travers is having him watched he decides to quit while he is ahead and flee to South America with the Countess, whom he now freely addresses as Anna. She obtains the forged passports and other papers they will need; but, on the day planned for their getaway, Diello learns from Travers that his former employer's widow has withdrawn the balance of £130,000 from her bank account, which she had opened at Diello's request so that he would have a place to hide the money the Germans gave him, and has left suddenly for Switzerland. The now penniless Diello tells Von Richter that he will get copies of the Overlord documents for him after all, in exchange for £100,000 in cash. He silences the safe alarm by removing a fuse; but, while he is taking his photographs, a cleaning woman replaces the fuse so that she can run her vacuum cleaner. The alarm goes off when Diello tries to replace the documents and he is forced to flee with Travers and his men in hot pursuit. He reaches Istanbul, where his ship for South America is waiting, and hands the roll of film over to Moyzisch before making his final escape both from the British and the Gestapo men who want to kill him now that his usefulness as a spy is ended. Von Richter has the information about Operation Overlord that he wants, but he angrily tears it up when Von Papen tells him that he has received a letter written by the Countess Staviska on the day of her flight denouncing Diello as a British agent. A brief epilogue reveals that Anna, who double-crossed Diello, and Diello, who double-crossed his British employer, were both double-crossed by the Nazis, who paid Diello the exorbitant sums he asked for entirely in counterfeit bills.

The previously mentioned Fox semidocumentaries had been straightforward melodramas, seriously intended, with a narrator on the sound track to remind audiences that they were watching a true story. *Five Fingers* opens with just such a narrator describing the political situation in neutral Turkey during the war, but Mankiewicz quickly punctures this balloon of solemnity with a scene between Von Papen and the Japanese ambassador at a diplomatic reception. The two men have been patiently enduring an after-dinner recital by a loud soprano when Von Papen excuses himself by whispering that he has a headache. "Besides," he adds, "I hate Wagner." "Count Von Papen," the other ambassador delightedly whispers back, "You are the only unpredictable German I have ever met." Rennie as Travers plays his usual droll self, but under Mankiewicz's direction the rest of the principal actors in the film approach their roles in a spirit of comic exaggeration. The result is that they more nearly resemble the character types in a Lubitsch comedy of the 1930's than the naturalistically conceived figures in typical postwar spy films such as Hathaway's *Diplomatic Courier* (1952). Even Diello and the Countess, as they spar and play their tricks, remind one of the crooked hero and heroine of Lubitsch's *Trouble in Paradise* (1932), that charmingly amoral comedy about two thieves who are last seen picking each other's pockets as they ride off together in a taxi. The other relevant comparison, of course, is between

Five Fingers and one of Alfred Hitchcock's comedy thrillers. Mankiewicz does not have Hitchcock's skill at staging physical action, but the whole atmosphere of cross and double-cross is distinctly in the Hitchcock tradition, as is Bernard Herrmann's witty and romantic score. The film was nominated for Academy Awards in two categories: Best Direction (which Mankiewicz lost to John Huston for *Moulin Rouge*) and Best Screenplay (which Wilson, and, by proxy, Mankiewicz, lost to Charles Schnee for *The Bad and the Beautiful*).

Charles Hopkins

FIVE GRAVES TO CAIRO

Released: 1943
Production: Charles Brackett for Paramount
Direction: Billy Wilder
Screenplay: Charles Brackett and Billy Wilder; based on the play *Hotel Imperial* by Lajos Biros
Cinematography: John F. Seitz
Editing: Doane Harrison
Interior decoration: Hans Dreier, Ernst Fegte, and Bertram Granger
Running time: 96 minutes

> *Principal characters:*
> John J. Bramble ....Franchot Tone
> Mouche .... Anne Baxter
> Farid .... Akim Tamiroff
> Field Marshal Rommel ....Erich Von Stroheim
> Lieutenant Schwegler .... Peter Van Eyck
> General Sebastiano .... Fortunio Bonanova

The first time Charles Brackett and Billy Wilder combined their talents to work as a writing team, one of whom also worked as producer and the other as director, was for *Five Graves to Cairo* at Paramount. This arrangement was a writer's dream come true, for it allowed them to control the production and the script. Their ensuing pictures included some of the brightest and most important films of the 1940's and the 1950's. Then Brackett moved to Twentieth Century-Fox to continue as a solo producer for a long list of films before he died, and Wilder is still working as an independent director, writer, and producer.

Five Graves to Cairo had been filmed twice before, both times as *Hotel Imperial*, the title of the Lajos Biros play from which it was adapted. The first time (1927) was as a silent, when it was one of Pola Negri's better features; the second time (1939) it presented Isa Miranda to American audiences in support of Ray Milland. Miranda never really made it as a star in the United States, although Milland was only six years away from winning an Oscar for *The Lost Weekend*. This second production had been planned two years previously as a vehicle for Marlene Dietrich and Charles Boyer to be called *I Loved a Soldier*, but Dietrich had walked out on the production and was replaced by Margaret Sullavan, who worked only a few days before she stumbled over a cable and injured her foot. The production was thereupon shelved and only revived in 1939 as a vehicle for the studio's new import, Miranda; it probably should have been left on the shelf, for it did not open the doors to a starring career at Paramount for her, and it was never anything more than a run-of-the-mill vehicle for Milland.

Brackett and Wilder only used the plot basis from *Hotel Imperial* as a jumping-off place for a brand new story line, which they called *Five Graves to Cairo*. Because World War II was in progress, the action of the piece was moved up to contemporary times, involving the conflict in Africa, with Rommel playing the key villain in an actual move he made in his North African campaign that nearly won victory for the Nazis. Brackett and Wilder turned the story into a tight, skillfully made thriller, loaded with suspense and as timely as the headlines of the day.

Five Graves to Cairo tells the story of a British corporal, John J. Bramble (Franchot Tone), the sole survivor of a tank battle during the fall of Tobruk. He manages to make his way to the Libyan border, only to discover that his regiment has moved on and the hotel where the English had made their headquarters is now held by the Nazis. The hotel's staff has run away except for the Egyptian owner, Farid (Akim Tamiroff), and his Alsatian maidservant, Mouche (Anne Baxter). Reluctantly at first, they give Corporal Bramble shelter, and he assumes the identity of a crippled manservant who was killed in a recent air raid. He and Mouche work to get information from Rommel (Erich Von Stroheim) and his officers. Bramble soon discovers that the man he is now impersonating had been in the pay of the Nazis, and Rommel divulges that seven years earlier the Germans had hidden huge supplies of gasoline, ammunition, and water in the desert; the key to the whereabouts of those hidden supplies lies in the position of the letters on the map spelling out the country's name, "Egypt." Those five letters become the titular five graves to Cairo, and it is Bramble's task to relay that information back to the British in Cairo. He manages only with the aid of Mouche, who gives her life to save him when his machinations are nearly discovered by Rommel and his officers. The British are able to locate the "five graves to Cairo" and usurp them, thanks to the information transmitted by Corporal Bramble, and Rommel and his officers are forced to make a hasty retreat from Africa.

The excellent dialogue and crisp story line elicit top performances from the cast. Franchot Tone, who never really got a great part from his home studio, Metro-Goldwyn-Mayer (outside of *Mutiny on the Bounty*, 1935), gives what is probably his finest acting performance in *Five Graves to Cairo*; and Anne Baxter, the only woman in the film, on loan-out from Twentieth Century-Fox, is spirited, sexy, and intelligent and gives the kind of performance that should have made her a top star. She did some of her best work in roles in which she had to use an accent (as in *Walk on the Wild Side*, 1962); she is always believable and dramatic. Erich Von Stroheim as Rommel gives one of the best performances of his long career. He fits his character to his own unique cinema personality and is wonderfully, Teutonically villainous, just he was later for Brackett and Wilder in *Sunset Boulevard* (1950). Akim Tamiroff plays the Egyptian hotelkeeper with a kind of catlike grace, and Peter Van Eyck, as a Nazi lieutenant who is attracted to Mouche, the maidservant, is a handsome addition to the cast, just as Fortunio Bonanova, as an Italian general snubbed and often snarled at by Rommel, is amusing and makes the most of the sharp, bitter dialogue assigned him.

The film should have won major nominations from the Motion Picture Academy members, but this was the year of *Casablanca*, also set in North Africa, which captured three Oscars and four other nominations. Academy members did at least acknowledge *Five Graves to Cairo* by giving it three nominations, recognizing its outstanding and dramatic black-and-white cinematography, its interesting interior decoration, and the superior job of film editing which never once lets the mood of tenseness lapse.

Brackett and Wilder were to go on to more popular collaborative efforts. Their films at Paramount—*Double Indemnity* (1944), *The Lost Weekend* (1945), *A Foreign Affair* (1948), and *Sunset Boulevard* (1950)—were especially honored. *Five Graves to Cairo*, however, began their collaboration, giving a promise for further work from two men who knew what they were doing and worked in complete harmony together.

DeWitt Bodeen

THE 5,000 FINGERS OF DOCTOR T.

Released: 1953
Production: Stanley Kramer for Columbia
Direction: Roy Rowland
Screenplay: Dr. Seuss and Allan Scott; based on an original story by Dr. Seuss
Cinematography: Franz Plancr
Editing: Al Clark
Music: Frederick Hollander
Running time: 88 minutes

Principal characters:
Arthur Zabladowski .... Peter Lind Hayes
Mrs. Collins .... Mary Healy
Dr. Terwilliker .... Hans Conreid
Bart Collins .... Tommy Rettig
Uncle Judson .... Robert Heasley
Uncle Whitney .... John Heasley
Sergeant Lunk .... Noel Cravat
Stroogo .... Henry Kulky

To the average adult, *The 5,000 Fingers of Doctor T.* may very well appear to be, as Bosley Crowther stated in *The New York Times* upon the film's premiere, "a strange and confused fabrication . . . with little or no inspiration or real imagination . . . abstruse in its symbols and in its vast elaboration of reveries, but also dismally lacking in the humor or enchantment such an item should contain."

To a small child, however, one whose eyes are not yet jaded and whose brain has not as yet become sophisticated enough to see through the rather elementary Freudianisms that are liberally spread over the film's eighty-eight minutes, viewing *The 5,000 Fingers of Doctor T.* can be an extremely frightening experience. For while most adults have worked through, exorcized, or repressed the many childhood fears brought to light in this film, children have not yet had the chance to do so. *The 5,000 Fingers of Doctor T.* illuminates many of the most basic childhood fears; forces children to come to grips with the possibility of these fears becoming reality; and finally provides an ultimate victory over their influence—a victory of good over evil, of courage over cowardice, of action over passivity, and of the young over the old.

The plot of *The 5,000 Fingers of Doctor T.* is very much like a child's nightmare, and the outlandishly surreal sets inspired by the well-known children's author/artist Dr. Seuss give the film the look of one as well. It opens with a young boy, Bart Collins (Tommy Rettig, who was later to star in television's *Lassie* series) wandering lost through a dream world of huge metallic balls and mounds set on a slick, gunmetal floor. As he moves over this oddly constructed universe, he is attacked from all sides by a group of darkly clad men wielding colorful nets just the right size for ensnaring small boys. As the pursuers close in on him, the picture fades out and in again to reveal the boy, asleep at a piano. As he screams for the nightmare to vanish, he is awakened by his piano teacher, Dr. Terwilliker (Hans Conreid), a mean, pedantic dictator whose only concern seems to be preparing his students for an upcoming recital, and who will not let "one dreary little boy" humiliate him. He further demands that Bart practice, practice, and practice until his technique is perfect.

After Dr. Terwilliker stamps out the door, Bart turns and addresses the camera directly, an act which draws us into his own level of experience, forcing us to confront his predicament head on. "Well, that's my problem," Bart tells us. "Dr. T. is the only enemy I've got." He further explains that he accepts this horrid situation only because it pleases his mother, who is having a difficult enough time of it since the death of his father. He goes on to say that sometimes it seems as though Dr. Terwilliker has his mother hypnotized, a fear emphasized by her ultimatum that he *will* learn the piano even if she has to keep him at the keyboard forever.

After this introduction to Bart's unenviable situation, to his lovely young mother (Mary Healy), and to a handsome plumber named Zabladowski (Peter Lind Hayes), the boy again lapses into dreamland as the film's main action begins.

Another fade takes us out of the Collins' home and into the Terwilliker Institute, a surreal environment whose labyrinthian corridors, trap doors, leering gargoyles, and other assorted oddities look familiar enough to anyone who has ever delighted in the remarkable world of the Dr. Seuss books. It is a world both frightful and wonderful, a Technicolor playground which doubles as a cage.

Bart is now a prisoner in Terwilliker's "Happy Finger Institute." He lives in a cell, is forced to wear the horribly absurd "Happy Fingers" beany (a skull cap topped by a bright yellow outstretched hand), and will, as of the next day, become an unwilling participant in the fulfillment of Dr. Terwilliker's lifelong dream. For tomorrow is to be the official grand opening of the Institute, and five hundred little boys, five thousand little fingers, will be forced to practice the piano twenty-four hours each day, 365 days a year.

Another inhabitant of Bart's nightmare world is the plumber Zabladowski, employed by Terwilliker to install fixtures in the five hundred cells to be occupied by the soon-to-be-arriving boys. Most horrifying to the boy, however, is the presence of his mother, who, under the tyrannical doctor's hypnotic spell, serves as the Institute's second-in-command. To make matters even worse, she is to wed the Doctor immediately following the grand opening.

With this horrific scenario in place, Bart's duty is clear. He must first enlist the aid of the kindly Zabladowski, after which the two will free his mother; foil both Terwilliker's grand opening and his marriage plans; liberate five hundred boys from the Doctor's iron clutches; and finally, see to it that his mother and the plumber discover their love for each other, thus insuring Bart a stable home life and a normal family.

Bart accomplishes all of the above-named tasks entirely through the use of his own resources. He bring's Terwilliker's world crashing down around the befuddled tyrant by inventing a "music fix," a hastily fashioned device that seems to draw sound out of the air like a room deodorizer. He frees the other boys from a life of slavery and finally brings Zabladowski and his mother together. He awakens to discover that again he has only been dreaming, but happily finds that Zabladowski is driving his mother downtown (we can only assume that their marriage is just around the corner). Upon their departure, Bart grabs his baseball and glove and races into the street, freed at last from the horrors of the piano and of Dr. Terwilliker.

During the course of the film the viewer is presented with a number of situations which provoke in children terrible fears and insecurities. As the young son of a pretty widow, Bart must both grow up himself and watch his mother get along without a man around the house, without a father/husband to guide and protect a weakened family structure through the hazards of daily life. Add to this the prospect of an unloving stepfather, and real fright results. Bart's worries along these lines are clearly manifested throughout the narrative. He sees that Dr. Terwilliker has a certain influence over his mother and concludes that he has hypnotized her, that he has turned her into an alien being unable to love or to think independently.

The film also brings to light the fact that children often see that adults do not take them seriously, that childhood perceptions are deemed discountable and illegitimate. Bart senses this when he tries to convince Zabladowski that Dr. Terwilliker is a tyrant, and it is only after the plumber is shown tangible proof that he is to be killed when his services are no longer required, that he decides to aid the boy.

Perhaps the most important message imparted by *The 5,000 Fingers of Doctor T.* is that while many situations are indeed frightening and are filled with uncertainty, anyone, including children, can take matters into his own hands, deal with problems and fears, and provoke effective, long-lasting change. Demons, once defined, can be exorcized. Wrongs can be righted. The world can be made whole once again.

We all need to be reminded of our own power from time to time, and film is just one mechanism by which we can do so. With so many films telling us that we are helpless tools in the palms of massive and uncaring power structures, it is comforting to see that *The 5,000 Fingers of Doctor T.* is more than a simple children's fairy tale. Rather, it operates, as do all great fantasies, on a variety of levels, the most important of which reveals us to ourselves and instructs us on how best to live our lives in times of great difficulty.

As a so-called "children's film," perhaps only the extraordinarily successful *E.T.* (1982) can be compared adequately to *The 5,000 Fingers of Doctor T*, for like the latter, the former is not merely about children, but seems to examine the very essence of childhood from a child's point of view rather than an adult's.

Daniel Einstein

FLAMING STAR

Released: 1960
Production: David Weisbart for Twentieth Century-Fox
Direction: Don Siegel
Screenplay: Clair Huffaker and Nunnally Johnson; based on the novel of the same name by Clair Huffaker
Cinematography: Charles G. Clarke
Editing: Hugh S. Fowler
Running time: 101 minutes

Principal characters:

Pacer Burton	Elvis Presley
Sam Burton	John McIntire
Clint Burton	Steve Forrest
Neddy Burton	Dolores Del Rio
Buffalo Horn	Rudolph Acosta
Will Howard	Douglas Dick
Roslyn Pierce	Barbara Eden
Two Moons	Perry Lopez

It is frequently argued that his two years in the army took all of the artistic fight out of Elvis Presley. Having changed the face of popular music more radically than anyone before or since, he entered the military a worthy successor to such rebellious heroes as Marlon Brando and James Dean, so the argument goes, and returned in 1960 tame and civilized, with his best work behind him. The truth is a bit more complicated. Presley's career undeniably went into eclipse in the early 1960's, but not without a whimper. Just as the music on his *Elvis Is Back* album can stand with anything he recorded in the 1950's, in *Flaming Star* Presley gave what must stand alongside his work in *Jailhouse Rock* (1957) as the best acting of his long, if erratic, film career; and both the album and the film were released in 1960, after he left the army. *Flaming Star* is noteworthy in another way as well: it marked the first (as well as best and last) attempt to market Elvis as an actor rather than as a singer. The effort failed, but on financial, not artistic, grounds.

As the film opens, we hear Elvis singing the title song over the credits; shortly thereafter comes "A Cane and a High Starched Collar," a song so undistinguished that Elvis' record company did not release it on an album until sixteen years later. From that point on, there are no more songs; instead of good songs, what we get is a good film.

Flaming Star finds Presley under the directional guidance of Don Siegel, one of the few directors of any personal distinction (Michael Curtiz, who directed *King Creole*, 1958, is another exception) to work with Elvis. By 1960, Siegel had one classic film already under his belt—the original *Invasion of the Body Snatchers* (1956); ahead lay a series of highly successful (and controversial) films with Clint Eastwood. Siegel's best work always has seemed to feature a lone, often antisocial protagonist, such as Neville Brand in *Riot in Cell Block 11* (1954), Mickey Rooney in *Baby Face Nelson* (1957), and Eastwood in *Escape from Alcatraz* (1979) and the "Dirty Harry" Callaghan films. In this respect, *Flaming Star* is certainly of a piece with the rest of Siegel's classics.

Flaming Star is a Western. It was not Presley's first Western—in *Love Me Tender*, his screen debut four years earlier, he played Clint Reno, a hot-headed young rancher in post-Civil War Texas. Pacer Burton, his role in *Flaming Star*, is also a hot-headed young rancher of the same time and place, but with a twist. His mother, Neddy (Dolores Del Rio), is a full-blooded Kiowa Indian, and Pacer's status as a half-breed—unable to accept completely or reject completely either side of his nature—creates the dramatic tension that shapes the film's narrative.

Pacer lives with his father, Sam Burton (John McIntire), his mother, Neddy, and his half-brother, Clint (Steve Forrest)—Sam's son by a previous marriage. The Burtons, as Siegel emphasizes repeatedly, are a close-knit family. Their first loyalties are always to one another. These loyalties are sometimes strained, however, by the Indian blood in the family. For although Sam and Clint are well liked by the surrounding ranchers and townsfolk, and Pacer is tolerated, the long history of mutual hostility between the Kiowas and the white settlers makes Neddy an outcast.

In the first scenes of *Flaming Star*, Siegel emphasizes the dichotomy between the Kiowas and the whites, and shows us that while Pacer is somehow a part of both worlds, he feels truly comfortable in neither. The white world is exemplified in a birthday party attended by Pacer, Sam, and Clint. There is laughter and singing, and the Burtons fit in easily with their friends, the Howards and the Pierces (although a reference to Neddy casts a momentary pall over the celebration). In a scene that follows shortly thereafter, however, we see the other side of Pacer's character. The Burtons are at home, on their ranch, when Pacer spots a lone Indian on horseback, several hundred yards away. Although he comes no closer and says not a word, Pacer turns to his family and says "The Kiowas have a new chief." When asked how he knew, Pacer cannot explain. He only knows that the Indian side of his nature permits him to interpret these obscure portents.

It soon becomes clear that circumstances will never permit the peaceful reconciliation of the two sides of Pacer's personality. The new leader of the Kiowas, Buffalo Horn (Rudolph Acosta), is a war chief, and the first of a series of raids he orders is directed at the Burtons' friends: the Kiowas attack and massacre the Howard family. Only Will Howard (Douglas Dick) survives. Wounded, he crawls out into the prairie, where he will reappear at a crucial point in the film.

The pressure is now on Sam and Clint Burton, who is by now engaged to Roslyn Pierce (Barbara Eden), to abandon Pacer and Neddy and join the whites in fighting the Indians. But Sam responds firmly. "This family will stick together," he says. "We'll resist whoever and whatever comes against us." A stormy confrontation with the Pierces ends when Clint shoots one of the clan for referring to his stepmother as a "Kiowa squaw." Typically, the hot-headed Pacer is dissatisfied with Clint's handling of the incident, swearing that the offender should have been killed.

This early indication that Pacer may be more Kiowa than white is reinforced when, with Sam and Clint gone, two men ride up to the Burton ranch asking for food. When they learn that Pacer and Neddy are Kiowas, their manner changes abruptly. They call Pacer "red boy," and demand sexual favors from Neddy. Pacer thrashes them and drives them off, but Siegel uses this incident to illustrate that his protagonist is inexorably being forced to deny or ignore the white half of his heritage.

The next day, Buffalo Horn returns to visit Pacer and Neddy. He demands that Pacer return to his people. "I don't know who's my people," Pacer replies, confused. "Maybe I ain't got any." Nonetheless, he and Neddy return with Buffalo Horn to the Kiowa camp to talk to the Indians and try to convince them to abandon their attacks against the white settlers. When a brave named Two Moons (Perry Lopez) asks Pacer contemptuously if the white man is treating him well, Pacer replies evenly "My father and my brother do." This is an important and revealing exchange. It indicates that while Pacer may be on the verge of rejecting the white half of his heritage, he is not ready to embrace the Indian half either. His family is of paramount importance.

The visit ends in a standoff. The Kiowas will not cease their depradations, and Pacer will not join them. On their way home, however, tragedy strikes. Neddy is ambushed by Will Howard, the survivor of the first Kiowa raid. A stunned Pacer kills Howard and takes his badly wounded mother home.

The white ranchers' reaction to the news of Neddy's injury further fuels the flames of Pacer's resentment. When he and Clint ride into town for help, the residents sneeringly suggest that they get a medicine man instead. The town doctor refuses to accompany them, and agrees to treat Neddy only when Pacer kidnaps his daughter. Neddy dies before they reach her, and Pacer is furious. "White men shot her and white men let her die," he hisses, vowing revenge. He takes Neddy's body to the Kiowa camp, where he intends to join Buffalo Horn and his warriors; but before leaving, he promises Sam and Clint that no harm will come to them.

This, however, is not to be. Just as a white man killed Pacer's Indian mother, a band of Kiowas ambush and kill his white father. Clint buries Sam next to Neddy's grave, and rides off seeking revenge of his own. He soon encounters the band led by Buffalo Horn and Pacer, and, after a long chase in which he is seriously wounded by a Kiowa arrow, Clint kills Buffalo Horn. Once again, fate (and the filmmakers) have given Pacer no easy way out. Betrayed by both sides, Pacer now abandons both sides and returns to his family—his brother Clint. "We're the only family we got left now," he cries, stricken.

The tragic denouement, now inevitable, soon follows. After seeing that Clint gets back into town safely, Pacer rides off to avenge his father's death. His parting words are "If it's gonna be like this the rest of my life, to hell with it."

The film's final scene is also one of its most powerful. Back in town, Clint wakes up and struggles to his feet as a voice announces "Rider comin' in. Looks like he's bad hurt." The rider is Pacer Burton, come back to deliver his own epitaph. "I've been killed already, I'm just stubborn about dying," he announces. "I saw the flaming star of death. I gotta last long enough to go into the hills and die. . . . You live for me." Thus only in death can Pacer embrace and unify the conflicting halves of his heritage. He will die like an Indian, but not before reaffirming his kinship to his white brother. It is a moving end to a strong film.

As in all of Don Siegel's films, the action in *Flaming Star* is tightly paced, as the director and his writers Clair Huffaker and Nunnally Johnson eliminate Pacer's options one by one. The cast works well together, with Steve Forrest and Dolores Del Rio turning in good performances as Clint and Neddy Burton, respectively. Even more affecting is John McIntire as Sam Burton; McIntire brings an unusual degree of melancholy warmth to his role.

But the best acting in the film is undeniably that of Elvis Presley. Though Pacer Burton exhibits many characteristics of the stock Elvis part—he specialized in playing hot-heads in the early part of his film career—Presley, doubtless with the help of Don Siegel, brings something extra to this role. Not only Pacer's anger but also his pain, his confusion, and, by the end of the film, his quiet resignation, come across as genuine. For the first time— and regrettably the last—in his career, Presley was an actor of subtlety.

Flaming Star was the second Presley film of 1960. The first was *GI Blues*, a tuneful if formulaic romp that was the top-grossing Elvis film up to that time. By comparison, *Flaming Star* was a financial flop. The film did not lose money, but Elvis fans had clearly expressed their preference; they wanted to see their hero in a singing role, and his manager, Colonel Tom Parker, quickly obliged, hustling Presley into *Blue Hawaii* (1961) and a succession of other profitable, if boring, ventures. It would be foolish, of course, to claim that Elvis Presley would have been another Marlon Brando; but the evidence in *Jailhouse Rock* and *Flaming Star* indicates that, with the proper directorial guidance, and given the proper roles, he might have become a very good actor indeed. Alas, this never happened.

Robert Mitchell

FLASH GORDON

Released: 1936
Production: Henry McRae for Universal
Direction: Frank Stephani
Screenplay: Frank Stephani, George Plympton, Basil Dickey, and Ella O'Neill; based on the cartoon strip by Alex Raymond
Cinematography: Jerry Ash and Richard Fryer
Editing: no listing
Running time: 97 minutes

Principal characters:
Flash Gordon	Buster Crabbe
Ming the Merciless	Charles Middleton
Dale Arden	Jean Rogers
Dr. Hans Zarkov	Frank Shannon
Princess Aura	Priscilla Lawton
Prince Barin	Richard Alexander
King Vultan	John Lipson
Prince Thun	James Pierce

Flash Gordon made his first appearance in 1934 in a comic strip by Alex Raymond. A Depression-weary America took an instant liking to this dashing science-fiction hero and his incredible adventures on the fantastic planet of Mongo. The tremendous public affection for this harmless bit of fantasy did not escape the notice of Universal. In 1936, the studio gave its veteran producer Henry McRae the then-incredible sum of one million dollars to create a thirteen-episode serial out of the best of Flash's comic-page derring-do.

McRae was able to stretch his lavish budget even further, thanks to the settings and costumes that artist Raymond had drawn for his strip. Aside from the outlandish monsters and a bit of futuristic machinery, Raymond had created a world that was littered with the artifacts and architecture of ancient earthly civilizations—primarily Chinese and Roman. Through the judicious use of props and stock film footage (from such films as *Frankenstein*, 1931, *The Invisible Man*, 1933, *The Invisible Ray*, 1936, and Twentieth Century-Fox's *Just Imagine*, 1930, among others), McRae was able to cut a number of corners on backgrounds and special effects. Curiously, this heavy interpolation of borrowed material into the *Flash Gordon* serial is not as distracting as it sounds; certainly the audiences of the day were happy with the results.

McRae turned the film over to director Frank Stephani, who wrote the screenplay along with George Plympton, Basil Dickey, and Ella O'Neill. The script followed the story developed by Raymond in his comic strip, and the film began with mysterious celestial disasters befalling the planet Earth. The disasters resulted from the approach of the planet Mongo, ruled by its diabolical emperor, Ming the Merciless (Charles Middleton), who is intent on destroying Earth, after first toying with it a bit. Ming causes comets and meteors to be hurled at the helpless Earthlings, two of whom—Flash Gordon (Buster Crabbe) and Dale Arden (Jean Rogers)—are forced to bail out of an airplane when it is struck by a bit of cosmic debris.

Flash and Dale land safely, but are captured by the brilliant-but-eccentric scientist, Dr. Hans Zarkov (Frank Shannon), who forces them at gunpoint to board his rocket ship. Zarkov plans to defeat Ming by crashing his vehicle into Mongo. The suicidal plan fails, however, as Ming's henchmen capture the trio before they can do any damage. The three are brought before Ming; the lustful tyrant takes a fancy to Dale, and Ming's daughter, Princess Aura (Priscilla Lawton), is similarly attracted to Flash. The remainder of the plot features one instance after another of Flash trying to save Dale, imperiled by one of Ming's monsters, only to be saved at the last moment (one episode would end with Flash facing what seemed to be certain death; the next would begin with his rescue) by the lovestruck Aura or by the brilliant Zarkov. Dr. Zarkov has a less complicated love life, but he is important to the plot, for it is he who persuades Ming not to destroy Earth immediately. Thus Zarkov and Flash have time to develop a plan to thwart Ming.

Meanwhile, Mongo teems with an incredible array of beasts and manlike creatures against which Flash must test his mettle. Needless to say, he is equal to the task. In a few instances, he not only defeats his adversaries but also succeeds in persuading them to join his crusade against Ming the Merciless. Among his new allies are Prince Thun (James Pierce) and his maned Lion Men, King Vultan (John Lipson) and his winged Hawk Men (who live in Sky City, a metropolis suspended by beams of light), and Prince Barin (Richard Alexander), who dresses like a Roman centurion and is in love with Princess Aura.

When Flash and his comrades launch their final attack, the forces of Mongo are defeated. Ming flees into the Sacred Palace of the Great God Tao, a holy-of-holies from which no one has ever escaped alive. Prince Barin marries Princess Aura, and Flash, Dale, and Dr. Zarkov return to the now safe planet Earth.

The plot may have been hokey, but the whole thing was irresistible, not the least because *Flash Gordon* featured inspired casting, especially in the choice of Crabbe and Middleton. Crabbe was an athlete before he was an actor. He won the Olympic four-hundred-meter freestyle swimming event in 1932, breaking the record held by another athlete-turned-actor, Johnny Weissmuller. His good looks and ambition took him to Hollywood, where, among his other roles, he took the perhaps inevitable shot at succeeding Weissmuller as Tarzan. He had made eight films before *Flash Gordon* made him famous. The virile Crabbe specialized in action and adventure films, including two more Flash Gordons, sandwiched around a Buck Rogers serial (based on another science-fiction hero from the comic strips) in 1939. He tried television briefly with *Captain Gallant of the French Foreign Legion* in the early 1950's, and retired from acting in 1965. None of his many roles brought him as much reknown as that of Flash Gordon.

Middleton was a veteran character actor who also reached the epitome of his career in the *Flash Gordon* serials, although he also played in such outstanding films as *Abe Lincoln in Illinois* (1940) and *The Grapes of Wrath* (1940). His Ming the Merciless appears to be the incarnation of evil; a more thoroughly dastardly character would be hard to find. In the other male roles, Shannon plays a relatively subdued Hans Zarkov; Alexander is a handsome Barin; Pierce is appropriately leonine as Prince Thun; and Lipson stands out as the barrell-chested King Vultan. The two female leads, Rogers (as Dale; she dyed her hair blonde for *Flash Gordon*, but appeared as a natural brunette in the sequel) and Lawton (as Princess Aura), are quite fetching.

Given the popularity of Flash and the other characters, a sequel was inevitable. 1938 found Ming the Merciless on the planet Mars (Universal capitalized on the Mars fever that gripped the nation that same year when Orson Welles terrified the populace with his radio broadcast of H. G. Wells's "The War of the Worlds"). Flash, Dale, and Dr. Zarkov investigate—Ming had been hitting Earth with a mysterious ray that deprived plants of nitrogen— and once again save their planet. *Flash Gordon's Trip to Mars* was the longest of the Flash Gordons, at fifteen episodes.

Flash came back for a final bow in 1940, in *Flash Gordon Conquers the Universe*. Crabbe and Middleton were back in their customary roles, but many other characters featured new actors. Carol Huges was Dale Arden, Roland Drew was Prince Barin, and Shirley Deane played Princess Aura. In this twelve-episode tale (which used a good deal of footage from Universal's 1930 feature *White Hell of Pitz Palu*), Ming is back on Mongo calling himself "the Universe"; hence the film's title, as Flash and his comrades fly once more into the breach to prevent the spread of a mysterious, Ming-inflicted plague called The Purple Death. Ming is defeated for what proved to be the last time.

Although the Flash Gordon serials were gone after 1940, they were not forgotten. Spliced together into single films, the three Flash Gordons appeared on television late shows throughout the 1950's and 1960's, inspiring a new generation of fans. One of these fans was director George Lucas, whose memories of the Flash Gordon serials prompted him to launch the epic *Star Wars* (1977) saga. *Star Wars*, in turn, sparked a boom in big-budget science-fiction films in the late 1970's, and the wheel came full circle in 1980, with the release of a new and lavish feature film entitled *Flash Gordon*. The 1980 version of the Flash Gordon saga was pleasant enough, and remarkably unpretentious, given the enormous size of its budget, but most critics agreed that it suffered in comparison with the original. Although they may never make anybody's ten-best list, the Crabbe–Middleton Flash Gordon films deserve to be remembered as an example of popular filmmaking at one of its apexes. Among the scores of cliffhanging Saturday matinee serials, *Flash Gordon* reigned as the undisputed king.

Robert Mitchell

FLYING DOWN TO RIO

Released: 1933
Production: Merian C. Cooper for RKO/Radio
Direction: Thornton Freeland
Screenplay: Cyril Hume, H. W. Hanemann, and Erwin Gelsey; based on a
  play by Anne Caldwell, adapted from a story by Lou Brock
Cinematography: J. Roy Hunt
Editing: Jack Kitchin
Dance direction: Dave Gould
Music: Vincent Youmans, Edward Eliscu, and Gus Kahn
Running time: 89 minutes

Principal characters:
Belinha de Rezende .... Dolores Del Rio
Roger Bond .... Gene Raymond
Fred Ayres .... Fred Astaire
Honey Hale .... Ginger Rogers
Julio Rubeiro .... Raul Roulien
Titia .... Blanche Friderici

In 1933, the overwhelming box-office success of Warner Bros. *42nd Street* revived the dormant film musical and inspired other studios to rush musicals into production. RKO's entry was *Flying Down to Rio*, a musical that combined exotic South American settings with the romantic theme of air travel. Even before the cast or director were decided upon, the studio dispatched a camera crew to Rio de Janeiro to film background scenes. Indeed, one of the strengths of the film is the artful blending of this background footage with the studio sets to establish the mood and look of the city. *Flying Down to Rio* will always be remembered, however, for the first important screen appearance of Fred Astaire (earlier in 1933 he had appeared very briefly in *Dancing Lady*), the spectacular aerial finale, and "The Carioca" in which Fred Astaire and Ginger Rogers danced together for the first time in a film.

Astaire had been a star in vaudeville and on Broadway with his sister Adele, but when she retired in 1932, he was forced to find a new career and a new professional identity for himself. He was intrigued by the possibilities of dance on film, but he wanted to be more than just a performer, and signed a contract with RKO, where he was able to supervise and control the choreographing, filming, cutting, and scoring of his own musical numbers. The studio executives apparently were not quite sure what to do with Astaire, however, since he did not fit any of the conventional ideas of a romantic leading man; so they decided to cast him in a secondary role in *Flying Down to Rio* as the leading man's wise-cracking friend. Together with Ginger Rogers (a late addition to the cast), Astaire handles most of the comedy and hovers watchfully on the edges as the stars, Dolores Del Rio and Gene Raymond, work out their romantic problems. But despite the handicap of such inane lines as "Hold onto your hats, boys, here we go again," and a hackneyed role as the hero's comic sidekick, Astaire, with his casual charm and debonair unpretentiousness, made such a favorable impression that many critics singled him out as the best thing about the film.

Although Astaire and Rogers do dance together briefly, this is not really an Astaire-Rogers film. There is no real relationship between them; both perform in nonromantic roles intended to provide the comic elements then standard in a musical. Their dance to "The Carioca" is engaging and spritely but not overwhelming. It is, rather, a portent of things to come in their later films—the delightful air of shared fun and spontaneity became one of their trademarks.

With its romantic setting of Rio de Janeiro and the glamour and novelty of air travel, the film has an energy and vitality that the tepid love story cannot diminish. As the film opens, Roger Bond (Gene Raymond) and his band, the Yankee Clippers, are playing at a Miami hotel. Roger, always on the lookout for a pretty girl though it has frequently gotten him and the band in trouble, notices a beautiful Brazilian, Belinha de Rezende (Dolores Del Rio), at a table with her aunt and some American friends. Attracted by Roger's blonde good looks, Belinha encourages his obvious interest in her. After her aunt leaves, she easily gets Roger to dance with her despite the warnings of his long-suffering friend, Fred Ayres (Fred Astaire), that it might cost the band their jobs. But Belinha's aunt Titia (Blanche Friderici) thinks Roger is a gigolo, and the hotel manager fires him for associating with the guests. The next morning, however, Fred tells everyone in the band including the vocalist, Honey Hale (Ginger Rogers), that Roger's Brazilian friend Julio Rubeiro (Raul Roulien) has gotten them a job in Rio de Janeiro at the Hotel Atlantico and that they will be flying down to Rio immediately.

By a happy coincidence, the Hotel Atlantico is owned by Belinha's ailing father whom she is returning home to visit. Roger, an enthusiastic aviator, immediately offers to fly her to Rio himself. During the flight Roger's airplane develops engine trouble and they are forced to land on a deserted island beach where Roger breaks down Belinha's already crumbling defenses by playing "Orchids in the Moonlight" on the specially built piano in his airplane. They quarrel, however, when Belinha says she must honor the engagement arranged by her family to a Brazilian. Belinha sleeps in the airplane and Roger on the beach. The next morning she refuses to speak to him, but when she sees some black faces peering at her from the jungle, she runs to him for help. Roger is struck down, however, by a missile that turns out to be a golf ball. A black golfer with a cultured British accent then appears and informs them that they are on the beach of the Port-au-Prince golf club, not a deserted island as they had supposed. Belinha catches another plane to Rio de Janeiro, and Roger completes the trip alone.

In Rio, Fred and Roger learn that the Hotel Atlantico has been denied an entertainment permit for its opening. (Although they do not know it, the problem is caused by the machinations of three Greek gambling operators— seen as menacing shadows—who plan to take it over.) Roger also discovers that his friend Julio is the man to whom Belinha is engaged. Since the hotel cannot have a regular floor show, Roger decides to save Belinha's father from ruin by staging a spectacular air show with hundreds of chorus girls riding on the wings of a fleet of airplanes. After the successful show, Julio, who now realizes Belinha and Roger truly love each other, hurries her onboard an airplane so she and Roger can be married by the pilot without delay. He then gracefully parachutes out of the airplane and out of their lives. Significantly, the film ends with a shot of Fred and Honey happily toasting the show's success with champagne as they watch Julio float to earth.

The aerial extravaganza that climaxes the film is still spectacular if slightly ridiculous, a fact which does not detract from its entertaining qualities. (Indeed, Ken Russell paid affectionate homage to this sequence in his 1971 film *The Boyfriend*.) As the flight of planes appears over the horizon, Roger's band strikes up "Flying Down to Rio." As the airplanes get closer, we see that chorus girls are performing on the wings of each airplane. They perform a series of synchronized, rhythmic movements in unison, reminiscent of a Busby Berkeley pattern, waving their arms and kicking their legs in a series of limited but effective patterns. In one breathtaking sequence, a few of the girls perform aerial acrobatics suspended beneath one of the airplanes; one misses the trapeze and falls through space but in the next shot she lands safely on the wing of an airplane flying below her. In another sequence several of the girls' scanty costumes are blown off to reveal scantier costumes beneath, and the girls then parachute to earth. Even to those who know that the entire sequence was shot in a hangar with the planes suspended from wires, there is an element of terror that adds to the effect, and it is a memorable, fantastic, and sometimes funny sequence.

One of the film's other memorable moments occurs when Astaire and Rogers, in the middle of a large production number of "The Carioca," step onto a small stage formed by seven white pianos to do a brief version of the dance and to "show 'em a thing or three," as Rogers' character buoyantly expresses it. The basic step in the dance is a backward and forward tilt with forehead pressed to forehead and hip to hip with the hands clasped over the head. Each partner is supposed to do a complete turn while still touching each other's forehead. "The Carioca" later became a craze and was taught at dance studios. The Astaire and Rogers portion of the dance is almost tantalizingly brief and ends on an amusing note as they bump foreheads and stagger dazedly around the dance floor for a few moments.

Astaire's first solo dance number in films occurs when he tries to teach some steps to the motley group of chorus girls hired for the Hotel Atlantico's floor show. The band keeps playing a song with an insistent beat that distracts him (a reprise of "Music Makes Me"), and, unable to control his dancing proclivities, he keeps breaking into a tap dance. Finally he surrenders and launches into a blazing tap exhibition of intricate steps. Astaire also does a brief tango with Dolores Del Rio to "Orchids in the Moonlight" but seems rather subdued by her stateliness, and it is not an important number in the film. Astaire's only vocal number, "Flying Down to Rio," begins the exciting aerial sequence that climaxes the film. It is a breezy, catchy tune that Astaire invests with all of his inimitable style, spontaneity, and vitality.

Before *Flying Down to Rio*, Ginger Rogers had appeared in nearly twenty films but had not yet caught the public's imagination. Her best previous roles had been as predatory showgirls in *42nd Street* (1933) and *Gold Diggers of 1933* (1933), and it seemed that she might be in danger of being typecast in such roles. As the band's vocalist in *Flying Down to Rio* she appears in a semitransparent black gown to sing the infectious "Music Makes Me" in her saucy style; and her costume seems to match both her vocal style and the somewhat suggestive lyrics. Her fresh, natural quality contributes to the fun of the song.

More than forty years later, *Flying Down to Rio* is still as charming, fresh, and enjoyable as the year it was released, primarily because of the presence of Fred Astaire and Ginger Rogers and its spectacular aerial climax.

Julia Johnson

FOLLOW THE FLEET

Released: 1936
Production: Pandro S. Berman for RKO/Radio
Direction: Mark Sandrich
Screenplay: Dwight Taylor and Allan Scott; based on the play *Shore Leave*
by Hubert Osborne
Cinematography: David Abel
Editing: Henry Berman
Dance direction: Hermes Pan
Songs: Irving Berlin
Running time: 110 minutes

Principal characters:
Bake Baker .... Fred Astaire
Sherry Martin .... Ginger Rogers
Bilge Smith .... Randolph Scott
Connie Martin .... Harriet Hilliard
Iris Manning .... Astrid Allwyn
Kitty .... Lucille Ball

In the series of musicals that Fred Astaire and Ginger Rogers made for RKO between 1933 and 1939, *Follow the Fleet* came after the elegant and glamorous *Top Hat* (1935) and was designed to present as much of a contrast as possible to it. This was done by casting Fred Astaire as a brash, gum-chewing sailor and Ginger Rogers as an entertainer in a dance hall in San Francisco.

In most of their films together Astaire and Rogers are strangers who meet accidentally. He immediately falls in love with her but she is distant and cool, if not openly antagonistic, and resists his attempts to ingratiate himself. Finally, persuaded by a romantic dance number, she yields. *Follow the Fleet* varies this pattern by having the two meet as old friends. Astaire plays Bake Baker, a former vaudeville performer who had joined the Navy when his partner, Sherry Martin (Ginger Rogers), refused to marry him, preferring to try to achieve success by herself. When Bake is granted shore leave in San Francisco, he decides to look up Sherry and renew their acquaintance. Although Sherry has told him she works in a "high-class place where all the money goes," when he goes with his shipmates to the Paradise Ballroom, a dime-a-dance hall, he discovers that she is a hostess there.

A further variation of the usual pattern lies in the initial reaction of the characters to each other. Sherry does not try to pretend indifference or conceal her joy when she sees Bake again. In fact, he has to wipe away a few of her tears. He, on the other hand, is more nonchalant and indifferent, although he confesses that he has missed her a little. She is sentimental and anxious to resume their old friendly relationship; he is brash, cool, and supremely self-confident.

There is also a secondary romantic story involving Sherry's sister Connie (Harriet Hilliard) and Bake's sailor friend Bilge (Randolph Scott) which tends to slow the pace of the film. Connie is, at first, a mousy schoolteacher, who comes to the Paradise Ballroom to see Sherry. Once she removes her glasses and puts on a glittery evening gown, however, she is beautiful enough to attract Bilge's attention. Because he does not want to get married, Bilge stops seeing Connie when she starts getting "serious." There are several quarrels and reconciliations between the two couples before they are happily brought together at the end. The major complication is the fact that Connie needs money to salvage and refurbish her father's ship for Bilge, because his dream is to be the captain of his own ship someday. To solve this problem, Bake and Sherry stage a show to raise the money.

In *Follow the Fleet* the musical numbers are not as well-integrated as those in some of the other films in the series, but this does not make them less enjoyable in themselves. They are magnificent set pieces that show off the versatility, range, and skillful teamwork of Astaire and Rogers. "We Saw the Sea" at once establishes the film's mood and the character of Bake. It is sung by Bake in his sailor's uniform with a chorus of sailors on a white battleship. After he sings the lyrics, the sailors pick him up and toss him about before letting him fall to the deck.

At the Paradise Ballroom, Sherry entertains the customers with the catchy song "Let Yourself Go," a jazzy tune intended to typify the big band/swing era of the 1930's. Later, Sherry and Bake dance to the song in a competition sponsored by the Paradise. Couples for the dance contest were recruited by dance director Hermes Pan from various ballrooms in Los Angeles, and the best were selected to compete against Bake and Sherry in the picture. Instead of invoking glamour and sophistication, the dance tries to create a contemporary, modern mood. There are shifts in the rhythm and tempo of the dance as Bake and Sherry try to outdo their competitors. In contrast to Rogers, Astaire uses his upper body a great deal, especially his arms, as the two sometimes balance on one foot, and at other times throw their whole bodies into a step. At one point Sherry leans back and Bake catches her and holds her just off the floor for a moment, a movement in keeping with the flashy, exhibitionistic effects appropriate to a dance contest. At the end they each drop to one knee, both arms outstretched, asking for and receiving the applause of the sailors at the Paradise. It is an exciting dance, and its mood and tone are perfectly matched to its place in the story.

In order to help Connie pay for salvaging her father's ship, Bake decides to put on a show in which he and Sherry will star. We see them rehearsing one number for the show, "I'm Putting All My Eggs in One Basket," which Bake first plays on the piano and then sings to Sherry. After he finishes, she sings a chorus to him, then he pulls her up onto the stage. The dance they do is a lighthearted comedy of errors, almost a parody of their inimitable timing and teamwork. "It was every old vaudeville trick in the world stuck into one number," dance director Pan has commented. Rogers, for example, with hunched shoulders and deep concentration, continues a step after Astaire has gone on to something else. When he stops, she bumps into him, sending him flying offstage. It happens again, but the next time Astaire steps cannily aside, letting Rogers' momentum carry *her* off the stage. At one point he stops her and starts her again in the right step. Another time, fists up like boxers, they mime a boxing match. Finally Astaire gives up in disgust, sits down, and begins reading a newspaper. As Rogers dances by alone, he suddenly springs up, catches her by the arms and whirls her around the stage. At the end, they cannot even take their bows together because they keep getting in each other's way.

The big dramatic and romantic duet of the film, "Let's Face the Music and Dance," has no relation to the rest of the story but is inserted as a number in the show being performed on the ship. It is a completely self-contained miniature drama with its own special resonance and meaning. The haunting song and the beautiful, elegant dance provide the glamour and sophistication so conspicuously lacking in the rest of the film. Indeed, it is the only time in the film Astaire appears in his trademark outfit—white tie and tails.

The curtain opens on a Monte Carlo gambling casino with Bake at the roulette table surrounded by beautiful women. He quickly loses all of his money and is deserted by the women. The curtain then closes and opens on a terrace overlooking the sea where we see Bake pointedly shunned by all the passersby. Alone now, he takes a pistol out of his pocket, looks around to be sure he is alone, and puts the gun to his temple. He is startled, however, by Sherry, who enters and stops at the edge of the railing surrounding the terrace, twisting a long scarf in her hands. When she steps up onto the railing as if preparing to leap, he runs over and stops her. Then, to let her know that he too is troubled, he shows her his gun and empty wallet before throwing them both away with exaggerated theatrical gestures. While she leans despondently against a pillar, he sings, "There may be trouble ahead, but while there's moonlight and music and love and romance, let's face the music and dance."

At first she tries to ignore the invitation, but as he dances in front of her, using his hands as well as his body to entice her into the dance, she allows herself to be caught up in the spell of the music. Every graceful movement, every gesture, is used to establish the mood of melancholy and romance in which this dance is steeped. Several times she stands away from him at arm's length as if in a reluctant parting, but he holds her by both hands, compelling her to return to him and to the dance. At one point they circle each other, turning first one shoulder then the other toward each other in a series of abrupt, dramatic movements. Both use their arms and hands a great deal to create beautiful, graceful patterns that become part of the flow of the dance as well as providing dramatic emphasis. Sherry's dress of metallic threads, weighted at the sleeves and the hem, winds and unwinds around her, itself becoming part of the dance. At the end, Bake and Sherry sink to their knees, slowly rise together, then exit bravely, their backs arched, one knee held high, their heads thrown back, personifications of gallantry and courage.

Despite the problems caused by the inclusion of the uninteresting romance between Bilge and Connie, *Follow the Fleet* shows Astaire and Rogers at their best with all the qualities audiences had now come to expect from them—spontaneity, freshness, charm, and exquisite dancing. Even in a sailor suit, Astaire is never less than graceful, and Rogers in her satin sailor costume has all of her usual charm.

Astaire has one solo, "I'd Rather Lead a Band," in which he sings and dances on board ship in his white sailor's uniform. The number is in three parts—Astaire dancing by himself, Astaire tapping out commands to a double line of sailors as he "reviews" them, and then, as they march in place to establish a "base rhythm," Astaire being stimulated by their beat to a new exhibition of dazzling tapping as the sailors march off, leaving him alone for the finale.

From ballet, tap, and ballroom dancing, Astaire created for himself what he calls an "outlaw style" that blends all three. In all of his solo dances and in the dances with Ginger Rogers one can see favorite elements of this "outlaw style" which he used to great effect. He especially liked sudden transitions from flowing movements to abrupt stops. The technique of abrupt stops, holding the pose for a moment before continuing with the next step, is used for dramatic emphasis and contrast in both "Let Yourself Go" and "I'd Rather Lead a Band." Astaire received no screen credit for either dance direction or choreography for this film, although he was largely responsible for them. He worked in close collaboration with Hermes Pan on the dances in *Follow the Fleet*, as he did in all of their other films together. Astaire was primarily responsible for the way in which the dances were filmed, in addition to their staging. In addition to the actual filming of the dances, Astaire also supervised the orchestration and editing of the numbers, so that he was totally in charge of all aspects of the dances. He disliked "reaction shots" (shots of people watching the dancers), and tried to maintain proper camera angles so that the dances were all filmed at eye level, thus giving the audience a perfect perspective; he did not use close-ups on head or feet.

Julia Johnson

FOOTLIGHT PARADE

Released: 1933
Production: Warner Bros.
Direction: Lloyd Bacon
Screenplay: Manuel Seff and James Seymour
Cinematography: George Barnes
Editing: George Amy
Music direction: Busby Berkeley
Song: Harry Warren and Al Dubin
Running time: 104 minutes

Principal characters:
Chester Kent .... James Cagney
Nan Prescott .... Joan Blondell
Bea Thorn .... Ruby Keeler
Scotty Blair .... Dick Powell
Silas Gould (Kent's partner) .... Guy Kibbee
Harriet Bowers Gould .... Ruth Donnelly
Vivian Rich .... Claire Dodd
Cynthia Kent .... Renee Whitney

The year 1933 was an important one for the film musical and for Warner Bros. The studio, which had pioneered the sound film in 1927 with *The Jazz Singer*, was in some financial trouble. Three smash hit musicals in that year solved their money problems, however, and marked the emergence of an important new talent in the world of the cinema musical: Busby Berkeley. *Footlight Parade* was the third, and in some ways the most impressive, of these films. Lloyd Bacon's fast-paced direction, James Cagney's superlative performance, and a good script with plenty of snappy dialogue and well-drawn characters combined with some of Berkeley's best musical extravaganzas to make *Footlight Parade* an excellent backstage musical.

The opening shot of the film is of an electric newsstrip on the Times Square Tower proclaiming that stage shows are dead—only talking pictures will be made in the future. Chester Kent (James Cagney), a producer of stage musical comedies, does not believe it, but he soon finds that his employers do not agree with him. They explain that they want no more such productions because they can make more money from films than from stage presentations. "Breadline, I hear you calling," Kent responds. Then he finds that his wife Cynthia (Renee Whitney) wants a divorce now that he cannot buy her the good clothes and good times that she is accustomed to having.

At this low point Kent decides to use his stage experience to make prologues, short stage musicals to precede the films in large motion picture theaters. He plans to have many units and book them into hundreds of theaters. We know that the idea is a success when we see a large sign advertising Chester Kent Prologues, and then a crowded waiting room.

Behind that waiting room we find that the company is, in fact, much like a factory. Dozens of prologues are being rehearsed simultaneously, and in the middle is Chester Kent. Under constant pressure to come up with new ideas, he also auditions performers, supervises rehearsals (sometimes demonstrating dance steps), works on promotion, and worries about a competitor who keeps stealing his plans. When Nan Prescott (Joan Blondell), his personal secretary, tells him she thinks his partners are cheating him, Kent says that he is too busy to investigate.

The pace never flags as we are introduced not only to Nan, who is a wisecracking blonde in love with Kent even though he does not notice it, but also to Bea Thorn (Ruby Keeler), Scotty Blair (Dick Powell), and Vivian Rich (Claire Dodd). Bea is a mousy office secretary; Scotty is an aspiring singer who is the protégé of the rich Mrs. Gould (Ruth Donnelly), the sister of one of Kent's partners; and Vivian is Nan's rapacious friend who has designs on Kent. Among this group there is a great deal of rapid-fire dialogue and witty banter that always makes a point, advances the plot, or furthers characterization.

Kent admires Bea, with her glasses and lack of makeup, because she has brains—she is not interested in show business; but when Scotty tells her that she is not alive, "not a bit feminine—all you need is the *Atlantic Monthly* tucked under your arm," Bea goes to Nan for help, and soon the drab secretary blossoms into a beautiful dancer and becomes a star in the company. Meanwhile, despite the efforts of Nan to warn him of Vivian's true character, Kent has fallen in love with Vivian and wants to marry her. All of these plot intricacies move briskly along under the direction of Bacon and are carried off with style and verve by the principal performers. Needless to say, all plot complications are resolved happily. Vivian is exposed as the cold-blooded gold digger she is, Kent finally realizes he loves Nan, and Bea and Scotty decide to sing and dance their way through life together.

The film vividly conveys the backstage atmosphere which is so important an element in the plot. It presents show business as tough, frantic, exhausting, and exciting. At one point Kent is shown falling asleep in his office after working all night; and always in the background are the constant rehearsals. Some of the numbers being rehearsed are full-scale production numbers seen at the end of the film, but one musical number, "Sitting on a Backyard Fence," is seen only in dress rehearsal in an empty hall. Unlike most Berkeley numbers, this one could conceivably have been done on an actual theater stage, except for one or two overhead shots.

In the film's denouement Kent must present three different prologues in as many theaters on the same night in order to secure a valuable contract with the owner of a large chain of theaters. To prevent his rivals from stealing his ideas, he keeps everyone in the rehearsal hall until the big night finally arrives. Then the company is loaded on buses and hurriedly shuttled from one theater to another. There are many shots of the chorus girls changing costumes on the buses, running in and out of theaters, and scurrying around backstage. All of this successfully conveys the tension, urgency, and pressures of an opening night. Director Bacon, as he had earlier demonstrated in *42nd Street* (1933), was an expert at capturing backstage atmosphere.

As might be expected in a film involving Berkeley, the musical numbers are the chief attraction. The three prologues, as directed by Berkeley, bear no resemblance to stage pieces; instead they are full-fledged musical numbers in which he utilizes all of his celebrated techniques. Although famous for his use of the moving camera, overhead shots, huge, elaborate sets, and dancers forming patterns, Berkeley never surpassed the numbers he staged for *Footlight Parade*. All are classics and show various aspects of his technique at its best. Each detail, as it unfolds, reveals his creative genius.

The first prologue is "Honeymoon Hotel," which in style and character is a variation of "Shuffle Off to Buffalo" in *42nd Street*. It opens in the standard Berkeley manner with Scotty singing the lyrics to Bea, followed by a close-up of a hotel doorman in a newspaper advertisement, taking the viewer into the actual number. The photograph turns into a real doorman who sings a line of the lyrics. Then the camera moves on to a clerk, a bellhop, a cocktail waitress, the house detectives, and the switchboard operator, each of whom sings a line of the lyrics. This is another typical Berkeley device. At this point Scotty and Bea arrive and are shown to their room, where they find a welcoming party consisting of Bea's parents and relatives. Next, a shot of the hotel in cross-section shows a pretty girl in a negligee in each room. After a scene showing Bea with Scotty in a double bed quarreling and making up, the camera moves in for a close-up of a magazine whose pages turn until they stop at a baby's picture. Although there are many indications that the Honeymoon Hotel is not very respectable, the number is performed with such a naïve air of fun and innocence that it is inoffensive.

The next number, "By a Waterfall," is one of Berkeley's most lavish and dazzling musical fantasies. As Chester Kent says, "If this doesn't get them, nothing will." Running nearly fifteen minutes, it uses two huge sets and was supposedly inspired by Kent's seeing black children playing in the water from a fire hydrant. The number begins modestly and builds gradually through one stupendous effect after another.

After singing the lyrics to Bea, Scotty goes to sleep. Seeing a few girls in bathing suits by a waterfall, Bea quickly changes so that she too can frolic in the water. Soon there are many girls by the waterfall, and then the camera moves in closer as the girls perform an intricate aquaballet. There are underwater shots, overhead shots, and close-ups, as Berkeley photographs the swimmers from almost every conceivable angle while they form kaleidoscopic patterns, break apart, and regroup. At one point the setting changes from the sylvan to an art deco Roman bath, and the dazzling variations continue. In addition to using a variety of shots, Berkeley continually changes the lighting for added emphasis and diversity. Sometimes the swimmers are dark silhouettes in the lighted pool, and then the effect is reversed, with the pool dark and only the girls lighted. At one point they form chains that become snakes, a Berkeley trademark, then butterflies, then a mandala in a continuous fluid series of movements. For the ending, the girls perch on a huge tiered fountain that revolves and spouts water, and the effect is that of a gigantic fountain composed of human bodies. The ending of the number brings us back from the realm of fantasy to reality as Bea sprinkles water on Scotty's feet to awaken him.

The final number, "Shanghai Lil," is the most dramatic and in many ways the most impressive number in the film. It is unique among Berkeley's creations because it is dominated and shaped by the vitality, singing, and dancing of its star, Cagney. The number tells a dramatic story before ending with some spectacular Berkeley patterns. In the time-honored tradition of backstage musicals, Chester Kent goes on at the last moment to save the show. Pushed down a short flight of stairs by the drunken leading man, Kent is literally forced into the number. We have already been prepared for his ability to handle the role because we have seen him rehearsing the various prologues and showing the chorus girls how to do the steps. The camera follows Kent as he threads his way among the tables of a barroom looking for his sweetheart, Shanghai Lil. The lyrics are half sung, half spoken by various people in the room as Kent makes his way to the bar, where he gets a bottle and sings about Shanghai Lil. There we see different types of people: a black, several Orientals, a number of sailors, and a British army officer. Each is assigned a single line of the lyrics.

Still searching for Shanghai Lil, Kent goes into a romanticized and extremely stylized version of an opium den filled with beautiful, long-haired girls reclining languorously on shadow-barred couches. Kent continues searching until, after a huge barroom brawl that seems almost choreographed, he comes out from behind the bar in a sailor's uniform while Shanghai Lil, played by Bea in a black wig and satin pajamas, appears from the other end. They sing the lyrics to each other, Bea does a tap dance on top of the bar, and Kent joins her. Suddenly a bugle call is the signal for sailors to form ranks and march off to their ship as crowds cheer. They go through various weapons drills before being joined by their Chinese girl friends. The situation is being reversed and it is Shanghai Lil who is looking for Kent and begging him to take her with him when he leaves. In the closing sequence the marching sailors, using placards, successively form pictures of the American flag, Franklin D. Roosevelt's face, and the National Recovery Act eagle. In the last shot we see Lil, now dressed in a sailor's uniform, marching off with Kent to board the ship.

Although Cagney is famous for his gangster roles, he himself is prouder of his musical films. *Footlight Parade* abundantly shows why. Indeed, the talents of Cagney and Berkeley dominate the film and make it a classic of musical cinema.

Julia Johnson

FOR WHOM THE BELL TOLLS

Released: 1943
Production: Sam Wood for Paramount
Direction: Sam Wood
Screenplay: Dudley Nichols; based on the novel of the same name by Ernest Hemingway
Cinematography: Ray Rennahan
Editing: Sherman Todd
Production design: William Cameron Menzies
Music: Victor Young
Running time: 170 minutes

Principal characters:
Robert Jordan	Gary Cooper
Maria	Ingrid Bergman
Pablo	Akim Tamiroff
Agustin	Arturo de Cordova
El Sordo	Joseph Calleia
Pilar	Katina Paxinou (AA)
Karkov	Konstantin Shayne

Many films have been adapted from Ernest Hemingway's stories and novels, such as *A Farewell to Arms* (1932 and 1957) and *The Old Man and the Sea* (1958). One of the most memorable of the Hemingway adaptations is *For Whom the Bell Tolls*, based on the author's brilliant 1940 novel of the same name. The film made its debut in July of 1943, after three years of prerelease publicity, second only to that of *Gone with the Wind* (1939). Since 1940 when Paramount bought Ernest Hemingway's controversial best-seller about an American university professor-turned-dynamiter on the side of the Loyalists in the Spanish Civil War, the studio faithfully kept the book's millions of readers informed of the film's production problems and progress. During the casting season, thirty thousand Hemingway fans mailed Paramount their selections for the various roles. In the end, the author's choices—Ingrid Bergman and Gary Cooper—won out, and it is difficult to imagine an improvement in either characterization.

The gripping story is set during the Spanish Civil War in 1937. Gary Cooper (who had previously starred in the film version of Hemingway's *A Farewell to Arms*) plays the rugged, unassuming Robert Jordan, a young Montana schoolteacher who goes to Spain to fight for democracy. During these brutal times, Jordan first dynamites tracks beneath a speeding railway train and then joins a brigand band of Spanish guerrilla fighters whose mission is to blow up a strategic bridge behind enemy lines. When Jordan goes into the rugged hills around La Granja and passes three days with the group in their cave hiding place, he meets Maria (Ingrid Bergman), a Spanish refugee girl with whom he falls in love. It is this love story that dominates the second half of the film until the end, when the ill-fated couple is tragically separated.

In outline, Dudley Nichols' screenplay is faithful—almost too faithful—to the slender plot that covers only four days in Jordan's foredoomed mission. Politically, however, the film maintains a safe middle-of-the-road position. For example, when Jordan is asked by his guerrilla companions why he fights for the Loyalists, he replies, "The Nazis and Fascists are just as much against democracy as they are against the Communists." That is the film's only political speech and its sole mention of Fascism by name. Franco's legions are called Nationalists; the assorted Loyalists are Republicans; and the introduction of a bungling French Communist commissar and a contrastingly practical emissary from Stalin splits ideological hairs to a point of ultimate confusion unless the viewer clearly recalls the corresponding passages in the book.

In general, it is perhaps most advisable to consider *For Whom the Bell Tolls* as a poignant, ill-starred romance depicted against a melodramatic background. Although the film leaves a great deal to be desired, director Sam Wood does manage to whip the action into a superb fury of excitement and suspense in his scenes of carnage, particularly in the climactic destruction of the bridge, and in the gallant, hopeless delaying action by El Sordo (Joseph Calleia) on a vulnerable mountaintop.

Fortunately, Paramount had the luck and enterprise to assemble a distinguished group of actors to play some of the most arresting characters to appear on the screen for some time. As the hero, Gary Cooper seems to embody the traditional yet romantic American male; he is courageous, tender, melancholy, taciturn, and forgivably gauche. A Hemingway prototype, Jordan is a man of action, and Cooper is excellent in this role. Ingrid Bergman, who was twenty-seven at the time of filming, is moving as Maria, whose father, the mayor, was murdered and who was herself raped by the enemy. Bergman's emotional range progresses from delicate to powerful. Her confession of the rape is an exquisitely calculated tearjerker, and her final farewell scene is shattering to watch; its intention and sources are so accurate that she seems to have really studied what a young woman might actually feel and look like in such a situation, nearly insane with grief and panic.

Joseph Calleia as El Sordo, the guerrilla chieftain, and Konstantin Shayne as Karkov, the Soviet journalist, are also well suited to their roles, but the film's highest acting accolades must go to Akim Tamiroff and Katina Paxinou. Tamiroff, a wonderful scene-stealer, plays Pablo, the peasant guerrilla leader who serves as a symbol of a man devastated by the fear of death. A onetime warrior who was responsible for terrible atrocities, Pablo has since become remorseful, and has taken to drink; he now opposes Jordan's mission to dynamite the bridge because such an action would force him to seek quarters elsewhere. Greece's leading actress, Katina Paxinou, with her beautiful aquiline features, is magnetic as Pilar, Pablo's indomitable woman. Possibly because she is the most fully realized character in the book, Pilar dominates the scenes in the guerrilla hideout in the mountains. Paxinou takes brilliant advantage of every facet of the character.

Cinematographer Ray Rennahan does exquisite justice to the High Sierras, with their mountain crags and hillside streams. Several hundred matte shots also add to the film's overall dramatic effects.

Although Dudley Nichols' screenplay follows close to the original Hemingway novel in parts, there are some major distortions and omissions. The film depicts the Spanish Civil War as a struggle between foreign powers as if there were no internal political struggles in Spain between Fascist and democratic factions. (In fact, Jordan says he joined the fighting as a protest against German and Italian forces using Spain's civil warfare as a testing ground for their own mechanized fighting units.)

At the time, the film's producers did not want to antagonize Franco and his sympathizers; in the film, therefore, the names necessarily had to be altered. In spite of studio officials' denials, Washington political columnist Drew Pearson and others continued to report various attempts by the Spanish government to block production of the Paramount film. One of Franco's agents in Washington made overtures to the State Department, and a representative in Hollywood approached Sam Wood on the subject. Yet, because only those directly involved with the production were permitted to see the film before its release, Wood was able to stall efficiently. Interestingly, Franco's objections were said not to have been based on the film itself, but on the advertising the picture would give the book, thus stimulating sales.

The political detachment of the film detracts from what could have been a more intense and better-motivated product. At the same time, the three-hour film (with no intermission) is overly long, and, in places, too talky. Nevertheless, *For Whom the Bell Tolls*, with its suspenseful action and depictions of love, death, terror, and passion, continues to generate excitement, and to this day holds up as solid entertainment.

Leslie Taubman

FORBIDDEN PLANET

Released: 1956
Production: Nicholas Nayfack for Metro-Goldwyn-Mayer
Direction: Fred McLeod Wilcox
Screenplay: Cyril Hume; based on an original story by Irving Block and Allen Adler
Cinematography: George Folsey
Editing: Ferris Webster
Music: Louis Barron and Bebe Barron
Running time: 98 minutes

Principal characters:
Dr. Morbius .... Walter Pidgeon
Altaira Morbius .... Anne Francis
Commander Adams .... Leslie Nielsen

From the time of Fritz Lang's *Metropolis* (1926) to the present, science-fiction films have expressed modern man's simultaneous fascination with and fear of the growing rapidity of man's technological innovation. This genre forms the screen upon which we can project our possible futures and see, through imaginative extrapolation, the results of our present acts. These projections are not, however, the purely mathematical or even logical outgrowths of our daily circumstances; they are an almost allegorical mixture of our cultural prejudices and our present fears.

When Boris Karloff cinematically immortalized Mary Shelley's Gothic figures in James Whale's *Frankenstein* (1931), he represented far more than the embodiment of that particular character. He personified the contemporary tension between man's newly found ability to control life and the still strong Judeo-Christian injunction against an individual's creations challenging those of the Creator Himself. Thus, beneath the film's technological trappings lies a bedrock of moral and psychological concerns expressed in the original Shelley novel.

An ethical antipathy to the forces of scientific change is found throughout films of the 1930's, even those that are not explicitly science fiction. In Charles Chaplin's *Modern Times* (1936), for example, the huge surreal machines which surround the Tramp are clearly antithetical to the film's sylvan, pastoral ending when Chaplin and Paulette Goddard walk away from the amoral city and into the United States' uncluttered agricultural past. Thus, throughout the era the tension between the machine and nature grew more pronounced and could only be resolved through escapism, as in *Modern Times*, or through the death of nature's near divinity, as in King Kong's unsuccessful epic battle against the Empire State Building and the airplanes which attack him.

During the 1940's and early 1950's, director/producers such as Val Lewton

(*Cat People*, 1942; *Isle of the Dead*, 1945; and *Bedlam*, 1946) focused this general phobia against technological change and began to apply it in ways that seemed more specifically to reflect their time's ambience. Thus, Byron Haskin's *War of the Worlds* (1953) stems not only from H. G. Wells's fascinating story but also from the McCarthy era's fear of Communist invasion. Likewise, Jack Arnold's *The Incredible Shrinking Man* (1953) seems to reflect the modern person's sense of diminishing self-worth in a growing mass society which was and is constantly threatened by the destructive power of atomic weaponry.

Throughout the middle and late 1950's, the period of open-air testing and of fallout shelter mania, science-fiction films found their format in the atomic potential for destruction. Typically, a hydrogen blast would unleash a mutated or primitive natural force which would revenge the systematic abuse of nature that had been seen in the 1920's, 1930's, and 1940's, as in *Godzilla* (1954). This A-bomb/monster combination was often too predictable and too facile, however, and it was not until *Forbidden Planet* (1956) that the psychological and moral tensions between past and future found an adequate vehicle.

Forbidden Planet, unlike its predecessors, drew from the two wellsprings of science fiction: a classic moral model and a modern psychological understanding. Thus, the story is a hybrid of two unlikely sources: William Shakespeare's last play, *The Tempest*, and Sigmund Freud's concept of a tripartite psyche consisting of the id, the basic primordial animalistic instinct; the ego, the conscious awareness of self and of others; and the superego, the moral moderator which enforces social and ethical norms in the conscious mind. This apparently infelicitous marriage is not as unlikely as it might seem; but to understand it fully we must turn to the film's plot.

Commander Adams (Leslie Nielsen) and his crew have been sent by earth to investigate an apparently ill-fated colonization effort of twenty years earlier. Upon landing he is greeted by a robot named Robby who escorts him to the home of the colony's two survivors, Dr. Morbius (Walter Pidgeon) and his extremely innocent and beautiful daughter, Altaira (Anne Francis). Dr. Morbius and his daughter, as he explains, are the only members of the original landing party who were saved from an unknown malevolent nocturnal power. When the spacemen are able to turn their attention from Altaira, they begin to wonder about Dr. Morbius' plush accommodations. As they discover, Dr. Morbius draws his physical wealth and, as will later be seen, his mental prowess from the mechanical remains of an ancient and highly evolved civilization, the Krell. He takes his material needs from a two hundred thousand-year-old powerhouse and has, through a Krell I.Q. machine, greatly increased his psychic powers. All this has led to an idyllic existence for twenty years; but now the spell is broken.

While Earl Holliman, as a space age cook, provides comic relief by convincing Robby to produce endless bottles of alcohol, the nocturnal monster stalks again. As we quickly discover, this invisible demon is a product of Dr. Morbius' sleeping mind. While unconscious, his most primal fears of the spacemen emerge as a telekinetically embodied monster which is fueled not only by Morbius' mind but also by the Krell powerhouse. At this point, the demise of the wise and superintelligent Krell race is explained. Having given themselves the power to materialize thought, they were, despite all their intellect, destroyed by the irrational urges that seethe at the bottom of even the most rational mind. Thus, Dr. Morbius' living nightmare can only end when he is destroyed by the amplified forces of his own basic fears.

Now some Shakespearean parallels become clear. Dr. Morbius is Shakespeare's Prospero, the magician who controls the action in *The Tempest*, and Altaira is his daughter, Miranda. Commander Adams is the handsome Prince Ferdinand. Robby is Caliban, the earthly—and here mechanical—spirit. The monster is Ariel, the effluvial sprite who does Prospero's bidding. Even minor characters, such as the cook, fit the mold: he matches Shakespeare's Stephano, the drunken servant. Thus, all these similarities tie the movie to the play and so provide a classic base of humanity, virtue, and the values of marriage.

Each major character also plays a Freudian role. Morbius and Altaira are, in this scheme, still father and daughter, although now in the archetypal Electra pattern (the female equivalent of the Oedipus complex) in which the overly fond father drives off a more appropriate suitor (Adams). Unable to realize this desire during his conscious moments, Morbius' id comes forth in the world of dreams. Within this sphere of wish-fulfillment—unhampered by the superego—the monster of his incestuous protectiveness comes forth and is, in this case, literally embodied by his Krell-enhanced capacity for telekinesis. Ultimately, Dr. Morbius is confronted with his own primal nature, and this confrontation, as in psychotherapy, leads to the crisis.

By bringing these elements together—Shakespeare and Freud, past and present, technology and psychology—*Forbidden Planet* epitomizes the inherent structure of the science-fiction tale. It brings into conscious recognition the forces that had always been at play in this backwater genre. In doing this with some quality, *Forbidden Planet* began the trend—especially in the United States—toward cinematic development of an often abused art form.

While the acting, especially that of Pidgeon, is better than the usual "B"-grade average, it still is not the film's saving grace; rather, the attention to the supporting technology is what helps to distinguish the film. The sets—the saucer/spaceship, Morbius' home, the Krell powerhouse—are all created with an attention to detail that gives them plausibility. This realism is complemented by the art work, which must create the impression of a new world and not, as was typical for this era, of a picture filmed in Arizona. The music, too, adds to this heightened effect, using electronic music effectively for almost the first time. Finally, Robby the Robot is himself a notable addition to the genre's repertoire of devices. Robby, the urbane, knowledgeable, almost human being, formed the prototype for a generation of robots to come, leading ultimately to H.A.L. in Stanley Kubrick's *2001* (1968).

Forbidden Planet, therefore, while not the most important picture of the 1950's, made a notable contribution to film. It helped to create a film precedent for the acceptance of psychology and special effects; it opened the way for the development of serious fantasy films; and it introduced the techniques which were to be realized most fully by the mammoth productions of the late 1970's: *Star Wars* (1977), *Close Encounters of a Third Kind* (1977), and *Alien* (1979).

Daniel D. Fineman

FORCE OF EVIL

Released: 1948
Production: Bob Roberts for Enterprise; released by Metro-Goldwyn-Mayer
Direction: Abraham Polonsky
Screenplay: Abraham Polonsky and Ira Wolfert; based on the novel *Tucker's People* by Ira Wolfert
Cinematography: George Barnes
Editing: Art Seid
Music: David Raksin
Running time: 78 minutes

Principal characters:
Joe Morse .... John Garfield
Leo Morse .... Thomas Gomez
Doris Lowry .... Beatrice Pearson
Ben Tucker .... Roy Roberts
Edna Tucker .... Marie Windsor
Freddie Bauer .... Howland Chamberlain
Ficco .... Sheldon Leonard

The critical and commerical success of *Body and Soul* (1947) paved the way for a second teaming of John Garfield and Abraham Polonsky, thus allowing Polonsky the opportunity of directing a film that he had written. Viewed upon release as somewhat of an arty gangster film, *Force of Evil* is something far more—a somber, unrelenting tale of corruption and attempted redemption.

Joe Morse, a young corporation lawyer (John Garfield), aligns himself with Ben Tucker (Roy Roberts), a smooth racketeer. Together they devise a scheme to turn a lucrative numbers racket into a legitimate business. They have discovered that superstition invariably causes thousands of nickel and dime bettors to pick 776 to win every Fourth of July. Joe and Tucker, cutthroat businessmen out to eliminate the competition, arrange for the number to hit, causing the collapse of all the small numbers "banks," which are unable to pay off. One such bank, however, is run by Joe's older brother, Leo (Thomas Gomez), a failed businessman with a weak heart. Joe owes his success to Leo, who sacrificed his own dreams by working to put Joe through school. Joe's rise from the slums to an office on Wall Street has left him with an enormous sense of responsibility and guilt. He must therefore coerce Leo into Tucker's Combination because he knows that when Leo's bank is wiped out with the rest, it will kill him.

In trying to persuade Leo to become one of Tucker's people, Joe meets his brother's secretary, Doris Lowry (Beatrice Pearson), a fresh-faced innocent in an otherwise corrupt world. Joe has never known anyone like her and is immediately attracted to her, while Doris, although disapproving of the kind of life he represents, is drawn to Joe and to the promise of excitement he offers. Meanwhile, two problems loom on the horizon for Tucker and Joe. A shadowy "special prosecutor" named Hall, whom we never see, is intent on trapping the Combination and its lawyer by tapping their telephones, and Ficco (Sheldon Leonard), Tucker's ex-partner from Prohibition days, arrives. He is a stereotypical gangster possessed of none of Tucker"s carefully acquired polish, and he is an unpleasant reminder of Tucker's past.

As the Fourth of July draws closer, Joe attempts to frighten his brother by arranging for the police to raid his bank. Everyone is arrested: Leo, Doris, Bauer, the frightened bookkeeper, and even the cleaning lady. Joe bails them out but Leo is adamant and will not join the scheme, clinging to his illusion of being a respectable paternalistic small businessman. When the number 776 hits and the small banks go under, Tucker, as a favor to Joe, allows Leo and his staff to remain in business, with Tucker running the show. When Freddie Bauer (Howland Chamberlain), terrified to see Tucker's gangsters in the office, attempts to quit, he is told that no one quits the Combination. Later, approached by one of Ficco's henchmen, Bauer is forced to arrange a meeting between Leo and Ficco. The "meeting" turns out to be a kidnaping engineered by Ficco, who is still attempting to force his way into the Combination. Leo is abducted, and Bauer, the timid Judas, is killed.

When Joe learns of the kidnaping, he bursts into Tucker's apartment demanding his brother's release. Ficco is there, now a full partner with Tucker. Joe is told that Leo has died of a heart attack and that his body has been dumped by the river. Suddenly the tension which has pervaded the film erupts into violence. A gun battle ensues, and Joe kills both men in the darkened apartment.

Leaving Tucker's apartment as the sun is rising, Joe finds Doris waiting. He runs through the empty streets until he reaches a great bridge and begins to descend flight after flight of stairs in search of his brother. He finds his brother's body where the gangsters left it on the rocks. Doris reaches his side as he turns away and leaves to surrender to the prosecutor.

Garfield's electric personality was never used to better advantage. Gomez's Leo is a remarkably defined character: a "good" man with a martyr complex that allows him to abandon his own dreams in favor of his brother's. In the kidnaping scene, for example, as he is dragged from the all-night diner to his doom, his crumpled body supported by his arms, Leo assumes the appearance of a shabby Christ. Pearson, who possessed the talent and "offbeat" beauty that might have made her a star, appeared in only one other film before disappearing from Hollywood. Chamberlain is the perfect victim as the frightened bookkeeper, first coerced into becoming a Judas goat and then slaughtered.

Force of Evil had some disturbing things to say about the law as an abstraction. Hall, the special prosecutor, is always mentioned but never seen. He is omnipresent and threatening, not unlike Ben Tucker. In initiating the wire-taps in his battle against organized crime, he presents an uncomfortable parallel to similar actions occurring during the Cold War hysteria which had already begun to cast a cloud over Hollywood. The filmmakers at Enterprise were aware of this; and, as a result, scene after scene reverberates with a palpable paranoia. The film's ending, centering on Joe's decision "to help," was, as director Polonsky admits, something of a compromise with Hollywood censors. Yet it rings true because the long descent to the bridge, "the bottom of the world," is representative of Joe reaching his nadir. He must commit himself to the destruction of the evil of which he has been a part if he is to survive at all. Far from being a noble act, it is one born out of desperation.

Force of Evil received little attention when it was released in 1948. Enterprise had lost a great deal of money in other ventures, chiefly Lewis Milestone's epic film *Arch of Triumph* (1948), and with the dissolution of that studio, M-G-M assumed distribution of the film and handling it as if it were a routine programmer. With time, however, it has grown significantly in stature. The richness of the film and its use of image and language indicate that it was somewhat ahead of its time and that audiences of the 1940's simply did not fully understand it.

Perhaps the very richness of the film is what made it so misunderstood, so inaccessible. It is a gangster film with allusions to the coming blacklist, but it is also a love story, not between a man and a woman but between two brothers who ultimately destroy each other. It is a film which dared to tell its audience that there are no easy answers—that perhaps no answers exist at all.

Michael Shepler

A FOREIGN AFFAIR

Released: 1948
Production: Charles Brackett for Paramount
Direction: Billy Wilder
Screenplay: Charles Brackett, Billy Wilder, and Richard L. Breen; based on
  stories by Robert Harari, Irwin Shaw, and David Shaw
Cinematography: Charles Lang
Editing: Doane Harrison
Costume design: Edith Head
Music: Frederick Hollander
Running time: 115 minutes

> *Principal characters:*
> Phoebe Frost .... Jean Arthur
> Erika von Schluetow .... Marlene Dietrich
> Captain John Pringle .... John Lund
> Colonel Rufus J. Plummer .... Millard Mitchell

The summer of 1948 saw the unexpected release of what is still considered the best "black" comedy to emerge from Hollywood, *A Foreign Affair*. It was the kind of film only Charles Brackett and Billy Wilder would have dared make on a postwar theme. It dealt with the twelve thousand American troops assigned to the American zone of Berlin, and with what came to be known as the "moral malaria" infecting them. It was remarkably witty and funny— in a sobering kind of way. *A Foreign Affair* remains one of the best of all the Brackett-Wilder comedies released by Paramount during the 1940's; and in addition to being funny, it provides food for thought, as well as a good photographic view of life as it was then being lived among the ruins of Berlin. Its exteriors were all shot in the actual occupation zone of that city.

As the movie opens, a congressional investigating committee arrives in Germany to track down the facts of what is really going on among American men stationed there. The most determined member is a spinster Congresswoman from Iowa, Miss Phoebe Frost (Jean Arthur), who is ready to be shocked by everything she learns and is equally confident that she can right all the wrongs she uncovers. Captain John Pringle (John Lund) is put in charge of showing her Berlin. He is disgruntled at first, because he himself has been involved in black market profiteering, and is reluctant to throw the first stone in an investigation. Gradually, however, she wins him over in spite of the fact that he has also been enjoying the favors of a onetime Nazi, Erika von Schluetow (Marlene Dietrich). Later, when Phoebe discovers what is going on between Captain Pringle and the lovely Erika, her annoyance and rage are boundless.

The pace never slows, in spite of such black comedy happenings as black market operations in full swing under the Brandenburg Gate by day and drunken gaieties in the cabarets by night—all patronized by the occupying armies. Driven to desperation when she tries to prove to Erika that American women are not the moral frumps that German women believe them to be, Phoebe makes the mistake of drinking too much champagne, which causes her to behave with abandon. She realizes that she has disgraced her country as well as herself; but before she returns home in shame, she wins the admiration of Captain Pringle, who recognizes that she is human after all. The audience now perceives that Phoebe is going to win Captain John, romantically. The sophisticated Erika, whose operations have been exposed, is sent to jail and placed under the guard of a handsome policeman. She proves that if a woman has something to sell in an occupied country, she can always find a willing buyer among the onetime enemy, even if it is behind bars.

Directed at a fast pace by cowriter Wilder, the motion picture's comedy never falters even under the blackest circumstances, and the cast of four principals constantly sustains the script. Lund as John Pringle has his best part ever at Paramount. The understanding Colonel is played with just the right degree of awareness by Millard Mitchell. Arthur as Phoebe Frost is cast in a role perfectly suited to her talents: she is officious and, at first, seemingly right out of the Bible belt. Then as she falls under the spell of Captain Pringle and becomes progressively more human, she turns from an ill-tempered spinster into a shy and very attractive woman.

Dietrich, as the onetime Nazi charmer, Erika, has one of her best parts. In addition to being well photographed by Charles Lang, she and Arthur have been given some very pungent dialogue as they spar for the favors of the hero. Dietrich, beautifully gowned by Edith Head, also has a chance to sing three songs in her own inimitable style. They are by Frederick Hollander, who wrote all of her best material when she was rising to fame as a top star at Paramount. In her husky style she sings "Black Market," "Illusions," and "In the Ruins of Berlin" with a wise, smiling amorality that is beguiling. Nobody else played a modern siren with the knowing sexuality that Dietrich always brought to her roles. In Germany during the 1920's she had played homewreckers and fast ladies of the evening with Emil Jannings, Willi Forst, and Fritz Kortner. The Hollywoodized Dietrich, however, proved to have unusual beauty, real chic, and a flair for high comedy rarely possessed by actresses known for their siren qualities. She had no singing voice, but she knew how to deliver a song, and Hollander knew exactly how to write for her. As she sings it, "Black Market" becomes almost a very evil ballad; the lyrics of "Illusions" have a kind of desperately resigned poignancy, while "Ruins of Berlin" is bold and boastful, exactly right as a song for one of the vanquished. When Josef von Sternberg brought Dietrich to Hollywood and made her an overnight star in *Morocco* (1930), he created a Dietrich image that had very little to do with the real actress. The last film she made for Sternberg was *The Devil Is a Woman* (1935), and that bears the full flower of the Sternberg image. By the time she made *A Foreign Affair* for Wilder, thirteen years had passed and that image had completely vanished. She went on, after *A Foreign Affair*, to play *Witness for the Prosecution* (1957) and *Judgment at Nuremberg* (1961), both of which had even less to do with the former Dietrich image.

Arthur, who has top billing in *A Foreign Affair*, actually displays a greater variety of acting talents than Dietrich does. She was under contract to Paramount during the silent era and rarely had anything to play except nice ingenues and breezy leading ladies. She established a very "becoming" image of herself with her healthy, good-natured characterizations of ordinary girls, made memorable by her husky, broken voice and completely honest portrayals. She could make almost any character she chose fit that mold, and she swiftly became a star. In one of her first talking features, *The Greene Murder Case*, she was able to confuse most people as to her identity as the real, more than slightly insane, murderess, simply because she was so affable, charming, and clever in her performance. Many a director has agreed that he would rather have Arthur play his leading female role than any other star, because audiences not only empathize with her, but they also really love her. Those same audiences, on the other hand, have always admired Dietrich, but only at a distance, because of her timeless, aloof glamour, which keeps them at a distance.

Viennese-born Wilder and Brackett, his collaborator in *A Foreign Affair*, were in an enviable situation as a team. They wrote their screenplays together; Brackett produced and Wilder directed, so they never really relinquished control over their property. A Brackett-Wilder motion picture is immediately identifiable because it is not only thoroughly professional, but also possesses an ironic humor that is inimitable. In *A Foreign Affair,* for example, when the camera pans down a Berlin street lined with its ruins, it is done to the melody on the soundtrack of "Isn't It Romantic?" They were fond of *A Foreign Affair*, although their most popularly successful collaboration was *Sunset Boulevard* (1950), and their own favorite film seems to have been *Double Indemnity* (1944).

More than thirty years have passed since *A Foreign Affair* was released. There is a new Berlin now, West and East, and the ruins have long since been cleared away. At any revival of this film, however, one finds audiences still intrigued by the fortunes of Congresswoman Phoebe Frost, Nazi sophisticate Erika von Schluetow, and American Army Captain John Pringle.

DeWitt Bodeen

FOREIGN CORRESPONDENT

Released: 1940
Production: Walter Wanger for United Artists
Direction: Alfred Hitchcock
Screenplay: Charles Bennett and Joan Harrison, with dialogue by James
   Hilton and Robert Benchley; based on the autobiography *Personal History*
   by Vincent Sheean
Cinematography: Rudolph Maté
Editing: Otho Lovering
Running time: 119 minutes

   Principal characters:
   Johnny Jones (Huntley Haverstock) .... Joel McCrea
   Carol Fisher .... Laraine Day
   Stephen Fisher .... Herbert Marshall
   Scott Ffolliott .... George Sanders
   Van Meer .... Albert Basserman
   Stebbins .... Robert Benchley

   Foreign Correspondent, released in 1940, signified a major turning point
in director Alfred Hitchcock's career. Although the film was his second to be
made in the United States, it constituted his first experience with a Hollywood-
type production. His first American film, based on Daphne du Maurier's
Rebecca, so retained the style and appearance of the director's English works
that it is difficult to think of it as having been made in Hollywood. Interestingly, this result was not due to any stylistic intention on Hitchcock's part but
was instead a reflection of the subject matter and of the production values
aimed for by producer David O. Selznick.
   Selznick had brought Hitchcock to Hollywood in 1940 with an $800,000
contract to make four important pictures. When the first project, *Titanic*,
based upon the story of the doomed luxury liner, had to be temporarily
abandoned, the director was given *Rebecca*, a property which he had earlier
attempted to purchase and produce in England. Hitchcock's second chance
to make this film of the Maurier novel was, of course, a major success,
earning the Oscar as Best Picture of 1940, but it also proved to Hitchcock
that working for Selznick would be a mixed blessing. In England, the director's creativity had been restrained by small budgets; in Hollywood, however, he could afford to explore more fully the technical tricks of moviemaking and experiment with projects that were not hampered by budgetary
limitations. There were, however, limitations imposed by Hollywood that
Hitchcock had rarely encountered in England, where he was in almost complete artistic control of his films. In the United States during the 1940's,
however, it was the producer who controlled the creative direction of the

project, and his intentions and wishes always superseded those of the director. When the producer was a man like David O. Selznick, control was imperious and complete. This was the situation with *Rebecca*, even though the film seems to be a reflection of the Hitchcock style.

Foreign Correspondent, Hitchcock's second American film, provided him with more artistic freedom than had *Rebecca* and at the same time afforded the director most of the assets available at a Hollywood studio. Hitchcock had discovered that some other producers were less likely to interfere in his films than was Selznick; thus he endeavored to make additional pictures on loan to other studios. *Foreign Correspondent*, loosely based upon journalist Vincent Sheean's autobiography, *Personal History*, the first of these additional films, was made for Walter Wanger and United Artists. Its budget of one-and-one-half million dollars, which represented the most money with which Hitchcock had ever worked, was principally spent on scenery consisting of a ten-acre Amsterdam public square, a large section of London, a Dutch countryside complete with windmill, and a large transatlantic airplane. These items were planned and constructed by an army of 558 carpenters and technicians. Additionally, fourteen screenwriters worked at various times on the screenplay, and more than 240,000 feet of film were shot and edited to 120 screen minutes. The film displays some of the finest visual design and cinematography evident in any of Hitchcock's productions, indicating that the director quickly learned the manner in which to make optimum use of a generous budget.

Unlike many of Hitchcock's other famous thrillers, *Foreign Correspondent* features no superstars. Gary Cooper, for example, refused the role of reporter Johnny Jones, and although Joel McCrea was eventually placed in the role and did a solid job, he simply lacked the box-office appeal of a major star such as Cary Grant or James Stewart. The problem was that the "thriller" was held in rather low esteem by 1940 Hollywood, and Hitchcock, who had not yet established himself as the master of suspense, was not able to recruit the big-name actors he desired.

Foreign Correspondent establishes a pattern of suspense and intrigue that would become a hallmark of many of Hitchcock's American thrillers. Johnny Jones (Joel McCrea) is a tough, hard-headed crime reporter who is reassigned by his editor to investigate the prospects of an outbreak of hostilities in Europe just prior to the beginning of World War II. He thus becomes a foreign correspondent, and temporarily changes his name to Huntley Haverstock. Arriving in Amsterdam, Jones meets Van Meer (Albert Basserman), a Dutch diplomat who has memorized a secret clause in an Allied treaty for his country. Traveling with the diplomat is the head of a pacifist group, Stephen Fisher (Herbert Marshall), and his daughter Carol (Laraine Day). Van Meer is to make a speech to the pacifist organization on the opportunities of averting war.

In one of the most memorable scenes of any Hitchcock film, Van Meer appears to be assassinated as he arrives to address the pacifists; the scene occurs in the Amsterdam public square filled with people carrying umbrellas in a pouring rain, and the murderer escapes in a chase beneath the umbrellas, the scene being presented through some excellent camerawork from above. An elaborate drainage system constructed beneath the set carried off the rainwater to maintain some degree of traction for McCrea and the other actors involved in the scene. The murderer is pursued by Johnny Jones into the Dutch countryside. At a windmill, the reporter discovers the real Van Meer, kidnaped by Nazis who have staged the assassination by murdering a double. The Nazis disappear with their captive while Jones is trying to convince the Dutch police that the diplomat is a prisoner inside the windmill.

Jones searches for Van Meer both in Holland and England with the aid of Carol Fisher, who is slowly falling in love with him. They discover that Carol's father, who has been masquerading as a pacifist, is in reality an agent for the Nazis and has been instrumental in kidnaping Van Meer and in trying to extract his secret information. Jones and Herbert Ffolliott (George Sanders), an English reporter, rescue the Dutch diplomat, but Fisher escapes with his daughter, who is now confused and disillusioned in her romance with Jones. As war is declared, the Fishers take a plane from England to America only to find that Jones and Ffolliott are also onboard, and as the reporters confront Fisher, the plane, mistaken by a German ship below for an English bomber, is shot down. The survivors attempt to stay afloat upon the wing of the plane while Fisher, realizing that he faces arrest in America, sacrifices his life to save the rest. An American ship approaches, frightening off the German one, and rescues the plane's passengers. Barred from telephoning their newspapers, Jones and Ffolliott pretend to make a personal call and then reiterate the story to the captain loud enough to be heard by Jones's editor on the other end of the line. As the film ends, Jones establishes himself as a top foreign correspondent and marries Carol.

Foreign Correspondent has achieved a well-deserved reputation as a masterpiece of suspense and intrigue, and was instrumental in upgrading the reputation of the thriller genre, being nominated for Academy Awards for Best Picture and Best Screenplay. The fact that the film won in neither category may be due to one significant fault in Hitchcock's effort: the film is overly long and drags in spots because of diversions in the story line incorporated to promote America's entry into World War II. The film attempts to merge two levels in an emotional appeal to the viewer. The first, that of the suspenseful cloak-and-dagger chase across Europe, is what Hitchcock does best; the second, however, is propaganda advocating an end to American isolation and an entry into World War II, and although Hitchcock manages a merger of these two themes more successfully than many other directors at the time, the intertwining causes the film to be less taut and

Magill's American Film Guide

more meandering than many of his later masterpieces.

The best reporter in *Foreign Correspondent* is, unquestionably, the camera. When the diplomat is assassinated, Hitchcock's camera is in the right place observing the fallen man's face; when a man is on the verge of dropping from a tower, the camera follows a hat making the plunge first; as the stricken airplane hurtles to the sea at the film's climax, the camera peers anxiously from the pilot's seat, indicating that it too has the reporter's gift of not revealing everything.

According to a number of sources, Hitchcock ordered several retakes of the wreck of the *Clipper* because it pleased him to see Joel McCrea and George Sanders floundering in the water, and when McCrea protested that the scene had ruined one of his suits, Hitchcock, who claims to dislike actors, sent him a new one the next day—made for a ten-year-old. In his role, however, McCrea proves both likable and capable. His interpretation of the reporter establishes the man as a credible citizen who, as the film ends, has the audience convinced that he will stride to one journalistic triumph after another. Laraine Day performs solidly in the role of Carol Fisher, her most ambitious part to that date, but Herbert Marshall appears somewhat miscast as the peace advocate who turns out to be a spy. Although he gives a good performance, he is too suave for his character and loses a little credibility. George Sanders, Albert Basserman, and Edward Ciannelli add much to the film, but it is Robert Benchley who carries off the acting honors in his portrayal of the broken-down American journalist Stebbins in London. He brought much of his own experience to the role and was specially chosen by Hitchcock, who enjoyed his brand of satiric humor. All of the scenes in which the humorist appeared were, at Hitchcock's request, written by Benchley himself.

In viewing the film as fundamentally a spy melodrama which places more emphasis on the pacing of the action than on where the action takes us, there are still awkward aspects. The meeting of the peace society contains prominently overdone elements; the crucial secret is, for the most part, meaningless, and the speeches are sometimes heavy-handed, particularly toward the end. Otherwise, the film moves swiftly, and although the plot is bare enough, Hitchcock, in the manner of a painter, loves details and loads his set with them without weighing down his action. He makes a character out of every extra; he likes to have a bland face or a sweet old lady personify evil, while the sinister fellow turns out to be the good guy all along. He sprinkles his scenes with people and mechanical devices which are not direct accessories to the plot so that the film conveys the realities of life, with dogs and casual passersby who are real and have nothing to do with any plot.

Above all, the film exemplifies Hitchcock's ability to use people, sound, and objects for the sole purpose of suspense. The use of objects, for example, is seen in *Foreign Correspondent* in the reversing windmill, the assassin's camera and the disappearing car. Hitchcock knows where to set the microphone and camera to catch the effect he has planned, and with all of the devices of this complex art completely at his fingertips, his characters never enter a deserted building or a dark alley without the viewer wondering if they will ever come out alive.

In short, *Foreign Correspondent* provides an example of all the techniques that make a film move in the lightest and fastest manner possible, utilizing all of the qualities that are available through a large budget and the art of Alfred Hitchcock. In fact, Hitchcock's only oversight in making *Foreign Correspondent* was in forgetting his invariable signature of personally appearing in the film. Fortunately, with a generous Hollywood budget, he had the means to reshoot a scene in a railway station in order to get himself into the picture.

Thomas A. Hanson

42nd STREET

Released: 1933
Production: Warner Bros.
Direction: Lloyd Bacon
Screenplay: Rian James and James Seymour; based on the novel of the same
  name by Bradford Ropes
Cinematography: Sol Polito
Editing: Thomas Pratt
Music direction: Busby Berkeley
Song: Harry Warren and Al Dubin
Running time: 85 minutes

> *Principal characters:*
> Julian Marsh .... Warner Baxter
> Dorothy Brock .... Bebe Daniels
> Peggy Sawyer .... Ruby Keeler
> Billy Lawler .... Dick Powell
> Pat Denning .... George Brent
> Anytime Annie .... Ginger Rogers
> Abner Dillon .... Guy Kibbee
> Lorraine Fleming .... Una Merkel

In 1933, Warner Bros. released three important musicals which revitalized
the moribund film musical and renewed its popularity with the moviegoing
public. The films are notable for their vitality, their originality in presenting
musical numbers on film, and the emergence of a major new talent in the
world of the film musical—Busby Berkeley. The first of these, *42nd Street*,
is the quintessential backstage musical. The familiar story of putting on a
play, with the star breaking her ankle at the last minute and the young
unknown stepping in to save the show, has been done many times, but seldom
with such zest and verve.

Under Lloyd Bacon's skillful direction that catches all the bustle and excitement of the backstage atmosphere, a group of engaging performers made
their niche in film history secure—Ginger Rogers as a shrewd chorus girl;
Warner Baxter as the tyrannical director of the show; Bebe Daniels as the
unhappy star who breaks her ankle just before opening night, giving Ruby
Keeler (in her screen debut) her big chance; and the baby-faced, mellow-
voiced Dick Powell, whose screen presence seemed tailored to fit Warner
Bros. musicals. But the biggest star, and possibly the most talented, was
Busby Berkeley, the man behind the cameras who conceived, staged, and
directed the musical numbers.

Berkeley's main contribution to the film musical was the staging of dances
especially for the camera, using all the cinematic resources at his command,

He is famous for the moving camera (which roved through, around, under, and over his dancers rather than remaining fixed in one position), and is particularly known for the overhead shot, in which the camera peers down at the dancers as they form everchanging patterns. Using dancers as elements in an abstract design to create his effects rather than as individuals who perform dance routines is one of his trademarks.

The backstage story concerns a famous Broadway director, Julian Marsh (Warner Baxter), who is preparing his last Broadway show, *Pretty Lady*. He is tired, ill, and broke, having lost all of his money in the stock market crash of 1929, and he realizes that this is his last chance to recoup his fortunes and retire with a respectable income. He is harsh, demanding, and driven to extract the last drop of energy out of his cast. Pacing and smoking nervously, he tells the cast that it will mean working day and night for five weeks until the show opens.

The show is backed by Abner Dillon (Guy Kibbee), a rich "sugar daddy" who is in love with the show's leading lady, Dorothy Brock. Dorothy tries to be sweet and friendly to Abner while keeping him at a distance because she is in love with her former vaudeville partner, Pat Denning (George Brent).

At the first casting call for the chorus of *Pretty Lady*, the stage is filled with eager hopefuls. Among them are Lorraine Fleming (Una Merkel), who gets a job in the chorus because she knows the stage director, and Anytime Annie (Ginger Rogers), a blonde with a monocle, a Pekingese, and a fake English accent; she has earned her nickname because she "only said no once and then she didn't hear the question."

Among the chorus girls is a naïve newcomer, Peggy Sawyer (Ruby Keeler). Recognizing her inexperience, the other chorus girls first direct her to the men's room, and then to the dressing room of Billy Lawler (Dick Powell), "one of Broadway's better juveniles" and the show's leading man, only to find him half dressed. Billy befriends the embarrassed and bewildered Peggy and later persuades Marsh to put her in the show.

Some of the best moments in *42nd Street* (aside from the musical numbers) are the vignettes of backstage life. There are numerous scencs of rehearsals with Marsh shouting at the dancers to "give it something," and to "work faster, faster," capturing some of the agonizing, endless work of rehearsing and the confusion and disorganization behind the glamour of the theater.

The character of the director, Julian Marsh, is particularly intriguing because it has some depth. We know he is a desperately tired man who has staked everything on making *Pretty Lady* a big hit. When told he is considered the "greatest musical comedy director in America today," he responds cynically that "You can't cash a reputation at the bank." In every scene he is chain-smoking, haggard, and wild-eyed, with shirt sleeves rolled up and tie askew. He screams and commands; he does not cajole or persuade. To encourage a tired Billy, he sarcastically tells him that all he needs is two license plates to look like a Model T Ford; the rest of the cast receives similar verbal treatment. When he informs them that the five-week rehearsal period will be the toughest five weeks they have ever lived through, we believe him.

The chorus becomes an impersonal group of girls driven beyond the limits of endurance. (At one point the image is reinforced by the superimposition of multiple images of legs and faces.) When Peggy faints during a rehearsal, Marsh screams at Billy to remove her quickly so that the rest can get back to work ("This is a rehearsal, not a rescue."). Outside the stagedoor entrance she is befriended by Pat, who is waiting for Dorothy, hoping that she will be alone so that he can see her. But later Dorothy tells him that they should not meet at all until they can meet openly; so he leaves for Philadelphia to be on his own.

At the final rehearsal before the out-of-town opening, a weary Marsh tells the cast that the finale looks like an amateur night and then dismisses them to get some rest. His troubles, however, have just begun. After a quarrel with Dorothy, Abner announces that he will withdraw his backing of the show if she is in it. As soon as Marsh solves that problem, he learns that Dorothy has broken her ankle.

The stage is now set for some of the film's best-known scenes. A reluctant Marsh chooses Peggy (on the recommendation of Anytime Annie, who unaccountably gives up her own chance for stardom) to go on and save the show. She is rehearsed remorselessly by Marsh, who yells at her, shakes her, and works her until she collapses. He encourages her by telling her that the jobs of two hundred people depend on her and that the audience has to like her. In the film's most famous line he says, "You're going out a youngster, but you've got to come back a star." Peggy also receives encouragement from Dorothy, who visits the theater on crutches and urges the trembling young woman to "go out there and be so swell you'll make me hate you."

Despite her exhaustion and imminent nervous collapse, Peggy does go on and, naturally, saves the show. In the last scene of the film, Marsh lingers outside the theater, listening to the comments of departing theatergoers. He smiles wryly as he overhears such comments as "Marsh gets all the breaks," and "With a kid like Sawyer how can he miss?" As the film ends he sits down wearily on the fire escape.

Throughout the film we have felt the tension mount as all efforts are concentrated on preparing for the opening night of *Pretty Lady*. We have been shown the enormous amount of work and discipline demanded of the cast and we have been tantalized by snippets of songs and dances seen in rehearsals. But not until the dress rehearsal do we see a number performed in its entirety. Although it is a bright, catchy song, "You're Getting to Be a Habit with Me," it is merely sung in front of the stage curtain by Dorothy with five male dancers; it is not a full-scale production number.

The pent-up emotions and tensions are released in three Berkeley production numbers that are seen as part of the show-within-the-show and that serve as an exhilarating climax to *42nd Street*. These numbers are a good introduction to the flair that Berkeley brought to the film musical. They are fresh, imaginative, and vigorous; and they display many of Berkeley's favorite devices—overhead shots, the moving camera, dancers creating patterns, and vignettes that tell short, dramatic stories.

In the number "Shuffle Off to Buffalo," a honeymooning couple walks along a train platform, waving good-bye to their friends. As the train pulls away, the Pullman car suddenly splits down the middle and opens up to reveal a cross section of the whole length of the coach. The compartments are filled with beautiful chorus girls in satin pajamas or nightgowns, singing and cracking jokes. Some of them are wearing curlers and cold cream as if to emphasize bachelor fears about marriage. The honeymooners dance down the length of the coach as the chorus girls sing sarcastically that "matrimony is baloney." But despite the knowing glances of the chorus girls and the pointed jokes about shy bridegrooms and eager brides, the humor is too innocent and naïve to be offensive. The number ends with a startling contrast: an old black porter falls asleep as he cleans the chorus girls' shoes. (Contrasts are a favorite Berkeley device.)

The next number, "I'm Young and Healthy," is more typical of Berkeley's work. Billy Lawler steps to the front of the stage and sings the lyrics to a young and obviously very healthy blonde in a low-cut ermine-trimmed gown and ermine muff. The angle shifts to an overhead shot of the two on a dark circular revolving stage, ringed by prone chorus boys. A line of blondes in brief costumes now encircle the glittering stage. Several overhead shots reveal the chorus forming kaleidoscopic patterns. The scene ends with the camera speeding down a tunnel formed by the open legs of the chorus girls to find at the end a smiling Billy and his blonde partner.

The best number is the title song, "42nd Street," which uses short, interwoven vignettes to convey a dramatic impression and tell a story. It starts simply, with Peggy Sawyer singing the lyrics in front of the curtain, which then parts to reveal "naughty, bawdy" 42nd Street. Peggy jumps down from what proves to be the top of a taxi as 42nd Street slowly fills with people. The camera weaves in and out among the "big parade," showing us a barber and his customer, midgets, a peddler with a pushcart full of fruit, automobiles, an Indian chief, and finally a room where a girl is arguing with a man. They quarrel, and she leaps from the window onto a ledge, and then to the street; the man follows, catching her and stabbing her. It is only a glimpse, and the camera does not linger as it turns to the street, now filled with dancing chorus girls who turn to reveal the New York skyline. We then see Billy and Peggy at the top of a skyscraper, waving to the audience before pulling down an asbestos curtain. The moving camera, the cross section of people, and the dramatic glimpses that build to a rousing climax are all Berkeley trademarks. The musical numbers in *42nd Street* are not as opulent or dazzling as those in later Berkeley films, but their comparative restraint and their vitality more than compensate for that.

The film musical was never quite the same after *42nd Street*. It confirmed the emergence of a major new talent—Busby Berkeley—and the emergence of the musical as a new art form. It was one of the top-grossing films of the year and is credited with rescuing Warner Bros. from bankruptcy.

Julia Johnson

FOUL PLAY

Released: 1978
Production: Thomas L. Miller and Edward K. Milkis for Paramount
Direction: Colin Higgins
Screenplay: Colin Higgins
Cinematography: David M. Walsh
Editing: Pembroke J. Herring
Running time: 115 minutes

Principal characters:
Gloria Mundy	Goldie Hawn
Tony Carlson	Chevy Chase
Mr. Hennesey	Burgess Meredith
Delia Darrow/Gerda Casswell	Rachel Roberts
Stanley Tibbets	Dudley Moore
Fergie	Brian Dennehy
Stiltskin	Marc Lawrence
Bible Salesman	Billy Barty
Bob Scott	Bruce Solomon
The Albino, Whitey Jackson	William Frankfather
Sally	Barbara Sammeth
Attacker	Don Calfa
The Turk	Ion Teodorescu
Manager	Chuck McCann
Pope	Cyril Magnin
Archbishop's brother	Eugene Roche
Japanese tourists	Rollin Moriyama and Mitsu Yashima

Colin Higgins, the writer and director of *Foul Play*, began his career making student films at UCLA and progressed to writing the scripts for the delightful cult film *Harold and Maude* (1972) and the quite profitable *Silver Streak* (1976). The financial success of the latter apparently gave him the opportunity to direct his next script, *Foul Play*. That script combines the detective thriller with the romantic comedy and reveals its author as an admirer and student of films of the past. It uses both general conventions of the thriller genre, such as the innocent person being caught up in a murder plot, reminiscent of the films of Alfred Hitchcock, and references to specific films, such as *Bullitt* (1968) and *Dial M for Murder* (1954). It is probably the best of the so-called "imitation" genre in which homage is paid to a style of filmmaking that has disappeared.

The film has two important scenes before the credits are finished. The first is a shocking image, the meaning of which does not become clear for some time; it does, however, establish the tone of the film. A religious figure (whom we later find is the Archbishop of San Francisco) looks in a mirror and sees someone who is dressed exactly as he is. Before he can utter a sound, he is killed by a knife, as a recording of Gilbert and Sullivan's *The Mikado* plays in the background. We then meet Gloria Mundy (Goldie Hawn) and find that she is a librarian who has recently been divorced. At a party, her friend Sally (Barbara Sammeth) is encouraging her to be more outgoing, to take a chance. Sally says Gloria should be more like the cheerleader she used to be than the repressed librarian hiding behind her glasses that she has become. Another guest at the party, Tony Carlson (Chevy Chase), reveals that he has been eavesdropping and tells Gloria that he agrees with Sally. Gloria is not amused.

Some time later, however, as Gloria is driving along the coast highway toward her home in San Francisco, she seems to heed the advice of Sally, Tony, and the theme song of the film, which we hear on the soundtrack, "Ready to Take a Chance Again." When she sees a young man standing by his disabled car, she picks him up. She finds that his name is Bob "Scottie" Scott (Bruce Solomon), and soon after he gets in her car, Gloria removes her glasses—without affecting her ability to drive. When he looks behind them, Scottie notices that they are being followed by a black limousine. He tells Gloria nothing about this, but when they reach the city he surreptitiously slips a roll of film into a box of cigarettes, asks her to keep it for him, and says he will meet her later at a movie theater.

Thus Gloria has unsuspectingly been drawn into the thriller plot. She does not even know that she possesses anything more than a box of cigarettes given to her by a hitchhiker who says he is trying to quit smoking; we in the audience know that the box is more important than that, but we have no idea why or to whom. We will soon find that certain people will go to any lengths to get the roll of film that the box contains.

At the movie theater, which is showing two old murder mysteries, Gloria has to go in by herself because Scottie is not there, but he soon joins her. He is wounded and bleeding, but she does not notice, and when he tries to tell her about the murder plot he has discovered, she thinks he is talking about the film they are watching. Finally he says to her, "Beware of the dwarf," and slumps over dead. By the time Gloria gets the manager (Chuck McCann) to stop the film and turn on the lights, the body is gone. She is then unable to convince anyone that the murder actually happened. Even her kindly old landlord, Mr. Hennesey (Burgess Meredith), tells her that Scottie was only playing a trick on her.

Gloria soon discovers that this "trick" was not an isolated incident. The next day, as she is closing up the library where she works, she is attacked by an albino (William Frankfather). She escapes by hitting him with her umbrella and dashing into a nearby singles bar. When the albino follows her, she asks the nearest man, Stanley Tibbets (Dudley Moore), to take her home. He is quite happy to agree, but he of course misunderstands the reason for her request. Gloria watches from Stanley's window until she sees the albino leave in the black limousine and then finds that Stanley has outfitted his apartment with every device he imagines a "swinger" should have, including flashing lights, a projector showing pornographic films, and life-sized inflated female mannequins. Gloria literally deflates a mannequin and figuratively deflates Stanley himself. She then returns home.

At her apartment, however, she is attacked by a large man with a scar on his face (Don Calfa) who wants her to give him whatever Scottie gave her. After he gets the box of cigarettes and sees that it has a roll of film in it, the man tries to strangle Gloria, but she stabs him with her knitting needles, in a scene reminiscent of Hitchcock's *Dial M for Murder*. She thinks she has killed him and calls the police. While she is telephoning, however, the man gets up and starts toward her with a poker in his hand. Before he can reach her, he is felled by a knife thrown by the albino. All this is too much for Gloria, and she faints.

When she awakens, Gloria finds Tony Carlson talking to her. It turns out that Tony is a policeman and that he and his partner, Fergie (Brian Dennehy), have answered her report of a murder in her apartment. Once again, however, there is no body. Neither Tony nor Fergie takes Gloria seriously, although Tony continues to be romantically interested in her. Tony, we find out, is currently on suspension in the police department for arresting the mayor for speeding and putting him in handcuffs. What this suspension entails, however, is never made clear, for he continues to work.

Gloria is still not safe because the cigarette box remains in her apartment, dropped by the scarfaced man after he was wounded. The next day she is abducted as she leaves the library in broad daylight. Although she is taken to an empty room where she is guarded by the Turk (Ion Theodorescu), she manages to escape and reach the police station. She is once again in the position of having no proof that anything happened.

The pieces of the puzzle finally begin to come together. Tony finds that Scott was an undercover policeman trying to find information about a tip that an assassination would take place in San Francisco. Then we gradually learn the whole plot. Delia Darrow (Rachel Roberts) and several other members of the Tax the Churches League have decided to assassinate the Pope as a protest against the government's nontaxation of churches. They murder the Archbishop of San Francisco and replace him with his twin brother (Eugene Roche), who is participating in the plot, and establish Darrow as Gerda Casswell, assistant to the Archbishop. The assassin is to be Stiltskin (Marc Lawrence), whose alias is The Dwarf.

While we and the protagonists are learning these facts, Tony and Gloria have fallen in love and spent a night together, but Gloria's adventures continue. The villains capture Fergie and through him lure Gloria to an out-of-the-way building. When he manages to warn her at the last minute, she escapes by ducking into the employee's entrance of a massage parlor. In one of the massage rooms she finds Stanley Tibbetts, waiting for a "massage." She enlists his help, but he cannot save her. After she is taken to the Archbishop's residence, Tony deduces that she is there and goes to help her. He kills Stiltskin but then is captured himself. Darrow explains to them that the Pope (Cyril Magnin) will be assassinated by the albino at the end of the first act of the opera he is attending at that very moment. Suddenly Hennesey, who had come with Tony, attacks the two villains. He dispatches the false Archbishop with a thrown bottle and bests Darrow in a wild karate fight.

Hennesey then releases Gloria and Tony, who set off on a wild race across the city to prevent the murder. It is a car race through San Francisco streets reminiscent of the one in *Bullitt* with an added touch being that the last part of the trip is in a commandeered limousine with two elderly Japanese tourists (Rollin Moriyama and Mitsu Yashima) in the back seat waving American flags and shouting "Kojak!" Tony and Gloria arrive at the opera house before the end of the first act of *The Mikado*, and after a frenzied chase and shootout behind the scenes, they kill the albino and save the Pope. This sequence is roughly patterned after the climax of Hitchcock's *The Man Who Knew Too Much* (1956), which takes place in the Albert Hall in London during a stirring concert. Finally Tony and Gloria embrace in the middle of the stage as the curtain is raised for the cast to take a bow. When they finally notice the applauding audience, they, too, turn and bow, as does a sheepish Stanley, who turns out to be the orchestra's conductor.

Critical reaction to *Foul Play* was mixed. Indeed, almost all reviewers praised some aspects of the film and criticized others. Moore's scene as the ultimate swinger with an apartment seemingly equipped with every possible sexual device was generally regarded as overdone and not in keeping with the rest of the film. Also excessive is the scene in which a dwarf Bible salesman, played by Billy Barty, visits Gloria's apartment. Gloria thinks that he is the dwarf she has been warned about and pushes him out her window. He falls into a garbage can, rolls down a hill, and ends up falling down a manhole. Indeed, the chief weakness of Colin Higgins' debut as a director is that he tends to excess in the effects and in the length of the scenes. The film could have been even more effective had it been more subtle and fast-paced.

Hawn has remarked that her role was not especially demanding, but both she and Chase are pleasant and likable in the film, and it is undoubtedly their performances that contributed the most to the enormous success of *Foul Play* at the box-office, placing it in the top ten of 1978. The film also led to a television series in the fall, 1980, season, but it was a short-lived failure. As an ironic footnote to the film, when *Foul Play* was scheduled for a prime-time television appearance in the spring of 1981, it had to be removed because the real Pope had just had an attempt made on his life in Rome. NBC network officials thought it ill-advised to show a film with *Foul Play*'s plot at that time. When the film was re-scheduled, however, after the Pope's recovery, it had very high ratings and went on to be a top-selling video tape item as well. Of all of the mystery/comedy films in the Hitchcockian mold produced in the late 1970's, *Foul Play* has remained the most successful.

Marilynn Wilson

THE FOUNTAINHEAD

Released: 1949
Production: Henry Blanke for Warner Bros.
Direction: King Vidor
Screenplay: Ayn Rand; based on her novel of the same name
Cinematography: Robert Burks
Editing: David Weisbart
Running time: 114 minutes

Principal characters:
Howard Roark	Gary Cooper
Dominique	Patricia Neal
Gail Wynand	Raymond Massey
Peter Keating	Kent Smith
Ellsworth Toohey	Robert Douglas
Henry Cameron	Henry Hull
Roger Enright	Ray Collins
The Dean	Paul Stanton

Hollywood likes to make films based on best-selling books because it can count upon virtually millions of people who have read or heard about the book wanting to see the film. Therefore, when Ayn Rand's novel *The Fountainhead* became a best-seller in 1943, Warner Bros. bought the screen rights to the work. *The Fountainhead* is, however, not the usual popular novel; it is a novel of ideas in which the thesis is often more important than the characters or the plot. The fact that Rand was hired to write the screenplay from her own book ensured that the studio could not follow the all-too-frequent practice of drastically changing the original material. Accordingly, *The Fountainhead* is a distinctly unusual film in which such customary Hollywood attributes as romance, spectacle, and characterization are subordinated to the development of the idea expressed, the importance of individualism.

In Rand's view it is individuals working without regard for the ideas and opinions of the public who produce "the constant stream of ideas" without which a culture cannot exist. She scorns "collectivism," the belief in subordinating oneself to the standards of the majority. In *The Fountainhead* she has constructed characters to represent various elements of this argument. Representing pure individualism is an architect, Howard Roark, and representing pure collectivism is a newspaper architecture critic, Ellsworth Toohey.

The film begins with Roark (Gary Cooper) being dismissed from a school of architecture by a dean (Paul Stanton) who tells him he cannot be so individualistic because there is "no place for originality in architecture." Roark then spurns the advice of a fellow student, Peter Keating (Kent Smith), that he compromise so that he can be successful. Keating says that he himself will give the public what it wants and predicts that he will soon be a successful architect. Roark instead goes to work for the only man he respects, Henry Cameron (Henry Hull), a character apparently meant to represent real-life architect Louis Sullivan, just as Roark himself is to some degree meant to suggest Frank Lloyd Wright, Sullivan's brilliant pupil. Cameron, although he is an independent man himself, does not encourage Roark on the road he has chosen because Cameron knows how difficult that road is; he urges Roark to compromise.

Roark, however, follows Cameron's example rather than his advice and takes over Cameron's office when the old man retires. He has very little success, just as everyone predicted. Indeed, Cameron comes to see him one day to urge that he give in to public taste. He contrasts Roark's lack of success with the newspaper *The Banner*, which has made its publisher a powerful man by giving the public the cheap, tawdry product it wants. Roark remains unmoved, and when Cameron asks if he knows what the people on the street think of architecture, Roark replies calmly, "I don't care what they think of architecture or anything else."

The next scene is perhaps the best in the film. Cameron has collapsed and Roark is riding with him in an ambulance. We see the city buildings through the ambulance windows as Cameron points out the folly of trying to make a totally new kind of building, the skyscraper, look like a Greek temple or some other design from the past. Cameron also notes one of his own buildings as they pass it, a building in which the form follows the function rather than copying the past. "Every new idea in the world comes from the mind of some *one* man," Cameron says, but once again he warns Roark of the difficulty of his chosen road; then he dies.

The next day Peter Keating visits Roark with the news that he has just been made a partner of Guy Francon, one of the city's most successful architects. While Keating is there, Roark gets a telephone call, but it is a wrong number that only emphasizes the contrast between the successful Keating and Roark, who has had no clients for eighteen months. Roark soon does get a chance for a commission, but he refuses when he finds that he would have to change his design to make it more conventional. He would, he tells the board asking him to compromise, rather work as a day laborer. We find that the attempt to get Roark to compromise was engineered by Ellsworth Toohey (Robert Douglas), the architecture critic for *The Banner*. He then recommends Peter Keating for the commission, because "artistic value is achieved collectively," and Keating's work has no individual personality stamped upon it.

Thus the main themes and characters have been established, but the plot and the argument are further thickened by the introduction of two more characters: Gail Wynand (Raymond Massey) and Dominique Francon (Patricia Neal). Wynand, the publisher of *The Banner*, has made himself rich and powerful by appealing to the taste of the masses even though he despises that taste. Dominique is the daughter of Guy Francon and is engaged to Peter Keating. We are introduced to her as she melodramatically drops a statue out the window of her high-rise apartment because she does not want to love anything in a world in which the masses rule. Wynand, who is in love with Dominique, offers Keating the commission for an important building if he will break his engagement, and Keating accepts. Dominique and Roark meet when she sees him working as a day laborer in her father's quarry in Connecticut. She does not know he is an architect but is attracted by his dynamic presence. She attempts to seduce him by asking him to come to her bedroom to replace some broken marble in the fireplace, but he ignores her obvious intention only to return at night and take her by force.

It is not until Roark has designed a building for Roger Enright (Ray Collins), a fiercely independent man who recognizes his talent and does not care what the public thinks of his building, that Dominique learns that Roark is an architect. She greatly admires his work, but she tries to persuade him to abandon architecture so that he will not be destroyed by the world as represented by Toohey, who gives the building a bad review in *The Banner* even though he knows it to be a great achievement. Roark, of course, refuses.

All the threads and themes come together dramatically in the last third of the film. Dominique has married Wynand although she does not love him, and Keating has come to Roark for help in designing a housing project. Roark agrees to design the project and let Keating receive all the credit on the strict condition that no detail of his plan shall be changed. The design is changed, however, over Keating's strenuous objections, and the resulting building is a monstrosity, a tasteless mixture of conflicting designs. Unwilling to accept this perversion of his work, Roark destroys the housing project with dynamite, then says he will explain nothing until his trial.

Wynand then tries to use the power he believes he has by supporting Roark in *The Banner* after firing Toohey, who continues to maintain that man can exist only to serve the wishes of others. Neither the public nor the staff of the newspaper will follow Wynand's lead, however; the paper is reviled and boycotted, and least credible of all, the staff of *The Banner* refuses to work until Toohey is rehired. After fighting for a while, Wynand finally gives in and denounces Roark, realizing that the "power" he achieved by following public opinion cannot be used against that same opinion.

Roark, therefore, must depend entirely upon his courtroom speech to the jury for his vindication. It is a long, didactic speech in which he states that all great creators stood alone and his idea is his property. He rejects collectivism, saying "The world is perishing in an orgy of self-sacrifice." Incredibly, even though we were led to believe that the entire city was against him, this speech convinces the jurors to find Roark not guilty.

After the trial, Wynand gives Roark a contract to design a massive building to commemorate his achievements, and then commits suicide. The film ends with Dominique, who had decided to leave Wynand for Roark even before he dynamited the housing project, riding a construction workers' elevator to the top of the new Wynand Building where Roark stands dramatically waiting for her.

The vindication of Roark's destruction of the project that did not follow his plans upset some critics and viewers, as well as the film's director, King Vidor. The film industry, after all, has very seldom let a director or a writer insist that his or her idea be followed to the letter; studio executives have nearly always made changes in films before, during, and after they were shot. Vidor says that he suggested to Jack Warner, the head of the studio, that he (Vidor) could burn the film if anyone changed it, but Warner did not agree. Also somewhat ironic is the fact that Rand specified in the script that Roark's buildings in the film should resemble those of Frank Lloyd Wright, since he was both modern and popular. "We must make the audience admire Roark's buildings," she wrote, even though that is the opposite of what Roark says throughout the film.

Another difficulty with the film is its incessantly didactic tone. The characters do not talk to one another; they state positions, giving much of the film the feeling of a dramatized debate rather than a drama of realistic characters. This difficulty is a great challenge for the actors, and one that none of them fully overcomes. Perhaps Hull, in the fairly small part of Roark's mentor Henry Cameron, is best because his character has some ambivalence. In the main roles, Cooper as Roark never seems quite comfortable having continually to utter such speeches as, "A building has integrity just like a man—and just as seldom," and Neal as Dominique has much the same problem, having at one point to say, "If it gives you pleasure to know that you are breaking me down, I'll give you greater satisfaction—I love you."

The film is by no means a total failure; it simply illustrates the difficulties of making a convincing film that is also explicitly didactic. Even such talented screen professionals as Cooper, Neal, and Vidor were not able to realize completely such an ambitious undertaking.

Julia Johnson

FOUR DAUGHTERS

Released: 1938
Production: Hal B. Wallis for Warner Bros.
Direction: Michael Curtiz
Screenplay: Julius J. Epstein and Lenore Coffee; based on the short story "Sister Act" by Fannie Hurst
Cinematography: Ernest Haller
Editing: Ralph Dawson
Music: Max Steiner
Running time: 90 minutes

> *Principal characters:*
> Ann Lemp .... Priscilla Lane
> Kay Lemp .... Rosemary Lane
> Thea Lemp ....Lola Lane
> Emma Lemp .... Gale Page
> Adam Lemp .... Claude Rains
> Mickey Borden .... John Garfield
> Felix Deitz .... Jeffrey Lynn
> Aunt Etta .... May Robson
> Ben Crowley .... Frank McHugh
> Ernest .... Dick Foran

A sentimental tale about small-town life, *Four Daughters* was widely heralded at the time of its release for its casting of three real-life sisters as the principal players. Soon after the film opened, however, Priscilla, Rosemary, and Lola Lane found themselves sharing the spotlight with a virtual screen newcomer, John Garfield. With his darkly cynical portrayal of a young fatalist, Garfield intensified an otherwise standard 1930's era soaper, giving a rough, thought-provoking edge to the film's gentle story.

Based on "Sister Act," a short story by Fannie Hurst, *Four Daughters* tells the story of Adam Lemp (Claude Rains) and his four daughters, Ann, Kay, Thea, and Emma (Priscilla Lane, Rosemary Lane, Lola Lane, and Gale Page, respectively), and of their life in a small Connecticut town. Lemp is a musician who frequently conducts his four musically inclined daughters in a family quintet. It is a close-knit, loving family, as evidenced by Ann's idealistic pledge to Emma that "neither of us shall marry, but just live like the happy family we are, forever." Ann, the youngest of the four daughters, feels threatened by the beaus who call on her sisters, for she does not want the family to break up. When a handsome stranger comes to town, however, even Ann is captivated by his charms.

Felix Deitz (Jeffrey Lynn) is a young composer from the West Coast who has come to town to vie for a thousand-dollar music prize. Adam invites Felix to board at the Lemp home, and all four girls are immediately taken with him, although he must put extra effort into winning over the family's spinster aunt, Aunt Etta (May Robson). The uplifting, engaging quality of the story is broken by the appearance of Mickey Borden (John Garfield), Deitz's orchestrator. Mickey has dark, tousled good looks, dresses carelessly, smokes constantly, and renounces almost everything that he encounters. His fatalistic views are the result of an orphaned youth spent in the big city. Mickey, who is uneasy in the quaint, small-town surroundings, immediately captures Ann's interest. She is attracted by his looks and startling demeanor, as well as the fact that she has never known anyone like him.

A key scene underlining the differences between the two takes place at the Lemp piano, where Mickey is playing a haunting piece. When Ann expresses her feelings about the music's beauty, Mickey retorts, "It stinks. It hasn't got a beginning or an end. Just a middle." When Ann asks why he does not complete the work, an angry Mickey responds, "What for? The fates are against me. They tossed a coin—heads, I'm poor, tails I'm rich. So what did they do? They tossed a coin with two heads." Although Ann is enamored of Felix, she is also determined to cheer the sardonic outsider. Indeed, Mickey does find himself touched by her sincerity and warmth. His near-optimism is depicted in a charming moment which finds Ann in the kitchen baking gingerbread men. With Mickey watching, she wipes away the sad, drooping mouth of the gingerbread man bearing his name and replaces it with a smile.

Mickey's changing attitude is shattered, however, when Ann accepts a marriage proposal from Felix. Her sisters are also caught off-guard by Ann's decision, for each had had a "crush" on the handsome composer. Ann's marriage plans force the other sisters to make decisions about their own lives. In a sense, it is the film's turning point. Kay, a promising singer, at last decides to pursue a scholarship in Philadelphia. Thea, who has always been impressed by money, agrees to marry wealthy Ben Crowley (Frank McHugh). Emma, however, who had been especially enamored with Felix, remains hurt and perplexed by Ann's plans. Mickey, who is equally upset, notices this.

When he at last reveals his own love to Ann, he also insists that Felix is the man Emma loves. Ann is doubly shocked. Caught up in Mickey's spell, she is also concerned for the feelings of her beloved sister. Thus, on the day she was to have married Felix, Ann elopes with Mickey. The Lemp family learns of the elopement as they are gathered for the wedding. They are so stunned by the news that it remains for family friend Ernest (Dick Foran), the town's florist, to deal with the wedding guests. Ernest's new, take-charge manner impresses Emma, who later realizes it is Ernest she truly loves (and will marry). Following the crisis, a jilted Felix leaves for Seattle.

The film now focuses on life for Ann and Mickey, which seems filled with constant disappointments, made worse by Mickey's belief that he cannot rise above the fates. Ann is encouraging and is hopeful that a Christmas visit back home will lift Mickey's spirits. The two are warmly welcomed by the family, and Felix, who is also visiting for the holidays, proves he is no longer angry with them when he offers Mickey financial assistance. Mickey, however, the "born loser," now realizes that he is wrong for Ann. Hoping to free her from his spell, he causes his own death by crashing his car into a tree.

Tragedy finally gives way to hope and new love in the spring. As the touching story comes to a close, Ann is reunited with Felix, and all four daughters, conducted by their father, again perform in the family home.

Four Daughters, which is effectively directed by the prolific Michael Curtiz, proved an immediate success following its August 9th opening at New York's Radio City Music Hall. Many critics of the day likened the film to an updated *Little Women* (1933). Nearly all were impressed with Garfield's performance and characterization, although several noted that his dark intensity nearly threw the charming film off balance. One of the year's most popular films, *Four Daughters* was nominated for five Academy Awards, including Best Picture, Best Director, Best Screenplay, and Best Supporting Actor. Garfield lost the Oscar to Walter Brennan, who won for *Kentucky*.

Four Daughters also inspired two sequels. *Four Wives* (1939), also directed by Michael Curtiz, included an appearance by Garfield as the ghost of Mickey Borden. *Four Mothers* was released in 1941. The huge success of *Four Daughters* and Garfield's portrayal also inspired a film which is nearly a clone of the original: *Daughters Courageous*, released less than a year after the first film, again starring Claude Rains, the Lane sisters, and Garfield, and directed by Curtiz. Garfield was once again paired with Priscilla Lane, and again, he played a world-weary cynic. This time around, he did not die—but neither did he get the girl. *Four Daughters* was also remade in 1954 as *Young at Heart*, a semimusical with Gordon Douglas directing. Doris Day, Dorothy Malone, and Elizabeth Fraser portray the film's sisters (this film featured only three), with Frank Sinatra cast in the Garfield role (the character was renamed Barney). This version, however, has an upbeat ending, with Barney, who does not die in the car crash, losing his cynicism; the final moments depict his happy reunion with Day. The story line changes were made because Sinatra had already "died" in his two previous films, *From Here to Eternity* (1953) and *Suddenly* (1954).

Garfield's career was forever marked by downbeat characterizations. In fact, the social unrest of the post-Depression era was often depicted by his work. Thus, in addition to providing a springboard for the actor's distinguished career, the *Four Daughters* characterization also came to personify his most famed roles. Particularly brilliant among Garfield's stirring depictions of men at odds with society and fate are *Humoresque* (1945), *The Postman Always Rings Twice* (1946), *Body and Soul* (1947), and *Force of Evil* (1948). His characters struggle against the darker side of human nature. The only traditional hero the actor ever portrayed was real-life Marine hero Al Schmid, in the patriotic *Pride of the Marines* (1945).

Generally regarded as the screen's first "angry young man," Garfield epitomized the man beset by inner conflict as well as a stacked deck. As Archer Winston once noted of the actor's grim characterizations, "He is fate's whipping boy, a personification of the bloody but unbowed head, and the embittered voice of the dispossessed." It is unfortunate that Garfield died from a heart attack in 1952 at the age of thirty-nine, not long after refusing to testify before the House UnAmerican Activities Committee, and at the low point of his career.

Pat H. Broeske

FRANCIS IN THE NAVY

Released: 1955
Production: Stanley Rubin for Universal-International
Direction: Arthur Lubin
Screenplay: Devery Freeman
Cinematography: Carl Guthrie
Editing: Milton Carruth and Ray Snyder
Running time: 80 minutes

> *Principal characters:*
> Lieutenant Peter Stirling/
> Slicker Donevan .... Donald O'Connor
> Commander Hutch .... Jim Backus
> Jonesey .... Clint Eastwood
> Francis' Voice .... Chill Wills

The New York Times critic Bosley Crowther once complained, half-jokingly, that 1950 was turning out to be the year of the mule. First there was Frankie Laine's pop record hit "Mule Train," and then came the movie *Francis*, which became the first in a long line of films based on the fictional adventures of Francis the Talking Mule. Based on the novel *Francis* by David Stern (who also wrote the screenplay for the series' opener), most of the Francis films were directed by Arthur Lubin and featured Donald O'Connor as the bumbling but enthusiastic Lieutenant Peter Stirling. Chill Wills provided the gravelly voice of the title creature.

The original *Francis* was set in the jungles of Burma during World War II. Peter Stirling (Donald O'Connor) stumbles across an old army mule named Francis who has the power of speech; Stirling is incredulous at first, but cannot deny the evidence before his eyes and ears, and the two become friendly. Francis is a patriotic mule and takes to spying on the Japanese, who never suspect that the traitor in their midst is a jackass. Francis relays the secrets to Stirling, who passes them on to his superiors.

All is well until Stirling is questioned about the source of his information. He tells the truth, and ends up in a psycho ward. Francis, it seems, wants to avoid the notoriety that would surely attend a talking animal and stubbornly refuses to talk to anyone but Stirling. It is from this situation that most of the film's laughs derive. Finally, however, Francis relents. He rescues his friend by talking to the General and holding a press conference in the bargain.

The film proved to be an immense popular success and begat successors annually for the next six years. *Francis Goes to the Races* appeared in 1951; *Francis Goes to West Point* surfaced in 1952; *Francis Covers Big Town* was 1953's entry; *Francis Joins the WACs* came along in 1954; 1955 brought *Francis in the Navy*; and the series ended with *Francis in the Haunted House* in 1956.

Each film follows a fairly set formula. The mule, a feisty animal with a love of practical jokes, involves himself and his human friend in some unlikely situation. Peter Stirling proceeds to flounder ineptly for the next hour or so, until Francis finally pulls his chestnuts out of the fire. Along the way, Universal inserts some of its older character actors and some of its new faces into the lineup for exposure. ZaSu Pitts, Gale Gordon, Jim Backus, Clint Eastwood, Piper Laurie, David Janssen, Mamie Van Doren, and Martin Milner all graced one or more of the Francis productions in this fashion.

Francis in the Navy is typical of the Francis series, except that O'Connor plays two roles—Stirling and his look-alike, Bosun's Mate Slicker Donevan. In his studio biographies, O'Connor often expressed his admiration for William Shakespeare's *A Comedy of Errors*, in which doubles and mistaken identities form the basis of the plot; and *Francis in the Navy* seems to have been tailored to provide O'Connor with an opportunity to interpolate this plot device into the Francis series.

It seems that Francis has somehow been transferred to the Navy, where he is about to be sold as surplus property. Stirling heads for the auction at San Diego's Coronado Naval Base, where he is mistaken (first by a pretty WAVE, and next by seemingly every sailor in the port) for Slicker Donevan, to whom he bears an uncanny resemblance. Since Donevan is given to spells of irrationality, Stirling's denials are routinely shrugged off by his solicitous pals. Donevan himself figures out what is going on and decides to take advantage of the situation by going on vacation for a few days.

Peter Stirling again winds up in a strait jacket, and Francis enjoys the whole spectacle immensely. The film ends with Stirling singlehandedly disrupting a complicated Navy training exercise as he attempts to handle Donevan's duties. "Francis, don't just stand there! Throw me a line," he cries. "I would, if I could think of one," deadpans the mule.

Arthur Lubin, who directed six of the seven Francis films, may not have been the world's greatest director, but he knew how to give the public what it wanted, specializing in lightweight, low-budget comedies. In the 1940's, he directed several Bud Abbott and Lou Costello films, including their best, *Buck Privates*, in 1941. In the 1950's, he repeated his successes with the Francis series. Likewise, O'Connor's tour of duty as Lieutenant Peter Stirling may not have been great acting—O'Connor's memorably acrobatic "Make 'Em Laugh" number in Gene Kelly's and Stanley Donen's *Singin' in the Rain* (1952) will probably stand as his finest screen moment—but he did his best with material that was at times admittedly thin. The star of the show was Francis the Talking Mule himself. The animal Francis was a remarkably expressive beast, with a penchant for rolling his eyes, twitching his ears, and smacking his lips in a very anthropomorphic fashion. Wills's gravelly voice suited the "character" perfectly.

After *Francis in the Navy*, however, most of the principals associated with the series seemed to tire of it and walked away *en masse*. In 1956, Charles Lamont picked up the Francis concept for one last film, with Mickey Rooney as Francis' new pal David Prescott and Paul Frees as the voice of the mule. The result, *Francis in the Haunted House*, was poor, even for the Francis series, which was never very deep to begin with; and that was the end of Francis, at least in his first incarnation.

Francis, however, did not entirely vanish in 1956. Lubin resurrected the basic concept in 1958 with his television series *Mr. Ed*, about a talking horse; the series lasted for six seasons and is still seen in syndication today. Finally, in the spring of 1980, *Variety* reported that O'Connor himself was on the verge of putting together a deal to produce an entirely new film entitled *Francis Goes to Washington*.

Critics found the first Francis film mildly amusing, although a bit too reliant on a single joke. Its successors only exacerbated this attitude. Critical scorn, however, did not hurt the popularity of most of the films or keep them from making money for their creators. Although never even within shouting distance of great art, the Francis films were good escapist entertainment. Further, they were all family films, an attribute not to be underestimated in an era that valued praying together, playing together, and staying together. The Francis series warrants our attention today primarily as an example of popular film fare of the Eisenhower Era.

Robert Mitchell

FRANKENSTEIN

Released: 1931
Production: Carl Laemmle, Jr., for Universal
Direction: James Whale
Screenplay: Garrett Fort and Francis Faragoh; based on John Balderston's
adaptation of the novel of the same name by Mary Wollstonecraft Shelley
Cinematography: Arthur Edeson
Editing: Clarence Kolster
Makeup: Jack Pierce
Running time: 71 minutes

Principal characters:
Dr. Henry Frankenstein .... Colin Clive
The Monster .... Boris Karloff
Elizabeth .... Mae Clarke
Victor ....John Boles
Dr. Waldman .... Edward Van Sloan
The Dwarf .... Dwight Frye

Carl Laemmle, Jr., the head of Universal—the studio that had produced such classic films as *The Hunchback of Notre Dame* (1939), with Lon Chaney, Sr., and the 1931 *Dracula*, starring Bela Lugosi—selected his new director, James Whale, to direct the screen version of Mary Shelley's classic novel, *Frankenstein*. British-born Whale had distinguished himself in the English theater, first as an actor and later as a director and producer. The screenplay for Universal's newest horror film was written by Garrett Fort and Francis Faragoh from a stage adaptation by John Balderston. The setting is a small windswept Bavarian village. Isolated from the village in an old abandoned mill is a laboratory where a scientist, Dr. Henry Frankenstein, conducts grisly experiments in his search for a way to create artificial life. Colin Clive, who played Captain Stanhope in the London stage production of *Journey's End* as well as the Hollywood film, was brought from England to play the role of Dr. Frankenstein.

As the film opens, Dr. Frankenstein, aided by a hunchbacked dwarf (Dwight Frye), is seen crouched near the edge of a cemetery watching the progress of a midnight funeral service. As soon as the mourners have left, the doctor and his assistant creep across the lonely moor to claim the object of their secret midnight excursion from its fresh grave. Next Dr. Frankenstein is shown stealing forth to cut down a corpse from the gallows, also to be cut up and used to assemble a new human form into which he hopes to inject the spark of life. To complete his gruesome work, the doctor needs a brain, so he sends the dwarf to a nearby medical school to steal one. In the gloom of the dissecting room, he inadvertently drops the glass bowl containing the brain he had been sent to procure. In order not to disappoint the doctor, however, he steals the brain of a criminal, a fact of which Dr. Frankenstein is never made aware.

Dedicated in his research to the point of obsession, Frankenstein shuts himself off from the outside world, working to the limit of his endurance. Alarmed over the doctor's complete disregard for his physical well-being, his fiancée, Elizabeth (Mae Clarke); his best friend, Victor (John Boles); and his old teacher, Dr. Waldman (Edward Van Sloan), descend on the mill where the experiments are taking place. The sequence that follows is a marvelous piece of theatrics. Frank Grove, Kenneth Strickfaden, and Raymond Lindsay get full credit for the creation and operation of the laboratory's electrical machinery. Here, within the horrified sight of his fiancée and friends, Dr. Frankenstein harnesses the awesome energy of a violent electrical storm which rages outside the old mill, jolting life into the inanimate monster strapped to the operating table.

Frankenstein's unholy creation is ably portrayed by Boris Karloff. Jack Pierce, Universal's head makeup expert, who worked on Dracula, was assigned the task of creating the monster. Pierce did research for more than three months before coming up with the final design. The application of the makeup for the role was an ordeal; nearly three and a half hours were required every morning to put it on, and nearly as long was required at night to remove it. Karloff struggled under the weight of sixty pounds of wardrobe accessories; the shoes alone weighed eighteen pounds apiece. Because the film was shot in midsummer, the heavy quilted suit often left him soaking wet. "Throughout the filming," he said, "I felt as if I was wearing a damp shroud, which no doubt added to the realism." Despite the physical handicaps that the makeup imposed, Karloff considered the role a challenge to his acting ability. Because the creature could utter only a few inarticulate cries, it was necessary for Karloff to act primarily with his eyes. He did not, however, yield to the temptation of melodrama by resorting to exaggerated gestures and expressions. This simplicity and restraint created a monster all the more frightening.

Following his "birth" in the laboratory, the monster is kept locked in the dungeon of the old mill, where he is tortured by the dwarf, whose mind is as twisted as his body. Tormented beyond endurance, the monster strangles the dwarf; afterwards, the concentrated effort of all concerned is needed to restrain him. While Dr. Frankenstein had been proud of his creation, he now knows he has reason to fear the creature, for it is no longer under his control. The full realization of the horror he has precipitated drives the doctor to the verge of a nervous breakdown. He returns to his estate to recover, after eliciting a promise from Dr. Waldman that he will destroy the monster while he is away. On the day that he and Elizabeth are to be married, the doctor is horrified to learn that the monster has strangled Dr. Waldman and escaped from the mill. Arthur Edeson's camera effectively follows Frankenstein's monstrous creation, his heavy-lidded, lizardlike eyes staring straight ahead, plodding like an automaton across the wild and sinister countryside. Karloff's superb performance arouses much more than spine-tingling fear. This alien creature with his terrible aloneness, his fear of fire, and his strange, pathetic cries, arouses compassion. The viewer knows that the creature must be destroyed but has empathy for his suffering.

After receiving the terrible news of Dr. Waldman's death, Dr. Frankenstein and Elizabeth return to the village, and the doctor joins the mob in their search for the creature. By this time, he has killed again, inadvertently drowning a little peasant girl, and the villagers, driven by fear and hate, have redoubled their efforts to hunt him down and destroy him. The doctor, however, becomes separated from the others and finds himself face to face with his hideous creation. The monster easily overcomes Frankenstein and carries him back to the mill, pursued by the villagers. Inside, Frankenstein regains consciousness and a struggle ensues. In the process, Frankenstein is hurled several stories to the ground and severely injured. The villagers, who by now have arrived, set fire to the mill. Amid the crackling of the flames, we hear the quavering, frightened cries of the dying monster. Following its destruction, a final scene shows Dr. Frankenstein recovered and in the process of marrying Elizabeth.

The studio was unsure how they should film the ending. In Shelley's novel and in previous stage presentations, Dr. Frankenstein dies; however, the studio felt that such an ending would leave the audience disappointed. Consequently, two endings were filmed, and, after a preview, the ending in which Dr. Frankenstein lives was decided upon. In another departure from the original text, the scene depicting the monster's murder of the little girl was deleted when the film was first released. The monster had been playing with the child on the bank of the river, watching her toss blossoms in the water. He had picked her up and thrown her in the water, expecting her to float as the blossoms did. Instead of a diabolical murder, therefore, the monster's act was an act of ignorance which, if it had appeared, would have aroused even more audience sympathy for the plight of the creature. Through the years, however, this scene has been reinserted, and the sympathetic interpretation of the monster has become popular.

Financially, *Frankenstein* was one of the most successful films of the 1931-1932 season, grossing more than $12,000,000 from an investment of $250,000. It set a pattern, even more so than *Dracula*, for Universal's subsequent treatment of the subject of horror. More significantly, however, it launched the career of Boris Karloff, whose portrayal of Frankenstein's monster catapulted him to international fame. In addition to his successes in subsequent Frankenstein films and over eighty other screen roles, Karloff also made extensive appearances on Broadway and on television; likewise, Colin Clive, who played the dedicated, inspired doctor with such believability and finesse, went on to appear in more than fifteen other films before his untimely death in 1937, and in *The Bride of Frankenstein* (1935) he again costarred with Boris Karloff.

The characters of Frankenstein and his monster have been portrayed on the screen many times since 1931. *Frankenstein*, in various forms, has proven to be saleable for almost fifty years. Such films as *Son of Frankenstein* (1939), *I Was a Teenage Frankenstein* (1957), and Mel Brooks's *Young Frankenstein* (1974) have all helped to enhance the popularity of the original story.

D. Gail Huskins

FREAKS

Released: 1932
Production: Metro-Goldwyn-Mayer
Direction: Tod Browning
Screenplay: Willis Goldbeck and Leon Gordon, with dialogue by Edgar Allan
   Woolf and Al Boasberg; based on the short story "Spurs" by Tod Robbins
Cinematography: Merritt B. Gerstad
Editing: Basil Wrangell
Running time: 64 minutes

Principal characters:
Phroso	Wallace Ford
Venus	Lelia Hyams
Cleopatra	Olga Baclanova
Roscoe	Roscoe Ates
Hans	Harry Earles
Frieda	Daisy Earles
Hercules	Henry Victor
Bearded Lady	Olga Roderick

Tod Browning's *Freaks* has achieved a reputation, in the fifty years since its introduction in 1932, as a masterpiece of horror and as a milestone in surrealistic filmmaking. This stature has been gained despite, or, more probably, as a result of, the fact that it was banned for more than thirty years in most civilized countries throughout the world. In fact, when it was initially completed at M-G-M in 1932, it quickly became known around the studio as the one mad blunder of the studio's reigning boy genius, producer Irving Thalberg. According to one, unverified, story, women ran screaming from the theater during a sneak preview, and the manager later complained that the film left him with a "cleaning job."

Upon the official opening of *Freaks* in New York City, *The New York Times* suggested that the film be screened at the Medical Center instead of at the Rialto theater. Other reviews generally panned the film, and it did poorly at the box office. Thalberg, who loved the film despite its reputation, felt that it had been victimized by poor presentation. He made a futile attempt to reissue it in 1933 under the sensational title *Nature's Mistakes* with such teaser captions as "Do Siamese Twins Make Love?" and "What Sex is the Half-Man-Half-Woman?" This version of the film carried a prologue mentioning that history, religion, and folklore abounded in tales of deformed misfits who have altered the course of world history. This version did no better than had the original, and M-G-M quietly gave up on it.

Freaks surfaced occasionally in Europe during the next thirty years, slowly gaining a macabre reputation, while continuing to be ignored in the United

States. It finally gained some legitimacy in 1962 when it was selected to represent the horror film category at the Cannes Film Festival. This was a somewhat dubious distinction since *Freaks*, although a masterpiece of the "cinema of the bizarre," is, in most respects, the antithesis of the conventional horror film.

The standard horror film centers upon mankind's responses to the nonrational or nonhuman element in the world that threatens to render life meaningless. The monster, whether it is the great white shark, King Kong, or aliens from outer space, is the representative of all that is irrational or inexplicable. It is through the destruction of these beasts that the audience is freed from its own fears of the nonhuman. We therefore tend to empathize and identify with the victims of the monsters and thus remain on the edge of our seats, finding release only through the monster's ultimate death.

Director Tod Browning creates an identity crisis for the audience of *Freaks* by attempting to reverse our expectations and by portraying his "monsters" sympathetically. In an ethical sense, Browning's freaks represent the best traits of mankind: humility and tolerance. The viewer must therefore turn against the conventional images of his own kind and identify with beings that would normally be thought of as abnormal or subhuman. *Freaks* becomes the ultimate challenge to the myth that beauty is the embodiment of goodness and truth and that ugliness represents evil. The film's plot is fairly routine, with most of the interest coming from the characters, who are played by real side-show freaks assembled by the director from circuses all over the world. They include bearded ladies, Siamese twins, dwarfs, pinheads, midgets, and human worms.

Freaks opens with a carnival pitchman addressing a crowd of people at a sideshow. He escorts the group of spectators over to a pit to see a hidden special attraction, but first, he describes the origin of the creature. The story is told through flashback. Hans (Harry Earles), a midget, is engaged to another midget, Frieda (Daily Earles), but becomes increasingly attracted to a trapeze performer named Cleopatra (Olga Baclanova), a normal-size woman. She is already having an affair, however, with Hercules (Henry Victor), the circus strong man. Interestingly, Browning depicts Hans and Frieda's romance so that it appears, despite its stiff gesture and squeaky voices, to be more mature and settled than the similar but tempestuous affair of the "normal" people, Cleopatra and Hercules. Through a series of contrasting scenes Browning establishes the inversion of values that forms the core of the film. Cleopatra perversely encourages Hans because she finds a secret pleasure in ridiculing him. When she finds out that Hans has recently inherited a considerable fortune, she takes him more seriously, but plots with Hercules to marry the midget, poison him, and inherit the money. Hans succumbs to her charms and Frieda is distraught.

At the wedding feast, Cleopatra and Hercules are the only "normals" in attendance. The banquet quickly becomes a ritual—a celebration of freak culture—as a dwarf dances across the table bearing a large communal wine bowl. He leads a macabre chant "We accept her, we accept her, gobble, gobble, one of us, one of us." He offers the wine bowl at last to Cleopatra to drink from as a rite of induction into the world of freaks. She registers horror and revulsion and later retaliates by riding Hans on her shoulders in front of his friends to humiliate him.

Eventually, Cleopatra's plot to poison Hans is discovered, and the enraged freaks hunt down the two villains and mutilate them in an unforgettable climactic sequence that gave the film its reputation for horror. On a rainy night, amidst a maze of wrecked circus trailers, with lightning flashing to illuminate the muddy ooze of the ground, grotesque crawling and hopping shapes wreak their vengeance upon the bodies of Hercules and Cleopatra.

Flashing forward again to the present, the carnival man finishes the story and pulls back the cover from the pit to reveal that Cleopatra is now a freak. This final touch, however, is the film's weak spot and represents a blunder on Browning's part. Cleopatra is not so much horrifying as a freak as she is comical in her resemblance to a giant half-formed fowl. This contrived ending destroys the credibility established by the film up to this point. Browning's thesis that the freaks are more normal than the Aryan strong man and the deceitful trapeze artist becomes quickly unraveled in the ludicrous, laugh-provoking image of Cleopatra as a half-plucked chicken.

If the director's intention was, as Browning avowed, to show that these misshapen creatures are not monsters or practitioners of black magic but ordinary human beings deformed through an accident of birth, the audience is left with a puzzle at the end. Either the sideshow pitchman made up the story, since if freaks are normal, according to Browning, they could not transform a human into a monster; or the storyteller is correct and the freaks are imbued with mysterious powers. This interpretation could be supported by the rites of initiation to the world of the freaks performed at the wedding feast. The alternate version of the film, *Natures Mistakes*, supports both interpretations with its introductory preamble which indicates that freaks are human beings but do have a mysterious code which binds them together, "The hurt of one and the hurt of all." Thus, instead of hammering Browning's message home, *Freaks*'s final scene blurs it.

The excellence of the film lies in the delicate balance which provides the context for the plot. On one side are the normal members of the circus with their ignorant, cruel mockery of the freaks. One the other side are the freaks, who are eager to befriend anybody who will accept them for what they are. These two extremes are bridged by Phroso the clown (Wallace Ford) and his girl Venus (Lelia Hyams) who accept and are accepted by the freaks. They tease Schlitze, one of the pinheaded women, about her new dress and joke with the bearded lady (Olga Roderick) about the birth of her baby. These scenes establish an emotional and sympathetic link between characters and audience that enhances the horror of the climax.

The climactic finale itself is effectively staged and beautifully shot with chiaroscuro lighting. The sequence begins as Hercules and Cleopatra go about the ritual of poisoning Hans. Suddenly, eyes begin to watch, peering in at windows, looking up from beneath the carnival wagons. As the freak forces gather, a storm breaks and rain comes pouring down. As knives appear, nothing can be heard except the storm and a melancholy tune played by a dwarf with a pipe. Through the streaming rain, the thick mud appears full of crawling shapes, and in the darkness Cleopatra and Hercules run screaming in terror.

The rest of the film is more or less conventional fare apart from the freaks. The most significant scenes are those which show the daily routine and individual adjustment of the freaks to their handicaps. They are almost clinically depicted. The armless woman drinks beer from a glass clutched by a prehensile foot, and the human worm, both armless and legless, manages to light his cigarettes with his teeth. The freaks are very much able to function as part of the real world and seem to make the best of their physical shortcomings. Browning's smooth direction portrays these creatures as both objects of sympathy and yet, also very subtly, as nightmarish incarnations of the audience's fears of the nonhuman.

The warm appreciation of the freaks' humanity is first evoked when we are introduced to them during an outing in the country. The camera inching through the forest encounters, in a distant clearing, a grotesque round dance of hopping, wriggling, and crawling things. Yet as the camera draws closer, these seemingly grotesque apparitions coalesce into childlike shapes, thus becoming transformed from agents of terror into objects of audience compassion within seconds. This evocation of humanity and sympathy is bolstered by the wedding sequence when Cleopatra humiliates Hans by riding him piggyback but becomes reversed in the final scenes when the mud illuminated by lightning swarms with the grotesque crawling and hopping shapes. Our final image of the freaks in the rain depicts creatures with all humanity erased and comes around full cycle to our initial introduction. Although this last scene may have been a mistake, it was perhaps an inevitable outcome of the precarious and delicate balance maintained by Browning throughout the film.

The acting of the "tall" (as opposed to normal) characters (Ford as Phroso, Hyams as Venus, and Baclanova as Cleopatra) is pretty much undistinguished although Wallace Ford does have several poignant scenes with characters such as the pinheaded women and the bearded lady. Cleopatra and Hercules in particular have been weakened as characters by acting which appears badly dated by modern standards.

Although *Freaks* has been compared to the surreal cinema of Spanish director Luis Bunnell, it is more properly Germanic in its theme. The humiliating situations, the ritual wedding feast torn apart through drunken hatred, the atmosphere of sexual jealousy, and the method of telling the story in flashback are all hallmarks of German directors such as Friedrich Murnan and Josef von Sternberg. Bunnel would have portrayed the freaks as embodying the latent spiritual deformity in man. Browning, however, endows them with man's nobler virtues and then subjects them to Cleopatra, one of Sternberg's diabolical women.

The film is baroque, then, and not surreal. It is certainly not a horror film although the final sequence in which the freaks capture and mutilate Cleopatra and Hercules is as monstrous as anyone might conceive. *Freaks* is a virtual textbook of the baroque and certainly influenced Federico Fellini's *La Strada* (1954); Max Ophuls' *Lola Montes* (1955); Edmund Goulding's *Nightmare Alley* (1947), featuring Tyrone Power in what many consider to be his finest role; and, of course, Ingmar Bergman's *Sawdust and Tinsel* and *The Naked Night* (1953). Although seldom allowed to be shown throughout its history, *Freaks* has, in fact, become a major influence on serious modern attempts at the baroque film and continues to tell us a great deal about ourselves as human beings.

Stephen L. Hanson

A FREE SOUL

Released: 1931
Production: Metro-Goldwyn-Mayer
Direction: Clarence Brown
Screenplay: John Meehan; based on the novel of the same name by Adela
   Rogers St. John
Cinematography: William Daniels
Editing: Hugh Wynn
Art direction: Cedric Gibbons
Costume design: Adrian

> *Principal characters:*
> Jan Ashe .... Norma Shearer
> Stephen Ashe .... Lionel Barrymore (AA)
> Dwight Winthrop .... Leslie Howard
> Ace Wilfong .... Clark Gable
> Grandma Ashe .... Lucy Beaumont

With her films supervised by her brilliant husband, Irving Thalberg, who
was head of production at M-G-M, Norma Shearer had the pick of story
properties at that studio. When a novel by Adela Rogers St. John, *A Free
Soul*, attracted her attention, Thalberg assigned it to her. In it, she plays Jan
Ashe, a modern San Francisco girl who has been brought up in an atmosphere
of freedom. She is motherless, but her father, Stephen Ashe (Lionel Barrymore), whom she adores, is a famous criminal lawyer. They are both free-
thinking rebels. Stephen has just proved his courtroom genius by freeing Ace
Wilfong (Clark Gable), a gambler and underworld character, from a murder
charge.

Stephen has one great fault: drinking. He is drunk when he brings Ace to
his mother's home for her birthday party, where Jan is waiting with her fiancé,
Dwight Winthrop (Leslie Howard). The aristocratic Grandma Ashe (Lucy
Beaumont) is appalled by her son's lack of taste in bringing someone like Ace
into her home and lets Stephen know that Ace is not welcome. Stephen,
already more than half drunk, says he will leave too, and Jan, in a sudden
spirit of rebellion, leaves with him and Ace, even though it means the end
of her engagement to Dwight Winthrop. Ace is flattered by Jan's attraction
to him, and they have an affair. He is very attracted to Jan, and she has never
known another man quite like him. Ace goes to Stephen to ask Jan's hand
in marriage, and he is amazed and angry when Stephen will not give his
consent to the marriage. Stephen tries hard to convince Ace that he is no
husband for his daughter.

When Ace's gambling den is raided, forcing Stephen to take refuge in Ace's
private quarters, he discovers Jan in a negligee with Ace. She is ashamed and

goes away with her father, who realizes that in his drunken way of life he is debasing his own daughter. He makes a bargain with her: if she will agree not to see Ace any more, he will give up drinking. They go away to the mountains together on a camping trip, and for the first time there is hope for both of them. When Stephen returns to San Francisco, however, he begins drinking again, and Jan, realizing that there is no point in her keeping her part of the bargain, goes back to being Ace's mistress.

Ace, triumphant, turns brutal, and Jan contemptuously leaves him, returning to her ex-fiancé, Dwight Winthrop. One night when they are together, they encounter Ace, who boldly tries to molest Jan. Although she fights him off, Ace is relentless, causing Dwight to draw a revolver and shoot Ace. Dwight is tried for murder, and Stephen defends him in a brilliant courtroom scene in which he says that it is not Dwight who should be on trial, but he himself, who is guilty of allowing his daughter to associate with a "mongrel" like Ace. He asks the court to free Dwight and judge *him* for the act of murder. His speech is so impassioned that he collapses and has a heart attack, dying in his daughter's arms. The jury frees Dwight, and Jan turns to him for consolation, acknowledging that it is he that she truly loves.

A Free Soul was Norma Shearer's seventh all-talking release at M-G-M. Her films were all modern stories, ranging from stylish dramas to drawing-room comedies, and all styled to make her "First Lady " of M-G-M. She had won the Academy Award for Best Actress in the year 1929-1930 for *The Divorcee*, and that same year she also earned a nomination for her work in *Their Own Desire*. (It was a practice in the early years that actors could be nominated more than once in the same year.) She was nominated again in the year 1930-1931 for her role as Jan Ashe in *A Free Soul*, but lost to Marie Dressler in *Min and Bill*.

Top honors went to Lionel Barrymore in his role of Stephen Ashe, for which he won his only Oscar. It was a popular award; his was a brilliant performance, much admired, especially in its day. Adela Rogers St. John based the character of Stephen Ashe on her own father, Earl Rogers, an attorney who was notable for his ability to take over the courtroom like a star about to give his finest performance. He seldom lost a case, and the courtroom was always packed when he worked. Rogers, like Stephen Ashe, was a very free soul, also well-known for his drinking exploits. William A. Brady had presented a play version of *A Free Soul* on Broadway by Willard Mack, with Mack in the role of Stephen Ashe and Kay Johnson playing Jan Ashe. In 1953, M-G-M filmed a new version of the story entitled *The Girl Who Had Everything*, starring Elizabeth Taylor, with William Powell playing Stephen Ashe. It played well and might have been more successful had there not been many viewers around who still remembered the electricity of the 1931 version.

DeWitt Bodeen

THE FRENCH CONNECTION

Released: 1971
Production: Philip D'Antoni for Twentieth Century-Fox (AA)
Direction: William Friedkin (AA)
Screenplay: Ernest Tidyman (AA); based on the book of the same name by
   Robin Moore
Cinematography: Owen Roizman
Editing: Jerry Greenberg (AA)
Stunt coordinator: Bill Hickman
Running time: 104 minutes

> *Principal characters:*
> Jimmy "Popeye" Doyle .... Gene Hackman (AA)
> Buddy Russo .... Roy Scheider
> Alain Charnier .... Fernando Rey
> Sal Boca .... Tony LoBianco
> Pierre Nicoli .... Marcel Bozzuffi
> Devereaux ....Frederic De Pasquale
> Mulderig .... Bill Hickman
> Lieutenant Simonson ....Eddie Egan
> Klein ....Sonny Grosso
> Weinstock .... Harold Gary

The French Connection, which won several Academy Awards, including
Best Picture and Best Actor (Gene Hackman), is a fast-paced thriller which
immediately captures the audience and never lets go. The true-to-life story
depicts the biggest narcotics seizure of all time, the 1962 confiscation of 120
pounds of pure heroin, which constitutes enough "junk" to keep every addict
in the United States supplied for eight months.

Now an American crime classic, the film is the semidocumentary story of
the actual detectives Sonny Grosso and Eddie Egan, who had worked together
for nearly a decade, mostly in Harlem, on New York's special narcotics squad.
Having smashed the multimillion-dollar international dope smuggling ring,
Gross's and Egan's exploits were captured in a best-selling book by Robin
Moore and translated onto the screen by a talented production team headed
by William Friedkin, the director of such diverse films as *The Night They
Raided Minsky's* (1968), *The Boys in the Band* (1970), and *The Exorcist*
(1973).

While a few scenes were set in Washington, D.C., and Marseilles, France,
the gangster picture was filmed almost entirely on location in New York: in
Bedford-Stuyvesant, the Lower East Side, Times Square, and Grand Central
Station. In gritty street pictures, Owen Roizman's camera captures the seamy
side of New York: the garbage, the pollution, and the city's brutal winter.
Composer-conductor Don Ellis' moody score, with its effective use of the

trombone, adds to the atmosphere.

Following the murder of a French detective in Marseilles by a professional killer, Pierre Nicoli (Marcel Bozzuffi), the dope-related mugging in Brooklyn of Detective Buddy Russo (Roy Scheider), and the suspicious flashing of large sums of money in an Eastside club, "supercops" Russo and Jimmy "Popeye" Doyle (Gene Hackman) play a long shot. Following some alleged heroin dealers into Brooklyn, the two plainclothesmen establish survcillance on a shady-looking candy store owned by Sal Boca (Tony LoBianco). Later, they trail Sal to the Manhattan apartment of Jewish Mafioso Joel Weinstock (Harold Gary), known to be the chief financial backer of illicit narcotics importation into the United States. Following that, Russo and Doyle persuade their boss, Lieutenant Simonson (Eddie Egan), to put Federal authorities on the case.

Meanwhile, the debonair French businessman Alain Charnier (Fernando Rey) and his wife; a leading French television personality, Henri Devereaux (Frederic De Pasquale); and the assassin Nicoli have arrived in New York and are seen meeting with Weinstock and Boca. Following assorted chases and shootouts, con-games and gundowns, the enormous consignment of smuggled drugs is uncovered, ingeniously hidden in Devereaux's specially designed Lincoln. As the story unfolds, Boca is exposed as the smugglers' Brooklyn contact, while Devereaux is inveigled into shipping his dope-laden car to America. Charnier is (unbeknownst to his innocent wife) the kingpin of the vast operation, and Nicoli is discovered to be his kill-happy strongarm.

By far the most memorable scene is the exciting chase through Bensonhurst, Brooklyn. Brilliantly executed, it is almost too gripping to enjoy. Spotting Nicoli, Doyle begins the hot pursuit. The hit man mounts the elevated station and takes over a moving train. Doyle, on the ground below, quickly commandeers a passing car and follows the path of the train. Amidst the fender-crunching, train-clacking, tire-shrieking noise, Nicoli ignores all station stops, terrorizes the passengers, and kills a transit motorman and policeman. Still down below, Doyle keeps one eye on the traffic and the other on the train as he weaves in and out at top speed, careens around pedestrians and track supports, and forces other cars off the road. Jerry Greenberg's editing is taut, hard, and relentless. With constricted stomachs, the audience feels that they, too, are participants in the furiously paced chase. It is reminiscent of Steve McQueen's car chase sequence in *Bullitt* (1968), which was also produced by Philip D'Antoni, but directed by William Friedkin.

Tough, violent, and brutal, *The French Connection* is not without some grim humor. In one scene Nicoli and Charnier elegantly dine in high style, while, outside in the bitter cold, Doyle disgustedly eats rubbery pizza and drinks muddy coffee. At another time, Nicoli tears a piece of bread from the loaf clutched by a man he has just shot in the face.

A melodrama with authenticity, the film provides insight into the nature of the police and the mobsters. Equally cold-blooded and callous, there are no good guys and bad guys, characters all black and white; instead, they are black and deep gray. Obscene, ferocious, and unheroic, Roy Scheider and Gene Hackman are excellent. Spanish actor Fernando Rey, in his first major American film, is suave and cool as the French mastermind with the silver-handled umbrella. Marcel Bozzuffi, who played the homosexual killer in *Z* (1969), is equally malevolent as Nicoli. Real-life detectives Egan and Grosso served as technical advisers during production, and each has a role in the film. Egan portrays Lieutenant Simonson, head of the two-hundred-man New York narcotics squad. Simonson was the police officer who had been Egan's actual supervisor during the original investigation. Sonny Grosso also has a minor role as Klein.

Ending on an ironic note, the action-adventure concludes as the hard-nosed detectives are transferred out of narcotics and the criminals escape with light sentences—or none at all. One difference between real life and this film is that the French assassin killed by Egan in the movie is actually now serving an eleven- to twenty-two-year sentence in prison.

So financially successful was the film that it spawned a sequel, *French Connection, II*, in 1974. That picture was not as well received critically as the original, but it did very well at the box office. It again starred Hackman and Rey, although most of the other principals were played by actors who had not been in the original production.

Leslie Taubman

FRIENDLY PERSUASION

Released: 1956
Production: William Wyler for United Artists
Direction: William Wyler
Screenplay: Michael Wilson (uncredited); based on the short stories of Jessamyn West
Cinematography: Ellsworth Fredericks
Editing: Robert Swink
Running time: 140 minutes

Principal characters:
Jess Birdwell	Gary Cooper
Eliza Birdwell	Dorothy McGuire
Josh Birdwell	Anthony Perkins
Mattie Birdwell	Phyllis Love
Little Jess	Richard Eyer
Sam Jordan	Robert Middleton
Gard Jordan	Mark Richman
Widow Hudspeth	Marjorie Main

Based on Jessamyn West's stories about a Quaker family living in southern Indiana during the Civil War, *Friendly Persuasion* is a "family film" in two senses. First, it has a broad appeal, presenting material that would interest both adults and children. Second, it focuses on a family's relationships, among its members as well as between the family and the rest of society. Winner of the *Palme d'Or* at the Cannes Film Festival, *Friendly Persuasion* received six Academy Award nominations, including one for Anthony Perkins, who was appearing in only his second film, as Best Supporting Actor.

Setting is crucial in *Friendly Persuasion*. The physical setting, the wooded hills of southern Indiana, creates a sense of pastoral peace. As nurseryman Jess Birdwell (Gary Cooper) and his family go about the idyllic pursuits of farm life, the film projects an admiration for the traditional, family-oriented security imputed to rural life in America. The film's social setting is also important. As Quakers, the Birdwell family stands somewhat apart from others in their community. For example, a traveling salesman makes good-natured sport of their nonstandard use of the pronouns "thee" and "thou" early in the film. In fact, the very seriousness with which they take their religion, demonstrated by the position of Jess's wife Eliza (Dorothy McGuire) as a leader of the local Quaker fellowship, makes the family out of the ordinary. Furthermore, Quakerism encourages full participation in the religion by all members of the family and discourages involvement in such "worldly" activities as music, horseracing, gambling, and violence. The historical setting of the film makes the last prohibition particularly difficult to observe. It is the turbulent era of the Civil War, and the Birdwell family as well as other Quakers are pressured to join the Union cause at least to protect their lives and property from the depradations of John Hunt Morgan's Confederate guerrillas, who are raiding into southern Indiana. This historical setting creates a tension with the peaceful physical setting in which the Quaker family tries to live its tranquil life.

The film's major narrative thrust concerns the gradual encroachment of war into the life of the Birdwells. The war first becomes apparent in the film when a Union soldier interrupts the Quaker meeting to appeal to the worshipers' patriotism and to urge the menfolk to enlist in the Union Army. The war and its effects become personified for the Birdwells especially in Gard Jordan (Mark Richman), the son of a neighbor who serves in the army. Wounded slightly on the battlefield, Gard comes home on furlough to win the heart of Mattie Birdwell (Phyllis Love) and the admiration of her brother Little Jess (Richard Eyer). As Morgan's Raiders move ever closer to the Birdwell property, they begin to see other signs of war such as billows of smoke from burning farmsteads in the distance.

The ultimate encroachment of war occurs when Josh Birdwell (Anthony Perkins) joins the local militia to help to repel the Confederate intruders. Josh's defection from Quaker teachings generates a family crisis. His decision is the result of his own inner crisis as he has agonized over whether his refusal to fight in the war results from his Quaker principles or from cowardice. Josh's struggle within himself recalls that of the protagonist of Stephen Crane's novel of the Civil War, *The Red Badge of Courage* (1895). On the battlefield Josh kills a Confederate soldier and is injured himself. When Jess sets out to find his son on the battleground, the older man also confronts a challenge to his Quaker beliefs. He finds his friend and neighbor Sam Jordan (Robert Middleton) dying from a Confederate sniper's bullet. Although the same sniper takes a shot at Jess, the Quaker allows the man to go in peace without exacting vengeance for his friend's death. Cooper's typical low-keyed acting is particularly effective and believable in his role as Jess. While Jess is away from the farm, the Confederates pillage the place. They are allowed to take what they want, Eliza resorting to defense with her broom only when the family's pet goose, Samantha, is threatened.

Although the film explores the serious issue of conflict of loyalties between religious principles and social responsibility, it also operates on a lighter level. The theme, sung by Pat Boone over the opening credits, sets up the expectation for a lighthearted film. That expectation is fulfilled in the first scene, the first of several which depict the running feud between Little Jess and Samantha, the goose who attacks the boy at particularly inopportune moments. Other scenes in the film such as the business call which Jess and Josh pay on the Widow Hudspeth (Marjorie Main) and her nubile daughters are almost totally comic. Much of the humor in the film, however, arises directly from the problems of being a good Quaker amidst the world's temptations. Members of the Birdwell family are shown humanly straying from the paths of Quaker righteousness in minor ways. For example, Jess cannot resist a horserace with his Methodist neighbor Sam Jordan even on the way to their respective churches. Mattie is vain, spending hours before her mirror despite the taunting of her brothers. Little Jess harbors thoughts of bloody revenge against his enemy Samantha. At a fair, members of the family are shown caught between the allurements of gambling, dancing, and music and the ever watchful eye of Eliza. (Significantly, Josh, who of course will later go to war, refuses to be swayed from his convictions at the fair, even when another fairgoer begins to abuse him physically.) These minor lapses from Quakerism, presented humorously for the most part, foreshadow the major lapses which occur with the advent of war.

Critical response to *Friendly Persuasion* was favorable and praised director William Wyler for his handling of what many felt to be unpromising material. The film manages to couple the quaint charm of rural American values with comedy and a serious theme, and the acting by the major characters responds nicely to the film's changing moods. *Friendly Persuasion* is a successful blending of dramatic tension with Currier-and-Ives nostalgia.

Frances M. Malpezzi
William M. Clements

FROM HERE TO ETERNITY

Released: 1953
Production: Buddy Adler for Columbia (AA)
Direction: Fred Zinnemann (AA)
Screenplay: Daniel Taradash (AA); based on the novel of the same name by
James Jones
Cinematography: Burnett Guffey (AA)
Editing: William A. Lyon (AA)
Art direction: Cary Odell
Sound: John P. Livadary and Columbia Studio Sound Department (AA)
Music: George Duning
Running time: 118 minutes

Principal characters:
Sergeant Milton Warden .... Burt Lancaster
Robert E. Lee "Prew" Prewitt ..... Montgomery Clift
Karen Holmes .... Deborah Kerr
Angelo Maggio .... Frank Sinatra (AA)
Alma (Lorene) .... Donna Reed (AA)
Captain Dana Holmes .... Philip Ober
Sergeant "Fatso" Judson .... Ernest Borgnine

James Jones's 1951 novel, *From Here to Eternity*, whose title was taken
from a line ("damned from here to eternity") in Rudyard Kipling's poem
"Gentlemen Rankers," is based on the author's own military experience and
presents a scathing portrait of barracks' life in a peacetime United States
Army company. In some respects it is hardly a novel at all, resembling a sort
of literary Rorschach Test. When the novel appeared, every reader seemed
to see something different in it and responded emotionally in diverse ways.
Most agreed, however, that it embodied a tremendously vivid and exciting
picture of men in mass groupings and added up to as powerful an expression
of love and hate for the United States Army as had every been published.
Written in sprawling and vigorous style, *From Here to Eternity* became a best
seller and won the National Book Award. In so doing it came to the attention
of Columbia's head, Harry Cohn, who eventually bought the rights to the
novel from Jones for $82,000 and set out to get an acceptable film treatment
written.

It was the feeling at Columbia that the explicit nature of the novel would
have to be toned down to make it suitable for the screen. This attitude
frustrated Jones greatly; his own treatment was rejected because it followed
too closely the obscene and sadistic flourishes of the novel. A somewhat
diluted version, written by Daniel Taradash, was finally accepted by the studio.
Even in its new state, however, *From Here to Eternity* is a powerful story,

and director Fred Zinnemann brought it to the screen with great skill and fidelity to the original source. In Zinnemann's refinement, however, there are touches of slick sentimentality that do not seem to come from the book; and many viewers have noted the absence of some of the novel's honest and rough-hewn vignettes that had to be shorn away during its transformation to the screen. Through its cold professional eye, though, Zinnemann's camera sees the persons of the drama more clearly and at the same time less bitterly than did Jones.

Following the selection of Zinnemann as director, the casting of the performers became a focal point of controversy among Cohn, Zinnemann, and Jones, as well as various other studio executives. Cohn recommended that the part of Robert E. Lee Prewitt, the young soldier who refuses to box for his company and is therefore persecuted, be given to Aldo Ray. Both Zinnemann and Jones had hoped that the part would be given to Montgomery Clift. Jones and Clift had become drinking companions and Clift had already worked for Zinnemann in the film *The Search* (1948). It was finally agreed that Clift would be given the role since he had a reputation for being well-equipped to interpret sensitive roles as demonstrated in such films as *A Place in the Sun* (1951) and *Red River* (1948). The part of Karen Holmes, the frustrated wife of Captain Dana Holmes, was originally given to Joan Crawford, but because of a disagreement over costume selection she quit, leaving the role open for English actress Deborah Kerr.

The remaining performers rounding out the cast were also excellent choices. The part of Sergeant Milton Warden went to Burt Lancaster who was perfectly suited to play the character of the solid career soldier who is aware of how to manipulate the system but is unwilling to do so merely for the sake of promotion. Frank Sinatra, who had to convince the studio heads that he could perform a nonsinging role, won the part of Angelo Maggio, the good-natured friend of Prewitt. In an uncharacteristic role, Donna Reed was cast as Alma (Lorene), the prostitute who befriends Prewitt.

On the wide screen and in stereophonic sound, *From Here to Eternity* draws the viewer into the world of the military. The film is more than noteworthy as being a significant example of a hardhitting and honest 1950's drama: a microscopic look at the undercurrents which ran through a peacetime military company stationed in Hawaii just before the attack on Pearl Harbor. The story line revolves around Private Prewitt, played in extraordinary depth by Montgomery Clift. The screenplay focuses more sharply than did the novel on Private Robert E. Lee "Prew" Prewitt, the "hardhead" who can soldier with any man, but who cannot play it smart because he is cursed with a piece of ultimate wisdom. As he puts it, "If a man don't go his own way, he's nothing." The character is essentially a loner who becomes further removed from the other men in the company because of his conscience. Transferred into Company G at Schofield Barracks in Hawaii, Prew is immediately informed by Captain Dana Holmes (Philip Ober) that he cannot go his own way. Captain Holmes, a boxing fanatic who wants his company to win the regiment championship, knows that Prew is a first-class middleweight, and insists that he box for his new outfit. Prew, who quit fighting after he blinded a friend with a "no more'n ordinary right cross," refuses. Furious, Holmes orders his noncommissioned officers—all of whom are on the boxing team— to give Prew "the treatment."

Prew endures this harassment for months on end. The sergeants trip him in bayonet drill and cheat him in rifle inspection, and for every fault they find, Prew has to pay with K. P., extra laps around the track under full pack, or hours of digging enormous holes in the ground so that the jeering noncoms can bury a single newspaper. His superiors even refuse his request to become the company bugler even though he is a polished musician (Clift spent a good deal of time learning to play the bugle so he could feel comfortable when the role called upon him to do so).

In addition to the story of Private Prewitt, there are other threads which are finely woven to fill in the picture of Army life between the world wars. There is the rowdy comedy of the soldiers' night out at the "New Congress Club" and the bittersweet story of Prew's love for a warm-hearted prostitute with visions of respectability. Although the novel bluntly called the girl a whore, the film manages to make the point merely by including her in some of the most accurately depicted brothel scenes in cinema. There is, by contrast, the fierce meeting of First Sergeant Warden (Burt Lancaster) and the captain's wife, Karen Holmes (Deborah Kerr), two people who think they know what they need and almost make life give it to them. Warden and Karen's love scene in the Hawaiian surf is one of the most famous moments in cinema history, and for some people the dominant romantic image of the film. Additionally, there are the stories of Private Maggio (Frank Sinatra), Prew's friend who is beaten to death in the stockade by "Fatso" Judson (Ernest Borgnine), the brutal captain of the guard, and of Prew's tragic revenge. The climax of the film is December 7, 1941, which, for all of its horror, finally ends this cycle of human misery. Fred Zinnemann, who fought tirelessly to hold the scenario as closely as possible to James Jones's original, deserves credit for molding the diverse lines of action at once large in scope, in power, and in passion, and also for conveying an intimacy of personal triumphs and tragedies. There is a clarity of purpose in his direction and a respect shown for the characters and the talented group of actors who portray them which effectively strengthens the story line.

The three male leads in the film turn in arguably the finest performances of their careers to that time. Burt Lancaster as the tough career military man is appropriately physical and obvious in his manner. He is the model of a man among men, absolutely convincing in his instinctive awareness of the subtle elaborate structure of force and honor on which a male society is based.

Sergeant Warden uses the military system to his advantage though he will not allow himself to bend to it and pull the right strings to become an officer, which would make his life easier. His love for Captain Holmes's wife is passionate and genuine. Their love affair eventually fails because of his refusal to make it easier on himself and succumb to the system. The film's big performance is given by Montgomery Clift. He does an ingenious job of acting a plain, slow-thinking individual who compares interestingly in scenes with Lancaster, who does everything with a glib, showy animal magnetism. Clift displays a marvelous capacity to contract his feelings into the tight little shell of Prew's personality. At the same time, he manages to convey that within this limited man there blazes a large spirit.

Frank Sinatra, in an Academy Award-winning performance, portrays Private Maggio like nothing he has ever done before. His face conveys the calm confidence of a man who is completely sure of what he is doing as he plays it straight from Little Italy. In certain scenes—performing duty in the mess hall, reacting to some foul piano playing—he shows a marvelous capacity for phrasing and a calm expression that is unique in Hollywood film.

Ernest Borgnine as Fatso, with his smiling villainy, is hard to forget. Deborah Kerr as Karen, playing a part far removed from the more refined roles for which she had been previously noted, brims with sensuality. As a woman married to the brutal military opportunist, she attempts to sieze a forbidden love, disregarding the consequences of such an act in the closed world of the military.

From Here to Eternity, under the care and direction of Fred Zinnemann, involves the viewer from beginning to conclusion, from the initial naïveté and innocence of Private Robert E. Lee Prewitt, on through the frustration and torment of the career soldiers and the women who become bruised casualties of this man's world. The performers convey that curious and captivating presence that director Zinnemann refers to as "behaving rather than acting," which he developed in such notable films as *The Search*, *The Men* (1950), and *The Member of the Wedding* (1953). Vienna-born Zinnemann, a former cameraman, uses the camera with easy familiarity and with a cool simplicity that seems surprised by nothing, but shows compassion for everything. The location cinematography took place at Schofield Barracks in Hawaii, which becomes a large, stark frame for some memorable scenes, such as the rite of taps for Private Maggio.

Great care and intent went into the making of *From Here to Eternity*. Zinnemann and Daniel Taradash share the credit for an outstanding script. Although the shift from one story to another is sometimes too abrupt, that is only a minor defect in a highly professional job of writing. Although this film is what Hollywood considers "a big picture" with slick production values, it is also something more. It attempts to tell a truth about life and the inviolability of the human spirit. It is not a total success but it does show powerfully that Americans care very much about a man's right to go his own way even though the times and the world may be contrary.

The public approved the effort and made *From Here to Eternity* a big box-office success for Columbia. The Motion Picture Academy followed suit by awarding the film seven Academy Awards, including Best Supporting Actor (Frank Sinatra), Best Supporting Actress (Donna Reed), and Best Picture. The New York Film Critics gave laurels to *From Here to Eternity* for Best Picture, Best Director, and Best Actor (Burt Lancaster). Montgomery Clift was nominated for Best Actor by the Motion Picture Academy, but the award went to William Holden that year for his performance in *Stalag 17*.

Jeffry Michael Jensen

THE FRONT PAGE

Released: 1931
Production: Howard Hughes for United Artists
Direction: Lewis Milestone
Screenplay: Bartlett Cormack and Charles Lederer; based on the play of the same name by Ben Hecht and Charles MacArthur
Cinematography: Glen MacWilliams
Editing: W. Duncan Mansfield
Running time: 101 minutes

Principal characters:
Walter Burns	Adolphe Menjou
Hildy Johnson	Pat O'Brien
Peggy Grant	Mary Brian
Bensinger	Edward Everett Horton
Murphy	Walter Catlett
Earl Williams	George E. Stone
Sheriff Hartman	Clarence Wilson

When Ben Hecht and Charles MacArthur wrote *The Front Page* in 1928, they used the basic premise that everyone is corrupt in one way or another, and, furthermore, that everyone enjoys it. The motley assortment of newspapermen and politicians who appear in the play are a cynical group who expend a great deal of energy in trying to outwit everyone else. They all are aware of who is playing games, and in many cases what the results will be; but the real fun will come in trying to be the first to acknowledge it publicly. The protagonists of *The Front Page*, scheming newspaper editor Walter Burns and his ace reporter Hildy Johnson, are the cleverest of the lot because they manage to outsmart the politicians as well as the other newspapermen. No other character in the play or film could possibly steal the show from these two cheerfully corrupt souls, who effortlessly manipulate everyone in the story.

The success of the Broadway production of *The Front Page*, directed by the legendary George S. Kaufman, was so great that it led to a proliferation of stories with newspapermen as protagonists both on stage and in the new "talkies." In most of these stories, the reporter, although he is working for a just cause, is pictured as a driven, almost inhuman individual; it is the female lead who begs him to "get out of the racket." Some of these stories chose to bypass the rich comedic vein unearthed by *The Front Page* to make more serious points. Paramount's *Gentlemen of the Press* (1929), for example, while containing most of the elements of *The Front Page*, is really more like a soap opera: editor Walter Huston's zeal for his job keeps him from his daughter's deathbed in one scene, and most of the people in the film remind him at one point or another that he is a heartless individual.

Hecht and MacArthur were very much a part of the Chicago of 1928 that they describe in the play; they could not have captured the nuances of the newspaper racket so skillfully had they not been, but it is obvious that, like the protagonists about whom they write, the authors feel a certain exhilaration for their characters and the unscrupulous schemes they perpetrate. Lewis Milestone directed this film version of *The Front Page*, and his dedication to the structure of film is evident in his attempts at staging. To avoid a slow, static rendition of a stage play, Milestone kept his camera on the move; he made sure that the audience realized that rooms have four walls (we never see four walls in a play); and he had the film cut quickly from shot to shot to give visual pace to the staccato dialogue, which had been a part of Kaufman's directorial technique for the play. Unfortunately, sound recording techniques in 1931 were not as sophisticated as they were later in the decade, and prints of *The Front Page* exhibited today have poor sound reproduction, forcing newer audiences to strain to hear the dialogue. Aside from that, however, *The Front Page* is a creditable effort to release the early talkie from its one-set, stagebound qualities, and it succeeds quite well.

As the story begins, we learn that ace reporter Hildy Johnson (Pat O'Brien) is leaving the newspaper racket, much to the chagrin of his unscrupulous editor Walter Burns (Adolphe Menjou), who wants Hildy to cover the hanging of Earl Williams (George E. Stone), a poor clerk who went temporarily mad and shot a policeman. Hildy no longer wants any part of the business as he is engaged to be married to Peggy Grant (Mary Brian). The other reporters, staying in the Press Room of the Criminal Courts building to cover the hanging, deride Hildy goodnaturedly about quitting, but he remains adamant. He, Peggy, and her mother are leaving for New York to begin life anew, far away from Chicago and its crooked politicians, gangsters, and cheap reporters.

When Williams escapes by accident, Walter realizes that he has the conclusive proof of ineptitude in the local government, and by disclosing this information to the public, can force the ouster of Sheriff Hartman (Clarence Wilson). Hartman is only the political puppet of the Mayor, who desperately needs Williams' immediate recapture since an election is forthcoming. Convincing Hildy that he will help the newlyweds after the capture of Williams, Walter persuades the reporter to cover the story for him. Hildy and the other newspeople fail to realize that Williams, a timid individual by nature, has not even left the Criminal Courts building. The sheriff mounts a citywide manhunt, and the reporters follow every lead hoping for a scoop. Hildy, alone in the Press Room, is surprised by Williams' entrance; he persuades the harried fugitive to hide in the Press Room, concealing him inside a rolltop desk. Hildy then summons Walter, who plans to return Williams officially to the police, not only getting the scoop but embarrassing the police as well.

Other reporters nearly discover Earl in the desk, and Walter's sudden appearance makes the sheriff suspicious. The police circulate stories of William's maniacal attack on his guards, and issue orders to "shoot to kill." Thus, the sheriff is in no mood to entertain a messenger from the Governor who brings a reprieve for Williams. Hartman attempts to bribe the messenger and sends him away, but the slow-witted messenger returns just as Williams has been exposed, and Walter and Hildy arrested as accessories. This new evidence is what Walter needs to expose the corruption within the city's administration. During all the excitement, Hildy realizes that he is a newspaperman for life, and he and Walter contemplate further double-dealings.

Howard Hawks remade *The Front Page* for Columbia in 1940. Changing the character of Hildy Johnson from a man to a woman and making Walter Burns more suave made *His Girl Friday* (1940) sparkle; the male-female relationship gave additional bite to many of the play's original lines. Charles Lederer, who worked on *The Front Page*, did the screenplay for *His Girl Friday* as well, and the Hawks film, curiously, retains much of the play's original integrity. In 1976, Billy Wilder, himself a cynical journalist, screenwriter, and director, remade *The Front Page* under its original title, starring Jack Lemmon as Hildy Johnson and Walter Matthau as Walter Burns. Despite the teamwork of Lemmon and Matthau, the film was surprisingly flat, and it was generally felt that the material had already been given the definitive screen treatment.

Ed Hulse

THE FUGITIVE

Released: 1947
Production: John Ford and Merian C. Cooper for Argosy; released by RKO/
  Radio
Direction: John Ford
Screenplay: Dudley Nichols; based on the novel *The Labyrinthine Ways* (or
  The Power and the Glory) by Graham Greene
Cinematography: Gabriel Figueroa
Editing: Jack Murray
Running time: 104 minutes

> *Principal characters:*
> The Fugitive ....Henry Fonda
> The Woman .... Dolores Del Rio
> The Police Lieutenant ....Pedro Armendariz
> El Gringo ....Ward Bond
> Chief of Police ....Leo Carrillo
> Police Informer ....J. Carrol Naish

The Fugitive, based on Graham Greene's novel *The Labyrinthine Ways*, is the first film that John Ford made with his independent production company, Argosy, which he had established in 1946. In partnership with Merian C. Cooper and financially supported by former wartime Office of Strategic Services comrades (William Donovan, Ole Doering, David Bruce, and William Vanderbilt), Ford hoped to free himself from the strict controls imposed on his earlier films by the major studios. Being an independent enabled Ford to indulge his artistic ambitions and to produce what he would later refer to as his only perfect film. *The Fugitive* was a commercial failure, however, and in spite of some favorable reviews at the time of its release, most critics now agree that it is one of Ford's worst films. Given his genius and the remarkable achievement of the majority of his work, it is instructive to examine the film in order to understand better why Ford's other films are so satisfying on so many different levels.

The central figure of the book is a priest in the state of mortal sin. Pursued by the authorities from village to village, the "whiskey priest" is also being tracked down by his own conscience through the labyrinthine ways of his own mind. Guilt wrenches him like a vice, leaving nothing but a yearning to do God's will—if only he were priest enough. When at last he dies, the hardship and the guilt have left very little of him still alive.

The film abandons the internal moral dilemma of the novel for a relatively routine plot that does not attempt to delve into the book's complex philosophical issues. It is set in an unspecified Latin American country which bears a strong resemblance to the Mexico of the 1920's and 1930's and its purges of the Roman Catholic churches and clergy. As it begins, a voiceover explains that the story is timeless, a story first told in the Bible. A man (Henry Fonda) approaches an imposing church on a hill and enters, pausing as he pushes open the doors and forming a shadow in the shape of a cross. He finds that the church has been vandalized and desecrated and notices that a woman (Dolores Del Rio) and her child are hiding inside. The man asks her why she is here, and she replies that she has no home and no husband to go to. Learning that the stranger is the former priest of this parish, the woman begs him to baptize her child. Although the priest is afraid, he agrees to perform the rite for her and for the other villagers. In the film, as well as in the original story, this priest proves, in spite of his giving way to temptation, that he is not a coward but a man overwhelmed by love for his fellow men. In a beautifully photographed sequence, the villagers enter the church and restore the baptismal font. The priest then blesses and baptizes the children of the village, beginning with the illegitimate child of the woman who had been hiding in the church.

By the next day the police have learned of the ceremony. They ride to the village, where they destroy the stalls and goods in the marketplace, thoroughly frightening the people. The lieutenant (Pedro Armendariz) rides into the church, where he finds the woman who befriended the priest. He recognizes her, and it is revealed that they had been lovers and that he is, in fact, the father of her child. He is startled to learn that she now works in the cantina, but is satisfied that his dedication to the revolution is more important than are his responsibilities to this woman and her daughter.

The police herd the villagers into the square, where the lieutenant urges them to reveal the identity of the priest. If they do not do so, the police will take hostages until the priest is found. When the lieutenant takes the mayor as the first hostage, the priest, disguised as a peasant, volunteers to replace the mayor. Ironically, he is refused as an unworthy substitute.

When the police leave, the woman helps the priest to escape the village. On his way, he passes El Gringo (Ward Bond), an American thief and murderer who has arrived by ship and is attempting to hide in the village; he too is a fugitive. Further on, the priest encounters a servile, cunning man (J. Carrol Naish) who insists on accompanying him to the port city. The man is an informer who has recognized the priest from a wanted poster and plans to betray him to the police. When they stop for the night, the informer gets drunk on the sacramental wine that the priest is carrying and passes out, enabling the priest to escape. Reaching the city, the priest buys a ticket for a departing ship, but before he can board, he is recognized by a small boy who begs him to give the last rites to his dying mother. The priest agrees to see her, thereby dooming his escape.

After administering last rites to the dying woman, he is asked to say a mass for all of the mourners but he needs wine for the mass and his supply is gone.

Because the state has prohibited the sale of wine, the priest must buy it from the corrupt cousin of the governor. Once he has paid for the wine, he is forced to drink brandy and share his wine with the black marketeer and the equally corrupt chief of police. He eventually escapes with the remaining brandy, but is arrested by the police for drunkenness. Once again the lieutenant does not recognize him, even though the informer, who is, by now, also jailed, tries to tell the lieutenant who he is. In jail, the priest must watch the hostage mayor march to his death.

The priest is subsequently released from prison and returns to the woman from the church. El Gringo is there and befriends the priest, paying for his supper. Soon the police arrive, and the woman hides the priest until she can persuade them to leave. The priest is seen as he tries to flee, but El Gringo shoots several of the policemen so that he can get away. The woman then helps the priest to cross the border where he is welcomed at a hospital.

The informer tracks him to the hospital and persuades him to return to the country because El Gringo is dying and needs his help. The priest agrees to go, but when they arrive, El Gringo says that he did not send for him. The priest tries to pray for him and urges him to confess his sins and repent, but El Gringo refuses, and as he dies, the police arrive to arrest the priest.

In prison, the lieutenant attempts to convince the priest to renounce his faith and to tell the people that he was a liar. The priest refuses. The woman brings him a crucifix, and the priest is marched to his death. At the sound of the guns, the lieutenant recoils as if hit himself and involuntarily crosses himself. In the last scene, the people are in the church praying when suddenly the doors open, and a man in the doorway announces that he is the new priest.

The Fugitive is the most consciously artistic film Ford ever made. Other films, among them *The Informer* (1935), *The Grapes of Wrath* (1939), *She Wore a Yellow Ribbon* (1949), and *The Quiet Man* (1952), are beautifully photographed with expressive camera angles and striking compositions; but in no other film is the attempt for artistic effect quite as obvious as it is in *The Fugitive*. The great Mexican cinematographer Gabriel Figueroa, who would later shoot many of Luis Buñel's Mexican films, produces a series of stunning visual effects. The people in the film are photographed like heroic Russian peasants, and whereas Russian director Sergei Eisenstein had, for example, glorified the citizens of his films in order to exalt the state, Ford glorifies his devout throngs to exalt the Church. Unlike Eisenstein, Ford is unable to combine those gorgeous but static images into a montage that is vibrant and alive. The audience is left with a film of visual richness, but one with a narrative that is full of implausible coincidences, pious but murky allegories, and actors portraying symbols rather than characters.

Given the limitations of the script, the actors are effective in their roles. Del Rio and Armendariz are particularly successful in lending some depth to parts that are essentially one-dimensional. Naish's obsequious hysteria is discordant when surrounded by other actors underplaying their roles. Fonda is almost immobile as the central character. One facet of Fonda's talent as an actor is the ability to convey a stillness, a quiet center to which other characters must respond. Ford uses that passivity in this film so that the fate of the priest is preordained from the beginning; as a fugitive priest who will not run from his duty in a hostile country, his martyrdom is inevitable. Thus, there is not the degree of dramatic tension in the film that there was in the novel since a certain inner conflict is lacking. The priest cannot save himself, and the audience loses interest in his passive journey toward death.

Ford is responsible for the failure of *The Fugitive*. The absence of studio control in his first independent effort became a license for self-indulgence, but Ford would not repeat his mistake. Other films made for Argosy would be commercial successes, and three or four would be masterpieces acclaimed by film scholars. *The Fugitive* contains some traits that would later be controlled in other films, but are freely expressed in this film, much to its detriment. The director's religious beliefs are evident in every frame. Pious Catholics may be inspired by the film; in fact, the Catholic magazine *The Sign* gave the film its 1947 award for the outstanding picture of the year. Yet general audiences are not persuaded by the religious aura, and many critics have objected to the heavy-handed symbolism of permitting Fonda's shadow to assume the form of the crucifix or of showing his sandled feet walking rough cobblestones to his execution. Other artistic objections center on the film's ending in a gratuitous miracle with the cross glowing in the darkness like a neon light. At the same time, Ford's chauvinist views of women are also given free rein, reducing Del Rio's character to a solemn caricature of woman as a combination of the Virgin Mary and Mary Magdalene.

Several critics have faulted Ford for not being more faithful to Greene's novel, saying that the film removes the "stink of humanity" which Greene had so powerfully conveyed in his book. The problem with the film is that Ford removes the humanity as well as the stink, and produces instead lugubrious, albeit beautiful, tableaux that lack the warmth and vitality which enliven so many of Ford's other films. It is ironic that when Ford consciously strived to produce an artistic film, he failed miserably, but when he tossed off "a piece of work," he gave the world such masterpieces as *The Searchers* (1956) and *The Quiet Man*.

Don K Thompson

FUNNY FACE

Released: 1957
Production: Roger Edens for Paramount
Direction: Stanley Donen
Screenplay: Leonard Gershe; based on his unproduced musical play of the
   same name
Cinematography: Ray June
Editing: Frank Bracht
Costume design: Edith Head and Hubert de Givenchy
Dance direction: Eugene Loring
Music: George and Ira Gershwin
Visual consulting: Richard Avedon
Running time: 103 minutes

Principal characters:

Jo Stockton	Audrey Hepburn
Dick Avery	Fred Astaire
Maggie Prescott	Kay Thompson
Professor Emile Flostre	Michel Auclair
Paul Duval	Robert Flemyng

Funny Face was a stage musical in the 1920's starring Fred Astaire and his
sister Adele, but the film of the same name made in 1957 used no more of
the original than the name, several of the songs by George and Ira Gershwin,
and Astaire as the star. In the film Astaire plays Dick Avery, a fashion
photographer. When Maggie Prescott (Kay Thompson), the editor of the
magazine for which he works, decides to do a series of photographs to show
that a woman can be beautiful as well as intellectual, Dick, Maggie, and a
group of decidedly unintellectual models invade a small Greenwich Village
bookshop, much to the dismay of the clerk there, Jo Stockton (Audrey Hepburn). She becomes especially upset when they begin moving books about
as if they owned the place. When they finally leave, Dick stays behind to give
her some help in straightening up the mess they have caused.

Dick finds that Jo is a student of "empathacalism," a philosophy founded
by a professor in France. Although he is not interested in empathacalism,
Dick is interested in Jo, but when he kisses her she responds coolly that she
has no desire to be kissed. She remains unmoved until after he leaves. Then
she begins to catch the mood, singing and dancing alone in the bookstore to
"How Long Has This Been Going On?"

Maggie is planning to choose a "quality woman" to photograph in Paris
wearing the new collection by the designer Paul Duval (Robert Flemyng).
Dick suggests that they use Jo, and when Maggie looks her over she says,
"She might do." "Might do what?" replies Jo. Dick convinces Jo that she can

be a model, even with her "funny face," and that the trip to Paris will give her a chance to meet Professor Flostre (Michel Auclair), the founder of empathacalism.

In Paris, Maggie, Jo, and Dick are shown on a split screen singing "Bonjour, Paris!" until they end up together on the Eiffel Tower. The next day, however, Jo does not show up at Duval's salon, and Dick has to search for her, finally finding her in a Bohemian café. After they argue and make up, they get down to the fashion business as Dick photographs Jo all over Paris in various Duval creations. For each photograph he tells her the mood he wants ("Today you're Anna Karenina," for example), and after each picture is taken we see it first in black-and-white negative, then in black-and-white positive, and finally in color. It is a visually striking technique. When he is photographing her as a bride outside a small church and she confesses that she loves him, he sings "He Loves and She Loves," and they dance together.

Professor Flostre, however, continues to be an obstacle to their romance. Jo goes to hear him lecture and then to see him privately although Dick has told her that he thinks Flostre's interest in her is more physical than intellectual. When she and Flostre are alone together, Jo finds that Dick was right. "I came here to talk with a philosopher, and you're talking like a man," she says before she hits him over the head with a statue and runs from the room.

Jo appears in Duval's fashion show, and she and the collection are a success, but Dick, not knowing that Jo has rejected Flostre's advances, is discouraged and determined to leave Paris without her. At the airport, however, he accidentally runs into Flostre and learns the true story. He goes back to find her, but she has left Duval's. At Maggie's suggestion he thinks of where she was happiest and immediately goes to the small church where they danced to "He Loves and She Loves." He finds her there; they sing "'S Wonderful" and glide away into the mist on a raft.

The plot of *Funny Face* is a perfectly serviceable one despite its gratuitous antiintellectualism in portraying empathacalism as inane and its followers as foolish or hypocritical. It even contains many excellent and well-acted nonmusical scenes, especially in the first half as bookish Jo is confronted with brassy Maggie and romantic Dick. *Funny Face* is, however, most importantly a musical, and its true highlights are in its musical numbers, many of which express the feelings developed in the plot.

The first important number finds Jo alone in the bookstore after the fashion magazine people have gone. She is dressed in dark and subdued colors in the middle of the equally dark and subdued colors of the books and the bookstore furnishings. Her discovery of a long brightly colored scarf left behind by the intruders and her memory of Dick's kiss start her singing and dancing to "How Long Has This Been Going On?" The visual effect of the one bright color moving about the room is striking. The voice, incidentally, is Hepburn's own, and is engaging if not superlative. (In *My Fair Lady* in 1964, of course, the producers chose to dub in Marni Nixon's singing voice for Hepburn in a famous Hollywood imbroglio.)

Probably the best and most inventive dance number is a solo by Dick to "Let's Kiss and Make Up," danced in a courtyard as Jo looks on from a balcony above. The two have quarreled, and Dick sings to her. Then as he begins dancing, a passing vehicle with a cow in it inspires Dick to continue the dance as a bullfighter, using his red-lined raincoat and his umbrella as props. It is a truly creative and expressive dance in which the bullfight motif never seems to be a gimmick.

The dance director, Eugene Loring, was a classically trained choreographer who had worked with Astaire before. Hepburn, although not known primarily as a dancer, had extensive training in ballet, while Astaire's experience was, of course, in stage and film musicals. Loring, therefore, as he has said, had "to try to think of Fred in a fresh way." For the dances of Astaire and Hepburn together he tried to use the strengths of each so that they would complement each other rather than clash or conflict. The dance he devised for "He Loves and She Loves" is a fine combination of the two, with Hepburn dancing in a bridal dress which somewhat resembles a ballet costume.

Also notable is a fun-filled seminovelty number called "Clap Yo' Hands." When Dick and Maggie find that Jo is with Professor Flostre instead of preparing for the fashion show, they invade the Bohemian quarters of the philosopher disguised as Southern folk singers who are there to entertain the Bohemian empathacalists. They do a rousing, gospel-style singing and dancing number with Dick wearing a false beard and using some Elvis Presley-like movements. Their performance is a hit with the empathacalists, but it does not succeed in getting Jo away from Flostre.

Funny Face gained a visual distinction from its "visual consultant," the noted photographer Richard Avedon; its producer and director, Roger Edens and Stanley Donen, had been part of the golden years of the M-G-M musical; and Hepburn and Thompson gave splendid acting and dancing performances. All these virtually guaranteed a good film, and the addition of the incomparable talents of Astaire made certain that the film would be the outstanding work it is.

Judith A. Williams

FUNNY GIRL

Released: 1968
Production: Ray Stark for Columbia
Direction: William Wyler
Screenplay: Isobel Lennart; based on her musical play of the same name with music by Jule Styne and lyrics by Bob Merrill
Cinematography: Harry Stradling
Editing: Robert Swink, Maury Weintrobe, and William Sands
Costume design: Irene Sharaff
Music direction: Herbert Ross
Running time: 151 minutes

Principal characters:
Fanny Brice .... Barbra Streisand (AA)
Nick Arnstein .... Omar Sharif
Rose Brice .... Kay Medford
Georgia James .... Anne Francis
Florenz Ziegfeld .... Walter Pidgeon

When the $8.8 million film version of *Funny Girl* had its premiere on September 19, 1968, it succeeded in doing what every reporter, journalist, and columnist had predicted it would—it catapulted Barbra Streisand into superstardom. It also led to an Oscar for her performance as Best Actress of the Year, tying Katharine Hepburn for *The Lion in Winter*. This was only the second time that a tie had occurred in an acting category, the first having been the one between Wallace Beery for *The Champ* and Fredric March for *Dr. Jekyll and Mr. Hyde* in 1931.

Streisand, the ugly-duckling Jewish girl from Brooklyn, had already wooed recording and television fans, and had scored personal acting successes, with her Miss Marmelstein role in Broadway's *I Can Get It for You Wholesale*, and her stage impersonation of Fanny Brice in the Broadway hit version of *Funny Girl*. When the stage version of *Funny Girl* opened at the Winter Garden Theatre in New York City, on March 26, 1964, where it was to run for a total of 1,348 performances, Bette Davis attended the opening night performance and exclaimed afterwards, "The girl has star quality."

Indeed, Streisand's star quality is her greatest asset and her greatest liability. The motion picture version of *Funny Girl* was tailor-made for Streisand's unique personality; most viewers did not care that what remained of Fanny Brice's story was little more than a glossy Cinderella story. The other films which Streisand has made since *Funny Girl* have likewise been tailor-made for her, each capitalizing on her star quality with varying degrees of artistic success, although most have also been box-office blockbusters.

Funny Girl property rights belong to producer Ray Stark, who is married to Fanny Brice's daughter, Frances, by Nick Arnstein. He had Isobel Lennart fashion a script for the musical play, to which Jule Styne and Bob Merrill added music and lyrics, respectively. While the play takes liberty with the actual facts of Fanny Brice's life, it is an affectionate and nostalgic recalling of America's Broadway past and a vehicle perfectly suited to the comic talents of Barbra Streisand. Stark produced the stage version, Garson Kanin directed it, and Carol Haney staged the musical numbers. When preparing the project for the screen, additional changes were made to more carefully create a showcase for Streisand's motion picture debut.

Herbert Ross, who was a former dancer and choreographer and who had directed Streisand in *I Can Get It for You Wholesale*, was called in to stage the musical numbers in the screen version; this staging is certainly the most important ingredient in the film version. (Ross would later direct Streisand in *The Owl and the Pussycat*, 1970, and *Funny Lady*, 1975, and Anne Bancroft and Shirley Maclaine in *The Turning Point*, 1977. Curiously, veteran director William Wyler consented to direct the film, the first time in his illustrious career (*Wuthering Heights*, 1939, *The Little Foxes*, 1941, *Roman Holiday*, 1953, and *Ben-Hur*, 1959) that he ever tackled a musical. Although a number of songs from the stage version were cut, Styne and Merrill created three new songs for the film—"Roller Skate Rag," "The Swan," and "Funny Girl"—and two longtime standards, "I'd Rather Be Blue" by Fred Fisher and Billy Rose and "My Man" by Maurice Yvian, were added.

The script for *Funny Girl* covers the early years of Fanny Brice's career and her marriage to and divorce from Nick Arnstein. The film opens with Fanny (Barbra Streisand) seated in front of her dressing room mirror in the Ziegfeld Theatre; as she looks at her reflection, her first words are, "Hello, gorgeous!" From this point on, the audience is made aware that this is going to be Streisand's show and nobody else's. The scene next flashes back to the old days on Henry Street where she fails to get a job at Keeney's Oriental Palace because she does not look like the other girls. Not one to give up, Fanny talks her way into a roller-skating production number and wins the applause of the audience as she hams it up with her comic skating; she also wins the job. This is one of Streisand's best scenes, putting to use her excellent talent for comedy and mimicry without being concerned about her "image." Fanny further pleases the audience with her rendition of "I'd Rather Be Blue," prompting suave gambler Nick Arnstein (Omar Sharif) to visit her backstage where he helps her get a fifty-dollar raise.

Fanny Brice soon comes to the attention of Florenz Ziegfeld (Walter Pidgeon), who hires her to appear in a musical "bride" number. Fanny argues with Ziegfeld that she is not pretty enough for this song, but Ziegfeld insists. On opening night, still not convinced, Fanny plays the bride with a pillow under her gown for obvious comic effect. It is a scene which makes excellent use of Streisand's abilities as a comedienne, even though, in reality, Ziegfeld would never have tolerated a star of his show getting away with such blatant insubordination. Ziegfeld would also never have had nearly nude showgirls in his Follies, as is depicted in this film.

Nick attends opening night and then accompanies Fanny to her mother's saloon for the after-theater party. Fanny goes on to become a star of the first rank, Nick continues with his gambling and con-artist games, and their paths cross in courtship which leads to love. The film's intermission finds Fanny aboard a tugboat heading to board Nick's European-bound ocean liner and singing "Don't Rain on My Parade."

Their marriage leads Fanny and Nick to a Westchester Tudor mansion, a daughter named Frances, and then bankruptcy and prison for Nick, who gets involved in a phony bond-issue deal. A scene in which Fanny leaves the jail after seeing Nick and faces a throng of loud, pushy reporters, is one of the best in the film, and perhaps Streisand's best on screen. With very little dialogue, she conveys the hurt and love she feels for Nick and the realization that the marriage cannot work out. Eighteen months after going to jail, Nick appears in Fanny's dressing room and kisses her good-bye. This leads to the film's finale in which Fanny tearfully sings "My Man."

Funny Girl is a sumptuous production. Streisand is swathed in exaggerated period costumes designed by Irene Sharaff, and the first-rate technical aspects, as well as settings and cinematography, all aim at making Streisand look good; and she does. What is missing in the film, however, is more story, more characterization, and more directing expertise by William Wyler, whose scenes are underplayed in comparison to the flamboyant musical numbers directed by Herbert Ross. Likewise, the supporting players are so eclipsed by Barbra Streisand that their roles seem insignificant. Kay Medford has a few good moments as Fanny's mother, and Mae Questel is briefly and delightfully seen as the nosy neighbor. The role of Fanny's showgirl-friend is so cut in the final print that actress Anne Francis, who played the role, demanded that her name be omitted from the credits. Even amiable Walter Pidgeon is made short shrift of as Ziegfeld. It is this catering to Streisand that prevents *Funny Girl* from being a good musical biography; instead it is simply superficial glossy entertainment.

Ronald Bowers

FURY

Released: 1936
Production: Joseph L. Mankiewicz for Metro-Goldwyn-Mayer
Direction: Fritz Lang
Screenplay: Bartlett Cormack and Fritz Lang; based on a story by Norman
   Krasna
Cinematography: Joseph Ruttenberg
Editing: Frank Sullivan
Running time: 94 minutes

   Principal characters:
   Joe Wilson .... Spencer Tracy
   Katherine Grant .... Sylvia Sidney
   District Attorney .... Walter Abel
   Sheriff Hummel .... Edward Ellis
   Bugs Meyers .... Walter Brennan
   Tom Wilson .... George Walcott
   Charlie Wilson .... Frank Albertson

   Fury occupies a niche in film history as an important social document of
its time and as a rather daring and ambitiously unique film which strongly
influenced Hollywood moviemaking. Through its analytical portrayal of mob
violence and individual lust for vengeance, *Fury* puts the human psyche under
a magnifying glass to observe it in much the way a scientist might stick a pin
through a fluttering specimen to hold it steady for the eye to see.
   The darkness and cynicism of Director Fritz Lang's vision are strongly
evident in this film, and these characteristics certainly reflect the influence
of his roots. Lang was a successful filmmaker in Germany before fleeing the
Nazis, first to France and then to Hollywood when M-G-M brought him over
in the early 1930's. During the 1930's, hundreds of German filmmakers em-
igrated to Hollywood to continue their careers as directors, actors, and technicians. Though they were rapidly assimilated into American culture and
Hollywood's studio system, they still contributed much that was unique to
American filmmaking, both overtly and through their influence on others
over the years. The two most notable and creative directors were Ernst
Lubitsch and Fritz Lang. The former was the master of a style of sexual
innuendo which came to be known in his comedies as the "Lubitsch touch";
and the latter, with his dark, depressing, sometimes apocalyptic vision, did
much to inspire and set the tone for what came to be known as *film noir*.
Lang's 1931 German film *M*, for example, is hailed as the first psychological
crime thriller of its kind and the prototype for the American crime/detective
films of the 1930's and 1940's. The haunting atmospheric qualities of these
films—the dark, wet streets, the long shadows, the obscure corridors and

alleys, the sense of tension and impending doom—all hail back to German Expressionism. In fact, *Fury*, which was Lang's first American film, fits the definition of Expressionism with remarkable precision: ". . . the external representation of man's inner world, particularly the elemental emotions of fear, hatred, love, and anxiety . . . the dual nature of man, the power of fate, and the fascination of monstrous or sub-human creatures. . . ."

In *Fury*, Lang's singularly stark vision of men and women as monsters is made most vivid through the use of grim stop-action close-ups of the voracious, contorted faces of a lynch mob. The scene is a pivotal one which takes place halfway through the film; later, the same material is treated more probingly and from different angles in a climactic courtroom scene in which the lynch mob is on trial for murder.

The film's story is that of Joe Wilson (Spencer Tracy), an ordinary, unpretentious "nice guy" who harbors honest middle-class aspirations and who becomes the innocent victim of an angry mob—strangers who have labeled him a kidnaper. The first few minutes of the film focus on Joe and his fiancée, Katherine (Sylvia Sidney), and on their dreams of happiness. Certain references are made which will have eventual significance—Joe's passion for salted peanuts, which he keeps in his coat pocket; his mispronunciation of the word "memento" and Katherine's correction of it; an engraved ring she gives to him; and his ripped coat, which she repairs with blue thread. Every scene and bit of minutiae is deliberate, laying the ironic groundwork for the coming tragedy.

A year passes (deftly presented in a two-minute transition through close-ups on the letters and pictures which Joe sends to Katherine), until finally Joe has saved enough money to rejoin his fiancée in the small Midwestern town where she now lives and to get married. As he travels across country he is stopped by a grizzled, gun-wielding deputy (Walter Brennan). A kidnaping has occurred, and the evidence is loaded against Joe. Again Lang uses an ominous close-up, this time of a telegram stating that traces of salted peanuts had been found in connection with the kidnaper. The news travels rapidly around town that the criminal has been captured, and we see a kind of insanity growing like wildfire as the townspeople trade gossip in the streets. The filmmaker's indictment is made in a sequence of exaggerated images of the malicious, blustery townspeople lustfully spreading the news: talkative ladies call each other on the telephone, groups of self-righteous men gather on the streets and in bars to moralize and condemn, city officials gloat over the good publicity their town is receiving for capturing the kidnaper. It is a clean-cut, overly tidy view of hypocrisy. In one shot, a brief fade-out is made from a pair of prattling women to a flock of strutting chickens. Another scene displaying Lang's slightly perverse sense of humor shows an eccentric German barber fantasizing about cutting throats.

The madness grows, and the mindless mob finally marches on the jailhouse and breaks down the door. When they cannot reach the keys to the prisoner's cell, they set fire to the building and stand back in a sort of holy, reverential silence to watch the holocaust. The glowing flames are reflected in the rapturous faces of the witnesses while the doomed man screams from the window of his cell. Three rapid, successive images show us the men's monstrous faces twisted with gleeful horror and fascination; a wide-eyed boy chomps on a hotdog while watching the spectacle, and a mother holds her baby up for a better look.

When it is discovered that Wilson was an innocent man and that what occurred amounts to murder, the townspeople become frightened and self-absolving. We see Joe's two brothers, enraged and grieving; then suddenly Joe's figure appears dark and forbidding in their doorway like a ghost. He has miraculously escaped the fire and no one else knows he is not dead. "All day I've been watching myself being burned alive," he says with a stony glare. "They like it!" He pulls down the shades and orders the lights doused. He has become a man of darkness, feeling nothing but hate and desire for revenge. "I am legally dead and they are legally murderers," he says, and he proceeds to lay out a plan to have the mob members tried, convicted, and executed. The tables have turned: Joe has now become the monster; he has undergone a Dr. Jekyll/Mr. Hyde transformation. Like that earlier horror story, *Fury* deals with the question of innate evil in man; only here it is presented in a societal rather than in a science fiction context. At the time the film was made, lynching was a real problem (the district attorney in the movie even gives a speech in which he gives the number of lynchings as 6,010 in "the last forty-nine years"), and for a movie to tackle a social issue with such forthrightness was uncommon in this era of escapist musicals and comedies. But for a man who saw and decried the Nazi terror, the implications of a mob banding together in madness against a single scapegoat, and of the debilitating hunger for revenge in a survivor, were profound. Lang takes this film further than other "lynch mob" movies, displaying an entire cycle of fury and despair in subjective, dramatic terms.

The courtroom scene is momentous. The editing is precise and taut as the tension builds. The intercutting between the in-court action and Joe's savoring of it via his radio in a dark, anonymous hotel room builds momentum. The clever district attorney allows the defendants to perjure themselves by providing one another with false alibis, and then presents the telling evidence— a film of the actual event taken by a newsman from a balcony. The twenty-two defendants are horrified as they watch themselves as savages. The idea of incriminating film footage being brought into a courtroom as evidence was unique at the time *Fury* was made, and Lang chose to use the device in spite of the fact that there was then no such judicial precedent. Indeed, he was probably the first to suggest it.

When proof is demanded that Wilson is really dead, Joe sends his half-melted ring to the judge along with an anonymous letter stating that the ring had been found in the charred rubble. In the climactic scene, Katherine, who does not yet know the truth, is to be the key witness for the prosecution. As she rides up the elevator with Joe's brother, she sees him put his hand into his coat pocket and bring out a couple of peanuts. She glances down and sees a rip which has been repaired with blue thread. When she enters the court-room, the district attorney asks if she is ready to take the stand. She falters but says "Yes." However, the judge himself takes the stand first to present the evidence he has recently received in the mail. As the district attorney reads the anonymous letter aloud he stumbles over the misspelled word "mementum," and Katherine glances up with a look of shock. Suddenly realizing the truth, she stares terrified and disbelieving at Joe's brother. He grips her hand pleadingly as she is called to the witness stand. In the middle of her shaky testimony one of the defendants leaps up screaming, "I'm guilty! We're all guilty!" and the trial is over.

Now the guilt has been transferred, and the brothers have trouble dealing with their own consciences. Joe becomes a haunted man. Katherine begs him to admit the truth and to leave his vengefulness behind. "I want to be happy again," she cries. But he is consumed by his own hate. "From now on I'm gonna do everything alone!" he screams. "I don't need any of you!" He wanders dark, deserted streets haunted by the twenty-two defendants. As he gazes in a shop window, reminiscent of the first scene of the film, twenty-two faces appear behind him reflected in the glass. As he walks down the street glancing fearfully behind, we hear the inexorable footsteps of the twenty-two pursuing him. He hears festive noises and voices coming from a bar and runs in to find the place deserted—only one man is mopping up. When the date on the calendar is ripped off, a page sticks and a bold-faced "22," framed ominously by the camera, leaps out at us. Joe runs home screaming for Katherine, and we next see him walking into the courtroom where the judge is about to pass sentence. "I came for my own sake," he tells the judge. It is not for the murderers, for they are still murderers. "They lynched what mattered to me . . . my liking people and having faith in them." He has been turned into a different person. Though many say that the ending of *Fury* is optimistic, it is so only to a certain extent. It is true that Joe escaped death and in the end was able to escape the evil within him, but he is scarred.

Lynn Woods

GAMBIT

Released: 1966
Production: Leo L. Fuchs for Universal
Direction: Ronald Neame
Screenplay: Jack Davies and Alvin Sargent
Cinematography: Clifford Stine
Editing: Alma Macrorie
Running time: 108 minutes

Principal characters:
Harold "Harry" Dean .... Michael Caine
Nicole Chang .... Shirley MacLaine
Ahmad Shahbandar .... Herbert Lom
Emile Fournier .... John Abbott

In the early 1960's, the spy movie was a popular craze, and Hollywood obliged the public at the box office. The James Bond movies were making enormous profits, and imitation Bond movies were quick to follow. After a rash of serious spy films, the logical follow-up was a rash of spy spoof films. The spy spoof often had the advantage of supplying its audience with the best of both worlds: it preserved the forms of a thriller and the action sequences sparked by dangerous situations, but it also allowed its audience to laugh at a sometimes absurdly cool spy film hero, never at a loss for the technique needed to command any situation.

The basic point of *Gambit* is the futility of imagining that the main character, Harold "Harry" Dean (Michael Caine), could mastermind anything. To point out the difference between Dean and a "real" superspy, *Gambit* tells its story two ways, first as Dean fantasizes it in *Mission Impossible* perfection, and then in bumbling reality.

Gambit begins as Harold follows Nicole Chang (Shirley MacLaine) into the Palace of Joy, a nightclub where she is a chorus-line dancer in blue feather boas. As she bumps and grinds, Harold joins his friend Emile Fournier (John Abbott) at a table. In a flashforward, Harold lays out his plan to Emile. In the plan, Harold is the daring and self-assured cat burglar and Nicole his elegant bait. Their target is the fabulously wealthy art collector, Ahmad Shahbandar (Herbert Lom). Harold foresees him as an Eastern pushover, complete with fez, monacle, and short-tempered arrogance. Shahbandar owns a priceless sculpture, an ancient Oriental piece of art, a woman's head to which Nicole's bears a striking resemblance. Harold is sure the millionaire will be intrigued by the close resemblance, especially since his late young wife also looked like the sculpture. An invitation for both to see the sculpture is inevitable, and the theft will take only minutes. The flashforward shows Harold heisting the sculpture effortlessly, paying off a wordless, mysteriously beautiful Nicole, and escaping easily.

The crime successfully "completed," the movie dissolves back to the Palace of Joy to reveal Harry about to begin step one of the plan. Fantasy meets the complexities of immediate reality, however, when Nicole proves anything but inscrutable. Her first conversational gambit is an offer to recite a German limerick. Not only is she chatty, warm, and not mysterious, but she is also spunky. She does not jump when Harold, whom she calls Harry, beckons; she does not accept his sketchy instructions without question. Mystified but game, she does accept his offer to travel, because she needs the British passport which he offers as a bribe.

Not only does Nicole prove to have a personality, but she also repeatedly shows a street savvy and quick-witted ingenuity which Harold lacks. Harold is doubly frustrated. His beautiful, precise plan is blown from almost the moment they arrive, and Nicole has an answer for every unforeseen dilemma.

Shahbandar in person is a shrewd, modern businessman: no fez, no monacle, and no squandering of money. He is suspicious of Nicole and Harold from the moment they arrive; "Have them watched," he orders. Then we see Harold, still rehearsing his foolproof plans with Nicole. More foul-ups take place as he loses his cohort Emile in the bazaar, and Nicole outsmarts him by finding Emile. Nicole, not Harry, arranges their invitation to Shahbandar's penthouse. Once there, she manages the art connoisseur chitchat at which Harold miserably fails.

When Shahbandar proudly shows the two his prize Oriental sculpture, Nicole realizes for the first time what Harold is planning. She threatens to walk out, but for Harold's sake, goes on with the plan. She and Shahbandar go out on the town, and Harold steals his way into the penthouse. Nicole then ditches her host, returns to the penthouse, and steals the head which Harry is not agile enough to reach, using her impressively limber dancer's legs. When Harry thanks her and confesses that he loves her, however, she impulsively hugs him and inadvertantly trips the electronic alarm. She is caught at the airport, but Harry escapes.

A trick ending has Nicole set free by Shahbandar, with a message to Harry to give up the game and return the head. Harry has not taken it, however; he has merely hidden it in a Buddha inside Shahbandar's penthouse. Harry plans to sell a forgery of the sculpture, prepared in authentic detail by Emile, in the wake of publicity over the theft. Nicole tells Harry that it is her or a life of crime, and Harry dramatically smashes the fake head to prove his loyalty. Somewhat belatedly, Nicole apologizes to Emile for destroying his beautiful forgery, and the two leave a distraught Emile alone in his studio. As soon as they are gone, Emile smiles and opens a closet revealing several more fake sculptures, showing that for Emile, the plot has worked after all.

As a spy spoof, *Gambit* particularly lampooned the humorless nature of a serious spy. Harry Dean's biggest flaw is his lack of humor and self-serious cool; as a result, he cannot do anything right. Nicole is down-to-earth, inclined to make a joke of Harry's pretensions to infallibility. With the flashforward structure, *Gambit* allows us, and Harry, to indulge in a fantasy of perfect control and mastermind prowess. Because the audience is made a party to Harry's fantasy, Nicole's education of him is also a refresher course for us. The masterspy is not a grand puppeteer, pulling the strings of various conquests. Rather, the man who thinks of himself as a puppeteer is likely to be in the position of a puppet, jerkily responding to unforeseeable events.

The film gave Caine a chance to play against his own spy image, created in several successful spy movies based on Len Deighton novels, most notably *The Ipcress File* (1965) and *Billion Dollar Brain* (1967), in which he played a character named Harry Palmer. (The similarity of the names is not lost on the audience.) Caine shows a good flair for comedy here which unfortunately has seldom been able to surface. For MacLaine, the role of Nicole was a twist on her usual "hooker with a heart of gold" role; here the streetwise cabaret dancer triumphs with more brains than kook. Abbott skillfully underplays Emile as the low-key cohort who takes all, so that the ending is indeed a surprise. Ronald Neame directs with a style echoing the gloss and snapshot editing of more serious thrillers.

Leslie Donaldson

GASLIGHT

Released: 1944
Production: Arthur Hornblow, Jr., for Metro-Goldwyn-Mayer
Direction: George Cukor
Screenplay: John Van Druten, Walter Reisch, and John L. Balderston; based
on the play of the same name by Patrick Hamilton
Cinematography: Joseph Ruttenberg
Editing: Ralph E. Winters
Art direction: Cedric Gibbons and William Ferrari (AA)
Interior decoration: Edwin B. Willis and Paul Huldschinsky (AA)
Running time: 114 minutes

Principal characters:
Paula Alquist	Ingrid Bergman (AA)
Gregory Anton	Charles Boyer
Brian Cameron	Joseph Cotten
Nancy Oliver	Angela Lansbury
Miss Thwaites	Dame May Whitty
Elizabeth Tompkins	Barbara Everest

   Gaslight is George Cukor's classic Victorian melodrama. Nominally a murder mystery, the plot is on the skimpy side, and the murder which opens the film is solved at the end, but the "whodunit" aspects of the plot are peripheral to Cukor's real concerns. *Gaslight* is a study in induced madness, and, paradoxically, the film sustains our interest because Cukor's direction intentionally subverts the traditional elements of mystery in the plot. Cukor unmasks the villain early on; and the tension in the film comes as a result of the audience watching helplessly as the villain very methodically sets about driving the heroine insane. *Gaslight* opens with a murder on a foggy night (in contrast to his interior shots, Cukor's exteriors are rather unimaginative, consisting primarily of swirling fog). The headline on a newspaper unfolds the story: "Thornton Square Strangler on Loose." The entire sequence spans less than two minutes, and provides the backdrop for the remainder of the film.
   Cukor next shifts the scene to Italy. It is a decade after the murder, and a young English voice student, Paula Alquist (Ingrid Bergman), is being courted by Gregory Anton (Charles Boyer), a French pianist. Although she is obviously in love with the man, she protests that she hardly knows him, and resolves to spend a week at Lake Como to think things over. On the train to Lake Como, Paula finds herself seated next to Miss Thwaites (Dame May Whitty), a garrulous Englishwoman addicted to murder mysteries. Elsewhere in the film, Cukor uses Miss Thwaites primarily for comic relief but here she serves as the link between the heretofore unexplained opening murder scene and the happy, if confused, Paula Alquist. The book Miss Thwaites is reading

on the train reminds her of a genuine murder that occurred in her neighborhood in London ten years earlier—the Thornton Square strangling. As
the old woman prattles on about the murder, Paula grows increasingly agitated. Thus Cukor reveals that there is some sort of connection between
Paula and Thornton Square, although the precise nature of this connection
will not be clarified until later in the film.

As the train pulls to a stop at the lake, an arm is suddenly thrust through
the open window of Paula's berth. Cukor quickly defuses the sinister implications of the incident; the arm belongs to Gregory Anton, who, unable to
bear the idea of being separated from his beloved, has preceded Paula to her
destination. She is happy enough to see him, and the jarring note is temporarily forgotten. It represents, however, Cukor's first hint that Gregory is
not the perfect lover that Paula takes him to be. *Gaslight*'s story is written
largely from Paula's point of view, which will grow increasingly distorted as
Gregory's machinations progress. Cukor reveals this distortion to the audience by his choice of camera angles, lighting, and pacing, all of which will
serve notice that, whatever Paula may believe, Gregory Anton is not be be
trusted.

At Lake Como, Paula agrees to marry Gregory, who reveals to her that
he has always wanted to live in London. By a curious coincidence, the dream
house that he describes to Paula bears an uncanny resemblance to the one
that Paula herself already owns, the house at 9 Thornton Square, which she
inherited from her murdered aunt, the victim in the film's opening scene.
Although she dreads living in this, of all houses, she accedes to Gregory's
pleas: "I've found peace in loving you. You shall have your house in Thornton
Square." With his two principals safely ensconced in their new surroundings,
Cukor devotes himself to the crux of his story—the persecution and near
destruction of Paula Anton by her husband. Shortly after they set up residence, Gregory, pretending to be solicitous of Paula's health, gradually closes
her off from the outside world. He is forever nagging her about her supposed
memory lapses. One key sequence in the film illustrates both Gregory's technique and that of George Cukor in explicating it.

Immediately prior to one of their rare excursions outside their house—a
trip to the Tower of London to see the Crown Jewels—Gregory gives Paula
a brooch. With a condescending smile, he chides her for losing things, and
makes a great show of putting it in her handbag. They visit the Tower, and
upon returning home, Gregory asks to see the brooch. An incredulous and
panicky Paula empties her bag, but to no avail. To her dismay, the brooch
is nowhere to be found, and Gregory, having made his point, contents himself
with only a mild reproof.

From the dialogue in this sequence, there is no evidence to support either
Gregory or his wife on the question of the loss of the brooch. We never see
Paula lose it, but she is off camera part of the time, and could have lost it

then. Nevertheless, by the end of the scene, Cukor has made it clear that it is Gregory, not Paula, who is responsible for the brooch's being missing. He keeps the camera focused on Gregory's face longer than usual, and his lighting emphasizes his eyes, which glint strangely. By tilting the audience's sympathy in this fashion towards Paula, the director undercuts much of the script's suspense, but the removal of any doubt about Gregory's guilt permits Cukor and the audience to concentrate on the melodramatic irony implicit in the situation: whether Paula is losing her mind on her own or being driven insane by her husband becomes secondary to the simple fact that she is, indeed, going mad.

Not the least of Gregory's weapons in his effort to rob his wife of her sanity is the house at Thornton Square itself. More than a mere set, the house becomes, in Cukor's hands, a third character. 9 Thornton Square is a marvelous three-storied building, and Cukor uses each of the stories in his narrative. The first floor of the house belongs to Gregory. It is where he administers most of his admonitions to Paula about her failing mental health, and it is also where Paula is forced to deal with Nancy Oliver (Angela Lansbury), a cheeky young girl whom Gregory has hired as a maid. Nancy clearly has eyes for her employer and makes no effort to disguise her contempt for Paula. Although she is unaware of Gregory's plotting, she serves his purpose well, constantly keeping Paula in a state of agitation.

The bedrooms are on the second floor, but Paula finds no refuge in her room. Left alone every night since Gregory claims to have rented a flat elsewhere, to which he purportedly goes nightly to practice his piano, Paula is beset by flickering lights, the gaslights that give the film its title, and mysterious noises that seem to emanate from the third floor. Indeed, the third floor seems, inexplicably at first, to be the symbol of Paula's horrors because on the third floor, behind locked and boarded doors, are all of her dead aunt's furniture and other possessions, providing a constant reminder of Paula's childhood trauma.

Gregory, meanwhile, steps up his assaults on Paula's sanity. His admonitions are no longer gentle, and he begins to accuse her of theft as well as mere forgetfulness. He browbeats her in front of Nancy and forbids her to see any of her neighbors, including Miss Thwaites, the woman she had met on the train to Lake Como. Indeed, Paula leaves the house at Thornton Square only once after her visit to the Tower of London, and that turns out to be a disaster. When she insists upon attending a party, Gregory reluctantly agrees to let her go, but quickly reduces her to hysteria once they arrive, and the pair returns home immediately, where Gregory threatens to have his wife declared insane and institutionalized.

What remains to be revealed is the motive for Gregory's villainy. The mechanism for this revelation is Brian Cameron (Joseph Cotten) of Scotland Yard. Cameron, as it happens, had been a fan of Paula's aunt, and when he catches sight of Paula at the Tower during the Antons' fateful visit, he is intrigued by the resemblance between aunt and niece. He finds himself drawn to the Thornton Square neighborhood, where Miss Thwaites fills him in as best she can. His interest piqued still further, Cameron reopens the ten-year-old murder case, which occurred, we now learn, during an apparently unsuccessful attempt to steal the victim's jewelry. Cameron puts Gregory under surveillance, and the policeman assigned to the task reports that Gregory leaves home every night, walks around the block, and then climbs onto the roof of his own house, which he thereupon enters through a trapdoor. Cameron, meanwhile, learns that Gregory had also been an admirer of Paula's aunt, and a jewel thief as well.

Piecing the facts together, Cameron rushes to 9 Thornton Square. He arrives as Paula is being tormented by flickering lights and moaning noises; and, winning her confidence with the story of his affection for her aunt, he tells her his theory about all of her problems. Gregory, he says, murdered her aunt, and is currently spending his nights above Paula's bedroom methodically ransacking her aunt's possessions in search of her jewelry, as well as driving Paula mad from fear in the process. Paula hardly knows what to believe, but when Cameron, in searching Gregory's desk, discovers the long-missing brooch, she is convinced. Having revealed the ultimate solution to the mystery, Cukor brings *Gaslight* to a close. Brian Cameron arrests Gregory, ironically, just after he finds the jewels that have led him on his bizarre quest; and, in a deliciously vengeful scene, Paula declines her husband's pleas for help. She is insane, Paula taunts; how could she possibly help anyone? The film ends on a comic note as Miss Thwaites, the neighborhood busybody, walks in just as Cameron and Paula are discussing what promises to be the start of a long relationship.

Gaslight is a claustrophobic film, and Cukor makes this claustrophobia work for him rather than against him. The tension generated by the house at Thornton Square, and the increasingly suffocating relationship between the two principals, more than replace the potential plot tension which Cukor diffuses early by revealing that Gregory Anton is manipulating his wife.

None of this would have worked, however, without top actors in the starring roles. Charles Boyer, an Academy Award nominee, plays Gregory Anton as a suave sadist, nearly always under control and able to turn every situation to his advantage. In turn soothing and bullying, he is able to take the young and naïve Paula to the edge of insanity with consummate ease. Ingrid Bergman, who won an Academy Award for her portrayal of Paula, is outstanding. Her physical beauty makes Paula an attractive character from the outset, and her acting skill insures that none of the impact of her psychic disintegration is lost on the audience. In the film's minor roles, Joseph Cotten has little to do but act stalwart as Brian Cameron of Scotland Yard. More noteworthy is the acting debut of Angela Lansbury; a Cukor discovery, Lansbury plays the tarty young Nancy Oliver with the aplomb of a veteran actor; she earned an Academy Award nomination as Best Supporting Actress for her efforts.

Gaslight owes its success to George Cukor, and to the performances he elicited from his cast, particularly Charles Boyer, Ingrid Bergman, and Angela Lansbury. The film thus stands near the top of its genre, a classic of melodrama.

Robert Mitchell

THE GAY DIVORCEE

Released: 1934
Production: Pandro S. Berman for RKO/Radio
Direction: Mark Sandrich
Screenplay: George Marion, Jr., Dorothy Yost, and Edward Kaufman; based
  on the play *The Gay Divorce* by Dwight Taylor
Cinematography: David Abel
Editing: William Hamilton
Dance direction: Dave Gould
Song: Herb Magidson and Con Conrad, "The Continental" (AA)
Running time: 107 minutes

> *Principal characters:*
> Guy Holden .... Fred Astaire
> Mimi Glossop .... Ginger Rogers
> Aunt Hortense .... Alice Brady
> Egbert Fitzgerald .... Edward Everett Horton
> Rodolfo Tonetti .... Erik Rhodes
> Waiter .... Eric Blore

In 1934, Fred Astaire and Ginger Rogers starred in *The Gay Divorcee*, beginning the series of classic musicals which they made for RKO. Both had appeared in secondary roles in *Flying Down to Rio* in 1933 and had danced briefly together in that film to "The Carioca." Accidentally cast opposite each other, they made an impact on the public strong enough for the studio to team them again in *The Gay Divorcee*, which firmly established their screen personalities and became the model for most of their films to follow. The use of the songs and dances to enhance or deepen moods or emotions, the accidental meeting of the two at which she is antagonized and he smitten, the spontaneity and freshness of the musical numbers, and the shaping of the films to the personalities and talents of the stars—these became trademarks of the Astaire-Rogers films.

The film is based on the *Gay Divorce*, a stage play in which Astaire had starred on Broadway and in London a few years earlier, but the censors insisted that the last word of the title be changed to *Divorcee*. In keeping with the customary procedure at the time, new songs were written for the film version; only one song from the original Cole Porter score was retained—"Night and Day." It was kept because it had been a big popular hit and had already achieved the status of a classic.

No one would claim that the story of *The Gay Divorcee* is very original, but Astaire and Rogers, in a triumph of style over content, transcend the somewhat preposterous coincidences underlying the plot to make their series of encounters into a fresh and meaningful romance.

The film opens in a Paris nightclub with Guy Holden (Fred Astaire), an American dancer, with his English friend, Egbert Fitzgerald (Edward Everett Horton), a fussy, bumbling lawyer, watching the floor show. The chorus girls sing "Don't Let It Bother You" as they do a dance with finger dolls. Later, Guy is forced to dance to the song in order to identify himself to the proprietor since neither he nor Egbert can find his wallet. Looking bored and unhappy, Guy reluctantly complies, at first merely going through the motions, but the tempo and beat of the music soon stimulate him in spite of himself into an intricate series of frenzied tap steps. He finally collapses disgustedly onto the floor just as the proprietor ostentatiously tears up the bill and Egbert finds his wallet.

Later, while waiting to clear customs in England, Guy comes to the aid of a pretty girl (Ginger Rogers) whose dress accidentally has been caught in a trunk locked by her flighty aunt. Unfortunately, he rips her dress while trying to free her, both embarrassing and annoying her. Ever gallant and already in love with her, he gives her his raincoat to hide the damage, but she leaves without telling him her name or where she lives. When the raincoat is later returned by a messenger without any indication of the girl's identity or whereabouts, Guy shakes off his disappointment and determines to find her "if it takes me from now on," expressing his determination by singing and then dancing "Needle in a Haystack."

This number establishes and defines Astaire's screen *persona*. Sitting on the couch in his silk dressing gown, he sings of his need to find his unknown love. As he continues the song, he walks to the window to look out, as if already beginning his search. His valet enters, and Astaire, still singing, debonairly tosses him his dressing gown, selects a tie, then goes to the fireplace and absentmindedly begins tapping the mantelpiece with his hand, lost in thought as he considers his strategy. Soon his feet have picked up the beat and then he is off, sailing over the couch, leaping onto a chair, clicking his heels together in midair. Not missing a step, he puts on his coat, leaps onto a chair where he catches the hat and cane thrown to him by his valet and strolls insouciantly out the door with a tip of his hat. Performed with great style and flair, these commonplace actions are incorporated into the ritual of the dance and seem to say that he can do anything, including finding his true love in a great city. Astaire liked to do getting-dressed-and-going-out routines, and here he gave the concept added meaning by using it to express feeling appropriate to both the character and the story.

He does find the girl but is able only to learn that her name is Mimi before she runs away once more. Then he does not see her again until he accompanies Egbert to Brightbourne, a fashionable seaside resort. When he unexpectedly sees her there, she immediately runs away, and he pursues her to a deserted beach pavilion bathed in moonlight. There he tells her of his longing for her by singing "Night and Day" with romantic intensity. The dance which then follows is a small drama in itself, portraying her reluctance, hesitation, increasing involvement, and eventual surrender to him. As the dance begins, she tries to leave, but he prevents her. Finally, as she turns to leave yet again, he catches her wrist, turning her toward him, and dances a few steps for her. She turns away once more, but the next time he catches her hand and pulls her toward him, she joins him in the dance. At one point she turns and walks away from him, as if making a final bid for freedom, and he pursues her. She seems to strike him, and he staggers back the length of the dance floor, but when he recovers his balance, he brings her back into the dance. At the end, another extraordinary moment occurs. As he lowers her gently onto a bench, she, half-reclining, gazes up at him, on her face an expression of rapt bemusement, and for a wordless moment the spell of the dance is prolonged.

The dances of Astaire and Rogers convey many different moods and feelings, but this great dance, portraying longing and desire, is one of their most intense and dramatic. Rogers was not yet the accomplished dancer she became later in the series, but that does not detract from the impact and the beauty of the dance. Unlike most of the later Astaire-Rogers dances, this one is shown from various angles, including a shot through some venetian blinds, devices with which Astaire would later almost entirely dispense. His favorite method of filming a dance number was to film it straight through, keeping the full length of the dancer in the camera frame and the flow of the dance intact. He liked the camera at eye level to keep the audience from being aware of it. Since film can present dance from the ideal perspective, the audience is thus able to follow intricate steps that would be lost on a theater stage.

Not yet sure that a musical could be filmed without a big production number for a climax, and perhaps uncertain of the ability of Astaire and Rogers to carry the film by themselves, the studio built a big production number around "The Continental," which won the first Academy Award for Best Song. A catchy tune, it is first sung by Rogers to Astaire as they watch the dancers from a balcony. Caught up in the song's insistent rhythm, they decide to join the dancers below, who gradually fall back, leaving them dancing alone in the middle of the floor. The two now proceed to do their own spirited version of the dance, dancing mischievously around each other with tilted, outstretched arms, seemingly unable to contain their high spirits. Rogers carries in one hand a long chiffon scarf which she uses for dramatic emphasis like a theatrical prop. The dance is another demonstration of the pair's almost perpetual spontaneity and freshness. The applause of the other dancers brings them back to reality, and they dash off the floor. Their exit is the signal for hordes of other dancers to enter and begin a protracted series of dance patterns and movements. The number was more than seventeen minutes long, a length unmatched then and for some time to come for a dance number. Not only does the piece contain many permutations of groupings and formations but variations in costumes and camera angles as well. In the midst of this madness Astaire and Rogers return for a brief interlude, which includes dancing up and down the steps before running up them and exiting through the revolving doors.

"The Continental" and one other number, "Let's Knock Knees" (in which Astaire and Rogers do not appear), are not really an integral part of the story but are set pieces to display formations of dancers or, in the case of "Let's Knock Knees," a novelty number for Edward Everett Horton, who plays Egbert Fitzgerald. Later in the series, big production numbers or novelty numbers unrelated to the plot or feelings of the characters would practically disappear.

The film ends exhilaratingly as Astaire dances Rogers around their hotel room to the strains of "The Continental"—over the sofa, over tables, up onto chairs—to express their delight in finally being together. At the end of this short dance, they stroll jauntily out the door, arm in arm, half dancing, half walking.

Although it is the music and the dancing which make the film so memorable, *The Gay Divorcee* is also impressive in its comic scenes. The comic plot revolves around the fact that, unknown to Guy, Mimi is getting a divorce from her wandering geologist husband and has hired Egbert as her lawyer. He advises her that the easiest way to get a divorce in England is for her to be found alone in a hotel room with a man, and Egbert promises to hire both the man (a professional corespondent) and the detectives who will find them. Thus the technical grounds for the divorce will be established. Complications ensue, however, when—after the "Night and Day" dance—Guy accidentally gives the proper password and Mimi mistakenly thinks he is the corespondent hired by Egbert. But with the help of an eccentric waiter at the hotel, all the plot complications are finally resolved.

The direction by Mark Sandrich and the script emphasize and give full value to the comic scenes. Imported from the stage production was Erik Rhodes as the effeminate Italian professional corespondent, Rodolfo Tonetti, whose slogan is "Your wife is safe with Tonetti. He prefers spaghetti." Although his role is a comic stereotype, he adds immeasurably to the droll and slightly ridiculous fun of the film as he continually garbles the password which he is to use to identify himself to Mimi: "Chance is the fool's name for fate." Edward Everett Horton as Astaire's bumbling lawyer friend, so inept that he forgets to arrange for the detectives who are essential to the divorce case, is an excellent foil for Astaire and for Alice Brady, who plays Mimi's twittering, flighty aunt Hortense to perfection. Eric Blore is also delightful as the waiter who has "an unnatural passion for rocks," a zeal which turns out to be extremely important in resolving the complications of the plot. Together with Astaire and Rogers, who also prove themselves to be fine light comedians, they give the film a mischievously amusing tone that seldom slackens.

The Gay Divorcee was a big box-office success (audiences often broke into applause at the end of the dance numbers), ensuring that there would be future Astaire-Rogers teamings. It also became the model for many of the scripts in the later films and firmly established the legendary style and charm of Astaire and Rogers.

Julia Johnson

GENTLEMAN JIM

Released: 1942
Production: Robert Buckner for Warner Bros.
Direction: Raoul Walsh
Screenplay: Vincent Lawrence and Horace McCoy; based on the book *The Roar of the Crowd* by James J. Corbett
Cinematography: Sid Hickox
Editing: Jack Killifer
Music: Heinz Roemheld
Running time: 104 minutes

Principal characters:

James J. Corbett	Errol Flynn
Victoria Ware	Alexis Smith
Pat Corbett	Alan Hale
Walter Lowrie	Jack Carson
Clinton DeWitt	John Loder
Billy Delaney	William Frawley
John L. Sullivan	Ward Bond
Buck Ware	Minor Watson
Harry Watson	Rhys Williams
Father Burke	Arthur Shields
Ma Corbett	Dorothy Vaughan
George Corbett	James Flavin
Harry Corbett	Pat Flaherty
Mary Corbett	Marilyn Phillips
Governor Stanford	Frank Mayo
Colis Huntington	Henry O'Hara
Charles Crocker	Henry Crocker
Judge Geary	Wallis Clark

A good case can be made for *Gentleman Jim* as the best motion picture ever made about boxing. Many of the others, such as *The Harder They Fall* (1956) and *The Great White Hope* (1970), are primarily social criticism. Some deal with the corruption of boxing and its connection with crime. A number of them, such as *The Champ* (1979) and *Body and Soul* (1947), deal with the attempt of a defeated fighter to make a comeback. *Rocky* (1977), *Rocky II* (1979), and *Raging Bull* (1980) are more character studies than studies of boxing *per se*; the actual matches are bloody slugfests, and Rocky, or whoever the hero is, wins only because he can take more punishment than his opponent.

Gentleman Jim, the story of James J. Corbett (1856-1933), who in 1892 became the second world heavyweight boxing champion when he defeated John L. Sullivan, focuses more than any other film upon the actual skill of boxing. Corbett himself relied not on brute strength but on blocking, timing, and fancy footwork; he initiated a technique for boxing which was almost dancing. Accordingly, the fights in *Gentleman Jim* are beautifully choreographed; instead of being gory contests of survival, they are like fencing matches, with skillful feinting, parrying, and riposting. Rocky, by contrast, has hardly any guard at all; he simply absorbs punishment until he can come back with a knockout blow. Again, whereas most other boxing films have only a few vignettes of boxing and one big fight at the climax, *Gentleman Jim* has a great many scenes in the ring and focuses throughout on boxing.

It is appropriate that Errol Flynn was cast as the dapper and dancing Jim Corbett. Flynn had made his mark in films as a swashbuckler noted for his graceful acrobatics and swordplay. He also had a way with satiric repartee and impudent humor. These qualities were precisely suited to *Gentleman Jim*, for while the other boxing films (except for *The Great John L.*, 1945) are grim psychological and/or sociological dramas, *Gentleman Jim* is a light-hearted romantic comedy. A meticulous period piece, it offers a colorful, nostalgic look at the late nineteenth century, with a blend of brawling and gentility. Its director, Raoul Walsh, had just completed another romantic comedy set in the 1890's, *The Strawberry Blonde* (1941), and was perfectly in tune with the period. Earlier, he had directed *The Bowery* (1933) with a similar setting. Born in 1887, Walsh grew up in the time of *Gentleman Jim*; as a boy, he had actually met both Corbett and John L. Sullivan and had seen Corbett fight.

Walsh began his career as an actor; he had played John Wilkes Booth in *Birth of a Nation* (1914) and had portrayed young Pancho Villa while at the same time directing the real Villa in a film of the Mexican revolutionary during the actual revolution. Alternating between acting and directing (and sometimes doing both in the same film, as in *Sadie Thompson*, 1928), Walsh had made such memorable films as *The Thief of Bagdad* (1924) and *What Price Glory?* (1926). He lost an eye in an automobile accident in 1929, while playing the Cisco Kid in the first sound Western, *In Old Arizona*, which he was also directing, and thereafter he abandoned acting for full-time directing. During the 1930's, he made a series of competent but mostly unmemorable films, but when he moved to Warner Bros. in 1939, he became a major director who turned out such classics as *The Roaring Twenties* (1939) and *White Heat* (1949) with James Cagney, *High Sierra* (1941), (the film that made Humphrey Bogart a star), and seven films with Flynn that are among Flynn's best.

Gentleman Jim, the third Walsh-Flynn combination, is perhaps the best of them all. Flynn and Walsh became close friends offscreen, and Walsh evoked from Flynn more complex and fully-rounded characterizations than he had achieved in the many films he had previously made with director Michael Curtiz, which depended more exclusively upon action. In addition, *Gentleman Jim* benefits from a superior screenplay by Vincent Lawrence and Horace McCoy (author of the novel *They Shoot Horses, Don't They?*). It is supposedly based on Corbett's autobiography, *The Roar of the Crowd* (1925), but because of legal problems with Corbett's estate, many of the details are fictitious, including the names of some of the characters and a romance with a high-toned society lady named Victoria Ware.

The film opens in San Francisco in 1887, where we see some men going to an illegal prize fight. Corbett and his pal Walter Lowrie (Jack Carson) turn up, but they lack the price of admission. With characteristic brashness, Corbett gets them in by pretending that Lowrie's pocket has been picked and that the police may have to investigate if he is not admitted. The gatekeeper does not notice that Corbett is already in. The fight, between two big gorillas, is a crude slug fest with no rules and one fighter even conceals a bolt in his fist. The event is broken up by police, who club the boxers over the head and haul the spectators off to jail. There, Corbett finds himself in the same cell with Judge Geary (Wallis Clark), who complains that Barbary Coast bruisers have ruined the fight game, and therefore his aristocratic Olympic Club will sponsor fights for gentlemen. Corbett, however, wants to see the end of the brawl and incites the fighters to start it up again in the cell by telling each of them an insult that he falsely attributes to the other. Later, he gets the judge off without scandal by telling another tall tale.

Back in the Comstock bank, where he and Lowrie work as tellers, Corbett is summoned before the management. He expects to be fired but finds himself promoted instead for having rescued the bank founder's friend Geary. When Victoria Ware (Alexis Smith), an elegant lady, comes to make a withdrawal for her father who is at the Olympic Club, Corbett offers to carry the silver dollars there for her. Pretending to be a bank executive, he summons a cab, actually driven by his father (Alan Hale), from whom he borrows some money while pretending to tip him. At the Olympic Club, Corbett refuses to be dismissed and brashly bluffs his way in. From Miss Ware, he mooches a meal at the dining room, avoids paying a tip by pretending he has no cash smaller than a twenty-dollar bill, and persuades the somewhat flabbergasted Miss Ware to show him around. A rich girl who has had everything, she is amused by Corbett's ingratiating impudence. During the tour, he wants to see the gymnasium. She protests that women are not allowed there, but he waltzes her in anyway. There, he talks his way into a match with the boxing coach, who taught the Prince of Wales to fight. Leaving Miss Ware holding a lighted cigar that he has mooched, he puts on the gloves and to everyone's surprise lands several stiff punches on coach Watson (Rhys Williams), who in turn cannot lay a glove on him. Impressed, Judge Geary talks Miss Ware into sponsoring Corbett for club membership.

The club members soon find Corbett a conceited boor who has himself paged all over the premises. In fact, Corbett is a Southside boy whose brothers are longshoremen. The Corbett family regularly gets into brawls, Irish Donnybrooks, and when his brothers taunt him for putting on airs, Corbett fights them in the backyard. Back at the Olympic Club, the high-toned members arrange to have Corbett fight the former heavyweight champion of England and Australia, who they expect (and hope) will give him a drubbing. Instead, the graceful, trim Corbett dances around the champion, parries and gets through his guard with ease, and knocks him out in the second round.

At a dance afterwards, Corbett waltzes with Miss Ware. Both amused and exasperated by his cockiness, she accuses him of having a swelled head and warns him of the champagne. He counters that he can outdrink anyone in the world. She smiles sarcastically, but despite his braggadocio, she likes him and takes him into the garden, where she advises him not to let the Nob Hill snobs repress him. Although she is engaged to Clinton DeWitt (John Loder), Corbett gets carried away by the romantic moment and kisses her, whereupon she calls him an impudent upstart and hopes someone will knock his block off. His pal Lowrie, meanwhile, has become offensively drunk, and when DeWitt tries to throw him out, Corbett goes too.

The two of them wake up horribly hungover in a strange town that turns out to be Salt Lake City. They have lost all their money, so to earn train fare home, Corbett lets a prize fight manager named Delaney (William Frawley) set him up to fight a local pug. Corbett wins and decides to go professional. Back in San Francisco, Miss Ware and DeWitt see him posing beside a portrait of John L. Sullivan, heavyweight champion of the world. When Sullivan himself (Ward Bond) turns up and Miss Ware admiringly feels his biceps, Corbett calls her vulgar and says that if she were his girl, he would spank her. She responds that the last thing in the world she would be is his girl. The relationship between them has deteriorated to a sarcastic antagonism that masks their real attraction to each other.

Going professional under Delaney's management, Corbett wins bout after bout and earns the nickname Gentleman Jim both for his fancy footwork and for his swaggering _nouveau-riche_ elegance. He even goes on stage as an actor, with considerable popularity, although Miss Ware mutters after one performance that she is amazed that anyone would pay to see him act. (In fact, Corbett did perform on stage, one of his roles being that of a boxer in an adaptation of George Bernard Shaw's novel _Cashel Byron's Profession_.) She is sardonically amused when Corbett informs her that he is considering playing Hamlet. Meanwhile, as he becomes affluent, Corbett buys his parents a new house on Nob Hill and sets his brothers up in business with their own saloon, in which the Corbetts boast that Jim can beat any man in the world, including John L. Sullivan.

Sullivan, however, refuses to fight Corbett, who he thinks is nowhere near his match. In order to get him to fight, Corbett swaggers into Sullivan's dressing room after seeing the pugilist perform on stage in a melodrama called _The Honest Woodsman_. He starts eating Sullivan's meal, twits him about his age, and by getting his goat, baits him into agreeing to a fight. For the forthcoming match in New Orleans, however, Sullivan insists on a side bet with Corbett of ten thousand dollars to ensure his showing up. Having spent all his money on his family, Corbett cannot raise the amount. He then meets Victoria Ware, who pages him (in mockery of his paging himself at the Olympic Club) at New York's Waldorf-Astoria. He is delighted to see her, but they quickly resume spatting after he invites her out and she insists that she is booked up for the next three weeks. Her father, who likes Jim, tells him not to worry; if he is shanty Irish, so were they; they simply have acquired a larger shanty. Victoria wants the ego knocked out of Corbett, however, and so she secretly puts up the money so that she can have the satisfaction of seeing Sullivan put him in his place.

Sullivan has a superstition against entering the ring first; Corbett also refuses to enter first, so they agree to enter together; but as they do so, Corbett holds back and tricks Sullivan into violating his taboo. When they shake before the fight, Corbett breezily warns Sullivan not to trip over his beard. As the fight begins, Sullivan tries to knock out Corbett with wild-swinging powerhouse punches that Jim easily dodges. While Sullivan slugs crudely, trying for a knockout blow, Corbett is an artist in the ring as he weaves, ducks, and virtually dances around Sullivan, dodging his heavy swings and landing quick, sharp counterpunches. The fight goes on for twenty-one rounds, with Sullivan getting progressively worn down, while Corbett remains fresh and nearly untouched. The bout is beautifully choreographed. When Corbett knocks Sullivan out in the twenty-first round, Victoria Ware surprises herself by coming cheering to her feet.

At a party afterwards, however, she presents Jim with a huge hat for his supposedly swelled head. A good sport, he laughs and tries it on. As he does so, he sees in the mirror John L. Sullivan enter hesitantly. Corbett greets him gently, "Hello, John—are you all right?" Sullivan sighs, "Just a little tired." He then gives Corbett his belt engraved for "The Heavyweight Championship of the World." Sullivan says quietly, "I've had it a long time, Jim—take good care of it." Corbett replies sincerely, "I'll do my best. The first time I ever saw you fight, I was just a kid—no man alive could have stood up to you. Tonight I was glad you weren't the Sullivan of ten years ago." Moved by Corbett's tribute, Sullivan asks, "Is that what you're thinking now?" Corbett insists, "That's what I thought when I entered the ring." Sullivan is touched by Corbett's graciousness and tells him, "it's tough to be a good loser and tougher to be a good winner. I know tonight I'm shaking the hand of the new champion and a gentleman." Moved in turn, Corbett says, "I hope when my time comes I can go out with half the friends you've got, and half the world's respect." "You will, Jim,' Sullivan assures him. "Already they're saying a great new age of boxing begins with you." "Maybe," answers Corbett, "but there'll never be another John L. Sullivan."

Corbett then goes out into the garden, where Victoria follows him, ashamed of her mocking gift after seeing his sportsmanship. She realizes there is a serious and considerate side to him, and his liking for Sullivan earns her respect. He feels sorry for Sullivan, who will never again be able to pound a bar and say that he can lick any man in the world. He then asks her if they like each other. She responds that she thinks perhaps he likes her more but that she loves him more. "Love," he says incredulously, but as they almost relapse into their antagonistic banter, he informs her that she is going to be a marvelous Corbett. As they kiss, his father and brothers break into another brawl, and Lowrie shouts again, as he did earlier in the film, "The Corbetts are at it again."

Flynn always called Gentleman Jim one of his favorite roles, and in the film he gives one of his finest performances. Because of his well-publicized offscreen shenanigans, Flynn was underrated and not taken seriously as an actor, but his performance as Jim Corbett is a splendid one, extraordinarily charismatic, full of humor, high spirits, dash, and charm. The script endows him with the gift of blarney and makes him at times a roguish, rascally liar who bluffs and swaggers his way up from obscurity but who wins fame, fortune, and the girl he loves by genuine skill. Walsh reports that Flynn was thoroughly professional and worked out strenuously in the gymnasium. A good athlete who handled his fists well, Flynn did his own fighting in the ring and worked with sportswriter Ed Cochrane, an authority on Corbett, and with fighter Mushy Callahan to recapture Corbett's style of fighting. His performance is immensely physical and energetic, and he receives fine support from Hale and Bond in possibly their best roles. Walsh directs with vigor and keeps the film moving at an almost dizzying pace. The production captures the look of the 1890's—a bit of its poverty and a good deal of its opulence. Heinz Roemheld's score consists mostly of traditional Irish reels and jigs plus some sentimental songs of the period. *Gentleman Jim* is an immensely engaging film, an example of the "movie-movie" at its best.

Robert E. Morsberger

GENTLEMAN'S AGREEMENT

Released: 1947
Production: Darryl F. Zanuck for Twentieth Century-Fox (AA)
Direction: Elia Kazan (AA)
Screenplay: Moss Hart; based on the novel of the same name by Laura Z.
  Hobson
Cinematography: Arthur Miller
Editing: Harmon Jones
Music: Alfred Newman
Running time: 118 minutes

  Principal characters:
    Phil Green .... Gregory Peck
    Kathy Lacey .... Dorothy McGuire
    Dave Goldman .... John Garfield
    Anne Dettrey .... Celeste Holm (AA)
    Mrs. Green .... Anne Revere
    Miss Wales ....June Havoc
    John Minify .... Albert Dekker
    Jane Lacey .... Jane Wyatt
    Tommy Green .... Dean Stockwell
    Professor Lieberman .... Sam Jaffe

In the 1930's and 1940's, Twentieth Century-Fox produced many socially conscious films, including *The Grapes of Wrath* (1940), *The Ox-Bow Incident* (1942), *The Snake Pit* (1948), and *Pinky* (1949). In 1947, Darryl F. Zanuck produced Moss Hart's adaptation of Laura Z. Hobson's best-selling novel *Gentleman's Agreement* as a major feature film which went on to win the Oscar as Best Picture of the Year. Although the film is somewhat dated and its initial impact is difficult to appreciate today, this social drama is generally acknowledged to be one of the first to attack openly prejudice against Jews, along with *Crossfire*, produced by RKO the same year.

Gregory Peck plays the protagonist, widower journalist Phil Green, a feature writer for *Smith's Weekly*, an important news magazine. At the suggestion of his liberal managing editor, John Minify (Albert Dekker), Green moves with his young son Tommy (Dean Stockwell) and mother (Anne Revere) from California to New York in order to work on a series of articles on anti-Semitism. In New York, he meets and falls in love with Minify's niece, Kathy Lacey (Dorothy McGuire), a beautiful, intelligent, and socially correct divorcée.

Green is unsure about his articles. He wants to approach the subject with an entirely new slant, but cannot come up with one which seems right. At first he wants to do the articles based on the experiences of his Jewish friend Dave Goldman (John Garfield), whom Green feels is similar to himself except that he is a Jew. However, when Goldman discusses what it is like to be a Jew, Green finally stumbles upon what he is sure will be the right angle to break the issue of anti-Semitism "wide open." Green decides to call his story "I Was a Jew for Six Weeks," and begins by telling the superintendent of his apartment building to add the name "Greenberg" to his mailbox. Although he never actually tells anyone that he is a Jew, he allows people to think that he is and to draw their own conclusions about him. When Kathy anxiously asks him whether or not he really is a Jew, Phil realizes with shock that even she is prejudiced.

In the course of his research, the journalist discovers prejudice in almost all aspects of his daily life. When Goldman cannot find a home for his family, Green learns that there is a sort of "Gentleman's Agreement" not to rent to Jews. He also learns that his Jewish secretary (June Havoc) is herself anti-Semitic—she has changed her name from Walorsky to Wales and refers to Jews as the "wrong ones"; and Tommy finds himself exposed to the cruelty of other children when he is taunted and called "dirty Jew" by his so-called school friends. Finally, feeling humiliated when he must leave a "restricted" New Hampshire hotel which abruptly cancels his reservations after learning that his name is "Greenberg" rather than "Green," Phil writes his series of articles. In the end, the series becomes a successful exposé which stuns many of his acquaintances. After reading the articles and thinking about her own views, Kathy finally overcomes her prejudices and rents her Connecticut cottage to Goldman and his family. Her act of courage touches Phil and they are reunited.

Gregory Peck is good, although a little stiff, as the crusading writer. Dorothy McGuire is also fine as his fiancée. Celeste Holm, who plays the vivacious, sophisticated Anne Dettrey, the open-minded fashion editor of *Smith's Weekly*, won an Oscar for Best Supporting Actress for her role. Sam Jaffe, who had only one scene in the film, is memorable as Professor Lieberman, the scientist who explains that Jews are practitioners of a particular religion and do not comprise a race. John Garfield, in a role which does not follow his usual "tough guy" screen image, gives a wonderfully underplayed performance as Dave Goldman. He is particularly moving when he speaks of his own children being barred from summer camp, or of the dying soldier whom a fellow GI called "Sheeney." In another scene he is arresting when he reacts to Kathy's description of the horror of an anti-Semitic party she attended by repeatedly asking, "But what did you *do*?"

Gentleman's Agreement was filmed in near-documentary style by cinematographer Arthur Miller. It was directed by the prolific Elia Kazan, who, in the manner of directors such as Sidney Lumet and Martin Ritt, is noted for his message pictures, usually photographed in black-and-white. He is also known for his concern for minority groups, as seen in such films as *Pinky*, which focused on Southern blacks, and *Panic in the Streets* (1950), which dealt with New Orleans Sicilians. Kazan won the Academy Award for Best Direction for *Gentleman's Agreement.*

Leslie Taubman

GENTLEMEN PREFER BLONDES

Released: 1953
Production: Sol C. Siegel for Twentieth Century-Fox
Direction: Howard Hawks
Screenplay: Charles Lederer; based on the musical comedy of the same name
by Joseph Fields and Anita Loos
Cinematography: Harry J. Wild
Editing: Hugh S. Fowler
Choreography: Jack Cole
Music: Jule Styne and Leo Robin
Song: Hoagy Carmichael and Harold Adamson
Running time: 91 minutes

Principal characters:
Dorothy ....Jane Russell
Lorelei Lee .... Marilyn Monroe
Gus Esmond .... Tommy Noonan
Sir Francis Beekman .... Charles Coburn
Detective Malone ....Elliott Reid

Gentlemen Prefer Blondes, a brassy musical comedy, would be unexceptional were it not for the presence of Marilyn Monroe. Though some people have considered her to be an untalented product of publicity and others have maintained that she was a great actress who never had the serious roles or serious consideration she deserved, neither extreme is true. Monroe had a screen presence which overcame her technical limitations in acting and singing when she was given a role suited to her screen *persona*. With her husky, whispery voice, wide-eyed innocent stare, round baby face, and pouting mouth, Monroe was perfectly suited to the role of Lorelei Lee, a seemingly scatterbrained but not-so-dumb blonde dedicated to securing her future by marrying a millionaire.

Engaged to a young millionaire, Gus Esmond (Tommy Noonan), Lorelei takes a ship to France where Gus is to meet her later. To make sure that Lorelei does not get into trouble, Gus sends along her friend Dorothy (Jane Russell), and his father sends along a detective, Malone (Elliott Reid). During the crossing they meet a rich elderly Englishman, Sir Francis "Piggy" Beekman (Charles Coburn), whom Lorelei blackmails into giving her his wife's diamond tiara. Malone finds this out, and when the girls reach Paris, they discover that Gus has cancelled their hotel reservations and their credit. They have to get jobs as showgirls in Paris, but all ends happily when Gus and his father come over and meet Lorelei. The film ends with a double wedding: Lorelei to Gus and Dorothy to Malone.

Lorelei originated in stories by screenwriter and author Anita Loos, who created the character when she was in love with editor and essayist H. L. Mencken. When she saw herself being neglected by him for a vacuous, unintelligent blonde, Loos was hurt and bewildered and decided to sublimate her jealousy by writing a story about an empty-headed blonde flapper of the 1920's whom she called Lorelei. *Harper's Bazaar* accepted her story and asked for more adventures of Lorelei. Eventually the magazine pieces were collected in a book, *Gentlemen Prefer Blondes*, which made Loos both famous and wealthy. The book remained popular over the years, being adapted first as a play, later as a silent film, then as a Broadway musical, and finally as the Twentieth Century-Fox film with Marilyn Monroe as Lorelei.

By the time the book reached the screen, it had lost some of its sharp characterization and wit, but it is often amusing, especially when Lorelei is explaining her philosophy of life to her friend Dorothy. When Lorelei advises her to find a rich man to marry, Dorothy replies that some people simply do not care about money. Lorelei is amazed by this naïve attitude. If a girl has to spend all her time worrying about money, she asks Dorothy, how can she have time to be in love? Marriage is a serious business to Lorelei. She may not be an intellectual, but she does know that her beauty will not last forever, and she intends to provide for her future. As she explains to one of her admirers, "A kiss on the hand might feel very good, but a diamond tiara is forever."

Lorelei is a shrewd judge of men's characters. When the outraged father of the naïve young millionaire she intends to marry warns her she is not fooling him, she responds instantly that she is not trying to, but that she could if she wanted to. She explains to him, with a logic that leaves him speechless, that a "man being rich is like a girl being pretty. You might not marry her just because she's pretty, but my goodness, doesn't it help?" Sometimes Lorelei seems dumb and other times astute. As she explains to Gus's father, she can be smart when it is important, but most men do not like that.

The film gains immediate momentum from a vividly colorful and sparkling musical number, "Little Girls from Little Rock," which Dorothy and Lorelei, in red sequined gowns slit up to the thighs and with feathers in their hair, perform in front of violet sequined curtains in a nightclub. Halfway through the number the credits for the film appear, and when the credits end, Lorelei and Dorothy return to finish the song. The motions and gestures of the number are based on burlesque movements, as they are also in the film's other musical numbers, but the bumps and grinds were toned down for the movie censor.

The other eye-catching number, "Diamonds Are a Girl's Best Friend," is strikingly staged and photographed and is the film's highlight. It opens in a manner reminiscent of Busby Berkeley: girls in full pink gowns and men in white ties and tails dance around human candelabra, formed by girls in black costumes. The colors, deep red and bright pink, clash excitingly. In the midst of the swirling couples, the audience suddenly sees Lorelei, sitting with her back to the audience, in a bright pink satin sheath and long pink gloves. Diamonds sparkle from her wrists, her ears, her throat. Suddenly she turns, facing the camera, and the men offer her cardboard hearts which she spurns, trilling in an operatic voice, "No, no, no," before launching into the lyrics in her own husky, whispery voice. Marilyn Monroe's singing and dancing are surprisingly effective, although the dancing consists largely of a few modified, gyrations very much as those used in "Little Girls from Little Rock." Still, within the context of the number, it is sufficient, and Monroe as Lorelei, clasping strings of diamonds to her face and surrounded by men in formal black evening attire, presents a striking picture.

The other musical numbers are more routine, both musically and dramatically, although Monroe's "Bye-Bye Baby," which she croons wistfully to her millionaire boyfriend as she sets off for Europe, is musically and emotionally effective. "When Love Goes Wrong" is Lorelei and Dorothy's best duet, sung in a bar after they have been forced to leave their luxurious hotel suite. Gradually, as the denizens of the bar gather round, two little boys begin clapping and everyone joins in for the big finale.

"Anyone Here for Love?" is a misconceived idea for Jane Russell's solo musical number as Dorothy. More interested in sex than money, Dorothy thinks she has found a gold mine when she discovers that members of the American Olympic team are aboard the ocean liner. She is quickly disillusioned when she learns that the men spend their time working out in the ship's gymnasium and must be in bed by nine o'clock. As she strolls around the gym watching the men practicing handstands, somersaults, weight lifting, and wrestling, she wryly sings the lyrics. The men's calisthenics are as carefully choreographed as a dance, but the effect is flat and unsatisfying.

Beside Marilyn Monroe the other actors are rather flat and colorless. Tommy Noonan as Gus Esmond, Lorelei's ineffectual millionaire boyfriend who is dominated by his father, seems perfectly cast, but Elliott Reid as Detective Malone, assigned to gather evidence against Lorelei by the elder Esmond, is dull as Dorothy's love interest. Charles Coburn is better in the role of Sir Francis "Piggy" Beekman, but his performance is only a collection of his now-famous mannerisms. Even Jane Russell, the brightest star in the cast besides Monroe, is somewhat wooden, though genial.

Director Howard Hawks, whose credits include *Bringing Up Baby* (1938), *Red River* (1948), and *To Have and Have Not* (1944), is obviously out of his element in *Gentlemen Prefer Blondes*, but as a star vehicle for Marilyn Monroe the film succeeds admirably and was in the top ten at the box office in its year.

Julia Johnson

THE GHOST AND MRS. MUIR

Released: 1947
Production: Fred Kohlmar for Twentieth Century-Fox
Direction: Joseph L. Mankiewicz
Screenplay: Philip Dunne; based on the novel of the same name by R. A. Dick
Cinematography: Charles Lang
Editing: Dorothy Spencer
Running time: 104 minutes

Principal characters:
Lucy Muir	Gene Tierney
Ghost of Captain Daniel Gregg	Rex Harrison
Miles Fairley	George Sanders
Martha	Edna Best
Anna (older)	Vanessa Brown
Mrs. Miles Fairley	Anna Lee
Coembe	Robert Coote
Anna (younger)	Natalie Wood
Sproule	Whitford Kane
Bill	William Stelling

The Ghost and Mrs. Muir was one of many fantasy films popular in the 1940's. Whereas fantasy and supernatural films of today tend to be lavish, special effects-laden, often violent productions, fantasy films in the 1940's were more subtle. A distinction should perhaps be made between "ghost" stories and "fantasy" stories, but 1940's films such as *Here Comes Mr. Jordan* (1941) and *It's a Wonderful Life* (1946), which had spirits prominently featured in the plot, can hardly be compared to the frightening films of later years, and are thus the more akin to fantasy. *The Ghost and Mrs. Muir* is not frightening at all. Instead, it is a tender love story between two people, one alive and one dead. The main characters never kiss or embrace, and there is nothing ghoulish about their relationship. The premise is merely a flight of fancy on which to build an entertaining love story.

The story opens at the turn of the century as Mrs. Lucy Muir (Gene Tierney) tells her mother-in-law and sister-in-law that she has decided to leave their home and begin a new life for herself. Lucy is a widow with a daughter named Anna (Natalie Wood), and almost a year after her husband's death she wants to manage her own life. So she takes Anna and their faithful housekeeper, Martha (Edna Best), and moves to a small British Coastal town, hoping to support herself on income from shares in a gold mine left to her by her husband.

When they go to a real estate agent named Coembe (Robert Coote) to find a suitable house, Lucy is at first discouraged by the high rents. She decides to look at one particular property, however, when she sees that its rent is less than half the price of other similar properties. Mr. Coembe is distressed and tries to discourage her, but Lucy stubbornly refuses to be dissuaded. They visit the house, which has a beautiful view of the ocean, and Lucy is immediately enthralled with it. Unfortunately, while Lucy and Coembe are there, they hear mysterious laughter and noises and are chased outside. Coembe finally confesses to Lucy that the house is haunted by the ghost of Captain Gregg, a well-known sea captain who committed suicide four years before. Since that time no one has been able to stay in the house for more than one night, and all of the tenants have complained about the ghost. Lucy, however, is adamant; she loves the house and wants to stay.

On her first night, after the others are in bed, she has her first encounter with the house's original occupant. As she tries to light a candle which will not stay ignited because the ghost keeps blowing out the match, Captain Gregg (Rex Harrison) appears for the first time. Lucy is at first frightened and ready to faint, but gradually she regains her composure and argues with Captain Gregg about his reported suicide. He tells her that his death was an accident and that the reason he haunts the house, called "Gull Cottage," is that he wants to turn it into a home for retired seamen (not sailors, he corrects). When he realizes Lucy's determination and spunk, he promises to let her stay unmolested in the house on a trial basis. His only stipulation is that she hang his portrait in the main bedroom, which Lucy now occupies. In a very well-done scene, Lucy goes to bed after trying to hang the portrait, but is embarrassed to undress in front of it. She covers it with an afghan, then proceeds to undress and get into bed. Just as she turns out the light, however, Captain Gregg's voice is heard, telling her not to "apologize to anyone for your figure."

There seems to be a truce between Lucy and Gregg just as her mother-in-law and sister-in-law arrive to take her back to London; the gold mine in which Lucy holds shares has petered out, and Lucy will have no money coming in on which to live. While Lucy listens despondently to their entreaties to return with them, Gregg, who is visible only to Lucy, tells her to send them away—that he will do something. She does what he asks, and her wishes are reinforced by some grandstanding ghost tricks on his part which make the women vow never to return.

As time passes, Lucy begins to write a book, *Blood and Swash*, which Gregg dictates to her, based on his own colorful life as a sea captain. When she completes the book she takes it to a London publisher, Mr. Sproule (Whitford Kane), who at first refuses to see her, thinking that she is just another silly widow writing a romance. When he does read the book, however, he likes it and promises Lucy that it will bring her a considerable amount of money in royalties. Now that Lucy's finances are secure she can buy Gull Cottage.

On the way out of the publisher's office, she meets a supercilious dandy, Miles Fairley (George Sanders), who shares a cab with her and sees her to the train station. Although she seems uninterested in him, she feigns admiration for his work when he reveals that he is the noted children's author "Uncle Neddy." Gregg is jealous when he meets Lucy, whom he prefers to call Lucia, in the train. They argue, but Lucy's temper and shouts of "blast" cause the dispute to end in laughter as they frighten away a gentleman passenger.

The growing affection between Lucy and Captain Gregg soon stops because Lucy becomes infatuated with Miles and thinks that she is going to marry him. She again argues with Captain Gregg, but this time she lets him know rather obliquely that she prefers a live man who can fulfill her needs over a dead one. Gregg agrees, and in the middle of the night he visits Lucy while she sleeps and whispers tenderly to her, telling her to forget him. He tells her that all memory of him will seem like a dream, and then he leaves her.

Soon after this Lucy removes the portrait of Captain Gregg from her bedroom, not really knowing why she put it there in the first place. Because Miles cannot come down and visit her, she decides to pay a surprise visit to him after obtaining his address from their mutual publisher. When she goes to his house, he is not there, but his wife (Anna Lee) is. She kindly tells Lucy not to feel too bad, because "this isn't the first time something like this has happened." A disconsolate Lucy returns home, and we see the years passing through shots of the surf hitting against a post in the sand bearing Anna's name.

Now the action advances to about twelve years later. Anna (Vanessa Brown) is now in college and she has come home with a fiancé named Bill (William Stelling). She wants Lucy to come and live with them, but Lucy refuses because she does not want to leave Gull Cottage. While they are having tea together, Anna reveals that she, too, had had "dreams" about Captain Gregg in which they talked about the sea and played games. Lucy has had recurring dreams about the Captain over the years, but she casts aside any thoughts that Anna has concerning his reality in their lives.

After this short sequence the passage of time is again shown by the pounding surf. By now Lucy is a white-haired old woman, and she is seen standing outside her bedroom on the porch which Captain Gregg had built to view the sea. Martha, also a white-haired old lady, brings Lucy inside and admonishes her to keep warm and drink her milk to abide by doctor's orders. Lucy rather brusquely sends Martha away, and as she begins to raise the glass of milk to her lips, she drops it and dies of a heart attack. Now, for the first time since they had parted many years before, Captain Gregg appears. He reaches for Lucy's hand, and superimposed photography shows a young and vibrant Lucy rising from the body of the old Lucy. The two walk hand-in-hand down the stairs, passing the unseeing Martha. The last frames of the film show the young Lucy and Captain Gregg walking off together in the mist, now joined in eternity.

The odd premise of the film would lead one to believe that it could only be successful as a comedy, but *The Ghost and Mrs. Muir* is not that. There are some mildly funny moments which are created by the reactions of some of the minor characters to Mrs. Muir's strong language or Captain Gregg's ghostly presence, but these are few. The film is a serious romantic drama in which a woman chooses one man over another and is literally as well as figuratively haunted by her scorned lover. Although Lucy is a widow at the beginning of the story, it is revealed that she was merely fond of her late husband. It is her love for Captain Gregg, which she cannot acknowledge, for which she grieves for the rest of her life.

There are numerous allusions throughout the film to Captain Gregg's presence as it was felt by Martha and Anna as well as Lucy. Martha uses such words as "landlubber" as soon as they settle in the house, and Anna marries a Navy man. When Lucy says that Anna's fiancé is a lieutenant, Martha scoffs, "Captain's more to my liking." For all of the women the illusion of Captain Gregg has a very real influence, but for Lucy, his influence cannot alter the fact that he is dead and she is not. She cannot accept him because they are divided by death, and it is only in her own death that they can be united.

The film is a favorite on television and even fathered an updated sequel. In that popular television series of the late 1960's, starring Hope Lange and Edward Mulhare, comedy rather than romance was the thrust of the story. The original film, however, is a bittersweet love story which strongly evokes the feeling and mystery of the sea.

Tierney's popularity was just beginning to decline when she made *The Ghost and Mrs. Muir*, and this was perhaps her last good role. She never was able to capture a distinct screen *persona*, a prerequisite for so-called superstardom, but she had been a popular leading lady in the 1940's. Her two most noteworthy roles were the leads in *Laura* (1944) and *Leave Her to Heaven* (1945), the latter of which brought her her only Academy Award nomination. Although she is American and Lucy Muir is English, Tierney admirably underplays the English accent required for the role. Her soft voice and almost Oriental-looking features give her the type of mysterious quality necessary to match her rival for Gregg's affections, the sea.

Harrison, an established star of British and American films and stage, does extremely well as the ghost of Captain Gregg, who is simultaneously handsome, suave, earthy, and stern, a character reminiscent of many other seamen on film. He is so earthy, in fact, that it is sometimes hard to believe that he is a ghost. Interestingly, he seemed more ethereal in *Blithe Spirit* (1945), in which he played the live husband of a haunting first wife.

In a time of widespread cinematic violence, gore, and scare techniques in films based on the supernatural, it is refreshing to watch an old film such as *The Ghost and Mrs. Muir* which entertains and does not resort to playing on the audience's primal fears.

Patricia King Hanson

GIANT

Released: 1956
Production: George Stevens and Henry Ginsberg for Warner Bros.
Direction: George Stevens (AA)
Screenplay: Fred Guiol and Ivan Moffat; based on the novel of the same name by Edna Ferber
Cinematography: William C. Mellor
Editing: William Hornbeck, Philip W. Anderson, and Fred Bohanen
Music: Dmitri Tiomkin
Running time: 198 minutes

Principal characters:
Leslie Lynnton Benedict .... Elizabeth Taylor
Bick Benedict .... Rock Hudson
Jett Rink .... James Dean
Luz Benedict (the older) .... Mercedes McCambridge
Vashti Snythe .... Jane Withers
Uncle Bawley Benedict .... Chill Wills
Luz Benedict (the younger) .... Carroll Baker
Jordan Benedict III .... Dennis Hopper
Juana Benedict .... Elsa Cardenas
Judy Benedict .... Fran Bennett

Giant belongs to the Hollywood era that saw the release of films such as *The Ten Commandments*, *Around the World in 80 Days*, *War and Peace*, and *The King and I* all in the same year. Emphasis was on spectacle, grandeur, extravagance, and length. Producer/director George Stevens, in keeping with the trend, ambitiously attempted to film a great American epic from Edna Ferber's sprawling best seller about a colorful, land-rich Texas family. The film's mixed critical reviews did not prevent its commercial success and kudos for individual performances and Stevens' overall work in the film. Some skeptical critics attributed the film's success to the last performance of James Dean, who became an object of adulation after his death in a fiery car crash. Dean portrayed Jett Rink, one of the three central characters in this saga that covers approximately twenty-five years of American, and especially Texan history.

Before Jett Rink is introduced, the two other central characters meet, fall in love, and set the stage for their future conflicts. The film opens with Texas cattle baron Bick Benedict, played with authority by Rock Hudson, being out of his element in Maryland, in the elegant, cultured society of the prominent Maryland surgeon, Dr. Horace Lynnton, whose prize stallion Bick has come to purchase. While visiting the Lynntons, he meets their lovely daughter Leslie (Elizabeth Taylor). Although Bick and Leslie sense an immediate attraction to each other, their totally dissimilar natures and backgrounds spark some spirited and lively scenes. Leslie Lynnton is the despair of her social-climbing mother because she has a sharp mind and a tongue to match. Mrs. Lynnton fears that Leslie, although she is engaged, may never marry the "right" husband. Bick is attracted to Leslie but is totally immersed in his ranch and completely convinced of the greatness of the Texas way of life. When Leslie tries to discuss certain controversial points of Texas history, such as how the large landowners obtained their vast holdings, Bick's response is hardly polite. Key areas of conflict are identified early in the film, even during this courtship stage, and foreshadow the power struggles and troubles to come.

These opening Maryland scenes are photographed in bright colors amid lush surroundings. There are shots of the green, rolling, fox-hunting country of Maryland, detailed close-ups of the lavish life style of the Lynntons, and lingering close-ups of the attractive Bick and Leslie as they fall in love. Stevens is painstaking in portraying small, sensitive details.

The scene now changes. Mr. and Mrs. Bick Benedict and the prize stallion, War Winds, are off to Texas to Bick's massive ranch, Reata, and to a bout of culture shock for the former Leslie Lynnton. Again, differences between Bick and Leslie are shown in Leslie's gracious greeting of a Mexican youth who has come to meet them at the train station. Bick tells her that she should not make such a fuss over a Mexican boy. They have their first quarrel as man and wife, but are reconciled on the drive to their home, which is a memorable visual experience. In contrast to the green, lush countryside of Leslie's Maryland home, Texas is introduced desolately as the speeding car kicks up the brown-gray dust for mile after mile of the vast, treeless ranch until the stark Gothic outline of the Big House emerges above the horizon.

Leslie is the outsider now. She must grapple with a new set of customs, beliefs, and people. First, there is Luz (Mercedes McCambridge), Bick's spinster older sister who finds it impossible to relinquish her tightly held rein on the Big House and on her younger brother. Luz is cordial to Leslie but treats her as a guest rather than as the new mistress of Reata. Other people whom Leslie meets are friends and neighboring ranchers. Leslie, who has spent her mature life engaging in adult conversations with men such as her father and other cultivated society folk, now is part of a completely different society. In Texas, the men talk only to other men about substantive matters. The women spend idle lives filled with shopping, endless coffee-klatching, and frivolous gossip. The prime example is Vashti (Jane Withers), the bulky awkward daughter of the neighboring ranch owner, who had hoped to land the dashing Bick and who marries one of her father's ranch hands out of spite.

Leslie's liberal instincts are stimulated by the plight of the Mexicans on the ranch and in the surrounding community. Her attempts to aid them only arouse Bick's anger, and this prejudice shown early in the film eventually will build to a climax in which Bick must come to terms with his own weaknesses and complacency.

The presence of the swaggering wrangler, Jett Rink (James Dean), adds a dimension of menace to the plot. The Benedicts of Reata are the "haves"; the insecure, upwardly striving, threatening Jett is a "have not." In his early scenes as a sullen ranch hand, he conveys an adulterous lust for Leslie, an arrogant hostility towards his employer Bick, and the hint of an unhealthy relationship with Luz. Jett's interference in Benedict affairs causes Luz, who is feeling spurned by her brother, to ride out in a fury on the stallion, War Winds. She suffers a fatal fall, and in a rage Bick runs Jett off the ranch. Luz, however, has willed Jett a seemingly worthless bit of land on the ranch and Jett will be heard from again. James Dean's performance, straight method acting, is photographed almost entirely in shadows. Together, Stevens and Dean have captured a sense of dramatic unity.

After Luz's death, a pattern of living emerges for Bick and Leslie. The slow pace is one method Stevens uses to reinforce his vision of reality. He wants to convey the feeling of twenty-five years slowly passing, of the adjustments and responses to change that his characters must make. Bick and Leslie become the parents of a son, Jordy (Dennis Hopper), and two daughters, Judy (Fran Bennett) and Luz (Carroll Baker), after her aunt. Now a new generation of Benedicts must deal with the conflicting values of their parents: Bick, who lives for the ranch and his traditions, and Leslie, still the liberal, fighting for causes and trying to impose some elegance and taste on the bleak Texas atmosphere.

Young Jordy, the pride and hope of his father, shows a marked distaste for the life of a rancher. In temperament, he takes after his mother, and, as he grows up, he longs to be a doctor. Jordy's twin sister Judy is a disappointment first to her mother for her tomboy ways, and, later, to her father for her growing attachment to an experimental farmer named Bob Dietz (Earl Holliman), whom she eventually marries. More arguments occur between Leslie and Bick as their preconceived expectations for the children do not take into account that they are individuals with individual needs and desires. Even Leslie becomes narrow-minded as she insists on molding her daughters into unsuitable, unwanted roles.

Part of the pattern of Texas living is the old cattle aristocracy making way for the new oil rich. In some of the most carefully crafted scenes in the film, Stevens shows Jett Rink's financial rise. Jett's character develops as Stevens portrays his enthusiasm in working his own piece of land. Jett at last has something that belongs to him, and he feverishly works his "worthless" land for oil harder than he ever worked for the Benedicts. At last, his gusher comes in, and a rapturous Jett is drenched by the black gold. His tie to the Benedicts, part resentment, part envy, and part desire to show off to Leslie, prompts him to race over to the Big House where the Benedicts are entertaining. Smirking over his success, he becomes a bit too familiar with Leslie, which causes Bick to strike him. Jett recovers quickly, delivers a sharp blow in return, and then furiously rides off.

Jett's increasing wealth and power in the state are often discussed by the other characters. Years later, still crude and insecure in spite of his wealth, he is back on the scene trying to woo young Luz. He has planned a huge party to celebrate the grand opening of one of his hotels. All Texas society, new and old, feels obliged to attend, including the Benedicts, despite their aversion to Jett. Dr. Jordan Benedict III and his Mexican wife Juana (Elsa Cardenas) make the trip, as well as graying Bick and Leslie. The Bob Dietzes and their young child are the only family members who do not attend the great affair. Juana has made an appointment with the hotel's beauty parlor under the name Mrs. Jordan Benedict. When she arrives, she is told that Mexicans are not served. She calls Jordy, who demolishes the beauty parlor in a rage and proceeds to the big banquet hall for a confrontation with Jett. Jett is surrounded by bodyguards who hold Jordy down for Jett's attack in front of a crowd of people which includes the other Benedicts. Bick, in spite of his conflicting emotions, rises to defend his son, and he too is felled by Jett.

Drunk and despondent over his failed attempt to impress Texas society, Jett has a touching scene in which he makes a pathetic speech to the deserted banquet hall. The speech is overheard by Luz, who earlier had defended Jett in defiance of her parents. Now at last she realizes that in Jett's eyes she is no more than a substitute for her mother.

After the disastrous banquet, Bick and Leslie drive Juana and her young son back to the ranch. They stop at a roadside restaurant where once again Juana is refused service. All the years of Bick's prejudice and conservatism now intermingle with his sense of family pride and Leslie's liberal influence. He engages in a wild brawl with the restaurant owner, amid the strains of the film's popular ballad "The Yellow Rose of Texas." The film ends back at Reata where Bick and Leslie compromise their old positions and look to their two grandchildren, one half Mexican, the other a blond toddler, to bring about needed changes and social justice.

A major criticism of *Giant* is that the film, like the Edna Ferber novel, has no focus, that it has combined melodramatic themes of family conflict, the alien outsider, and racial prejudice, without any true resolution. Another criticism is that the disdain for the crass, bigoted, materialistic society on the move is not balanced by a sensitive understanding of the individual motivations of the people in that society. These points may be valid, or only partially so; but such deficiencies are redeemed by the strengths of George Stevens' work. He is able to elicit more than competent performances from Rock Hudson and Elizabeth Taylor, especially before they are required to age. James Dean ended his career with a stunning characterization that received almost universal praise. Dean, Rock Hudson, and Mercedes McCambridge received Best Actor and Best Supporting Actress nominations, respectively. Other nominees from the film were Dmitri Tiomkin for the scoring; William Hornbeck, Philip W. Anderson, and Fred Bohanen for film editing; Ralph S. Hurst for art and set decoration; Moss Mabry and Marjorie Best for costume design; and Fred Guiol and Ivan Moffat for the screenplay.

Despite its faulty plot, George Stevens is able to bring to this film a visual sweep, careful attention to sound, and many striking small touches. Examples of Stevens' sensitive direction include the shot of the drunken Jett walking to the dais at his banquet, the beautifully framed long shot of the horse that has just thrown Luz on her return to Reata, and the warm pillow-talk conversations between Bick and Leslie. For his efforts in delineating a sensitive landscape of the human condition, Stevens the producer received an Academy Award nomination for Best Picture and won the Best Director Award for 1956.

Maria Soule

GIGI

Released: 1958
Production: Arthur Freed for Metro-Goldwyn-Mayer (AA)
Direction: Vincente Minnelli (AA)
Screenplay: Alan Jay Lerner (AA); based on the novel of the same name by Colette
Cinematography: Joseph Ruttenberg (AA)
Editing: Adrienne Fazan (AA)
Art direction: William A. Horning and Preston Ames (AA)
Set decoration: Henry Grace and Keogh Gleason (AA)
Costume design: Cecil Beaton (AA)
Music direction: André Previn (AA)
Music: Frederick Loewe and Alan Jay Lerner
Song: Frederick Loewe and Alan Jay Lerner, "Gigi" (AA)
Running time: 116 minutes

Principal characters:
Gigi .... Leslie Caron
Honoré Lachaille .... Maurice Chevalier
Gaston Lachaille .... Louis Jourdan
Madame Alvarez .... Hermione Gingold
Aunt Alicia .... Isabel Jeans
Liane d'Exelmans ....Eva Gabor

A stylish, elegant musical set in turn-of-the-century Paris, *Gigi* is based on the novelette by the French author Colette. The film depicts the coming of age of a young French girl, Gigi, and her development from a tomboy into a lovely young woman. Though Gigi is being educated to become a courtesan in a fashionable world of luxury, scandal, expensive mistresses, and lavish entertainments, the approach of director Vincente Minnelli and scriptwriter Alan J. Lerner is so light and delicate and the ending so appropriately romantic that the story never seems at all sordid or the atmosphere decadent.

Although the novelette had previously been filmed in France in 1950 and presented as a Broadway play in 1951, Lerner—with Minnelli's encouragement—based his adaptation almost entirely on the original work, delicately expanding it to enhance the tone of Colette's story. His only significant addition was the character of Honoré Lachaille, which was written especially for Maurice Chevalier. Barely hinted at in the novelette, the character was introduced by Colette herself for the French film, thereby justifying its inclusion in Lerner's script.

Rather than being a drama with songs inserted in it, *Gigi* is truly an integrated musical, with the songs so deftly interwoven into the story that they are perfect expressions of the characters' feelings and thoughts and often develop the plot. Indeed, they are so much a part of the story that they are not quite as impressive when removed from their context in the film. The unusual vocal style used in nearly all of the songs also serves to integrate them into the rest of the film. Parts of these songs are delivered in a recitative manner—a rhythmic, rhymed delivery halfway between singing and ordinary speaking. Instead of suddenly breaking into song, a character may subtly slip from normal speaking into recitative, and then into singing.

Many scenes were shot in Paris—in the Bois de Boulogne, at Maxim's famous restaurant and the Palais de Glace. Scenes were also shot using the interiors and exteriors of various residences. This location shooting and the fact that the leading performers are French adds immeasurably to the Parisian charm and feel of the film. Director Vincente Minnelli relied heavily on the drawings of the French caricaturist Sems (whose work appears under the credits) to guide his choice of costumes, settings, and even faces to establish a visual style appropriate to the period. This careful attention to the overall visual design of the film results in a most satisfying re-creation of period and place.

The film begins charmingly with a sequence in the Bois de Boulogne showing pretty women and elegant men in stylish carriages. Having established the atmosphere and mood of fashionable, turn-of-the-century Parisian society, the camera moves in closer to show an elderly, elegantly dressed man-about-town who turns to the camera and introduces himself as Honoré Lachaille, a "lover and a collector of antiques." As he gazes at a group of young girls playing nearby, his speech glides into the song "Thank Heaven for Little Girls." He interrupts the song to tell us that this is a story about a particular little girl, Gigi. The camera then follows Gigi (Leslie Caron) as she leaves the group of girls and runs home to the little upstairs apartment she shares with her grandmother, Madame Alvarez (Hermione Gingold).

Gigi is a tomboyish schoolgirl dressed in long black stockings, plaid suit, and sailor hat. We find that this is the day of the week she has lunch with her great-aunt Alicia (Isabel Jeans), who "never sets foot out of her apartment or her past." A great courtesan in her heyday, she is determined to train Gigi in the arts of pleasing a man in order that she too can become a successful courtesan. Gigi's lessons range from how to eat and how to pour coffee properly ("bad table manners have broken up more households than infidelity") to how to choose cigars and evaluate the quality of jewels.

Gigi is bored and impatient with her lessons. Forbidden by her grandmother to accept invitations from children of her own age, she is also lonely and isolated. When she questions the need for some of Aunt Alicia's lessons, she is told that "love is a work of art and like art must be created." But Gigi is still not convinced. As she walks home after her lessons she vents her frustration in the song "I Don't Understand the Parisians," which expresses her inability to understand their preoccupation with love.

On her way home she meets Gaston Lachaille (Louis Jourdan), who is going to the Palais de Glace (an indoor ice-skating rink) to meet his mistress, Liane (Eva Gabor). Gaston is a rich and bored friend of the family who likes to visit Gigi and "Mamita," as he calls Madame Alvarez, to enjoy a cup of camomile tea. With them he is not bored and can relax. Mamita says of his visits, "It's always a pleasure to watch the rich enjoying the comforts of the poor." Gigi reluctantly agrees to accompany Gaston to the Palais, where he finds Liane skating with a handsome instructor of whom he is immediately jealous. When he asks Gigi's opinion of Liane, Gigi says bluntly that she is pretty but common and coarse. Gaston is at first taken aback by this directness but then decides it is refreshing and entertaining.

Later that evening when Gaston escorts Liane to Maxim's, he is bored and also suspicious and uneasy because of Liane's exuberant gaiety. In a musical interior monologue he tells himself that "she's so gay tonight" that "she's not thinking of me," and ends the evening by pouring a glass of champagne down the front of her dress.

The scenes at Maxim's are cleverly staged to emphasize the ostentatious display and gossipy throngs that made it such a popular place at which to be seen. As Gaston and Liane enter, the noise of the crowd stops for a moment, isolating the couple in silence; then, as they walk to their table, everyone turns to look at them and chants in unison the current gossip about them. As they are seated at their table, the natural sounds of the crowd resume. Each time another couple enters, the process is repeated.

The next morning Gaston confides his suspicions about Liane to his Uncle Honoré, unconsciously echoing Gigi's opinion of her as he sums up his relief that the affair is over: "The woman was common." Honoré persuades Gaston that to save face he must confront Liane and the skating instructor. Gaston does so, and gets rid of the lover by paying him to leave; he then informs Liane that their affair is over. Later, she tries to commit suicide—in "the usual way: insufficient poison," Aunt Alicia acidly remarks. Liane's attempted suicide is the talk of fashionable Paris, and the story appears in all the newspapers. The whole affair makes Gaston depressed and edgy, and he thinks of going to the country until it subsides. But Honoré warns him that his honor is at stake; rather than being despondent, he must act cheerful and high-spirited.

Gaston obediently embarks on a round of extravagant party-giving which bores him extremely. One evening, however, he comes to visit Mamita and Gigi and asks to be allowed to share their simple dinner; he spends the evening with them before leaving for Trouville, a fashionable seaside resort. Gigi has never seen the ocean and makes Gaston promise to take her and her grandmother with him if she beats him at cards. Indulgently, he allows her to win, although he knows she has cheated him; he even permits her to drink champagne over her grandmother's objections. Tipsy and in high spirits, all three dance and sing "The Night They Invented Champagne." Gigi is especially exuberant as she cavorts with a rose in her teeth and finally jumps into Gaston's lap.

Gaston keeps his promise and takes Gigi and Mamita to Trouville, where we see Gigi giggling, playing tennis, swimming, and riding a donkey along the beach with Gaston. Gigi's high spirits and natural behavior are contrasted with that of the other young women we see, all of whom are correctly dressed, reserved, and decorous.

Honoré is also visiting Trouville in pursuit of his usual quarry, women; but when he sees Mamita, he remembers his youthful love affair with her. The two had almost married, but Honoré, not wanting to become entangled permanently, had involved himself with another woman to offend Mamita. They reminisce in song about their youthful romance in "I Remember It Well," in which each recalls the past somewhat differently.

When Gigi and Mamita return from Trouville, Aunt Alicia, realizing the possibility of fixing Gaston's interest in Gigi, buys her a new wardrobe and intensifies her lessons, teaching her how to drink wine, how to enter and leave a room, and how to sit down gracefully. Later, when Gaston returns from a trip to Monte Carlo, Gigi models one of her new dresses for him; but instead of being pleased, he is upset and tells her she looks "like a giraffe with a goiter." He leaves angrily but soon returns with an offer to take her out for a drive. Mamita intervenes at this point, telling Gaston that Gigi cannot be seen with him lest she be compromised and her reputation ruined. Now angrier than ever, he leaves again and goes for a solitary walk. In a long soliloquy that leads into the title song, "Gigi," he finally realizes what his feelings toward Gigi really are. He begins his musings in an angry, frustrated mood in ordinary speech and then alternates between bitterness and pleasant memories as he slips into recitative and finally into song. The continual changes in the delivery and tempo reflect his alternating moods and effectively vary the soliloquy.

At the end of his musings, realizing what he wants, he goes back to Mamita and offers his usual business arrangement: he will provide lavishly for Gigi and she will become his mistress. This is entirely satisfactory to Mamita, but Gigi is upset, and especially so when Gaston confesses that he is in love with her. She is horrified that he would want to involve her in the sort of scandalous notoriety that would make her suffer, for she does not want that kind of life. But she finally accepts his offer because she would rather be miserable with him than without him.

We now see how Aunt Alicia's lessons benefit Gigi as, beautifully dressed in white satin, she is escorted to Maxim's by Gaston. Again, there is no sound as everyone turns to stare at Gigi and Gaston. After they are seated, the noise of the crowd resumes and Gigi selects his cigar for him, comments knowledgeably on another woman's pearls, deftly pours his coffee, and when he gives her an emerald bracelet, admires his taste.

Throughout the evening Gaston is obviously ill at ease, and his feelings are crystallized by Honoré's remarks when he comes over to compliment him on Gigi's looks after she has left to put on her bracelet. Gaston grows increasingly restive because of Honoré's fulsome and cynical comments, especially when Honoré remarks on Gigi's freshness and youth, saying "It's the sophisticated women who get boring so quickly. . . . But someone like Gigi can amuse you for months." When Gigi returns, Gaston abruptly seizes her by the hand and drags her, protesting and crying, out of Maxim's. Still not having given her a word of explanation, he leaves her with her grandmother and walks broodingly away, lost in thought.

As the music for the title song comes up on the sound track, Gaston paces back and forth past some of the picturesque settings of his earlier soliloquy. Both the music and the settings recall his earlier thoughts about Gigi. One pose, in which, deep in thought, he is silhouetted against a floodlit fountain, is visually striking and indicates his inner turmoil. At last he strides purposefully up the stairs of Mamita's apartment, a determined look on his face. Both Mamita and Gigi are startled and apprehensive when they see him, but all ends happily when he asks for Gigi's hand in marriage. The film ends on the same buoyant note on which it opened, with Honoré in the Bois de Boulogne. As we watch the strolling couples, one of them comes closer to the camera and we see that it is Gaston and Gigi.

The delightful performances in *Gigi* add charm and warmth to the elegant visual style and atmosphere of the film. Maurice Chevalier displays his relaxed charm and wit in the role of Honoré Lachaille, the rather detached philosopher and cynical commentator on the society of which he is so conspicuously a part. Leslie Caron as Gigi convincingly manages the transition from awkward tomboy to beautiful young woman, and Louis Jourdan as Gaston is appropriately handsome and charming. The supporting cast was especially well chosen. Hermione Gingold as Mamita perfectly blends practical common sense with a genuine concern for Gigi's future, and Isobel Jeans as Aunt Alicia is the consummate embodiment of the successful courtesan from another era who has never forgotten her past triumphs.

Gigi is a film in which almost every element is not only excellent but also fits perfectly with the others. In addition to the acting, other notable elements are the script by Alan Jay Lerner, the songs by Lerner and Frederick Loewe, the costumes by Cecil Beaton, and the cinematography of Joseph Ruttenberg. But perhaps the greatest credit should go to director Vincente Minnelli for uniting all these in a seamless whole.

Musicals, even very good ones, tend to emphasize the musical numbers at the expense of the story so that they become virtually independent of their setting. M-G-M demonstrated this in its compilations called *That's Entertainment* (1974) and *That's Entertainment, Part 2* (1976), which are largely a series of separate musical numbers from dozens of the studio's musicals. But

Gigi is a different kind of musical in that all the elements have the same general tone, and develop the characters while they advance the story.

The Motion Picture Academy recognized the overall excellence of *Gigi* with nine Oscars, including the one for Best Picture of the Year. Maurice Chevalier also received a Special Academy Award for his contributions to the world of entertainment for more than half a century.

Julia Johnson

GILDA

Released: 1946
Production: Virginia Van Upp for Columbia
Direction: Charles Vidor
Screenplay: Marion Parsonnet; based on a screen story by E. A. Ellington
Cinematography: Rudolph Maté
Editing: Charles Nelson
Running time: 110 minutes

   Principal characters:
   Gilda .... Rita Hayworth
   Johnny Farrell .... Glenn Ford
   Ballin Mundson .... George Macready
   Obregon .... Joseph Calleia
   Uncle Pio .... Steven Geray
   Casey .... Joe Sawyer

In 1946, Columbia president Harry Cohn was quoted as saying that Rita Hayworth was the fourth most valuable property in the business. Cohn, almost universally despised by the people who worked for him during his thirty-odd-year reign at Columbia, was nonetheless regarded as a reliable barometer of the motion picture industry, and if he said Rita Hayworth was the fourth most valuable star in Hollywood, then she *was*. And Cohn never let anyone forget that he was responsible for Hayworth's success.

Born Rita Cansino in 1919, the dark Latin beauty made her first motion picture appearance in 1926 in a ten-minute short subject produced by Vitagraph in Brooklyn, New York, and starring her family, The Dancing Cansinos. Rita's first feature film appearance was a dancing role filmed for Fox's 1935 *Dante's Inferno*, starring Spencer Tracy. She was given a Fox contract for her efforts and, in fact, two subsequent appearances (in *Under the Pampas Moon*, 1935, and *Charlie Chan in Egypt*, 1935) reached the screen before the official release of *Dante's Inferno*.

After appearing in minor roles at Fox and as an ingenue in numerous "B" Westerns for independent producers, Rita signed a contract with Columbia in 1937, where she was assigned to the Irving Briskin unit. Briskin, then making inexpensive program pictures, was charged with giving exposure to Columbia contract players, and toward this end, Rita did a series of memorable roles in largely unmemorable pictures such as *Girls Can Play* (1937), *Paid to Dance* (1937), and *Special Investigator* (1939). It was at Columbia that Rita's last name was changed from Cansino to Hayworth, and that she received the buildup and grooming necessary for stardom and obtainable at major studios. Her first major role at Columbia was the second female lead in Howard Hawks's *Only Angels Have Wings* (1939), and following favorable reaction to her performance, Rita was loaned to both M-G-M and Warner Bros. It was on loan to Twentieth Century-Fox, however, that Rita demonstrated her value as a star in the remake of *Blood and Sand* (1941), with Tyrone Power playing the Rudolph Valentino role. Hayworth, playing the fiery Dona Sol, gave a spectacular performance and returned to her home lot a star. She was immediately cast opposite Fred Astaire in *You'll Never Get Rich* (1941) and *You Were Never Lovelier* (1942). Loaned to Fox again for *My Gal Sal* (1942), and *Tales of Manhattan* (1942), Rita returned to Columbia in 1944 for two of her best pictures, *Cover Girl* (1944), starring Gene Kelly, and *Tonight and Every Night* (1944), with Janet Blair and Lee Bowman.

In 1945, Columbia decided to change Rita's image. Since her triumph in *Blood and Sand*, Cohn had cast her in big-budget musicals playing a warm, all-American girl. After a sultry pinup picture of Rita, clad in a nightgown and kneeling on a bed, had been distributed to millions of soldiers during the war, the decision was made to exploit Rita as a love goddess. Her long, luscious red hair, originally dyed for her role in *Blood and Sand*, and her voluptuous figure had been displayed in dozens of studio publicity stills, and Cohn decided to blend her appearance and fiery Latin image in a new film, *Gilda*. Although Cohn had envisioned the new potential here, not even he could have realized the effect that *Gilda* would have on Hayworth's career.

Gilda was one of the earliest postwar thrillers which, in predating what French critics would later describe as *film noir*, painted a darker side of life than Hollywood films had been accustomed to portray. Its story, heavily rewritten during production, was seamy and turgid, and director Charles Vidor, working closely with its stars, Hayworth and Glenn Ford, was able to deliver a film of smoldering sensuality.

Gilda begins with the narration of Johnny Farrell (Glenn Ford), a two-bit American gambler down on his luck in South America. While collecting his winnings from a crap game in a seedy section of Buenos Aires, Johnny is attacked by two thugs who attempt to rob him. He is saved by the timely intervention of Ballin Mundson (George Macready), a fashionable gentleman who frightens the would-be bandits off with a sword cane. Mundson introduces himself to Johnny as the owner of a luxurious gambling casino. Johnny is naturally suspicious of the stranger who invites him back to the casino, but he nevertheless goes. Mundson is looking for a man whom he can trust to assist in running the casino since he has other commitments which demand much of his time. Johnny finds himself curiously drawn to Ballin; they share many of the same attitudes and dislikes, and the young American accepts Mundson's proposal. The audience later learns that Ballin is the front man for a Nazi-backed cartel in Europe. In his new position at the casino, Johnny finds himself annoyed by the presence of Uncle Pio (Steven Geray), one of the casino's most philosophical employees.

Ballin returns to Buenos Aires after one of his mysterious trips with a new wife, Gilda (Rita Hayworth). When Johnny meets Gilda, he becomes aware of traits in her that he knows all too well, and while taking a dislike to her, he nonetheless respects her as Ballin's wife and assigns himself the task of watching her to make certain that she does not embarrass Ballin. A love-hate relationship soon develops between Gilda and Johnny, which is noted by Ballin. Ballin, however, soon finds himself in grave danger after killing one of his partners in crime; his cartel is exposed, and, refusing to give himself up, he flies his private plane into the sea, apparently comitting suicide.

Johnny marries Gilda, but not for love; he blames her for Ballin's suicide and is determined to see that she remains faithful to his memory. Gilda tortures herself over Johnny's hatred of her, and exhibits bizarre behavior, even attempting to make a spectacle of herself in the casino by doing an abortive striptease.

Ballin, having convinced everyone of his death, thereby averting a manhunt, returns to the casino to kill his trusted friend and loving wife, who have both betrayed him. Crazed by passion, he almost succeeds with the murders until the intervention by Uncle Pio, who stabs Ballin with his own stiletto. At this point in the film, plot and characterizations change abruptly, and Johnny and Gilda, now free from Ballin forever, are portrayed as, at last, being able to pursue their own happiness together.

The perplexed critics who reviewed the film on its initial release were puzzled by the abrupt shift in Gilda's character and the muddled motivations of the others as well. They found the plot, with good justification, to be confusing and pointless; but the film is rich in suggestive dialogue and steamy love scenes between Hayworth and Ford. Despite its poor reviews, *Gilda* was a huge success with the public, grossing more than three million dollars. It changed Rita Hayworth's career dramatically; and she found herself in later years forced, in picture after picture, to live up to the image created for her in this film.

Ed Hulse

GIRL CRAZY

Released: 1943
Production: Arthur Freed for Metro-Goldwyn-Mayer
Direction: Norman Taurog
Screenplay: Fred F. Finklehoffe; based on the musical play and book of the
   same name by Guy Bolton and Jack McGowan
Cinematography: William Daniels and Robert Planck
Editing: Albert Akst
Choreography: Charles Walters
Music: George Gershwin and Ira Gershwin
Running time: 99 minutes

> *Principal characters:*
> Danny Churchill, Jr. .... Mickey Rooney
> Ginger Gray .... Judy Garland
> Bud Livermore .... Gil Stratton
> Henry Lathrop .... Robert E. Strickland

   Girl Crazy is a Mickey Rooney/Judy Garland musical out of the "let's put on a show" mold. In several respects it is the best of the formula musicals which paired the two. The score by the Gershwins includes many of their classics. Norman Taurog, who replaced Busby Berkeley midway through the shooting, directed with more depth than Berkeley had in earlier Rooney/ Garland movies, with more sensitivity to the strengths of his leading players, and with less delight in creating "camp" musical numbers. Where Berkeley tended to stress the geometry of big production numbers with Rooney and Garland as figureheads who lead the band, Taurog set up simpler musical numbers which permitted greater subtleties.

   In *Girl Crazy*, Rooney and Garland finally grow up, despite the best intentions of a formula which saw them as kids on stage in film after film. For Judy Garland especially, *Girl Crazy* marks a change in presentation, although the script sees her, once again, as a teenager. This time she is Ginger Gray, the daughter of a college president. The character Garland once described as "Dorothy Adorable," once given free rein in *Babes on Broadway* (1941), *Babes in Arms* (1939), or the Andy Hardy movies, has, however, grown more complex. Ginger Gray shows the contradictory and ironic charm of the later Garland characters, both vulnerable and quick to laugh at herself in a way that the roles as "Dorothy Adorable" hardly suggest.

   The musical number which marks a transition point for this musical is "I Got Rhythm." It was the number which, according to several accounts, caused Berkeley to lose control of the movie. His idea for it involved very large ensembles with anonymous girls in fringe cracking whips and plenty of trick camera shots. Obviously this style buried the principal characters, who by this time were both important stars on the lot. Furthermore, the style reflected an approach to musicals that was becoming passé at M-G-M. Musicals such as those at which Berkeley excelled, which were collections of flashy production numbers only vaguely involving character development, were on their way out. M-G-M—especially the Freed production unit which handled big-budget musicals with big-name casts—was quickly adopting the style of the so-called "integrated" musical. In the integrated musicals, songs, dances, and plot all reflected and extended character development; each element deepened the understanding of the others. Berkeley films such as *Babes on Broadway* and *Babes in Arms* had used the "let's put on a show" format as an excuse for Garland, Rooney, and dozens of chorus people to concoct variety shows. They might do a melodramatic farce, a takeoff on Franklin D. Roosevelt, or a minstrel show—anything that might be performed on a stage. Meanwhile, offstage they were just kids who wanted to be onstage. Their roles were fleshed out just enough to allow the romantic subplot a conventional credibility. Berkeley followed this pattern in filming the "I Got Rhythm" sequence for *Girl Crazy*. But this time, there was enough disagreement with that concept among his coworkers to have Berkeley taken off the picture.

Although Taurog's direction and staging of the musical numbers reflected the beginnings of a new style in film musicals, the plot of *Girl Crazy* is altogether conventional. It involves reeducating a wayward youth in the simple values of a small-town, middle-class community. The young man, Danny Churchill, Jr. (Mickey Rooney), has lost sight of these values because he has too much money. The need to teach spoiled rich people what is truly valuable in life was a constant convention of Americana films made at M-G-M and other studios in that period. Also true to convention, Danny's means of education is a woman who has the integrity and proper sense of values he lacks, and who has faith that the man she loves will regain his appreciation of them.

Danny Churchill, Jr., is a college playboy who is sent to a boy's school in the West. There life is different for Danny, away from the comforts and influence his money has always supplied. No taxis meet him at the station; he walks. Once at the college, he is stricken at learning that he must rise daily at 6:00 A.M. Worse, he must suffer ignoble lessons in horseback riding. At first Danny's pride creates his problems, since he refuses to admit that he has anything to learn. Gradually, however, with the help of Ginger Gray (Judy Garland), his character improves. Danny's feelings for Ginger and for the school are completely changed for the better by the time a financial crisis hits the college. Money has run out, and the school is faced with closing. Ginger and Danny raise the money to save the school by staging a Western jamboree. Once again, Rooney and Garland "put on a show." The new school will be coeducational, and Danny and Ginger are classmates as the picture ends.

The filming of this variation on the familiar "let's put on a show" plot is what sets *Girl Crazy* apart from the earlier musicals. Not only are Rooney and Garland featured in virtually every scene, but they usually dominate the frame in Taurog's composition. The difference in style becomes glaringly apparent in the final production number, "I Got Rhythm," which Berkeley shot before leaving the picture. It is the only number which uses its main characters as solutions to geometry exercises. The numbers which Taurog shot are much less busy. Garland sings "Embraceable You," "But Not for Me." "Bidin' My Time," and other lesser-known Gershwin songs. Newcomer June Allyson appears in one specialty number at the film's beginning, and the popular band leader, Tommy Dorsey, plays in several numbers.

Leslie Donaldson

GIRL FRIENDS

Released: 1978
Production: Claudia Weill with Jan Saunders for Cyclops Films; released by Warner Bros.
Direction: Claudia Weill
Screenplay: Vicki Polon; based on an original story by Claudia Weill and Vicki Polon
Cinematography: Fred Murphy
Editing: Suzanne Pettit
Running time: 87 minutes

Principal characters:
Susan Weinblatt	Melanie Mayron
Anne Munroe	Anita Skinner
Martin	Bob Balaban
Ceil	Amy Wright
Rabbi Gold	Eli Wallach
Eric	Christopher Guest
Beatrice	Viveca Lindfors

Girl Friends is a small, quiet film that builds its whole effect out of individual scenes or moments rather than through an unmistakable exposition and a clear-cut plot line. At the beginning of the film we meet the two main characters, Susan Weinblatt (Melanie Mayron) and Anne Munroe (Anita Skinner); from then on we experience the happenings and crises of their lives just as they do, as separate events that sometimes arise out of or lead into the next event, and sometimes do not. *Girl Friends* is not, however, a difficult or obscure film; it merely stresses the emotions and reactions of the main characters rather than the shaping of the plot.

Both Susan and Anne are artistic young women sharing an apartment and a friendship as they attempt to find their way in life after college. Susan, from whose viewpoint most of the film is seen, makes her living photographing weddings and bar mitzvahs, but she also takes more serious and artistic photographs and tries to sell them to magazines and galleries. Anne writes poetry and reads it for Susan's approval.

When Anne becomes involved with Martin (Bob Balaban), we do not see him at first; we see only Anne discussing her feelings with Susan. Anne is initially quite tentative; "I think I almost might love him," she says, and in later discussions with Susan, she is ambivalent about whether she wants to be independent or wants to be taken care of by Martin. A minor climax in the film comes in an artful sequence of three scenes. Susan and Anne have picked out a new apartment, and Susan plans to paint one wall red. Then we see Anne in a laundromat as Susan bursts in with the news that three of her

pictures have been bought by a magazine. Sure that she is now on the way
to success, Susan exclaims that she will not have to photograph weddings any
more. "One more wedding," says Anne—she and Martin are getting married.
Susan tries to act happy, but she says, "How can you be sure when you're
so unsure?" Next we see black-and-white pictures of Anne's wedding as we
hear the voices of the people at the festivities. Then, as the voices continue,
we see Susan, alone, painting a wall red.

Susan has an unsatisfying experience with Eric (Christopher Guest), a man
she meets at a party. (We see her leave his apartment in the middle of the
night and take a taxicab home.) Then after a visit to Anne and Martin during
which she sees the pictures they took on their honeymoon in Morocco and
hears that they plan to go to Italy, Susan becomes depressed and goes to a
hairdresser (Albert Rogers) for a new look. When he tells her that the style
she has selected will not work with her face, she responds, "Will anything?"
She emerges with frizzy hair but no new success in her work and no contentment in living alone. Visiting Anne and Martin again, she sees an argument break out between them and learns that Anne is going back to school
because she feels so isolated.

Susan picks up a young woman hitchhiker, Ceil (Amy Wright), on the way
home and offers to let her stay in her apartment since she has no other place
to go. Ceil turns out to be an irritant as the weeks go by, making no effort
to find her own place, but Susan does nothing about the situation. She has
gone back to photographing weddings and bar mitzvahs and has a long enjoyable talk with the rabbi (Eli Wallach) with whom she works. It ends with the
rabbi kissing her and arranging to have lunch with her. When Anne comes
to see her soon afterward, Susan describes her relationship with the rabbi as
"bordering on mad passion." Anne is not at all sympathetic, however, because
he is married and much older than Susan. As it turns out, the rabbi cancels
the lunch because he is going to a football game with his family.

Tearful and upset, Susan finally tells Ceil to move out. At this point she
needs something good to happen to her; so she summons up her courage and
guile and manages to show her work to an important gallery owner, Mr.
Carpel (Roderick Cook). He does not accept her work but does recommend
her to another gallery owner, Beatrice (Viveca Lindfors), who likes her work
and arranges an exhibition of it. Soon she is happily anticipating her exhibition
and spending most of her time with Eric, whom she has begun seeing again.

A planned dinner for the four of them at Anne and Martin's, however,
precipitates another crisis. Eric does not want to go and at the last minute
says he is going to stay home and watch a football game. When Susan arrives
late, Anne explodes, causing an argument that brings out many of the latent
feelings of both women. Susan felt betrayed when Anne left to get married
and now half envies her security. Anne thinks Susan selfish because she sees
her so seldom and half-envies Susan's freedom. Not long after that Susan and

Eric have an argument. Susan says that she likes herself best when she does not need him and leaves.

When Susan's exhibition opens not long after, everyone she knows comes except Anne; even Eric appears. When Martin reports that Anne left for the country that morning and that he does not know why, Susan goes to the country and finds Anne playing solitaire and ignoring the ringing telephone. Anne says that she has just had an abortion without telling Martin, and Susan says that she is afraid to move in with Eric. The two proceed to get drunk together in their first moment of camaraderie since they lived together. Then a car arrives, and we hear Martin's voice ask, "May I?" as the camera freezes on Susan's face.

A great strength of *Girl Friends* is the fact that it explores various themes— chiefly the requirements of friendship and the conflicting desires for freedom and security—without being didactic and without making each character represent a certain position. Susan gives Anne a pep talk to convince her that she can take care of herself and does not need to rush into a marriage with Martin only because he will take care of her. When Anne does marry, however, Susan has trouble convincing herself of the benefits of independence.

Girl Friends was originally planned to be a short film about the two young women living together and facing the same problems, but the creators— intrigued with the idea of exploring what would happen to the two of them, especially Susan, if Anne moved out and married—expanded the story. The chief creators of the film are Claudia Weill and Vicki Polon. After the two worked out the story line together, drawing upon Weill's earlier experience as a free-lance still photographer, Polon wrote the entire screenplay, and Weill produced and directed the film. They wisely decided to keep the film less than ninety minutes long and thus avoided dissipating the fragile effect of the work.

Working on an extremely small budget, the filmmakers were fortunate to assemble an outstanding cast in which even the small parts are well played. Mayron as Susan has the largest role and superbly portrays the young Jewish woman's vulnerabilities and strengths without making her a stereotype. Nearly everyone else in the film could be singled out for praise, especially Wallach as the rabbi. He is appropriately gentle and fatherly, but in the scene in which he tells Susan that he originally wanted to be an actor and demonstrates to her how Marcel Marceau would do the lighting of the two cigarettes scene from *Now, Voyager* (1942), he reveals more of his character rather than of his acting ability.

Weill should get major credit for her directing, which artfully uses the camera without any tricky shots, and for evoking such good performances from the actors to provide a film that lingers in the mind.

Timothy W. Johnson

GO FOR BROKE

Released: 1951
Production: Dore Schary for Metro-Goldwyn-Mayer
Direction: Robert Pirosh
Screenplay: Robert Pirosh
Cinematography: Paul C. Vogel
Editing: James E. Newcom
Running time: 92 minutes

Principal characters:
Lieutenant Michael Grayson	Van Johnson
Sam	Lane Nakano
Frank	Akira Fukunaga
Ohhara	Henry Oyasato
Chick	George Miki
Kaz	Ken K. Okamoto
Masami	Harry Hamada
Tommy	Henry Nakamura

At the outbreak of World War II, Americans of Japanese ancestry were unwelcome in this country. In 1942, Franklin Delano Roosevelt's infamous Executive Order 9066 caused the separation of Japanese Americans from their communities and their relocation into special camps. Approximately 120,000 citizens, guilty only of their Japanese ancestry, were resettled in these "relocation centers." Japanese characters in radio and film series suddenly became Chinese; "Jap" and "nip" villains in Hollywood war films were portrayed by Chinese actors.

Americans of Japanese ancestry were not necessarily disloyal. Many, in fact, fought in the war as members of the 442nd Regimental Combat Team. With the exception of its officers, all of the soldiers in the regiment were Nisei—American-born Japanese. Their extraordinary battle accomplishments are depicted in a sincere, taut, realistic film, *Go for Broke*, released in 1951, six years after the war. The title comes from the 442nd's battle cry, which is Hawaiian dice-shooting slang meaning "shoot the works." The 442nd compiled a record unequaled by any unit during the war. The regiment, composed of three thousand men and six thousand replacements, all volunteers from the continental United States, Alaska, and Hawaii, was honored with more than nine thousand combat citations—more unit and individual awards in proportion to time spent in combat than any other military outfit.

Although Van Johnson appears as Lieutenant Michael Grayson, a young Texas platoon officer in charge of a group of Nisei soldiers, the stars of the film are a small group of men who prepare for and participate in battle. They meet at Camp Shelby, Mississippi, for training. Grayson, who is biased and bigoted, is wary of the Nisei's loyalty and courage and resists his assignment as group commander. He is particularly hard on his men, both during training and after they are shipped overseas to Italy and France. All of the traditional GI "types" are present among Grayson's charges: the smart sergeant, Sam (Lane Nakano); resident clown, Tommy (Henry Nakamura); lazy time-waster, Chick (George Miki); and loud "Irishman", Ohhara (Henry Oyasato). Once the bullets fly, however, they all faithfully defend their flag. A highlight is the team's rescue of the 26th Texas Division, where Grayson has been transferred to act as liaison officer between the companies, from annihilation in the Vosges Mountains, France. Finally, they are decorated in a ceremony at the White House. Grayson finally realizes the true mettle of the men and is proud to have served with them.

Go For Broke is a tightly directed, straightforwardly absorbing and non-romantic presentation of the horrors of war, and a commentary on racial tolerance as well. The soldiers of the 442nd Regimental Combat Team may be of Japanese ancestry, but they are Americans first. Their loyalty to their country is not measured by religion or skin color or ancestry but by the combat record of their regiment.

Although the story line is loose and actually unimportant to the overall impact of the film, the major thrust of the plot concerns the soldiers' attempts to prove that they are good soldiers, and, more importantly, good Americans. The characters are stereotypes of soldiers, perhaps, but not of Japanese. Each man has his own reason for entering the army, but eventually all are unified in their desire to be good combat soldiers. One particularly effective scene near the end of the film illustrates this point. When a startled group of Germans surrender to the 442nd, they ask what kind of soldiers they are—"Chinese?" No, they reply, "Americans."

The film was shot primarily with amateur actors, which was a first for a major Metro-Goldwyn-Mayer production. To the credit of screenwriter/director Robert Pirosh and producer Dore Schary, Chinese or non-Oriental actors were not hired for *Go for Broke*. The soldiers are portrayed by actual "Heroes of the 442nd Regimental Combat Team" re-creating their combat experiences on the screen. More than six hundred veterans answered the studio's newspaper and radio casting call. No previous acting experience was required, and Pirosh coached the men for a month before shooting began. The film's consultant was Mike Masaoka, the first volunteer with the 442nd when it was activated in 1943. Masaoka was one of five brothers who served; four were wounded, and one was killed in action.

In 1949, Pirosh had won a Best Story and Screenplay Academy Award for the Schary-produced *Battleground*, a grim re-creation of the Battle of the Bulge as experienced by the soldiers of an American airborne infantry division. The goal in *Go for Broke* was similar: to present a gutsy, dramatic, but decidedly unglamorous view of war with flavorful GI talk and realistic battle scenes; and to highlight the accomplishments of the 442nd. The soldiers in both films are not superficially heroic but are men, human beings with fears, hopes, complaints, and senses of humor. The film is sometimes a bit too idealistic. Flowery commentary accompanies marching and landing sequences, and racist Texans far too broadly accept the Nisei. These are minor flaws, however; *Go for Broke* is a generally excellent production. The soldiers are not martyrs, just good and dedicated GI's.

Go for Broke is Pirosh's first film as a director and easily his best effort. He is a successful Hollywood screenwriter; in addition to *Go for Broke* and *Battleground*, he wrote *A Day at the Races* (1937), *I Married a Witch* (1942), *Up in Arms* (1944), and *What's So Bad About Feeling Good?* (1968). Several of the *Go for Broke* actors had limited screen careers. The most prolific was Nakamura, the pint-sized Nisei who plays the outfit's comedian, who is as tough a soldier as any of his comrades. He was featured in *Westward the Women* (1952), *Athena* (1954), *Unchained* (1955), and *Blood Alley* (1955). Nakano, who is particularly fine as the sergeant, also played in *Japanese War Bride* (1952). Akira Fukunaga had a role in *Beachhead* (1954), and Harry Hamada was in *The Frogmen* (1951).

The film received laudatory reviews, with Nakamura's performance singled out. It was a box-office success, and with a gross of $2,500,000, it was ranked a respectable twentieth on *Variety*'s list of 1951's top-earning films. Pirosh received another Best Story and Screenplay Oscar nomination, but, unlike for *Battleground*, he did not win, losing to Alan Jay Lerner for *An American in Paris*.

Rob Edelman

GO TELL THE SPARTANS

Released: 1978
Production: Allan F. Bodoh and Mitchell Cannold for Mar Vista Productions;
　released by Avco Embassy
Direction: Ted Post
Screenplay: Wendell Mayes; based on the novel *Incident at Muc Wa* by Daniel
　Ford
Cinematography: Harry Stradling, Jr.
Editing: Millie Moore
Music: Dick Halligan
Running time: 114 minutes

　　Principal characters:
　　　　Major Asa Barker .... Burt Lancaster
　　　　Corporal Courcey .... Craig Wasson
　　　　Sergeant Oleonowski .... Jonathan Goldsmith
　　　　Captain Olivetti .... Marc Singer
　　　　Lieutenant Hamilton .... Joe Unger
　　　　Cowboy .... Evan Kim
　　　　General Harnitz .... Dolph Sweet
　　　　One-eyed man .... Tad Horino

Go Tell the Spartans is set in Vietnam, 1964, when the United States had
only twelve thousand "military advisers" in the country, and a large issue in
the American presidential election campaign was whether Americans were
going to be sent to do what the Vietnamese should be doing for themselves.
The film tells the story of one mission by a Military Advisory Assistance
Group stationed in Penang, but in this specific episode we see the enormity
or futility of the entire American involvement in that country. As is usual in
war films, the members of the unit represent a wide variety of backgrounds
and attitudes, but *Go Tell the Spartans* transcends didactic intent and stereotyped characters. It is a fully realized human tragicomedy firmly rooted in a
particular moment of American history.

In command of the Advisory Group is Major Asa Barker (Burt Lancaster),
a weary veteran of World War II and the Korean War. His aide is Captain
Olivetti (Marc Singer), a gum-chewing young officer with a somewhat cynical
view of his duties and the American effort. Olivetti's chief interest is in
furthering his military career; he expects to be at least a Brigadier General
before he is forty years old.

The film opens with telling details and quickly but artfully establishes its
milieu and cast of characters while deceptively introducing the central focus
of the plot. After Barker restrains the overzealous, even bloodthirsty, Vietnamese interpreter, Cowboy (Evan Kim), from further torturing a prisoner,

he goes to his office where two duties await him: a request for a "complete position paper" on a Vietnamese town of which he has never heard, and a group of new men that he is to receive into the outfit and assign to jobs. He takes care of the position paper first. Because he does not have enough men to investigate the location and because he does not believe in trying to establish and defend static positions, he directs Olivetti to write up and send in a paper stating that the town, Muc Wa, contains only two hundred people and is of no strategic importance.

After supposedly disposing of Muc Wa, Barker meets the new men, one by one. Lieutenant Hamilton (Joe Unger) is patriotic but naïve and expresses his fervent wish to kill Communists for his country. His idealistic statements are greeted with jaded cynicism by Barker and Olivetti. Sergeant Oleonowski (Jonathan Goldsmith) is a battle-weary veteran who has been transferred from the Delta region of Vietnam and who also served under Barker in Korea. Corporal Courcey (Craig Wasson) is the one who most puzzles Barker. He is a college graduate and a draftee who has volunteered for Vietnam even though that increases his period of service by six months. He either cannot or will not give the Major a credible explanation for his decision.

The new men are given whatever jobs Barker can concoct for them since the duties of the Advisory Group are ill-defined and the training and capabilities of the men are ill-suited to those duties that are defined. Hamilton and Courcey, for example, are assigned to the mosquito patrol, which consists of exposing their arms to mosquitos and counting the number of bites. This absurdity is, however, exchanged for another when General Harnitz (Dolph Sweet) arrives by helicopter to tell Barker that he knows his position paper on Muc Wa was faked and that, in fact, Barker's Group has been assigned the task of establishing and defending a garrison at the abandoned outpost. Barker knows that he has neither the men nor the equipment for such a mission and that the garrison will be an inviting target for the Viet Cong, but he must follow the orders.

Hamilton is assigned to command the Muc Wa unit with Oleonowski and Courcey and two other Americans completing the advisory team. Hamilton begins an idealistic speech about defending freedom to the Vietnamese he is to lead, but he stops when the ragged collection of Vietnamese mercenaries, regular soldiers, and farmers bursts into laughter at his words when they are translated by Cowboy, who is also part of the Muc Wa unit.

At Muc Wa they find very little except a French cemetery, the result of another attempt by outsiders to defend the location. At the cemetery gate is a sign that Courcey translates as "Stranger, when you find us lying here, go tell the Spartans we obeyed their orders." It is a quote from fifth century B. C. Greek historian Herodotus about the battle of Thermopylae in 480 B. C. in which three hundred Spartans died defending a pass, and it will prove only too relevant to current events once again.

When a group of Vietnamese appear at the river near the garrison, Cowboy insists that they are Viet Cong, but Hamilton says, "They don't look like Communists to me," and Courcey gives them chocolate and tries to make friends with them. Oleonowski, who has virtually taken over command of the unit because of Hamilton's inexperience and severe attack of dysentery, is infuriated that the people have been brought into the garrison. The audience is given no clue as to whether they are Viet Cong. Indeed, throughout the film the audience is often left wondering whether such characters as Oleonowski are overly cynical or merely realistic. Later Cowboy shoots the group of Vietnamese and claims that they were Viet Cong stealing weapons from the garrison, but the situation is so murky that the audience cannot be absolutely sure that he did not fake the evidence because of his own paranoia or bloodthirstiness.

When a patrol led by Oleonowski is attacked and he returns to Muc Wa leaving a wounded Vietnamese on the other side of the river, Hamilton insists on personally going to get the man. When he reaches him, the man is dead, and Hamilton is killed as he tries to return. This is somehow the last straw for the battle-weary, burnt-out Oleonowski; he exclaims that he is "tired of dinks" and kills himself. (Throughout the film the Vietnamese are referred to as "dinks" or "slopes" and the Viet Cong as "Charlie.")

Barker now has to visit a Vietnamese Colonel (Clyde Kasatsu) to convince him to supply additonal troops and mortar support to Muc Wa. The discussion takes place in the Colonel's ornate and lavishly appointed house. Only by promising the Colonel a large number of extra mortar shells is Barker able to obtain his promise of support. When Muc Wa is attacked and needs air support, however, the air support is refused because there is a rumor of a coup in Saigon, and the South Vietnamese want to save all their military strength for possible use against their own political opponents. Major Barker finally gets the support through a colorful and graphic threat he telegraphs to General Harnitz, but after the battle is over the High Command decides that the garrison should be abandoned, or "exfiltrated," because intelligence shows that the Viet Cong are increasing their pressure on the outpost.

A helicopter, with Barker aboard, arrives to evacuate the "defenders" of Muc Wa. When Courcey sees that only the Americans are going to be allowed on the helicopter, he insists on staying with the Vietnamese. The Americans, he says, cannot simply leave the Vietnamese behind—they brought them to Muc Wa. Barker, inexplicably, stays behind also, and the two have a long discussion as they prepare to leave the camp. Barker says that Courcey is a tourist, out to visit a war. As they leave that night with the Vietnamese, they are ambushed and both Courcey and Barker are wounded. The next morning Courcey awakens to find himself the only survivor. He walks to the cemetery, is almost shot by a strange one-eyed man he had seen there before (Tad Horino), and turns and says, "I'm going home, Charlie."

Go Tell the Spartans is excellent in virtually every aspect. Lancaster gives one of the very best performances of his long career, but he does not overshadow the realistic and often moving acting by the ensemble of relative unknowns. Particularly noteworthy are Goldsmith as the veteran burned out not only by fighting but also by trying to determine an American's place in this Asian war; Singer as the Captain who thinks he can keep a realistic outlook on the war and still use it to advance his military career; and Wasson as Courcey, the Corporal who discovers the difficulty of being a tourist in a war.

Underlying all these human stories, of course, are the larger issues of the war, which the United States was never able to resolve satisfactorily. The American soldiers are unable to understand the war or their place in it. When one Vietnamese brutalizes another, Oleonowski tells the other Americans to ignore the incident. "It's *their* war," he says. A medic who is aiding a wounded Vietnamese remarks that the wounded man could change places with the "slope" who shot him and he would not know the difference. Indeed, the Americans are never able to tell which Vietnamese are on which side until the shooting starts.

In the midst of this confusion, however, the American command decides to establish and defend an outpost at Muc Wa, endangering many Americans and Vietnamese to do so, but the Vietnamese Colonel must be bribed with ammunition to support the effort, and at the crucial time power struggles among Vietnamese on "our" side are more important than the effort against the Vietnamese on the "other" side. Compounding the irony and absurdity is the ultimate decision to abandon Muc Wa.

Ted Post's direction is never pretentious and never pedestrian. He and cinematographer Harry Stradling, Jr., aided by Dick Halligan's effective music, keep the emphasis upon what is happening rather than on landscapes or ostentatious effects. It is, perhaps, this lack of ostentation, the largely unknown cast and director, and the refusal of the filmmakers to sugar-coat uncomfortable issues that kept *Go Tell the Spartans* from achieving the fame of such Vietnam-related films as *Apocalypse Now* (1979) and *Coming Home* (1978), but the virtues of *Go Tell the Spartans* were noticed by many critics, several of whom said it was one of the ten best films of 1978 and two of whom, Stanley Kauffmann and John Simon, said it was the best film they had then seen about the Vietnam war.

Timothy W. Johnson

THE GODDESS

Released: 1958
Production: Milton Perlman for Columbia
Direction: John Cromwell
Screenplay: Paddy Chayefsky
Cinematography: Arthur J. Ornitz
Editing: Carl Lerner
Running time: 104 minutes

Principal characters:
Rita Shawn	Kim Stanley
Dutch Seymour	Lloyd Bridges
John Tower	Steve Hill
Mrs. Faulkner	Betty Lou Holland
Nurse	Elizabeth Wilson
Emily Ann Faulkner (later Rita Shawn)	Patty Duke

Being a so-called movie goddess, the idol of millions, hardly points the way to happiness. Paddy Chayefsky's original screenplay *The Goddess* details the life-story of such a star, doomed from childhood to loneliness and discontent. It is told in the realistic style expected of director John Cromwell, who has nevertheless created some haunting moments that are almost sheer poetry in their revelations of a human soul in torment. The story is divided into three parts: Portrait of a Young Girl, Portrait of a Young Woman, and Portrait of a Goddess. Much of the power of the film is generated by Kim Stanley, making her screen debut as the goddess.

The opening scenes set in a small town in the South have a kind of early Tennessee Williams starkness about them. Rita Shawn, as a little girl named Emily Ann Faulkner (Patty Duke), is a fatherless child whose mother, Mrs. Faulkner (Betty Lou Holland), is loquacious and giddy, and works in a five-and-dime store. In school Emily has no close friends; there is something uncommunicative about her that makes other children withdraw in her presence. They do not invite her to participate in their games or to be their companion or friend. Yet there are special days when she needs to communicate. One of these is the day of her graduation from grade school. She tries to tell schoolmates, even strangers, of her accomplishment, but no one will listen. She goes to the store where her mother works, but her mother is busy between sales gossiping with other store attendants, and tells her daughter abruptly to go home; she will see her later. Emily obediently goes to the house where she lives with her mother, and a pet cat commands her attention. Emily pours some milk into a sauce dish and crawls under the kitchen table with the cat. She strokes it fondly, and then whispers in confidence, "Today I graduated."

Emily's life as a teenager (Kim Stanley) is not much different. She is still lonely, and none of the girls her age is a close companion. Her mother now has discovered Jesus, and nightly goes off to sing hymns in praise of the Lord. There is only one change in the even tenor of Emily's days: boys are interested in her. They are drawn to her, because she radiates sexuality to them. She is known as a "hot date" and has no difficulty getting partners at any dance. Although she is not a great beauty, there is something magnetic about her that makes men want to sleep with her. She teases and leads them on, but in the case of one young man, John Tower (Steve Hill), she takes him as a lover and then becomes his wife.

It is not a happy marriage; they have nothing in common, other than the fact that John finds her irresistible sexually, and she does not mind him. John does get her away from the ugly little Southern town, however, and she meets an up-and-coming young prizefighter, Dutch Seymour (Lloyd Bridges). Life with Dutch becomes fun because he moves in a constantly changing social scene. Indifferent to John, she leaves him and marries Dutch. It is inevitable that she meets with theater people, and because of her sensitivity and imagination, she comes alive as an actress. The camera opens a new world to her, and she blossoms while the lenses focus upon her.

Dutch is forgotten and abandoned as his wife climbs to stardom as Rita Shawn. A studio head, signing her to a starring contract, informs her significantly that she will be expected at his house later that evening. Now on a higher echelon is that same existence spelling only further, more acute loneliness for her. She becomes a sex goddess, and her fans worship her. Living on a Hollywood hill in a big modern Hollywood house, she sends for her mother, who predictably is no friend and companion—she never was. She is only a reminder of all that Rita never had as a child. The mother by now has become a religious fanatic and is all too aware of her daughter's sinful ways, but masochistically blames herself.

Rita continues to sleep her way around town, but she also withdraws more and more into another fantasy world, and not even doctors and pills are of any help to her. When her mother dies, she breaks down completely. The only companion she has now is the secretary-nurse (Elizabeth Wilson) paid to stay with her and keep her sedated. On film and to the world, Rita is still a goddess, but it is no longer easy for her to work before the camera. Broken and ill, she is kept alive by sedation and drugs. There is no hope, and it is obvious that the day will soon come when she is no longer a goddess on a pedestal.

The Goddess is one of the better than truer portraits of Hollywood. Actually, there are not many shots taken in Hollywood itself, since the motion picture was filmed largely in the East; but the spirit of a Hollywood that once existed breathes in the film, and Rita Shawn is not unlike some of the past real goddesses of Hollywood, such as Clara Bow and Marilyn Monroe. Some critics named Ava Gardner as the star who had inspired Chayefsky's story, but Gardner was, and is, a beauty, while the point is constantly made that Rita Shawn is not beautiful. She has sexual allure, and her charisma makes her famous. Like all goddesses who epitomize sex, Rita has probably never known a completely happy sexual relationship; men desire her body and use it, but it brings her nothing but a restless lack of fulfillment.

Stanley is in many ways perfectly cast for the part. She is cleverly photographed in the scenes where she is young so that her own personal maturity does not always show, and she does give the illusion of a kind of sexual beauty; in the last half of the picture, when Rita Shawn is mature, she is obviously at home in the part. Ironically, the film might be, in a sense, autobiographical. Stanley starred brilliantly on the Broadway stage, and was regarded by many as the best new actress in the theater. *The Goddess* marked a delayed film debut, and she got stunning notices, but she only played once again in films, in the London-filmed *Séance on a Wet Afternoon*, which won her an Academy Award nomination in 1964 as Best Actress. She flew to London again in 1972 to play with Katharine Hepburn and Paul Scofield in *A Delicate Balance*, but when she had to go before the cameras, she could not do it, and had to be replaced. She had often experienced neurotic spells during her acting career, and after filming *Séance on a Wet Afternoon*, she suffered a complete breakdown. She retired then to New Mexico, her native state, and for a time lived in Taos, eventually getting well enough to teach retarded children. She now lives in Santa Fe and is a full-time drama instructor at the College of Santa Fe. She directs productions for the campus playhouse, known as the Greer Garson Theatre, where one of her most successful productions was William Inge's *Bus Stop*, which in 1955 had won her the New York Drama Critics' Award as Best Actress.

The Goddess has been a much-admired film. Critically, it is still regarded favorably and always draws plaudits in any retrospective devoted to films about Hollywood or the motion pictures of John Cromwell. Cromwell returned to directing with *The Goddess* after a three-year absence from film production. Cromwell was apparently blacklisted by Howard Hughes, for whom he directed *The Racket* in 1958, but he kept busy by going back to the theater, where he never had any difficulty working as director or actor. He had been one of the first top stage directors to come to Hollywood at the beginning of talkies at Paramount in 1929. He worked constantly during the 1930's, 1940's, and into the 1950's, mostly at Paramount, RKO, and Twentieth Century-Fox, and was especially happy working for David O. Selznick, directing such films as *Little Lord Fauntleroy* (1936), the elegant remake starring Ronald Colman of *The Prisoner of Zenda* (1937), *Made for Each Other* (1938), and Selznick's big World War II special about the war at home, *Since You Went Away* (1944). Cromwell, now in his nineties, is still highly respected in the film world, to which he returned as a character actor for Robert Altman's recent *The Wedding* (1979), playing the senile priest who cannot remember the words of the wedding ceremony. He did wonders for Stanley in her film debut in *The Goddess*. An actor himself, he always put actors at ease, and they gave their best for him.

The Goddess has attracted new admirers over the years, and will undoubtedly continue to be one of the most highly regarded of those films about the Hollywood scene. It is one of the truest and the most poignantly tragic.

DeWitt Bodeen

THE GODFATHER

Released: 1972
Production: Albert S. Ruddy for Alfran Productions; released by Paramount (AA)
Direction: Francis Ford Coppola
Screenplay: Mario Puzo and Francis Ford Coppola (AA); based on the novel of the same name by Mario Puzo
Cinematography: Gordon Willis
Editing: William Reynolds and Peter Zinner
Music: Nino Rota
Makeup: Dick Smith and Philip Rhodes
Running time: 175 minutes

Principal characters:

Don Vito Corleone	Marlon Brando (AA)
Michael Corleone	Al Pacino
Sonny Corleone	James Caan
Clemenza	Richard Castellano
Tom Hagen	Robert Duvall
Kay Adams	Diane Keaton
Captain McClusky	Sterling Hayden
Jack Woltz	John Marley
Barzini	Richard Conte
Sollozzo	Al Lettieri
Tessio	Abe Vigoda
Fredo Corleone	John Cazale
Connie Corleone Rizzi	Talia Shire
Carlo Rizzi	Gianni Russo
Mamma Corleone	Morgana King
Johnny Fontane	Al Martino
Luca Brasi	Lenny Montana

A quintessential gangster film that elevates the longstanding popular genre to the highest level of art, *The Godfather* portrays a Mafia organization that is a malevolent extension of the ethics of capitalism and the free enterprise system. Its Sicilian-American "family" serves as a metaphor for corrupt big business and government. At one point in the film, the heads of the underworld sit around a large conference table as if they comprise a corporate board of directors. At another point, Michael Corleone (Al Pacino) says that his father, Don Vito (Marlon Brando), is "no different from any other powerful man." "You're being naïve," responds his Anglo-Saxon girl friend, Kay Adams (Diane Keaton), "Senators and Congressmen don't have people killed." "Who's being naïve now, Kay?" Michael replies.

Nearly three hours in length, and played without intermission, the massive epic costing $6,300,000 had a large ready-made audience since it was based on Mario Puzo's best-selling novel. Italian-American Puzo adapted his own work for the screen, keeping the action close to that of the book. His cowriter on the script, and the film's director, was another Italian-American, Francis Ford Coppola. Coppola had previously been responsible for the screenplays of *Reflections in a Golden Eye* (1967) and *Patton* (1970).

Reminiscent of Orson Welles's *Citizen Kane* (1941) and Luchino Visconti's *Rocco and His Brothers* (1961) and *The Damned* (1969), *The Godfather* is a powerful story tracing the history of a Mafia clan, showing how its members live, how they work, and how they die. Because they feared a negative image, the Italian-American Civil Rights League saw to it that Paramount hired a League member to assist on the production and insisted that the words "Mafia" and "Cosa Nostra" be removed from the script. We see the close-knit Corleone family as folksy people, with their wives, their babies, and their subculture, with its ritualistic funerals, baptisms, and weddings replete with "vino," the tarantella, mandolin music, and Sicilian folk songs. We also experience the flavor of Italian home life and witness the ethnic preoccupation with food, as pasta is prepared in the kitchen.

The patriarch of the clan is the Godfather himself, Don Vito Corleone. Ostensibly a gentle man, the aging Don is seen inhaling the fragrance of a rose, stroking a cat as it sits on his lap, and proudly dancing with his daughter at her wedding. A scene depicting the playful Don doting on his grandson in the garden is particularly charming, with its natural, seemingly improvised quality. The Don is only seemingly benign, however. Just as in the garden scene when the Don inserts a bit of orange rind into his mouth to scare and tease the child, the film shows that the Godfather is really a monster. He is a man made rich by corrupt unions and gambling houses and by wielding enormous power as he metes out favors and punishments, orders men to be murdered, and makes offers one "cannot refuse." Indeed, the Don is the chieftain of one of the five most ruthless families of the criminal underworld. Thus the film serves as a powerful metaphor for the separation between private and public lives.

A period piece set between 1945 and 1955 in New York City; New Jersey; and the Long Beach, Long Island, family compound, *The Godfather* begins with the wedding of the Don's daughter Connie (Talia Shire) to Carlo Rizzi (Gianni Russo). At this point, the family's cultural roots are revealed as are the principal characters and their relationships.

It is a custom for the father of the bride to grant favors to all who ask, and during the wedding reception, the Don attends to business: he sees to it that the assaulters of one supplicant's daughter receive proper "justice" and that his godson, the famous singing idol Johnny Fontane (Al Martino), receives a part in a Hollywood movie. Overseeing these activites is Tom Hagen (Robert Duvall), the Don's non-Italian adopted son and "consigliere" (adviser) whose law degree gives the dynasty a respectable façade and a veneer of class. At the wedding we are introduced also to the Godfather's three sons: Fredo (John Cazale), shy, vulnerable, and weak; Michael (Al Pacino), the Ivy League-educated, sensitive, and withdrawn marine captain and war hero; and Sonny (James Caan), the sexually athletic, hot-blooded extrovert.

When the rival "capo" Sollozzo (Al Lettieri) wants to introduce heroin dealings into the Mafia operations, Don Vito refuses—not for moral reasons, but because he does not want to jeopardize his relations with his political contacts. In the course of the ensuing bloody gang war for control of the entire Mafia empire, the Godfather is gunned down by two rival henchmen as he walks across a street; he is severely wounded but not killed. Taking over the reins is his volatile oldest son, Sonny; the big, boisterous, violent successor soon becomes a victim of his own unleashed passions, however. Following his assault on Carlo for beating his sister Connie, Sonny is ambushed with Carlo's help and killed at a highway toll bridge.

With Don Vito now retired, Michael, the youngest and favorite son, becomes the next chieftain. Though he originally wanted to have his own legitimate identity away from the Corleone "business," the murder attempt on his father and Sonny's assassination changes Michael's mind and plans. He becomes inextricably involved after he kills Sollozzo and McCluskey (Sterling Hayden), a corrupt police captain. After hiding out in a village in Sicily, and after the brutal killing of his young Italian wife, Apollonia, by a rival gang, Michael returns home as the hardened new Don.

No longer naïve, Michael is now shrewd, devious, and ruthless. Following his marriage to Kay Adams and the death of his father, Don Vito, Michael expands his family's operations into prostitution, narcotics, and legal Nevada gambling enterprises. In the end, he coldbloodedly orders Barzini (Richard Conte), a prime enemy and rival boss, to be murdered, and has his loyal hit man, Clemenza (Richard Castellano), assassinate the weak and treacherous Carlo Rizzi. Closing the door on his wife Kay, Michael, now a methodical murderer, also lies to her; in the film's final shot, he tells Kay that he is not responsible for the brutal death of his sister's husband Carlo. Michael then accepts the kiss of his ring from his followers.

A "blockbuster" of a film, with tremendous mass appeal, *The Godfather* was a critical and commercial success. Along with such movies as *Gone with the Wind* (1939), *The Sound of Music* (1965), and *Jaws* (1975), it became and has remained one of the all-time box-office favorites. Not only did the film have an excellent screenplay, extraordinary direction, and outstanding production values, it also had a brilliant cast.

Marlon Brando's portrayal of the Godfather is a genuine *tour de force*. Along with Dick Smith's unique makeup (Smith was also responsible for Cicily Tyson's makeup in *The Autobiography of Miss Jane Pittman* on television, as well as Dustin Hoffman's in *Little Big Man*, 1970), the forty-seven-year-old non-Italian Brando was transformed into a sixty-two-year-old Sicilian-American. With an elaborate mouthplate that extended his jowls to create a pugnacious bulldoglike jaw, dirty teeth, drooping eyelids, graying temples, and a pencil-thin moustache, Smith and Brando create the look of a paunchy (padded), slightly feeble, stiffly moving man, dressed in fedoras and overcoats or in his formal wear with its stand-up collar. With his harsh, guttural, rasping whisper, his slightly mumbling Italian accent, his mannerism of scratching his cheek with one finger, and his mirthless smile, Brando's characterization combines terror and tenderness as he moves from the demeanor of invincibility, to deterioration, to death in the idyllic garden. A performer of great control (although, as usual, he often forgot his lines and needed to rely on hidden cue cards), Brando is riveting. Although the part of the Don is not a particularly large one, the Godfather's presence dominates the picture; for his role, Brando won the Oscar for the Best Actor of 1972.

Ironically, Brando nearly failed to get the part. Numerous others were talked about for the role—Laurence Olivier, George C. Scott, Frank Sinatra, Lee J. Cobb, Carlo Ponti, and many others. Most important, however, Brando was considered a virtually "unbankable" star. His reputation for temperament on the set was noted in *Mutiny on the Bounty* (1962) and *One-Eyed Jacks* (1961), and though still a technically brilliant actor, he had not given a really satisfying performance in years. Some of his "clinkers" included *A Countess from Hong Kong* (1967) and *Candy* (1968).

Coppola wanted to use the star, however, and Brando himself was extremely eager for the role, so he tested for the part. At the audition, Brando used such props as a cup of expresso, an Italian stogie, and a plate of apples and cheese; he also put shoe polish under his eyes and stuffed wads of tissue paper in his cheeks. Brando was hired with a minimal salary, but he was given a percentage of the film's considerable profits. Brando's performance in *The Godfather* is so stunning that it revitalized his reputation and brought him back to eminence, allowing him to go on to other interesting parts in *Last Tango in Paris* (1973), *Superman* (1978), and Coppola's own *Apocalypse Now* (1979).

Interestingly, when Brando won the Academy Award, he sent an Apache Indian militant named Sasheen Little Feather to speak at the ceremonies on his behalf. Announcing through her that he was declining the Oscar as a protest against film and television treatment of the Indian, Brando once again made cinema news. His proclamation, and decline of the award, were greeted with "boos" at the televised ceremonies and scathing comments in the press.

The Italian-American actor Al Pacino, young and relatively unknown at the time (his only previous film was *The Panic in Needle Park*, 1971), is magnificent in the pivotal role of Michael Corleone. Originally, both Warren Beatty and Jack Nicholson were considered for the part, but the brooding, callow, and ferocious Pacino creates a multifaceted character of tremendous variety and depth. Michael convincingly moves from a nervous young G.I. to a menacing Mafia leader.

James Caan, who had starred previously in Coppola's *The Rain People* (1969), is effective as the high-spirited, ill-fated Sonny, whose explosively hot temper leads to his downfall. John Cazale, another Italian-American, is sympathetic as the timid, feckless, and slightly dim-witted Fredo; he is particularly amusing as he attempts to be a Las Vegas "stud" and particularly affecting as he sits next to his father's bullet-riddled body and helplessly wails. Robert Duvall (who, along with Brando, would star in Coppola's *Apocalypse Now*) is believable as Tom Hagen, the Don's counselor, valet, and advance man. Hagen makes it clear that he is totally unapologetic about who he is and about what he is doing.

Shot mostly at New York locations (Brooklyn, the Bronx, Manhattan, and Staten Island), *The Godfather* is beautifully photographed by Gordon Willis. The camera moves back and forth between light and dark scenes, as when we see the Godfather in the darkened, closed room with patterned shadows on the walls created by the shutters, and then are transported to the bright exterior light of the wedding. Thematically, the lighting reflects the dual nature of the family and of a man who is warm and generous and is also a murderer. Some interiors have the burnt-umber look of old photographs, and the outdoor tableaux of the garden party and the Sicilian interlude are bathed in warm sunlight. Unlike the visual style of most films of the period, *The Godfather* makes little use of jarring close-ups, fast cuts, or zoom shots.

Warren Clyner's art direction and Dean Tavoularis' production design are superb and accurate down to the smallest, well-researched details. The (post-World War II) period is excellently re-created with such details as the handbills and street posters of Dean Martin and Jerry Lewis, the old-time autos and taxis, the movie marquee announcing Ingrid Bergman and Bing Crosby in *The Bells of St. Mary's*, and the song "Have Yourself a Merry Little Christmas." The musical score is also outstanding. Written by Nino Rota, who also composed the music for Fellini's *La Strada* (1954), *8½* (1963), and *La Dolce Vita* (1959), as well as for *The Taming of the Shrew* (1967) and *Romeo and Juliet* (1966), *The Godfather*'s musical theme has since become a classic.

William Reynolds' and Peter Zinner's brazen editing is equally effective. With the score here by J. S. Bach, the camera cuts back and forth between Michael at the baptismal ceremony for his sister Connie's baby (where he literally becomes a godfather) and the bloody extermination of the rival families that Michael has arranged to take place. The scenes of violence make effective use of special effects and stunts. For example, Sonny's death scene, in which a 1941 Lincoln Continental wired with 110 explosive charges is blown up, cost $100,000 to film.

A richly textured and dramatic portrait of racketeers and the underworld,

The Godfather shows the viewer violence as a way of life. The violence is realistic and gory, graphically depicting a strangulation, a hoodlum's hand being pinned to the table with a knife, a machine-gunning, and a mass murder. In one chilling scene, the movie mogul, forced into signing the singer for his movie, slowly awakens to find the severed and bloody head of his prize stallion in his bed; the scene is accompanied by the man's horrified screams. Interestingly, there is little sex in the film.

More than merely a taut action melodrama, *The Godfather* is a compelling psychological character study of inner motivations and relationships, as well as a sociological study of a deplorable aspect of American society. Characters are not reduced to stereotypes, nor are they sentimentalized. We see that the family is made up of racists, liars, hypocrites, and killers. We may empathize with them to some degree, but we do not condone their life style.

It is the artistry of Francis Ford Coppola that pulls the enormous production together. Although as a director he had never had a hit film before this one (he had done the low-budget *You're a Big Boy Now*, 1966 and the big-budget flop *Finian's Rainbow*, 1968), Coppola manifests his overall unifying vision in *The Godfather*. Elaborate, haunting, frightening, and gripping, *The Godfather* is a towering achievement. The Academy Award-winning film was eventually sold to television for ten million dollars, and was followed by an equally magnificent sequel, *The Godfather, Part II* (1974).

Leslie Taubman

THE GODFATHER, PART II

Released: 1974
Production: Francis Ford Coppola for Paramount (AA)
Direction: Francis Ford Coppola (AA)
Screenplay: Francis Ford Coppola and Mario Puzo (AA); based on the novel
  The Godfather by Mario Puzo
Cinematography: Gordon Willis
Editing: Peter Zinner, Barry Malkin, and Richard Marks
Art direction: Dean Tavoularis and Angelo Graham (AA); set decoration,
  George R. Nelson (AA)
Costume design: Theadora Van Runkle
Music direction: Carmine Coppola
Music: Nino Rota, with additional music by Carmine Coppola (AA)
Running time: 200 minutes

Principal characters:

Michael Corleone	Al Pacino
Tom Hagen	Robert Duvall
Kay Corleone	Diane Keaton
Vito Corleone	Robert De Niro (AA)
Fredo Corleone	John Cazale
Connie Corleone Rizzi	Talia Shire
Hyman Roth	Lee Strasberg
Mama Corleone	Morgana King
Merle Johnson	Troy Donahue
Tessio	Abe Vigoda
Carlo	Gianni Russo
FBI Man	Harry Dean Stanton
Senator	Roger Corman
Sonny Corleone	James Caan
Frankie Pentangeli	Michael Gazzo

Like a great nineteenth century novel that relates the progress of a family and society, *The Godfather, Part II* continues the saga of the Corleone family while exploring the nature of power in the United States. Spanning six decades and three generations, this personal and historical drama is not only a sequel to the monumental *The Godfather* (1972), but also serves as a prologue to that production. The film begins where *The Godfather* left off and follows the career of the youngest Corleone son, Michael (Al Pacino), in the mid-1950's, as he continues the reign established by his father, Don Vito. At the same time, the film is intercut with the background story of the youthful Don Vito (played by Marlon Brando in the original film). The story chronicles the rise and fall of the Italian-American empire; the making of a Mafia chief; the rise of Don Vito; and the prime and decline of Michael.

Whereas *The Godfather* begins with a wedding, *The Godfather, Part II* begins with a funeral. It is 1901 in Sicily. After the child Vito witnesses the murder of his family by the local Black Hand, the nine-year-old orphan is shipped off to the ghetto of New York's Little Italy; the Ellis Island immigration clerks name the boy Vito "Corleone," after the Sicilian village of his birth. At first a scrawny pox-ridden waif, young Vito grows up to be an honest laborer in a grocery store, but soon wanders into petty crime where he picks up the phrase, "I made him an offer he couldn't refuse." Following a return to Sicily to carry out his twenty-year-old vendetta, Vito attains a position of power, and he finally emerges as a Mafia leader with his own "family."

Just as Vito sheds his innocence and transforms from a delicate, sensitive youth into a ruthless Mafia operator, so, too, does his son Michael. In a 1940's flashback sequence set in the Corleone Long Island compound (a setting from *The Godfather*), we see the young Dartmouth-educated Michael reveal to all the second generation Corleones that he has enlisted in the Marines. When his brother Sonny (James Caan in a brief appearance repeating his role from the earlier film), curses him, saying the family is the only cause worth fighting for, the idealistic Michael disagrees. In the course of the film, however, the war-decorated, would-be professor of mathematics inherits Vito's empire and becomes the new Godfather. "If anything in this life is certain," says the now-ruthless Michael, "if history teaches us anything, it's that you can kill anyone."

Don Michael's enterprises consist of operations in Las Vegas, Miami, and Havana (the latter an aborted attempt to take over the rackets in Cuba before Castro's revolution), and three of his many enemies include his own brother Fredo (John Cazale), a Jewish crime czar, and a family informer. In the end, the merciless Michael has all three killed simultaneously. Ultimately, Michael himself is "destroyed," not by a rival gang or by a Senate investigation of criminal activities, but by himself. He becomes trapped by his own emptiness, a prisoner of his own paranoia.

Although both *The Godfather* and *The Godfater, Part II* are concerned with the themes of power and corruption, family loyalties, and revenge, *The Godfather* is dominated more by violence and suspense, while *The Godfather, Part II* is quieter, more solemn, more introspective, and more concerned with intense and difficult human emotions. Al Pacino is chilling as the soulless Don Michael who cares for nothing but power and whose only concern is the "business." An actor of enormous range and power, Pacino is almost, but not quite, pitiable as Michael—he is simply too repellent.

Robert De Niro gives an astonishingly controlled performance as the deceptively mild-mannered and soft-spoken Vito as he magnificently conveys the character's underlying iron will and moral corruptibility. Replacing Marlon Brando, the original Godfather, De Niro maintains the same whispery, gravelly voice, grimaces, and mannerisms. (Interestingly, De Niro was signed to play in *The Godfather* for the small part of Carlo Rizzi, the brother-in-law who sets Sonny up for the kill; when a larger part came along for the actor, however, in *The Gang That Couldn't Shoot Straight* [1971] Coppola released him.) Robert Duvall, with his understated strength, does well as Tom Hagen, the Corleone's adopted son and *consigliere*, as does John Cazale as Fredo, Michael's older but weakling brother, Mariana Hill as Fredo's slatternly wife, and Talia Shire (Coppola's sister) as Connie, the Corleone's spoiled sister. Diane Keaton is especially good as Michael's second wife Kay, the WASPish, New England woman who eventually leaves her husband. As she tells Michael bitterly of her so-called "miscarriage," "It was an abortion, Michael, just like our marriage is an abortion."

Other interesting casting in the film includes former teen idol Troy Donahue as Connie's sycophantic gigolo husband; producer-director Roger Corman (who gave Coppola his start in the film business) as a senator, and playwright Michael Gazzo (*Hatful of Rain*) as a *capo* informer. In his screen debut, although well into his seventies, Lee Strasberg, the Artistic Director of the Actors' Studio, is excellent as Hyman Roth, powerful syndicate boss; with his nervous cough, deceptive charm, and Talmudic façade, Strasberg does extremely well as the aging, ailing financial mastermind. "Michael, we are bigger than U.S. Steel," Roth says, as he and Michael embark on their uneasy alliance to seize control of Havana with Batista's cooperation.

The film's fifteen-million-dollar budget allowed for lavish production values. Dean Tavoularis' production design is exquisite; noteworthy scenes include the arrival of immigrants past the Statue of Liberty and the cattle-pen chaos of Ellis Island, the expertly detailed re-creation of the picturesque but teeming Little Italy at the turn of the century, the Festa of San Rocco, the Corleone estate parties, the whorish pre-Castro Havana of the eve of the revolution, and the Kefauver Committee hearings on criminal activities in the Senate Caucus Room. Theodora Van Runkle's costume designs, which span decades of changing styles, are also magnificent.

Cinematographer Gordon Willis continues the admirable work he did on *The Godfather*, here characterizing Vito's early life with soft, delicate, and warm pastels. The Sicily sequence is sun-bleached; the New York of 1900, with its sepia tones, resembles Jacob Riis's documentary-style photographs; the family fortress in Lake Tahoe is photographed in low-key lighting with many shadows; and Michael's world is revealed to us in dark, somber, mahogany tones.

Nino Roto and Carmine Coppola's music combines sensuality and terror; the score includes the familiar "Godfather" waltz theme, "Senza Mamma," "Napule Ve Salute," "Mr. Wonderful," and "Heart and Soul." The editing of Peter Zinner, Barry Malkin, and Richard Marks is fascinating as the film moves back and forth in time. The first time, for instance, that we move from present to past, from Michael to Vito, we see Michael putting his son (the boy who is playing with Don Vito in the garden when he dies in the earlier film) to bed, and Michael's face is at the left; then there is an elegant dissolve to Vito, whose face is at the right of the frame as we see him putting his son Fredo to bed. The film receives additional richness from the use of English subtitles for the spoken Sicilian dialects and the Italian and Spanish languages.

To be sure, *The Godfather, Part II* has a few minor flaws: twenty-two minutes longer than the original, the sequel runs a lengthy three hours and twenty minutes without intermission. One scene between Michael and Mama Corleone (Morgana King) tends to be too sentimental, and the fact that young Vito at Ellis Island has smallpox has no dramatic bearing on the story, since Vito does not seem to bear either literal or figurative scars from the disease.

Nominated for eleven Oscars and winner of six, *The Godfather, Part II* is considered by many to be the greatest gangster saga ever filmed. Dense with characters, locations, plots, subplots, and political, social, and psychological ideas, and replete with alliances, betrayals, renunciations, and ambushes, the exhilarating picture is romantic, violent, and tragic. It both enriches and expands the Corleone story and the American myth, for ultimately, the film deglamorizes violence as it shows a family in disintegration, corrupt senators and businessmen, and the connection between criminals and capitalists.

Francis Ford Coppola, who had total control over the filming of *The Godfather, Part II*, has created a masterpiece, a film that may rightly be called a triumphant chapter in screen history; one can no longer say a sequel is never as good as its predecessor. Coppola has made a film that is both art and popular entertainment, a work of the stature of *Birth of a Nation* (1915), *Gone with the Wind* (1939), and *Citizen Kane* (1941).

Leslie Taubman

GOING MY WAY

Released: 1944
Production: Leo McCarey for Paramount (AA)
Direction: Leo McCarey (AA)
Screenplay: Frank Butler and Frank Cavett (AA); based on a screen story
 by Leo McCarey (AA)
Cinematography: Lionel Lindon
Editing: Leroy Stone
Song: Johnny Burke and James Van Heusen, "Swing on a Star" (AA)
Running time: 130 minutes

Principal characters:
Father Chuck O'Malley .... Bing Crosby (AA)
Father Fitzgibbon .... Barry Fitzgerald (AA)
Father Timothy O'Dowd .... Frank McHugh
Genevieve Linden .... Risë Stevens
Carol James .... Jean Heather
Ted Haines, Jr. .... James Brown
Ted Haines, Sr. ...., Gene Lockhart

Going My Way is a film that clearly embodies the essentially optimistic spirit that pervaded Hollywood films during the World War II years. The film is also typical of the work of its director Leo McCarey. Although McCarey received two Academy awards for direction—one for *Going My Way* and the other for his classic "screwball" comedy *The Awful Truth* (1937)—his films are generally regarded as being too sentimental for modern tastes. However, at the time of its release in 1944, *Going My Way* was well received by critics and was such a box-office hit that it spawned a sequel, *The Bells of St. Mary's* (1945). Like most of the films that McCarey directed, *Going My Way* is consistently romantic, idealistic, and centered not around epic events of Herculean endeavors, but around the attempts of rather average people to cope with the problems of daily living. McCarey was not a director with a strong visual style, but, as *Going My Way* reveals, he had a talent for showing the humor and poignancy in life. To a nation embroiled in the uncertainty of war, the optimism and good humor of this film provided a welcome escape from its fears.

As with the films of John Ford, *Going My Way* is a product of the Irish-American background of its director. The familiar stock figures of the Irish widow, the Irish cop, and the Irish priest are all included in the film, but these characters are not simply the creations of a screenwriter; they are based on types that were actually very common in the Irish immigrant ghettos of Eastern cities.

The film is concerned with the experiences of a young Irish-American priest, Father Chuck O'Malley, who is sent by his Bishop to a poor New York City parish to help an old Irish-born priest keep his church from impending financial disaster. This situation, it is implied, has been caused by the latter's increasing inability to perform his duties successfully. *Going My Way* focuses comfortably on this decidedly uncomfortable relationship.

Unlike many previous films dealing with priests as major characters, such as *San Francisco* (1936) and *Boys Town* (1938), *Going My Way* presents characters that contrast sharply with the usual movie priest, who was most often a figure of bland and boring piety, with an all-consuming interest in saving souls. The collective sameness of that Hollywood image of the Irish and Irish-American priesthood does not reflect the real diversity that was present in the Catholic clergy. Father O'Malley (Bing Crosby) and Father Fitzgibbon (Barry Fitzgerald) provide the basis of a classic confrontation between two distinct and conflicting personalities. After his abundant sports gear has preceded him, Father O'Malley appears for his initial meeting with Father Fitzgibbon in a rumpled St. Louis Browns sweatshirt. O'Malley receives a telephone call from an old school friend, Father Timmy O'Dowd (Frank McHugh), and literally climbs over Father Fitzgibbon so he can get to the phone to join Timmy in a yowling rendition of their school song. Father Fitzgibbon is immediately convinced that his new assistant should certainly not be *his* assistant, and should probably not even be a priest. O'Malley's continuing display of a curious blend of naïveté and shallow humor force the defensive Fitzgibbon to employ his last and only line of defense—a very sharp wit.

Father Fitzgibbon is more than a character tailored to capitalize on the droll physicality and staple Irish *persona* of actor Barry Fitzgerald. Father Fitzgibbon embodies the vulnerability, frustration, and fear of aging that concerned director McCarey; McCarey had confronted these issues more directly in an earlier film, *Make Way for Tomorrow* (1937). Fitzgibbon's strong ties to the traditions of his rural homeland and his resulting inability to accept those of the new one make him incapable of dealing with the problems of an urban American ghetto. Although he is well-intentioned, Father Fitzgibbon refuses to recognize the delinquency of the boys in his parish and can only spout trite formulas to a runaway girl in need of help. He finds his memories of the past more comforting than the realities of the present or his prospects for the future. After serving St. Dominic's for more than forty-five years, Fitzgibbon knows he is regarded as inept. Driven to distraction when Father O'Malley starts a boys' choir, he goes to the Bishop to ask that he be assigned a new assistant. Fitzgibbon returns from the Bishop aware that O'Malley has actually been in charge of St. Dominic's since his arrival. Humiliated, Fitzgibbon impulsively runs away, but he is returned by a local policeman who chides him for acting like a child. He is lovingly accepted back by the housekeeper, and by O'Malley.

The reconciliation that follows between O'Malley and Father Fitzgibbon is both the turning point in the film and its most touching scene. Its beauty lies in the fact that the communication between the two is accomplished primarily through gestures rather than dialogue. The ritual of drinking "a wee bit of the crature" together, and O'Malley's singing of "Too-raa-loo-ra," suggests that the two are reconciled not only as individuals but also as generations of Irishmen, immigrant on the one hand and American-born on the other. The drinking together, done at O'Malley's suggestion, reflects his sensitivity to Fitzgibbon's strong ties to old-country traditions.

The song links Fitzgibbon to Ireland and to his memories of a mother he has not seen in almost half a century. Within the scene, past and present are united, cultural bonds recognized, and emotional issues resolved. At the end of the scene, Fitzgibbon indulges in a perfectly timed bit of comic business that turns the sentimentality of the scene upside down with a gently mocking nudge. Balancing the poignant and the comic, this reconciliation scene exemplifies McCarey's direction at its best. Excellence of ensemble acting is the key to the success of *Going My Way*. O'Malley's singing of "Too-raa-loo-ra" also reveals how McCarey could use music as an important means of expressing a character's personality and his emotional response to the moment.

In the final scene of the film, as the parish celebrates the dedication of a new chapel, Father Fitzgibbon is reunited with his mother. He is a changed man whose capacity for life has been renewed by his contact with O'Malley. Although Fitzgibbon, on hearing the news that O'Malley has been assigned to another parish, exclaims that he does not know how he can go on without him, one is left with the feeling that Fitzgibbon is now capable of carrying on very well without O'Malley. O'Malley is replaced by the irrepressible Father Timmy O'Dowd, a condition which promises to make Father Fitzgibbon's life a demonstration of that old Irish saying that contention is better than loneliness.

Even though *Going My Way* cannot be acquitted of the charge of sentimentality, it emerges as a very personal expression of a filmmaker whose optimism and humanistic spirit affirms the potential goodness in man. *Going My Way* creates a world of music, laughter, tears, and cherished friendships in which the challenge of life is something as simple, and as vastly complex, as the challenge and responsibility of caring.

Gay Studlar

GOLD DIGGERS OF 1933

Released: 1933
Production: Warner Bros.
Direction: Mervyn LeRoy
Screenplay: Erwin Gelsey and James Seymour; based on the play *Gold Diggers*
    by Avery Hopwood
Cinematography: Sol Polito
Editing: George Amy
Song: Harry Warren and Al Dubin
Music direction: Busby Berkeley
Running time: 94 minutes

Principal characters:
Carol .... Joan Blondell
Polly Parker .... Ruby Keeler
Trixie Lorraine .... Aline MacMahon
Brad Roberts (Robert Treat Bradford) .. Dick Powell
Fay .... Ginger Rogers
J. Lawrence Bradford .... Warren William
Thaniel H. Peabody .... Guy Kibbee
Barney Hopkins .... Ned Sparks

The year 1933 saw the emergence of an important new talent in the world
of the film musical, Busby Berkeley. He produced extravagant musical numbers which were staged for the camera rather than for the theater. His first
success was *42nd Street* (1933), and a few months later *Gold Diggers of 1933*
arrived to confirm that he was a master of the cinematic musical. In this film,
and others like it, the story is not especially important and serves merely as
a setting for the true interest, the musical numbers. These numbers, directed
by Berkeley, are so dazzling and imaginative that they delight audiences today
as much as when the film was first released. The story, directed by Mervyn
LeRoy, is simple and unexceptional.

Three out-of-work show girls, Polly, Carol, and Trixie, played respectively
by Ruby Keeler, Joan Blondell, and Aline MacMahon, learn that a Broadway
producer is casting a new show, a musical about the Depression showing its
sad, happy, and cynical sides. When the girls discover that the producer has
no money, a young composer and singer they know named Brad (Dick Powell)
agrees to put up fifteen thousand dollars to finance the show if Polly has a
featured part in it. On opening night Brad is forced to substitute for the
leading singer. The next morning the newspapers reveal that he is the son of
a wealthy conservative Boston family. Horrified at his connection with show
business and his rumored engagement to Polly, the family sends Brad's older
brother J. Lawrence Bradford (Warren Williams) and their lawyer (Guy Kib-

bee) to extricate him from Polly's clutches. Instead, the brother and the lawyer fall in love with Carol and Trixie and give their blessings to Brad and Polly.

Although this slight story provides many opportunities for snappy dialogue and much wisecracking, it is the musical numbers in the show that are the true glory of *Gold Diggers of 1933*. The four big production numbers in the film, "We're in the Money," "Pettin' in the Park," "The Shadow Waltz," and "My Forgotten Man," are representative of Berkeley's best work and show his artistic imagination and innovations. Each of the four begins on an actual stage before taking off into flights of fantasy that could never have been achieved in a real theater. The numbers each begin with the principal performers singing the lyrics to the song: Ginger Rogers in "We're in the Money"; Powell in "Pettin' in the Park" and "The Shadow Waltz"; and Blondell in "My Forgotten Man." After performing their solos they either disappear or merge into the ever-changing, evolving rhythm of the number.

The film opens with a close-up of Fay (Ginger Rogers) singing "We're in the Money," an optimistic, breezy antidote for Depression fears ("We never see a headline about a breadline today"). Fay, the chorus girls, and the stage are decorated with oversized silver dollars. As the number progresses, the camera pulls back to show Fay, seemingly with dozens of arms, rising at the head of a long line of chorus girls, a favorite Berkeley device. She even does a chorus of the song in Pig Latin, a fad of the time.

The next number, "Pettin' in the Park," does not come until the film is more than half over. It displays Berkeley's methods at their best—overhead shots, unexpected but linked images and scenes, transformations, and elaborate sets and costumes. It begins on a stage with Brad singing the lyrics. When the camera leaves him it also leaves behind the pretense that the number is being performed in a theater. As the camera pans across park benches, we see a variety of couples, white, black, Oriental, old, and young. Soon, girls on roller skates appear, followed by roller-skating policemen chasing a roller-skating midget dressed like a baby. At one point the camera shoots between the legs of a long line of policemen as they skate over the midget.

Berkeley then continues variations on the "Pettin' in the Park" theme in winter and summer settings. In a snow scene the chorus girls form changing circles as Berkeley uses his famous overhead shot to record the shifting patterns. Then a bouncing snowball becomes a child's rubber ball in a summer scene. Couples are lying on the grass cuddling. When it begins to rain, the girls run behind a screen, and we see them silhouetted as they change. The midget slyly raises the blind, expecting to see scantily clad girls. Instead, they are wearing metallic costumes with metal tops. The number ends with the midget giving Brad a can opener to open the back of Polly's costume.

"The Shadow Waltz" is another example of Berkeley at his best. It also begins as if it were being performed on an actual stage, with Brad again singing the lyrics. A close-up of Polly holding a flower takes us into the number. That image dissolves into one of many blondes in spiraling white hoop skirts playing white violins on a curving staircase. The violin motif goes through an imaginative progression, including overhead shots of the girls in patterns resembling opening and closing flower petals and ending with an overhead shot of a giant violin formed by many small violins. The violins are outlined with neon tubing for a more spectacular effect against the dark background. The girls are next seen reclining around a circular pool. The camera follows them around the edge of the pool until it comes to Brad and Polly, who drops a flower into the pool. The ripples cause the picture to break up and the number ends as it began, with a flower.

The film ends with "My Forgotten Man." Although it continues the pattern of starting out on an actual stage with one or two of the main performers singing the lyrics, it is unlike Berkeley's other work in several ways. It focuses on a serious social issue of the time, jobless war veterans, something not usually done in a musical. It is also different because there are no such typical Berkeley devices as overhead shots or swaying lines of chorus girls. It does tell a short, dramatic story, however, as Berkeley liked to do.

The number opens with a deserted street corner lit by a single street lamp. Carol, dressed in a tight slit skirt, leans against the street lamp and delivers the lyrics in a dramatic soliloquy. Then the scene shifts to a black woman in a tenement window who sings the lyrics. While she is singing there are vignettes of old, tired, worn, and hopeless women in other tenement windows. Then lines of uniformed men appear, marching to war while crowds cheer, throwing confetti and waving flags. Next, some men are marching in the rain while others are carried in the opposite direction, wounded, After this, the lines of men are not in uniform; they are in breadlines with tired, unshaven faces. In the final sequence, men in uniform are silhouetted at the back of the stage while Carol sings "My Forgotten Man" to men from the breadlines who form a circle, stretching their hands toward her. The total effect is very moving.

In Berkeley one sees a truly artistic imagination at work. Besides the appeal of individual images, he usually links the individual parts together in imaginative ways. Sometimes he tells a story; at other times, he uses a progression, such as the violin sequence, or transformations, such as the snowball becoming a rubber ball. Thus the reaction of the viewer as each new image comes on the screen is first surprise, then comprehension as the connection becomes clear, and then amazement at Berkeley's inventiveness.

One of Berkeley's chief artistic devices is the creation of patterns with his dancers. He uses overhead shots to show geometric or kaleidoscopic patterns that are constantly forming, breaking up, and reforming, into stars, flowers, circles, or abstract figures. He uses dancers as elements in a design or pieces in a jigsaw puzzle rather than as individuals, to create startling effects.

Although some critics of the time felt that a musical should not deal with serious social issues, *Gold Diggers of 1933* was one of the top-grossing films of the year. It remains an entertaining and funny backstage story, with musical numbers created by Berkeley at the peak of his creative powers. Audiences now find it as enjoyable as audiences in the 1930's did.

Julia Johnson

GOLDEN BOY

Released: 1939
Production: William Perlberg for Columbia
Direction: Rouben Mamoulian
Screenplay: Lewis Meltzer, Daniel Taradash, Sarah Y. Mason, and Victor
   Herman; based on the play of the same name by Clifford Odets
Cinematography: Nicholas Musuraca and Karl Freund
Editing: Otto Meyer
Music: Victor Young
Running time: 98 minutes

Principal characters:
Lorna Moon	Barbara Stanwyck
Tom Moody	Adolphe Menjou
Joe Bonaparte	William Holden
Eddie Fuseli	Joseph Calleia
Mr. Bonaparte	Lee J. Cobb
Siggie	Sam Levene

When Columbia first announced its purchase of Clifford Odets' Group
Theatre play *Golden Boy*, it seemed a strange choice, because that studio
had never favored dramas of strong social significance. Odets was not hired
to adapt his own play for film; instead, four top writers carefully deleted the
play's social comment from the screenplay that was being prepared. Some
of the controversial characters were completely eliminated; the romance was
built up; and the hero's conflict was simplified. A happy ending was devised
as a substitute for the play's conclusion. All things considered, the screenwriters did a good job, for *Golden Boy* as a movie proved to be much stronger
entertainment than the play. Today the play is dated, but the movie is still
as pertinent as it was at the time of its initial release.

When the production was first announced in the trade magazines, it featured
an appealing painting of Jean Arthur, who was announced as its star. Producer
Harry Cohn was biding his time, hoping to borrow John Garfield from Warner
Bros. for the title role, but Jack Warner and Harry Cohn were feuding, so
Garfield could not be secured for the part. Things began to fall into place,
though, when Rouben Mamoulian was signed as director. Mamoulian was a
versatile man who could never be typed in any one kind of film. Whatever
the background of the story he was directing, its cinematic mood was always
beautifully sustained. He was faced with two strong dramatic story lines to
resolve: the romance between an unworldly youth and a sophisticated girl;
and the internal struggle of the boy who had to choose between fulfilling
himself artistically through his music, and the opportunity to achieve quick
success as a boxer. Mamoulian had one advantage in telling the story on the

screen that could never be realized in the theater: he could show the prizefight sequences realistically. In the theater these scenes had to take place offstage; in the film they are superbly done, and convey an electric charge of quick ringside excitement and suspense.

Mamoulian demonstrated superb taste in casting his picture. He was fortunate in being able to get Barbara Stanwyck for the heroine, Lorna Moon, the girl friend of the fight manager Tom Moody, who is perfectly played by Adolphe Menjou. Stanwyck had just finished her last scenes as the heroine in De Mille's *Union Pacific* (1939), and she came over to Columbia with almost no break from her Paramount duties. Lee J. Cobb had been in the original stage play in a minor part, but was cast by Mamoulian in the more important role of Mr. Bonaparte, the boy's father, who dreams of his son's becoming a great violinist and who strongly opposes his son's boxing career because of the threat it holds of injuring the boy's hands. Joseph Calleia was exactly right for the mobster, Eddie Fuseli, and Sam Levene, as the taxi driver Siggie, provided the humor the story needed.

The most difficult role to fill was that of the young hero, the golden boy himself, Joe Bonaparte. Sixty-five youthful actors were tested for the part, and Mamoulian, a perfectionist, found fault with all of them. He finally tested an unknown, a youth of twenty-one, who was under contract to Paramount but had done virtually nothing on the screen except a few appearances in such routine pictures as *Prison Farm* (1938) and *Million Dollar Legs* (1932). His name was William Holden, and Mamoulian detected something in his screen test that was just what he wanted to portray in the character of Joe Bonaparte. Harry Cohn opposed the casting, but Mamoulian went to bat for young Holden; so did Barbara Stanwyck. Grudgingly, Cohn agreed to Holden's playing the part, but when he made the deal to borrow the boy from Paramount, he insisted on buying half of his contract. Because Holden was only under stock contract at that time and Paramount was paying him fifty dollars a week, it meant that Columbia was getting him for a weekly twenty-five dollars.

Holden's performance is workmanlike, believable, often brilliant, and deserving of the stardom he subsequently gained. Joe Napoleon is a sensitive youth whose father has sacrificed much to make him an accomplished musician. The boy is dual-natured, for he has mastered the difficult violin and is on the threshold of a career as a virtuoso. Yet, in exercising at the gym, he has gained a reputation as an amateur boxer, and when an impecunious manager, Tom Moody, sees him fight in the ring, he envisions a winner and signs the boy to a contract, promising him a quick rise to fame and fortune. Moody, also aware of the boy's innocence concerning women, instructs his own mistress, Lorna Moon, to lure the boy and entice him to stay in the fight world rather than pursue his music. Lorna does as Moody wishes, but she falls in love with Joe, even as she is urging him to stay with his fighting career.

Joe introduces Lorna to his family. When she understands what Joe's life has been and comprehends his genuine love of music, she switches her loyalties to persuade him to give up his fighting career. A gangster, however takes over the boy's contract for betting purposes, causing Lorna to be so disillusioned and disgusted that she agrees to marry Moody.

In the big fight, Joe's opponent is a young black prizefighter. Joe knocks him out with such a punch that he breaks his own hand and kills the black boy. Joe, overwhelmed by this tragedy, throws away his gloves and all thoughts of a career in the ring. In a well-played scene, he goes to the black fighter's father, who is mourning his dead son. The father tells him tearfully that he does not blame Joe for his boy's death. He had never wanted his son to fight, and he is sorry that it had to be a boy of Joe's caliber who killed him.

Lorna breaks with Moody and his way of life and comes to Joe. They are reunited, with his father's blessing. This ending was generally applauded by film critics. Even the few who were disappointed did admit that the double suicide of the boy and the girl in the play had been meaningless and that the movie reconciliation was done with taste and tenderness and did not signify a "tacked-on" happy ending.

Golden Boy was one of Columbia's all-time best films, and the fact that it gained only one Academy Award nomination—to Victor Young for Original Score—should not be held against it. It was released in 1939, frequently cited as the greatest year for the talking film, and was in competition with *Gone with the Wind*; *The Wizard of Oz*; *Wuthering Heights*; *Mr. Smith Goes to Washington*; *Goodbye, Mr. Chips*, and other films that are still favorites among both moviegoers and moviemakers. *Golden Boy* remains well-liked, however, and gains new admirers whenever it is revived, for it is one of Mamoulian's finest contributions to the cinema.

DeWitt Bodeen

GONE WITH THE WIND

Released: 1939
Production: David O. Selznick for Selznick International; released by Metro-Goldwyn-Mayer (AA)
Direction: Victor Fleming (AA)
Screenplay: Sidney Howard (AA); based on the novel of the same name by Margaret Mitchell
Cinematography: Ernest Haller and Ray Rennahan (AA)
Editing: Hal C. Kern and James E. Newcom (AA)
Production design: William Cameron Menzies (AA Special Award)
Art direction: Lyle Wheeler (AA)
Special effects: Jack Cosgrove
Costume design: Walter Plunkett
Music: Max Steiner
Running time: 219 minutes

Principal characters:
Scarlett O'Hara	Vivien Leigh (AA)
Rhett Butler	Clark Gable
Ashley Wilkes	Leslie Howard
Melanie Hamilton	Olivia de Havilland
Mammy	Hattie McDaniel (AA)
Gerald O'Hara	Thomas Mitchell
Ellen O'Hara	Barbara O'Neil

Gone with the Wind is unique among motion pictures. From the time of its initial release until 1980—forty-one years later—it was and is the most popular and profitable (in terms of uninflated dollars) film ever made. Margaret Mitchell's first and only published novel was a literary phenomenon. Shortly after its appearance in May of 1936, it became an unprecedented best seller, and it continues to enjoy impressive sales.

In July of 1936, independent producer David O. Selznick paid $50,000 for the screen rights to *Gone with the Wind*, the highest price paid to an unknown author for a first novel up to that time. The initial problem was to adapt the 1,037-page book to the screen. Selznick considered playwright and screenwriter Sidney Howard "a great constructionist" and hired him to write the script. Selznick believed strongly that "in connection with adaptations of books, the trick is to give the *illusion* of photographing a book. The only omissions from a successful work that are justified are omissions necessitated by length, censorship, or other practical considerations." To photograph the novel literally would, of course, have yielded a film that ran seven or eight hours or more; thus artful pruning, telescoping, and rearrangement of the story and characters were mandatory.

Gone with the Wind is set in the Old South, moves through the Civil War, and then on to the Reconstruction period. Its heroine, Scarlett O'Hara, who, as the book begins, lives on the plantation called Tara, loves idealistic and sensitive Ashley Wilkes of nearby Twelve Oaks. The young, high-tempered Scarlett spitefully accepts the impetuous proposal of Charles Hamilton, upset that his sister, shy and sedate Melanie, is going to marry Ashley. When Charles dies of pneumonia after going off to war and Atlanta is seized by the Northerners, Scarlett is poverty-stricken. She is forced to struggle for her family and also for the aristocratic Ashley, who has not been trained to work with his hands. Yet, Scarlett is determined to keep Tara: she does manual labor, marries her sister's fiancé Frank Kennedy for his money, and, after his death in a Ku Klux Klan raid while avenging Scarlett's honor, marries Rhett Butler, the black sheep of a good family, a blockade runner and an unscrupulous profiteer. Scarlett has had a child by each of her husbands, but Bonnie, her child by Rhett, is killed in a riding accident. Because of Scarlett's lasting love for Ashley, Rhett finally deserts her, but she realizes at last, after the death of Melanie and the indifference of Ashley, that Rhett, similar in spirit to her, was her real love.

Before and during the filming of *Gone with the Wind*, various writers had a hand in working on the script. After Sidney Howard completed his draft, Oliver H. P. Garrett, Ben Hecht, Jo Swerling, John Van Druten, F. Scott Fitzgerald, John Balderston, and others worked from a few days to several weeks on the constantly changing script. Finally, Selznick went back to what was basically Howard's version, but he personally kept modifying it, even during shooting.

Remarkably, Margaret Mitchell's book remained relatively intact, or, more precisely, gave the illusion of remaining the same during its transfer to film. However, Scarlett's first two children were eliminated; Rhett's candid confessions of his blockade activities were minimized; the book's Belle Watling character was cleaned up; love scenes, particularly the so-called "Orchard Love Scene" or "paddock scene," were toned down; any mention of the Ku Klux Klan was dropped; Rhett's contempt for Ashley was not depicted; nor was the book's implication that Rhett began living with Belle Watling after Scarlett vowed to have no more children even remotely suggested in the film. Also, of course, some characters were dropped or fused and many scenes and events eliminated.

Because of complications in the areas of casting, screen adaptation, and distribution contracts, Selznick was unable to begin actual shooting with the principals until January, 1939, although the burning of the warehouse district in Atlanta was filmed on the night of December 10, 1938. Only four actors were ever considered for the role of Rhett Butler: Clark Gable, Gary Cooper, Errol Flynn, and Ronald Colman. Gable was under contract to M-G-M, and Coleman was mentioned only in the early weeks. Flynn was a relatively strong contender as far back as December, 1936. Warner Bros. had both Flynn and Bette Davis under exclusive contract, and for a while it looked as though Warners and Selznick were going to work out a package deal for Davis and Flynn that would also include Olivia de Havilland as Melanie, but the negotiations and interest bogged down. Gary Cooper was under contract to Samuel Goldwyn at the time, and discussions seemed to be getting nowhere. Besides, the public was almost unanimous in its choice of Clark Gable. Selznick finally worked out an arrangement to get Gable and partial backing from M-G-M in exchange for distribution rights and fifty percent of the profits. Since Margaret Mitchell wrote the bulk of *Gone with the Wind* between 1926 and 1929, the apocryphal story about her having Gable in mind for Rhett while she was writing the novel has no validity. Gable was an obscure stage actor in the late 1920's and did not start to come into his own in films until 1931 and 1932.

Whereas there was relative agreement on the ideal actor to portray Rhett Butler, there were considerable differences of opinion regarding the choice for Scarlett O'Hara. Incredibly, casting the part of Scarlett fascinated the world. Thirty-one women were actually screen tested—including a good many unknowns and amateurs—from September, 1936, until December, 1938. Among the better-known personalities tested were Tallulah Bankhead, Susan Hayward, Paulette Goddard, Anita Louise, Frances Dee, Lana Turner, Diana Barrymore, Jean Arthur, Joan Bennett, and a dark-horse contender, a British actress named Vivien Leigh. Selznick had always favored finding a relative newcomer for the role, someone fresh who would not be identified with previous performances. Other well-known actresses who were high in the running at one time or another, but who for various reasons did not test, include Margaret Sullavan, Miriam Hopkins, Joan Crawford, Norma Shearer, Loretta Young, and Katharine Hepburn. In November, 1938, Selznick stated in a memo that Hepburn has "yet to demonstrate that she possesses the sex qualities which are probably the most important of all the many requisites of Scarlett." At one point Paulette Goddard was about to be signed for the part, but she could not produce a license proving that she and Charlie Chaplin were married. Selznick was afraid of negative public opinion, since she and Chaplin had been living together for quite some time. By December 12, 1938, the choice had narrowed down to Paulette Goddard, Jean Arthur, Joan Bennett, and Vivien Leigh; shortly thereafter Vivien Leigh signed a contract to play the role.

For the part of Ashley, Leslie Howard had been considered early, but Selznick's main concern was that he was considerably older than the young man in his twenties depicted in the novel. Melvyn Douglas gave what Selznick described as "the first intelligent reading of Ashley we've had, but I think he's entirely wrong in type." Regarding Ray Milland, Selznick stated that he was "very definitely a sensitive actor, possessing the enormous attractiveness and at the same time the weakness that are the requirements of Ashley." Before signing Leslie Howard for the role, Selznick had also considered Robert Young, Douglas Fairbanks, Jr., Jeffrey Lynn, and Lew Ayres.

Olivia de Havilland became the first choice for the role of Melanie with other possibilities being Janet Gaynor, Dorothy Jordan, Andrea Leeds, and Julie Haydon. Although Warner Bros. was initially unwilling to loan her to Selznick, they finally relented in late 1938. Interestingly, neither Gable nor Howard wanted to be in the film, and only after much coaxing, persuading, and money did they relent. Gable felt he could never live up to the public's advance expectations of the role, and he was not drawn to the character or the period. Leslie Howard had no desire to play yet another weak and sensitive soul and did not even bother to read the novel.

Principal cinematography began on January 26, 1939, under George Cukor's direction. Immediately there were problems. Within two-and-a-half weeks Cukor was off the picture. The exact circumstances behind his exit are not totally clear. Selznick was quoted in 1947 as saying: "We couldn't see eye to eye on anything. I felt that while Cukor was simply unbeatable in directing intimate scenes of the Scarlett O'Hara story, he lacked the big feel, the scope, the breadth of the production." Speculation in the industry at the time centered about M-G-M being dissatisfied with the speed at which the scenes were being photographed, Cukor objecting to revisions of Sidney Howard's script, changes in the dialogue by Selznick being delivered on the set continuously, and Clark Gable's unhappiness over Cukor's supposed preoccupation and fastidiousness with the characters portrayed by Leigh and de Havilland.

The day following Cukor's exit, Victor Fleming, a good friend of Gable, was taken off the completion of *The Wizard of Oz* (1939) at M-G-M and signed to direct *Gone with the Wind*. Fleming was the antithesis of Cukor, and the leading ladies were unhappy. There were tensions and disagreements throughout the production. At one point Fleming collapsed and veteran Sam Wood replaced him. When Fleming returned, Selznick kept both directors—in addition to second unit directors—shooting different scenes concurrently. This was possible due to William Cameron Menzies' carefully detailed production design. Finally, following five months of arduous and complicated filming, the picture was finished.

After several more months of editing, effects cinematography, some retakes, and scoring, *Gone with the Wind* had its world premiere in Atlanta, Georgia, on December 15, 1939. Its success was even greater than anyone had anticipated. In addition to being voted the Best Picture of 1939 by the Academy of Motion Picture Arts and Sciences, *Gone with the Wind* was the unprecedented recipient of nine other Oscars, including Best Actress, Best Director, Best Screenplay, and the Irving G. Thalberg Memorial Award for consistent excellence of production, which went to the producer David O. Selznick. Selznick, without question, was the dominant force behind *Gone with the Wind.* He was involved in every single detail of the film, and in every sense of the word it is primarily his film—not a committee film, not a director's film, and not a star's film, but a spectacular example of a creative producer's work.

When finally shown in Europe after World War II, *Gone with the Wind* had a tremendous impact since it represented for the French a story about surviving a defeat, and Japan has been particularly addicted to the picture over the years. Extraordinarily successful full-scale theatrical reissues in America in 1947, 1954, 1961, and 1967 followed. For the 1967 run it was blown up optically to "the splendor of 70mm wide screen and full stereophonic sound." The splendor was dubious; *Gone with the Wind* is at its best in the format originally photographed and shown, and that format was retained for its network television debut on NBC in November, 1976, where it promptly drew the largest audience of any program shown on one network in television's history. In 1977, from a list of more than one thousand entries, *Gone with the Wind* was voted by members of the American Film Institute the greatest film made in the United States, with *Citizen Kane* (1941) and *Casablanca* (1942) placing second and third in the poll.

Whether or not it is "the greatest" film, *Gone with the Wind* is certainly the most enduring and endearing. Very few motion pictures have been able continuously to captivate the mass audience in theaters and on television over the decades. The film represents the high-water mark and quintessence of the big super-attraction of Hollywood's golden age. The mosaic is composed of an "epic" narrative, varied and rounded characters enduring overwhelming obstacles, family crises, unrequited and idealized love stories, war, turmoil, nostalgia, and Technicolor.

Many people are still extremely drawn to the essentially soap opera aspects of some of the material. This is particularly true of events which take place during the last quarter of the film, where, because of the need to telescope drastically a great many chapters of the book, tragedy and climax seem to pour forth without relief—Scarlett's miscarriage, Bonnie's death, Melanie's death, and Rhett's abandonment of Scarlett. Although Selznick's production is characteristically meticulous, some of the settings are highly romanticized and have, in many instances, a picture postcard quality, particularly the settings for Twelve Oaks.

The remarkable and enduring performance of Viven Leigh makes every scene in which she appears come alive, bringing dimension and magnetism to the role of Scarlett, along with beauty, tenacity, fire, humor, intelligence, and, above all, great charm. Gable, despite his fears, superimposes his disarming screen presence and personality on the novelist's Rhett Butler for a colorful and believable blend. Leslie Howard's Ashley is exactly right, albeit he is too old for the character; and Olivia de Havilland's performance underlines, perhaps a shade too much, the inherent sweet and altruistic characteristics of Melanie.

There is much in terms of characterization with which audiences can or wish to identify. Scarlett is both self-centered and realistic. She can stand on her own; she is resourceful, aggressive, passionate, and realizes too late that she has loved the wrong man far too long. Rhett is the personification of the free spirit who flouts public opinion, knows what he wants, and goes after it. He is a man's man and a lover: shrewd, realistic, and earthy, but also capable of tenderness, compassion, and tears.

To further dissect and analyze the myriad ingredients that have made *Gone with the Wind* the most popular film over the decades would be useless. It is sufficient to state that it has that rare quality of still being able to capture the imagination of a great many people. That is more than we can expect and more than we receive from most films.

Rudy Behlmer

THE GOOD EARTH

Released: 1937
Production: Irving Thalberg for Metro-Goldwyn-Mayer
Direction: Sidney Franklin
Screenplay: Talbot Jennings, Tess Slesinger, and Claudine West; based on the novel of the same name by Pearl S. Buck and the stage play by Owen Davis and Donald Davis
Cinematography: Karl Freund (AA)
Editing: Basil Wrangell
Running time: 130 minutes

Principal characters:

Wang Lung	Paul Muni
O-Lan	Luise Rainer (AA)
Uncle	Walter Connolly
Lotus	Tilly Losch
Old Father	Charley Grapewin
Cuckoo	Jessie Ralph
Aunt	Soo Yong
Elder Son	Keye Luke
Younger Son	Roland Lui

When Pearl S. Buck's novel *The Good Earth* was published in 1931, it won the Pulitzer Prize for Literature and stayed on the best-seller lists for nearly two years. The fifty-year chronicle of the House of Wang familiarized a whole generation of Americans with China, that mysterious and exotic country on the other side of the world. It is not, however, the kind of novel from which great American films are made, or so thought Louis B. Mayer, head of Metro-Goldwyn-Mayer. Irving G. Thalberg, however, Mayer's production chief, regarded it as a viable screen property. Mayer admonished him by exclaiming that if Americans would not buy tickets to films about American farmers why should they pay to see one about Chinese farmers. Thalberg's literary bent prevailed nevertheless, since Mayer had great respect for Thalberg's prestigious track record as a producer: Greta Garbo's *Anna Christie* (1930) and her *Camille* (1936); *Private Lives* (1931); *Strange Interlude* (1932); *Mutiny on the Bounty* (1935); *The Barretts of Wimpole Street* (1934); and *Romeo and Juliet* (1936).

As early as 1934, M-G-M sent talented director George Hill to China to shoot some two million feet of location footage and to bring back actual Chinese props, including two water buffalo and farm implements. Hill had earned a sizable reputation with such films as *Min and Bill* (1930), *The Big House* (1930), and *The Secret Six* (1931), and *The Good Earth* was expected to be his masterpiece. Tragically, he committed suicide in 1934, however, and the directorial assignment was passed on to Victor Fleming. Illness later prevented Fleming from working on the film, and the project was ultimately directed by Sidney Franklin, who had directed *Private Lives* and *The Barretts of Wimpole Street* for Thalberg. M-G-M painstakingly re-created the Chinese locale in the San Fernando Valley, using more than one thousand actors and spending a final budget of $2,816,000, an extraordinary amount of money for any production during those years.

The central theme of Buck's novel is that the earth is the fundamental giver of life, and this philosophy is made manifest through her depiction of the lives of a family of simple farm folk. The film opens almost elegiacally on the morning of the wedding day of Wang Lung (Paul Muni), as we see him prepare to go into town to take as his bride a slave girl named O-Lan (Luise Rainer). He finds O-Lan crouched near a stove in the kitchen of the Great House; she is a simple, awkward, quiet young peasant woman who stoically accepts her fate as the wife of this poor farmer. These opening scenes are utterly convincing and of the utmost importance in creating audience credibility. On the walk back to Wang's farm, O-Lan follows behind her husband-to-be the dutiful number of paces, and when he throws away the pit to a peach he has eaten, she retrieves it. Following the wedding feast, Wang discovers O-Lan planting the seed, for she knows that from the soil it will produce life.

Their life together as husband and wife is one of hard work, loyalty, and respect for each other. Their "good earth" is their strength and salvation, and they must produce sons to help them in the fields. When O-Lan becomes pregnant for the first time, she continues to work in the fields right up until the time she is to give birth. When she faints in the fields, Wang carries her back to their humble home. She refuses to allow him to go for a midwife, and says he must return to the harvest. Alone, with quiet dignity and strength, she gives birth to their first son.

As the family prospers, Wang buys more farm land, including rice fields, and O-Lan bears two more children—another son and, to Wang's great disappointment, a daughter. Their modest prosperity is destroyed by drought, and when starvation sets in, Wang's uncle (Walter Connolly) pleads with his nephew to sell the land. Wang replies, "Before I sell it, I'll feed it to my children." One of the most poignant scenes in the film occurs when O-Lan cooks soil to feed her family. The drought finally forces them to seek refuge in the city like thousands of neighboring farmers. There they are confronted by a political rebellion in which O-Lan is trampled unconscious by a mob fleeing the police. When she awakes she discovers a little purse of jewels. She keeps two pearls for herself and gives the others to Wang, who uses them to buy the Great House and the surrounding land.

Wang prospers as a wealthy landowner but changes from a simple farmer to a socially ambitious man. He becomes enamored of an exotic, lusty teahouse dancer, Lotus (Tilly Losch), whom he takes as his second wife. O-Lan accepts this fate stoically and mutely as she accepts all in life. It is here, as the focus of the film shifts from the land to the passionate entanglement of Wang and Lotus, that the film flounders. When Wang discovers Lotus with his son (Keye Luke), he beats the young man, but is interrupted by the cry that locusts are about to destroy his property.

Once again the "good earth" is of the foremost concern, and the film regains its impetus and believability. In the novel, the locust plague is described in three pages, but in the screenplay it is built into a scene of climactic importance and visually re-created with expert tension and reality. O-Lan joins her husband in the fields to help save their crops from devastation by the swarming insects. The crops are saved, but that evening O-Lan is too ill to attend the wedding feast of her younger son (Roland Lui). Wang comes to her and gives her the two pearls which she had saved. He holds her in his arms and implores her not to die, saying he will do anything, including selling the land, if it will make her well again. She responds, "No, I would not allow that. For I must die sometime, but the land is there after me." The film ends with Wang standing by the tree which grew from the peach seed O-Lan had planted many years before. Realizing that his prosperity has been the result of her steadfast courage, he says, "O-Lan, you are the earth."

Thalberg did not live to see *The Good Earth* completed; he died in 1936 at the age of thirty-seven. During his years as a producer he had never allowed his name to appear on the screen. At Mayer's insistence, *The Good Earth* carries this dedication:

> "To the memory of Irving Grant Thalberg,
> We dedicate this picture,
> His last great achievement."

The Good Earth received almost unanimously glowing reviews, with special commendations for the sepia-toned cinematography of Karl Freund, who received an Academy Award for his work. Freund was a master cinematographer who had worked on such German classics as *The Last Laugh* (1924), *Variety* (1925), and *Metropolis* (1926); much of the visual authenticity in these films was the result of Freund's cinematography.

Rainer's portrayal of O-Lan, which earned an Academy Award for Best Actress, remains one of the cinema's extraordinary performances. As in the novel, O-Lan is a combination of character and symbol, and Rainer's ability to bring her courage and pain and loyalty alive on the screen in a performance consisting almost entirely of pantomime (she had less than two dozen lines of dialogue) is eloquent. It brought Rainer her second Oscar in two years—the first time an actress had won twice in a row (her first Award was for *The Great Ziegfeld*, 1936). *The Good Earth* was not only the third of the nine films Rainer was to make in Hollywood, but was also the high point of one of Hollywood's oddest and shortest careers.

Although the other important acting roles in *The Good Earth* were played by non-Oriental performers, they are for the most part very believable. Muni looks appropriately Chinese, and in the beginning and the end of the film his acting is admirable. In the middle segment, however, which details his life as a prosperous landowner and his love affair with Lotus, his Americanisms detract from his performance. Losch, however, is entirely convincing as the seductress. Overall, *The Good Earth* is exemplary in its depiction of Chinese characters by American performers, unlike the almost laughable *Dragon Seed* (1944), also produced by M-G-M, which unsuccessfully presented Katharine Hepburn, Walter Huston, and other Americans as Chinese farmers. *The Good Earth* is memorable for Rainer's performance and for its attempt to be authentic. It is a fitting epitaph to the career of Irving Grant Thalberg.

After Thalberg's death, the Motion Picture Academy initiated the Irving G. Thalberg Memorial Award for "the most consistent high level of production achievement for an individual producer." This award, different from the more famous Oscar statuette, is given once a year, and only to the very best producers who have sustained their record of excellence over a long period of time.

Ronald Bowers

GOOD NEWS

Released: 1947
Production: Arthur Freed for Metro-Goldwyn-Mayer
Direction: Charles Walters
Screenplay: Betty Comden and Adolph Green; based on the musical comedy
  by Lawrence Schwab, Lew Brown, Frank Mandel, B. G. De Sylva, and
  Ray Henderson
Cinematography: Charles Schoenbaum
Editing: Albert Akst
Song: B. G. De Sylva, Lew Brown, Ray Henderson, Betty Comden, Adolph
  Green, Roger Edens, Hugh Martin, and Ralph Blane
Running time: 83 minutes

> *Principal characters:*
> Connie Lane .... June Allyson
> Tommy Marlowe .... Peter Lawford
> Pat McClellan .... Patricia Marshall
> Babe Doolittle .... Joan McCracken
> Bobby .... Ray McDonald
> Danny .... Mel Torme
> Peter Van Dyne III .... Robert E. Strickland
> Professor Burton Kennyon .... Clinton Sundberg
> Beef .... Loren Tindall

The 1940's and 1950's are often thought of as the Golden Age of the Hollywood musical. It was, in fact, one studio and one production unit within that studio that produced nearly all the landmark films of that era, such as *Meet Me in St. Louis* (1944), *Singin' in the Rain* (1952), *The Band Wagon* (1953), and *Gigi* (1958). That studio was Metro-Goldwyn-Mayer, and the production unit responsible for these films was headed by Arthur Freed. Freed was a lyricist in the early days of the sound film and with Nacio Herb Brown wrote such songs as "Singin' in the Rain," which was used in a number of films before becoming the title song of the 1952 film. As a producer, Freed surrounded himself with such great and famous talents as Fred Astaire, Vincente Minnelli, Michael Kidd, and Gene Kelly to create the musical masterworks of two decades. Another important contribution of the Freed unit was a great number of minor musicals without big stars that aimed for and achieved modest but real virtues and remain entertaining and rewatchable today because of their excellent craftsmanship.

One of these unpretentious but rewarding films is *Good News* (1947), which features Peter Lawford and June Allyson. It was also the directorial debut of Charles Walters, who had previously been a choreographer and would go on to direct such famous films as *Easter Parade* (1948) and *High Society* (1956).

In addition it was the screenwriting debut of Betty Comden and Adolph Green, who later wrote such classics of the genre as *Singin' in the Rain* and *The Band Wagon*.

Except for Allyson, none of the principals was at first enthusiastic about the project. *Good News*, which was first a Broadway play in 1927, had already been filmed in 1930; Comden and Green thought the college football comedy too trivial for them to work on; and Walters was naturally nervous about directing his first film. Lawford did not want to play the lead because he thought his British accent would sound foolish for the role of the all-American football hero. Eventually all these problems and objections were overcome or forgotten, however, and none of them show in the finished film.

The plot does sound trivial, with the two main issues being who the football captain will take to the prom and whether he will be able to play in the big game. It is, however, the easygoing and light-hearted way in which the whole film is presented, the engaging quality of the main performers, and the success of the musical and specialty numbers that make the plot an agreeable confection rather than a ridiculous trifle. It is regarded by many as the definitive college musical.

The setting is a familiar one for a Hollywood musical film: a college in which the main activities are romance, football, and music. Tait College is in fact so much fun, we are informed in the opening song, that no one wants to graduate. After a title that tells us "This story takes you way, way back to another era—1927" and the opening song, we are quickly introduced to Pat McClellan (Patricia Marshall), an egotistical transfer student from a finishing school who continually drops French words into her conversation and is an immediate hit with the male students—"burning up the campus inch by inch," as one of them says. Then, in the football locker room, we meet some of the other main characters: Bobby (Ray McDonald), an inept athlete who is trying out for the team only because girls are attracted to football players; Beef (Loren Tindall), a huge but slow-witted player whose passion for Babe Doolittle (Joan McCracken) interferes with his ability to concentrate on football, and Tommy Marlowe (Peter Lawford), the captain of the team and favorite of all the women. When Bobby asks him if he has seen Pat, he merely responds that he lets the girls come to him. Bobby's request that Tommy explain his technique leads neatly into the next song-and-dance number. The secret, according to the song "Be a Ladies Man," is to walk, talk, and dress "collegiate." It is an energetic number in which Tommy and Bobby are joined by other students, including Danny—played by Mel Torme, the best singer in the film.

The scene then shifts to the sorority house where most of the young women are engaged in frivolous activities, except for Connie Lane (June Allyson), who is under the sink repairing the plumbing. (We will find later that she is also the assistant librarian of the school and an assistant to the French professor.) Pat is also there, but instead of working on the plumbing she is staring at herself in the mirror and saying, "You wonderful creature, why does everyone love you?" The main part of the plot is then set in motion when Pat lets it be known that she is interested in marrying a wealthy man, and the other girls tell her that Peter Van Dyne III (Robert Strickland) is worth twenty-five million dollars. Pat ends the conversation by saying "quel frommage," and Connie has to point out to her that she has just said "what cheese."

At the dance that evening Pat is the focus of attention of all the men and Tommy of all the women except Pat; she is interested only in Peter Van Dyne and his fortune. It is a new experience for Tommy to be rejected by a girl, and he cannot understand it. Pat's attentions to Peter lead into her singing to him "Lucky in Love," which is then continued by various other students at the dance, with some variations. Connie sings that she "never will be lucky in love," and Tommy sings, "Up to *now* I've been so lucky in love."

At the end of the song Pat rebuffs Tommy in French, which inspires him to make his first trip to the library the next day. There he meets Connie, who tells him what the French word means, and when he decides to take a French course to keep up with Pat, Connie tells him the best teacher in the department is Professor Kennyon (Clinton Sundberg), but he is "a tough bird and he hates football players." The discussion between Tommy and Connie leads into a half-spoken, half-sung specialty number, "The French Lesson," written by Comden, Green, and associate producer Roger Edens, in which Connie teaches some French words to Tommy. The ironic aspect of this scene is that Lawford spoke French fluently, while Allyson did not speak the language at all. Before the number, therefore, Lawford had to teach Allyson the words that she would teach him on screen.

Tommy learns a speech in French to say to Pat, but she still spurns him, causing the other students to fear that his being unlucky in love will interfere with his football playing and cost Tait the opening game. Babe therefore tells Pat that Tommy is worth *thirty* million dollars. Meanwhile, however, Tommy has asked Connie to the prom and she is floating on air. "Just think," she says, "I am going out with a football hero." After the game, however, Pat rushes up to Tommy and asks him to take her to the prom. He accepts immediately and does not remember his date with Connie until later; he calls and breaks their date at the last minute. Just before he calls, Connie has put on her prom dress and asked Babe how she looks. Babe gives her what is meant to be the ultimate compliment, "You sure don't look like a librarian."

More complications ensue as Tommy becomes so infatuated with Pat that he neglects his studies and fails his midterm examination in French, thus becoming ineligible for the big game the next Saturday. When he is offered a make-up exam, the other students convince Connie that she must coach him for the good of the school, even though she despises him for what he has done.

The coaching session rekindles their love, but it takes an intentionally failed exam, a change of heart, some manipulation by Professor Kennyon, and a complicated scheme devised by Connie to get Pat out of the way before they are back together in an imaginative love scene that begins with the two shouting at each other. Then Tommy tells Connie that he loves her and will do anything she asks. "Down on your heels," she replies. "Up on your toes." "What's that?" he asks, and the whole student body in the background responds "That's the way you do the Varsity Drag," leading cleverly into the big song-and-dance finale, "The Varsity Drag."

The key to the success of *Good News* is that it is unassuming; it never tries too hard and never pretends to be more than it is. The principal players are not top-flight stars, but they have engaging screen personalities and adequate musical talent. McCracken, in a supporting role, gives an especially good dancing performance in "Pass That Peace Pipe," a musical number performed in the college soda shop.

Clifford Henry

GOODBYE COLUMBUS

Released: 1969
Production: Stanley R. Jaffe for Paramount
Direction: Larry Peerce
Screenplay: Arnold Schulman; based on the novella of the same name by
 Philip Roth
Cinematography: Gerald Hirschfeld
Editing: Ralph Rosenblum
Running time: 105 minutes

Principal characters:
Neil Klugman .... Richard Benjamin
Brenda Patimkin .... Ali MacGraw
Mr. Patimkin .... Jack Klugman
Mrs. Patimkin .... Nan Martin
Ron Patimkin .... Michael Meyers

   Philip Roth's award-winning 1959 novella, *Goodbye, Columbus*, is a bittersweet tale of a summer romance between a sensitive young man and a pampered, wealthy, sexually aware girl. Both partners are Jewish, and, in the uncertain, hyperactive world of Philip Roth's America, both hold onto each other for a kind of security. While Neil Klugman (Richard Benjamin) believes in poetry, honest sex, and sincere *angst*, Brenda Patimkin (Ali MacGraw) devotes her attention to sex, platitudes, and the comfort of her father's enormous home in Westchester. It all fails in the end: Neil learns that Brenda does not have much going for her despite her lithe body, and he will, one assumes, value the balmy summer experience for what it was worth. The novella is about values clashing amid a dissipated ethnic tradition of the late 1950's. The film translation of Roth's story has been updated to 1969 by director Larry Peerce.
   The sun is out every day at the country club where Neil and Brenda first meet; the summer greenery of the richly endowed home of Mr. Patimkin (Jack Klugman) shimmers with inviting warmth; there is no intrusion by a war in Vietnam or civil disturbances. All is quiet and peaceful; and while everybody else eats lots of fruit and fried chicken at the Patimkin house, Neil and Brenda meet, slip away, and make love in various places. MacGraw does a fine job of convincing one that spoiled late adolescents who attend Radcliffe are not meant to be cherished by spiritually aware young men such as Neil, who, more than anything else, seek sex and love and meaning in a reasonably sterile suburban world. The film does a relatively good job of conveying the substance of Neil's and Brenda's awkward relationship. The camera records Richard Benjamin's various facial expressions, which transparently reflect his feelings: his throat pulses with aroused desire when he first encounters the

beautiful Brenda in the pool at the country club. He mumbles when he just does not know what to say to this creature who so excites him.

Neil's world is portrayed in an overly stereotyped way; it includes a protective Jewish family whose mutterings about jobs and girls and chicken soup become tedious and distracting. However, the dialogue between Neil and his assorted relatives, although occasionally strained and ridden with clichés, does point out just how different Neil is from Brenda. He has attended a city college in New Jersey and served an unheroic term as a private in the army; his current vocation places him in a library in the city. He has to deal with his aunt and uncle, as well as with his status-conscious cousin who sits around the country club pool, her skin peeling away like red paint while she tries to read *War and Peace*. Neil comes from a different world, but he is, the audience is reminded, a boy with promise.

Brenda knows a life of overabundance, living in a suburban mansion, wearing fur coats, and enjoying frequent buying trips to Bloomingdale's. Her family's wealth, which comes from her father's plumbing supply business, has transformed the family. The elder son, Ron (Michael Meyers), is a nice guy, a dumb former jock who spent his glory years on Ohio State's basketball court; the youngest daughter is her father's pet, and is extremely spoiled. The mother spends most of her time wrapped up in mudpacks, tissue paper, and eyeshadow.

All of these characters are literally thrown together for the audience. The director's intent was to filter all of this subject matter through Neil's expanding perspective. Although the real strength of Roth's story lies in Neil's first-person narration, the film changes the structure. The audience is shown everything, and it is occasionally hard to determine just what Neil is seeing and feeling. There are, for example, several scenes when Neil is not present, moments when the camera focuses on Brenda and her father at the lavish wedding of Brenda's brother. It is, to be sure, a tender moment between father and daughter; both realize, perhaps for the first time, that they know very little about each other. The father wants his daughter to be the princess she believes she is, but the scene's sadness revolves around his real ignorance of her life (in this case, the furtive and passionate relationship between Neil and Brenda).

At the same time, however, the film succeeds in its attempt to introduce some marvelous characters caught up in the materialism of American life. In the case of the Patimkin family, abundance leads to a sense of fear that their recently acquired wealth will crumble. Mr. Patimkin yearns for everything to remain the same. He sweats and grimaces over his son's fate (always, it seems, to be employed as a lackey at the plumbing supply store), his wife's fears about her daughter's marital prospects with an unpromising boy like Neil, and his own ability to preserve and protect his pampered flock.

When *Goodbye Columbus* strays from Neil's point of view, therefore, the audience is presented with a portrait of the upper middle class and, specifically, the descendants of poorer people from New York's Lower East Side. This is certainly what Roth intended his readers to see while judging the perceptions of Neil as he makes his way through the country clubs, the ostentatious wedding, and the mind of a materialistic girl. In the short span of one summer, Neil Klugman is introduced to a dream girl who in the end is as vacuous and selfish as the head librarian at Neil's reference desk at the library. Even as the librarian, his small eyes screwed up with dislike and fear of a small black child who wants to look at the "big pictures" in a book of Paul Gaugin's paintings in the library's art collection, Brenda Patimkin is fearful of real and honest values. Although one may wish to dismiss the deftly placed clichés in the script as attempts to inject a few laughs at the expense of the Patimkin family and everything it represents, *Goodbye Columbus* is a well-played critique of romance, love, and sexual attitudes shaped by the harsher dictates of a material culture.

Lawrence J. Rudner

THE GOODBYE GIRL

Released: 1977
Production: Ray Stark for Warner Bros.
Direction: Herbert Ross
Screenplay: Neil Simon
Cinematography: David M. Walsh
Editing: John F. Burnett
Music: Dave Grusin
Running time: 110 minutes

Principal characters:
Elliott Garfield	Richard Dreyfuss (AA)
Paula McFadden	Marsha Mason
Lucy McFadden	Quinn Cummings
Mark	Paul Benedict
Donna	Barbara Rhoades
Oliver Fry	Nicol Williamson

The basic plot of *The Goodbye Girl* is borrowed more or less from a delightful comedy, *The More the Merrier* (1943), which starred Jean Arthur, Joel McCrea, and Charles Coburn and which was remade as *Walk, Don't Run* (1966), starring Cary Grant. Neil Simon "urbanized" the story and changed the characters to the extent of placing them in show business (one is a dancer, one an actor), locating them on New York's Upper West Side, and removing the older man character and replacing him with a child.

By a stratagem that only works in movies and seldom happens in real life, Elliott Garfield (Richard Dreyfuss) arrives from Chicago at the apartment of Paula McFadden (Marsha Mason) the night after her boyfriend has taken off, leaving her with a daughter, Lucy (Quinn Cummings), to support and no money. Lease and key in hand, he asks them to leave, but she has no place to go. After much yelling and bickering they compromise; Paula and Lucy will share Paula's bedroom, Elliott will have Lucy's. While Paula resumes dancing lessons and takes a job pitching in an auto show, Elliott starts rehearsing *Richard III* for the off-Broadway stage. The director, Mark (Paul Benedict), wants him to perform Richard as an outrageous homosexual, an interpretation which causes the show's immediate demise. Elliott then takes a series of jobs, during which time he and Paula stop antagonizing each other and fall in love. Another off-Broadway engagement leads to a movie role, and as Elliott leaves for Hollywood, he proposes to Paula, declaring that he will be back as soon as the film is finished.

Although much of *The Goodbye Girl* is funny and does work, the rapidity of the repartee is wearing. Nobody can deliver comebacks as quickly as these two, and the ping-pong dialogue seems to work against the script's conventions. To compound this problem, Simon has saddled his heroine (and real-life wife) with an equally adroit daughter, the kind of poisonous brat Virginia Weidler played in 1940's comedies such as *The Philadelphia Story* (1940). The audience never gets a rest from the nonstop clashing of egos and the gratuitously hostile repartee which is the couple's defense against feeling.

Fortunately, Dreyfuss and Mason are expert performers, and if the audience frequently wants them to relax and shut up, it is not their fault. Simon substitutes rapid-fire patter for character development, so Elliott and Paula keep bashing away at each other. Both are propelled mostly by bad temper, which makes them something less than attractive to be around for 110 minutes. Their flagrant abrasiveness is initially funny, but often becomes irritating. It is hard to see what they see in each other at first. In fact, they are both such self-involved characters that believing that they could ever pay sufficient attention to anyone else to become emotionally involved is a difficult undertaking.

Simon has sand-bagged Paula with a number of annoying traits. Called upon to deliver a sales pitch at the auto show, she cannot remember her lines for two minutes. Simon also credits her with the worst taste in decorating history. When Elliott and Paula settle down to domestic bliss, she redecorates the apartment, with the result that it looks like a Middle Eastern seraglio; Paula orders Elliott to move heavy furniture around repeatedly while she makes up her mind about its placement.

Simon has the soul of a matchmaker. He wants everybody fixed up and happy by the final reel: Jane Fonda and Robert Redford, Charles Boyer and Mildred Natwick in *Barefoot in the Park* (1967); Walter Matthau and Jack Lemmon in *The Odd Couple* (1968); George Burns and Matthau in *The Sunshine Boys* (1975); and now Dreyfuss and Mason. There have to be reasons for people to get together, however, and in *The Goodbye Girl*, he does not provide enough of them. In place of character Simon gives us jokes, for sentiment he gives us petulant tears, and for warmth we get more jokes—and sex. Simon is nasty about the very things he wants us to believe are lovable; underneath all the screaming are two vulnerable people who just need a little push from fate to become the most adorable couple since Janet Gaynor and Charles Farrell in *Seventh Heaven* (1927).

Director Ross has gotten spirited performances from his stars. Mason, who won a Golden Globe Award as Best Actress for her performance, may be a bit too cuddly-cute for comfort—she was much better, for example, in her brief role in *Blume in Love* (1973) as the woman who was impulsively, sloppily involved with George Segal immediately after his divorce—but she is still enjoyable to watch. Dreyfuss' interpretation of Elliott, however, which won him an Academy Award, is both complex and involving. When he first appears, he is raucous and pushy. We think that we are going to hate him, but then he changes on screen. Forced to mature in order to win Paula, his character gives up the childishness which has been Dreyfuss' forte throughout his acting career in such films as *American Graffiti* (1973), *The Apprenticeship of Duddy Kravitz* (1974), and *Close Encounters of a Third Kind* (1977). Paula is immature enough for both of them, so Elliott *has* to grow up, and he does it with charm and grace. Dreyfuss also provides *The Goodbye Girl* with its one scene of genuine humanity. Publicly embarrassed in his New York debut when *Richard III* flops resoundingly, Elliott gets royally drunk. For once his self-absorption is not exasperating: it is developed out of his character so that the audience can feel his humiliation and sympathize. Dreyfuss' habitual intensity is an organic part of Elliott, and he uses it to round out the man, not as an element applied from outside to add interest to the individual whom he is playing.

Judith M. Kass

THE GRADUATE

Released: 1967
Production: Lawrence Turman for Embassy Pictures
Direction: Mike Nichols (AA)
Screenplay: Calder Willingham and Buck Henry; based on the novel of the same name by Charles Webb
Cinematography: Robert Surtees
Editing: Sam O'Steen
Running time: 105 minutes

> *Principal characters:*
> Benjamin Braddock ....Dustin Hoffman
> Mrs. Robinson .... Anne Bancroft
> Elaine Robinson ....Katharine Ross
> Mr. Braddock .... William Daniels
> Mrs. Braddock ....Elizabeth Wilson

The Graduate is one of the most important films of the late 1960's. Through it, Hollywood discovered that the "misunderstood youth" of years past, from the Holden Caulfields to the James Deans, were no longer teenagers. Alienation had gone to college, and for much of the next decade, those who made films about youth in America concerned themselves with the problems and priorities of men and women between the ages of twenty and thirty. This is not to suggest that *The Graduate* was simply another kind of exploitation movie. Although critics were by no means unanimous, the film and its principals were widely acclaimed. Director Mike Nichols was hailed as a major new talent in American film; Anne Bancroft was justifiably lauded for her portrayal of the neurotic seductress, Mrs. Robinson; and, perhaps most importantly, Dustin Hoffman's illustrious film career was launched by his stunning performance as Benjamin Braddock—the graduate of the film's title.

Benjamin Braddock (Dustin Hoffman) is an upper-middle-class young man from Southern California who has just graduated from an Eastern college, and is not yet ready to face adult life, which he regards as a game with rules that do not make much sense. The film opens with a close-up of Benjamin's impassive face (Nichols uses these close-ups continually throughout the first part of the film); his blank expression mirrors his feeling of emptiness while Paul Simon and Art Garfunkel's "The Sounds of Silence" plays on the sound track, reinforcing the impression of Benjamin's alienation from his surroundings.

This alienation carries over into Benjamin's family life. His parents (William Daniels and Elizabeth Wilson) have arranged a welcome home party for him, inviting all of their own friends rather than his. Their intentions are not malign; they simply want to show off a son of whom they are justifiably proud, but Benjamin wants no part of the occasion. He is worried about his future, and wants to be alone with his thoughts. With his parents insisting that he put in an appearance, however, Benjamin runs the gauntlet of inane small talk, including one guest's now-famous remark that the future lies in "plastic."

Unable to tolerate any more, Benjamin retires from the party to his bedroom, where he is followed by Mrs. Robinson (Anne Bancroft), the wife of his father's business partner. Although Benjamin would rather be alone, Mrs. Robinson insists that he take her home, and he relunctantly agrees to do so. Just as reluctantly, he complies with her request that he accompany her inside the house, have a drink, and remain with her until her husband returns. Mrs. Robinson's conversation grows increasingly intimate, which thoroughly flusters Benjamin, and she plays on his confusion. Alternately seductive and maternally imperious, she lures him up to her daughter's bedroom, where she begins to disrobe. Significantly, we see Mrs. Robinson's nudity reflected in the glass which covers her daughter's picture, foreshadowing the role that the two women will play in the film. Benjamin is terrified, but Mrs. Robinson remains calm, offering herself to him, now or at any later time. Benjamin rushes down the stairs, only to meet Mr. Robinson (Murray Hamilton), who, while Benjamin literally whimpers in terror, proceeds to administer a fatherly chat. His advice is that Benjamin should sow a few wild oats.

The scene shifts to the Braddock house on the occasion of Benjamin's twenty-first birthday. As usual, his parents have thrown a party for him, again inviting only their own friends, and Benjamin is called upon to perform for them—in this case, to model his new scuba gear. Completely dressed in it, he moves ponderously through the crowd to the pool, where he jumps in and sinks gratefully to the bottom in peace. Nichols reinforces the adsurdity of the scene by shooting it entirely from Benjamin's perspective—through the goggles of his diving suit.

Time passes, and Mrs. Robinson's offer of seduction begins to look more attractive to Benjamin. At once eager and apologetic, he calls her, and she agrees to meet him in the bar at the Taft Hotel. Under her patient prodding, Benjamin agrees to get a room, thoroughly embarrassing himself in the process since he is certain that the desk clerk knows what he is about to do. In the room, Mrs. Robinson is calm and almost businesslike, which further aggravates Benjamin's case of nerves. He bangs his head against the wall in frustration, and decides to end the affair before it begins. Mrs. Robinson defeats this resolve by accusing him of being a virgin. Outraged, he defends his virility by consummating the liaison.

The summer passes with Benjamin spending most of his time diving into his parents' pool or into bed with Mrs. Robinson. Nichols shoots this sequence in a series of montages that begin and end with the now-familiar close-up of Benjamin's blank stare against a white background—alternately a pillow in the Taft Hotel and an inflatable rubber raft in his parents' pool. The effect is intentionally disorienting, and suggests that both pursuits are as empty of meaning as the expression on Benjamin's face, while the sound track underlines this impression with a reprise of "The Sounds of Silence."

Thus far in the film, Benjamin has never really talked to anyone. He has merely been spoken to; and he has responded in as perfunctory a way as possible. His intimacy with Mrs. Robinson has never gone beyond the physical, as evidenced by the fact that he never calls her by her first name, which indeed is never learned throughout the film. Now, however, he feels a need for communication, and his attempts to initiate a conversation with the more carnally inclined Mrs. Robinson result in some of the film's funniest moments. Once the conversation starts, however, it focuses on the Robinsons' marriage and their daughter Elaine (Katharine Ross). This sets the stage for the second, more serious part of the film.

Although Mrs. Robinson is adamantly opposed to Benjamin's dating Elaine, and although Benjamin is also unenthusiastic about the prospect of such an encounter, he finally gives in to the matchmaking pressure from his parents and Mr. Robinson, and agrees to take Elaine out one time. As the evening begins, Benjamin is deliberately offensive, driving recklessly and taking Elaine to a tawdry strip joint. Humiliated, Elaine runs away in tears, while Benjamin, realizing he is fond of the girl, pursues her, calms her down, and kisses her. In a conversation in which he shows genuine feeling for the first time in the film, he explains that he has been confused and worried about his future. Without naming Mrs. Robinson, he tells Elaine of an unsatisfactory relationship that he has been having with an older woman. She seems to sympathize, and they spend the rest of the evening happily, their affection for each other grows, and Elaine agrees to see Benjamin the next day.

When Benjamin arrives at the Robinsons' house the next day, however, a furious Mrs. Robinson meets him before he can get out of his car and threatens to reveal their affair if he continues to show any interest in Elaine. Benjamin rushes into the house and attempts to talk to Elaine, with Mrs. Robinson in hot pursuit. Elaine, seeing them together, realizes that her mother is the older woman with whom Benjamin is having an affair, and refuses to speak to him. Up to this point, the film's emphasis has been on humor; however, when Benjamin finds his true love, the film shifts gears perceptibly. Nichols abandons most of his broad satiric swipes at suburbia and the scene shifts from Los Angeles to Berkeley, where Elaine has gone back to school. In short, the film, though it never ceases to be funny, becomes more earnest in its later scenes.

Benjamin follows Elaine to Berkeley, tracks her around campus, and finally confronts her with his presence, only to discover that she has a buttoned-down, pipe-smoking fiancé named Carl Smith. Although Elaine is uneasy in Benjamin's presence, she is not sufficiently angry to order him away. Confused by her feelings for Benjamin, Elaine appears one day in his room and demands an explanation for his actions with her mother. He tells Elaine that he loves her. In their conversation it is divulged that Mrs. Robinson has told her daughter that Benjamin raped her; reluctantly, however, she believes him when he tells her the true story. As the days pass, although Elaine declines to commit herself to marriage with Benjamin she seems to be moving in that direction.

Matters soon come to a head in the Robinson family, however. Mr. Robinson is divorcing his wife, and Elaine, without Benjamin's knowledge, has left school to marry Carl Smith. When he finds out that she is gone, he embarks on a frantic Berkeley to Los Angeles to Berkeley to Santa Barbara drive to find her. His car runs out of gas a few blocks from the church where the wedding is in progress. Running into the church, Benjamin finds the ceremony just completed. Torn between Benjamin on the one hand and her parents and new husband on the other, Elaine finally chooses Benjamin, and the couple fight their way through the crowd in the church, with Benjamin swinging a large cross, in a bit of heavy-handed symbolism, to clear the path and then to bar the door once they are outside. Benjamin and Elaine run to a conveniently departing bus, where they rush to the back amid puzzled looks from their fellow passengers. The pair is strangely silent at this climactic moment, and the film ends much as it began—with "The Sounds of Silence" on the sound track, and a close-up of Benjamin staring wordlessly ahead. This time, however, he is grinning broadly.

Much of the effectiveness of the film lies in the masterful work of the principal actors, all three of whom won Academy Award nominations for their work. Katharine Ross as Elaine brings dimension to a role that could easily have been played as just another "girl next door" stereotype. Anne Bancroft is outstanding as the predatory Mrs. Robinson, who, of the three major characters in the film, is the least sympathetic. Bancroft, however, conveys not only her character's bored cynicism and self-loathing, but her wit as well. Despite her calm expression, the twinkle in her eye when she first encounters Benjamin in the bar of the Taft Hotel indicates that she finds Benjamin's discomfiture as amusing as the audience does. The best acting in the film, however, is the work of Dustin Hoffman. Benjamin is the only character that is required to change during the course of the film. A very passive young man until he meets and falls in love with Elaine, he erupts into a frenzy of activity during the second half of the film. Whether he is squirming with embarrassment at one of his parents' parties or frantically swinging the cross at Elaine's wedding, Hoffman is utterly convincing. His performance is the cohesive element that bonds the two parts of the film and keeps it coherent; it captured the imagination of a generation, and propelled Hoffman to instant stardom in his first screen role.

For all its success, however, *The Graduate* is not a perfect film. Mike Nichols goes for some too-easy laughs at the expense of the plastic Los Angeles suburbanites; and, more importantly, he changes the tone of the film too abruptly when the scene shifts from Los Angeles to Berkeley. His mistakes are ones born of enthusiasm, however, and can be excused. Although *The Graduate* failed to win the Academy Award for Best Picture, Nichols did win the Award for Best Director.

The Graduate was a seminal film in that some of Nichols' innovations, such as the focus on the new, older youth culture, and the use of pop/rock music on the sound track as commentary on the action, were so successful that they have now become commonplace. *The Graduate* is truly a landmark in American cinema.

Robert Mitchell

GRAND HOTEL

Released: 1932
Production: Irving Thalberg for Metro-Goldwyn-Mayer (AA)
Direction: Edmund Goulding
Screenplay: William A. Drake; based on the novel and play *Menschen im Hotel* by Vicki Baum
Cinematography: William Daniels
Editing: Blanche Sewell
Running time: 115 minutes

Principal characters:
Grusinskaya	Greta Garbo
Baron Felix von Geigern	John Barrymore
Flaemmchen	Joan Crawford
Preysing	Wallace Beery
Otto Kringelein	Lionel Barrymore
Dr. Otternschlag	Lewis Stone
Senf	Jean Hersholt

Grand Hotel was the precursor of many films in which characters from all walks of life are thrown together by chance in the same hostelry, airplane, oceanliner, storm-swept island, or other location removed from the rest of civilization. The so-called disaster film of the 1970's can trace much of its origins to this film. Like many of its successors in the multistory, multicharacter genre, *Grand Hotel* was adapted from a best-selling novel. Vicki Baum's book, and later play, *Menschen im Hotel*, was a familiar story to audiences when it was brought to the screen in 1932. In order to bring an immediate and fresh impact to the screen, director Edmund Goulding opened the film with shots of a vast switchboard and busy operators which set the tone and pace for *Grand Hotel*. The feeling of fast-moving and varied action was further reinforced by the magnificent setting of a multileveled lobby which resembled a towering beehive. For the next two hours, the audience sees a constant intermingling of characters and stories which were foreshadowed in the opening shots.

The characters are quickly introduced to enable the audience to become immediately enmeshed in the individual stories. Greta Garbo plays Grusinskaya, an *émigré* ballerina for whom everything since the fall of St. Petersburg seems "threadbare" and lonely until she meets Baron Felix von Geigern (John Barrymore), who brings her out of her cocoon. The Baron is really an erstwhile aristocrat-turned-jewel thief who goes about his career of crime with a heart of gold that will not stoop to petty maliciousness. At one point he steals a wallet belonging to Otto Kringelein (Lionel Barrymore), but when he hears the old man bemoaning his loss, the Baron somehow "finds" the lost billfold. Kringelein is the meek and musty bookkeeper whose life has been spent working with figures and eking out an existence. Early in the film it is revealed that he is going to die, and it is his impending death that brings him to a plush suite in the hotel where he has decided to live what is left of his life the way the "other half" does. Wallace Beery plays Preysing, an overbearing industrialist who is on the verge of bankruptcy but who cashed out on his humanity years ago. Joan Crawford plays Flaemmchen, his stenographer of questionable repute, who at last finds a friend and protector in the dying Kringelein. These are the main characters around whom the film revolves but there is also the added equivalent of the Greek chorus in the person of the world-weary Dr. Otternschlag, wonderfully enacted by Lewis Stone. It is his famous line that is the epithet of the hotel: "people coming, people going—always coming and going—and nothing ever happens."

In some ways, that remark is an accurate observation reflecting not only the subplots within the main story line but also the main plot itself; yet in other ways, it is a statement that seems to deny the throbbing life within the hotel. First, it is true that there is tremendous hustle and bustle; but although much emotion is expended in the scenes, the characters—with the possible exception of Kringelein—do not often strike a responsive chord of truth in the audience. There are interesting and sometimes enchanting incidents, but for the most part they are nothing more than the inconsequential business of vain, unlikable people.

As the Baron, Barrymore does an exceptional job of creating a charming and engaging larcenist and lifting him out of the ranks of what is essentially an ordinary leading-man role; but played by someone of less stature and skill, the Baron could have come across as silly. The character of the ballerina Grusinskaya borders on the absurd, and again, it is only because of Garbo's performance that she does not become grotesquely comical; Garbo instills her with a sprinkling of humor that saves the characterization. Wallace Beery makes the swaggering businessman Preysing appropriately mean and despicable; yet, because we are not shown any redeeming quality in the character's makeup, he is easy to dismiss as completely unreal and, therefore, not truly threatening. As his secretary and doxy, Joan Crawford plays a woman whose brash exterior only hides an insecure personality.

It is Lionel Barrymore's portrait of Kringelein, however, that gives an essentially superficial movie an element of depth and sensitivity. His interpretation of the abject and querulous clerk who blossoms amid the luxurious surroundings and companionship of the huge hotel is magnificent. He displays the complex mixture of comedy and tragedy abiding in everyone; and when he and Crawford board a train together for Paris and whatever new adventures they can find together, the audience wishes the best for them. Lionel Barrymore won more acclaim for this role than any other; he was so convincing that in his last scene the tears Crawford shed—not called for in the script—

were the actress' natural reaction to his moving performance.

For its time, *Grand Hotel* is technically impressive. From the sweeping opening shots of the switchboard and the expansive marble-floored lobby to the intimate close-ups in the private rooms, the film is rich in texture and tone. Interestingly, *Grand Hotel* won the Academy Award for Best Picture, but received no other awards or nominations. The fact that neither actors, director, nor technical staff were acknowledged for their contributions to what was considered a landmark picture caused considerable commotion. In fact, this was the only such case in the more than fifty-year history of the Motion Picture Academy.

Because the film contained such a large number of prominent actors, the press was eager to play up what they termed "the Battle of the Stars" during production. One such instance involved John Barrymore, who was purportedly unbearably demanding when it came to such things as lighting. According to Hollis Alpert, author of *The Barrymores*, however, Barrymore only gave a witty response to the lighting director's question about how he wished to appear: "I'm a fifty-year-old man and I want you to make me look like Jackie Cooper's grandson." (Cooper, of course, at the time, was merely a child.) Most authoritative sources agree that, in reality, all the stars involved in *Grand Hotel* made an extra effort to accommodate one another, despite publicity to the contrary.

Grand Hotel was an attempt by M-G-M to attract a larger profit at the box office by putting more established stars in a single film. This practice was to go in and out of fashion in the following decades. One other film which attempted to do the same thing was M-G-M's own remake of *Grand Hotel* entitled *Weekend at the Waldorf* (1945), which boasted such top box-office attractions as Lana Turner and Van Johnson, but it was unable to equal the impact of the original version.

Juliette Friedgen

THE GRAPES OF WRATH

Released: 1940
Production: Darryl F. Zanuck for Twentieth Century-Fox
Direction: John Ford (AA)
Screenplay: Nunnally Johnson; based on the novel of the same name by John
   Steinbeck
Cinematography: Gregg Toland
Editing: Robert Simpson
Running time: 128 minutes

Principal characters:
Tom Joad	Henry Fonda
Ma Joad	Jane Darwell (AA)
Pa Joad	Russell Simpson
Grandpa Joad	Charley Grapewin
Rosasharn	Dorris Bowdon
Casy	John Carradine
Muley	John Qualen

The Grapes of Wrath, based on John Steinbeck's widely read novel about
the plight of migrant workers during the Great Depression, is director John
Ford's most famous work. It bears the characteristic stamp of many of his
classic films; it is the story of a hapless society told with strong visual narrative
technique. In this case, the microcosm of migrant workers is represented by
a single family, the Joads from Oklahoma.

The film opens with the view of a small figure walking down the road
against an expansive Oklahoma landscape. It is Tom Joad (Henry Fonda),
recently paroled from prison. He is returning after four years to the home
of his family, who are tenant farmers. Things have changed during his absence.
The dust bowl conditions, combined with the advent of mechanized farming,
have caused their ruthless landlords to force the Joads, as well as hundreds
of their neighbors, off their lands. Tom rejoins his family just as they are
preparing to leave for California, where handbills have proclaimed that there
is plenty of work harvesting fruits and vegetables. The Joads—Tom, Ma (Jane
Darwell), Pa (Russell Simpson), Grandma and Grandpa (Charley Grapewin),
Uncle John, Tom's sister Rosasharn (Dorris Bowdon) and her new husband,
and other brothers and sisters—set off in an overloaded, dilapidated truck
for the "promised land" of California.

The trip itself takes its toll on the family: the elder Joads, first Grandpa,
then Grandma, die en route, and pregnant Rosasharn's husband deserts her.
Moreover, once in California, they find that the working conditions there in
no way compare with the glowing accounts of the handbills. Thousands of
migrants like the Joads have answered the call, and jobs are scarce. All are

forced to live in squalid transient camps and work for starvation wages, when indeed any work is to be had. Eventually, the Joads find jobs on a ranch where some of the workers are on strike and are attempting to organize a union. During an altercation between the striking workers and a band of deputies, Casy (John Carradine), a friend of the Joads who traveled west with them, is killed. In retaliation, Tom kills one of the officers. The family flees, ending up at a clean, democratically run government camp. Contrasted with all the other places they have stayed, this camp seems almost like paradise. However, as a fugitive who has broken parole, Tom realizes the inevitable. He must leave the family and strike out on his own. In one famous scene, he bids farewell to Ma, promising to fight for social justice. As the film ends, the family continues its ever-moving search for work.

As with any film adaptation of a popular literary work, one of the first questions raised is that of the film's fidelity to its source. From the first, *The Grapes of Wrath* was praised for its faithfulness to Steinbeck's book. Indeed, despite the careful pruning of curse words from the dialogue and the compression necessary to reduce a six-hundred-page novel to standard feature length, Steinbeck's characters and events come to life on the screen with remarkable vitality. Nunnally Johnson's screenplay, which has retained Steinbeck's themes concerning human dignity and the fundamental importance of the family, along with the performances of an outstanding cast, constitute the major achievement of the film. The screenplay, however, does deemphasize some of Steinbeck's material. The angry political message of the novel, as well as its religious satire, are considerably muted on the screen. In addition, by means of a single omission and transposition the screenplay has fundamentally altered the structure of the novel and the artistic vision of its author. This was accomplished by deleting in its entirety Steinbeck's controversial ending involving the death of Rosasharn's infant and by reversing the order of two major episodes in the novel: the government camp sequence and the strike sequence in which Tom kills Casy's assassin. By concluding with the comparatively upbeat government camp episodes, the film tends to imply an optimism—not present in the novel—about the power of the American government to solve the deplorable socioeconomic problems illustrated by the odyssey of the Joads. This faith in democracy is also implicit in Ma Joad's final speech in the film: "We're the people that live! We'll go on forever because we're the people!"

The acting by the major players in *The Grapes of Wrath* is superb. Henry Fonda's portrayal of Tom Joad, who angrily insists on decency and human dignity, is one of the memorable achievements of his career. Jane Darwell's performance as the courageous Ma Joad, who struggles to preserve the family unity as the key to its survival, is sensitive and compassionate—among the strongest in the film. One of her most effective scenes is that which takes place in the predawn darkness while the family prepares for their journey

West. Ma is seen sorting through a small box of mementos. In this wordless solo scene the actress conveys a sense of the human dimensions of the past now irretrievably lost as the family leaves the farm, never to return. Charley Grapewin is effective as Grandpa Joad, who first bubbles with enthusiasm at the prospect of being able to pick grapes in California, but later balks at leaving home. Clutching a fistful of soil, he cries, "It's my dirt—no good, but it's mine!" The testimony of Muley (John Qualen) to the land—"We were born on it, and we got killed on it, died on it; even if it's no good, it's still ours"—is delivered with such skill that it becomes one of the most poignant moments in the film.

The success of the film is also due to its remarkable visual impact. Gregg Toland's evocative black-and-white cinematography gives the film an epic quality reminiscent of the great photographic record of rural America during the Depression sponsored by the United States Farm Security Administration. His strikingly photographed landscapes give graphic expression to the involvement Steinbeck's characters have with the land, and the documentary quality of the visual images succinctly underscores the hopeless conditions of the migrant workers. Productive collaboration between the photographer and the director has resulted in many images that linger in the memory: the inexorable progress of the house-demolishing tractors in Oklahoma; the journey west along Highway 66 with its montage of signs ("We fix flats," "Water 15¢ gal.," "Last chance for gas and water"); the nighttime reflection of the three riders in the truck's windshield through which can be seen the passing desert; and the subjective camera record of the arrival of the Joads at the first migrant camp as it tracks through the campground crowded with jobless, hungry people.

The Grapes of Wrath was a popular and critical success when it was first released. Both Jane Darwell and John Ford won Academy Awards for their contributions. Although it lost the Academy Award for Best Picture to Hitchcock's *Rebecca*, the film was named the outstanding film of 1940 by many other groups, including the New York Film Critics. It is historically important as one of the first Hollywood films to portray honestly and realistically one of the least admirable aspects of American society. Although the implications of the film's ending may seem too simplistic for modern audiences, *The Grapes of Wrath* remains a powerful dramatization in personal terms of a major socioeconomic problem, the rumblings of which were beginning to be heard in the 1930's.

David Bahnemann

GREASE

Released: 1978
Production: Robert Stigwood and Allan Carr for Paramount
Direction: Randal Kleiser
Screenplay: Bronte Woodward; based on Allan Carr's adaptation of the
    Broadway musical of the same name by Jim Jacobs and Warren Casey
Cinematography: Bill Butler
Editing: John F. Burnett
Running time: 110 minutes

Principal characters:

Danny Zuko	John Travolta
Sandy	Olivia Newton-John
Rizzo	Stockard Channing
Kenickie	Jeff Conaway
Principal	Eve Arden
Coach Calhoun	Sid Caesar
Frenchy	Didi Conn
Vince Fontaine	Edd Byrnes
Teen Angel	Frankie Avalon
Vi	Joan Blondell
Mrs. Murdock	Alice Ghostley
Johnny Casino and the Gamblers	Sha Na Na

Among the popular arts of the 1970's (cinema, television, and pop music), few subjects provided a greater source of inspiration than the rediscovery of the 1950's—1950's fads, foibles, and most of all, 1950's music, rock-and-roll. This rediscovery began to be manifested nationally in 1973, with George Lucas' marvelous *American Graffiti* (set in 1962, but filled with the music and teenage life-style of the previous decade). *American Graffiti* led to television's popular series *Happy Days*, and the rush to nostalgia was on. Before all of these, however, came *Grease*, a musical comedy that was a long-running Broadway hit, making its stage debut in 1972. When the film version was released in 1978, the genre of 1950's-worship reached its apex.

Actually, the play, by Jim Jacobs and Warren Casey, was a natural for the movies, and producers Robert Stigwood (a record company mogul who specialized in coordinating hit films with their wildly successful sound track albums) and flamboyant Allan Carr (who adapted the play for film) were just the men to preside over the transition. They took two hot properties from the 1970's—John Travolta (hard on the heels of his triumph in 1977's *Saturday Night Fever*) and Olivia Newton-John (an Australian-born pop singer in her film debut)—and mixed them with a host of 1950's television and rock stars. The result was a box-office smash: an affectionate, slightly cynical, and highly selective remembrance of things past.

Grease is set in a 1950's never-neverland where all the kids speak with Flatbush accents yet live in California. Most of the action centers around Rydell High (named after Bobby Rydell, a teenage idol of the late 1950's and early 1960's), and the film is a grab bag of 1950's clichés, all seen from the slightly skewed perspective of a later decade. The plot goes something like this: Danny Zuko (John Travolta) meets a girl named Sandy (Olivia Newton-John) on the beach during summer vacation. To Danny's surprise (he is used to thinking of girls as nothing more than sex objects), he develops a genuine affection for Sandy. Their romance is doomed, however; summer is over, and they must go their separate ways, since Sandy is Australian and must return home.

The scene then shifts to Rydell High, where the first day of class is beginning. Danny is reunited with his "gang," the T Birds. The T Birds consist of Danny's pal Kenickie (Jeff Conaway), along with Doody (Barry Pearl), Sonny (Michael Tucci), and Putzie (Kelly Ward), who act like the Three Stooges in motorcycle jackets. The T Birds' big ambition for their senior year is to get a car. The T Birds' female auxiliary is the Pink Ladies, led by the tough-talking Rizzo (Stockard Channing). Rizzo's second bananas are the gorgeous Marty (Dinah Manoff) and Frenchy (Didi Conn), the sweet but dumb girl who drops out of high school to become a beautician. Unbeknownst to Danny, however, the Pink Ladies are about to add a new recruit to their ranks—Sandy, his summer love, who enrolls at Rydell when her parents move from Australia.

In the film's first production number, "Summer Nights," director Randal Kleiser cuts back and forth between the T Birds and the Pink Ladies, as Danny and Sandy tell conflicting versions of their summer romance to their respective cliques. Danny's account is leering and suggestive, as he exaggerates his sexual prowess; Sandy's more demure account is a humorous counterpoint. Travolta and Newton-John are in good voice, and the cast dances (actually, struts and sways) nicely; the whole effect starts the film on a very positive level. Romantic complications arise, however, when Danny and Sandy meet. Unable to transcend the macho image he has built up among the T Birds, Danny treats Sandy very brusquely, and she is rightfully offended. He quickly realizes his mistake, but Sandy is not quick to forgive. Danny spends the rest of the film trying to win her back.

Meanwhile, a number of subplots develop. Sandy has a falling-out with Rizzo, who finds her innocence both naïve and offensive. In "Look at Me, I'm Sandra Dee," Rizzo parodies Sandy's attitudes by equating them with those of the famous virgin queens of 1950's filmdom, such as Sandra Dee and Doris Day, who virtuously fight off their lustful male pursuers in the movies. Later in the film, Rizzo defends her more wanton ways with the song "There Are Worse Things I Could Do," in which she argues that her frank acknowledgement of her sexual appetite is preferable to the hypocrisy that typified that era's approach to such matters. Things end happily for Rizzo, however; after a pregnancy scare, she ends up engaged to the T Birds' Kenickie.

Kenickie acquires a beat-up old jalopy, and the T Birds set out to convert it into a fearsome street machine. With the help of some "borrowed" parts and their auto mechanics teacher at Rydell, Mrs. Murdoch (Alice Ghostley), they do so. Toward the end of the film, Danny wins a hotly contested drag race against a car driven by one of the hated Scorpions, a rival gang.

In an effort to win Sandy back, Danny places himself in the hand of Coach Calhoun (Sid Caesar) of the "Phys Ed" Department. As an athlete, Danny is neither particularly strong nor coordinated; he is, however, aggressive to the point of belligerence. The sequence in which Coach Calhoun attempts to find a sport suited to Danny's particular "talents" is hilarious. When Danny does eventually end up on the track team, his efforts at self-improvement win Sandy back, at least temporarily. She agrees to accompany him to the big dance.

The National Bandstand sequence is the film's longest dance number and its most effective. The whole thing comes about when Vince Fontaine (played by Edd Byrnes, Kookie of television's popular 1950's series *77 Sunset Strip*) decides to bring his national dance contest to Rydell High. Naturally, all of the hot dancers are there, and just as naturally, Danny wins. Unfortunately, his winning partner is not Sandy. As Johnny Casino and the Gamblers (played by the rock group Sha Na Na, 1950's revivalists who function as the spiritual godfathers of the whole film) crank out "Born to Hand Jive," one of Danny's old girl friends, Cha Cha DiGregorio (Annette Charles), cuts in. Sandy leaves the dance floor in a huff as Danny, confused but ultimately too caught up in the beat to care, continues to dance. Couples jockey for favorable camera angles, and when the contest is over, Danny and Cha Cha have won.

Sandy decides that she loves Danny anyway, and finally hits upon a scheme to win him permanently. She enlists the aid of her friend Frenchy, who is back at Rydell High after discovering that beauty school was not all it seemed to be (she took the advice of another 1950's idol, Frankie Avalon, who, as Teen Angel, appeared to her in a vision and urged her to become a "Beauty School Dropout"). Frenchy turns Sandy into the sartorial equivalent of a T Bird. She acquires teased hair, a tight sweater, and black stretch pants and sports a cigarette dangling carelessly from her lips. When she confronts Danny in this guise, he is stunned. He falls to his knees in awe, and begins to belt out "You're the One That I Want" in a duet with Sandy. Thus everything ends happily. The kids get together for a few "bop-sh'bops," and Danny and Sandy drive off into the sunset—literally. Their car has not only been transformed into the wildest looking dragster ever; it has also somehow been given the power of flight.

Obviously plotting is not *Grease*'s strong point; nor is the screenplay by Bronte Woodward anything special. At times, the film seems intent on simply throwing as many 1950's images (everything from hula hoops to an animated toothpaste commercial featuring Bucky the Beaver) as possible into the mix and letting the chips fall where they may. That the film works, despite its occasional excesses, can be credited to the fine cast headed by Travolta and Newton-John as well as to the producers who put the cast together.

Randal Kleiser, whose only previous screen credit was as one of the writers on an atrociously received Italian gangster opus filmed in the United States called *Street People* (1976), keeps the pace of the film fast and furious. Production numbers are well staged and successfully integrated into the flow of the narrative, and Kleiser elicits terrific performances from his entire cast, which consists of a blend of newcomers and well-established character actors.

Travolta's acting prowess was not challenged by the role of Danny Zuko—like the other characters in the film, Danny seems to exist on a level somewhere between a comic strip and a situation comedy—but Travolta gives a terrific performance nevertheless. He is full of exhuberance and wit; his singing voice is pleasant, if unremarkable; and as a dancer, he possesses a feline grace that is beautiful to watch. Newton-John is perfectly cast as the bland/sweet Sandy; her fresh-faced innocence is ideal for the part. Whether her range is limited to such roles may be a legitimate question, but in *Grease*, her abilities match the role precisely.

There are nearly a dozen important supporting roles in *Grease*, and all of the actors in them do their share to make the film a success. Among the veterans, Arden (who for years played a high-school teacher in television's *Our Miss Brooks*) plays Rydell's cynical principal to the hilt; Caesar is appropriately beleaguered and bemused as the overmatched Coach Calhoun; Blondell is good in a brief role as Vi, a harassed waitress at the T Birds' favorite eatery; Byrnes is fine as the Dick Clark look-alike, Vince Fontaine; and Avalon, as Teen Angel, delivers a knockout "Beauty School Dropout" number.

The younger members of the supporting cast more than match their older colleagues. Channing is hilarious as Rizzo, the bad girl who discovers that she needs love after all; Conn gives an affecting performance as the hapless Frenchy, whose career as a beautician ends after she inadvertantly dyes her own hair pink; Charles looks appropriately exotic as Cha Cha, the hot number from St. Bernadette High; and Conaway does well as Kenickie, the hot rodder who yearns for Rizzo.

Despite (or perhaps because of) *Grease*'s huge popularity with the public, the film drew a fair share of disparagement from the critics. Those who disliked *Grease* seemed to base most of their objections on the fact that the film presented a distorted view of the 1950's. As far as it goes, this criticism is entirely valid (producers Stigwood and Carr even hedged their bets on the drawing power of 1950's music, commissioning Barry Gibb of the Bee Gees to write the disco-ish title song); as noted above, the film was written from the perspective of a decade that was (or at least felt itself to be) considerably hipper than the 1950's ever pretended to be. *Grease* laughs at, as well as with, the 1950's. No one would deny that the 1950's were much more complex than *Grease* would indicate.

The counterargument, of course, is that *Grease* does not pretend to be anything but the broadest parody; it is a musical comedy, not a documentary, and it is as a musical comedy that it must be judged. The energetic performances of Travolta, Newton-John, Channing, and the rest of the cast convinced an enormous audience (the film quickly became one of the top money earners of all time) that, as a musical comedy, *Grease* was very good indeed.

Robert Mitchell

THE GREAT DICTATOR

Released: 1940
Production: Charles Chaplin for United Artists
Direction: Charles Chaplin
Screenplay: Charles Chaplin
Cinematography: Karl Struss and Rollie Totheroh
Editing: Willard Nico
Music: Meredith Willson
Running time: 127 minutes

Principal characters:
Adenoid Hynkel/Dictator of Tomania/
A Jewish Barber .... Charles Chaplin
Hannah .... Paulette Goddard
Benzini Napaloni/
Dictator of Bacteria .... Jack Oakie
Schultz .... Reginald Gardiner
Garbitsch .... Henry Daniell
Herring .... Billy Gilbert

Five years had passed between Charles Chaplin's *Modern Times* (1936) and *The Great Dictator*. Chaplin was the last holdout against the talking film; *Modern Times* was essentially silent, dependent on his genius for pantomime, except for a comic song made up of rhyming pig-Latin lyrics. Thus, *The Great Dictator* marks Chaplin's talking film debut. In it, the dialogue is as important as the masterful pantomime, for Chaplin had something to say, and he felt that he had to say it in words. Although the dialogue is funny throughout the film, the six-minute speech which he delivers near the end of the film is definitely an example of the misuse of dialogue, for it is didactic and misfires completely in a picture that is already too long. Nevertheless, *The Great Dictator* is a great tragicomedy and one of the best creative films Chaplin ever made.

Chaplin plays a dual role: a Jewish barber and a dictator. In World War I the barber had suffered an injury that affected his mind. He has regained his sanity twenty years later and has returned to his shop in the Jewish ghetto of a great city in Tomania. He is unaware that while he has been away, a dictator named Hynkel has risen to power. Hynkel, a persecutor of Jews, has built up a strong police force. The irony of the situation is that the little Jewish barber and the great dictator Hynkel are look-alikes. Almost immediately the little barber becomes a victim of the police when he attempts to resist them. He is beaten and incarcerated, and then escapes and flees to a bordering country.

Meanwhile, however, he finds himself attracted to a pretty little laundress named Hannah (Paulette Goddard), whom he defends against Nazi oppression. The ghetto people realize that Hynkel must be destroyed, and there is a very funny sequence in which four of them meet to eat puddings containing coins to determine by lot which of them shall become a martyr and slay the dictator.

Hynkel, completely mad, delivers a wild, senseless speech that is a conglomeration of German, Yiddish, and pig-Latin. Later, when he is alone, he performs a solo ballet with a huge balloon representing the world. He bounces it protectively, leaping and pirouetting to catch it once more in his embrace, then he twirls it lovingly. Accidentally, in his fervor, he breaks it and is reduced to childish tears; his world is shattered.

The border country where the barber and Hannah have sought refuge is one that Hynkel has recently annexed, and the inhabitants mistake the barber for Hynkel himself. He finds himself pushed forward upon a speaker's platform, where he is expected to address the crowd. He chooses, rather than an inflammatory, screaming speech, to make an impassioned plea for reason and mercy. The crowd is moved and applauds him, and it is on this note of triumph that the picture ends.

Chaplin is wistful and moving as the small, persecuted barber, much as he had always been as the beloved little tramp. But it is as Hynkel that he enjoys his greatest triumph. Satire and ridicule have always been the sharpest weapons against wrong, and Chaplin portrays Hynkel with all the genius of his comic skill. Hynkel becomes an insane fool who can inspire only derisive laughter in any thinking person. Yet Hitler, of whom Hynkel is obviously a portrait, could not be laughed into nonexistence. *The Great Dictator* was released on the eve of World War II; one could still laugh then at Chaplin's satiric portrait of the Nazi dictator. All too soon, however, a war that embraced the world was raging, and there were times when it seemed that the mad power that bloomed even in mythical Tomania was hardly a funny thing since the satire struck too close to home.

Some of the wildest humor in the picture comes in the sequence in which Hynkel is visited by Napaloni, the dictator of Bacteria, with which Tomania has formed an alliance. Jack Oakie plays Napaloni as a wonderful caricature of Mussolini, and if making fun of one dictator is funny, deriding two is twice as hilarious.

At Academy Award time *The Great Dictator* was nominated for Best Picture, and Chaplin received nominations as Best Actor and Best Writer of an Original Story; Jack Oakie was nominated for Best Supporting Actor of the Year; and Meredith Willson's original score gained a nomination as well. But there were no Oscars awarded to *The Great Dictator*. When the awards were made in February of 1941, the world was seething with news of Hitler's newest devastations abroad, and America was very soon to be drawn into the conflict. As World War II raged, Chaplin wisely withdrew *The Great Dictator* from circulation, and it did not reappear until after the war, when the Allies had won and Hitler and Mussolini were dead. The full bittersweet power of Chaplin's tragicomedy could draw a smile again. Hitler could be an object of mirth. *The Great Dictator* was not shown in Rome until 1961, long after Mussolini's empire had fallen and there was a whole new generation of Italians who had not lived under Fascist rule. Then *The Great Dictator* became the reigning hit of the movie season in Rome, and the Romans thought Jack Oakie the funniest man they had ever seen. They literally rolled in the aisles and jumped up and down with glee at his interpretation of Napaloni, Dictator of Bacteria.

Chaplin chose an excellent cast to support him. Paulette Goddard had been Chaplin's leading lady in *Modern Times* and his wife from 1933 to 1942, and Hitler's two aides, Goebbels and Göring, arc effectively parodied by Henry Daniell as Minister of Propaganda Garbitsch (Goebbels) and Billy Gilbert as Minister of War Herring (Göring). There is also an amusing impersonation by Reginald Gardiner as a high-ranking Tomanian named Schultz.

By 1940, Chaplin had become a world figure, dominating film comedy with his superb gift of pantomime. Internationally known and loved, his gift for laughter transcended language barriers; thus, it is not difficult to understand how he went on making silent films when nobody else bothered with them. Warner Bros.' *The Jazz Singer* first initiated the "talkie" in 1927, and by 1929, there remained only three great holdouts against the talking film. Two of them, Lon Chaney and Greto Garbo, appeared in talkies in 1930, but Charles Chaplin did not relent until 1940, when *The Great Dictator* was released. In 1928, the very year after *The Jazz Singer*, he released *The Circus*; it was the first year of the Academy Awards, and the silent film still made nearly a clean sweep at the awards. Along with Emil Jannings and Richard Barthelmess, Chaplin was nominated as Best Actor for his performance in *The Circus*. Even though Jannings won the Oscar, a special award was given to Charles Chaplin "for versatility and genius in writing, acting, directing and producing *The Circus*."

One of his best and most poignant features, *City Lights*, came out in 1931. It was a moving silent picture, gaining no attention from the Academy voters, but becoming one of his best-liked and biggest moneymaking films. He did not release another comedy until 1936 when *Modern Times* appeared. Again, the Academy gave him no recognition. As the one successful silent star, he was an oddity, and possibly could not have been considered as competition for Paul Muni, Gary Cooper, Walter Huston, William Powell, and Spencer Tracy, the five nominees in 1936 for Best Actor. But in 1940, with the release of his first all-talking feature, *The Great Dictator*, the Academy took notice again of Chaplin's genius, rewarding him with five nominations. In 1947, Chaplin's most impudent black comedy, *Monsieur Verdoux*, received an Academy nomination for Best Original Screenplay.

In subsequent years right wing forces came to the fore, especially in the film industry. *Limelight*, released in 1952 (the year Chaplin left the United States), was not allowed to play in the Los Angeles area mainly because of the protests of the American Legion. When *Limelight* was finally presented in Hollywood in 1972, it received an Oscar for Best Original Score. That was the year after the Academy, in 1971, gave Chaplin a Special Honorary Oscar, which he accepted in person on Awards night. It was his last important public appearance; and the ovation given him by the audience proved that he was regarded as one of the screen's few authentic geniuses.

DeWitt Bodeen

THE GREAT ESCAPE

Released: 1963
Production: John Sturges for United Artists
Direction: John Sturges
Screenplay: James Clavell and W. R. Burnett; based on a book of the same
name by Paul Brickhill
Cinematography: Daniel L. Fapp
Editing: Ferris Webster
Music: Elmer Bernstein
Running time: 168 minutes

Principal characters:
Hilts .... Steve McQueen
Hendley ....James Garner
Bartlett .... Richard Attenborough
Velinski .... Charles Bronson
Blythe .... Donald Pleasence
Sedgwick .... James Coburn

The Great Escape details the true story of the largest mass escape of POW's
during World War II. Utilizing an all-star cast and a running time which
approaches three hours, director John Sturges creates a compelling tribute
to the human spirit. The film is rather complex and can be broken down into
three distinct parts: the elaborate preparations leading to the escape; the
escape itself; and the eventual recapture of most of the prisoners.

The prison camp in the story is populated by the most notorious troublemakers encountered by the Germans in their various camps all over Europe.
The Germans, having isolated the most volatile elements among their captives, intend to scrutinize them intently. Bartlett (Richard Attenborough),
the British officer who is the leader of the escape committee, is able to recruit
experts for every phase of the well-planned mass exodus. He uses master
tailors to create civilian clothes; visas and identity cards are forged by cal-
ligraphers and artists; mine workers dig the escape tunnels. There is a sense
of harmony in their efforts.

The only discouraging voice is that of Hilts (Steve McQueen), a captured
American flyer, who is a loner and would prefer to escape on his own. After
several attempts and as many terms in solitary confinement, he manages to
get out, only to be captured and returned. At this point Bartlett realizes his
need for Hilts, since he is the only prisoner who knows exactly how far it is
to the forest and what lies immediately beyond. Persuaded finally to work
for the group, Hilts assists in the escape plans. The escape is partially successful, with more than two-thirds of the planned escapees making it out of
the tunnel before their escape is detected.

From this point the film breaks its unified focus to concentrate on the various routes taken by the more significant prisoners. The ingenuity of the individuals to make good their escape is punctuated by scenes of the Gestapo capturing or killing other escapees. Bartlett is recaptured, and, in a move of savage revenge, he and a large number of other prisoners are trucked to an isolated spot and machine-gunned. Hilts, who manages to commandeer a motorcycle, gives the Germans a wild race for the Swiss border, but he fails in a final attempt to breach the fence that separates him from neutrality and freedom. Returned to the POW camp, he is once again placed in solitary confinement as the names of those escapees killed by the Germans are read to the assembled prisoners.

What is unique about *The Great Escape* is the sense of camaraderie expressed through various characters in the film. There is a feeling of community enveloping the prison camp which is not found in such films as *The Bridge on the River Kwai* (1957), *Stalag 17* (1953), or *King Rat* (1965). Each of these other films concentrates on one aspect of men in prison. *The Bridge on the River Kwai* dealt with the obsessions of a man trying to maintain his sanity in a world of total chaos. *Stalag 17* was more optimistic, showing how individuals can survive in an environment of pain and suffering. *King Rat* utilized a similar theme, but, rather than showing the humor in the situation, it concentrates on unscrupulous characters who take advantage of human misery. This lack of harmony found in most POW films is avoided in *The Great Escape*. There is no concern with finding the traitor selling information to the captors for extra rations of food, there are no exploiters, and there is no real concern about poor living conditions. Rather, the focus of the film drives home a single goal: escape.

The selection of the cast is important in the success of *The Great Escape*. Steve McQueen's portrayal of Hilts functions as an extention of the loner *persona* of the 1950's and is thus somewhat of an anachronism in the film's 1940's setting. James Garner as the "scavenger" is perfectly suited to the role of the wheeler-dealer, and Richard Attenborough is flawless as Bartlett, the organizer of the escape. The secondary characters also seem perfectly suited for their roles.

James Clavell, one of the screenwriters for *The Great Escape*, later wrote another prisoner-of-war film, *King Rat* in which he concentrated on the darker side of the human condition. There are glimpses of this bleak outlook in the conclusion of *The Great Escape* in which most of the cast is either killed or recaptured; however, *The Great Escape* was made during the period of epic length motion pictures, and director John Sturges preferred to concentrate on entertainment rather than on stark realism to carry the dramatic story line.

There is a sense of the humor and joy of life in *The Great Escape* that transcends the ramifications of the escape. Based on a true situation and embellished with Hollywood's characteristic flair, the film functions both as a document of World War II and as a proclamation through its characters' of ingenuity and irrepressible instinct for survival.

Carl F. Macek

THE GREAT GABBO

Released: 1929
Production: James Cruze for Sono Art-World Wide Pictures
Direction: James Cruze
Screenplay: F. Hugh Herbert; based on an original story by Ben Hecht
Cinematography: Ira H. Morgan
Editing: no listing
Running time: 91 minutes

> *Principal characters:*
> Gabbo .... Erich Von Stroheim
> Mary .... Betty Compson
> Frank .... Donald Douglas
> Babe .... Marjorie "Babe" Kane

In recent years, *The Great Gabbo* has become something of a cult favorite with young film enthusiasts, thanks largely to the bravura playing of Erich Von Stroheim and the "camp" nature of the musical numbers. The film should not be regarded merely as a cult curiosity, however, for it contains, after all, Von Stroheim's first appearance in a sound film and was directed by James Cruze, a major force in silent films with such classics as *The Covered Wagon* (1923), *Beggar on Horseback* (1925), *The Pony Express* (1925), and *Old Ironsides* (1926) to his credit.

Cruze's direction is surprisingly good. It only seems second-rate because of the ludicrous nature of the plot and the melodramatics of the dialogue, for which, presumably, blame should be assigned to Ben Hecht, who certainly should have known better. Cruze is particularly brave in the handling of a sound montage sequence—something very unusual for this period—while the Great Gabbo's insanity comes to the surface. The montage does not really work but that is chiefly due to the primitive nature of early sound, and Cruze deserves top marks for attempting such a difficult sequence and for almost pulling it off.

Von Stroheim heads the cast, in the title role of a ventriloquist whose egotism leads to his eventual downfall and madness. The Great Gabbo is a part perfectly suited to the actor/director who, in the silent era, had gained the title of "The Man You Love to Hate," and who was to continue portraying this type of role for the rest of his career. In fact, *The Great Gabbo* is well worth comparing with the later Republic production of *The Great Flamarion* (1945), in which Von Stroheim gives a similar performance. Incidentally, the Great Gabbo's ventriloquist act was based on that of Marshall Montgomery, "America's premiere ventriloquist," who really did eat, drink, and smoke while his dummy, Otto, did the talking. In the film, Von Stroheim did the same trick, but he relied on an unidentified actor to provide the "voice" of

Otto, and at least one critic complained that Von Stroheim's throat displayed not the least sign of movement during the dummy's recitations.

Supporting Von Stroheim in the role of Mary is Betty Compson, in reality Cruze's wife and a busy actress in the early years of sound, continuing a screen career that had started in the late teens. (The role of Mary was originally to have been played by silent star Pauline Starke, but when Compson suddenly became available, Starke was dropped and her film career came to an abrupt end.) Compson is adequate for the part she plays, but the same cannot be said of Donald Douglas as the romantic lead, Frank, who is effetely bland and totally lacking in dramatic ability. Rounding out the cast is Marjorie "Babe" Kane, sister of the popular early talkie star Helen Kane, who sings a few songs in the manner of her sister and delivers a few lines of dialogue with bravado.

The Great Gabbo opens in a small neighborhood theater, where the egocentric ventriloquist is performing, assisted by his partner Mary who serves as little more than "window dressing" for the act, but who constantly tries to please her employer. When Mary accidentally drops a tray on stage during Gabbo's act, she is fired by him.

In time, the Great Gabbo has become one of the stars of the Manhattan Revue, which also features Mary and her new singing and dancing partner, Frank. For effect, the Great Gabbo and his dummy, Otto, eat dinner every evening together in a smart restaurant. To emphasize Gabbo's lofty position, a footman is required to carry Otto from the pair's chauffeur-driven car to their table. When Mary sees the two of them at the restaurant, she comes over and talks to Gabbo through the dummy. The vertriloquist falls in love with her, and his affection for Mary, together with his ego problems, begin to affect his act. When Gabbo overhears Frank and Mary talking outside their dressing rooms and learns that the two are secretly married, he becomes completely insane, and wanders onstage during their final dance number, destroying the performance. He is fired by the management, and the film ends with Gabbo slowly walking away from the theater as workmen remove his billing, "The Great Gabbo," from the marquee. (It should perhaps be noted that throughout the film, the rise and fall of the Great Gabbo is watched by a minor vaudeville husband-and-wife team who had played on the same bill with Gabbo and Mary when they were unknown.)

Although the dramatic sequences are shot in black-and-white, the musical numbers are filmed in color (although no color prints of *The Great Gabbo* appear to have survived). The film features seven such numbers, "The New Step," "I'm in Love with You," "I'm Laughing," "Ickey" (the last two of which were performed by Otto), "Every Now and Then," "The Web of Love," and "The Ga-Ga Bird." The last is seen briefly as part of the montage sequence, but otherwise does not appear in the film as it exists today, and may possibly have been cut prior to the feature's original release. The most ludicrous of the musical numbers is "The Web of Love," which features Mary and Frank (she as a fly and he as a spider) prancing and dancing around on stage while grotesquely garbed chorus girls perform curious gyrations on a large spider's web in the background. The number itself is bad enough, but it is made even more unintentionally funny by having the two principals carry on a stilted conversation as they pause in grotesque positions. The humor is further helped by its being blatantly obvious that doubles are performing for the principals in the long and medium shots of the number, while offstage another performer is singing while Compson mouths the song. Compson's somewhat nasal and common speaking voice was noted for its rich soprano when she sang in early musicals, thanks to the anonymous singers standing just out of camera range and taking care of that chore for the star, in the days before dubbing was invented.

The Great Gabbo received mixed reviews on its initial release. *Variety* (September 18, 1929) wrote, "All the superlatives in a heavy vocabulary can be expanded and yet *The Great Gabbo* will just remain the picture prodigy of the independent ranks and a talker drama, from the standpoints of theme originality and absorbing qualities, above the average show window display of the big companies." Mordaunt Hall in *The New York Times* (September 13, 1929) found the film "highly original," and thought Von Stroheim "punctilious in the earnestness with which he attacks his role." *Photoplay* (December, 1929), however, considered *The Great Gabbo* "a bitter disappointment. . . . Cruze seems to have lost his sense of humor, and the lighting and scenario are terrible."

Today, *The Great Gabbo* stands as both a curiosity and an interesting historical document, a perfect example of a failed early talkie, made with the best intentions and the best of talent.

Anthony Slide

THE GREAT GATSBY

Released: 1949
Production: Richard Maibaum for Paramount
Direction: Elliott Nugent
Screenplay: Cyril Hume and Richard Maibaum; based on the novel of the same name by F. Scott Fitzgerald and the play of the same name by Owen Davis
Cinematography: John F. Seitz
Editing: Ellsworth Hoagland
Running time: 91 minutes

Principal characters:

Jay Gatsby	Alan Ladd
Daisy Buchanan	Betty Field
Nick Carraway	Macdonald Carey
Jordan Baker	Ruth Hussey
Tom Buchanan	Barry Sullivan
Wilson	Howard da Silva
Myrtle Wilson	Shelley Winters
Dan Cody	Henry Hull

The 1949 film of F. Scott Fitzgerald's classic novel *The Great Gatsby* succeeds in being a good film even though it is not entirely successful in conveying many of the essential qualities of Fitzgerald's work. This is not surprising. Cinema and literature are such different forms that it is rare indeed for a masterpiece in cinema to be the result of an adaptation of a masterpiece in literature. The great films are usually made from original screenplays, as was *Citizen Kane* (1941), or from second-rate novels, as was *Gone with the Wind* (1939). Indeed, each of these films is better than any one of the films made from the works of such great writers as Ernest Hemingway, Thomas Hardy, and Gustave Flaubert.

In adapting a masterwork of literature for the more popular medium of cinema, the screenwriter must usually shorten and simplify the original work, since a film containing all the incidents of the average novel would be five to ten hours long. In the process of shortening and simplifying, nuances are lost, and in the process of making a written work into a primarily visual one, distinction and style in language will not survive. Because nuances and verbal style are less important in second-rate books, such books usually withstand the process of adaptation better than do first-rate books.

The film of *The Great Gatsby* is no exception to these precepts. The novel loses a good deal in its translation to film, but enough of the basic elements survive and the quality of the filmmaking is high enough that the film is worthwhile and rewarding if one does not expect it to be as good as the novel.

The film opens in 1948 with Nick Carraway (Macdonald Carey) and his wife Jordan (Ruth Hussey) visiting the grave of Jay Gatsby. Jordan's reminiscences immediately take us back twenty years to the time when young America was "joy-riding on home-made hootch." After a montage of scenes of the lindy hop, bootlegging, and gangsters, we are told by the narrator that Jay Gatsby came out of the 1920's and "built a dark empire for himself because he carried a dream in his heart."

We soon find that Gatsby (Alan Ladd) has bought an old mansion on Long Island that is directly across the channel from the home of the wealthy and prominent Buchanans. He has paid two hundred thousand dollars for the house and plans to spend many thousands more to renovate it, using the same decorator who did the Buchanans' house. After Gatsby gazes across the channel at the Buchanans' residence, there is an abrupt transition to a lively party in progress at Gatsby's now lavishly-redecorated house.

At this party is Nick Carraway, who soon finds that he may be the only person specifically invited. One of the many revelers explains to him that no one is invited to Gatsby's, they just come. It is not long before Nick learns why he has been singled out. First, however, he meets Gatsby and listens to his life story. Actually, Gatsby first tries to tell a false story, but Nick lets him know that he does not believe it, so Gatsby—in a long flashback—explains how he rose from humble origins to ostentatious wealth.

Gatsby began life as plain Jimmy Gatz, but he came to the attention of Dan Cody (Henry Hull), a millionaire who hired the young Gatz to work on his yacht as it went three times around the world. Cody both lived and preached the motto that a person can take anything he wants if he has money. Gatz learned the lesson well. After Cody's death and his own army service, Gatz—who began calling himself Gatsby—amassed a fortune through bootlegging.

Nick then finds out why Gatsby is interested in him. Nick is a second cousin of Daisy Buchanan (Betty Field), and Gatsby wants Nick to arrange a meeting between Daisy and Gatsby by inviting them both to tea some time. Gatsby even offers to assist Nick's business as a bond salesman. He finally becomes quite blunt: "Every man has his price, Mr. Carraway. What's yours?" Nick, however, refuses to agree to arrange the meeting.

We gradually find out, chiefly through two flashbacks, the story of Daisy and Gatsby. They met and fell in love during World War I in Louisville, Kentucky, when Gatsby was a young lieutenant. Daisy wanted to marry Gatsby then, but he insisted on waiting until he had enough money. By the time the war was over, however, Daisy had married the rich, polo-playing Tom Buchanan (Barry Sullivan). Remembering Dan Cody's view that money can buy anything, Gatsby decided to become rich and successful enough to win Daisy back.

Daisy, we find, is not happy. Although she loved Tom when they were married, she now—rightly—suspects him of infidelity. Her two closest friends are Jordan Baker and Nick. We have learned from the opening scene that Jordan will become Nick's wife, but that is still in the future and is not suspected by either one of them. They are, in fact, quite different in outlook and temperament. Nick is principled, but Jordan has tried to cheat in a golf tournament, and when she learns that Gatsby wants to meet Daisy she agrees to arrange it if Gatsby gives her a new Dusenberg roadster.

Gatsby, of course, accepts Jordan's offer, and soon a date for tea at Nick's is set up. They do not tell Nick anything about the plan, and they do not tell Daisy that Gatsby will be there. Nick finds out what is happening when Gatsby arrives one rainy afternoon with five servants and several baskets of food. Then Jordan arrives with Daisy, and she and Gatsby finally meet again (with suitable, if not subtle, music on the sound track).

As always, Gatsby is eager to impress and boasts of keeping his house "full of celebrated people." When he and Nick and Daisy go over to his house, he shows Daisy his closets full of custom-made shirts. Gatsby easily convinces Daisy that she should leave her husband and come back to him. There are delays, but finally there is a confrontation in a hotel in New York; Nick, Jordan, Gatsby, Daisy, and Tom are all there. Daisy tells Tom she is leaving him, but Tom refuses to accept her decision and counters by telling Daisy what he has found out about Gatsby's illegal activities. With the situation still unresolved, the group returns to Long Island, traveling in two identical yellow roadsters—Daisy and Gatsby in one, with Daisy driving, and Tom, Nick, and Jordan in the other.

Tom has been having an affair with Myrtle Wilson (Shelley Winters), the wife of a gasoline station owner. As Daisy and Gatsby drive toward the station on their way back to Long Island, Myrtle—thinking Tom is in the car—rushes out on the road. Daisy hits her but does not stop. When Tom, Nick, and Jordan, drive by a few minutes later and see that there has been an accident, they find that Myrtle is dead. After this horrifying event, everything changes. Gatsby tells Daisy he will say he was driving the car, and when Tom arrives, Daisy tells him what happened and that Gatsby will take the blame. She is hysterical about going to prison and is willing to let him. Nick is disgusted by her reaction and tells Gatsby to forget her.

Later, Myrtle's husband, Wilson (Howard da Silva), comes to Tom's house with a gun looking for the man who took the affection, and then the life, of his wife. Muttering "you and Myrtle," he is about to shoot Tom, but Tom says it was someone else and tells him to look for another yellow roadster— the one with a damaged fender. The climactic scene takes place at Gatsby's swimming pool. Gatsby tells Nick that he has decided to quit trying to be a gentleman. "Look what I've done to myself and everyone else to get where I am," he says. The telephone rings and continues to ring, but Gatsby has dismissed his servants and refuses to answer; he does not know it is Tom, who has been persuaded by Daisy to call to warn him about Wilson. Soon Wilson appears and shoots and kills Gatsby. Then, in a final scene, Nick says he is going to become a writer and Jordan asks to go along and help.

Even though this film of *The Great Gatsby* may have missed some of the shadings of Fitzgerald's examination of the price of pursuing success regardless of the cost, it presents its subject quite well for a mainstream Hollywood film. The acting is neither deep nor brilliant. The characters portrayed are essentially shallow, and when they attempt to show off, they tend to be flashy rather than radiant. The one exception is Nick Carraway, the observer with integrity, who is played by Carey in a convincingly understated manner. The direction, too, is effective if not imaginative.

The Great Gatsby has been popular with adapters. It was presented as a play staged by George Cukor in 1926, as a silent film in the same year, and as a sound film in both 1949 and 1974. Perhaps because of the lavish (although not profitable) 1974 production starring Robert Redford in the title role, the 1949 version of *The Great Gatsby* has been seen by few people in recent years. The 1974 film was scorned by critics, and, in a sense, this scorn has brought a greater respect for the earlier film.

Sharon Wiseman

THE GREAT LIE

Released: 1941
Production: Hal B. Wallis and Henry Blanke for Warner Bros.
Direction: Edmund Goulding
Screenplay: Lenore Coffee; based on the novel *January Heights* (*Far Horizons*) by Polan Banks
Cinematography: Tony Gaudio
Editing: Ralph Dawson
Costume design: Orry-Kelly
Music: Max Steiner
Running time: 102 minutes

Principal characters:
Maggie Patterson	Bette Davis
Peter Van Allen	George Brent
Sandra Kovac	Mary Astor (AA)
Aunt Ada	Lucile Watson
Violet	Hattie McDaniel

After her great triumph in a bravura role as a murderess in *The Letter* (1940), Warner Bros. decided to give Bette Davis a sympathetic heroine to portray. She alternated the kinds of ladies she played with a great deal of finesse, always a proof in films of versatility. The vehicle chosen for her was from a Polan Banks novel retitled for the screen *The Great Lie*; it was one of those stories patently manufactured for a female star and appealing to the female members of the audience. In this case, there were really two important female parts—the heroine and the bitch, who turns out to be not such a bitch after all.

Most of the big scenes in the story take place between the two women, as they had in *The Old Maid* (1939), which Bette Davis made with Miriam Hopkins. That was a duel, as everything always was when Hopkins costarred with a member of her own sex; but in *The Great Lie* the two women are played by Davis and Mary Astor. They are enemies in this story, but in real life they admired each other and worked together, sometimes sitting on the sidelines while the lights were being adjusted, reworking their dialogue together.

The story of *The Great Lie* begins when the hero, Peter Van Allen (George Brent), wakes up after ten days of partying to realize that at some time during the drunken celebration he had married Sandra Kovac (Mary Astor), a celebrated concert pianist. Peter deplores his action, because, while Sandra is a handsome woman, he happens really to be very much in love with another girl, Maggie Patterson (Bette Davis). His attorney contacts him, and Peter is startled by another shock: his marriage to Sandra is not legal, because she had not received her final divorce decree from her previous husband.

Peter gets in his private plane and flies directly to Maggie's well-appointed plantation home in Maryland. Maggie is understandably angry; Peter and she have loved each other for years, and now in a rash, drunken moment, he has spoiled her future as well as his. Peter does not tell her about the invalidity of his hasty marriage to Sandra, because he realizes that he has a duty to Sandra to perform first. He goes to Sandra and asks her to marry him on the day her divorce does become effective. Sandra, however, has a concert date in Philadelphia that night, and although Peter suggests that she break it, she goes to Philadelphia. In her dressing-room after the concert, she receives Maggie, who asks her to relinquish Peter because her uncle, who has an important job in Washington, can get him a flying job with the government. Sandra coldly tells Maggie that she intends to hang onto Peter.

When Maggie returns home, Peter is waiting for her, and tells her that his marriage to Sandra is not valid. Maggie is overjoyed, and they are immediately wed at her plantation home. They have only a brief but happy honeymoon, however, which is interrupted when Peter is summoned by the government to fly to South America on a survey flight. Maggie sees him off in Washington and receives a call there from Sandra, who tells her that she is going to have a baby, Peter's child. The worst is yet to come, however; news is flashed that Peter's plane has crashed in a South American jungle and all hope for any survivors has been abandoned.

Sandra now no longer has any interest in bearing Peter's child, but Maggie comes to her with a curious proposal, one that involves the titular "great lie." Her suggestion is that Sandra and she go away together to a lonely ranch she knows about in Arizona, where Maggie will tend and play nurse to Sandra during the period of pregnancy. When the child is born, it will be turned over to Maggie to rear. Nobody will ever know that the baby's mother is really Sandra because Maggie will rear the child as Peter's and hers. Maggie will also pay for everything.

The proposal is too bizarre for Sandra to ignore. She has no use for Maggie, and Maggie dislikes her, but they agree to live together for the months involved, bound in this conspiracy out of their mutual love for one man. They move to the lonely Arizona ranch, and Maggie becomes nurse, companion, and policewoman to Sandra, forcing her to take care of herself, to eat properly, and to exercise regularly. The baby, a healthy boy, is born and is named Peter. Sandra is disinterested in the child and goes off to Australia on a concert tour, while Maggie returns to Maryland with the baby. Then suddenly comes the explosive news: Peter Van Allen has survived the crash and is on his way home, alive and well. There is never any doubt in his mind that Maggie is the mother of his son. She is reluctant to confess the truth, and as the days pass, she is more than ever determined to live out "the great lie."

Sandra returns from her concert tour, but does not yet intend to change events, and for a time she keeps the secret. Then, without warning, she descends upon the Maryland plantation, telling everyone that she has come to see the wonderful baby; but in private she tells Maggie that she intends staying at the Maryland house until Maggie tells Peter the truth. She admits that this is only the first step in her plan; once she has regained custody of the child as her own, she intends to get Peter back as her lawful husband. Maggie bravely tells Peter the truth in front of Sandra, affirming that Sandra now wants her baby, and Peter, stunned, admits that he can understand her feeling; but it must also be understood that he loves Maggie, and he will stay with her. Sandra looks at the two of them and realizes that she has lost the battle. When she tells them that she is leaving, Peter asks what is to be done about the boy. Sandra looks at them both with cynical insolence, saying "I'm leaving him with his mother," and walks out of their lives.

The Great Lie was immediately successful at the box office. The plot is admittedly soap opera, but director Edmund Goulding stages it with style, and the basically artificial, contrived story comes across with great believability. Davis plays with great sincerity, and Astor's performance as Sandra is a personal triumph. She is beautiful and authoritative and offers a stunning portrayal of a temperamental musical artist. It came as no surprise when Academy members voted her the Oscar for Best Supporting Actress. There are several scenes showing her in concert, and Astor plays them so superbly that there was no doubt in many a viewer's mind that it was she herself who had played Tchaikovsky's Piano Concerto so brilliantly. Astor was no stranger to the piano keyboard, so her fingering and gestures while playing are exactly right, but the execution of the concerto itself was dubbed by a professional concert pianist. That year the Tchaikovsky concerto was heard ceaselessly on radio, and numerous recordings of it were sold.

DeWitt Bodeen

THE GREAT McGINTY

Released: 1940
Production: Paul Jones for Paramount
Direction: Preston Sturges
Screenplay: Preston Sturges (AA)
Cinematography: William C. Mellor
Editing: Hugh Bennet
Running time: 81 minutes

Principal characters:
Dan McGinty	Brian Donlevy
The Boss	Akim Tamiroff
Catherine McGinty	Muriel Angelus
The Politician	William Demarest
Thompson	Louis Jean Heydt
The Dancer	Steffi Duna
La Jolla	Esther Howard

Early in the summer of 1940, there was considerable anxiety at Paramount concerning a soon to be released feature then entitled *Down Went McGinty*. The film was a political satire, a genre which had never been a proven favorite with moviegoers. The hero was Brian Donlevy, whom audiences had passionately hissed as the bestial Sergeant Markoff in the studio's popular remake of *Beau Geste* (1939); and the author-director was Preston Sturges, an eccentric, unorthodox and unheralded talent. Baffled as how to "sell" the picture, Paramount dispatched Donlevy on a three-week, twenty-city promotional tour; circulated endorsements by popular Paramount personalities such as Claudette Colbert, Bob Hope, and Dorothy Lamour ("I'd wear my best sarong for McGinty any day"); and, on the eve of release, they changed the title to *The Great McGinty*, hoping that the more positive title might help at the box office. Such pains were unnecessary, as *The Great McGinty* became one of the most celebrated "sleepers" in Hollywood history. It was a surprise critical and box-office success that survives today as the cinema's most pungent lampoon of politics and, arguably, the purest satire of the highly original, sadly erratic Preston Sturges.

Actually, Paramount had reasonable cause for apprehension regarding *The Great McGinty*. It was solely the brainchild of Sturges, a wealthy playboy, Broadway playwright, and Paramount contract writer whose work on such films as *If I Were King* (1938), the Bob Hope vehicle *Never Say Die* (1939), and *Remember the Night* (1940) were largely rewritten by less talented but more disciplined contractees before going before the cameras. The cynical tone of the piece worried the front office, but Sturges' offer was economically appealing: he would sell his script to the studio for virtually nothing if he were allowed to direct it. Paramount agreed, then handicapped Sturges with a modest $350,000 budget and a three-week shooting schedule. Sturges cast Donlevy after the jaunty actor passed him on the lot and said "Hi 'ya." (He also remembered Donlevy's being fired by an unhappy producer during rehearsals for Sturges' Broadway play *Young Man of Manhattan* in 1930.) The only other "name" in the cast was Paramount's fine Russian character actor Akim Tamiroff, who portrayed the Boss. The part of Mrs. McGinty went to a fresh studio starlet, Muriel Angelus.

The Great McGinty opens in a seedy Banana Republic saloon, where a drunken embezzler named Thompson (Louis Jean Heydt) is pouring his heart out to a hootchie dancer (Steffi Duna). The ex-cashier bemoans the crime that forced him to forsake his family and fortune: "One crazy minute," he laments, just before the bartender (Brian Donlevy) escorts him to the men's room. "Go ahead—heave-ho," grins the bartender—but instead the drunk tries to shoot himself. The bartender dutifully intervenes, but continues to heap scorn on the remorseful man. The hootchie dancer asks what right he has to do that. He replies: "*I* was the governor of a state, baby."

There is a flashback to an election eve scene during the Depression, in which the bartender, then hobo Dan McGinty, is one of many people in a soup line provided as a ploy by the Politician (William Demarest), who is looking for hungry souls willing to vote for his candidate for two dollars apiece. McGinty agrees, and returns late that evening—after voting thirty-seven times. The Politician takes him to the Mayor's headquarters, where McGinty stuffs himself with a hero sandwich, orders a boilermaker, and swaps insults with the Boss. The Boss is impressed, and roars: "He thinks he's *me*!"

McGinty is soon in the Boss's employ. Sporting an outrageous checkered suit and derby hat, he collects protection money from a brothel madame, La Jolla (Esther Howard), and others. With Irish charm and ham fists, he rises fast, quickly becoming an alderman. Soon the Boss asks him to run as a reform candidate for Mayor. "In this town I'm *all* the parties!" bellows the Boss to a questioning McGinty. "You think I'm going to starve every time they change administrations?" McGinty warms to the idea of being Mayor until the Boss demands that he marry ("Women got the vote, and they don't like bachelors"), at which time he stomps out. "I know all about it," he sneers, speaking of matrimony. "My parents was married." However, McGinty's pretty blonde secretary Catherine (Muriel Angelus) is smitten with him, and, wary of wolves, proposes a loveless marriage: "We'd never have to see each other except to be photographed on the steps of the City Hall . . . I could run the house for you and make speeches at the women's clubs." After surveying her legs, McGinty agrees, but does not find out until after the wedding that Catherine has failed to inform him about her little boy and girl.

McGinty becomes Mayor, and for a time the convenient marriage agrees with him—"At least we ain't got nothin' to fight about like people that's in love with each other." However, he soon falls in love with his wife, becomes a doting father to the children, and feels their loving influence tempting him to become an honest, caring politician. Catherine encourages this idealism, and assures him that he will someday be sufficiently strong to escape the corrupt influence of the Boss.

McGinty soon wins the race for Governor and confronts the Boss with a full repertoire of schemes for new dams, buildings, and bridges. He offers to pay back the $400,000 that the Boss spent to get him elected, and announces plans for a child labor bill and a sweatshop and tenement reform. The outraged Boss blames McGinty's idealism on his "cheapskate" wife. McGinty hits him, whereupon the Boss tries to shoot McGinty. The Boss is thrown in jail, and that night, after he reveals the details of McGinty's past deals, McGinty lands in jail with him.

Next, the Politician, disguised as a policeman, frees McGinty and the Boss from prison, and McGinty calls Catherine from a pay phone as he flees to escape the country. He tells her to get a divorce, informs her of a safe deposit box where he has left some securities for just such an emergency, and apologizes: "You can't make a silk purse out of a pig's ear."

Back in the bar, the Governor-turned-bartender concludes his story. The hootchie dancer pronounces him a liar. "O.K., sister," he replies. "Have it your way." McGinty rings up the embezzler's tab, pilfering some of the money, and is caught by the saloon proprietor—who is the Boss. "You cheesy cheapskate!" he roars. "You fat little four-flusher!" replies McGinty, as the two begin another slugfest. "Time out, gents," bemoans the Politician, now a waiter. "Here we go again!"

Released on August 25, 1940, *The Great McGinty* was an instant success. *Time* hailed it as ". . . shrewd, silly, adroit . . . an actor's dream. Brian Donlevy makes the dream come true." The *New York Times* placed the film seventh on its 1940 "Ten Best" list, and an Academy Award went to Preston Sturges for Best Original Screenplay. *The Great McGinty* established Donlevy as a popular leading man of the 1940's, and launched the career of Sturges, who, acclaimed by Paramount as "The Miracle Man," proceeded to create such satirical classics as *Sullivan's Travels* (1941), *The Miracle of Morgan's Creek* (1944), *Hail the Conquering Hero* (1944), and others, before his strange genius burned itself out in the late 1940's.

The Great McGinty remains a marvelous experience. Sturges' blend of subtlety and pratfall humor is perfect. Donlevy's satiric performance as McGinty is a joy, whether he is snarling at the Boss ("Take your finger out of my face!"), reading his children a bedtime story about "Muggily-wump the Tortoise," or warning his wife about the trials of being an honest governor ("There's no money in it, you understand—just a salary"). Akim Tamiroff is a marvelous incarnation of the traditionally greasy, amoral, backroom politician. Muriel Angelus plays Catherine McGinty with style and charm, and the colorful players who would become Sturges' favorites—William Demarest, Frank Moran, and Harry Rosenthal—spark the picture with the atmosphere, spirit, and fireworks of a raucous Tammany parade.

Americans have always been cynical about politics. *The Great McGinty* remains Hollywood's most delightful celebration of that cynicism, an emotion that, in this post-Watergate age, makes *The Great McGinty* all the more enjoyable.

Gregory William Mank

THE GREAT ZIEGFELD

Released: 1936
Production: Hunt Stromberg for Metro-Goldwyn-Mayer (AA)
Direction: Robert Z. Leonard
Screenplay: William Anthony McGuire; based on his original screen story
Cinematography: Oliver T. Marsh, George J. Folsey, Karl Freund, Merritt
  B. Gerstad, and Ray June
Editing: William S. Gray
Art direction: Cedric Gibbons
Costume design: Adrian
Music direction: Arthur Lange
Running time: 180 minutes

Principal characters:
Florenz Ziegfeld, Jr. .... William Powell
Anna Held .... Luise Rainer (AA)
Billie Burke .... Myrna Loy
Billings .... Frank Morgan
Sampston ....Reginald Owen
Sandow .... Nat Pendleton
Audrey Lane .... Virginia Bruce
Fannie Brice ....Herself

The Great Ziegfeld won the Oscar as Best Picture of 1936 over nine other
nominated films. Although most of these other films, including *A Tale of Two
Cities*, *Dodsworth*, *Anthony Adverse*, and *Mr. Deeds Goes to Town*, have
increased their respective standing with film historians over the decades, many
critics regard *The Great Ziegfeld* as overblown. At the time of the film's
release critical reaction to the film was mixed, with most reviews dwelling on
the length and cost of the production. In its era, *The Great Ziegfeld* was a
staggeringly extravagant production. Estimated to have cost about two million
dollars, it had a larger budget than any other film made by M-G-M up to that
time, with the exception of the silent *Ben Hur* (1926). It also boasted a running
time of three hours, which was longer than any film previously released in
the United States.

The statistics of the film and the twenty-three opulent musical production
numbers have made it the butt of much industry criticism, but much of this
negative response seems undeserved. The film is too long, and there are too
many musical numbers, but *The Great Ziegfeld* does an excellent job of
blending a dramatic biographical story line with a musical extravaganza, a
successful merging that has rarely been equaled. Robert Z. Leonard, who
was nominated for an Oscar for his work, directed the film as two separate
works with the musical numbers used to interrupt the drama. This method

proved necessary because Florenz Ziegfeld, who had died only a few years before the film was made, had been the impresario of so many stage extravaganzas himself—with his "Ziegfeld Follies" being particularly well known—that to have made the film any other way would have been a mistake. The audience expected to see opulent production numbers in the famous Ziegfeld manner, and any toning down of this aspect of the film would have been a disappointment. Yet, Ziegfeld the man was an interesting figure, and his life story deserved a dramatic retelling. The solution was a drama with many musical numbers rather than a straight musical in which music is a part of the story and advances the plot.

The Great Ziegfeld begins in the mid-1890's when Florenz Ziegfeld, Jr. (William Powell), the son of a music teacher, is a carnival barker promoting a German strong man named Sandow (Nat Pendleton). Sandow is not much of an attraction on the midway until one of his feats causes a woman to faint. Ziegfeld, who is a master at publicity, capitalizes on Sandow's new status. The two tour the United States and earn a great deal of money. Their luck changes, however, when they announce that Sandow will wrestle a tiger, and the animal dies before the match can begin. After this, Ziegfeld decides to go to Europe, and on the voyage he runs into an old friend and carnival rival named Billings (Frank Morgan). The two are always in competition, and Ziegfeld always manages to better his friend. Billings is on his way to Europe to sign a new star to an exclusive American contract, but, not wanting Ziegfeld to ruin things, he refuses to say who the woman is.

After a brief side trip to Monte Carlo, where he loses all of his money, Ziegfeld goes to London, where Billings is also staying. When Ziegfeld asks a doorman who the greatest attraction in London is, he finds out that it is a French singer named Anna Held (Luise Rainer), and it is she whom Billings wants to sign. Ziegfeld is a man of great taste and style, and, as always, he easily charms Anna into signing with him, despite the fact that he has no money with which to pay her. Money never seems to stand in his way, however, and soon Anna Held is the toast of the New York stage. Extravagance and publicity, two of Ziegfeld's specialties, help to promote Anna with the New York carriage trade at the turn of the century. One example of Ziegfeld's flair for publicity, and one which is based on an actual publicity stunt, concerns Anna's milk baths. She became famous throughout America for supposedly taking baths in milk every morning to preserve her well-known beautiful complexion. The film debunks the myth that Anna actually did bathe in the milk by showing that she thinks the baths are silly and does not understand Ziegfeld's craving for publicity. Whether she bathed in milk or not, however, the real Anna Held was an early equivalent of a "super star," with her life and actions followed eagerly by thousands of adoring fans.

Anna marries Ziegfeld, and at first they are very happy both because she is a star and because he is becoming increasingly successful. He never seems to be out of debt, however, as his lavish life-style and craving for bigger and better productions use up his money faster than he can earn it. The main problem between Ziegfeld and Anna, though, is his well-known attraction to beautiful women. Although she suspects infidelity for some time, it is not until she sees him in a compromising position with a drunken showgirl named Audrey Lane (Virginia Bruce) that she leaves him.

The viewer is aware that several years have passed when Ziegfeld is next seen; he is now more subdued and grayer. At a party he meets Broadway star Billie Burke (Myrna Loy), a calm woman who is the antithesis of the emotional Anna. The real Billie Burke is best known today as a twittering, flighty comedienne of such 1930's and 1940's films as *Topper* (1937) and *Girl Trouble* (1942), but in the teens and the 1920's she was a well-known dramatic stage actress. In *The Great Ziegfeld* Billie and Ziegfeld meet when she is escorted to a party by Billings who, as usual, is trying to keep Ziegfeld from hiring her. In actuality, it was British writer W. Somerset Maugham who introduced the pair when he took Billie to a New Year's Eve party in 1913. After Billie and Ziegfeld marry in 1914, they are very happy and live on a large estate with their young daughter, on whom they both dote. Ziegfeld's extravagances now are confined to his family and the stage, and he is no longer the playboy that he was in his younger days.

Ziegfeld's fortunes begin to fail in the mid-1920's, when several of his shows, even the Follies, begin to falter. He does recapture his success temporarily, however, when he has four hit shows running concurrently on Broadway in the 1929 season: *Whoopee!*, *Rio Rita*, *Show Boat*, and *The Three Musketeers*. Predictably, because of the date, Ziegfeld goes broke when he invests his money (for the first time according to the film) in stocks which fail in the market crash of 1929. In the last sequence, Ziegfeld is a sick, broken man who is hoping to make a comeback but does not have the money to finance his dreams. Billings, who is also broke, comes to visit his old rival and promises to finance the new show that Ziegfeld wants, but even Ziegfeld realizes the sham. He dies as he dreams of "higher stairs" for his production numbers.

The dramatic narrative tells the life of Florenz Ziegfeld in a well-presented, well-acted manner. Yet, it is less than half of this very long film. What the film's admirers prefer are the musical production numbers, which are some of the most lavish ever filmed. It is unfortunate that a film which cost so much did not have color to accentuate the beauty of the sets and costumes. With moving sets and dozens of beautiful women wearing magnificent costumes by Adrian, color might have made the numbers even more reflective of the live stage shows which they were supposed to represent. The musical numbers were so lavish, in fact, that many critics felt that even Ziegfeld could not have done as well himself.

In addition to the blockbusters, there are several "small" numbers which are noteworthy in the film. The scene of Anna Held dressed in a long black gown and huge plumed hat singing "It's Delightful to Be Married," as she strolls among eight beautiful chorus singers who have similar costumes in white, is one of these. Anna Held herself was known for considerable charm and sauciness which came through on the stage, and this number captures that charm perfectly. Another delightful number is Fannie Brice's burlesque act. In the film, Ziegfeld goes to Brice's show to see if she might be suitable for his Follies. The real Fannie Brice appears in one of her famous numbers, singing "Mr. Yiddle, on your fiddle, play some ragtime." Later, after a nice comedy scene in which Brice mistakes Ziegfeld for a cut-rate furrier, she auditions for the Follies. This is one of the major disappointments in the film; as Brice begins to sing her theme song, "My Man," wearing a knitted shawl, and with tears running down her cheeks, the scene shifts to Ziegfeld's office, and only the music can be heard in the distance.

Of the major production numbers, the most famous, and one of the most famous numbers ever filmed, is "A Pretty Girl Is Like a Melody." This sequence, which was included in *That's Entertainment* (1974), is often referred to as the "wedding cake" number because of the huge wedding cakelike set used. The number begins when Dennis Morgan (billed as Stanley Morner, and, although an accomplished tenor himself, he lip-syncs the voice of singing star Allen Jones) sings the song in front of a huge curtain. As the curtain opens, a large set appears, revealing dozens of "pretty girls" seated, standing, or dancing along a revolving staircase. The camera follows the movement of the graduated circular staircase so imperceptibly at first that it barely seems to move. Then, as the stairs go higher and the set narrows, it moves faster, sweeping past dancers in a variety of beautiful costumes. At the end, there is only one women sitting on top of the staircase; she is dressed in a full skirted costume which seems to blend into the set. A final sweep of the entire set is made and then the lavish circular curtain closes. Ray June photographed this section of the film (which had several cinematographers for different sections). Interestingly, there is no applause on the sound track or shots of the audience applauding as there are at the end of other numbers in the film. This is fitting, however, as the number is so magnificent that the actual film audience broke into applause, thus replacing what might have been seen and heard on the film. Although they are individually excellent, the large number of musical numbers is the one aspect of the film which tends to make it rather tedious. There are large sections of the film consisting of song after song, which tend to fatigue audiences. This is especially evident in the series of numbers (of which the "A Pretty Girl Is Like a Melody" number is a part) which represents the Follies at its peak.

There is a surprising lack of historical continuity in the film, at least to the extent that the audience does not know what year or even what decade is being represented without a great deal of background knowledge. Actually, "A Pretty Girl Is Like a Melody" was introduced in the 1919 Follies, yet in the film this number precedes Ziegfeld's discovery of Fannie Brice by a few weeks. Brice, however, first appeared in the 1910 Follies. This changing of facts and dates runs throughout the film and tends to be an annoyance to purists, although it does not seem to interfere with the success of the film as a piece of entertainment,

In addition to Brice, several other well-known Follies performers are portrayed in the film, including Will Rogers and Eddie Cantor. Also, Ray Bolger and Harriet Hoctor perform specialty numbers which are enjoyable, if not historically accurate. There are a number of other performers who are mentioned either by their real names or fictitious ones who represent the dozens of well-known personalities who began their careers with Ziegfeld.

The film was nominated for Oscars in several categories but won in only two: Best Picture, and Best Actress for Rainer. Rainer gave a good performance as Anna Held, but it is a curiously small part for a nomination in the Best Actress category, especially considering the length of the film. Rainer had one of the strangest careers in Hollywood. She came to Hollywood after studying under theatrical impresario Max Reinhardt in the mid-1930's and quickly won the Oscar for *The Great Ziegfeld*, followed by another Best Actress Oscar the next year for *The Good Earth*. After these two monumental films, however, her career fell apart and she made only one film after 1938, *Hostages* (1943). She then retired and never acted again. By modern standards her acting seems rather melodramatic. In the scene which was considered her masterpiece, when she calls Ziegfeld on the telephone to congratulate him upon his marriage to Billie Burke, she displays near hysteria, which is almost laughable today. Yet, in 1936, this was very poignant and probably contributed more than anything to her winning the Oscar.

Powell was nominated for an Oscar for his role as the butler in *My Man Godfrey* the year that *The Great Ziegfeld* was released, but he lost to Paul Muni for *The Story of Louis Pasteur*. The role of Ziegfeld was perhaps more challenging than that of Godfrey for Powell, but somehow the light comic touches which he displayed in both films are more effective in *My Man Godfrey*. Also, the film's last scene, which is far too melodramatic, leaves a lingering impression of over-acting which detracts from Powell's overall excellent performance.

The other principal of the film, Loy, gave her standard, underplayed performance. Although she was quite good in the role of Billie Burke, Loy has been criticized because she did not resemble the real Burke in voice or mannerisms. This is an unfair criticism, however, because the real Burke was so well known in the 1930's that any attempt at imitation would have seemed like a caricature, something that would have been inappropriate in a dramatic story such as this. Actually, when one looks at Billie Burke in a film such as *The Wizard of Oz* (1939) where she played Glenda, the Good Witch, Loy's quiet, restrained performance does not seem off the mark. The flighty Burke is the actress who is most frequently remembered, however, and thus many critics find fault with the soft-spoken, gentle Loy.

The rest of the cast, mainly members of M-G-M's stock company, turn in their usual professional performances, especially Morgan who gives his characteristic comic/serious second-banana role sparkle. The other major parts, acted by Owen, Pendleton, and Bruce, also add color to the production's dramatic aspects.

Despite some mixed critical reaction to the film, *The Great Ziegfeld* did well at the box office, ending up in the top five moneymaking films of 1936. It also indirectly gave birth to two later M-G-M films, *Ziegfeld Girl* (1941), about a group of aspiring performers working in the Ziegfeld Follies, and *Ziegfeld Follies* (1946), directed by Vincente Minnelli in which a white-haired Powell has a small part as the spirit of Florenz Ziegfeld. In the latter film, Ziegfeld looks down from heaven on a series of unrelated musical and comedy numbers, showing how the master showman would put on another production if he could. Although Powell's part is the only dramatic aspect of the film, *Ziegfeld Follies* still merits attention for several well-known production numbers, including a famous song-and-dance routine featuring both Fred Astaire and Gene Kelly.

Patricia King Hanson

THE GREATEST SHOW ON EARTH

Released: 1952
Production: Cecil B. De Mille for Paramount (AA)
Direction: Cecil B. De Mille
Screenplay: Fredric M. Frank, Barre Lyndon, and Theodore St. John; based on the screen story by Fredric M. Frank, Theodore St. John, and Frank Cavett (AA)
Cinematography: George Barnes, Peverell Marley, and W. Wallace Kelley
Editing: Anne Bauchens
Costume design: Edith Head, Dorothy Jeakins, and Miles White
Music: Victor Young
Running time: 151 minutes

> *Principal characters:*
> Holly .... Betty Hutton
> Sebastian .... Cornel Wilde
> Brad .... Charlton Heston
> Angel .... Gloria Grahame
> Buttons the Clown .... James Stewart
> Phyllis .... Dorothy Lamour
> Klaus .... Lyle Bettger
> Henderson .... Lawrence Tierney
> Detective .... Henry Wilcoxon
> John Ringling North .... Himself
> Emmett Kelly .... Himself

Considering producer/director Cecil B. De Mille's fondness of Barnumlike spectacle, his decision to make a movie on the circus would seem to be a particularly apt choice. A long-cherished personal project, the planning of *The Greatest Show on Earth* took some three years prior to the several months of actual shooting. Never one for half measures, instead of the usual "cast of thousands" De Mille hired the entire Ringling Bros.–Barnum & Bailey Circus in addition to his several starring players. Beginning at the circus' winter quarters in Sarasota, Florida, the film chronicles the show's annual cross-country circuit, albeit with a few De Mille plot complications en route.

Reduced to its barest premise, the film's theme is "The show must go on." If circus life is naturally a communal affair, De Mille lets us know in no uncertain terms that it is also a very capitalistic endeavor. Just as the high-wire artists risk life and limb, so the circus is like a tightrope walker, inching toward success, yet always in danger of plummeting to ruin. The person around whom all this drama revolves is the boss, Brad (Charlton Heston). Viewed as a benign dictator, determined, omniscient, always putting the circus ahead of personal satisfaction, he appears to be very similar to De Mille's image of himself.

De Mille seemed to love weaving complicated yarns with a number of subplots, and this film is no exception. There is a professional, and later romantic, rivalry between the two trapeze artists, Holly (Betty Hutton) and Sebastian (Cornel Wilde). Their conflict revolves around who will occupy the center ring, each trying to outdo the other. Their stunts become ever riskier, causing Brad no small amount of trouble, until Sebastian suffers a crippling accident. Another subplot centers on Angel (Gloria Grahame), the elephant girl, and the trainer, Klaus (Lyle Bettger). Insanely jealous, Klaus almost kills Angel when he finds that he is losing her affections to Brad. Dismissed from the circus, he derails the circus train in revenge and is killed in the process. As a result of the wreck, the mysterious past of Buttons the Clown (James Stewart) is revealed. He is really a doctor who is wanted by the FBI for the euthanasia killing of his wife. Seemingly at the end of its tether, the circus is led by Holly, who has learned her lesson, to the nearest town for another performance. In addition to the train wreck, the circus also endures a disastrous fire, sabotage by a rival circus, petty infighting, and the vagaries of the weather. It is a testimonial to De Mille's skill as a storyteller that each of these various incidents and intrigues finds its place without pulling the story apart in many directions.

Whether De Mille's films depict the parting of the Red Sea or the journey of Cleopatra's barge down the Nile, they are usually built around larger-than-life moments. There are two such spectacle sequences in this film. The fire sequence is by far the more vivid of the two. The fire, well paced from the first spark until it gradually becomes a blazing inferno (although using a liberal amount of back-projection), is startlingly real and gripping as both man and beast panic in the flames. If De Mille in one of his epics had chosen to depict Hell, he could not have done better than he has here. The train wreck, similar to an earlier sequence in *Union Pacific* (1939), is done very effectively with miniatures. For the aftermath, elaborate sets were built to depict the wreckage. Unfortunately, the scenes following the wreck do not ring true. Nobody except the villain is killed or seriously hurt, and the animals are quickly and easily put back into their cages.

Although the spectacle is handled with the director's customary flair, it must be admitted that the film as a whole does suffer from serious defects in dramatic credibility which are paralleled in much of De Mille's work. Stern-minded moralist that he was, De Mille never depicted characters beyond a very simple level. And having his roots in the tradition of barnstorming theatricals, De Mille's nineteenth century sensibilities never allowed for much psychological ambiguity in his characters.

Existing alongside De Mille's three-ring circus of a movie is another show-within-a-show, a modest and effective depiction of the real circus. Most people, it seems, never outgrow a fascination for the circus, and fortunately neither did De Mille. Actual circus acts probably have never been more lovingly filmed, portrayed with all the glitter and excitement of the real circus. The finest moments of the film are those events which one usually does not see, such as the massive circus tent being raised in the early hours of the morning, and the tedious rehearsals of the performers. It is here that the film achieves a poetry which transcends its more banal plot.

However one rates De Mille, there can be no doubt that he was wholly responsible for his films. Working independently through Paramount, De Mille went his own way, oblivious to the rest of the cinema world. Although sometimes trite, old-fashioned, and bombastic, there is an innocent charm about several of his films which may well outlast many of the more recent so-called "thinking man's spectaculars." At a certain point, an invigorating vulgarity is preferable to smug pretentiousness. As his Westerns in particular prove, De Mille was squarely in line with another American primitive, novelist James Fenimore Cooper. Like Cooper's characters, De Mille's characters gain in mythic resonance what they lose in dramatic sense. When not lured away by the religious epic, De Mille made films about America, including *The Greatest Show on Earth*, which was awarded the Oscar for Best Picture of the year. Although it is often guilty of reactionary excesses, De Mille's vision remains determinedly optimistic.

Mike Vanderlan

THE GUARDSMAN

Released: 1931
Production: Metro-Goldwyn-Mayer
Direction: Sidney Franklin
Screenplay: Claudine West and Ernest Vajda; based on the stage play of the
 same name by Ferenc Molnar
Cinematography: Norbert Brodine
Editing: Conrad A. Nervig
Running time: 83 minutes

Principal characters:
The Actor .... Alfred Lunt
The Actress .... Lynn Fontanne
The Critic .... Roland Young
Liesl, the Maid .... Zasu Pitts
Mama .... Maude Eburne
A Creditor .... Herman Bing
A Fan .... Ann Dvorak

Production chief Irving Thalberg had a dream of bringing the best actors
from the Broadway theatre to M-G-M in a series of starring film productions
that would immortalize their performances and add an extra luminescence
to the studio's own stable of contract players. Through his diligent efforts,
Helen Hayes became a highly esteemed, Academy Award-winning star for
M-G-M. Thalberg also wanted renowned stage star Katharine Cornell at
Metro, but she resisted all his offers. Alfred Lunt and Lynn Fontanne, however, the most esteemed acting team in the country, were interested in Thalberg's offer. Each of the Lunts had had some film acting experience in silent
films individually, but now that they were married and had become the num-
ber-one acting attraction in the Broadway theater, Thalberg wanted them to
bring their talents to the cinema. One of their biggest theatrical attractions
had been Ferenc Molnar's *The Guardsman*, in which they had costarred for
the Theater Guild. When the Lunts signed a contract with Thalberg for a
single feature with options for more, it was agreed that this play would be
adapted into a film for their talking film debut. So confident was Thalberg
that they would be memorable on the screen that he also bought for M-G-M
the film rights to Robert E. Sherwood's comedy, *Reunion in Vienna*, in which
the Lunts had performed brilliantly onstage, and Thalberg hoped it might be
their second vehicle for his studio.

When the Lunts came to Hollywood to film *The Guardsman*, they were
given the red carpet treatment, and on release, the film was greatly admired
by critics and audiences alike. Although they were both honored with Academy Award nominations for Best Actor and Best Actress, respectively, they

did not want to do any more films for M-G-M or for any other film company. The Broadway stage was their home, and they wanted to continue their careers together as stage actors. Their dream of performing for people who would never be able to see them on Broadway was reached by touring their productions nationwide and internationally. Although they were at ease in front of the camera, the theater was their true domain. Thalberg bowed to their decision and turned *Reunion in Vienna* (filmed in 1933) over to two other extraordinarily fine theater stars who had made their mark in films— John Barrymore and Diana Wynyard.

The Guardsman, the only film that the Lunts made, is a prize that still shines. In 1931 it was admired; in 1979, when it was revived at an M-G-M retrospective at the Vagabond Theater in Los Angeles, it left audiences who had never seen it or the Lunts before delighted. It is romantic comedy at its most sparkling, beautifully directed, written, and photographed, and acted with a finesse that only the finest actors have mastered. It was a small production, made with only the two stars and five supporting players. As an exercise in what actors can do when given a good script, it remains unique. It has Continental flavor, sophistication, wit, grace, and sexual energy.

The plot opens in the theater in Budapest, where the reigning favorite actors of the day are concluding a performance of Maxwell Anderson's play *Elizabeth the Queen* (which the Lunts, incidentally, had performed magnificently for the Theater Guild). Thalberg was unsure about asking playwright Maxwell Anderson for the right to buy the final moments of the play, but Anderson had once been under contract to M-G-M and said that he had begun writing the play there in his studio office, while waiting for an assignment, so he willingly let them use his scene free of charge.

Lunt, as Lord Essex, takes his final leave of Queen Elizabeth, played by Fontanne, going to his execution, while she slumps back on her throne, "queen of emptiness." With a roll of drums, the curtain comes down, and then the actors come out together to take their bows to an admiring audience. They retreat behind the curtain into the wings, where Fontanne quickly removes her wig and basic makeup as Elizabeth; they then join hands and go out to bow to an audience that continues to applaud. There is a surprised gasp, and the audience is heard to exclaim upon the actress' true youth and beauty. The Actor and Actress carry on a running conversation under their breath while they smilingly receive the plaudits of their admirers. He tells her to smile at the officers, for he knows she likes men in uniform; she returns his bantering sallies, never losing her smile, even when she is forced to warn him between her teeth, "You're on my dress; you're on my dress."

In the dressing-rooms, their bantering becomes quarrelsome and, on his part, jealously accusative. Alone in his own dressing-room later, the Actor encounters the Critic (Roland Young), and with histrionic despair he confesses that he can sense an unknown rival's approach. His wife now sits in darkened rooms, weeps softly, and plays Chopin. He knows that a new man is coming into her life, or she is at least yearning for one, whom she will welcome with open arms when he puts in an appearance. Driven to desperation, the Actor decides to test the love and fidelity of his wife. He concocts an elaborate scheme whereby he will go off for an overnight trip to a neighboring city which has invited him supposedly to fill in with a performance of Hamlet. He will make all his farewells, leave his wife, and then surreptitiously return to make himself up as a Russian guardsman and woo his own wife, hoping she will resist him, but determined to give his all to entice her to be faithless.

The Critic, who is a delighted voyeur, is privy to the impersonation. The Actress is tempted; she resists, but allows the Guardsman to see her home from the opera. He kisses her passionately, and she hurriedly retires with a gasp of fear into the house, locking the door. The Actor is delighted that, good as his performance has been, she is loyal and has been able to turn him down. Then the window opens above, and she tosses down a key, and with a despairing look at the Critic, the Actor goes in to seduce his own wife.

The final sequence deals with his return the next day from his supposed engagement, his confession of the impersonation, and her defense that she knew all along who he was, that he did not fool her for one moment, and that she simply played the comedy through as he cued her in. In the very final shot of the picture, however, Fontanne is shown as she presses her loving, repentant husband to her breast and looks over to the Critic and smiles enigmatically. Did she really know that it was her husband who seduced her, or did she willingly succumb to the advances of a strange lover for one night of love? The look in her eyes and the smile that curls her lips invites the audience to decide.

The Guardsman is a flawless transcription of a play to cinematic form, and the performances are all exceedingly good. For its day, it was considered extremely racy, but not even the Hays office could object to a husband seducing his own wife, and the audiences, whether of 1931 or 1979, have always been entranced with the film. M-G-M remade the film in 1941 as *The Chocolate Soldier*, a curious combination of the play *The Guardsman* enacted with the music of the Oscar Straus operetta, as sung by Nelson Eddy and Rise Stevens. The result is only a hazy shadow of the skillful 1931 comedy starring the Lunts. Fortunately, since, their version of *The Guardsman* is a wonderful and timeless treasure, the Lunt film survives in very good prints.

DeWitt Bodeen

GUESS WHO'S COMING TO DINNER?

Released: 1967
Production: Stanley Kramer for Columbia
Direction: Stanley Kramer
Screenplay: William Rose (AA)
Cinematography: Sam Leavitt
Editing: Robert C. Jones
Running time: 108 minutes

Principal characters:
Christina Drayton .... Katharine Hepburn (AA)
Matt Drayton .... Spencer Tracy
John Wade Prentice .... Sidney Poitier
Joey Drayton .... Katharine Houghton
Monsignor Ryan .... Cecil Kellaway
Mrs. Prentice .... Beah Richards
Mr. Prentice .... Roy E. Glenn, Sr.
Tillie .... Isabell Sanford
Hilary St. George .... Virginia Christine

Because of producer/director Stanley Kramer's films such as *The Defiant Ones* (1958), *On the Beach* (1959), *Inherit the Wind* (1960), and many others which have dealt with themes of social injustice, his work has often been called "thesis" or "message" cinema. Although not every one of his films has neatly fallen into this category, most of them have, and the body of his work is thus message-oriented. Usually the messages of the films have been presented as highly dramatic statements, often with tragic endings, but his highly successful 1967 film *Guess Who's Coming to Dinner?* is more of a light entertainment with a serious theme as its basis.

The plot concerns the problem of interracial love and marriage, represented by the reactions of one liberal upper-middle-class family to the announcement by their daughter that she is going to marry a black man. In the film, Katharine Hepburn and Spencer Tracy play the parents in their last appearance together. The film also marked Tracy's last motion picture; he died shortly after its completion. Although the film received raves when it was released, did extremely well at the box office, and received many Academy Award nominations, almost fifteen years later, it is the work of Tracy and Hepburn which is the best part of a badly dated film. It has been said by some cinema historians that there is no type of film which becomes more dated than a social message film, and *Guess Who's Coming to Dinner?* proves that axiom.

The main characters are established early in the film. Tracy plays Matt Drayton, a veteran crusading San Francisco newspaper publisher who prides himself on being a champion of justice; Hepburn plays his equally liberal wife, Christina, a gracious woman who owns a fashionable *avant garde* art gallery in downtown San Francisco. When their pretty, blonde, twenty-one-year-old daughter Joey (Katharine Houghton) returns from the University of Hawaii where she has been attending college, she announces that she has brought her fiancé, Professor John Wade Prentice, back with her. She describes the man in such glowing terms that her mother is delighted about the news, but she is shocked at first to learn that the fiancé is not white. When Prentice (Sidney Poitier) enters the room where Christina and Joey are talking, the audience as well as Christina recognize immediately that the family's liberal views will be severely tested. To complicate the problem even further, both Joey and Prentice agree that they will not marry unless they have their parents' permission and approval. If they wanted to defy their parents, the story would be different, but the fact that they want their parents' blessings makes the situation more difficult for everyone, since it forces both sets of parents to face the situation head on.

The story takes place in the space of less than twelve hours because Prentice must leave for an important assignment in New York that evening and Joey wants to go with him. Her decision to go or stay rests with the parents. Most of the action occurs in the Drayton's beautiful French colonial house. During the course of events, all of the major characters come to the house, including Prentice's parents (Beah Richards and Roy E. Glenn, Sr.).

The first one to wholeheartedly accept Joey and Prentice's marriage is Christina, who is soon too swept up in the romance of the whirlwind courtship to wish them anything but good. Matt, however, is something less than enthusiastic throughout most of the film. When he returns from his office in the afternoon, the black maid, Tillie (Isabell Sanford), greets him at the door with "All hell done broken loose." He never actually says no to the marriage, but his struggle eventually to say yes takes up the major portion of the film. This allows the characters to develop in different ways, with each showing his true feelings.

The reactions of various types of people are shown through key characters. Christina's friend Hilary St. George (Virginia Christine) is openly polite and unctuous to Joey and Prentice, but when Christina sees her to her car, Virginia tells her how "heartsick" she is that Christina has to go through such a thing. In one of the better scenes of the film, an equally unctuous Christina tells Hilary, who manages the art gallery, to go to the gallery, write herself a large check, and never come back. Hepburn's smiles and Christine's shocked expression illustrate a classic rebuff to a hypocrite. Another character who visits the Drayton's home is their old friend Monsignor Ryan (Cecil Kellaway), who is totally happy and enthusiastic about the marriage. Naïvely, perhaps, like Christina, he refuses to see any problems for the two which cannot be overcome by love. Prentice's parents seem to parallel the reactions of Joey's parents: his mother is delighted, and his father is merely perplexed and a little disgusted.

There are a number of speeches in the film which delve into the problem of parent-child relationships, as well as the issue of race, but most rely heavily on platitudes. The message which comes through today is that people should understand one another's feelings, rather than the message regarding tolerance which the filmmakers intended. Mr. Prentice and Matt are somehow pitted against their respective families because they are merely being practical, if somewhat cynical, in their views of Joey and Prentice's marriage. Mrs. Prentice accuses her husband and Matt of being dried up old men who cannot understand the passions of youth. "What happens to men when they get old?" Mrs. Prentice asks.

In the large major sequence of the film, Matt delivers a speech which dissects the major issues of the story and slowly analyzes everything that has transpired. He eventually gives his consent to the marriage, but only after he makes everyone think about their own blind reactions to it. He did not "dry up" as Mrs. Prentice says; he still has passion for his wife and love for his daughter. What he wants is for them all to come emotionally back to earth and realistically see the problems which the two will face. If Joey and Prentice still want to get married, then he is in agreement. The film ends as the entire group goes to the airport to see Joey and Prentice off, while on the soundtrack we hear the old song "Glory of Love."

Although the film received a near-record ten Academy Award nominations and won two, one to William Rose for Best Screenplay and one to Hepburn for Best Actress, it is not a particularly outstanding film. There are some beautiful moments of humor and sentimentality in the story, and the acting is excellent, but the script fails to live up to the serious nature of the film's theme. Perhaps the lessening of the social consciousness impact of the film is caused by its typical Hollywood glossy look. Since the white family is well-to-do and the black family middle-class (Mr. Prentice is a retired mailman), some of the problems of racism are skirted. Additionally, Poitier's performance as a "super black" stretches credulity. Prentice is brilliant, handsome, and charming, a physician graduated *cum laude* from Harvard who has written numerous books and scholarly articles, has been a professor at Yale, and now will be the Assistant Director of the World Health Organization. Racial differences aside, it seems difficult to believe that the parents of a naïve, almost frivolous twenty-one-year-old girl would not want him for a son-in-law.

Another problem with the script concerns the differences between Joey and Prentice that do not have anything to do with race. He is forty and a widower, and the problems of the differences in their ages and intellectual development are never discussed. Thus, in some respects the audience's sympathies lie with Matt when he accuses them of not being realistic. To his credit as an actor, Poitier does give a good performance in a characterization which

is almost completely preordained by the parameters of the script. He underplays the character's accomplishments instead of stressing them.

Houghton, who is Hepburn's niece in real life, made her acting debut with
Guess Who's Coming to Dinner? She seems right for the part of the starry-
eyed Joey, but she never pursued her acting career and has since retired from
films. Others of the cast, including Sanford, who starred in the long-running
television comedy series *The Jeffersons*, and veteran actor Kellaway in one
of his last roles, give characteristically solid performances. The stars, however,
give brilliant performances which make the film. While Hepburn won an
Oscar for her performance, it is Tracy, who was ill and close to death during
the filming, who gives the best performance. He is the only person who seems
to change during the film, evolving from shocked parent to angry curmudgeon
to understanding father. As always in his nine films with Hepburn, it is the
banter between them which adds sparkle to the script. In the last long speech
of the film, however, Tracy, the man of reason, is at his most brilliant. Many
of his films displayed long rational, wise speeches, and it was a fitting end to
his career that one of his best was included in *Guess Who's Coming to Dinner?*
Tracy was posthumously nominated for an Oscar for his performance, but he
lost to Rod Steiger for *In the Heat of the Night*. He did, however, win the
British equivalent of the Oscar, the "Stella," for his performance.

Janet St. Clair

GUN CRAZY

Released: 1949
Production: Frank King and Maurice King for United Artists
Direction: Joseph H. Lewis
Screenplay: Mackinlay Kantor and Millard Kaufman; based on the short story
 "Gun Crazy" by Mackinlay Kantor
Cinematography: Russell Harlan
Editing: Harry Gerstad
Musical direction: Victor Young
Song: Victor Young and Ned Washington, "Mad About You"
Running time: 87 minutes

> *Principal characters:*
> Annie Laurie Starr .... Peggy Cummins
> Bart Tare .... John Dall
> Packett .... Barry Kroeger
> Judge Willoughby .... Morris Carnovsky
> Bluey-Bluey .... Stanley Praeger
> Dave Allister .... Nedrick Young

Like many "B"-movies, *Gun Crazy* is nourished by an American myth, in this case one of alienated youth on the run, obsessed by flight, guns, freedom, and love, and throwing away tomorrow for an incandescent today. The image of the fugitive couple has created its own subgenre, including Fritz Lang's *You Only Live Once* (1937), Edgar Ulmer's *Detour* (1945), Nicholas Ray's *They Live by Night* (1949), Jean-Luc Godard's *Breathless* (1959), Arthur Penn's *Bonnie and Clyde* (1967), Robert Altman's *Thieves Like Us* (1974), and Terrence Malick's *Badlands* (1974), not to mention variations on the theme from producers such as Roger Corman.

The audience knows this story before they enter the theater. In the 1940's and 1950's they paid to see it performed explicitly, in "B"-movies without pretensions to high culture. Whatever such films lacked in subtlety they often made up in speed, energy, and assurance. Producers, after all, knew what the audience expected. Even in the most formula-ridden of those films there resided a further possibility. Because the raw materials of the films were so emotional, so rooted in unconscious fears and desires, it sometimes happened that moments—even in a lowly "B"-movie—would ignite. In *Gun Crazy* the whole picture catches fire.

The film deals with two lovers who have nothing but each other. It suggests the hunger for oblivion that lurks in their love and the allure that romantic desolation holds for them. The simple story throws these elements into sharp relief. A young man, Bart Tare (John Dall), who loves to shoot, meets a ruthless blonde markswoman, Annie Laurie Starr (Peggy Cummins), who works in a carnival. Immediately spellbound, he persuades her to go off with him. Their money soon runs out, however, and to hold her, he joins with her in a series of robberies. Eventually the woman kills a bystander and the couple is hunted down by the young man's boyhood friends, who have become lawmen, in a swamp blanketed by fog.

It is less a story than a ritual, in which the world is well lost for love and all taboos exist only to be broken. As in most "B"-movies, the characters seem simpler and larger than life. Cummins gives the definitive portrait of a *film noir* seductress, for whom sex is the deadliest weapon. She is as dangerous as Barbara Stanwyck in *Double Indemnity* (1944), but is portrayed much less realistically. We know nothing of her background or hopes. She exists in bold outline, like a Pop Art figure. Despite a lofty English accent, Cummins is all flash and greedy appetite, with overtones of sadistic dominance. Like the Stanwyck character, she is acutely aware of her limits in a man's world. With a gun in her hand, however, Annie Laurie is as good as any man.

Bart also seems simple at first. Played with weakness and uncertainty, he is torn between love for Annie Laurie and revulsion at his descent into crime. Once he tries to leave the woman, then hurries back. The truth is he cannot leave her, any more than he can dismiss the aggression buried in himself. The lovers' relationship makes sense as one accepts that the woman is the projection of all the boy's own destructive nihilism. Things he cannot even think of on his own are possible while he lives through her.

They meet in a marksmen's duel that sets the style of their romance. These characters are always defined by action; they are what they do. Thus their initial duel becomes a one-scene seduction, climaxing when she puts on a crown of candles, looking like a side-show Athena, and, one-by-one, the fascinated young man shoots out her lights. This electrifying meeting only sets the stage for the delirium to follow. During the robberies, the otherwise doubtful Bart is quick and confident. Especially for him, the robberies are sexual events. The staging and camera movement generate a mad exhilaration. The scenes do not exploit sex and violence; the effect is more subversive and despairing. Sex and violence are fused into a single action, a dance of death for young lovers.

Director Joseph H. Lewis' staging has been justly praised. Perhaps it reaches a peak in the long, single-shot bank robbery. The camera looks forward from the back seat of the couple's car as they drive to the bank. The man goes in to rob it while the woman waits behind the wheel and spends a tortured minute as a bank guard on the street comes over to chat with her. The boy races out and they start their getaway, hurtling down side streets, barely missing other vehicles. For those few minutes the film lives in a heightened "real time." We experience the lovers' claustrophobic tensions and the thrill of their release. We are irresponsible with them; we are seduced.

Lewis counterpoints the swiftness of the film with constant reminders of falling and stumbling. As a boy, Bart reaches for a stolen gun and slips into the grasp of a policeman. Later, Annie Laurie slips during a robbery at a meat packer, stumbles during a dance on a night out, and falls during the swamp scene. Each break in the forward momentum tightens the tension. More tension is produced by a series of contrasting angles, from deep-focus long shots to big, crowded close-ups, often with the driving couple in profile.

The MacKinlay Kantor-Millard Kaufman screenplay is resonant enough to allow a variety of interpretations. Thus we can see Bart as an "artist" with a "talent" forced into an outsider's role by the demands of a materialistic society, personified by Annie Laurie, the bitch-goddess. Every detail in the script counts in several ways. The fog in the last scene is atmospheric, but also ironic. In the impenetrable mist, Bart sees his doom most clearly. Yet for the audience all interpretation comes after the film ends. As it unwinds, one only *feels* it. Nothing interrupts the flow. The sheer velocity of the couple forces us to suspend thought.

As an enterprise, *Gun Crazy* is steeped in poverty, yet it also flaunts that poverty and gains character from it. The King brothers, its producers, were specialists in low-budget films whose previous hit was *Dillinger* (1945). The characters in *Gun Crazy* are poor, and the story springs from the working class, idealizing a couple with nothing to look forward to. The leanness of the narrative is a low-budget necessity. Most of all, however, the film is haunted by the image of its director. Lewis was a major talent, influencing a generation of American and French filmmakers through such works as *Gun Crazy*, *The Big Combo* (1955), and *So Dark the Night* (1946). Yet he was never assigned a major film; all he could do was turn minor ones into gems.

Ted Gershuny

GUNFIGHT AT THE O.K. CORRAL

Released: 1957
Production: Hal B. Wallis for Paramount
Direction: John Sturges
Screenplay: Leon Uris; based on an article by George Scullin
Cinematography: Charles Lang
Editing: Warren Low
Music: Dmitri Tiomkin
Running time: 122 minutes

Principal characters:

Wyatt Earp	Burt Lancaster
Doc Holliday	Kirk Douglas
Laura Denbow	Rhonda Fleming
Kate Fisher	Jo Van Fleet
Johnny Ringo	John Ireland
Billy Clanton	Dennis Hopper
Ike Clanton	Lyle Bettger
Ed Bailey	Lee Van Cleef
Virgil Earp	John Hudson
Morgan Earp	De Forest Kelley
Jimmy Earp	Martin Milner
Betty Earp	Joan Camden

The story of Wyatt Earp and Doc Holliday has attracted filmmakers for decades. *My Darling Clementine* (1946), directed by John Ford, is generally regarded as the best film about the two, and *Doc* (1971), directed by Frank Perry, is probably the least reverent treatment of the story. Falling somewhere between the two in quality and realism is *Gunfight at the O.K. Corral*, directed by John Sturges in 1957. Realism is not, however, necessarily an important criterion in a genre such as the Western, which is usually meant to be closer to myth or legend than to history. What each director and writer chooses to do with the characters and events is much more important than whether they present the known facts with perfect fidelity.

For this treatment of the story of the legendary pair, producer Hal B. Wallis signed Burt Lancaster and Kirk Douglas, even though both had acquired reputations for sometimes being difficult to deal with. To write the script he hired the novelist Leon Uris. The script followed a fairly standard Western formula of building slowly to a final showdown at the end, just as the film's title promised. Within that framework, and ultimately of more interest than the victory of the good guys at the end, are Doc Holliday's ambivalent relationships with both Wyatt Earp and Kate Fisher.

The film is divided into three sections, each in a different location and each beginning with a shot of the boot hill, or cemetery, of the town in which that section takes place. The first section is set in Fort Griffin, Texas, where we are introduced to Doc Holliday (Kirk Douglas), who is alternately throwing knives in a door and drinking whiskey. A gambler who used to be a dentist, he is now afflicted with a tubercular cough and is involved in an almost sadomasochistic relationship with Kate Fisher (Jo Van Fleet). He expects her to be loyal to him and to be with him when he needs her, but otherwise he largely ignores her and her needs. Douglas had researched the character of Doc, finding that he was "a meticulous dresser," but actually, no ladies' man. "He slept until noon . . . and consumed oceans of whiskey." These characteristics are used by Douglas in his portrayal of the man even though the script, as has been noted, made no attempt at historical accuracy.

At the first meeting of Doc and Wyatt Earp (Burt Lancaster), neither admires the other. Earp is a Dodge City lawman trying to track down Johnny Ringo (John Ireland) and Ike Clanton (Lyle Bettger), and he goes to see Doc only for information on their whereabouts. Doc refuses to tell him anything, but he does receive some valuable information from Wyatt. Ed Bailey (Lee Van Cleef), a man who is waiting for Doc at the saloon to avenge the death of his brother, carries a small pistol in his boot. When Doc goes to the saloon, that information saves his life. He kills Bailey with a knife when he sees him draw the pistol from his boot. Although Doc is in the right according to the frontier code, it soon becomes evident that he is in danger of being lynched as a result of popular opinion. Kate appeals to Wyatt for help, but he responds, "I don't want any part of him; I don't even like him." When Wyatt sees that the probability of Doc's being lynched is real, however, he helps him escape with Kate. It is nothing personal, Wyatt explains; he just does not like lynchings. Doc then says he will go to Dodge City to express his thanks properly, but Wyatt tells him that he can best express his thanks by staying out of Dodge City. Nevertheless, a bond has now been established between the two men that will find them standing side by side at the O.K. Corral by the end of the film.

The scene then shifts to Dodge City, Kansas, some time later. Wyatt receives the news that Doc and Kate have just arrived. He goes to tell Doc that he must leave immediately, but Doc says that he has just been run out of Abilene and has no money. Finally Wyatt agrees to let Doc stay if he will promise "no knives, no guns, no killings." Not long after, Wyatt accepts Doc's offer to help him chase some bank robbers, and Doc saves Wyatt's life. At this same time, Wyatt has begun a romance with Laura Denbow (Rhonda Fleming), a woman gambler who arrived in Dodge City on the same day that Doc did. The romance is presented in an unconvincing fashion, but it does give Wyatt another reason for his plan to give up being a lawman and move to California. Meanwhile, Kate has grown tired of Doc's callousness toward her and has taken up with Ringo, who "blew into town" while Doc was out after the bank robbers. Doc goes to Ringo's room and confronts her, but he refuses to fight Ringo because of his promise to Wyatt. He even lets Ringo throw a drink in his face without reaching for a gun.

Wyatt's plans of retiring to a life of peace are disrupted when he learns that his brother Virgil (John Hudson), a lawman in Tombstone, Arizona, is in trouble. He tells an upset and disappointed Laura that he must help his brother, and, as he rides off to Tombstone, Doc joins him. When the scene shifts to Tombstone, we find that all the Earp brothers—Morgan (De Forest Kelley) and Jimmy (Martin Milner), as well as Wyatt and Virgil—have assembled to combat the Clanton gang, which is trying to run stolen cattle through Tombstone. After the Clantons try bribery and every other means that they can think of, they decide that the only way to overcome the Earp brothers is to provoke them into a shootout. They plan to shoot Wyatt one night, but when his brother Jimmy goes on the rounds that night instead, the Clanton gang shoots him down in cold blood. Wyatt has been the voice of reason throughout the film and has frequently been taunted about his "holy" attitude, but finding Jimmy lying in the street is too much: it is now a personal battle between the Earps and the Clantons. A gunfight at sunup at the O.K. Corral is arranged.

The confrontation is to be between the three Earp brothers and six of the Clanton gang, including the youngest Clanton, Billy (Dennis Hopper). Earlier Wyatt had tried to talk Billy out of being a gunfighter, telling him no gunfighter lives to see his thirty-fifth birthday and all are lonely; "they live in fear and die without a dime or a woman or a friend." He thought he had convinced the young man, but he finds that he had not. Wyatt goes to Doc for help, but he finds him unconscious and being looked after by Kate, who tells him that Doc is dying. Virgil's wife Betty (Joan Camden) also tries to talk the brothers out of the showdown by pointing out that as lawmen, "Your duty is to people, not to your own pride."

Nothing, however, can keep the Earp brothers from their vengeance. They head for the confrontation walking tall, as have countless Western movie heroes. Along with the three Earp brothers is Doc Holliday, who has gotten up from what seemed to be his deathbed because, as he tells Kate, he wants to die with the only friend he ever had. Although the actual shootout apparently took only a few seconds, it is extended on the screen to several minutes. The Earp brothers and Doc kill all of the Clanton gang except young Billy, with Doc finally getting his own revenge by shooting Ringo. Billy, who is wounded, makes his way to a nearby building, followed by Wyatt. Although Wyatt gets a chance to shoot Billy then and there, he waits, apparently hoping that Billy will remember what he has told him and throw down his gun. Instead, Billy painfully raises his gun to aim at Wyatt. At just that moment Doc looks in the window, sees what is happening, and kills Billy with one shot. A disappointed Wyatt drops his gun and badge by Billy's body and walks out.

There remains only one last sequence in which Wyatt and Doc meet in the saloon. We learn that Wyatt's brothers, although wounded, will be all right and that Wyatt plans to leave for California immediately. He tells Doc that he should go to the hospital in Denver, but Doc only responds, "So long, preacher." Then he joins the card game in progress at the saloon and Wyatt rides off across the desert landscape, accompanied by a song sung by Frankie Laine that has punctuated the major sections of the film throughout.

Gunfight at the O.K. Corral fits the classic formula of the Western in that it presents a conflict between civilization and anarchy in which there is some ambivalence in the heroes. Wyatt Earp is particularly ambivalent. He wants three conflicting things: to get married and settle down, to uphold the law, and to avenge his brother's death. Although Wyatt's feelings are mixed, he spends most of the film being so righteous that other characters sarcastically call him "preacher," and his romance with Laura is neither directed nor written well. As a result, Doc Holliday is a more complex and interesting character than Wyatt. Doc's character also has many facets: his upper-class family background, his past career as a dentist, his need for Kate along with his inability to give her anything, his ability to win fights even though he never provokes them, and his strange affection for the upright lawman, Wyatt Earp. Douglas conveys all this well. The other notable performance is by Van Fleet as Kate. She makes us see the hurt that Doc inflicts as well as the reasons that she cannot leave him permanently.

The music by Dmitri Tiomkin often goes overboard in underscoring and emphasizing emotions and events, but that was the style of music for "big" films in the 1950's. In addition, the ballad sung by Laine during various interludes in the film might seem better had the device not been used more effectively in *High Noon* (1952). Despite some weaknesses in the script and the less than imaginative direction by John Sturges, the performances of Douglas, Van Fleet, and Lancaster as well as the superb color cinematography by Charles Lang, make *Gunfight at the O.K. Corral* a solid, entertaining Western that was quite popular at the box office.

Marilynn Wilson

THE GUNFIGHTER

Released: 1950
Production: Nunnally Johnson for Twentieth Century-Fox
Direction: Henry King
Screenplay: William Bowers and William Sellers; based on an original story
  by William Bowers and Andre de Toth
Cinematography: Arthur Miller
Editing: Barbara McLean
Running time: 84 minutes

Principal characters:
Jimmie Ringo .... Gregory Peck
Peggy Walsh .... Helen Westcott
Sheriff Mark Strett .... Millard Mitchell
Molly .... Jean Parker
Mac .... Karl Malden
Hunt Bromley .... Skip Homeier
Charlie .... Anthony Ross
Mrs. Pennyfeather .... Verna Felton
Mrs. Devlin .... Ellen Corby
Eddie .... Richard Jaeckel

The Western has been called America's most enduring contribution to the cinema. No other genre has better captured the American spirit or provided more insight into American mythology. For the purpose of definition, the Western period is generally limited to the years from 1860 to 1890—thirty years in which the great American frontier was settled. Even if the period of the California gold rush and the first wagon trains to Oregon were included, the entire Western era lasted less than fifty years. Nevertheless, this short period has provided the world with endless tales and adventures, many of which have become part of American mythology.

The Gunfighter is about only one of those myths. Unlike the dozens of other films which have chosen to focus on the gunman, however, this film is different. It is an adult Western, dealing with adult concerns. This is in itself very unusual, as Westerns often rely on a more simplistic formula, in which complex themes and motivations are reduced to a child's level of comprehension. As a result, the Western has often been ignored by critics and film historians. *The Gunfighter*, however, is neither simplistic nor traditional. It explores the psyche of a man who has lived by the gun and is now tired of that life. *The Gunfighter* is in fact the first psychological Western.

As the film begins, Jimmie Ringo (Gregory Peck), a professional gunman, has returned to the town of Cayenne after many years' absence. He is weary of killing and wants no more of it. Instead, he has come to pick up his long-estranged wife Peggy (Helen Westcott) and his son and take them to a place where they can live quietly and peacefully. His wife, however, has long ago learned to live without him, free from notoriety. Nevertheless, Ringo waits in a saloon hoping that she will arrive before the train comes and takes him away forever.

As word of Ringo's presence in town gets around, he is visited by Sheriff Mark Strett (Millard Mitchell) a friend and former gunman himself, who warns him to get out of town before there is trouble. Ringo is tired of running but promises to leave as soon as his train arrives. In the meantime, he agrees to stay out of sight inside the saloon. Children begin to gather at the windows to catch a glimpse of the famous gunman. Among them is his own son, who is unaware that this man is his father. Inside, Ringo's only companion is the bartender Mac (Karl Malden), who confides that he is very excited about meeting the famous Jimmie Ringo.

Not everyone, however, is content with merely looking at him or talking to him. As he has experienced time and time before, there is always one man who wants to challenge the gunman's reputation. In this case, it is Hunt Bromley (Skip Homeier), a brash young punk. Eager to avoid a confrontation with yet another young gun looking for a reputation, Ringo tries to ignore him; but Hunt is determined to prove himself by goading Ringo into action. Taunting him with remarks such as "He don't look so tough to me," he finally forces Ringo to defend himself, and the young man is left dead.

Outside the saloon, the presence of Ringo has become the subject of everyone's conversation. Women lament the state of their town when a known killer is allowed to remain within its boundaries. Nevertheless, the excitement far outweighs the concern. There are those who want Ringo dead. One man is waiting at a window with a rifle, ready to shoot him down the moment he steps out into the street. It seems that this man believes that Ringo is responsible for the death of his son and wants to take revenge, all of which leads to a very tense atmosphere.

Finally, Ringo's wife goes to the saloon to talk with him. She acknowledges the change in her husband but knows he is doomed to live out his life as a gunman, unable to shake off the label of "fastest gun alive." When Ringo leaves, he is shot from behind by yet another young man eager to be known as a "fast gun." His arm shattered by the bullet, Ringo knows he is helpless and doomed. Before leaving, however, he pronounces what amounts to a sentence of death on the young man, warning him to be prepared for others eager to prove themselves against the man who shot Ringo.

Unlike other Westerns, which never questioned the thoughts and feelings of gunfighters, *The Gunfighter* provides insights and stimulates speculation. As Ringo, Peck brings intensity and seriousness to the role. His low-key performance is perfect for a man tired of the notoriety his trade has brought him. Director Henry King wisely focuses the action primarily within the spatial confines of the saloon. He knows that the action must center on this one man, as it has throughout his entire career.

In addition to its deserved reputation as one of the first psychological Westerns, the film is also noteworthy for the sociological implications of its release time. The year 1950 was a time of turmoil for both the country and the film industry. Senator Joseph McCarthy was attacking the film industry for harboring Communists, and the war in Korea was just beginning. For many who had fought in World War II and had enjoyed five years of peace, the desire of Ringo to rest and settle down was one with which they could identify. Few were eager to rush back into war.

As a result of this film, many other psychological or adult Westerns, such as *High Noon* (1952) and *Shane* (1953), were produced; but there were those who deplored a trend which seemed to be destroying many of the traditional aspects of the genre. As Robert Warshow pointed out in his famous essay "The Westerner," published in 1954: ". . . The spectator derives his pleasure from the appreciation of minor variations within the working out of a pre-determined order. One does not want much novelty."

The Gunfighter inspired new interpretations of traditional Western myths. Ringo was allowed to think and act according to a code other than the long-accepted one of the Western hero. Audiences were allowed to see what happened to all those men after they had ridden into the sunset. The Western never fully returned to the simple stories and attitudes of the pre-1950's. Furthermore, filmmakers learned that it was often easier to deal with controversial themes within a genre such as the Western than in straight dramatic stories. Directors and writers were beginning to explore more complex themes, and Westerns offered them a vehicle in which to present them. America had outgrown the simple Western.

James J. Desmarais

GUNGA DIN

Released: 1939
Production: George Stevens for RKO/Radio
Direction: George Stevens
Screenplay: Joel Sayre and Fred Guiol; based on Ben Hecht and Charles
   MacArthur's adaptation of the poem of the same name by Rudyard Kipling
Cinematography: Joseph H. August
Editing: Henry Berman and John Lockert
Art direction: Van Nest Polglase
Music: Alfred Newman
Running time: 117 minutes

> *Principal characters:*
> Archibald Cutter .... Cary Grant
> MacChesney .... Victor McLaglen
> Ballantine .... Douglas Fairbanks, Jr.
> Gunga Din .... Sam Jaffe
> Guru .... Edward Ciannelli
> Emmy .... Joan Fontaine
> Higginbotham .... Robert Coote
> Colonel .... Montagu Love

Gunga Din, George Stevens' cinematic adaptation of Rudyard Kipling's famous poem, is one of the greatest pure adventure films of all time. If there is, as it happens, little of Kipling in the end product, the film suffers not at all as a result. Writers Ben Hecht and Charles MacArthur took the title, the setting, and the last few lines from Kipling's Barrack Room Ballad, and turned them into a full-fledged epic.

The setting is mysterious India; the time, late in the nineteenth century. The sun has yet to set on the British Empire, and, as *Gunga Din* opens, we meet the film's heroes ("protagonists" is a much too intellectual word to describe them) Sergeants Cutter (Cary Grant), MacChesney (Victor McLaglen), and Ballantine (Douglas Fairbanks, Jr.) of the Imperial Lancers. Stevens introduces the three men with a bang: they are the instigators of a knockdown-dragout brawl with some of the locals over a map to an emerald mine. Bodies fly out windows, plummet from rooftops, and tumble down stairs as the three comrades, grinning all the while, singlehandedly subdue what seems like half the population of the teeming subcontinent. The scene would have done quite nicely as the climax for a lesser adventure film, but Stevens is just getting started.

Stevens and his writers quickly introduce the conflicts which propel the film forward. First, and most importantly, the three friends are in danger of breaking up. Sergeant Cutter is forever pursuing the chimera of lost treasure, and

Sergeant Ballantine is on the verge of an even worse sin: he intends to get married and leave the service altogether. Sergeant MacChesney is determined to keep his friends together by whatever means. Gunga Din (Sam Jaffe), the lowly Indian water boy (who plays a less important role in the film than its title would seem to indicate), desperately wants to join the British Army. To top everything off, the natives are restless. The Thuggees, members of a dreaded murder cult, have resumed their depredations in the hills.

The Thugs are led by their Guru (Edward Ciannelli), a hooded figure with a piercing gaze that reveals a perpetually crazed glint in his eye. They worship the many-armed goddess Kaili (a note at the end of the credits explains that this is historical fact) and practice murder as a religious sacrament, digging graves for their intended victims before carrying out the murder. Inactive for years, the Thugs have risen once more, swearing to rid their country of the colonial British. Their first target is the village of Tantrapur, which they overrun with ease.

Cutter, MacChesney, and Ballantine lead a detachment of Lancers to retake the village. When they reach Tantrapur, they find it to all appearances deserted, but it does not stay that way for long. Screaming their defiance, the Thugs attack. Once again, Stevens stages a long battle scene, replete with hand-to-hand combat and the usual acrobatic derring-do on the part of the heroes. Cutter is particularly nonchalant amidst the carnage that rages around him.

The good guys win, of course, and head for home to report. Gunga Din tags along like a puppy at their heels, never missing an opportunity to express his wish to be a soldier. The sergeants are amused by his presumption—the idea of a native water boy in the lordly Lancers is preposterous—and urge him to content himself with his lot. Cutter does permit Din to keep a bugle that he has found. "Very regimental, Din," he says, patting the diminutive Indian on the head approvingly.

Cutter and MacChesney are more concerned about Ballantine, who is apparently serious about marrying his girl friend Emmy (Joan Fontaine) and going into the tea business. His potential loss is made all the more unbearable when their Colonel (Montagu Love) replaces Ballantine with Sergeant Higginbotham (Robert Coote), a humorless prig whom Cutter and MacChesney loathe. They contrive to make Higginbotham unbattle-worthy by spiking the punch at Ballantine's pre-wedding ball with elephant medicine; and the Colonel is forced to reassign Ballantine to the regiment for the brief duration of his enlistment.

Meanwhile, Archibald Cutter is interested in treasure again. Rumors of a golden temple have reached the fort, and Cutter is anxious to investigate. Annoyed when MacChesney forbids the treasure hunt, he picks a fight with his powerfully built friend. The quarrel ends quickly. MacChesney decks Cutter with a single punch, and Cutter wakes up in the brig. Undeterred, he persuades Gunga Din to help him escape. Annie, MacChesney's pet elephant, is the vehicle of Cutter's deliverance; guided by Din, she knocks over the whole stockade. Cutter hops aboard, and he and Din head off in search of the golden temple.

They find the temple, but unfortunately, it turns out to be the Thug head-quarters. Din's eyes pop as the Thug rituals unfold ("Kill, kill, kill," the cultists chant), but Cutter keeps his head. "The Colonel's got to know," he says, and sends Din for help. Cutter distracts the Thugs by walking into their midst singing a merry tune. "You're all under arrest," he announces calmly to the hundreds of killers. "Her Majesty's very touchy about having her subjects strangled." Despite this show of bravado, Cutter is quickly over-powered and imprisoned by the Thugs.

Meanwhile, Gunga Din has apprised the Lancers of Cutter's predicament. MacChesney prepares to set off alone; when Ballantine insists on coming, MacChesney scowls "I ain't takin' any bloody civilians with me." Grinning wolfishly, he insists that the only way Ballantine can join the rescue mission is to reenlist. The stratagem works; as the once-again Sergeant Ballantine explains to his furious bride-to-be, "I hate the blasted army, but friendship, well that's something else." With that, he, MacChesney, and Gunga Din ride off to save Cutter.

They reach the temple and immediately are captured by the Thugs. "Where's the troop?" demands Cutter. "Another fine mess you've gotten us into," replies MacChesney; but the Lancers are not dead yet. When the Guru himself arrives to interrogate Cutter ("I want to know about your army." "Why don't you enlist?"), the sergeants quite improbably manage to capture him and lock his followers outside the temple. The situation seems stalemated. The Lancers will not release the Guru, and the Guru will not call off his men. He reveals that he is using the three sergeants as bait to ensnare their entire regiment. "Two come to rescue one, then the others follow," he reasons, until he has rid the entire country of the British.

As he had hoped, the sound of bagpipes signals the approach of the British Army. The Guru, his plan nearing fruition, breaks the impasse by leaping to his death from the top of the temple, but the Thugs storm in after the Lancers. Gunga Din grabs a bayonet and makes short work of one attacker. "Good work, soldier," cries Cutter approvingly, and Din glows with pride. Their triumph is short-lived, however; MacChesney and Ballantine are captured, and Cutter and Din are stabbed and left for dead.

The sergeants watch helplessly as the British march towards certain death. Suddenly, Gunga Din appears on the screen once more. Although seriously wounded, he still has the strength to bring his beloved bugle to his lips and blow a warning. A Thug bullet cuts him down, but the water boy has saved the regiment. The British form ranks and slowly but surely fight off their attackers. In the meantime, Cutter, who was not dead after all, rescues MacChesney and Ballantine.

The last scene strikes the only false note in the film—false because it ends a marvelous lark with a note of almost sanctimonious solemnity. Gathered round the campfire after the battle, the Colonel makes Gunga Din a posthumous corporal. Then, with the sound track swelling portentously, the Colonel recites Kipling's famous lines: "Though I've belted you and flayed you/ By the living God that made you/You're a better man than I am, Gunga Din." The sound track then leads into "Auld Lang Syne," and an image of Gunga Din is superimposed on the screen. Wearing a clean white British uniform, he snaps off a crisp salute, grinning wildly.

It would not do to overanalyze *Gunga Din*; the film is, after all, entertainment. It is great entertainment, however, and credit must go where it is due. The film's success must be attributed to its writers, its fine cast, and to Stevens, its director. Hecht and MacArthur fashioned a terrific adventure story out of a few lines of poetry. It is full of a lot of nonsense, of course, but fantasy allows such license. The script by Joel Sayre and Fred Guiol is full of excitement, loyalty, and heroism—everything but romance. Emmy, Ballantine's unfortunate intended, is given a very small part by the writers; evidently women have no place in this particular fantasyland.

The male characters, however, are interesting, even if they are substantially broader than they are deep. Grant as the witty, impetuous Cutter and McLaglen as the gruff and burly MacChesney ham it up ferociously. Fortunately, Fairbanks, as Ballantine and Jaffe as Gunga Din, underplay their roles—the screen would not have been big enough to hold them otherwise. Mention must also be made of Ciannelli who plays the Guru of the Thugs. He radiates an evil fanaticism that must be seen to be believed.

Stevens weaves these fine performances into some of the most furious action sequences ever filmed. RKO spent the then-incredible sum of two million dollars to produce *Gunga Din*, and Stevens used their money well. The sets are lavish and exotic, under the artistic direction of Van Nest Polglase, and the traditional "cast of thousands" look is exploited effectively. Indeed, the first two fight scenes, wherein the three sergeants subdue hordes of their enemies with an incredible nonchalance, are expertly staged and are as witty in their own way as anything the dialogue has to offer.

Gunga Din was remade twice (Tay Garnett's *Soldiers Three* in 1951 and John Sturges' *Sergeants 3*, with Frank Sinatra, Peter Lawford, Dean Martin, and Sammy Davis, Jr., in 1962); and generous portions of the film's substance and spirit have shown up in such unlikely quarters as Richard Lester's 1965 Beatles epic, *Help!* This far-reaching influence is testimony enough, if testimony is needed, to the durability and greatness of Stevens' *Gunga Din*.

Robert Mitchell

THE GUNS OF NAVARONE

Released: 1961
Production: Carl Foreman for Columbia
Direction: J. Lee Thompson
Screenplay: Carl Foreman; based on the novel of the same name by Alistair MacLean
Cinematography: Oswald Morris
Editing: Alan Osbitson
Special effects: Bill Warrington and Wally Veevers (AA)
Music: Dmitri Tiomkin
Running time: 157 minutes

Principal characters:
Captain Mallory .... Gregory Peck
Corporal Miller .... David Niven
Andrea Stavros .... Anthony Quinn
C.P.O. Brown .... Stanley Baker
Spyros Pappadimos .... James Darren
Major Franklin .... Anthony Quayle
Maria Pappadimos .... Irene Papas
Anna .... Gia Scala

At its time of production, *The Guns of Navarone* was one of the largest-budgeted war films ever made. Its resounding box-office success established it as a precedent in its genre for many years following. Produced and scripted by Carl Foreman, the widescreen color film, superbly photographed by British camerman Oswald Morris, details the nearly suicidal attempt of a hand-picked band of saboteurs to rescue a force of two thousand British soldiers beseiged on Kheros, an isolated island in the Aegean Sea off the coast of Turkey.

The movie's prologue, produced by UFA, the cartoon company, sets the stage. The only approach to the island is by sea through a narrow channel near Navarone. At the top of four-hundred-feet-high sheer cliffs set in a deep natural cave impregnable to air attack are a pair of huge 210 mm guns manned by a Nazi force. Allied Intelligence learns that the Germans plan to blitz the trapped soldiers very soon, and the saboteur force, headed by Major Franklin (Anthony Quayle), has six days, later reduced to five, to destroy the guns as the British fleet sets out to evacuate the men. Along with Franklin, the band is composed of Captain Mallory (Gregory Peck), a famous mountaineer; explosives expert Corporal Miller (David Niven); Andrea Stavros (Anthony Quinn), a Greek Resistance fighter who has vowed to kill Mallory after the war because the Captain was indirectly responsible for the wartime deaths of his wife and children by Nazis; and two trained killers, C.P.O. Brown (Stanley Baker), the so-called "Butcher of Barcelona," and Spyros Pappadimos (James Darren), an American soldier reared in urban slums but a native of Navarone.

The team sets out in a converted fishing vessel and before long destroys an inquisitive German patrol boat. In a tumultuous storm, the boat is wrecked at the foot of the Navarone cliffs, largely unguarded by the Germans because they are considered impossible to scale. Mallory slowly leads the group up the treacherous face of the cliffs and takes command when Franklin is injured. Traveling across the island, they link up with two Resistance members, Spyros' sister Maria (Irene Papas) and a schoolteacher, Anna (Gia Scala), who was struck dumb by Nazi torture.

In the small village of Mandrakos, the force is captured by Germans, but Stavros engineers a trick whereby the group escapes in Nazi uniforms, leaving Franklin behind with deliberately false information which Mallory knows he will reveal to the enemy in his delirium. On the evening before the assault on the guns, Miller denounces Anna as a traitor who has been revealing their positions to the Germans. Before Mallory can kill her (they had previously shared a romantic interlude), Maria shoots her. The SS uses a truth drug on Franklin, who tells them of an assault landing; and the Germans pull out the Navarone forces to meet the invaders. Mallory and Miller sneak into the fortress and lay the explosives, knowing some of them will be discovered. The others stage diversionary actions, during which both Pappadimos and Brown are killed. The survivors escape to the sea in a boat secured by Maria, who leaves with Stavros to continue fighting in the Resistance. Mallory and Miller watch the British ships make their approach. The huge guns begin to fire, but the two men's horror turns to triumph as the last charge, carefully hidden under an elevator, finally goes off, triggering a massive series of explosions during which the guns fall harmlessly into the sea.

The production of the 5.6-million-dollar film was something of an epic in itself. Foreman had acquired the rights to the novel by Alistair MacLean as early as 1958, but refused even to contemplate production until his screenplay was letter-perfect. He wisely chose to shoot on locations as authentic to the novel's setting as possible and visited nearly every country in Europe looking for a site. He finally settled on Cyprus, where the local government, ranging from Bishop Makarios to Governor-General Sir Hugh Foote, promised lavish aid in the form of troops and military equipment from local British bases, with an eye to the prestige a large movie company filming a major production could provide the tiny island. However, Foreman, nearing production, was soon innocently involved in Cyprus' political problems, which concerned the colony's increasingly urgent desire to leave the Commonwealth. Foreman was accused of being a British agent. Despite assurances to Columbia of the movie company's safety by all three factions in Cyprus vying for power, Foreman pulled out and relocated to Rhodes, where the Greek government assured him of full cooperation, providing troops, destroyers, helicopters, planes, armaments, and military advisers, mainly for the impetus the project would provide to the fledgling Greek film industry.

Production finally began in early 1960. Well into the shooting, director Alexander MacKendrick fell ill and had to be replaced. Foreman himself took over for two weeks until J. Lee Thompson was hired. The shooting dragged on for seven months, which included time spent in London's Shepperton and Elstree Studios (where the harrowing shipwreck and storm sequences were shot in a tank). The film received a series of Royal Premieres in London and opened in June, 1961, in the United States, where it became the top-grossing film of the year for Columbia, which had financed the project (although it was produced by Foreman's British company). According to *Variety*, by the end of 1978, the film had returned rentals to the distributor of over $13 million, earning it a place on the all-time top-grossing films list.

The movie did not do as well critically, with reviewers chiefly finding fault with impassive acting, illogical plotting, and long, dialogue-laden passages containing Foreman's themes of personal *versus* "national" responsibility. Indeed, Foreman and Thompson are best in the wordless stretches of the film: the explosive fishing boat encounter with the German U-boat, the storm and shipwreck, and the agonizing scaling of the rain-swept cliffs. These fine sequences served up an exciting one-two punch that the film does not match until the finale. The thematic elements of the movie, including the Good German/Evil Nazi dichotomy, have since become standard themes for the genre. The film established a continuing vogue of producing films from Alistair MacLean's other war and espionage adventure novels. None, however, has enjoyed the success of *The Guns of Navarone*. Foreman's casting for the film, which had every agent in Hollywood with a candidate scurrying to the telephone, helped immensely to put the film over, catching Peck, Niven, Quinn, and Baker in ascending popularity, and throwing in Papas for a bit of class.

Foreman, Thompson, MacLean, and Columbia announced a sequel to the film as early as 1967. The project shifted hands several times, with Foreman gradually losing interest. MacLean's sequel scenario eventually was published as a novel which became a best seller. The poorly made and received film that finally appeared, from American-International in 1978, *Force 10 From Navarone*, was technically not a sequel although it opened with the original film's rousing finale and involved two of its characters, Mallory and Miller (played by Robert Shaw and Edward Fox, respectively), on a World War II mission to destroy a bridge and dam in Yugoslavia.

The Guns of Navarone won Golden Globe Awards for Best Motion Picture (Drama) and Best Score; it was voted Best Picture in the annual *Film Daily* poll; and it was nominated for seven 1961 Academy Awards, including Best Picture, Direction, Screenplay, Editing, Music, Sound, and Special Effects. It deservedly won in the last category while losing in most of the others to the major Oscar-winner of that year, *West Side Story*. The New York Film

Critics nominated *The Guns of Navarone* for Best Motion Picture and Best Director.

David Bartholomew

HAIL THE CONQUERING HERO

Released: 1944
Production: Preston Sturges for Paramount
Direction: Preston Sturges
Screenplay: Preston Sturges
Cinematography: John F. Seitz
Editing: Stuart Gilmore
Running time: 101 minutes

Principal characters:
Woodrow Truesmith .... Eddie Bracken
Libby .... Ella Raines
Mr. Noble .... Raymond Walburn
Sergeant .... William Demarest
Mrs. Truesmith .... Georgia Caine
Libby's Aunt .... Elizabeth Patterson
Committee Chairman ....Franklin Pangborn
Bugsy .... Freddie Steele
Doc Bissell .... Harry Hayden

By 1944, Preston Sturges had written and directed five films for Paramount, spoofing everything from politics to motherhood. Nothing was safe from his satirical eye. Described by other studio employees as "eccentric" or "screwball," Sturges nevertheless had the respect of the front office, who had seen his gamble on *The Great McGinty* (1940) turn into a box-office smash and who acceded to his demands because his films were proven moneymakers. Sturges once described his credo for making good films to one of the Hollywood trade papers, and it bears repeating as representative of his sense of humor:

1. A pretty girl is better than an ugly one. 2. A leg is better than an arm. 3. A bedroom is better than a living room. 4. An arrival is better than a departure. 5. A birth is better than a death. 6. A chase is better than a chat. 7. A dog is better than a landscape. 8. A kitten is better than a dog. 9. A baby is better than a kitten. 10. A kiss is better than a baby. 11. A pratfall is better than anything.

Hail the Conquering Hero, considered by many to be Sturges' finest film, certainly contains all of the elements that his fans had come to expect: the usual cast of lovable bumblers and stuffed shirts, and an equal blend of sly wit with raucous slapstick.

In this film, Woodrow Lafayette Pershing Truesmith (Eddie Bracken) is the son of a World War I hero who joins the Marine Corps at the start of World War II, only to be washed out shortly thereafter because of his chronic hay fever. Ashamed to go home to face the family and friends who expected great things of him, Woodrow takes a job in a shipyard. He perpetrates a hoax by having departing Marines send letters to his mother (Georgia Caine) from the South Pacific. In one of these letters he writes to his girl friend Libby (Ella Raines) that he has found someone else. The dejected Woodrow plans to stay away from his hometown.

One day, while having a few drinks in a bar, Woodrow meets a group of Marines back from the Pacific theater and tells them of his deception. Bugsy (Freddie Steele), one of the men, has a deep and profound respect for mothers, and Woodrow's plight nearly brings him to tears, so he decides to make Woodrow a hero for his mother's sake. He makes a phone call to Woodrow's mother, telling her that her hero son will be returning home for a visit. The Marine Sergeant (William Demarest) convinces Woodrow that they can put him in uniform temporarily, sneak him into his home town, and give his mother the joy of seeing her son a true hero. Woodrow is uneasy about the whole idea, but the Marines put him in uniform and whisk him aboard a train before he can change his mind.

News spreads fast, and when Woodrow and his "honor guard" step off the train at Oakridge, they find the entire town at the station to greet the returned warrior. Blustery Mayor Noble (Raymond Walburn) leads the ceremony, which includes brass bands and political hoopla. The embarrassed Woodrow attempts to explain the hoax, but the crowd mistakes his words for modesty, and Truesmith fever sweeps the entire community. The mortgage of his mother's home is burned as a gallant gesture to her son's heroics, others propose that monuments be erected in his honor, and some begin promoting Woodrow for mayor. Woodrow later tries to sneak away, mortified at the results that his little hoax has wrought, but Bugsy and the others foil his attempts to escape, using his mother's pride as the means of keeping him home.

Finally, Mayor Noble learns of the deception, and, furious, attempts to expose the youth; but the heartsick Woodrow beats him to it, making a public confession before the townspeople at a special meeting. He denounces himself as a liar and a coward and then leaves in shame. At that point the Sarge takes command, telling the assembled townspeople that it was the group of Marines who plotted the hoax; Woodrow was an unwilling participant from the start, and his public confession is itself a heroic act that took as much courage as any victory on the battlefield. Woodrow, meanwhile, makes his way dejectedly to the train station, where he plans to return to the shipyard. The crowd marches to the station, however, and catches up to him just as his train arrives. Old Doc Bissell (Harry Hayden) comforts him by telling him that acting out a little lie to save one mother from humiliation is a fault of which any man could be proud. The townspeople are impressed by Woodrow's honesty, and they ask him to stay and run for mayor.

Hail the Conquering Hero certainly shows Sturges at his best, combining the best elements of comedy and pathos in a delightful film. Bracken (a Sturges favorite who had also performed well in *The Miracle of Morgan's Creek* for the director that same year) gives one of his finest performances as the harried Woodrow Truesmith, bringing to the role his own special brand of goofiness. Lovely Raines does not have much to do but makes the most of her screen time as a beautiful companion for Woodrow. The Sturges stock company of character actors (Walburn, Demarest, Franklin Pangborn, and others) are shown to good advantage as well, and the scene in which Woodrow returns home to find a mob waiting for him is memorable for Walburn's flustered attempts to deliver a speech while master of ceremonies Pangborn fails to hold the bands in check, creating total pandemonium for the returning Woodrow. The group of Marines, headed by Demarest, lends much to the manic atmosphere of the film as they whirl a reluctant Woodrow from event to event. Steele as Bugsy, the shell-shocked Marine whose devotion to mothers borders on the obsessive, is particularly good.

The most notable aspect of the film, however, is the dexterity with which Sturges moves the story along, combining slapstick with sentiment. Scenes that could easily have been maudlin are saved by honest, straightforward delivery, and they are made to seem more poignant by contrast to the wilder comedic scenes.

After his contract with Paramount ran out in the middle 1940's, Sturges left the studio system for the pleasures of independent filmmaking, but his subsequent efforts were far inferior to the seven films that he directed for Paramount. He died in 1959 at the age of sixty, before the new critical acclaim for his motion pictures reached the filmgoing community. He was thus robbed of the satisfaction that the rediscovery of his work would have afforded him.

Ed Hulse

HAIR

Released: 1979
Production: Lester Persky and Michael Butler for United Artists
Direction: Miloš Forman
Screenplay: Michael Weller; based on the play of the same name by Gerome Ragni, James Rado, and Galt MacDermot
Cinematography: Miroslav Ondricek
Editing: Stanley Harnow and Alan Heim
Choreography: Twyla Tharp
Music: Galt MacDermot, Gerome Ragni, and James Rado
Running time: 118 minutes

Principal characters:

Claude	John Savage
Berger	Treat Williams
Sheila	Beverly D'Angelo
Jeannie	Annie Golden
Hud	Dorsey Wright
Woof	Don Dacus
Hud's fiancée	Cheryl Barnes
Fenton	Richard Bright
The General	Nicholas Ray

Hair, a "tribal love rock musical," is based upon the stage play which was produced by Joseph Papp at the off-Broadway New York Public Theater in 1967 and on Broadway in 1968. Shocking to many because of its antiwar, and free-love sentiments, drug orientation, and nudity, the relatively plotless musical contained such eyebrow-raising numbers as "Sodomy" and "Colored Spade." More than ten years after its Broadway run, in which such future stars as Diane Keaton and Keith Carradine had small parts, director Milos Forman translated the musical from stage to screen. Although the play created a sensation with its anti-establishment antics, the film version is rated a mild P. G. for its one brief nude swimming scene. Considerably less defiant than the play, the movie presents a nostalgic, idealized, glossed-over view of the 1960's.

The expanded plot, with its more realistic narrative, takes place in 1968 and concerns a naïve, short-haired, clean-cut Oklahoma Kid named Claude, winningly played by John Savage, who stops in New York City for a three-day fling before his induction into the army. In Central Park, he meets a romping group of hippies, including the frizzy-haired leader, Berger (Treat Williams), long-haired blonde Woof (Don Dacus), the arrogant black Hud (Dorsey Wright), and the pregnant, childlike waif Jeannie (Annie Golden), who does not know if Woof or Hud is the father of her child. The troupe attempts to show Claude the free-living-and-loving side of life.

When the shy Claude is smitten by a beautiful debutante named Sheila (Beverly D'Angelo), Berger takes him to the girl's family's estate in Short Hills, New Jersey. Claude and Sheila fall in love and the ingenue is coaxed into joining the group. After Claude leaves for his basic training at the Nevada desert boot camp at which veteran film director Nicholas Ray plays the general, the tribe decides to follow him. Joining them on the cross-country trip is Hud's "straight" girl friend (Cheryl Barnes) and their small son, whom Hud had temporarily abandoned after "dropping out." Upon their arrival in Nevada, Sheila seduces a sergeant out of his uniform; Berger then dons the outfit, sneaks into the military camp, and changes places with Claude, who leaves base for a reunion with Sheila. In the film's final, bittersweet moments, Claude does not return to the camp in time and Berger is accidentally shipped off to Vietnam in his place. We soon learn that Berger subsequently was killed in the war. The dream of the flower children, unfortunately, does not last.

A rock fantasy musical like other films of the late 1970's such as *The Wiz* (1979), *Sgt. Pepper's Lonely Hearts Club Band* (1979), and *Grease* (1978) this high-energy production makes use of realistic locations such as the "be-in" in Central Park and the protest at the Lincoln Memorial in Washington, D. C., for example. These open-air locales add to the film's fresh, breezy spontaneity and charm. The exuberant cast of newcomers, the outrageous costumes, the dazzling staging, and the innovative choreography by Twyla Tharp, who appears with her ensemble and several members of the American Ballet Theater, create an exhilarating and euphoric picture. Even the horses canter in step to the music.

The now-classic twenty-seven songs, which are fluidly integrated into the plot, include the title song, "Age of Aquarius," as well as "Good Morning Starshine," and "Let the Sunshine In." At Sheila's formal and staid "coming-out" party, Berger goes berserk, dances on the table, and belts out "I Got Life." Barnes, as Hud's fiancée, performs a touching, riveting, and magnificent Aretha Franklin-like rendition of "Easy to be Hard." There is also the rousing antiwar song "3-5-00," led by two cast members from the original stage production, Melba Moore and Ronnie Dyson. Another number, "Black Boys, White Boys" is shot and edited so that a group of male military personnel, creating homosexual overtones, and a group of wildly dressed girls are both shown singing the song.

Written by Michael Weller, author of the play *Moonchildren*, also about youth in the 1960's, *Hair* is the seventh film directed by Forman, the 1975 Academy Award-winning director of *One Flew over the Cuckoo's Nest*. After seeing the play *Hair* on off-Broadway in 1967, Forman tried unsuccessfully to produce it in his native Czechoslovakia. Interestingly, the East-European expatriate, now an American citizen, does indeed capture the atmosphere of

1960's Americana, its flower children, protest marchers, and peaceniks.

Forman's direction is very effective, as is the cinematography of Miroslav Ondricek, also a native of Czechoslovakia. The camera is whimsical in its careening movement and innovative angles. The film's lyrical, visual splendor is particularly evident in the "Hare Krishna" production number, a surrealistic LSD sequence in which the characters float in the air at an imaginary wedding ceremony that juxtaposes Eastern and Western religions.

There are some who feel that the twelve-million-dollar film, which took two years to make, is outdated and was made ten years too late. There are also those who feel that the irresponsible, hedonistic characters are not commendable. Indeed, they take money from tourists and commandeer a car from Sheila's uptight, conservative ex-boyfriend. Others feel that the politics in the film is mindless and shallow, and that the film does not really examine the era or represent any ideological statement. Without becoming sentimental or platitudinous, however, *Hair* does indeed contain social observation about the 1960's and at times creates an affecting drama. Most importantly, the film is a celebration of discovery and friendship. Full of vitality and bouyancy, *Hair* is a refreshing tribute to the flower-power era and to the love and peace generation of the not-so-long-ago 1960's.

Leslie Taubman

HALLELUJAH!

Released: 1929
Production: King Vidor for Metro-Goldwyn-Mayer
Direction: King Vidor
Screenplay: Wanda Tuchock, Ransom Rideout, Richard Schayer; based on the story of the same name by King Vidor
Cinematography: Gordon Avil
Editing: Hugh Wynn
Art direction: Cedric Gibbons
Music direction: Eva Jessye
Song: Irving Berlin
Running time: 109 minutes

Principal characters:
Zeke	Daniel L. Haynes
Chick	Nina Mae McKinney
Hot Shot	William Fountaine
Parson	Harry Gray
Mammy	Fanny Belle de Knight
Missy Rose	Victoria Spivey
Spunk	Everett McGarrity

Hailed as the first all-Negro musical, *Hallelujah!* has long overshadowed its immediate predecessor, Paul Sloane's *Hearts in Dixie*, released earlier in 1929 by Fox. Technically, however, *Hallelujah!* really is the first in that category, since there is not a white actor in the entire film, while *Hearts in Dixie* features Richard Carlyle as a white doctor. Both are dramatic portrayals of the life of the poor black in the South. However, *Hallelujah!*, a King Vidor film, concentrates on a continuous flow of music to highlight each scene. The Texas-born Vidor, who had been directing since the age of twenty-three and had long wanted to make the movie, was prestigious enough to persuade his company, M-G-M, to join him in financing the film. Vidor produced the film from his own original story, which was further polished by several other writers. He had written the part of Zeke for Paul Robeson but wound up with Daniel L. Haynes, an understudy in the stage version of *Show Boat*, when Robeson was unavailable. Similarly, Ethel Waters and Honey Brown were being considered for the role of Chick before it went to Nina Mae McKinney, an energetic seventeen-year-old performer who had been appearing onstage in Lew Leslie's *Blackbirds* review in New York. Most members of the cast were making their film debuts, including eighty-six-year-old ex-slave Harry Gray, cast as the parson-father of Zeke.

Hallelujah!, which was Vidor's only musical, was filmed on location in Tennessee and Arkansas; interiors were then made at the new Culver City studios of M-G-M, where the sound on disc was recorded by Western Electric

Sound System for the location sequences. Along with the well-known spirituals and work songs were two original compositions by Irving Berlin, "Waiting at the End of the Road" and "Swanee Shuffle." Music supervision was by Eva Jessye, who also directed the Dixie Jubilee Singers heard throughout. In the shuffle number, McKinney shows enough style and talent to have made her an instant star, if such a thing were possible in the early sound days of Hollywood.

Whether *Hallelujah!* is a true representation of the plight of blacks in the 1920's or is a disguised series of stereotypes reacting to melodramatic situations is certainly debatable. Either allegation can be looked upon as having varying degrees of truth, although the film is full of life and movement and many individual scenes can be enjoyed on a high level. Chick's sexuality is evident in every scene, as are Zeke's baser instincts, which often overcome a strong will. The baptism in the river, ending with Zeke's pawing of the hysterical Chick, and the revival meeting, which almost resembles an orgy, point up the raw energy which Vidor brought to his project. Additionally, they serve to illustrate the struggle between religious and sexual fervor which dominates the film.

Hallelujah! opens with cotton pickers singing "Swanee River" as the Johnson family finishes the day's work. Zeke (Daniel L. Haynes), the eldest son, jokes with his Mammy (Fanny Belle de Knight); he lives happily with her and his father, a parson (Harry Gray), younger brother Spunk (Everett McGarrity), three little brothers (Milton Dickerson, Robert Couch, and Walter Tait), and an adopted sister, Missy Rose (Victoria Spivey), with whom he is in love. The three youngest boys need no excuse to begin dancing. That night, the Parson is called upon to unite Adam and Eve, a couple with eleven children who want to make their union permanent. As Rose plays "Here Comes the Bride" on a shaky-sounding organ, Zeke forces her to kiss him. He apologizes, but it obviously is not necessary. The newlyweds celebrate with a cakewalk.

Mammy sings the youngest boys to sleep and then retires with a "Thank God" for everyone getting through another day safely. The next day, Zeke and a chorus sing about cotton as he and Spunk bring their load to a mill, where it is processed and baled. There, Zeke joins in a rendition of "Waiting at the End of the Road." He sees the cotton loaded onto a riverboat before overhearing a crap game in progress and then encountering Chick (Nina Mae McKinney), a young dancer on the docks. He impulsively stops her and says she is just what he had in mind. She responds, "Get outta here, small change, you don't look like big money to me." Zeke lures her with the money he has just made by selling the cotton while a band blasts away at a saloon, where Chick introduces a song-and-dance number, "Swanee Shuffle." A couple dances to the song and then a huge man shuffles it before Chick and a group of singing waiters bring the proceedings to a rousing conclusion. During a slow dance with Chick, Zeke mentions that he has a hundred dollars with him; she replies that it would be easy to double it. Soon Zeke is gambling away all the money with Hot Shot (William Fountaine), Chick's partner.

Demanding to see the dice Hot Shot used, including the loaded pair in his pocket, Zeke forces the gambler to act. As Hot Shot pulls a gun after Zeke draws his knife, Spunk enters the premises. In a grapple for the gun, Hot Shot fires two shots, which hit Spunk. Grabbing the weapon, Zeke fires wildly three more times and then finds a sobbing Spunk on the floor. His brother is dead by the time Zeke reaches home with his body. The wake is a sorrowful, song-filled affair as Zeke mourns, prostrate in the field. Filled with religious fervor by the Parson, Zeke chants that the Lord is all, while Rose clings to him.

Next, a title proclaims, "And Zekiel became a Preacher." In the next scene, a congregation waiting for Zeke to step down from his gospel train sings "Get on Board." Children in a procession sing as Zeke proceeds on a mule. Heckling from the sidelines are Hot Shot and Chick, who remember Zeke from Greensville. The new preacher roughs up his two critics. At an outdoor meeting, the congregation does "Give Me That Old Time Religion" as Chick continues to jeer "Make me cry." Zeke acts as a conductor on a train, with Repentance the last station for sinners before Hell. He and the congregation sing "Waiting at the End of the Road." A sobbing Chick runs to the platform with the other converts.

The spiritual "Goin' Down to the Water" is sung while Zeke presides at baptisms in the river. A self-proclaimed wicked woman, Chick is filled with emotion as she is immersed. Zeke carries her back to his tent and tries to seduce her until Mammy intervenes, calling her a hypocrite. Troubled, Zeke asks Rose to marry him when they stop at the next station. Chick is singing "Give Me That Old Time Religion" when Hot Shot enters her house, over-riding her objections with the statement that sinning is in her blood. She knocks him down and begins hitting him with a poker, stating that she will do that to anybody who stands in her path to glory. Rushing to a revival meeting where Zeke is preaching, Chick joins in the singing and dancing. Zeke is drawn to her and follows her outside, then he carries her off. Rose then runs out and yells for Zeke. She returns to the church, where her wailing for him is mistaken for praying by the others.

Months later, Zeke is working at a saw mill to provide a modest cottage for Chick. The latter is entertaining Hot Shot, who makes a quick exit before Zeke arrives home. While Chick sings "St. Louis Blues," Zeke asks about the buggy out front. Suspiciously, Zeke pretends to sleep while Chick slips out with Hot Shot. He fires two shots at them, then races furiously after the buggy. It loses a wheel and Chick is thrown into a ditch. She tells Zeke of her fear of the Devil, who is coming for her as she dies. Pursuing Hot Shot through a swamp, Zeke kills him. On a rock pile, Zeke works as others sing.

Probation comes and Zeke strums a banjo while singing "Goin' Home" (on a barge, on top of a train, and in the fields). Once home, he is instantly forgiven, particularly by Rose, who still loves him.

Hallelujah! was not universally well received by the critics. Many confined their reviews to discussions of the film's treatment of blacks without discussing the work as drama, and therefore commented negatively on its impact. Later critics, however, have recognized its merits as a musical and have considered it as an important part of film history both for its sociological and cinematic values.

John Cocchi

HALLOWEEN

Released: 1978
Production: Debra Hill for Compass International
Direction: John Carpenter
Screenplay: John Carpenter and Debra Hill
Cinematography: Dean Cundey
Editing: Tommy Wallace and Charles Bornstein
Music: John Carpenter
Running time: 93 minutes

Principal characters:
Doctor Loomis	Donald Pleasence
Laurie	Jamie Lee Curtis
Michael Myers (younger)	Will Sandin
Michael Myers (older)	Nick Castle
Annie	Nancy Loomis
Linda	P. J. Soles
Tommy	Brian Andrews
Lindsay	Kyle Richards

Despite the fact that *Halloween* is credited with initiating a disturbing trend toward graphic screen violence, it stands as a hallmark within the horror genre. With its relentless, visceral delivery resulting in effective shock appeal, *Halloween* joins a select group of low-budget films, including George A. Romero's *Night of the Living Dead* (1968) and Tobe Hooper's *Texas Chainsaw Massacre* (1973), that extended the boundaries of the horror film. (Although *The Exorcist*, 1973, had a similar effect, it achieved its fame largely through a big budget and a name cast.)

In terms of manipulative screen horrors, *Halloween* redefined audience expectations. In years to come, however, it is probable that the film will be best known as a showcase for John Carpenter's terse and invigorating directorial style. *Halloween* served as Carpenter's springboard to recognition among audiences and throughout the industry. Its manipulative, grisly nature aside, *Halloween* is also extremely well made, and although many critics have been contemptuous of the onslaught of bloody successors triggered by the film and of the (mostly) nihilist views of Carpenter's films, there is unanimity that the director is an excellent craftsman.

Filmed during twenty days for a scant $320,000, *Halloween* had grossed in excess of sixty million dollars by 1981. The most successful independent film ever made to date, it remains a perennial favorite at the box office and on television. Released in 1978 with phenomenal success, it spawned near-record numbers of imitators during the late 1970's and into the 1980's. Sporting such uneasy titles as *He Knows You're Alone* (1980), *Don't Go in the House* (1980),

When a Stranger Calls (1979); and a penchant for holidays, as evidenced by *Prom Night* (1980), *Graduation Day* (1981), and *Happy Birthday to Me* (1981); and killers brandishing sharp-edged weapons such as knives, hatchets, razors, and chainsaws, these films evoked a kind of mad scientist syndrome, with the filmmakers wielding the scalpels. *Halloween* popularized the notion that a successful horror film can be a young filmmaker's ticket into the industry. It is notable that of the many who attempted to cash in on the bloody screen trend, however, none have shown Carpenter's skill at creating critically admired, commercially viable products.

In *Halloween*, Carpenter offers an inventive treatment of the familiar plot about an escaped maniac who terrorizes and murders teenage girls. A skilled trickster, he utilizes his mastery of the fluid camera to convince audiences that every space and every shadow is threatening. Moreover, through the use of a subjective camera which records events from the killer's point of view, each character seems a potential victim. These unnerving qualities serve to underline Carpenter's belief that "film is a feeling medium."

A graduate of the cinema school at the University of Southern California (where he did music, editing, cowriting, and some codirecting on the 1970 Academy Award-winning short film, *The Resurrection of Bronco Billy*), Carpenter garnered initial industry attention with his 1974 feature film, *Dark Star*. A space saga parody about "spaced-out" astronauts, the film did not succeed at the box office at the time of its release, but has since become a popular cult film on the midnight circuit. Carpenter's collaborator on the film and also its star was Dan O'Bannon, who went on to coauthor the story and screenplay for the blockbuster *Alien* (1979).

Carpenter made *Assault on Precinct 13* in 1976. One of his most wrenching works, the film is a grim depiction of a crime spree in a Los Angeles ghetto; after taking a blood oath, gang members launch a kamikaze attack on a nearly deserted police precinct. Independently made on a $200,000 budget, the film bears several now-familiar Carpenter trademarks. Liberally doused with blood, the film presents violence with an ironic, doomed edge; in fact, the violence is unleashed with the shocking death of an eight-year-old child who is shot at point blank range while ordering an ice cream cone. Once the warfare begins, there are additional sardonic inferences, including the fact that two of the film's "good guys," those defending the precinct, are Death Row prisoners. Known for paying homage to veteran directors he admires, Carpenter gives innumerable Hawksian traits to *Assault on Precinct 13*, a film which essentially transplants Howard Hawks's *Rio Bravo* (1959) to the ghetto. Carpenter himself has labeled this film an "urban Western," and he edited the film under the name of John T. Chance, the name of John Wayne's character in *Rio Bravo*.

Although *Assault on Precinct 13* is today recognized as a shattering foray into the crime genre, reaction was lukewarm at the time of its release. It was not until 1977, when the film emerged as the surprise hit of the London Film Festival, that *Assault on Precinct 13* and Carpenter were "discovered." As a result, producer Irwin Yablans, whose company had distributed the film, approached Carpenter about directing the first motion picture from his newly formed Compass International. Yablans had a concept called "The Babysitter Murders," which ultimately evolved into *Halloween*.

Mirroring familiar low-budget genre traits, *Halloween* abounds in ominous shadows, nubile teenaged girls, and illicit sex. The film opens with a brutal murder, and the story then jumps ahead fifteen years (this time-shift ploy was much imitated by succeeding "knife" films), when the lunatic has returned to continue his terror spree. While the basic format is certainly predictable, *Halloween* is not without distinctive strains. In the character of the murderous Michael Myers there are mythical qualities suggesting he is not human, but rather, the embodiment of evil. Dr. Loomis (Donald Pleasence), the psychiatrist who observed Michael for fifteen years, alludes to the theory throughout the film. "This isn't a man," he tells an investigator, describing a "blank, pale, emotionless face and the blackest eyes" that stand for "purely and simply evil." To the ire of many reviewers, *Halloween*'s murders appear to be precipitated by illicit sex or the intention of illicit sex. Indeed, the film's heroine is a virgin who survives because her repressed sexuality gives her the strength to fight back against the relentless killer.

To a lesser degree, *Halloween* also examines the role fate plays in lives. This intriguing nuance surfaces when Laurie (Jamie Lee Curtis) helps her real estate agent father by dropping off a key at the notorious Myers house, the scene of the brutal knifing fifteen years earlier. Unknown to Laurie, Michael (Nick Castle) is hiding inside the house watching her as she makes her brief stop. Later that day, during a classroom discussion about fate ("fate caught up with several lives here," drones the teacher), Laurie finds herself inexplicably uneasy. Staring out the classroom window, she briefly glimpses a figure in the distance watching her. Now, fate will catch up with her life.

Set in the seemingly quaint town of Haddonfield, Illinois, *Halloween* opens on Halloween night, 1963, with a suspenseful sequence that speaks for the film's suspenseful pulse. Watching through the windows of a wood frame house, we are voyeurs as a teenage girl and her boyfriend engage in petting; their passions lead them upstairs to the bedroom. Later, after the boyfriend has left the house (with an obligatory "I'll call you soon"), the audience realizes that the voyeurism is actually the killer's point of view. As the camera moves indoors one sees through his eyes, around corners and through doorways. In the kitchen a menacing knife is pulled from a drawer; then the camera climbs the stairs to the bedroom. Once inside, vision is somewhat impaired, for like the killer, the audience is seeing through the eyes of a confining Halloween mask, which is similar to a view through binoculars. A quick survey of the bedroom reveals soiled bedsheets and a teenaged girl, partially nude, brushing her hair at a vanity table. Turning in surprise, she recognizes her assailant: it is her brother Michael (Will Sandin), and she is unable to fend off his furious stabbing. Afterward, the killer descends the stairs and wanders out the front door. As the sequence comes to a close, a shocked couple arrives home to discover their young son clutching a bloodied knife and standing motionless in his Halloween clown costume.

The story line then shifts to Smith's Grove, Illinois, on October 30, 1978. Dr. Loomis, who has deemed it necessary to keep Michael institutionalized, is distraught when Michael manages to escape in the institution's car. Again the setting shifts, back to Haddonfield. It is now Halloween day, and Michael has returned home.

Throughout the day Loomis attempts to retrieve his patient, convinced that he will return to Haddonfield, and he vainly tries to make local officials understand the imminent danger. Meanwhile, Laurie begins to sense that she is being stalked. Her nervousness grows when she sights a person watching her; he wears a plain face mask which lends an eerie, dreamlike quality as viewed from a distance. Tommy (Brian Andrews), the youngster she frequently babysits, endures the torment of classmates that day who insist that "the bogeyman" is going to come after him. Later that night, when Laurie babysits Tommy, both will realize their nightmares.

Laurie's friend Annie (Nancy Loomis) also has a babysitting job, across the street from Tommy's house. Unlike Laurie, however, Annie is rather negligent of her young ward, Lindsay (Kyle Richards), and plans a sexual tryst with her boyfriend. Another girl, Linda (P. J. Soles), and her boyfriend also have a sexual encounter at the house where Annie is sitting; "Everyone's having a good time tonight," Laurie says glumly, peering through venetian blinds at the house across the street which is the site of the planned romances. Of course, it is Laurie (and Tommy and Lindsay) who will have the best times that night, for they will manage to survive the relentless attack.

Annie, Linda, and Linda's boyfriend are gruesomely murdered. Although Laurie is wounded, stabbed in the shoulder, and dazed by the events, she fights back. Ultimately, it is she who drives the knife through Michael; but still he comes at her, with the attack ending only when Loomis arrives in the nick of time and coolly shoots the murderer. Stabbed and shot, Michael's body tumbles from the bedroom window onto the ground below. Turning to her rescuer in a state of near shock, a bloodied Laurie asks, "That's the bogeyman?" "As a matter of fact," says Loomis, "that was." The supernatural thread becomes joltingly real when the camera returns for a final glimpse of Michael, only to reveal that his body is gone.

In addition to directing and cowriting *Halloween* (along with his partner, writer-producer Debra Hill), Carpenter scored the film's erratic music, a simple but effective piano melody that repeats constantly, signifying pending suspense. (In films such as *The Fog*, 1980, and *Escape from New York*, 1981,

Carpenter's scores are heavily synthesized.) Applauded by audiences for its edge-of-the-seat suspense but condemned by some critics for its violence, *Halloween* is a taut thriller that serves as Carpenter's industry calling card. It also stands as a memorable introduction for Jamie Lee Curtis, the daughter of Tony Curtis and Janet Leigh, who makes her film debut in *Halloween*. This casting ploy garnered press because, in a sense, she was following her actress mother's footsteps, since Leigh played the famed victim of the shower assault in Alfred Hitchcock's *Psycho* (1960). Curtis has since gone on to "scream queen" status, with roles in horror vehicles such as *Prom Night*, *Terror Train* (1980), and *Road Games* (1979). Within the genre she is known for her gutsy characterizations (always the heroine, she never "dies") and commendable work.

Carpenter's credits since *Halloween* have included the inventive ghost film, *The Fog*, about a band of bloodthirsty leper pirates, and *Escape from New York*, a commercially popular film which looks at the future through a grim, clouded crystal ball (among other things, Manhattan Island is a maximum security prison in the year 1997). Carpenter is equally skilled working within the framework of television. In 1978, he made the television film *Someone Is Watching Me* (released theatrically in Europe as *High Rise*), a thriller inspired by Hitchcock's *Rear Window* (1954) which starred Lauren Hutton. In 1979, Carpenter's longtime interest in rock and roll and the legendary Elvis Presley culminated with his three-hour television film *Elvis*. A ratings blockbuster (toppling much-publicized competition from network showings of *One Flew Over the Cuckoo's Nest* and *Gone with the Wind*), *Elvis* starred one-time Disney studio star Kurt Russell in the title role. Russell's performance was one of the television season's biggest surprises, and his role as the surly antihero Snake Plissken in *Escape from New York* was one of the most widely lauded of 1981. Russell is presently at work on a third Carpenter project, a remake of the Howard Hawks film *The Thing* (1951).

Carpenter, who served as executive producer for the sequel *Halloween II* (1980), tends to work with a familiar ensemble. Producer Hill often teams with him; Curtis has starred for him twice, the second time in *The Fog*; Castle, who plays *Halloween*'s deadly Michael Myers (the credits label the character "The Shape"), coauthored the script for *Escape from New York* with Carpenter. Carpenter's wife, Adrienne Barbeau, noted for her success in television, including the long-running series *Maude* as well as for her voluptuous figure, also appears regularly in his films.

Prior to achieving his status as a versatile, inventive filmmaker, Carpenter authored the screenplay "Eyes," which, after some dozen rewrites, became the 1978 film *Eyes of Laura Mars*. This film, which departs widely from Carpenter's original script, is not at all in keeping with his since-evolved style. "I like to be as simple as possible. I don't like to show off," says Carpenter; thus, his films have concise story lines and economical technical sleekness.

As a result, many critics argue that his work lacks defined characters with whom the audience can sympathize or relate. To date, however, the Carpenter flair for fast-paced, high-action storytelling—sometimes at the expense of characterizations—is a signature of an industry original. If this director's "great" film is yet to come, his track record is an exciting one.

Pat H. Broeske

THE HANGING TREE

Released: 1959
Production: Martin Jurow and Richard Shepherd for Warner Bros.
Direction: Delmer Daves
Screenplay: Wendell Mayes and Halsted Welles; based on a novelette of the same name by Dorothy M. Johnson
Cinematography: Ted McCord
Editing: Owen Marks
Music: Max Steiner
Song: Mack David and Jerry Livingston
Running time: 106 minutes

Principal characters:
Doc Joe Frail	Gary Cooper
Elizabeth Mahler	Maria Schell
Frenchy Plante	Karl Malden
Rune	Ben Piazza
Grubb	George C. Scott

The Hanging Tree is a thoughtful, unvarnished Western which exhibits many of the classic traits associated with the genre—notably that of the mysterious stranger attempting to hide his past, the unbridled greed that accompanies gold fever, and the hanging tree itself—long an imposing symbol of frontier justice. Adapted from Dorothy M. Johnson's novelette, which received the Spur Award from the Western Writers of America, *The Hanging Tree* presents real, sometimes unlikable characterizations against the rugged setting of a gold mining camp in the 1870's.

The story line involves a frontier doctor who is as cynical as he is compassionate and equally skilled with both scalpel and gun. Doc Frail (Gary Cooper), who has hung up his shingle on the outskirts of Skull Creek, a Montana mining camp, is a laconic loner known for his poker skills and fast gun. In dispensing medicine, Frail can be both greedy and kind. To those without money, there are no fees, but Frail has no qualms about asking high prices from those who can pay. Through town gossip, it is revealed that Frail, who has been moving from frontier town to frontier town, is attempting to escape his reputation. Back in his home state of Missouri, Frail killed his brother after finding him with his wife; later, Frail's wife committed suicide. Before riding away, an embittered Frail burned his home to the ground. He now seemingly has no need for personal relationships.

As with many other films within this genre, outsiders do invade his life. The first is a would-be sluice robber who is shot, although never seen, by an angry mob of prospectors. After taking the bullet out of Rune (Ben Piazza), who has called himself a "wood's colt," indicating he has no home, the doctor pockets the tell-tale bullet and threatens to use the bullet as evidence against Rune unless the youth agrees to become his manservant. Rune has no choice but to obey. Eventually, he comes to sense the doctor's need for companionship, despite Frail's attempts to keep his distance from any possible friendship.

The doctor's detached demeanor falters when he treats Elizabeth (Maria Schell), a young woman who has been blinded by the sun after wandering for days in the wilderness. A Swiss immigrant, she was aboard a stagecoach with her father when bandits attacked. The only survivor, she was thrown clear of the wreckage. She is rescued from her wanderings by Frenchy (Karl Malden), a vociferous and rather lecherous prospector who seems to look upon the girl as his property. Indeed, after locating the girl, Frenchy victoriously parades her before the other miners. She is a pathetic sight: she is almost in shock, her clothes are in tatters, and she has been severely sunburned, bruised, and blinded. Because she requires constant medical care, she is taken to Doc Frail's cabin. There, she begins to show signs of improvement.

In her disturbed state, Elizabeth is also in need of friendship and support. In a touching scene, the blind girl, who is becoming more attractive-looking with each day, clings desperately to the doctor's strong hands. Frail will not allow himself to feel affection for the grateful girl, but he is concerned for her health. After becoming convinced that her blindness is due to shock from witnessing the murder of her father, he turns to unorthodox treatment. Taking her to the edge of a cliff, he forces her to look down. Insisting that her eyes are physically healed, the doctor maintains that if she still cannot see it is because she refuses to see "things as they are." His treatment is successful. Following her cure, an indebted Elizabeth stays on at Frail's cabin, where she cooks and cleans. Although she becomes increasingly fond of him, he will not declare any feeling for her. The living arrangement comes to an end after town gossip increases and Elizabeth is verbally assaulted. As a result she moves into her own cabin, but she is still determined to repay Doc Frail. The best way to do so, she surmises, is with her own grubstake, but her efforts to solicit grubstake funds prove futile until Frail anonymously provides the money. Elizabeth then takes Rune and Frenchy as partners.

Working alongside Rune and Frenchy in the muddy riverbeds, Elizabeth discovers that the work is back-breaking and filthy. Although their spirits grow downcast, they are revived—for obvious reasons—when they uncover a glory hole in the aftermath of a dramatic storm. The hole is uncovered when a gnarled old tree is toppled, and its roots are discovered to be entangled with nuggets. The entire community is excited by the discovery, and the frenzy grows after Frenchy invites the entire town to the saloon, where he buys bottles instead of glasses. Inevitably, the mood grows dangerous, particularly after a massive bonfire is lit in the town's main street. Frenchy, propelled by the excitement and his new lofty status, leaves the saloon and breaks into Elizabeth's cabin, where he attempts to rape her. The assault is interrupted by the arrival of Frail, who finds a bloodied Elizabeth lying unconscious on the floor with a drunken Frenchy standing over her. Drawing his gun, Frail begins shooting. After driving Frenchy to the edge of a nearby cliff, Frail empties his gun into the prospector, then uses his foot to lift the body and send it toppling over the cliff.

Grubb (George C. Scott), a zealot whose faith-healing tactics had previously agitated Frail, now leads the angered, drunken miners in an assault on the doctor. He is swiftly carried to the camp's hanging tree, and the noose is lowered around his neck. The frenzied crowd's excitement changes direction, however, when Elizabeth confronts them. With Rune at her side, she offers the miners her nuggets. Met by a stifled response and with Rune's agreement, she next offers them the deed to their mine in exchange for Frail's life. As one of the miners loudly proclaims, Elizabeth is trying to buy Frail's life because she loves him, while Rune is declaring his friendship for the man who blackmailed him. During the film's final moments, Elizabeth and Doc Frail embrace, with Rune at their side. Dominating the scene is the now life-giving hanging tree.

Although 1959 was marked by the blockbuster spectacular *Ben-Hur*, the low-key *The Hanging Tree* proved to be one of the year's sleepers. All exteriors were shot in a mining camp built near Yakima, Washington, and the location filming, enhanced by the breathtaking mountain landscapes, greatly add to the rustic flavor of the Technicolor production. Cinematography by Ted McCord, who had also filmed *East of Eden* (1955) and *The Treasure of the Sierra Madre* (1948), is top-notch. Performances are effective: Cooper is a perfect choice for the role of the tight-lipped doctor, and Schell is excellent in a role that deviates from her usual parts, particularly since her character toils alongside the men, thus denying a glamorous appearance. As Frenchy, Malden provides an enthusiastically menacing portrayal that marked the first of his screen villains. The role of the crazed Grubb also provided Scott with a memorable and highly dramatic film debut.

Critics of the day were generally enthusiastic about this literate Western, although some were upset by the film's "phychological" implications, such as the doctor's unorthodox treatment of Elizabeth's blindness. The film's song, a powerful ballad sung by Marty Robbins (written by Mack David and Jerry Livingston), proved popular and garnered an Academy Award nomination. The film's rather unexpected popularity resulted from many facets, including a superb production crew which included composer Max Steiner. Skillfully bringing all the elements together was director Delmer Daves. Daves's Westerns, as first evidenced by *Broken Arrow* in 1950, are marked by social realism and a personal rather than epic stature. The still-effective *The Hanging Tree* typifies Daves's quality-minded thought-provoking approach.

Pat H. Broeske

THE HARDER THEY FALL

Released: 1956
Production: Philip Yordan for Columbia
Direction: Mark Robson
Screenplay: Philip Yordan; based on the novel of the same name by Budd Schulberg
Cinematography: Burnett Guffey
Editing: Jerome Thoms
Running time: 108 minutes

Principal characters:
Eddie Willis	Humphrey Bogart
Nick Benko	Rod Steiger
Beth Willis	Jan Sterling
Toro Moreno	Mike Lane
Buddy Brannen	Max Baer
George	Jersey Joe Walcott

In the tradition of fight films, which usually focus on the fighter as protagonist, *The Harder They Fall* is atypical. Unlike *Body and Soul* (1947), *Champion* (1949), or *Rocky* (1977), this film is not a character study nor does it ever allow the audience the pleasure of vicariously sharing the triumphs of a boxer as he rises to the top. *The Harder They Fall* is a study of corruption within the fight game and has an unyielding harshness in exposing a machine of deceit in which each individual has a place, and in which the fighter himself is more spectacle than man. The duped Toro Moreno is not the principal character (although he is an effectively realized presence as played by the hulking and somber Mike Lane), and the carnival atmosphere in which he is "sold" is reminiscent of nothing so much as the carnival which goes up during the rescue of the ill-fated Leo in Billy Wilder's *Ace in the Hole* (1951).

Toro is imported from South America by a fight promoter, Nick Benko (Rod Steiger), to be developed into a money-making contender, but although he looks and believes himself to be formidable, Toro is really awkward, has a "glass jaw," and "could not punch his way out of a paper bag." Backed by an efficient team of experts both in and out of the ring, Toro becomes a popular contender, unaware that Benko is having all of his fights fixed. A former sports writer, Eddie Willis (Humphrey Bogart), whom Benko has hired as a publicist, initially has misgivings about selling this sham of a boxer; but he throws himself into his work on the theory that Toro, too, will receive a substantial share of the money for which they are all working. Ultimately, Toro must fall from innocence and subsequently take a terrible beating from the champion, Buddy Brannen (Max Baer), the only fighter he has been up against who cannot be fixed. When Willis goes to Benko to collect Toro's share of the money, however, he finds that Benko has cheated him out of almost all of it. Remorseful over his involvement, Willis gives Toro his own share, twenty-six thousand dollars, and puts him on a plane to Argentina. Ignoring threats from Benko, he then begins an exposé of the syndicate and its power over boxing in America.

If there is a protagonist in this socially conscious drama, it is Eddie Willis, and the audience is immediately alerted to his relative moral superiority by the casting of the role. Bogart had much earlier established an image in most of his classic films—that of the hard-shelled idealist who ultimately turns out to be a white knight in black armor. In *The Harder They Fall*, his last film, Bogart looks more world-weary than ever (perhaps the result of his illness), and the film's responsiveness to the audience's faith in his essential integrity adds much feeling to the final sequences. This is an excellent example of the idolization of a star adding dimension and meaning to a film.

With the exception of Willis, the major characters are either ruthless and unsympathetic manipulators like Benko or pathetic fools like Toro. Willis' wife Beth (Jan Sterling), although she is intelligent and sympathetic, has only a marginal role in the story, while Toro's trainer, George (Jersey Joe Walcott), although he appears at times to be a sensitive man, never reproaches himself for his self-demeaning participation in the elaborate setup. The film's strongest and most characteristic scenes are of confrontations between callous men, relentlessly planning strategies and proclaiming their self-interest without pretense. Benko is continually in a rage over his associates' mistakes and weaknesses. His egotism, which is often the dramatic focus of individual scenes, gives these scenes forcefulness and intensity.

The unsparing cynicism and appealing lack of sentimentality in the film are visually enhanced by effective direction, cinematography, and editing. The characteristic sharp black-and-white contrasts of the 1950's are persistent in the texture of the film, giving an impression of vivid realism to the scenes in the ring, in the dressing rooms, and in the hotel suites and streets of the small towns through which Toro is paraded with his *entourage*. Director Mark Robson's work on the film reflects his early experience as an editor in the almost musical precision with which he realizes a succession of short scenes which build dramatically to convey the unsparing manipulation of Toro, his opponents, and the public.

The film reflects credit most of all on Philip Yordan, who not only wrote it but also served as its producer. Yordan is one of the great screenwriters of the modern cinema and has never received the attention or honors which he deserves. He has the ability to create highly unusual relationships in conventional genre films, as in *The Big Combo* (1955), in which Jean Wallace spends most of the time mesmerized by her attachment to the "bad" gangster, Richard Conte, while the "good" cop, Cornel Wilde, pathetically carries a torch for her. Yordan has the insight to create an offbeat romance between the puritanical plantation owner Charlton Heston and the "fallen woman" Eleanor Parker in *The Naked Jungle* (1954), so that when the ants attack there are intimations that they are the physical manifestation of Heston's own neurotic self-destructiveness. Yordan's special gifts are displayed in the reflective and sensitive war film *Men in War* (1957), which suggests the complexity of its characters with a minimum of dialogue. At the same time, Yordan can write very beautiful dialogue, as in the celebrated central love scene between Joan Crawford and Sterling Hayden in *Johnny Guitar* (1954), in which the two characters express their romantic bitterness in mocking phrases which both conceal and reveal their true feelings. Yordan benefited from the artistic personalities of the directors of these films, especially Nicholas Ray and Anthony Mann, for whom he had a special regard; but even in the work of less imaginative collaborators, Yordan's gift for subtly poeticizing his material is always evident.

The Harder They Fall is one of the most striking examples of this gift. The source material is in some ways narrow, highly explicit in its social concerns and moral themes, and very much of its time. The stylistic richness of Yordan's writing lifts the film above these liabilities, with the result that it retains a surprising power on repeated viewings.

Blake Lucas

HAROLD AND MAUDE

Released: 1971
Production: Colin Higgins and Charles Mulvehill for Mildred Lewis and Colin
   Higgins Productions; released by Paramount
Direction: Hal Ashby
Screenplay: Colin Higgins
Cinematography: John A. Alonzo
Editing: William A. Sawyer and Edward Warschilka
Music: Cat Stevens
Running time: 91 minutes

   Principal characters:
   Harold Chasen .... Bud Cort
   Maude .... Ruth Gordon
   Mrs. Chasen .... Vivian Pickles
   Uncle Victor .... Charles Tyner

   Harold Chasen is a very rich twenty-year-old obsessed with death and the
staging of faked suicides. Maude is a willingly impoverished seventy-nine-
year-old dedicated to a life-affirming and cheerful approach to her existence.
The relationship that evolves between these two highly divergent characters
is the focus of one of the 1970's most enjoyable comedies.
   Harold (Bud Cort), a pale and gangly youth, spends considerable time
trying to gain the attention of his manipulative socialite mother by staging
grisly "suicides." They are both horrendous and hilarious. However, they
usually fail to impress Mrs. Chasen (Vivian Pickles), who instead goes blithely
about her self-appointed task of turning Harold into a man with "responsibilities." One of her ploys is to find a girl friend for Harold, and to this end,
she engages a computer dating service. In one magnificently ridiculous sequence, she corners Harold to fill out the dating service's questionnaire, and
as Harold sits mutely by, Mrs. Chasen directs the questions to Harold but
answers them to her own specifications. Three dates ultimately are sent to
the Chasen mansion over a period of time. Two are driven away by the
suicides that Harold stages to bedevil them; but the third beats Harold at his
own game. She becomes more involved than he in staging a fake *hara-kiri*.
   Another of Harold's death-oriented pastimes is his regular attendance at
the funerals of strangers. At one of these he encounters Maude (Ruth Gordon), who also shares his strange passion. At first he is somewhat reluctant
to strike up a friendship with her; but it is not long before Harold is charmed
by the old woman's vitality and unconventional ways.
   Harold soon becomes a regular visitor at the renovated railroad car that
Maude calls home. It is during these visits that Maude, by sharing her zest
for living, begins to teach Harold the meaning of life and love. She first

awakens his awareness of the world by getting him to use his five senses. She exposes him to yoga breathing, tactile sculpture, and the tastes of oatstraw tea and ginger pie, and teaches him to play the banjo. In conversations, she shares her philosophy of life with him. She believes in individual freedom and has little patience with the repressive forces in society that seek to impose conformity and spiritual death.

It is quickly apparent that Harold is learning a positive attitude toward life. At the same time, however, his mother, undaunted by the failure of the computer dating approach to make a man of Harold, now decides that a stint in the Army will succeed where she has failed. She turns Harold over to his Uncle Victor (Charles Tyner) for a preinduction pep talk. An earlier reference has characterized Uncle Victor as having been General MacArthur's "right-hand man." When he first appears on the screen, the audience sees that he has lost his right arm—only an empty, starched sleeve that performs a mechanically controlled salute remains. In one of the more cynically biting scenes, Uncle Victor takes Harold on a visit to an old soldier's home at which he extols the virtues of Army life while decrepit and handicapped inmates falter and collapse on the ground.

Harold and Maude, however, devise a scheme to keep Harold out of the Army. In full view of Uncle Victor, Harold "murders" Maude to convince his uncle that he is too psychopathic even for the Army. The ruse succeeds; Harold's Army career comes to an abrupt end.

By this time, Harold has fallen in love with Maude. She graciously accepts his tokens of affection and they become lovers. In one fleeting, poignant scene, the audience glimpses a number tattooed on Maude's arm. Thus dramatically we are made to know that Maude has survived a concentration camp and yet remains a lover of life who relishes her freedom and her individuality.

Harold soon produces pandemonium when he announces his intention to marry Maude. In rapid succession the straitlaced and horrified reactions of his mother, his psychiatrist, a minister, and his Uncle Victor are shown. All are so appalled by the unconventional alliance that none bothers to address the fact that Harold has found love and aliveness with Maude.

Over all objections, Harold pursues his plans to marry Maude. He intends to propose to her on the occasion of her eightieth birthday celebration. When he arrives at her home, he finds, to his horror, that Maude has taken an overdose of sleeping pills and is quietly awaiting death. When the frantic Harold demands an explanation, Maude simply explains that she had always planned to be gone by the time she reached eighty. In this way she will avoid lingering illness and incapacity. An ambulance rushes Maude to the hospital. Harold, tears streaming down his face, accompanies her. He tells her that he loves her; she replies that she loves him too and that he should "go out and love some more." Doctors attempt to save her, but they are too late. Maude's death has proven to be her last act of self-determination.

In the final scene, Harold is seen speeding his minihearse through the rainy countryside. The car plummets over a cliff, bursting into flames as it hits the rocky beach below. Enough time elapses to allow the audience to believe that Harold has now committed a real suicide, but the camera pans upward to reveal Harold standing on the cliff, playing the tune on his banjo that Maude had taught him. Having learned the meaning of real living and loving, he walks away performing a little jig as he continues to play his tune.

Hal Ashby's sensitive direction of the film saves it from becoming either an unbelievable farce or a maudlin love story. He balances the two seemingly contradictory but interrelated themes of the film: life is to be lived and enjoyed and yet it will ultimately end in death. The delicacy with which he delineates these themes gives the viewer a sense of the rhythm of life, along with an acknowledgment that death is an integral part of life. Death need not be dreaded if, in fact, life has been lived well and to the fullest.

Harold and Maude was Ashby's second directorial effort, following *The Landlord* (1970). These two films were the seminal beginnings of a distinguished career that has subsequently included such memorable films as *The Last Detail* (1973), *Shampoo* (1975), *Bound for Glory* (1976), and *Coming Home* (1978).

Ashby's direction evokes some impressive acting performances. Bud Cort is appealingly whimsical in his portrayal of Harold. From the ashen and depressive eccentric of the early scenes, he flowers believably into a cheerful and robust young man. Ruth Gordon's performance maintains the credibility of Maude's quirky but delightful character throughout. Another gem is Vivian Pickles' interpretation of Harold's unflappable and self-absorbed mother.

While the film is a comedy, it is also a biting social satire of an era. Its condemnation of the Army, as personified by Uncle Victor, represents the concerns of a generation that was questioning United States involvement in Vietnam. Other previously sacrosanct institutions are also examined in a satirical fashion: the policeman is seen as officious, doltish, and inhuman; the psychiatrist is a shoddy copy of an outmoded Sigmund Freud; and the clergyman is a ridiculous man who attempts to deal with both relationships and sexuality without ever having had, one surmises, the benefit of firsthand experiences. The forces of society that are inclined to straitjacket us are weighed against the value and dignity of human life. In effect, the film encourages the viewer to examine the possibilities of his own life. Rather than accepting the preformulated definitions and answers handed down by traditional authorities, the film urges the viewer to experiment and then savor the results.

Mention should be made of Cat Stevens' musical score. The sprightly and ephemeral quality of his melodies eloquently express the mood of the film.

When *Harold and Maude* opened in December, 1971, reviews were somewhat mixed. Some critics hailed it as a joyously innovative piece of film-making, while others felt that the story line was inconsistent in seeking to glorify life yet ending with Maude's suicide. In the last analysis, the earlier criticisms have proven somewhat superfluous since *Harold and Maude* has developed a life of its own, becoming a minor cult film. From 1971 to mid-1978 it continued to draw such sizable audiences in neighborhood art and revival theaters that a new print of the film was released in mid-1978. Thus, despite the initial lukewarm response of some critics, *Harold and Maude* continues to please the critics that matter most—the paying audience.

Isabel O'Neill

HARRY AND TONTO

Released: 1974
Production: Paul Mazursky for Twentieth Century-Fox
Direction: Paul Mazursky
Screenplay: Paul Mazursky and Josh Greenfield
Cinematography: Michael Butler
Editing: Richard Halsey
Running time: 115 minutes

Principal characters:
Harry	Art Carney (AA)
Shirley	Ellen Burstyn
Sam Two Feathers	Chief Dan George
Jessie	Geraldine Fitzgerald
Eddie	Larry Hagman
Burt	Phil Bruns
Ginger	Melanie Mayron
Hooker	Barbara Rhoades
Norman	Joshua Mostel

Harry and Tonto is something of an updated sequel to Vittorio DeSica's masterpiece, *Umberto D* (1955). That film, which was the story of an old man who is ultimately thrown out of his apartment for lack of money, ends with the man facing the remainder of his life with only his faithful dog as a companion. *Harry and Tonto* begins when a man in his seventies, Harry (Art Carney), is forced out of his New York apartment building with only his cat, Tonto, as his companion. Urban renewal has precipitated the destruction of Harry's apartment in order to make way for a parking lot. Obstinately fighting eviction to the end, Harry is forcibly carried out of his one-room apartment by the police while he is still sitting in his favorite easy chair. From then on, Harry begins his picaresque adventures, meeting all sorts of people and experiencing freedom on a trip across the United States. Harry misses his dead wife Annie, but he optimistically begins the journey with Tonto, his best friend and confidant.

At first Harry's son Burt (Phil Bruns) tries to convince Harry to move in with his family in the suburbs, but Harry has no desire to live there, so he decides to fly to Los Angeles, where another son, Eddie (Larry Hagman), now lives. Harry cannot get a flight, however, because the airline will not go out of its way for cats; and because his driver's license expired ten years earlier, Harry and Tonto continue their trip by bus. They decide to stop in Chicago to visit Harry's daughter Shirley (Ellen Burstyn), who is a lonely and cynical bookstore owner, toughened and embittered by four failed marriages.

When Harry finally arrives in Los Angeles, he and Tonto visit the other son, Eddie, who is a stereotype of a Southern California swinger who lives in a singles' complex replete with sauna. We discover, however, that Eddie is only pretending to be a successful bachelor; actually, he is a man with no direction in life who even needs to borrow money from his father. The three children, although young, are confused and unhappy, whereas Harry, who is old, has now found a new independence which brings his life purpose. His odyssey from New York to Los Angeles has shown him that it is his vital spirit that is important, not the past.

The story would seem to be fairly predictable and ordinary, but the screenplay and the acting add the dimension needed to make the film a gem. Carney is wonderful as the cranky, bursitis-suffering Harry. Although Carney was actually much younger than Harry in the film, he makes Harry "a character" without being a caricature. Additionally, the other members of the cast, who are virtually all supporting players, give dimension to their roles. While Harry and Tonto are on their journey, they meet many interesting people, all of whom represent different elements of society and illustrate some things that are wrong with it. Harry is old, but willing to accept the idiosyncrasies of the people he meets. Thus, he does not judge Ginger (Melanie Mayron), the sixteen-year-old runaway, but merely spends a platonic night with her in a motel. Neither does he judge a hooker (Barbara Rhoades) who offers her services to him explaining that she has had previous experience with men of his age.

Although he used to be a professor of Shakespeare, Harry seems to get along fine with the oddballs he meets on the road. He also seems to be the only one who can understand his plump grandson Norman (Joshua Mostel), who is interested in brown rice, yoga, and Zen, and who has taken a solemn vow of silence. Harry is flexible enough to accept Norman's silence early in the film, just is he is able to accept the senility of Jessie (Geraldine Fitzgerald), his first love, whom he visits in a nursing home later on. Jessie was once a beautiful woman and used to dance with Isadora Duncan; now she is senile and cannot even remember Harry's name.

The various characters add color to the film and illuminate varied aspects of our society, but it is Harry who is the center of attention and dominates the film. Carney won an Academy Award for *Harry and Tonto*, one of his first films. Although he had been a successful television actor for years, playing Ed Norton on *The Honeymooners* with Jackie Gleason, he had been in only a handful of films before *Harry and Tonto*. This was also his first starring role in a motion picture, although he had built up a considerable reputation as a lead actor on Broadway even while he was performing on *The Honeymooners*. Since the film, Carney has starred and costarred in several films, most notably *The Late Show* (1977) and *House Calls* (1978). He has a sardonic appeal which is equally pleasing in comic or dramatic roles, and often, as in *Harry and Tonto*, the blending of the two elements produces effective characterizations.

There are a number of well-known actors in small roles in the film, most notably Ellen Burstyn, who won an Oscar for Best Actress the same year as *Harry and Tonto* for *Alice Doesn't Live Here Anymore*. Chief Dan George is also very good as Sam Two Feathers, an Indian herbal medicine man whom Harry meets in jail. Two Feathers is a 106-year-old man who, like Harry, refuses to give up, and is thrown into jail in Las Vegas for practicing medicine without a license. Of the rest of the cast, only Hagman as Eddie and Fitzgerald as Jessie are well-known names. Some minor roles are acted by people of interest to the audience, such as Mostel, who is comedian Zero Mostel's son, Sally Marr, who is Lenny Bruce's mother, as a cat lover, and director Paul Mazursky as a male hustler. Mazursky seems to favor these little "in" jokes and bits of casting and they are frequently evident in his films.

Although *Harry and Tonto* is basically a comedy rather than a social message film, it does offer some insights into the condition of old people in the United States. The opening montage of elderly people (not actors) sitting on city benches makes its own subtle statement about the plight of the elderly. Additionally, Harry's strength and dignity, even after the death of his beloved Tonto, show what inner reserves people can have if they are able to maintain their own sense of dignity.

Leslie Taubman

HARVEY

Released: 1950
Production: John Beck for Universal-International
Direction: Henry Koster
Screenplay: Mary C. Chase and Oscar Brodney; based on the play of the same name by Mary C. Chase
Cinematography: William Daniels
Editing: Ralph Dawson
Running time: 103 minutes

Principal characters:
Elwood P. Dowd .... James Stewart
Veta Louise Simmons .... Josephine Hull (AA)
Miss Kelly .... Peggy Dow
Dr. Sanderson .... Charles Drake
Dr. Chumley .... Cecil Kellaway
Myrtle Mae Simmons .... Victoria Horne
Marvin Wilson ....Jesse White

Harvey represents a successful film adaptation of the Pulitzer Prize-winning play by Mary C. Chase. After a successful run of five years on Broadway, the screen rights were purchased by Universal Studios for $1,000,000, then a record. To help insure the success of the movie version, the studio made very few changes in the script and retained the talented Josephine Hull and others from the original cast, adding James Stewart, who had also appeared in the stage version in summer stock. He was not, however, the originator of the amiable alcoholic Elwood P. Dowd, as many people believe. The Broadway play actually starred Frank Fay. Hull was primarily a stage actress, but this second screen role (her first was in *Arsenic and Old Lace*, 1944) won her an Oscar for Best Supporting Actress in 1951.

The movie is still a favorite because of the strength of the original play and because of its wonderful cast. Besides Stewart and Hull, most of the other characters were portrayed by well-known character actors playing the roles they knew best: Cecil Kellaway as Dr. Chumley, Jessie White as Wilson, and Charles Drake as Dr. Sanderson. While such a film would probably not be made today, it stands as a classic comedy in which fantasy triumphs over the Victorian repressions of society.

The basic plot concerns the problems caused by Elwood P. Dowd's friendship with a rabbit, six feet, three inches tall, named Harvey. This situation immediately leads the audience to suspect the state of Elwood's mind, but what generates the comedy is the fact that Harvey is more real than is at first suspected, at least within the context of the plot. Harvey is a pooka, a mischievous spirit, who had introduced himself to Elwood on Fairfax Street one night. Harvey represents the forces of fantasy and magic which counterbalance the repressed, straitlaced "normal" world that Elwood has left behind. As he later states, he wrestled with reality for forty years, and then, when he met Harvey, he won.

Elwood is a forty-two-year-old Taurus who has inherited money, thus explaining how he can spend his days in leisurely amiability. He lives in the family mansion with his sister Veta (Josephine Hull) and her daughter Myrtle Mae (Victoria Horne). The family is not concerned about Elwood's obvious fondness for martinis, but they are upset because his invisible companion is embarrassing and interferes with Veta's plans to find Myrtle Mae a suitable husband.

As the picture opens, Veta has planned a meeting of the Wednesday Forum to introduce Myrtle Mae to society. For years the two women have been recluses because of Elwood, but Veta has finally decided to risk a party while her brother is out for the afternoon visiting his many friends about town. Elwood and Harvey unexpectedly come home, however, and as they arrive the viewer is treated to a hilarious rendition of a spring song about flowers and rabbits going hop, hop, hop. The ladies are enchanted by this entertainment, but they are very upset by Elwood's introduction of Harvey. The juxtaposition of the song lyric with the movie theme illustrates the wry humor that pervades the film. As the women make their hurried exits, the first points are scored in the central conflict over just whose sense of reality and propriety should be questioned. The stage is also set for Veta's reaction. She has "had it," and calls the family lawyer to arrange for her brother's commitment.

By this time it is clear that Elwood, while perhaps a little peculiar, is far from dangerous. In fact, he is a truly gentle man, extremely courteous and likable. What frightens the women and what bothers Veta is his total acceptance of his fantasy and his insistence on drawing them into it. This is the crux of the movie's theme: the inability or refusal of most people to let down their defenses and admit the extraordinary into their lives. As Elwood, Stewart is an engagingly whimsical missionary. To filmgoers of today, the role seems perfect for Stewart's easy drawl and shy, boyish mannerisms, although at the time his choice for the role was criticized because of his age and the popularity of his predecessor on the stage, Frank Fay. The charm works wonderfully on film, however, and it is easy to believe that for Elwood, every day is a beautiful day.

Moving to the Chumley Rest Home, the plot takes some rather predictable turns. Responding to Veta's agitated state, Marvin Wilson (Jesse White), a young staff psychiatrist, assumes that she is the new case, and she is taken away by Wilson babbling about rabbits and pookas. During her initial meeting with Dr. Sanderson (Charles Drake) Veta had blurted out an admission that once or twice she had seen Harvey, a fact which explains her great sensitivity to the problems his friendship with Elwood has created. It also explains why she rigidly refuses to put up with Elwood any longer—she fears for her sanity. While she is confined at the Home, several minor romantic plot lines are developed. Wilson is introduced as a possible match for Myrtle Mae, and although it is obvious that he is not "suitable" within the context of the film it is very probable that their attraction will develop into something more serious. Dr. Sanderson and his nurse, Miss Kelly (Peggy Dow) constitute another obvious couple; but he, like so many of the rational characters in the film, takes life too seriously to notice romantic possibilities. One of Elwood's positive accomplishments is helping to bring both of these couples together.

Eventually, the mistaken commitment of Veta is discovered and she returns home ready to sue Chumley (Cecil Kellaway) and have Wilson arrested. Chumley goes in search of Elwood, certain that he can help him back to sanity. Elwood, meanwhile, has been searching for Harvey all over town, and finally runs into him at Charley's, a local bar. When Chumley finds them, it is clear that he should have heeded Veta's warning concerning what he was up against. Even an eminent psychiatrist is no match for a pooka, and after a few drinks Chumley not only argues with Harvey but with the man at the next table as well, and is expelled from the bar. Harvey, it seems, is visible and real to those who are free enough to admit his existence, although there is admittedly a certain danger in letting go of one's normal inhibitions. The effect of Harvey on Dr. Chumley reflects essentially the same appeal that the movie holds for audiences. Harvey's presence epitomizes the desire to escape the reality of our everyday problems and to begin to indulge our fantasies. The comic twist is that a pooka is also mischievous, and makes it difficult to live comfortably in both worlds.

Later, back at the Home, Elwood and Dr. Chumley have quite a discussion about the wonderful things Harvey can do for his friends. Chumley begins to wish that his fantasies would become reality through Harvey's remaining with him, and this appears to be the plan. There is, however, still the matter of Elwood's commitment to deal with, and, despite the doctor's acknowledgment of Harvey's existence, a drug injection is recommended to rid Elwood of his delusions. The always charming Elwood consents because Veta asks him to do so. Fortunately, at a crucial moment a cab driver interrupts the procedure and helps Veta understand that this injection will not only get rid of Harvey, but will make her brother all too normal: he will become miserable, crabby, and mean. She stops the doctors just in time, saving both Elwood and Harvey. She has realized that Elwood's pleasant nature is too valuable to lose.

There is only one major theme in this story about a man and his rabbit, but it takes many forms. Veta, although she is as lovable as her brother, represents a social and sexual repression which is the antithesis of the fantasy and freedom represented by Elwood and Harvey. Her solution to the problem of sexual feelings is to go out for long walks, while Elwood's is to encourage closeness and feeling through pleasant compliments and flowers. Veta is the perfect foil for Elwood's ramblings. As she becomes hysterical, he remains calm and sincere, undermining her attempts to be rational and to take life too seriously. The magic inherent in Elwood is his ability to help people see their problems as small and manageable. Veta strives throughout to maintain her rationality by denying Harvey's existence, although deep inside she knows that he is real. By the end of the film, she must either accept him openly or deny the benefits of his existence by drugging her brother.

A final statement about magic, added to the movie version, constitutes a nice touch. Chumley wants Harvey to stay with him, putting Elwood's pleasant nature to the ultimate test. Of course he agrees, as long as Harvey had no objections. In the stage version, Chumley merely tries to "steal" Harvey by injecting Elwood with his formula, thus preventing Harvey's return to his old friend. Magic, however, as every reader of fairy tales knows, can be used for good or for selfish purposes, the former being preferable. Chumley's desires, as we suspect all along, are too personal and dull, in sharp contrast with Elwood's friendly nature; and as the film ends, Harvey rejoins Elwood. Fortunately, Elwood observes, they may just have time for a nightcap before the bars close.

Christine Gladish

THE HARVEY GIRLS

Released: 1946
Production: Arthur Freed for Metro-Goldwyn-Mayer
Direction: George Sidney
Screenplay: Edmund Beloin, Nathaniel Curtis, Harry Crane, James O'Hanlon, and Samson Raphaelson, with additional dialogue by Kay Van Riper; based on the book of the same name by Samuel Hopkins Adams
Cinematography: George J. Folsey
Editing: Albert Akst
Song: Harry Warren and Johnny Mercer, "On the Atchison, Topeka and the Santa Fe" (AA)
Running time: 101 minutes

Principal characters:
Susan Bradley	Judy Garland
Ned Trent	John Hodiak
Judge Sam Purvis	Preston Foster
Alma	Virginia O'Brien
Deborah	Cyd Charisse
Em	Angela Lansbury
H. H. Hartsey	Chill Wills
Sonora Cassidy	Marjorie Main
Chris Maule	Ray Bolger

George Sidney's place in the rank of directors of musicals is clearly below that of such luminaries as Busby Berkeley or Vincente Minnelli. Nevertheless, he has brought some memorable moments to the screen in films such as *Anchors Aweigh* (1945), *Annie Get Your Gun* (1950), *Bye Bye Birdie* (1963), and *The Harvey Girls*. In *The Harvey Girls*, Sidney is blessed with wonderful songs by Harry Warren and Johnny Mercer and by the ineffable presence of Judy Garland in the lead. The music and the star, however, occasionally fall victim to a script that is totally unimaginative. The result is a film that mirrors Sidney's career: uneven, but with moments of brilliance.

Harvey Girls were young (and sometimes not so young) women who were recruited by Fred Harvey to staff his chain of restaurants strung throughout the American frontier along the route of the famous Atchison, Topeka and Santa Fe railroad. As the film opens, a trainload of Harvey Girls are heading toward Sand Rock, Arizona, to help open Harvey's latest dining room. Their motto is: "Where Harvey Girls appear, civilization is not far behind."

The film's star is Judy Garland, who plays Harvey Girl Susan Bradley, a prettier than usual mail order bride. She intends to marry one H. H. Hartsey, who placed an advertisement for a wife in an Ohio newspaper read by Susan. Susan is befriended by Alma (Virginia O'Brien) and Deborah (Cyd Charisse)—a farm girl and a would-be dancer, respectively—who have joined the Harvey organization in their quest for love and adventure.

Far and away the film's finest sequence comes when the train arrives in Sand Rock and the assembled cast breaks into Warren and Mercer's Academy Award-winning song "On the Atchison, Topeka and the Santa Fe." The song introduces the townsfolk and the Harvey Girls to one another, thus advancing the plot. The tune was an instant classic, and Sidney's staging matched the brightness of the melody. While there is a great deal of movement in this scene, however, Sidney never allows things to get out of control. It is a *tour de force*.

Unfortunately, at this point the plot, which is the weakest part of the film, begins to thicken. H. H. Hartsey (Chill Wills) turns out to be a nervous yokel who is as afraid of Susan Bradley as she is of him, and they quickly agree to terminate their "relationship." Hartsey reveals that a local saloon operator named Ned Trent (John Hodiak) wrote his flowery proposal as a joke. Furious, Susan corners Trent in his Alhambra Saloon and publicly denounces him. The sparks that fly from this encounter inevitably kindle the flame of romance in their hearts, and the rest of the film is an overly melodramatic account of their courtship, lightened only by a few excellent musical sequences.

"The Train Must Be Fed" is a witty and well-staged exposition of the Harvey philosophy, performed by Sonora Cassidy (Marjorie Main) and the girls in ensemble. "It's a Big Wide World," sung by Garland, O'Brien, and Charisse (whose voice was dubbed by Betty Russell), relates the three women's struggles to find true love—a quest which O'Brien further explicates later in the delightful "The Wild Wild West," in which she bemoans the lack of romantic action on the part of the he-men on the frontier, especially her love interest, Chris Maule (Ray Bolger).

Sidney is at his best in these scenes. He is at his worst when the music stops and the melodrama resumes. Trent's two-faced partner, Judge Sam Purvis (Preston Foster), and his wicked henchmen try to burn out the Harvey House, pegging it as competition for the Alhambra. Trent's growing affection for Susan tempers his own ruthlessness, however, and he decides to leave town with his other paramour, a dancehall girl named Em (Angela Lansbury), but finally opts to remain in Standing Rock and marry Susan. The story ends as the two meet in a running embrace.

Garland does her best with Susan Bradley, and she has her moments. She projects spunk, intelligence, and, of course, a good singing voice; but the script (a large team effort by Edmund Beloin, Nathaniel Curtis, Harry Crane, James O'Hanlon, and Samson Ralpaelson, with additional dialogue by Kay Van Riper) does not give her much with which to work. The rest of the cast is in much the same boat: they are ultimately defeated by the script. Perhaps O'Brien fares best; her wry, down-home wit and mannerisms work against the script's strained seriousness to good effect.

Sidney's ultimate problem in *The Harvey Girls* is that his script and his music simply did not go together. Warren and Mercer wrote bouncy, terrifically hummable tunes that unfortunately were out of place in the stock Western script. Since the music is better than the script, it would have made sense to come up with a different story line.

Still, it is possible to be too critical of *The Harvey Girls*. The film was quite popular in its day and merits our attention even now. At its best—particularly in the "On the Atchison, Topeka and the Santa Fe" scene, for which the film will ultimately be remembered—it is very good indeed. It is also one of the best-loved of all the "big" M-G-M musicals and is frequently shown on television.

Robert Mitchell

A HATFUL OF RAIN

Released: 1957
Production: Buddy Adler for Twentieth Century-Fox
Direction: Fred Zinnemann
Screenplay: Michael V. Gazzo and Alfred Hayes; based on the play of the
    same name by Michael V. Gazzo
Cinematography: Joe MacDonald
Editing: Dorothy Spencer
Music: Bernard Herrmann
Running time: 109 minutes

> *Principal characters:*
> Celia Pope ....Eva Marie Saint
> Johnny Pope ....Don Murray
> Polo Pope .... Anthony Franciosa
> John Pope, Sr. ....Lloyd Nolan
> Mother ....Henry Silva
> Chuch .... Gerald O'Loughlin
> Apples ....William Hickey

Drug addiction has never been a very useful subject for Hollywood since it lacks the histrionic possibilities of alcoholism and psychological disorders, and there is not much chance for a realistically happy ending. In the mid-1950's, however, when the problem first really burst upon the American public and when Hollywood's Production Code loosened enough to actually permit mention of the subject onscreen, there was a quick rash of exploratory dramas, all tautly enlightening and harrowingly detailed and none very popular. The most praiseworthy of these and, also, the most highly praised in its own time, was *A Hatful of Rain.* It was initially a 1955 Broadway play by Michael V. Gazzo (who is better known today as a character actor specializing in such ethnic oriented roles as a traitorous Mafioso lieutenant in *The Godfather, Part II,* 1974). Gazzo's play probingly detailed the grim difficulties imposed on a lower-middle-class Italian household when a young husband, Johnny Pope (Don Murray) becomes a heroin addict as a result of becoming hooked on morphine while recovering from Korean War wounds in a GI hospital. His addiction has caused him to lose laborer's job after laborer's job, hindered his efforts to improve his education, and led him to roam the streets at night looking for a fix. This, in turn, causes his sweetly concerned but not overly intelligent wife, Celia (Eva Marie Saint), to become convinced that he is seeing another woman. Meanwhile, his frantic older brother, Polo (Anthony Franciosa), is supplying him with the money he had intended to loan to their father (Lloyd Nolan) to help him set up a small business. The father is exceedingly small-minded and blames his son bitterly for not having the money to give him. Additionally, Polo not so secretly is in love with Johnny's despairing and noticeably pregnant wife.

It is to Gazzo's credit that he manages to draw these unwieldy strands together. He suggests, for example, that in the father's gruff obtuseness and detached *machismo* lie the real seeds of his son's addiction. He builds this idea through a number of powerful scenes to an inevitible conclusion. The now fully aware wife, with her husband's permission, calls the authorities to have him sent away for a cure that may well not work. It was a realistic conclusion to a drama of fine individual moments but also of numerous fits, starts, and breaks in continuity that many observers felt belied the place where it had been nurtured and somewhat developed: the Actors Studio. Staffed almost completely with Actors Studio graduates and performed very much in the Method manner, it soon became the most acclaimed example of what that much-maligned school could produce.

Twentieth Century-Fox producer Buddy Adler saw the play and, confident that all Production Code difficulties could be met, bought the film rights. He had long been searching for another project for himself and director Fred Zinnemann. The two had already been responsible for the Oscar-winning *From Here to Eternity* (1954). Zinncmann thought it all over and flew to New York to work with Gazzo on the script. As might be expected, Zinnemann had his own views on the work. "This is not a case of history of a dope addict," he told one interviewer. "We're concerned with a family, nice people, who love one another and are suddenly confronted with a terrible revelation, a real problem . . . this is the real poignancy of a life cut short." To give the story more universal appeal, Zinnemann and Gazzo dropped any ethnic orientation and changed the family's social rank to housing development status (since *Marty* in 1955, Italian ghetto dwellers had become somewhat clichéd anyway). To give the story more realism, Zinnemann and Murray, who was to play the addict, spent a month working with the Narcotics Squad. "We didn't just want to see how these people looked," Zinnemann said. "Or how they acted when they needed the drug or took the drug. We tried to find out about their emotions—why they took drugs, how it felt to crave it, the land of relief that drugs gave them." Zinnemann and Murray even "roamed the streets between nine at night and five in the morning . . . when these poor people come to life and died all over again."

For further authenticity, Zinnemann did something that even in 1957 was still a bit rare. He went on location, shooting for two winter weeks on Manhattan's Lower East Side because "I wanted to shoot the exteriors in the worst possible New York weather—rain, fog, snow. And the interiors in impossibly cramped settings that would create a sense of intimacy with the people who lived in that crowded flat." This same quest also led Zinnemann to settle on a cast of New Yorkers to play the roles. Only Nolan, as the irascible father, had more of a Hollywood background than a Broadway one. Murray was a

New Yorker recently risen to film prominence in *Bus Stop* (1956) and *Bachelor Party* (1957); Saint, cast as Celia, the wife, had won an Oscar for *On The Waterfront* (1953), another film with strong Actors Studio connections, and had played the wife in *A Hatful of Rain* when it was still an Actors Studio project. From the original Broadway cast itself, Zinnemann chose Franciosa to repeat his part as the brother, Polo. If the cast shared a New York City authenticity, however, they also possessed an apple-cheeked wholesomeness, a middle-America charm that Zinnemann planned to use for its ironic effect.

Zinnemann seemed to see the conflict as similar to those in such films as *High Noon* (1952), *The Search* (1948), and *From Here to Eternity*. In these films, as well as in Zinnemann's later works, his characters were torn by an unexpected outside force that had slowly made them examine themselves and come to a moral decision. The sheriff in *High Noon* has to stand up to a sudden menace but finds that the very people that he has been trying to defend are not worth it. Nevertheless, he does defend them. Corporal Pruitt in *From Here to Eternity* grows to loathe the peacetime Army and all that it stands for, but when Pearl Harbor occurs, he sacrifices himself for the cause. In *A Hatful of Rain*, however, it is not really an outside force that erodes the family; it is the hero's addiction, which he can neither resolve (he has already tried unsuccessfully to quit) nor face up to before his wife and father. All of the dramatic situations in the play follow from this one fault. The subtle morality of the hero's dilemma, however, was much less obvious to audiences than the sheriff's or Pruitt's had been in the earlier films. Also, with the wholesomeness came one other factor that served Zinnemann less well—intelligence. Murray, Franciosa, and Saint simply seem too smart, too aware a trio to have fallen into the dilemmas that the plot specifies. Saint in particular comes across as too doggedly intuitive and rationally observant to spend as much time as she does worrying about another woman. Murray's character seems too outgoing and bright not to have sought outside help for his problem long earlier. Zinnemann greatly admired his actors' instincts and improvisational abilities, but the alertness and agility that were a part of those performers' attributes did not help the film as it should have.

What did help was the location. New York portrayed at its bleakest permeates the film. The parks are nothing but gritty snow impaled upon grey wisps of grass. The streets bear a more obvious grime, an impersonal dirt that neatly continues the theme of institutional dullness permeating the cramped apartment and the metallic housing project hallways, not yet littered with 1960'a graffiti and all the more dingy for it. There is an almost ghostly shot of a policeman's horse late at night gently nudging the drunken Johnny down the street that neatly sums up the foreboding impersonality of the city.

Despite the problems mentioned above, Zinnemann obtains insightful performances from his cast. Franciosa's portrayal of the glib extrovert was so definitive that it typed him immediately as far as Hollywood was concerned.

Murray conveys the desperate sincerity of a man who has always counted upon being everyone's favorite and is as much afraid of losing their good opinion as he is of facing the illness. Finally, Nolan is wonderfully querulous and testy, an essentially unpleasant and unobservant man stripped to the bone by age and disappointment.

A Hatful of Rain still seems much less like a Zinnemann film and more like the sort of moral issue discussion that television was to attempt at about the same time in New York-based series such as *The Defenders* and *Naked City*. The film never tries to slip public service information into the dialogue as the television shows often did, but it does have the almost too careful look of something that is being done for the public good. Although we do not see needles and the rest of a drug addict's paraphernalia, the way that these things are hidden and the "it-is-not-his-fault" nature of the hero's addiction help suggest that the real core of the problem has not been approached. Instead, a compelling story with a realistic setting has been built around the problem in order to hook the audience better into considering it—even though the story itself is not very indicative of the subject matter. It is a practice that television drama with its lack of big budgets and location panoramas was then doing quite well. *A Hatful of Rain* was more honest and even more realistic than sponsor-oriented television could then be, but it stands today more as a sign of what films could do at that point in time than as a study of a desperately real and timeless problem.

Lewis Archibald

THE HEART IS A LONELY HUNTER

Released: 1968
Production: Thomas C. Ryan and Marc Merson for Warner Bros.
Direction: Robert Ellis Miller
Screenplay: Thomas C. Ryan; based on the novel of the same name by Carson McCullers
Cinematography: James Wong Howe
Editing: John F. Burnett
Running time: 123 minutes

Principal characters:
John Singer .... Alan Arkin
Mick .... Sondra Locke
Spiro Antonapoulos .... Chuck McCann
Mr. Kelly .... Biff McGuire
Mrs. Kelly .... Laurinda Barrett
Blount .... Stacy Keach
Portia .... Cicely Tyson
Doctor Copeland .... Percy Rodriguez
Willie .... Johnny Popwell

In 1940, at the age of only twenty-two, Carson McCullers wrote *The Heart Is a Lonely Hunter,* her first novel and according to some critics her best. Almost thirty years after the novel's initial appearance, screenwriter Thomas C. Ryan updated the Depression setting of the novel to the present time and adapted it to film. Because the novel was a very difficult one to adapt, the film was not considered a total success. Whereas McCullers' writing is beautifully poetic, the film is unable to capture the true spirit of the original work. Also, some of the problems which existed in the Depression were not easily transformed to the late-1960's. Whatever the problems with the screenplay, however, the film did earn rave reviews for its star, Alan Arkin.

In the film, Arkin plays the story's main character, deaf-mute John Singer. Singer is a kind and gentle silver engraver living in a small Southern town. He is a lonely man, and his only real friend is a fat, bearlike, simple-minded Greek named Spiro Antonapoulos (Chuck McCann). Spiro is also a deaf-mute, and he and Singer gently communicate through dactylology (sign language), silently expressing themselves in words that can only be understood by the two men. Because Spiro, who is mentally retarded, becomes more and more disturbed, he must be sent to a mental institution. With his only companion gone, Singer decides to move to another town which is closer to the sanatorium where Spiro will be staying. In the new town, Singer finds a room with the Kelly family, who need money to offset the expenses of a recent hip injury suffered by Mr. Kelly (Biff McGuire). The Kellys' daughter Mick

(Sondra Locke) has to give up her own room to house the boarder, so she resents Singer at first, but he tries to win her friendship. Eventually he does, by encouraging her love of classical music, and they share some happy moments as Mick plays the piano and tries to explain to Singer what music is like. Mick is supposed to represent McCullers as a young girl, and her characterization by Locke is a very moving portrayal of a sensitive girl trying to find her own identity.

While he is staying with the Kellys, Singer also befriends Blount (Stacy Keach), who is a heavy drinker, and Dr. Copcland (Percy Rodriguez), a black physician. Dr. Copeland's character is the most changed from the original novel, possibly because the Back to Africa movement, which was well-known during the 1920's and 1930's, and of which the novel's Dr. Copeland was a part, meant little in 1968. What was a significant subplot in the book becomes rather weak and insignificant in the film, although Rodriguez tries his best in the part. Copeland is dying from cancer, but he is keeping his illness secret from his daughter Portia (Cicely Tyson), an educated woman who has become estranged from her father because of her father's objections to her husband Willie Hamilton (Johnny Popwell), a field hand.

In the course of the film, Singer goes to visit Spiro, who is now suffering from a kidney infection. They go for an outing, but when Spiro becomes almost wild in his behavior, Singer goes home very despondent. Not long after this, Portia becomes reconciled with her father when she learns, through Singer, that he is dying. This brings Singer one victory, but it is later offset by Mick's renewed animosity toward him. Depressed because of a bad first sexual experience, Mick refuses to accept Singer's friendship, and Singer again begins to feel lonely for his only friend Spiro. Shortly after this, however, when he goes to visit Spiro, he learns that the Greek died a few weeks before. After sadly visiting Spiro's grave and saying good-bye in sign language, Singer goes home and commits suicide, feeling that there is not one whom he can call a friend anymore.

Almost as an epilogue to the story, a few months after Singer's death, Mick goes to his grave with flowers and meets Dr. Copeland. There she tells him that it was really Singer who helped her to grow up and that his gentle strength will help her to face the future. Locke is very good in the role of Mick and received some of the film's better notices. After a career which consisted of small supporting roles in numerous films in the late 1960's and early 1970's, she finally came to prominence in a series of films with Clint Eastwood, most notably *The Gauntlet* (1977) and *Bronco Billy* (1980). Unfortunately, the subtleness which characterized her performance in *The Heart Is a Lonely Hunter* has been missing from her more successful ventures as Eastwood's leading lady, and her career seems to have reached a leveling-off point.

Arkin is the "be-all, the end-all and, whenever he is in sight, the cure-all of *The Heart Is a Lonely Hunter*," according to *Newsweek* critic Joseph Morgenstern, an opinion that pervaded most of the reviews of the film. An extremely versatile actor, Arkin, although not of the "superstar" ranks, has been a very successful leading man and character actor. He has taken on a very wide spectrum of roles, and throughout his career he has gone back and forth between leads and supporting parts with equally successful results. He has also been successful on the Broadway stage and earned a Tony award for his first starring role, *Enter Laughing*.

Others in·the film who give good performances are McCann as Spiro and Tyson as Portia. Although their roles lack the depth of Arkin's, they at least make the best of their parts. It is unfortunate that a novel with the power of McCullers' did not have an adaptation which did more of what the original did. Some reviewers felt that it should not have been updated, and perhaps it might have been better produced as a period piece. Unlike McCullers' *The Member of the Wedding*, which had less of an attachment to a particular time period, *The Heart Is a Lonely Hunter* should have been left in the Depression in order to convey more of the feeling of a Southern town in a time when things were economically difficult for everyone.

The film was shot on location in Selma, Alabama, by veteran cinematographer James Wong Howe. This was his fiftieth film, and the beautiful scenes of rust-colored footage pay tribute to one of the great geniuses of the film medium. *The Heart Is a Lonely Hunter* did not do very well at the box office, probably because the rather melodramatic production was not the type of thing which readily appealed to a mass audience. It did win the Best Actor Award for Arkin with the New York Film Critics, and it also brought Arkin an Academy Award nomination for Best Actor and Locke a nomination for Best Supporting Actress.

Janet St. Clair

HEARTS OF THE WEST

Released: 1975
Production: Tony Bill for Metro-Goldwyn-Mayer
Direction: Howard Zieff
Screenplay: Robert E. Thompson
Cinematography: Mario Tosi
Editing: Edward Warschilka
Running time: 102 minutes

Principal characters:
Lewis Tater	Jeff Bridges
Howard Pike	Andy Griffith
Miss Trout	Blythe Danner
Kessler	Alan Arkin
A. J. Nietz	Donald Pleasance
Fat Man (Swindler)	Richard B. Schull
Thin Man (Swindler)	Anthony James
Pa Tater	Frank Cady

Hearts of the West is a favorite cult film which was financially unsuccessful upon its release, but which has gained a large number of devoted followers who admire its subtle comedy and good-natured criticism of the film industry. The film's comic tone is established with its opening: the M-G-M trademark lion in black-and-white followed by a screen test, also in monochrome, of a bumbling actor identified as Lewis Tater (Jeff Bridges). Lewis completes his scene and turns to the camera, smiling for his close-up.

The balance of the film, in color, delightfully unfolds the picaresque odyssey of Lewis Tater, beginning with a scene in the bedroom of his Midwestern home. Here, circa 1930, Lewis writes florid Western prose, surrounded by the colorful pulp magazines that inspire him. His father (Frank Cady) and brothers, all practical farmers, scorn Lewis' ambitions. As an act of defiance, Lewis vows to attend a correspondence school of Western writing in person. Arriving in a one-horse Nevada town by train, Lewis discovers that the "school" consists only of eight post-office boxes. Bewildered, he ends up spending the night at a nearby hotel. The two swindlers (Richard B. Schull and Anthony James) who operate the bogus school learn of his presence, and one of them slips into Lewis' room during the night to rob him. Lewis awakes with a start and overpowers the intruder. After escaping in the swindlers' car, Lewis runs out of gas in the desert. Searching the car for provisions, he finds only a metal box containing a revolver and school stationery. Lewis sets out on foot in the desert, unaware that the swindlers are not far behind. Later, Lewis is almost trampled by cowboys on horseback. One of the cowboys, Howard Pike (Andy Griffith), gives Lewis a ride back to their camp. There

Lewis discovers he has stumbled onto the location of a low-budget Western movie. In awe, he observes the egotistical director Kessler (Alan Arkin) choreograph a fight scene. Then the aspiring writer meets the attractive Miss Trout (Blythe Danner), a script supervisor.

When Lewis gets a ride to Los Angeles with the stuntmen, Howard tells him what it is like to "ride up front" with the director and stars. After finding a room in a boarding house, Lewis works washing dishes at the Rio Café until Tumbleweeds Productions calls on him to be an extra. Several humorous episodes follow: Lewis ruins a scene, injures himself after volunteering to do a dangerous stunt, and narrowly escapes the swindlers, who trace him to the Rio Café. Back in his room, Lewis discovers thousands of dollars in cash underneath the gun and college stationery in the metal box, and he finally realizes why the swindlers still pursue him: he possesses the entire proceeds of their bogus school.

Even with the swindlers searching the local studios for him, fortune seems to be in Lewis' favor. Kessler offers him a chance to become the leading villain in his next production; Miss Trout, attracted by his charming innocence, romances him; and he completes his first novel, *Hearts of the West*. Trusting Howard's advice, Lewis gives him the manuscript to read. After Kessler fires him when they cannot agree on salary, Lewis takes his manuscript to producers around town, promising to contribute two thousand dollars toward the budget.

Lewis' good fortune turns sour as he delivers the money and a copy of the manuscript to publisher A. J. Nietz (Donald Pleasance). Nietz admits he likes the story, but that it is identical to another manuscript he has already bought, and introduces Lewis to the alleged author, Howard Pike. In the ensuing scuffle, Howard reveals that he was once the famous Western star Billy Pueblo, now out of money, and that he sold the script to pay alimony.

Lewis, turning to the only person he still trusts, goes to Trout's apartment. When he finds Kessler there in a drunken state, he leaves with the false impression that Kessler and Trout are romantically involved. Trout races to Lewis' apartment to find him. The swindlers, having found Lewis' address from Tumbleweeds, see the light on in his apartment and decide to follow Trout when she departs. Trout's next stop is the Rio Café, where she implores the surly Howard to help her. Finally one of the stuntmen tells her that Lewis is hiding in his apartment. Just as Trout arrives at the room, the swindlers burst in demanding their money, and when Lewis argues that the money was ill-gotten in the first place, one of the swindlers shoots him in the elbow. Howard, in full Western costume, bursts in with guns blazing, locking the thieves in a closet. Lewis admiringly tells Howard, "You looked just like Billy Pueblo." As the ambulance drives away, a bystander asks, "Who is that kid?" Howard replies, "Lewis Tater. He's a writer. Just sold his first novel."

In *Hearts of the West* Bridges exhibits a flair for comedy not seen in his earlier roles, making the exaggerated ingenuousness of Lewis Tater convincing. Standout scenes include his extemporaneous composition of melodramatic Western prose as he walks the desert; his ill-fated movie stunt; and his salary meeting with Kessler. Bridges handles the potentially difficult role with delicacy and makes his character affable enough to carry the story.

The other actors fit perfectly into the ensemble. Arkin, in a departure from previous parts, accurately conveys the egotistical fanaticism of the director Kessler. Danner is engaging as the pragmatic script supervisor with a weakness for Lewis' trusting soul. In the likable heel Howard Pike, Griffith creates his strongest characterization since Lonesome Rhodes in the Elia Kazan/Budd Schulburg film *A Face in the Crowd* (1957). Schull and James lend able support as the comic villains.

Hearts of the West is a film about filmmaking. Its light tone is similar to Stanley Donen and Gene Kelly's *Singin' in the Rain* (1952) and Peter Bogdanovich's *Nickelodeon* (1976). Thematically, however, it is unique because it is the only comedy to deal with the corruption in the business and with the ephemeral nature of fame and success, while at the same time affirming the power of idealism over egotism and corruption.

As the first solo production of Tony Bill since his highly successful co-production of *The Sting* (1973), *Hearts of the West* was not destined to enjoy the same box-office success. Director Howard Zieff's first film, *Slither* (1974), which was not financially successful either, is similar to *Hearts of the West* in its offbeat characters and in its theme of corruption involving the innocent. In both movies, Zieff displays a keen sense of character and of comic timing which has unfortunately been lost in his more recent films such as Barbra Streisand's *The Main Event* (1979) and Goldie Hawn's *Private Benjamin* (1980), both financially, if not critically, successful. With more personal projects, Zieff could possibly fulfill the promise of the earlier films, but *The Main Event* and *Private Benjamin* were pet projects of their respective stars.

Perhaps the box-office failure of *Hearts of the West* is due to the major weakness in its story: an unconvincing ending. Although writer Rob Thompson's original characters, comic situations, and natural dialogue ring true, the last-minute rescue by Howard Pike stretches credibility even in a comic context. In the preceding scene with Trout, Howard expresses disgust at her concern for Lewis. No dramatic foundation for his sudden change in attitude in the following scene is built. The renewed trust and respect between Howard and Lewis comes all too quickly and without development.

Even with its flawed denouement, *Hearts of the West* remains a rarity in recent films: a pure entertainment movie that, for the most part, realizes its purpose.

Stephen Myers

HEAVEN CAN WAIT

Released: 1943
Production: Ernst Lubitsch for Twentieth Century-Fox
Direction: Ernst Lubitsch
Screenplay: Samson Raphaelson; based on the play *Brithday* by Laszlo Bus-Fekete
Cinematography: Edward Cronjager
Editing: Dorothy Spencer
Art direction: James Basevi and Leland Fuller
Interior decoration: Thomas Little and Walter M. Scott
Running time: 112 minutes

Principal characters:
Martha	Gene Tierney
Henry Van Cleve	Don Ameche
Hugo Van Cleve	Charles Coburn
E. F. Strabel	Eugene Pallette
Mrs. Strabel	Marjorie Main
His Excellency	Laird Cregar
Albert Van Cleve	Allyn Joslyn
Bertha Van Cleve	Spring Byington
Randolph Van Cleve	Louis Calhern
Jasper	Clarence Muse
Mademoiselle	Signe Hasso

Heaven Can Wait begins in an anteroom of hell, to which the recently deceased Henry Van Cleve (Don Ameche) reports to accept his assignment to one or another infernal circle. The doorkeeper ("His Excellency") is not convinced, however, that Van Cleve is a good candidate for eternal damnation and demands a review of the facts in the case of Van Cleve's life.

The story that unfolds is that of a spoiled though amiable child of a late nineteenth century New York family of established wealth, who sows as many wild oats as he can within the bounds of discretion imposed by the reigning Victorianism. He elopes with his cousin's betrothed; loses her as a result of his continuing dalliances; recaptures her with his limited though unabated charm; enjoys a thoroughly happy married life; rears a son; plays the field again after his wife's death; and finally himself succumbs under the strain of sudden ministrations from a beautiful nurse—managing all the while to avoid a single day's work or any endeavor which could be even remotely construed as socially useful.

Though Van Cleve may exclude all extraromantic considerations from his life, he does not come across to the viewer as some Dionysian reveler; he has not thrown it all away in some *l'amour fou*; he has not lost his soul in some Faustian compact in which passion has been his reward. The very structure of the film militates against any such perception: for the greater part, Van Cleve is simply the husband in a marriage that endures thirty years. His extramarital affairs are alluded to rather than seen; his transgressions are invariably discreet; his submission to society's standards is such that his life comes to seem rather prosaic, an impression that is deliberately reinforced by the casting. Yet the film stands in judgment of the sins of Henry Van Cleve (Don Ameche). Of what sins could so infinitely mild a hedonist be guilty, or even capable?

However, it is precisely his mildness that is the issue: Van Cleve—and, to a certain extent, the world the film depicts—stands accused of triviality. In a sense, this is not a new development in Lubitsch: the characters in his films frequently are both in and of circumscribed worlds from which he maintains an ironic, if affectionately inconsistent, distance. In *Heaven Can Wait*, however, Lubitsch deals with the most vulnerable players and limited characters of his career, and he is correspondingly gentle with them—his attraction to them is real.

Partly as a matter of self-protection, though, Lubitsch does reverse one career-long pattern. Traditionally, his sophisticated leads are the objects of audience identification, and his bumbling supporting characters the objects of audience derision. In *Heaven Can Wait*, this arrangement is reversed. As Henry's foxy grandpa, Hugo Van Cleve (Charles Coburn) serves as an island of sanity in a sea of fools. While other characters spout clichés among themselves, his undercutting asides are a kind of direct address to the audience— a characteristic function of Lubitsch leading players. Significantly, though, Hugo Van Cleve cannot refrain from indulging his grandson, whose elopement he abets. A similarly mediating role is played by the black manservant Jasper (Clarence Muse) of the Strabels (Eugene Pallette and Marjorie Main), the parents of Martha (Gene Tierney). Jasper serves as an emissary between the cartoonlike, choleric couple, and then between them and their outcast daughter. When we first meet the Strabels at home, they are engaged in mortal breakfast-table combat which culminates when Mrs. Strabel prematurely reveals to her husband, E. F. Strabel, the outcome of that morning's episode of the Katzenjammer Kids. Hugo and Jasper stand fastidiously above such nonsense, but ultimately they are committed to their respective households, thereby serving as refractions of Lubitsch's own critical affection.

Indeed, the tug of war between affection and gentle derision permeates every aspect of the movie. The interplay between Henry Van Cleve and Martha is, as James Agee called it in his near-rave review, a "mosaic of kidded clichés." It is as if Lubitsch were placing quotation marks rather unobtrusively around much of the material. When the angry Martha flashes her eyes or the lovesick Henry coos with fervent emotion, the quotation marks grow suddenly more obvious. A similar commentary is implicit in the sets, which move in ravishing color (*Heaven Can Wait* is the only film whose use of color was known to have excited D. W. Griffith) from the stuffy parlors of the 1890's to the sleek Art Deco living rooms of the 1920's. The modification of dress, speech, and posture as the film moves across the decades is wonderfully handled and encloses the characters deeper within prevailing conventions.

That Lubitsch is touched by the trivial life even as he feels superior to it becomes clearer in the later parts of the picture. Tokens of the past become precious. The dying Van Cleve tells his nurse of a dream he has just had: the boat ferrying him across the River Styx becomes a luxury liner with an orchestra playing the Merry Widow Waltz, so popular when he was young. Without losing any of its seriousness, death itself becomes encased in the prevailing archaic genteel frivolity.

At the moment of Van Cleve's actual death, Lubitsch transforms one of his most famous touches—the closed door that symbolizes sexual encounter, guaranteed in earlier Lubitsch films to produce amusement—into a sign of mortality. A beautiful new nurse walks down the hall to come on duty, enters Van Cleve's room and closes the door behind her, the camera remaining, as always, discreetly outside. After a moment, the Merry Widow Waltz starts up, the camera tracks slowly back from the door, then pans downward as the scene dissolves back to hell. This is not merely Van Cleve meeting death: it is also the sick and aging Lubitsch confronting mortality as directly yet discreetly as he had always encountered life.

This may explain why Lubitsch made a film that sought to redeem a man from the charge of triviality. (Van Cleve is indeed redeemed; the doorkeeper sends him up to heaven.) Lubitsch is so inextricably wedded to this society that he cannot conceive of heaven and hell operating on any other basis. Indeed, Van Cleve is greeted in hell's anteroom by an aged, just-deceased old girl friend who makes the ghastly error of showing him her legs and is dispatched immediately to the infernal fires, thus illustrating that taste still matters. These are not transient trivialities; they are ultimate trivialities.

In a sense, the man whom Lubitsch is redeeming from these charges is himself. *Heaven Can Wait*, in this regard, is to Lubitsch what *Sullivan's Travels* (1941) is to Sturges. At a time when artists were supposed to be concerned with the horrific issues of war and Fascism, Lubitsch and Sturges chose to defend the claims of the comic muse, of frivolity and triviality and style, and, by implication, of the validity of their life's work. *Heaven Can Wait* thus becomes the *apologia*, as if one were needed, for Ernst Lubitsch's career.

Harold Meyerson

HEAVEN CAN WAIT

Released: 1978
Production: Warren Beatty for Paramount
Direction: Warren Beatty and Buck Henry
Screenplay: Elaine May and Warren Beatty; based on the play of the same
name by Harry Segall
Cinematography: William A. Fraker
Editing: Robert C. Jones and Don Zimmerman
Art direction: Paul Sylbert and Edwin O'Donovan (AA); set decoration,
George Gaines (AA)
Music: Dave Grusin
Running time: 110 minutes

Principal characters:

Joe Pendleton	Warren Beatty
Betty Logan	Julie Christie
Mr. Jordan	James Mason
Max Corkle	Jack Warden
Tony Abbott	Charles Grodin
Julia Farnsworth	Dyan Cannon
The Escort	Buck Henry
Krim	Vincent Gardenia
Sisk	Joseph Maher

At a time when films as diverse as *Invasion of the Body Snatchers* (1956),
A Star Is Born (1937), and *The Big Sleep* (1946) were being remade, and
when sequels such as *Jaws II* (1979) and *Rocky II* (1979) seemed a safe
proposition, a remake of *Here Comes Mr. Jordan* (1941) must have appeared
to be a sure success. Accordingly, Warren Beatty, hedging his bets, collaborated with Elaine May on the screenplay for the remake and with Buck
Henry on the direction, but relied upon himself as the film's star and producer.
The film, entitled *Heaven Can Wait*, aided by a very clever poster campaign
(anyone writing to Paramount could get one free), became a box-office smash
and garnered eight Academy Award nominations. It won only one Oscar,
however, for Paul Sylbert's and Edwin O'Donovan's Art Direction with
George Gaines' Set Decoration.

The story concerns Joe Pendleton (Warren Beatty), a second-string quarterback for the Los Angeles Rams who has an automobile accident. He is
supposed to survive the incident, but an overzealous heavenly Escort (Buck
Henry) collects his soul and his body is cremated. When the mistake is
discovered, Joe and Mr. Jordan (James Mason), the man in charge of sending
souls on to their final reward, scour the world in search of a body in good
enough shape for Joe to consider occupying it. They arrive at millionaire Leo
Farnsworth's mansion just as his wife Julia (Dyan Cannon) and his confi-

dential secretary Tony Abbott (Charles Grodin) are about to murder Leo.
The proceedings are interrupted by the arrival of Betty Logan (Julie Christie)
representing an English town about to be displaced by one of Leo's refineries.
Joe, who is invisible and watches the scene, is charmed by Betty Logan and
by the notion that he can inhabit Leo temporarily and do her a favor. Joe
decides to occupy Leo's body until he can straighten things out. Betraying
his egalitarian roots, Joe invites the press and Betty to a board meeting of
Farnsworth's corporation where he makes a virtual shambles of the millionaire's business empire by agreeing not to dispossess the inhabitants of Pag-
glesham; further, he agrees to stop snaring dolphins along with the tuna that
one of his factories cans, and finally to quit dealing in nuclear energy plants.
Joe next decides to get Farnsworth's body in shape in order to try out for the
Rams. He summons Max Corkle (Jack Warden), his old trainer from the
Rams, and convinces Max that he is Joe by massacring a familiar song on his
saxophone. He then embarks on an intensive training program which involves
the entire Farnsworth household staff, and ultimately buys the Rams so that
he can play in the playoffs and take the Rams to the Super Bowl. He becomes
increasingly attracted to Betty and declares his love for her just as Abbott
and Julia murder Farnsworth. Joe, once again without a body, enters the
body of Tom Jarrett, a Rams player who is about to die during a game. This
is Joe's final incarnation; Mr. Jordan makes it clear that he will not remember
his previous embodiments, and this is borne out by his refusal to recognize
his saxophone when Max tells him that he knows that he is Joe rather than
Tom. Outside the stadium, Joe, in Tom's body, finds Betty looking for Max.
Without consciously knowing who he is, she senses Joe's presence in the
quarterback's body and they leave together.

   Heaven Can Wait was treated by reviewers as a comedy, but it is not.
Rather, it is a modest little morality tale, the heart of which is Joe's Capraesque
speech to Farnsworth's board of directors about saving dolphins and respect-
ing people's rights. The darts it throws in the guise of being a social comedy—
at treacherous wives, bumbling functionaries, and suave professionals—are
very soft. In fact, *Heaven Can Wait* is so plot-heavy, repeating such gags as
Joe's dislike of hats, Farnsworth's love of naval uniforms, and a daily flag-
lowering ceremony involving a cannon, that there is precious little room for
the message. The statements which the film makes concerning ecology get
unintentional reinforcement from the filmmakers during a sequence in which
Joe travels by helicopter to downtown Los Angeles. There is so much smog
that one can scarcely see the buildings, and we suddenly understand and
visualize Betty Logan's concern when she says that Farnsworth's refinery will
ruin her home town.

   Although Beatty obviously conceived of the film as a starring vehicle for
himself and Julie Christie, the film is stolen by its supporting players, notably
by Joseph Maher as the butler, Sisk, who remains unflappably courteous

whether talking to his employer in a darkened closet (where Joe has taken Mr. Jordon and the Escort for a conference) or grimly joining Joe in calisthenics when he trains to rejoin the Rams. James Mason is equally self-possessed as Mr. Jordan, calmly explaining that other people cannot see or hear him; and Buck Henry is owlishly indignant as the inept supernumerary who eagerly collects Pendleton's body too soon. Charles Grodin as Tony Abbott is a model of sneaky rectitude as he talks to Joe from behind his inamorata's curtains during a midnight rendezvous with Dyan Cannon, or in anticipation of their arrest for murder, tells her to "Pick up *The Fountainhead* and pretend to be reading." Cannon as Julia Farnsworth is deliciously two-faced, screaming in the bushes one minute and frantically guzzling scotch from a decanter the next, her candid blue eyes never once indicating that she is ever telling the truth. Jack Warden as Max Corkle has the most colorful role as the cheerful trainer who is both comedic—talking into thin air in the misguided notion that Mr. Jordan is listening—and sentimental—telling Joe at the end that he can tell who he really is because of that ever-present saxophone.

Oddly enough, Beatty miscast himself. He does not represent that blend of flippant sincerity and blithe chicanery that Cary Grant brought to roles such as *His Girl Friday* (1940) and *The Awful Truth* (1937). Beatty is too frantic and too smart; a man capable of absorbing all the corporate data he ingests in a few hours as Farnsworth would not be a football player in the first place. And as a football player, he appears both too old (at age forty-one) and too underdeveloped physically. Julie Christie is bright, pliant, and attractive as Betty, but she is not necessary to the plot; Joe as Farnsworth would have discovered the error of Farnsworth's ways and delivered his populist manifesto without her prompting.

Heaven Can Wait is benign, genial, and slightly addled. It does not so much contain and present ideas as it does present people who talk about theirs. *Here Comes Mr. Jordan* did not bother with a message; it was an unabashed fantasy, whimsical escapist fare for people who wanted to believe in romance and happy endings. That is what *Heaven Can Wait* should be, but it is that only when Beatty and Henry relax. The film is pleasant nonsense which occasionally becomes preachy and unnecessarily strident.

Judith M. Kass

HEAVEN KNOWS, MR. ALLISON

Released: 1957
Production: Buddy Adler and Eugene Frenke for Twentieth Century-Fox
Direction: John Huston
Screenplay: John Lee Mahin and John Huston; based on the novel of the
  same name by Charles Shaw
Cinematography: Oswald Morris
Editing: Russell Lloyd
Sound: Basil Fenton-Smith
Music: Georges Auric
Running time: 106 minutes

> *Principal characters:*
> Sister Angela .... Deborah Kerr
> Marine Corporal Allison .... Robert Mitchum

Heaven Knows, Mr. Allison strikes a responsive chord primarily because
it is a film without apparent artifice. Its ability to reach out and touch audiences
lies in its simplicity, which is one of the key aspects of its greatness. The story
line is simple: a rough marine corporal and a young Irish nun are thrown
together on a remote Pacific island during World War II. Their story is one
of struggle, strength, and courage in the face of two formidable adversaries—
the enemy Japanese and a growing and impossible love for each other.

In the opening sequence, a lone dinghy is swept toward shore over a vast
stretch of rolling waves. From the first shot, director John Huston places the
audience in dual roles as observers and participants. We too are carried over
the crest of the sea to the unknown beach of a tropic paradise. An exhausted
marine (Robert Mitchum) begins a cautious search of the seemingly deserted
island. The audience moves with him through the lush rain forest in a series
of tense tracking shots, with sunlight filtering in through the overhanging
palms. Light comes up with sparkling brightness as the marine discovers some
abandoned huts, and there is a quiet, tense pause as a rustling sound is heard
inside the white church. In a golden glow, a nun (Deborah Kerr), dressed in
the habit of her order, emerges, sweeping through the church doors. Being
the only survivor on the island, at first Sister Angela regards the marine with
fear, then happy recognition as he collapses from exhaustion in the interior
of the semilit church.

The young and delightful Sister Angela makes every provision she can for
the comfort of her new companion. In a series of idyllic scenes, we see the
unlikely twosome collecting coconuts, happily exchanging stories, and preparing a makeshift vessel they hope will carry them to safety. Both are bound,
it seems, by bonds of service, being dedicated to their respective paths—the
Marines and the Catholic Church. This idea is reinforced as Sister Angela

weaves palm fronds into a mainsail for the raft that is to carry them over the unstable waters of the wartorn Pacific. The hot sun shines brightly on the pair as they work industriously together. Allison regards her with reserve and respect while at the same time revealing to us, but not to her, a growing feeling of affection.

A rumble of bombers is heard in the distance, and Japanese planes are soon over the island blasting everything: buildings, trees, immaculate beaches, and the mainsail and boat. Allison throws himself upon the running Sister Angela, covering her with his body as the island is showered with bullets. Remarkably, they emerge alive and unhurt, but their hopes of leaving the island are as smashed as the little church, which is now a smoldering wreckage. Allison pokes through the debris and retrieves the charred altar crucifix for Sister Angela. It is interesting to consider that the crucifix holds no personal meaning to Allison, yet his gesture of salvaging it and giving it tenderly to Sister Angela shows his developing regard for her calling. There is an interesting counterpoint developed as well, for shortly after this moment, a Japanese destroyer rounds the island point, and its portent is ominous. The crucifix, therefore, is now more than merely a personal symbol. It becomes a universal object, signifying hope, faith, and transcendence in darkest hours.

As the Japanese invade the island, Mr. Allison and Sister Angela are forced to flee to a deserted cave, a natural hideaway. Together, they subsist there. She engages in prayer and meditation while the fascinated marine looks upon her with expressive adoration. He spends hours carving a comb for her which he places with bright red flowers below the crucifix on the cave rockshelf and ventures out under cover of night to spear fish for her. Unfortunately, the raw fish sickens her, and her hair is cut too short to require a comb. Clearly, Allison will need to develop faith to understand her.

By the time the Japanese leave the island the marine and the nun have become deeply attached to and dependent upon each other. Allison is clearly in love with her, but her feelings for him are those of friendship. They jubilantly celebrate, and the charming little song "Don't Sit Under the Apple Tree" is sung by Allison with more than casual gaiety. They do a jig under the moonlit sky and share a good supper of cooked rice and canned goods. Later Sister Angela finds a bottle of sake in a flour sack and Allison proceeds to get drunk, ruining what had been a happy occasion. With drunken bravado, Allison becomes physically aggressive and brutally truthful about their chances of survival. When he tries to embrace her, she rushes in fear and panic into the pelting downpour of a tropical storm.

This is the critical sequence for which Huston has carefully prepared. For Sister Angela, the intoxicated amorous marine is more menacing than the Japanese. His overture toward her prompts her to run from the dark side of her inner self, her suppressed feelings, and subdued sexuality. On the spiritual path to which she has dedicated her life and heart, she has had to renounce and possibly repress natural emotional and physical desires. Now she flees from her friend and protector in a hysterical panic of identity. Her flight through the storming rain forest, with Allison in delirious pursuit becomes our means of sharing the frustrations of both characters.

Allison forages through the jungle searching and calling for her. Finally, at dawn, he finds her lying shivering and delirious in a mud slick, her white habit saturated with rain and earth. Tenderly and apologetically, he grabs her to him, carries her back to the cave, and undresses her. Her condition is serious as she shakes with fever and delirium. He must get her warm clothing and food, but the Japanese have returned. In the suspenseful sequence which follows, he ventures into the Japanese encampment and succeeds in obtaining the necessary provisions, but in the process, he is discovered and forced to kill a Japanese soldier. When Sister Angela regains consciousness, her eyes fall on her dirty habit which hangs up drying, and she realizes that Allison has changed her clothes and cared for her during her illness. Her appreciation lends a new degree of understanding to their relationship, and she humbly assumes responsibility for the killing of the Japanese soldier, perceiving her effort to escape Allison's advances as the direct cause of the incident.

It is important to stress that Allison has consistently expressed the desire to look after Sister Angela, and it is important to remember that early in the film she mentions that she has not yet taken her final vows. The possibility exists, if they survive, that the regard she feels for him may develop into the romantic, that they could conceivably marry given time and circumstance. Huston never lets us forget, however, that first and foremost, the combination is unlikely, and that the first priority is service and survival.

In the action-packed and bittersweet conclusion, Allison is apparently divinely inspired to sabotage the enemy weapons, facilitating a relatively safe American landing, but under direct fire he sustains a serious shoulder wound. His courage and Sister Angela's supportive attitude are short-lived, however, as the Americans land on the island. The audience regards the American force with mixed feelings, for they, not the Japanese, are clearly going to separate the couple. Allison is carried downhill on a stretcher, with Sister Angela walking beside him and putting a cigarette between his lips, as the camera rests for a moment on the charred crucifix and comb she holds tightly. As they approach the beach and an awaiting ship, our perceptions of the meaning of this departure are displayed in a shower of tropical light. On a romantic level, we feel a deep and sad resignation that silently emanates from the principal characters. On a higher spiritual plateau, we experience a mood of hope, acceptance, and contentment. The words of Sister Angela echo in our minds. "Wherever I go, wherever I may be, you will always be in my heart, dear Mr. Allison, always." This suggests a transcendental love that will forever be sustained by thought, experience, and ultimately, memory. That this love will live in the hearts of both Sister Angela and Allison is reinforced by the eternal motion of the gently moving sea in the background.

Although the sea is a vehicle used to unite and possibly separate the pair, Huston uses the device to leave ultimate interpretation to the audience. The component that makes this an affecting and successful picture is the consistent clarity of the storytelling with no trace of heavy-handedness. The muted romanticism is evoked by the film's controlled tempo. Huston deals with a theme that has fascinated him before and since, that of isolation as a micro-cosm (*The Treasure of the Sierra Madre*, 1947, *The African Queen*, 1951, and in one of his more successful later films, *The Man Who Would Be King*, 1975). He is at his best in handling twists in human relationships when people are forced away from the mainstream of society.

Heaven Knows, Mr. Allison is moving, exciting, and well made. Huston and John Lee Mahin complement each other brilliantly in their collaboration on the script. Basil Fenton-Smith also merits praise for contributing an unmuffled soundtrack, much of it recorded live against great obstacles on the island of Tobago. Under Huston's direction, Mitchum and Kerr create very human characters. Without the support of other players, they sustain rapt audience attention for the duration of the film with a dynamic chemistry which recalls and compares favorably with that of Humphrey Bogart and Katharine Hepburn in Huston's similarly styled *The African Queen*. Kerr received a deserved Oscar nomination, but Mitchum, an often neglected actor, was again overlooked.

Huston has always been regarded as a rugged individualist whose own flamboyance has overshadowed his *oeuvre*, but he has succeeded in demon-strating that his films are a rugged and colorful reflection of his own *persona*. This film shows the flash of genius that erratically surfaces in his finer work. *Heaven Knows, Mr. Allison* belongs with the best of the Huston canon.

Elizabeth McDermott

THE HEIRESS

Released: 1949
Production: William Wyler for Paramount
Direction: William Wyler
Screenplay: Ruth Goetz and Augustus Goetz; based on their stage adaptation
 of the novel *Washington Square* by Henry James
Cinematography: Leo Tover
Editing: William Hornbeck
Art direction: John Meehan, Harry Horner (AA)
Set decoration: Emile Kuri (AA)
Costume design: Edith Head and Gile Steele (AA)
Music: Aaron Copland (AA)
Running time: 115 minutes

> *Principal characters:*
> Catherine Sloper .... Olivia de Havilland (AA)
> Dr. Austin Sloper .... Ralph Richardson
> Morris Townsend .... Montgomery Clift
> Lavinia Penniman .... Miriam Hopkins

The Heiress is the story of Catherine Sloper (Olivia de Havilland), a plain young woman in her mid-twenties who lives in a grand house in Washington Square, New York City, in the 1850's. She lives with her father, the prominent Dr. Austin Sloper (Ralph Richardson), and his sister, Aunt Lavinia (Miriam Hopkins). The film is an adaptation of Henry James's novel, *Washington Square*. First produced in New York and London as a stage play under the novel's original title, it was not a critical success; consequently, it was not made into a film until several years later.

The Heiress is recognized for many things, including its performances and outstanding art direction. The story takes place mainly in one location, the Sloper home—a limited setting ideally suited for the theater; however, in a screen version it becomes a challenge to keep the audience engrossed and the film visually exciting. *The Heiress* succeeds on both counts. Directed by William Wyler, the excellence of the performances and the intricacies of the character development work to create a film which succeeds through the power of its subtlety. *The Heiress* is a period piece in the true sense; not only the costumes and sets are evocative, but every nuance of dialogue and behavior is consistent with the formality and elegance of mid-nineteenth century New York.

The simple plot revolves around Catherine's love affair with Morris Townsend (Montgomery Clift), a young man whom her father considers a fortune hunter interested only in her inheritance. Since the action is very limited, the success of the story depends upon close attention to detail and complex characterizations. It is essential to get a sense of the drives and needs of each character as they interact within the stifling social regimentation of the period. Dr. Sloper and Catherine form the most complex relationship which gradually unfolds, revealing the raw emotions which lie beneath their facade of propriety. Dr. Sloper is a model of respectability and elegance. The unresolved pain he experienced at his wife's death years ago permeates his life. Ralph Richardson's performance succeeds in creating a character who, without straying from accepted behavior, becomes racked by bitterness and hatred. It is necessary to perceive the poisonous effect of that pain in order to understand the doctor's failure as a father in his relationship with Catherine. His suppressed hatred toward the child that caused his wife's death at childbirth reveals itself little by little, and it is the appearance of Morris which finally brings that hatred to a head.

To Catherine, Morris' arrival in her life is a dream come true. He is handsome and charming and professes to love her. The doctor uses his own low opinion of Catherine in judging Morris' motives, and he is determined to keep them from marrying. In view of Dr. Sloper's attitude towards Catherine, it is easy to see how vulnerable she is and how deeply she yearns to be loved. The first third of the story prepares the audience for Catherine's exploitation. Her starvation for affection is seen in her desperate attempts to please her father; but another side of her character is revealed through her relationship with her aunt, who accepts and loves her. With Aunt Lavinia, Catherine is clever and vibrant and reveals an innate charm; yet a story she amusingly tells her aunt becomes an awkward fiasco when she attempts to retell it to her father. The damage of his influence becomes increasingly evident. When Catherine is first introduced, she still has the spark of what she might be away from her father's emotional domination; the remainder of the story traces the extinguishing of that spark.

The first time Catherine appears in the film she is buying fish, an obvious contrast to the first introduction of Dr. Sloper and his elegant home. Thinking the fish will please her father, she is instead reprimanded for not letting the servant carry the fish. This, like all of Catherine's attempts at pleasing him, is met with criticism and with negative comparisons between Catherine and her late mother. Dr. Sloper's memory of his wife as a beautiful, talented, and charming lady pits Catherine against a ghost to whom she can never live up in his eyes. Catherine has never known her mother except as an ever-present reminder of her own inadequacies. For example, when Catherine wears a red dress because she thought her mother wore one like it, her father responds mainly to its expensiveness, quietly adding that her mother, unlike Catherine, was fair and dominated the color.

Morris Townsend is more the embodiment of all Catherine's dreams than a real man, and to stress this point, he is often photographed in such a way that he is faceless. When he first approaches Catherine at a party, he is a finely dressed torso with a voice; and throughout the film, his face is hidden when the two embrace. The audience sees only Catherine's blissful face against Morris' neck and dark shoulder. Morris convinces Catherine that her awkwardness and shortcomings are charming and lovable to him. Even as his mercenary nature surfaces, Catherine's blindness to his motives is understandable. She is not stupid; she simply wants desperately to believe him. Montgomery Clift as Morris combines good looks with a perfect ability to behave appropriately. His charm is inexhaustible as he skillfully maneuvers his way into the hearts of Catherine and her aunt. Clift's is a difficult role, since he must be slightly shady at the same time that he charms the audience (as well as Catherine) into wondering whether it might not be a good idea that he marry Catherine. His words and behavior are convincing as he deftly counteracts every suspicion directed toward him; but his questionable motives become more evident when he is dealing with Dr. Sloper, with whom his compliments sound false, his promises empty. The doctor and Morris are transparent to each other; their mutual hostility results from the similarity of their feelings towards Catherine. Morris, as a mercenary suitor who desires Catherine's wealth more than her, does not seem any worse than a father who hates his daughter for not being her mother.

The Sloper house is extremely important as a living environment to which each character reacts as if playing against another real character. The house is frozen in time and serves as Dr. Sloper's shrine to his wife; the furnishings are all as she left them more than twenty years earlier, the only change being a visible expansion of the doctor's medical practice downstairs. The most conspicuous furnishing is the spinet, which is introduced as a symbol of everything Mrs. Sloper was and Catherine is not. When first seen, it is being tuned—unnecessarily, since it has not been played since it was last tuned six months earlier; it is religiously kept in perfect shape in memory of its last player, Mrs. Sloper.

To Morris, the house is a lure whose elegance and lavishness are more desirable to him than Catherine. Viewed through his eyes, it is a showplace of wealth and taste, as close-ups are utilized to show off its fine craftsmanship. Morris adapts to the house in a way that Catherine never seems to. He is at home amongst the rich furnishings and is able to sit down at the spinet and play and sing. To Catherine, on the other hand, the house represents the embodiment of her mother's memory. Like the presence of the spinet, the house constantly reinforces her inability to fill her mother's place. There is no evidence of Catherine's presence in the main rooms other than her embroidery loom which eventually becomes an overt object of her father's disdain for her. The house represents enclosure to Catherine; and it will eventually become her prison.

When Doctor Sloper takes Catherine to Europe in the hope that she will forget her marriage plans, Morris is extended the honors of the house by

Aunt Lavinia. He eases comfortably into the rich life as he helps himself to the doctor's cigars and brandy, all the time properly yearning for Catherine. Upon returning from Europe, the doctor realizes he has failed in his attempt to keep Catherine from Morris. He threatens disinheritance and unmercifully confronts her with his feelings that she is dull and unattractive, and desirable to Morris only because of her prospect of thirty thousand dollars a year. His climatic bite is that she does, however, embroider neatly.

Catherine's shock at her father's release of hostility makes her need for Morris more desperate. She meets him to plan their elopment and naïvely tells him of her threatened disinheritance; they plan to leave that night. The scene that follows is certainly one of the most torturous of the film. As Catherine waits for Morris at the front window, it becomes increasingly evident that he will not come. Her aunt, knowing the truth, wishes that Catherine had just been a little wiser and not mentioned the disinheritance. Catherine suffers the harsh realization that she has been deceived and manipulated by those who supposedly love her.

In the time that follows, the doctor falls ill. It is a hardened Catherine who refuses to go to his deathbed. De Havilland's performance excels here as she makes the transition from a naïve and hopeful young woman to a bitter and cynical heiress. When the story picks up five years later, Catherine is an icy, hard woman. Sitting in her own home now, the loom has taken a more prominent place. There is some mystery as to her psychological state at this point. Morris has returned from California after five years and with Aunt Lavinia's help comes to see Catherine. He begs understanding for deserting her, claiming it was in her best interest. His current flattery is as charming as always; he proposes again and seems truly delighted when Catherine appears to weaken and agrees. It is soon evident, however, that *she* is now toying with *him*. He leaves to gather his belongings and Catherine sits down to finish her embroidery. When her aunt realizes that Catherine has no intention of marrying Morris, she asks how she can be so cruel. Catherine's response is that she has been taught by masters. The ultimate revenge occurs as Morris arrives at the appointed moment and futilely bangs on the bolted front door. Catherine once again mounts the stairs, her eyes bright with perverse satisfaction.

The Academy recognized de Havilland's performance in *The Heiress* with the Oscar for Best Actress; the art directors, John Meehan and Harry Horner, also received Oscars for their work. Edith Head received the award for costume design, and Aaron Copland for his musical score. The blend of these talents as well as the direction and script make *The Heiress* a beautiful film which brings to life believable characters from a different time.

Dena Roth

HELL'S ANGELS

Released: 1930
Production: Howard Hughes for Caddo Company/United Artists
Direction: Howard Hughes
Screenplay: Joseph Moncure March; based on Howard Estabrook's and Harry
  Behn's adaptation of a story by Marshall Neilan and Joseph Moncure March
Cinematography: Tony Gaudio, Harry Perry, and E. Burton Steene
Editing: Frank Lawrence, Douglass Biggs, and Perry Hollingsworth
Chief of aeronautics: J. B. Alexander
Chief technical engineer: E. Roy Davidson
Running time: 119 minutes

> *Principal characters:*
> Monte Rutledge .... Ben Lyon
> Roy Rutledge .... James Hall
> Helen .... Jean Harlow
> Karl Arnstedt .... John Darrow
> Baron von Kranz .... Lucien Prival

Hell's Angels was the first major production of the multimillionaire playboy, businessman, and aviator, Howard Hughes. The idea for the film was conceived by Marshall Neilan in 1926, and Hughes acted upon it immediately, acquiring more than fifty World War I planes and hiring a hundred pilots, including America's leading stunt flyers led by Frank Clarke. Hughes even established his own airfield, "Caddo Field," at the site of what is now known as Van Nuys Airport in the San Fernando Valley.

Filming began on *Hell's Angels* as a silent production in October of 1926 with a cast headed by the Scandinavian actress Greta Nissen. However, with the advent of sound, Hughes scrapped all of the silent footage of the principals and completely reshot those scenes, with Jean Harlow, in her first starring role, replacing the accent-ridden Nissen. Silent footage of the air sequences already shot was retained, with sound effects being added where appropriate. The final climactic air battle was filmed over the San Francisco Bay area, because Hughes found the cloud formations there more suitable. Shooting was eventually completed on December 7, 1929, which meant that *Hell's Angels* had been in production longer than any film up to that time and probably longer than any since. In all, more than twenty thousand people were said to have appeared in the finished film; more than three million feet of film was actually shot; and Hughes advertised *Hell's Angels* as a four-million-dollar spectacle, which it may well have been. Certainly the celebrities who crowded Grauman's Chinese Theater on May 27, 1930, for the premiere were not disappointed.

Because of Howard Hughes's determination to keep *Hell's Angels* out of general distribution and because of the many stories which have circulated through the years concerning its production, the film has taken on almost legendary proportions. In reality, for all its magnificent flying sequences, the production is a disappointment, badly hampered by early talkie acting techniques and overblown melodramatics.

The highspots in *Hell's Angels* are two lengthy flying sequences. The first features a zeppelin raid on London, with the ship appearing, like a gigantic, silent, black whale of death, through the white clouds. The Germans onboard smile a lot and flash their white teeth, and, with a sophistication lacking in recent films in which everyone speaks English, the Germans speak in their native tongue. Titles, in the manner of silent films rather than the subtitles one has come to expect in foreign-language films, explain the action.

The workings of the zeppelin are shown in intimate detail, from the lowering of the observer's car from which a target can be pinpointed to the bomb placements and the great ship's engines. As the British flyers gain on the zeppelin, the captain orders that any extra weight be jettisoned to allow the ship greater speed and higher altitude. With a cold-blooded belief in God, Kaiser, and country, members of the crew silently jump to their deaths to lighten the ship's load. One lone British flyer also demonstrates suicidal patriotism by flying his plane directly into the zeppelin, causing it to burst into flames. With an almost uncanny similarity to the *Hindenberg* disaster of a few years later, the zeppelin plunges to a fiery grave.

The other flying sequence dominates the latter half of the film and shows the two brothers—Roy and Monte Rutledge (James Hall and Ben Lyon)— flying a captured German bomber over enemy territory to destroy an ammunitions dump, thus allowing the Allies to make a major advance. The aerial shots in this sequence are breathtaking, and one soon forgets the very un-European desert scenery clearly visible below. The two brothers, Roy at the controls and Monte at the machine gun, achieve their objective, and appear about to reach safety when they are shot down by Baron von Richthofen. At all times, there is a sense of reality, with only the ammunitions dump appearing to be a miniature.

Roy and Monte are the heroes of the story. Roy, the elder brother, is honest, dependable, and brave, while the younger Monte is the very opposite—lazy and cowardly. The opening scenes of the film, cut from the Astor Pictures reissue of *Hell's Angels*, show the two boys at Oxford, where they form a friendship with a German youth, Karl Arnstedt (John Darrow). Monte's true character is shown in a sequence in which he becomes involved with the wife (Jane Winton) of Baron von Kranz (Lucien Prival) while the trio are on vacation in Munich. He later pretends not to know the woman when challenged to a duel by her husband.

At the outbreak of the war, Roy immediately enlists in the Royal Flying Corps, while Monte is recruited only after another light amorous adventure.

At a charity ball given by a Lady Randolph, Monte becomes infatuated with Roy's fiancée, Helen. As played by Jean Harlow, Helen shows little evidence of being an English socialite and debutante. Harlow does, however, imbue the character with the right degree of sensual arrogance and easygoing sexuality. Her first appearance has her emerging from the bushes with a young officer, his hair in disarray. Later, she invites Monte back to her rooms, which she describes as "a new toy," a description which fits Monte equally well. "Would you be shocked if I put on something more comfortable?" she asks, as she goes into the bedroom to emerge in a very revealing dressing gown. Later, in France, where Helen is working at Lady Randolph's canteen, she is revealed to Roy as the flirtatious loose woman that, for all her wealth and social position, she really is.

After the brothers are captured by the Germans, Monte's cowardice again comes to the fore. Confronted by Baron von Kranz, he is willing to give the Germans details of the Allies' advance in return for his own life. Lucien Prival as Baron von Kranz gives a marvelous performance, with mannerisms apparently borrowed from Erich von Stroheim. In desperation, Roy pretends to be willing to help the Germans in exchange for a revolver with one bullet with which to silence Monte, who would be a witness to his dishonor. As Roy tries to reason with Monte, Monte screams for the Germans to listen to him, and Roy shoots him in the back. As he lies dying in Roy's arms, he tells his brother, "Don't cry, it was the only thing you could do." As the Baron discusses with an aide what is to be done, Roy is marched away for execution, and through an open window, we hear his final defiant cry: "I'll be with you in just a minute, Monte." No sooner have the shots of his execution been heard than there is the sound of shelling. The final scenes are of the Allies on the march—"Come on, we've got them now," shouts a soldier—indicating that Roy's and Monte's deaths were not in vain.

There are many interesting subplots in an epic such as *Hell's Angels*. One involves Karl, who is on the zeppelin during its raid on London and deliberately steers the ship over the river rather than have his fellow countrymen bomb Trafalgar Square. Karl in the observer's car is the first to go when the captain orders the zeppelin to be lightened. A curious silent sequence begins with a title, "Somebody always gets it on the night patrol," and shows scenes of the British planes in flight, followed by a beautifully composed shot of a crashed plane on the beach.

For its flying sequences, Howard Hughes deserves every credit for a masterly job of direction, but the story and dialogue have dated badly. Perhaps in a way *Hell's Angels* shows Hughes to be a man with more money than sense, a man lacking the cinematic sense necessary if the talkies were to succeed.

Anthony Slide

HERE COMES MR. JORDAN

Released: 1941
Production: Everett Riskin for Columbia
Direction: Alexander Hall
Screenplay: Sidney Buchman and Seton I. Miller (AA); based on the play
   Heaven Can Wait by Harry Segall (AA)
Cinematography: Joseph Walker
Editing: Viola Lawrence
Running time: 93 minutes

Principal characters:
Joe Pendleton/Bruce Farnsworth/
Ralph (K.O.) Murdock .... Robert Montgomery
Mr. Jordan .... Claude Rains
Max Corkle .... James Gleason
Messenger 7013 .... Edward Everett Horton
Bette Logan .... Evelyn Keyes
Julia Farnsworth .... Rita Johnson
Tony Abbott .... John Emery

Stories which carry an audience to other worlds or realms of experience
are enthusiastically received regardless of trends, fads, or the prevailing national mood. This is seen in the enormous popularity of two versions of the
same story which have been successfully released almost forty years apart.
Here Comes Mr. Jordan, a celestial fantasy first released in 1941, was remade
thirty-seven years later as *Heaven Can Wait*, and both films garnered more
than the usual number of nominations for Academy Awards. The 1941 version
received seven nominations, winning two awards, and the 1978 version received nine nominations and one award.

Here Comes Mr. Jordan is a variation of the usual simple motif of a benevolent angel being sent on a mission to earth. The film begins its rather
complicated and enjoyable tale by turning the tables and having a human
being journey to heaven to rectify an angelic error. Joe Pendleton (Robert
Montgomery), a saxophone-playing heavyweight title contender, is prematurely snatched from a plummeting plane by an overzealous heavenly messenger named 7013 (Edward Everett Horton) who has wanted to spare him
the pain of the crash. Joe protests that nothing could ever happen to him as
long as he has his lucky saxaphone with him; but 7013 insists that Joe is really
dead and that confirmation of this fact can be made with Mr. Jordan (Claude
Rains), the man in charge of transporting souls to eternity. Mr. Jordan, however, admonishes 7013 for being overzealous in trying to establish a new
record and admits that Joe, indeed, should still be among the living. He is
not scheduled to join his deceased parents for another fifty years, becoming

heavyweight champion in the interim. Naturally, Joe is anxious to return to his body. This would be relatively simple, but Joe's manager, Max Corkle (James Gleason), has already had Joe's body cremated. Mr. Jordan offers to let Joe be reborn but Joe refuses. Thus, the only alternative is to find a new body for Joe, and he agrees to this as long as they can find one that is in the prime condition that his former body was in when 7013 prematurely called it in.

Their search begins, but it is not until the 134th candidate that a body is found which Joe is willing to accept, and then reluctantly. It is the body of unscrupulous millionaire Bruce Farnsworth, who is, at that very moment, being drowned in his bathtub by his wife (Rita Johnson) and her lover, Farnsworth's private secretary, Tony Abbott (John Emery). At first, Joe is not interested in putting himself into such company; he changes his mind, however, upon the arrival at the Farnsworth mansion of Bette Logan (Evelyn Keyes) who has come to plead with the millionaire to reveal the truth about a fraudulent stock scheme that he has orchestrated and which has resulted in her father's imprisonment. Joe sees that if he were to step into the millionaire's body he could help the young woman. Thus, he agrees to take Farnsworth's body only on the condition that it is temporary until he can get the Logans out of trouble. Immediately, a dripping Joe Pendleton in Bruce Farnsworth's body steps out of the tub where the millionaire has died as Mr. Jordan explains why the audience still recognizes Joe, "You still are Joe Pendleton, just doing business from within Farnsworth's body." Julia Farnsworth and Mr. Abbott can barely mask their consternation when the obviously healthy Farnsworth comes down the stairs. Farnsworth directs Abbott to show Miss Logan to him, and then dismisses him with "and stay out of my bathroom."

Joe, as a more kindly version of Farnsworth, promises a very skeptical Bette Logan that he will indeed take care of the terrible mess her father is in, and he does just that, causing no end of protests from the dour-faced executives of Farnsworth Industries. However, just as Joe is beginning to enjoy unraveling Farnsworth's treacheries, he learns of news that could only be important to Joe Pendleton, the boxer. Ralph (K.O.) Murdoch, Joe's rival for the title bout, automatically becomes a contender since Joe is dead. Joe turns to Mr. Jordan to get him another body that can fight Murdoch; however, Jordan reminds Joe that he has agreed to remain Farnsworth for a certain length of time and that the time has not yet expired. Joe, nevertheless, will not be deterred: he sends for his ex-manager, Max Corkle, and in a hilarious scene convinces Max that he is really Joe Pendleton looking at him through Farnsworth's eyes. Corkle agrees to train him in order to get Farnsworth's body in shape to challenge Murdoch.

Meanwhile, Bette Logan purportedly visits Farnsworth to thank him for saving her father; it is obvious, however, that their feelings for each other have not remained neutral. Aware that he will not always be Farnsworth, Joe asks Bette if she can recognize someone by their eyes, a question that will have great meaning for them both later. The heavens, however, have decided that Farnsworth shall not fight the championship match, and Mrs. Farnsworth and Mr. Abbott finally succeed in bringing about his untimely demise. Again Joe must transmigrate and find a body "in the pink" as he calls it on short notice—a body that is at the point of death. Although Joe has missed the chance to fight Murdoch since Murdoch is now in the ring with the defending heavyweight champ, the fates have not deserted him. Murdoch is the target for racketeers who have bet a great deal of money on his losing the fight. Unheard by the noisy crowd, a gunshot is fired and Murdoch falls. The referee begins the count and the gangsters are confident, but then Murdoch slowly gets back on his feet. As the crowd roars its approval, he continues the fight to win the title, but it is not Murdoch. With the help of Mr. Jordan, it is Joe Pendleton doing business from inside Ralph Murdoch's body. Although Joe has won the title, it appears that he lost the girl. However, as he leaves the locker room after the fight, he rounds a corner only to run into Bette Logan who is looking for Max Corkle. At that moment, Mr. Jordan erases Joe's memory of all that has happened, and as their eyes meet, they experience the feeling of having known each other. The heavyweight champion/ex-millionaire/ex-prize fighter and the pretty girl walk away arm in arm to get to know each other better.

Here Comes Mr. Jordan is a story to delight and refresh, but its real strength lies in the performance of Robert Montgomery. His sustaining sense of awe concerning all that is happening neither falters nor becomes overdone, and he never allows the audience to entertain the idea that the film is fantasy. Claude Rains's performance as Mr. Jordan is immaculate, and Edward Everett Horton makes one hope that none of his descendents are still in the heavenly messenger business. James Gleason as feisty Max Corkle comes close to scene-stealing, and all the male characters are solid, well-written roles.

As clever and quick as the male actors' dialogue is, the dialogue is proportionately bland and unimaginative for the women; and one wonders how anyone as special as Joe Pendleton could be sparked by anyone as dull and shallow as Bette Logan. Each male character has his own style of patter which adds dimension to what could have been a silly story; unfortunately, the women are uninteresting.

The story remained essentially the same in the 1978 version entitled *Heaven Can Wait* with appropriate updatings, but the ingredient that was so prominent in the original that seemed to escape the newer one was innocence. Whereas Robert Montgomery's Joe Pendleton is never quite at ease stepping into the role of a millionaire, Warren Beatty's Joe Pendleton fits all too slickly into the role of wealthy playboy, his rough edges disappearing completely under his cashmere clothing. Nevertheless, if *Here Comes Mr. Jordan* is given a new film treatment in another thirty years, assuredly it will be met with the same generous response from audiences of all ages. It is a timeless story.

Juliette Friedgen

HESTER STREET

Released: 1975
Production: Raphael D. Silver for Midwest Films Production, Inc.
Direction: Joan Micklin Silver
Screenplay: Joan Micklin Silver; based on the story "Yekl" by Abraham Cahan
Cinematography: Kenneth Van Sickle
Editing: Katherine Wenning
Running time: 90 minutes

Principal characters:
Jake .... Steven Keats
Gitl .... Carol Kane
Bernstein .... Mel Howard
Mamie .... Dorrie Kavanaugh

Hester Street is the painful story of a cultural clash and the painfulness of change. It is an ambitious effort to dissect and scrutinize one central activity in the development of the American character—the assimilation of hundreds of thousands of immigrants into the uniquely American *mélange.* Director Joan Micklin Silver has sharply focused on one street, one neighborhood, and one family of Russian Jews in order to explore the painful process of Americanization and its effect on the lives it devoured. In her first feature film effort, Silver utilizes her considerable experience in educational film-making to present this small, ironic story.

The setting is New York's teeming Lower East Side in 1896. The principal character is Yekl, who, in his eagerness to embrace his adopted culture, has changed his name to Jake (Steven Keats). Jake is a tailor slaving in a sweat shop to make a meager living and to save for the arrival of his wife and young son from the Old Country. He is, however, also experiencing a growing fascination with a very American dancer named Mamie (Dorrie Kavanaugh). She is all brass and boldness, and epitomizes Americanization at its most base as well as its most free. Gitl (Carol Kane), Jake's wife, is as much bound to her tradition and religion as to the confining wig she will not be without and the Yiddish language to which she clings. She epitomizes all that Jake would like to reject. Through their conflict, Silver lays bare the throes of the cultural clash that repeatedly rent the nation during those years of mass influx of Eastern Europeans that came close on the heels of the Industrial Revolution.

To further polarize the issues, a young Yeshiva student, Bernstein (Mel Howard), is introduced as a boarder who lives the old life of religious study and discipline, and who is in sympathy with the bewildered Gitl. Divorce follows the agonizing attempts of Jake and his pious, pitiful mate to recapture whatever definition of marriage they held before the uprooting. Jake goes to the irrepressible Mamie, who, he learns, is not all glitter and fun. Gitl and Bernstein create an asylum for each other in the midst of their rapidly changing environment. The ending is not a typical "happy-ever-after" one, although the viewer does come away with a sense of continuity if not optimism concerning the outcome.

Jake's character embodies the vulgarity of Americans as seen through the eyes of Europeans. Emerging from what one assumes is the controlled paucity of spirit of the Orthodox life-style, he behaves with a recklessness, a brash and transparent cockiness, and a kind of hedonism. His one sympathetic moment comes during a family picnic where his warm, open play with his young son reveals his tender side, his longing for the irresponsibility of youth; but his basic character is one of show without substance, future without past. Jake is so lacking in sympathy that one clearly feels confronted with the director's own biases toward a post-Vietnam America. There is an unmistakable nostalgia for the old ways, a longing to return to the simplicity and order of another time and place, and an aversion to gloss and youthful irreverence. Steven Keats is only adequate in the role of Jake, lacking the depth necessary to reveal the tremendous conflict and momentum of change we anticipate in the character. With the exception of the picnic scene, his acting is generally flat and predictable.

There is considerably more affection invested by the filmmaker in the character of Gitl. Yet behind her wide-eyed passivity and frailty, a subtle contempt undermines the obvious sympathy she would otherwise invoke. She represents the universal resistance to change thrown against the terrible force of American progress and pride. The fact that Silver creates a sympathetic solution for her in the end (if one considers Bernstein a solution) detracts from the emotional potential of *Hester Street*. Yet the character shows small signs of flowering toward the end, of resisting strictures in such a way that she does not seem to give in to the dominant culture as much as to begin taking advantage of it.

Carol Kane as Gitl is appropriately gentle, and her facial expressions are studied and effective; her work earned her an Academy Award nomination, a special distinction considering the unpretentious nature of the film. Yet one wishes for greater irony and power in her acting out of her trauma. It is an exceedingly difficult role, requiring obvious restraint and the kind of covert emotionalism that seizes an audience before it knows it. The difficulty of both of the major characterizations is accentuated by the sparse, documentarylike quality of the film. The black-and-white starkness of the environment and the camera's narrow range demand of its actors a wider range and greater depth. Bernstein is adequately portrayed, wearing his restraint like a dull but serviceable overcoat; Mamie constitutes a convincing foil, forcing us to cringe at our repressed shamelessness. The yenta neighbor is a warm, comic addition who occasionally bridges the extremes.

Generally, the balances and counterbalances in Silver's characters seem to indicate some underlying dislike for the American character, for its excesses and wanton disregard of history and tradition. The direction of *Hester Street* seems largely experimental, which is the result, in part, of Silver's crossing of the usually well-defined line dividing educational from feature film. The film is neither, and it is both. The slightly shaggy homemade movie quality creates an ambivalence that gives a sense of charm and substance on the one hand and of inadequacy on the other. The detail is rich and memorable, and except for the frequent lapses in the camerawork, the film achieves the intimate reality essential to its purpose.

The liberal use of Yiddish, supplemented by subtitled clues to the dialogue, works reasonably well, setting a mood as well as lending authenticity. The dialogue is somewhat strained and sometimes difficult to follow. Several factors contribute; the interspersing of Yiddish is only one of them. The sound itself leaves much to be desired; it is disappointingly flat and often uneven. Another technical failing that mars the final product is the poor lighting; although some may argue that the lighting effects are deliberate, they fail nonetheless to achieve any sustained impact. Likewise, the editing lacks that extra measure of imagination needed to excite and pace the audience through this microcosmic story. Overall, the film moves slowly—the combined result of poor editing and the complexity of Silver's screenplay.

However, *Hester Street* is saved by its faithfulness to detail and its fearless exploration of issues basic to an understanding of Americans as a people; therein lies the importance of the film. As an instrument of self-exploration, predating the mass phenomenon of *Roots*, and as a critical examination of ourselves and our collective psyches, this small film is an affirmation of courage—a small beginning effort to focus on a small but intriguing part of our heritage. It pricks the collective conscience and demands response in an age of increasing individual isolation and declining commitment to any national institution.

Hester Street offers a moment of history suspended and magnified, in which Silver has allowed us a tiny glimpse of how we came to be a country of such confusion and contradiction. We see it in Jake's disdain for the confines of his old life and his ill-disguised fear of it. Gitl's passivity feeds her intransigence and leaves her powerless; yet it rewards her with happiness in the end. Mamie's brash hedonism belies her underlying insecurity and disillusion. The setting's gray yet teeming tone gives them all something to conquer, to rise above, to bloom against. In his or her own way, each does.

Such is the kaleidoscopic nature of the American personality. There is some pretension and obvious hazard in attempting to identify such a collective entity. The merit must lie in the concept of a working model, dynamic and open to continuing analysis. In that way we are able to grapple with our consciences, our values, and the quality of our lives. The process is painful, but that kind of self-criticism is basic to our culture. As the yenta cajoles Gitl into a new corset, she tells her: "If you want to be American, you gotta hurt."

Hester Street's insight demands that those hard questions be examined; and one of the strongest sources of that insight is its authenticity. With more attention to art and more technical facility, Silver's first feature film would have achieved the grace to make it more than memorable. The maturity of her wisdom and perception is still far ahead of her filmmaking. However, the prognosis for her future work, based on this effort, is exciting and positive.

Sally V. Holm

THE HIGH AND THE MIGHTY

Released: 1954
Production: A Wayne Fellows Production for Warner Bros.
Direction: William A. Wellman
Screenplay: Ernest K. Gann; based on his novel of the same name
Cinematography: Archie Stout
Editing: Ralph Dawson
Running time: 147 minutes

Principal characters:

Dan Roman	John Wayne
May Holst	Claire Trevor
Lydia Rice	Laraine Day
Sullivan	Robert Stack
Sally McKee	Jan Sterling
Ed Joseph	Phil Harris
Gustave Pardee	Robert Newton
Ken Childs	David Brian
Flaherty	Paul Kelly
Garfield	Regis Toomey
Jose Locola	John Qualen

The High and the Mighty is a unique film, outdated and perhaps doomed by its own success. Yet even today, it remains the standard by which its successors must be judged. Made in 1954 by William A. Wellman from the best-selling novel by Ernest K. Gann, it became the first slick modern disaster film and, in the process, established the basic formula for these films—one that would be followed for the next thirty years.

While it is true that earlier films, among them *Stagecoach* (1939) and *Lifeboat* (1944), had employed a similar theme of exploring relationships among a group of lost souls thrown together on a doomed journey, the elements of disaster were secondary and usually employed to advance development of character. *The High and the Mighty* elevated the element of disaster to the preeminent position among the concerns of its plot—a twist that would not go unnoticed by the host of imitators that followed. The series of Airport films (*Airport*, 1970, *Airport 1976*, and *Airport '77*) are the ones most obviously influenced by Wellman's film, but *Abandon Ship* (1957), *A Night to Remember* (1958), and *The Poseidon Adventure* (1972) also owe obvious debts to the formula set by *The High and the Mighty*.

It could be argued perhaps that Wellman and screenwriter Gann might, in fact, be obligated to Edmund Goulding's 1932 *Grand Hotel* for its collection of troubled characters and personal crises. Although Wellman admittedly does provide a cabinload of lost souls and examines to some degree their reactions to one another and to the imminent catastrophe in terms of their past experience, this is primarily padding inserted to delineate and to enhance the crisis. Through this means, Wellman is able to get lively footage out of his scenes of an airliner in distress.

As would obviously be expected in a film which contains multiple personal dramas enacted against a life-and-death background, the *Grand Hotel* type of embellishments suffer by comparison. Gann and Wellman, however, have introduced the assorted individual dramas with professional smoothness beginning with the moment that each passenger arrives to pick up his tickets at the Hawaiian airport's reservation counter for the flight to San Francisco. The travelers are then introduced to us by the reservations clerk, who shapes our initial impressions about their characters. To his credit, Gann in his script avoided most of the obvious clichéd situations that would be tempting to any writer dealing with a large number of characters in a situation such as this. No romance develops during the flight, for example, and when the plane door is opened to jettison the excess baggage, no one falls out or is in any danger of doing so.

As the passengers are seated on the plane, we learn more about them and quickly discover that each is burdened with a great deal of excess emotional baggage. The pilot, Sullivan (Robert Stack), is a nervous man harboring secret fears and is bordering on a nervous breakdown. His second-in-command, Dan Roman (John Wayne), although much calmer than his captain, harbors dark memories of losing his own captain's license because he was the pilot of a plane that crashed killing everyone on board except himself, including his wife and child.

Among the passengers, Lydia and Howard Rice (Laraine Day and John Howard) are returning home with the intention of getting a divorce. Gustave Pardee (Robert Newton) is a loud-mouthed theatrical producer, and Ken Childs (David Brian) is a cowardly playboy. Flaherty (Paul Kelly) is a demoralized atomic scientist who worries throughout the flight about political misuse of the force that he and others like him have unleashed in the world. Also, as might be expected, there is a woman of easy virtue, May Holst (Claire Trevor, repeating her *Stagecoach* role), who possesses the proverbial "heart of gold" with which such women are often imbued in films like this one. A number of other troubled characters, as well as Jose Locola (John Qualen), a sympathetic figure with no problems who only got on the plane to go to San Francisco, complete the passenger list.

As the plane flies out over the Pacific the individual dramas unfold. In the background, however, some disquieting things are happening. One of the stewardesses notes a recurring vibration that is so subtle at first that it does not do more than spill a few drops of coffee out of a cup. The passengers do not notice, however, because a jealous husband is wielding a gun and threatening to shoot Ken Childs for having an affair with his wife. He is soon calmed down by copilot Roman and returns to his seat.

The vibration now begins to alarm Roman, who starts searching the plane for the cause. Things start to go wrong in rapid succession. First, an engine catches fire and goes out of commission, ripping a hole in a gas tank in the process. The fuel leak severely limits the amount of fuel available to cover the 2,400-mile run and reach San Francisco. The specter of a night crash-landing on the ocean begins to loom larger. To lighten the load and ease the strain on the fuel supply, Roman opens one of the cabin doors and begins to jettison as much luggage as possible. In the midst of this crisis, Captain Sullivan finally goes to pieces under the stress but has some sense knocked into him by his copilot Roman, who has been through it all before.

It now becomes a race against the declining fuel supply for the plane and crew, with their flying efficiency diminished, to make San Francisco. With the plane in trouble, personal dramas are resolved. The plane's captain learns to conquer his fear; a pair of honeymooners develop confidence in their mutual ability to face life. The wealthy Lydia Rice makes up her mind to forget the divorce and go to the Alaska mining country and give her kept husband a chance to try to stand on his own two feet. There are equally suitable resolutions for the prostitute, the atomic scientist, the jealous husband with a pistol in his pocket, and a horde of others, although one is not fully confident regarding the permanence of these changes once the airliner lands.

The plane barely reaches San Francisco with its fuel tanks reading empty when it touches down. After all of the passengers depart to make good on their various "new starts," Roman stands under the plane contemplating all that has happened. He is approached by Garfield (Regis Toomey), who, after checking the plane, informs the copilot how little fuel was actually left. Suspecting that Roman's cool competence was a factor in the plane's survival, he tells him to come to his office tomorrow to discuss his reinstatement as a captain.

The High and the Mighty utilizes a sure-fire film situation: a group of people from diverse backgrounds with individual human problems faces and reacts to a common deadly crisis. Although most of the airplane's passengers and their problems might in retrospect seem bizarre and to some degree contrived, Trevor, through sheer acting ability, does create a certain credibility for the highly specialized plight of an erstwhile tarnished lady; but the other passengers are pretty much only along for the ride.

Wayne delivers his normal characterization as the rock-steady copilot who makes the right decision when the pilot cracks under stress. He maintains his cool composure but at the same time exhibits the courage to knock some clear sense into the Captain's muddled head. For his part, Stack as the captain gives a convincing performance of a highly neurotic man walking a tightrope between nervous sanity and a complete breakdown. *The High and the Mighty* marked a turning point in Stack's acting career. Prior to this film, he seemed relegated to playing light romantic roles and secondary leads. After his performance as the captain, however, he went on to star in *Written on the Wind* (1956), for which he received an Academy Award nomination, and to play the lead in the long-running television show, *The Untouchables*. Both of these roles were made possible by the new image that he established as a dramatic actor in *The High and the Mighty*. Both director Wellman and Gann have an excellent knowledge of the mechanics of flying and a relatively good idea of the psychology of the men who fly the planes. There are some occasional technical errors, but the only major one is the opening outward of a passenger door while the plane is in flight. The sets, instrument panels, and particularly the airports look businesslike and professional. The aerial cinematography is stunning and is enhanced by the use of color and CinemaScope.

When *The High and the Mighty* turns from the emotional problems and entanglements of its passengers, it is an absorbing drama of a race against time. There is no denying that the parts of the film dealing directly with the crippled plane's dilemma are tremendously effective. The film suffers in retrospect only because viewers seeing it today for the first time have been exposed to its many successors which have taken its stock characterizations and situations and rendered them trite. Although the airline disaster formula was formalized by Wellman and Gann, it has not been changed imaginatively or sufficiently by later directors. Thus a new viewer could be excused for thinking of it as *Airport 1954*—a victim of the style it created.

Stephen L. Hanson

HIGH NOON

Released: 1952
Production: Stanley Kramer for Stanley Kramer Productions; released by
 United Artists
Direction: Fred Zinnemann
Screenplay: Carl Foreman; based on the story "The Tin Star" by John W.
 Cunningham
Cinematography: Floyd Crosby
Editing: Elmo Williams and Harry Gerstad (AA)
Music: Dmitri Tiomkin (AA)
Song: Dmitri Tiomkin and Ned Washington, "High Noon" (AA)
Running time: 84 minutes

> *Principal characters:*
> Will Kane .... Gary Cooper (AA)
> Jonas Henderson .... Thomas Mitchell
> Harvey Pell .... Lloyd Bridges
> Helen Ramirez .... Katy Jurado
> Amy Kane .... Grace Kelly
> Percy Mettrick .... Otto Kruger
> Frank Miller .... Ian MacDonald

The Western as a genre film is no longer in vogue, although its popularity
has been extremely durable. Until the 1970's it honestly could be said that
almost every top-rated star had appeared in at least one Western at some
time during his career. Perhaps it has been the abundance of Westerns on the
television screen that has decreased their popularity as theatrical films, but
whatever the reason, the Western remains anathema to modern producers.
In 1952, however, the Western was at the height of its popularity, and Stanley
Kramer's production of *High Noon* is deservedly rated as one of the best
Westerns ever filmed. It boasts a beautifully written, tight script by Carl
Foreman; superb direction by Fred Zinnemann; and an Academy Award-
winning performance by Gary Cooper.

High Noon tells a very simple story. Will Kane (Gary Cooper) has been
marshall of Hadleyville, a small Western town, and on a particular Sunday
morning in 1870 he has turned in his badge and is waiting to be replaced
officially by a new and younger marshal. He has married Amy (Grace Kelly),
a Quaker girl he truly loves, and he now wishes to move to a new town, settle
down, open a store, and have a family. In the midst of Kane's wedding party,
however, word comes that Frank Miller (Ian MacDonald), a killer he had
long ago captured and testified against, with the result that Miller was sentenced to the penitentiary, has been pardoned, and is on the train due to
arrive in Hadleyville at noon. It is now 10:40 A.M., and on the otherwise
deserted station platform three of Miller's cohorts are waiting for him to

arrive so that the four can ride into town and avenge themselves by killing Kane.

Amy Kane implores her husband to leave town at once with her because she is a Quaker and deplores violence of any kind. The newly appointed marshal is on his way, and theoretically it is now his responsibility to deal with the situation since Kane has already turned in his badge. Many of the townspeople are leaving temporarily in order to be gone when Miller shows up, including the judge who had sentenced him (Otto Kruger). The young deputy, Harvey Pell (Lloyd Bridges), who has been Kane's friend and helper, deserts the former marshal because he resents having been passed over in favor of an unknown stranger for the vacated post. Even Kane's ex-girl friend, Helen Ramirez (Katy Jurado), urges Kane and his bride to leave before Miller arrives. Kane is tempted, but he is an honest man with a high sense of morality, and he sees this showdown as a challenge he must meet even if he is killed.

The train arrives on time; Miller is met by his gang and they set out for Hadleyville's main street and the office where Kane waits alone. It is one of Cooper's finest performances, as he conveys Kane's fear, tension, and frustration, while the clock ticks off the minutes after twelve. In the dramatic conclusion, Kane's wife is the only person to help him, having put aside her beliefs to raise a rifle in protection of her husband. This denouement is one of the most famous scenes in the Western film and one that has been copied frequently. The final scene of the film shows Kane and his wife leaving town riding off to their new life.

The role of Amy Kane was only Grace Kelly's second screen performance, and, although not long or exacting, it won her an M-G-M contract. Gary Cooper is perfect as Kane, a role similar to that which established his reputation as a Western hero in *The Virginian* (1929). The entire supporting cast of *High Noon* is perfectly chosen; every actor acquits himself honorably, particularly Ian MacDonald as the antagonist, Frank Miller. *High Noon* brought Cooper his second Oscar; he had won his first in 1941 for *Sergeant York*, and had been nominated for *Mr. Deeds Goes to Town* (1936); *The Pride of the Yankees* (1942); and *For Whom the Bell Tolls* (1943).

High Noon is one of the few films to observe the dramatic unities. Interestingly, however, when the screenplay was first written and shot, it had a subplot that periodically took the action away from Hadleyville by cutting to scenes of the newly appointed marshal (James Brown) being delayed on his journey to the town. Zinnemann was quick to see, however, that those scenes lessened the film's tension rather than building it, so the episodes were dropped, thus eliminating Brown's role in the picture altogether. Editors Elmo Williams and Ned Washington were in complete accord; thanks to them and to Zinnemann, the suspense in *High Noon* mounts with every moment until it becomes almost unendurable. Zinnemann was nominated for an Oscar as Best Director, although the award went to John Ford for *The Quiet Man*; but Williams and Washington both won Oscars for Best Film Editing. Dmitri Tiomkin and Ned Washington's original ballad "High Noon," sung throughout the film by Ted Ritter, won the Oscar for Best Song, and Tiomkin also earned an Oscar for his scoring of the film.

If one were to list the all-time best Western films, *High Noon* would merit a high place on the list, in the company of such Western classics as *The Covered Wagon* (1923), *The Iron Horse* (1924), *Stagecoach* (1939), *The Ox-Bow Incident* (1942), *The Gunfighter* (1950), *Cimarron* (1931), *Red River* (1948), *Shane* (1953), *Will Penny* (1967), and *The Virginian* (1929). The West remains an integral part of the American heritage; perhaps the pendulum of popularity will someday swing back to favor the Western again.

DeWitt Bodeen

HIGH SIERRA

Released: 1941
Production: Hal B. Wallis for Warner Bros.
Direction: Raoul Walsh
Screenplay: John Huston and W. R. Burnett; based on the novel of the same name by W. R. Burnett
Cinematography: Tony Gaudio
Editing: Jack Killifer
Music: Adolph Deutsch
Running time: 100 minutes

Principal characters:
Marie	Ida Lupino
Roy Earle	Humphrey Bogart
Babe	Alan Curtis
Red	Arthur Kennedy
Velma	Joan Leslie
Doc Banton	Henry Hull
Pa	Henry Travers
Louis Mendoza	Cornel Wilde
Jake Kranmer	Barton MacLane
Big Mac	Donald MacBride

By 1941, the possibilities of the gangster film had been fairly well exhausted; at the same time, world events were proving to be far more dramatic and compelling. Warner Bros., generally acknowledged to be the leading purveyor of "socially significant" gangster films, had an impressive roster of hardboiled male stars. The titans were James Cagney, Paul Muni, and Edward G. Robinson as well as George Raft and the newly arrived John Garfield. By contrast, the tried and true heavy, Humphrey Bogart, found himself for the most part relegated to supporting roles in which he invariably played a despicable and doomed character.

The studio found itself running into difficulty when it attempted to cast the leading role in Raoul Walsh's new film, *High Sierra*. The top male stars of Warners' "murderers' row," after having established themselves in crime films, had gone on to prove their talent in a wide variety of roles; consequently, none of them was particularly eager to become a public enemy again. Raft complained that he was tired of getting killed in the last reel. Finally, at Walsh's suggestion, the studio settled on Bogart for the role of the Dillinger-type Roy Earle. Ida Lupino received top billing and performed admirably, but the film belonged to Bogart, for whom the role was a major step forward in his career.

The complete film was a fairly faithful adaptation of W. R. Burnett's novel, chronicling the last weeks in the life of Roy Earle, an aging bank robber newly released from prison through the efforts of an old pal, Big Mac (Donald MacBride), who needs him to rob a resort hotel in California. Big Mac is dying, and Roy, out of gratitude for his release and loyalty to his old pal, agrees to this one last "caper." Doubts arise, however, when he meets the other members of the gang composed of Babe (Alan Curtis) and Red (Arthur Kennedy), young hotheads whose prior criminal expertise is limited to filling-station and liquor-store holdups; Marie (Ida Lupino) a dance-hall girl along for the ride; Louis Mendoza (Cornel Wilde), a desk clerk at the hotel and the gang's inside man; and a corrupt policeman named Jake Kranmer (Barton McLane).

On the cross-country drive to California, Roy has met and befriended the Goodhue family and their granddaughter, Velma (Joan Leslie), a beautiful lame girl. They have migrated to California hoping to find a doctor who might perform an operation to correct Velma's handicap. This decent family reminds Roy of his own upbringing. He falls in love with the girl and, without her knowledge, finances the operation. Once the job is over he hopes to marry Velma and settle down to the kind of peaceful, untroubled life which has so long eluded him.

Gradually, as the gang marks time before the robbery, Roy begins to depend on Marie, who is more levelheaded than Red or Babe. Marie has fallen in love with Roy; and a symbol of the bond which is gradually forming between them is the stray dog, Pard, rumored to be jinxed, who loves them both.

The holdup is a success, but during the getaway Red and Babe's car goes off the road and explodes. Mendoza is implicated and soon names Roy as the leader of the gang. Roy heads for Los Angeles to deliver the goods to Big Mac, who is to supply a "fence" for the jewelry taken from the hotel safe; but when he arrives, he finds Big Mac dead of a heart attack. The greedy ex-policeman Kranmer attempts to take the money and jewels from Roy, who is forced to kill him.

Roy, Marie, and Pard are on the run. Still obsessed by his dream of a life with Velma, Roy stops off at the home of the Goodhues intending to propose to Velma, only to find that she has become engaged to the young playboy who had jilted her when she was still a cripple. His hopes shattered, the embittered Roy leaves. For the first time he realizes how Marie feels about him.

However, the net has begun to close around him. Half-acknowledging his love for Marie, he puts her and Pard on a bus, promising that he will come to her when things have cooled off. A well-coordinated manhunt is on for "Mad Dog" Earle, as the press melodramatically labels him. Unable to spend any of the money stolen from the hotel, he attempts a drugstore holdup and is spotted by the police. In the ensuing chase, Roy abandons his car at the foot of Mount Whitney and climbs to a high vantage point from which he holds the police at bay with a machine gun.

Hearing the news of the impending capture, Marie gets off the bus and makes her way to the base camp at the foot of the mountain. Unable to reach the outlaw, the police send a sharpshooter to climb around behind him. At dawn the police once more urge Roy to surrender. His reply is, "Come and get me!" Pard, hearing Roy's voice, jumps from his wicker basket and races toward him. Seeing the little "jinxed" dog and knowing that Marie must be with him, Roy forgets himself, stands up, and calls out to Marie; he is shot down by the sharpshooter's bullets. Alone again, Marie takes consolation in the knowledge that at least Roy's agonizing life of crime is at an end.

Two brilliant filmmakers, Raoul Walsh and John Huston, here combine to make a memorable film. Of the same generation as the more highly lauded Ford and Hawks, Walsh, with his unpretentious, uncluttered style, seemed to lack some of the obsessions which made his two contemporaries stand out and, for a time, overshadow him. Walsh was, however, quite probably the finest action director, in whatever genre, to emerge during the period. His reputation remained secure for the four decades in which he was active as a Hollywood director, and, since the release of his final film in 1961, there has yet to appear any new director to claim Walsh's crown.

For this last in a long line of gangster films, Walsh and Huston created an essentially decent man who, because of the Depression, went wrong. There is nothing of the Big City or organized crime about Roy Earle. He is no little Caesar; instead, in the tradition of Jesse James, he is a farm boy-turned-outlaw who retains some of the humane traits he had before he entered a life of crime. It is to their credit that Walsh and Huston are able to establish the character of Earle with a minimum of dialogue. In one of the initial scenes we walk with the just-paroled ex-convict, enjoying, through his eyes and ears, the sights and sounds of a world without bars or guards. The two shots of the rugged High Sierras behind the opening credits and again at the very end of the film convey a sense of ineluctable fate.

It is doubtful that Walsh, Huston, and Bogart thought they were making a great film; they had simply done their best with another gangster story. That it would prove financially successful there was little doubt; yet it was more than that. Emerging just as America was about to enter World War II, *High Sierra* was a fitting denouement to a decade of gangster films; in future, the antisocial hero would take a back seat. Actors such as Humphrey Bogart (*All Through the Night*, 1942) and Alan Ladd (*Lucky Jordan*, 1942) were soon involved in transitional films in which they abandoned crime in favor of patriotism. Finally, *High Sierra* is notable as the first true "Bogart picture," elevating him to stardom and providing him with the opportunity to prove that he could play highly sensitive roles with skill and even brilliance.

Michael Shepler

THE HIRED HAND

Released: 1971
Production: William Hayward for Universal
Direction: Peter Fonda
Screenplay: Alan Sharp
Cinematography: Vilmos Zsigmond
Editing: Frank Mazzola
Running time: 93 minutes

Principal characters:
Harry Collings .... Peter Fonda
Arch Harris .... Warren Oates
Hannah Collings .... Verna Bloom
Dan Griffen .... Robert Pratt
McVey .... Severn Darden
Janey Collings .... Megan Denver

The Hired Hand is not a typical Western, although it shares the time, place, and basic good-guys-versus-bad-guys aspects of its genre. What separates it from the others is its highly stylized approach and its attempt to portray the significance and meaning behind the action. After his success in the role of Captain America in *Easy Rider* (1969), Peter Fonda offered this film as his directorial debut and added to the Western some of the mystical, surrealistic overtones that had characterized that more popular film. Like *Easy Rider*, *The Hired Hand* deals with basic American values; it differs significantly in that it affirms these values rather than questioning the contemporary cultural malaise.

The plot is not very complex. In the first sequence, Harry Collings (Peter Fonda) and Arch Harris (Warren Oates) avenge the death of their friend Dan Griffen (Robert Pratt), who has just been shot down by the sadistic McVey (Severn Darden). Instead of killing McVey, they shoot him in both feet—an example of the often oblique symbolism employed throughout the film. Tired of wandering, Collings returns to his wife and daughter whom he had deserted seven years before. Hannah (Verna Bloom) is understandably cool and suspicious, at first only accepting him as another of the hands she has hired, but eventually accepting his return as her husband. Harris, now a threat to her security, soon leaves. Later, a messenger from McVey gives proof that they have captured Harris. Collings must leave to meet McVey at once or they will cut off another finger for each day's delay, eventually taking his life. It is a hard decision to make, with the guilt of Hannah's past betrayal still weighing on him; but he must try to save his friend's life. Promising to return, he leaves, only to be killed in the ensuing showdown with McVey. Harris survives, however, and returns to the farm to take Collings' place as Hannah's hired hand.

On the surface the film portrays the values of the Old West: loyalty, courage, responsibility, hard work, and pain. Fonda and screenwriter Alan Sharp have blended a romanticized vision of these idealized attributes with a story whose characters live in a very real, harsh world. The result is a latter-day morality play. Each of the characters embodies certain qualities, and their interactions illustrate and emphasize the human values that reaffirm life. Collings, Hannah, and Harris form a triad whose lives illustrate the basic struggle of life on the frontier. Sin, guilt, and atonement can easily be read into the plot as Collings' return does not totally expiate his sin of having left Hannah. His return creates another moral conflict since he must end his association with Harris in order to stay with her. Only his death and Harris' return to Hannah restores order.

At the center of the triangle is Hannah Collings. Compared with other Western heroines, Hannah is refreshingly realistic. She looks as if she has spent many years working hard, and her face mirrors the struggles she has had to survive. Underneath, however, there is a softer, more feminine woman whom Bloom beautifully exhibits in shy and touching ways. When Collings is finally accepted back into the house, she dresses and primps like the young bride she once was, clearly trusting Collings and accepting her wifely role again. Although other hired hands have shared her bed, we sense that this one is different, more significant. Collings' actions at this point are also indicative of his inner feelings and his commitment to a new life. The entire sequence in which both go through a ritual cleansing and preparation establishes the import of their renewed relationship. Completing the triangle, Oates plays Harris as an interesting blend of strength and sensitivity. Like Collings, he is weary of traveling and is envious of the home Collings has rediscovered. In a beautifully played scene marking Harris' realization that he must leave, he and Hannah experience a natural attraction for each other. Both characters realize at once what is happening but both instinctively retreat. Collings is important to both of them, and neither wishes to upset the newly reestablished union.

On the surface, the main weakness of the film is the characterization of Collings. While trying to reduce the character to a simple, everyday cowboy, Fonda has left little substance to the man. Only his choices and decisions carry any significance, while his daily activity is something of a puzzle. Fonda, as Collings, delineates a character so painfully nonverbal and seemingly unemotional that it is difficult to understand fully his motive in returning to his wife or her attraction for him. Presumably, Collings' seven years' absence and his close association with Harris, who seems more likable, have taught him the meaning of the loyalty, responsibility, and love which he clearly lacked earlier. The key is that we are not supposed to read too much into the character's individual actions, but to appreciate the wider human implications of the drama. The people are simple and the dialogue sparse on purpose.

The visual effects support these mythical dimensions. The lingering dissolves, the slow motion, and the superimposed multiple images remove the action from reality. Technically, the audience is treated to a lushly beautiful picture of a harsh, rugged landscape, but many have agreed that this does not compensate for the film's slow pace. In fact, many critics have felt that the editing contributed to the film's failure. Many of the techniques used are now rather commonplace, however, and this might make their predominance in the film seem less intrusive to a more sophisticated audience. The fact that the film appeared immediately after the psychedelic fervor of the late 1960's may have hurt its reception, since many critics felt that its mystical overtones and solemn acting were pretentious; but time may blur some of those objections. Although it will probably never be widely acclaimed, over the years *The Hired Hand* has attracted a cult following whose members appreciate its beauty and uniquely simple charm.

Christine Gladish

HIS GIRL FRIDAY

Released: 1940
Production: Howard Hawks for Columbia
Direction: Howard Hawks
Screenplay: Charles Lederer; based on the play *The Front Page* by Ben Hecht
   and Charles MacArthur
Cinematography: Joseph Walker
Editing: Gene Havlick
Running time: 92 minutes

Principal characters:
Walter Burns	Cary Grant
Hildy Johnson	Rosalind Russell
Bruce Baldwin	Ralph Bellamy
Earl Williams	John Qualen
Molly Malloy	Helen Mack

Howard Hawks's *His Girl Friday* is a culmination of the "screwball" comedy tradition of the 1930's. Hawks had a habit of coming last to a genre; but his contribution was never the least; it was always an excellent entry. This film, a reworking of Ben Hecht's and Charles MacArthur's *The Front Page*, is charged with new life through Hawks's masterful direction and major script changes. In this version, he adds a sophisticated battle of the sexes by turning the "male" Hildy Johnson into a Hildegarde, and pitting her against her boss and former husband, Walter Burns. The new love triangle replaces the old plot of political corruption and newsroom nonsense, but the changes cause only minor discomfort. The story, like the original, is all surface and no substance. The dialogue rather than the plot gives the picture its distinction.

Rosalind Russell as Hildy Johnson turns the newsroom upside down as she throws her well-padded shoulders around. Accepted by the newsmen as "one of the boys," she is fast-talking, with a quick retort for every wisecrack. A hard competitor, she is extremely successful in a man's world. Russell's acting is always adequate and at times captivating. Her most dramatic scene, for example, is with the condemned criminal Earl Williams (John Qualen) midway through the film when, as Hildy, she builds a "story" out of Williams' use of a gun to kill, turning it into a philosophical argument about "production for use." The character of Walter Burns is made-to-order for Cary Grant. Unlike the romp through the woods that Hawks gave Grant and Katharine Hepburn in *Bringing Up Baby* (1938), the stunts in *His Girl Friday* are verbal. The insults fly like daggers, and with Hawks, Grant, and Russell throwing them, they are rarely misdirected.

The pace is sometimes frenzied, yet the film does not suffer from its weak thread of a plot. As the story opens, Hildy returns to the *Morning Post* to flash her new engagement ring in her ex-husband's face and to bid him, the newspaper business, and the city farewell. She is marrying Bruce Baldwin (Ralph Bellamy), a bland insurance salesman from Upstate New York; he represents security, stability, and a white picket fence in Albany. Nothing could be duller, unless it is Bruce himself. While Hildy staunchly insists that Bruce is what she wants, Burns and the audience believe that she desperately wants to be convinced otherwise. From the beginning, Bruce is an open challenge for Burns's mischievous mind, and it is obviously no contest.

Although Hildy is ready to leave on the next train for Albany, Burns delays her departure with a plea that she cannot refuse. His star reporter, he claims, is unavailable to cover the imminent death-row story on Earl Williams. Still desperately hoping for a pardon, Williams faces execution at dawn. Hildy, Burns argues, is the only reporter "man" enough to enter the prison and get the story.

Hildy stalls Bruce from one train to the next, promising not to miss the last one. But Burns is determined to get rid of Bruce for good. Through a series of contrived mishaps which he masterminds, Bruce lands in jail twice and is nearly killed in a car accident with his "mother," all in one night.

As the evening wears on, the Governor's pardon of Williams is intercepted and concealed by a corrupt mayor who feels that his reelection depends on the execution. Meanwhile, after an interview with Hildy, the somewhat confused Williams dramatically escapes from death row, then suddenly appears in the prison newsroom where he finds Hildy alone. True to her profession, Hildy hides Williams in a rolltop desk to protect him as well as her scoop. Complications set in when Williams' alleged girl friend, Molly Malloy (Helen Mack), is interrogated for information about Williams' whereabouts. Under the pressure, Molly breaks down and leaves through the second story window, falling to her death on the pavement below.

The film does not skip a beat as, in true Hollywood "screwball" fashion, the mayor, the criminal, the love triangle, and the mother-in-law all converge in the newsroom for the grand finale. Phones ring, guns fire, and everyone shouts at once. The corrupt mayor and his henchmen are exposed and Hildy and Burns team up for another round of marriage.

Hawks's presentation of the battle of the sexes is as old as Shakespeare, and the treatment of Hildy and Burns is typical of the egocentric type of hero that the director enjoyed. However, love and respect get the better of their self-centered interests and ultimately the two join forces against the wooden, lifeless people who, they consider, make up most of the population of the world.

The directorial style of *His Girl Friday* is as straightforward as Hawks's dialogue. His direct cuts and lack of montage keep the film from being dated and keep extraneous movement to a minimum. Time dances frantically by; the comedy is copious and varied; the gags are rapid-fire. The sarcastic banter between Hildy and Burns is the soul of the film, and it is this clever repartee that captures the audience. Representative of Hawks's comedy at its best, *His Girl Friday* is a treat not to be missed if the opportunity arises.

Joanne L. Yeck

HOLIDAY

Released: 1938
Production: Everett Riskin for Columbia
Direction: George Cukor
Screenplay: Donald Ogden Stewart and Sidney Buchman; based on the play
 of the same name by Philip Barry
Cinematography: Franz Planer
Editing: Otto Meyer and Al Clark
Running time: 94 minutes

Principal characters:
>Linda Seton .... Katharine Hepburn
>Johnny Case .... Cary Grant
>Julia Seton .... Doris Nolan
>Ned Seton .... Lew Ayres
>Nick Potter .... Edward Everett Horton
>Susan Potter .... Jean Dixon
>Edward Seton .... Henry Kolker

One of the best comedies of the 1930's, *Holiday* sparkles with undiminished radiance even today. Sophisticated and witty, it is a romantic comedy with serious undertones. Underlying the intelligent, urbane banter and the critical view of the rich is the struggle of two kindred spirits to overcome social and psychological obstacles.

Having met and fallen in love with Julia Seton (Doris Nolan) during a vacation at Lake Placid, Johnny Case (Cary Grant) does not know that she is a member of a socially prominent and wealthy family. A charming, clever, free-spirited soul with no social position, Johnny is attracted to Julia at once because she is sweet and intelligent; he assumes that she wants the same kind of life he does although he knows nothing much about her. When, after the vacation, he first visits the Seton house, he is astonished at all he sees as the butler escorts him through the palatial marble-floored hall with its tapestries, paintings, and statuary. When the butler leaves him gingerly perched on the edge of an antique chair, he performs a flip-flop to keep from being over-awed. Once Julia arrives, he finds that their romance is not going to be as simple as he had expected, and the audience begins to see that he and Julia may not be so well-matched after all. Johnny laughingly chides her for not telling him she is rich. "Aren't you funny to talk about it?" she responds. "Is it so sacred?" he asks, and when she tells him quite seriously that she expects him to make millions himself, he responds equally seriously that he will not be doing that. The basic conflict between them is thus established.

The atmosphere is very different, however, when he is introduced to Linda (Katharine Hepburn), Julia's sister. He and Linda like each other immediately, and beneath their light banter we can see that they are kindred spirits, although it takes them a while to recognize it.

Linda Seton is, in fact, the film's central character. As critical of the society in which she lives as Johnny Case is, she is also a product of that society. To it she owes the poise and elegance that a background of money and secure social position can provide, but her sensitivity and intelligence are always at odds with the constricted and pompous circle of family and acquaintances who surround her. Linda has tried painting, acting, and nursing without success. Her problem, as she confides to Johnny, is deciding whether she wants to be Joan of Arc, Florence Nightingale, or John L. Lewis. There are elements of self-pity and theatricality in Linda's character, but she is basically honest and sincere, although puzzled about how to break out of the life she is living. One reason she is instantly attracted to Johnny is that he is a nonconformist.

Significantly, it is to Linda that Johnny explains his philosophy of life. He wants to take a holiday for a few years to find himself and to find out why he is working—surely it is not just to pay bills and pile up more money. There are new, exciting ideas around, he says, and he wants to discover how he fits into the changing world. The catch, as he explains to Linda, is that he wants to retire young and work when he is older. There is an element of pleading in Johnny's voice as he talks to the sympathetic Linda. He almost seems to be reassuring himself at the same time that he asks for her support and confidence.

Linda is not the only Seton who does not fit into the family's marble-pillared world. Her younger brother Ned (Lew Ayres) is also unhappy; but he is less courageous. Having given in to his father's pressure to work in the family bank, he has taken refuge in alcohol to forget that he is a talented musician and wants to pursue music as a career. Their mother, they tell Johnny, "tried to be a Seton for a while and gave up and died."

Representing this nonconformist side of the Setons is a part of the mansion completely different in spirit from the echoing marble halls—the playroom. It is Linda's refuge—a warm, intimate room filled with dreams, childhood mementos, Ned's musical instruments, and a portrait of their mother over the fireplace. Linda invites Johnny up to the playroom, and she and Ned go through an amusing little charade with Johnny to prepare him for the cross-examination he can expect from their father. Julia, however, is not amused and tries to stop them. When Linda says, "Money is our God," Julia is seriously upset and tells Johnny that it is not true. Amused, Johnny responds, "I ask myself what General Motors would do and do the opposite."

Having found out that Johnny has a promising financial future, Mr. Edward Seton, the father (Henry Kolker), decides to overlook his lack of social standing and give his consent to the marriage of Julia and Johnny; but all the conflicts culminate at their engagement party. Linda is so happy that Julia has found such a good man—"Life walked into this house," she says—that she wants to give a small engagement party for them with "no white ties, no formal invitations." As she speaks these words, however, the scene dissolves to a close-up of an engraved invitation and then to a huge formal party— Edward Seton and Julia have not agreed with her idea. Because giving an intimate party was so important to her, Linda stays in the playroom and refuses to come downstairs.

The only people invited who are not connected with the Setons are Johnny's good friends, Nick and Susan Potter (Edward Everett Horton and Jean Dixon). When they appear, they are self-conscious and obviously out of place. Stared at by the butler, they nervously produce their invitations to prove that they have been invited. Seeking to escape, they accidentally end up in the playroom with Linda. An immediate rapport is established among the three, and when Ned wanders in they all begin playing and singing and laughing together.

Soon Johnny, wearing white tie and tails, appears, sent by Julia to persuade Linda to come downstairs. He joins the group after being properly chastised for allowing the marble pillars to overwhelm him. Linda and Johnny attempt an acrobatic trick and end up falling on the floor just as Mr. Seton and Julia enter. Mr. Seton, losing his temper, tells Linda that she has caused enough trouble and orders her downstairs. Turning to Johnny, he tells him how extremely pleased he is with the success of his stock market manipulations and offers him a desk at the Seton bank. Johnny chooses this moment to try to explain his idea of taking a long holiday and to turn down the offer. Neither Julia nor her father can understand him, and Julia has to persuade her father to leave to prevent an open quarrel. After an inconclusive conversation Julia leaves; but Johnny stays to talk to Linda, and they begin waltzing to a music box. It is a very quiet, tender moment in which they are drawn closer together. Then Johnny goes back to the party for the announcement of his engagement to Julia.

Johnny then spends several days vacillating between compromising his principles and leaving Julia for good. Julia will not bend; she insists that he accept her father's position. Finally Johnny tells her, "I love feeling free inside more than I love you"; and he leaves to join the Potters on a trip to Europe. When Julia admits that she does not love Johnny, Linda sees her opportunity to escape and join the man she loves. She arrives at the ship just in time to see Johnny do a flip-flop, and the film ends with their first real kiss.

Johnny's friends, Nick and Susan Potter, are very important to the development of *Holiday*. They are in the very first scene, in which Johnny comes to tell them that he is going to marry Julia; and they are in the last, when Johnny comes to the ship to tell them that he is going to Europe with them. Although they are older than Johnny and are both intellectuals (Susan is a former teacher and Nick a university professor) the film never makes them seem ridiculous. In fact, they are a human, witty, interesting couple. When they look and feel out of place at the formal engagement party, we know that their values are right and that the others' are wrong. When they meet Linda, they immediately side with her against the stuffy side of the Seton family.

Perhaps the only question we might ask is why Johnny does not realize that Linda rather than Julia is right for him long before he does. Indeed, Linda herself does not realize until near the end that Julia is, as Ned tells her, "a very dull girl." Everyone, he says, is taken in by her looks.

Closely following the play by Philip Barry, the script by Donald Ogden Stewart and Sidney Buchman artfully blends wit, feeling, and romance. Although the dialogue always seems natural, it is carefully constructed to have a certain rhythm and to be very revealing of character. Also skillful is the naturalness of the exposition. Most of the characters are just meeting each other, so we learn about them as they learn about one another. There are no scenes in which a character explains something solely for the benefit of the audience. The chief virtue of the script, however, is the creation of four interesting and believable characters: Linda, Johnny, Nick, and Susan.

Brilliantly bringing the script to life is a cast perfectly directed by George Cukor, who wisely realized that the acting had to be slightly stylized but without affectation. Katharine Hepburn as Linda ranges from playful and witty when she first meets Johnny Case and his friends, the Potters, to intense and serious as she finds Johnny a sympathetic person and unbends to him; it is one of her best performances. As Johnny, Cary Grant is also at his best in portraying the charm and spirit of a young man with his own ideas about what is meaningful in life. Edward Everett Horton and Jean Dixon as the Potters and Lew Ayres as Ned excel in crucial supporting roles; indeed there is not a weak performance in the film.

Holiday set box-office records in 1938 and has been recognized ever since as a great achievement of three artists of the cinema, George Cukor, Katharine Hepburn, and Cary Grant.

Timothy W. Johnson

HOLLYWOOD BOULEVARD

Released: 1936
Production: William LeBaron for Paramount
Direction: Robert Florey
Screenplay: Marguerite Roberts; based on the story of the same name by Max
  Marcin and Faith Thomas
Cinematography: Karl Struss
Editing: William Shea
Running time: 83 minutes

Principal characters:
John Blakeford	John Halliday
Patricia Blakeford	Marsha Hunt
Jay Wallace	Robert Cummings
Jordan Winslow	C. Henry Gordon
Flora Moore	Esther Ralston
Alice Winslow	Frieda Inescort
Dr. Sanford	Albert Conti
Detective	Thomas Jackson

Hollywood Boulevard is by no stretch of the imagination a major motion picture, but it does typify the type of film directed by Robert Florey, a man of intelligence and craftsmanship who was responsible for some of the American cinema's best second features and later went on to direct many popular television series, including *The Loretta Young Show* and *Four Star Playhouse*. Born in Paris, France, in 1900, Florey came to the United States in 1921 as a correspondent for the French film magazine, *Cinemagazine*; he later became foreign publicity director for Douglas Fairbanks and Mary Pickford and handled Rudolph Valentino's tour of Europe in 1923. Florey graduated to directing from the position of assistant director, and in 1928 codirected with Slavko Vorkpapich one of the most important American avant-garde shorts, *The Life and Death of 9413—A Hollywood Extra*. Among Florey's more than sixty features are *The Coconuts* (1929, and the first Marx Bros. feature, codirected with Joseph Santley), *Murders in the Rue Morgue* (1932), *The House on 56th Street* (1933), *King of Alcatraz* (1938), *The Desert Song* (1943), *God Is My Co-Pilot* (1945), *The Beast with Five Fingers* (1946), and *Monsieur Verdoux* (1947, codirected with Charles Chaplin). Florey died in Los Angeles on May 16, 1979.

Hollywood Boulevard is unquestionably the best film ever made with a Hollywood filmmaking setting, far superior, for example, to *The Day of the Locust* (1975) or to Florey's earlier *The Preview Murder Mystery* (1935). It provides fascinating glimpses of Hollywood in the 1930's, of the Hollywood-land Sign, the Hollywood Brown Derby, Grauman's Chinese Theater, The

Trocadero, and Sardi's, as well as glimpses of filmmaking at Paramount, obviously staged but nevertheless realistic. More importantly, *Hollywood Boulevard* provides a useful social commentary on the Hollywood scene, its hypocrisy and its compromises.

After a montage of Hollywood landmarks seen under the credits, the film opens in the Brown Derby restaurant, where waiters are seen nailing a caricature of a new Hollywood star, Fred MacMurray, to the wall, and as they do the caricature of a fading star, one John Blakeford, falls to the floor. The two waiters discuss Blakeford, indicating that he is probably now walking Hollywood Boulevard, because "When they put the skids under you in this man's town, you're out," as one waiter succinctly puts it. The mood is set, and in the next scene we do indeed see John Blakeford (played in a suave and urbane manner by John Halliday) walking Hollywood Boulevard. He watches a new star put her footprints in the cement at Grauman's Chinese Theater and overhears a disparaging remark about himself from a child in the crowd. He purchases a newspaper after the newsboy has told him it contains a picture of himself, only to find that the photograph is next to a story about his being sued by his tailor.

When Blakeford visits The Trocadero, a popular Hollywood restaurant and night club of the period on the Sunset Strip, he learns the painful truth from the manager that he is heavily in debt to the establishment and his presence is no longer welcome there. It is also at The Trocadero—in the men's room—that he is approached by a wealthy publisher of scandal magazines, Jordan Winslow (C. Henry Gordon), and offered a considerable sum of money for his life story. Blakeford believes it is because he is a star, but Winslow is only interested in the scandalous love affairs in Blakeford's life. Winslow, unfortunately, is not aware that one of those scandalous love affairs was with his own wife, played in a typically cold and ladylike fashion by Frieda Inescort.

Hollywood Boulevard next moves up the coast from Hollywood to Santa Barbara, where the audience meets Patricia Blakeford's daughter, charmingly portrayed by Marsha Hunt—then new to the screen—who is first seen surrounded by flowers, a shot which accentuates her loveliness and innocent quality. Patricia meets a young writer, Jay Wallace, not too well acted by Robert Cummings, who appears to be giving an impersonation of James Stewart. Wallace gets assigned to a film starring temperamental star Flora Moore (Esther Ralston), another of Blakeford's ex-loves, and while the two are at a Hollywood nightspot, Wallace accidentally punches Blakeford—the punch was intended for a prying photographer—creating further publicity about the fading star and his love life.

Patricia visits her father and begs him for the sake of herself and her mother to end the magazine series. Blakeford has a contract with Winslow, however, which the publisher is unwilling to break, particularly now as he is also secretly financing a film starring Blakeford which will be successful thanks to the publicity from Blakeford's life story. Now Blakeford has met Mrs. Winslow and recognizes her. She goes to his house at night to beg him not to reveal her past, and when Blakeford tries to explain the predicament he is in, she shoots him. At this point, Winslow arrives and, learning the truth, agrees to cancel the series if Blakeford will say the shooting was accidental. No sooner have the Winslows left than Patricia arrives to apologize for her rudeness on her last visit. Unaware of her father's bullet wound, she rushes from the house to join Jay Wallace and drive to Arizona to be married.

She passes friends of Blakeford's as she departs, and when they find the wounded actor and call the police it is not long before Patricia is arrested on suspicion of trying to kill her father. Meanwhile Wallace has discovered that Blakeford had left the Dictaphone, on which he was recording his memoirs, still running while Mrs. Winslow visited him. Armed with the recording, Wallace visits the Winslows, and they and Patricia and the police all troupe to Blakeford's bedroom, where the wounded man announces his shooting was an accident.

If the plot sounds clichéd, the dialogue is even more so. At one point, Blakeford remarks, "Does it occur to any of you that we're acting like the characters in a play—and a very bad play?" Among the more interesting comments in the dialogue are "Only the young could be so bitter" and "Revenge is a pretty cheap emotion." The young writer, Jay Wallace, announces the title for the story he is writing about Hollywood will be "Too much too soon—too bad."

Interestingly, it was director Florey who provided the original story for *Hollywood Boulevard*, and, in fact, based the Cummings character on himself. When Cummings talks of writing a script for a monster movie, Florey is recalling his own first script for the original 1931 production of *Frankenstein*. Much of Florey's story and many of the Hollywood scenes that Florey shot were cut before the release of *Hollywood Boulevard*, as was a cameo by Harold Lloyd, leaving only one cameo appearance—by Gary Cooper—in the film.

What makes *Hollywood Boulevard* particularly fascinating is its use of silent stars, and there are more than twenty such players in the production, including Mae Marsh as Patricia's mother, Francis X. Bushman and Maurice Costello as directors, Charles Ray as an assistant director, Herbert Rawlinson as the manager of Grauman's Chinese Theater, Ruth Clifford as a nurse, and Betty Compson as a film star. No other film featured such an array of talent from the silent era, and the only regret is that too few of the stars receive adequate recognition on the screen. Only two, Creighton Hale (who was once Pearl White's leading man) and Jack Mulhall play themselves.

Hollywood Boulevard was well received by contemporary critics as a minor feature. *Variety* (September 23, 1936) thought it had "one of the best scripts ever possessed by a behind-the-scenes-in-Hollywood picture." Today, the film entertains and even enlightens as a social commentary. This is not a bad record for a "B"-picture of forty years ago.

Anthony Slide

HOME OF THE BRAVE

Released: 1949
Production: Stanley Kramer for United Artists
Direction: Mark Robson
Screenplay: Carl Foreman; based on the play of the same name by Arthur Laurents
Cinematography: Robert de Grasse
Editing: Harry Gerstad
Running time: 88 minutes

Principal characters:
Peter Moss	James Edwards
Major Robinson	Douglas Dick
T. J.	Steve Brodie
Doctor	Jeff Corey
Finch	Lloyd Bridges
Mingo	Frank Lovejoy
Colonel	Cliff Clark

For almost a century after Reconstruction the American black was consigned to the back of the bus, a third-class citizen in a society dominated by Jim Crow. Hollywood reflected and exaggerated this reality. Into the 1940's, most film parts for blacks were as servants or Pullman porter types, characters who seldom developed beyond the shuffling, one-dimensional "mammie/ Uncle Tom" stereotypes.

After the Great Depression and World War II, white movie audiences were no longer solely content with the mindless, entertainment-oriented musicals and melodramas which dominated the prewar cinema. A market emerged for films which examined inadequacies in the American system, particularly in the areas of race relations and religious discrimination. With television encroaching upon and soon undermining the box office, the studios had no choice but to comply with the wishes of their public.

Crossfire and *Gentleman's Agreement*, both released in 1947, focused on anti-Semitism. Two years later, no less than four major productions, each of which was well made and critically acclaimed, indicted racial discrimination while preaching tolerance and communication. Each featured protagonists who were black and three-dimensional, each being as honest, as tormented, and as complex as their white counterparts. Each film focused on characters who existed in a society that was inherently racist and who suffered solely because they were born with sepia skins.

In *Lost Boundaries* a light-skinned doctor and his family pass for white and are hypocritically shunned by their neighbors when the truth about their race is discovered; *Intruder in the Dust* features a black man who is falsely accused of murder; in *Pinky* a light-skinned nurse, who has passed for white while living in the North, returns to the racist ambience of her Deep South roots; and, finally, there is *Home of the Brave*. The first to be released, the latter picture is based on a critically acclaimed 1946 Arthur Laurents Broadway play about a young Jewish soldier. A black private named Peter Moss (James Edwards) is substituted in the film, which chronicles his mental breakdown after he is ignored and maligned by some of his fellow GI's while patrolling a Japanese-held island during World War II.

The plot is revealed in flashback. As Moss is examined by an understanding psychiatrist captain (Jeff Corey) after returning from the mission in a state of shock and paralysis, he relates a series of incidents culminating in his illness. In particular, he is bothered by a brazen bigot called T. J. (Steve Brodie), who mercilessly harangues Moss because of the color of his skin. He eventually breaks down when he sees his one real friend, Finch (Lloyd Bridges), killed. It is clear, however, that Moss's troubles are caused as much by the racism to which he was exposed while growing up in America as by the abuse he suffers during the mission. By the age of ten, he tells the captain, he was used to being called a "dirty nigger." After all, "If you're colored, you stink." Yet he is ultimately just another man fighting for his country and should be accepted as such. The film concludes on an upbeat note: Moss, now fully recovered, plans to open a bar with Mingo (Frank Lovejoy), a sympathetic white soldier. The partnership will work because the men respect each other as equals.

Home of the Brave, produced by Stanley Kramer, is one of the producer/director's first "message" films. It is the ancestor of Kramer's *The Defiant Ones* (1958) and *Guess Who's Coming to Dinner* (1967), integrationist features stressing unity between the races. Kramer's contribution is more noteworthy than director Mark Robson's, who that year also directed the hard-hitting *Champion* (1949) for Kramer, and whose uneven filmography ranges from the touching *Bright Victory* (1951) and gritty *The Harder They Fall* (1956) to the dull *Return to Paradise* (1953) and the atrocious *Valley of the Dolls* (1967).

To ensure a maximum amount of publicity and profits and to avoid pre-production protests, *Home of the Brave* was shot in secret. The working title of the project was later used for a film which Kramer produced a few years later and which now is a classic Western—*High Noon* (1952). No "marketable" stars were featured: Douglas Dick, Cliff Clark, and Corey were the only other members of the cast in addition to Edwards, Lovejoy, Bridges, and Brodie.

Yet the historical impact of *Home of the Brave* is monumental. The film, hopelessly dated by today's standards, is intended for white audiences since it depicts blacks in relationship with whites instead of as themselves, and since it ends on a note of well-intentioned although superficial idealism. Although well acted, and adequately scripted by Carl Foreman, the production is far too stagy. The film was, however, the first to deal directly and bluntly with racial discrimination and was also the first in which such words and phrases as "nigger," "nigger lover," and "boogie" were uttered on screen. *Home of the Brave* was praised for its forthrightness and honesty in 1949, with Edwards' acting singled out for commendation. The production was named to the National Board of Review's list of ten best films of the year. While it was banned in South Africa, the response to the film in America was heartening. For example, prointegration protesters picketed a segregated theater in Austin, Texas, in which the film was being screened.

The production, release, and acclaim of *Home of the Brave* marks the turning point in the manner in which black Americans have been depicted by Hollywood. This reception allowed for the acceptability of filming screenplays which explored and condemned racial prejudice. Of the four "message" films, *Pinky* was by far the biggest hit. It was the second highest grossing feature of the year, taking in $4,200,000. *Home of the Brave*, which cost only $511,000 to produce, was ranked a respectable twenty-seventh for the year and earned a tidy profit: box-office receipts totaled $2,500,000. *Lost Boundaries* was forty-eighth, with $2,000,000, while *Intruder in the Dust* (curiously, the best of the lot due largely to Juano Hernandez' bravura performance) was not among the top ninety-two films listed in *Variety*; it garnered less than $1,500,000.

A year after *Home of the Brave* was released, a young actor named Sidney Poitier appeared in his first film, *No Way Out*. That drama focuses on a young black doctor whose budding career is almost ruined by a racist hoodlum who accuses him of murdering the gangster's brother when the pair are wounded and hospitalized after an attempted robbery. Poitier's looks and charm enabled him to become the first black actor to achieve full-fledged Hollywood stardom. That success eluded Edwards, although the appearance and demeanor of the *Home of the Brave* star was certainly acceptable to white audiences. In the same year that the film was released, Edwards gave a sparkling performance as a perceptive young prizefighter in *The Set-Up*; the actor was then a prime candidate to become the model of the integrationist black who was to emerge on screen during the next decade. During the early 1950's he was effective as a patriotic soldier fighting the Korean War in *The Steel Helmet* (1951), and as a sightless GI befriended by a blind, bigoted white man in *Bright Victory*. He refused, however, to testify concerning his politics before the House UnAmerican Activities Committee and, as a result, lost a prominent role to Poitier in *Red Ball Express* (1952). He appeared inauspiciously in features ranging from *The Member of the Wedding* in 1952 to *The Sandpiper* (1965). His last part was in 1970, a bit as George C. Scott's valet in *Patton*. He died that same year.

Rob Edelman

THE HOME TOWNERS

Released: 1928
Production: Warner Bros.
Direction: Bryan Foy
Screenplay: Addison Burkhart and Murray Roth; based on the play of the same name by George M. Cohan
Cinematography: Barney McGill
Editing: no listing
Running time: 94 minutes

Principal characters:
Vic Arnold	Richard Bennett
Beth Calhoun	Doris Kenyon
P. H. Bancroft	Robert McWade
Mr. Calhoun	Robert Edeson
Lottie Bancroft	Gladys Brockwell
Joe Roberts	John Miljan
Mrs. Calhoun	Vera Lewis
Wally Calhoun	Stanley Taylor

Late in October, 1928, Warner Bros. released a third all-talking feature, *The Home Towners*. The studio had learned from its two previous experiences, *The Lights of New York* (1928) and *The Terror* (1928), that if a picture is going to talk, the dialogue must be worth listening to. *The Home Towners* was adapted from a successful Broadway play by George M. Cohan, and all of its players had had years of experience in the theater. As the weekly *Variety* critic noted, *The Home Towners* is probably the first instance in the use of dialogue where tempo is achieved. Every reel of *The Home Towners* is entertaining, and the situations build to natural climaxes, which could hardly be said for either *The Lights of New York* or *The Terror*.

Performances benefited also because Robert McWade, playing P. H. Bancroft, was translating to the talking screen a role he had successfully created on the New York stage. Bancroft is a do-gooder who comes from South Bend, Indiana, all the way to the big city to serve as best man at his best friend's wedding. The friend is Vic Arnold (Richard Bennett), a man in his late forties, of considerable means, who is about to marry a woman only about half his age, Beth Calhoun (Doris Kenyon). Bancroft suspects the worst, that the woman has to be a fortune hunter. To his mind no young lady of her years would consider a man of Vic Arnold's maturity. Bancroft's genial wife, Lottie (Gladys Brockwell), tries to keep her husband from interfering in affairs that are not his, but Bancroft's mind is that of the suspicious small-towner who believes that women seeking husbands have got to have an ulterior motive: in this case, the groom's considerable wealth.

Bancroft is well-meaning, but he is not content until his suspicions color Vic Arnold's thinking, and Beth, in a cool rage, returns her engagement ring. Almost at once, Bancroft learns that Beth and her family are richer than Arnold has ever been. Contrite, Bancroft now tries to patch up the differences he has caused, creating new suspicions and aggravating his own wife to a point that she almost washes her hands of him. The situation is finally resolved, however, and the wedding takes place, with the principals reunited, contrite, and ready to let bygones be bygones.

Onstage it was a typical Cohan domestic comedy, with believable characters in a believable predicament, and lots of good, hearty, middle-class American humor. All this was transferred to the screen. One would never know that Bryan Foy, who directed this very lively and human comedy, had also been the director for *The Lights of New York*. This time he was successful because he had a good script and better than competent actors. He wisely created an almost literal transcription of the successful Cohan comedy; he had enough sense not to try and improve it, but simply to stage it for the camera much as it had been played in the theater.

McWade's performance of a small-town American, complete with all his faults and prejudices, distrustful of any "citified" sophistication, is neatly balanced by Richard Bennett as the city friend who for once trusts his heart and is nearly brought to disaster by loyalty to an oldtime friend who has not kept up with the changing times.

Brockwell's performance as Lottie Bancroft is highly commendable, and Brockwell, one of the best players in silent films, a star at one time in her own right on stage and screen, was bound for a new career in talking pictures, where her talents as a character actress could well have been utilized. Unfortunately, the very next year after *The Home Towners*, in 1929, she was killed in an automobile accident in Hollywood.

The Home Towners was a talkie debut for Kenyon, who had been a star in silent specials at First National with her husband, Milton Sills. Widowed, she filmed *The Home Towners* the year following her husband's tragic death. Any criticism her performance evoked, largely that her voice was pitched too high to be natural, was to be corrected when the Vitaphone process of recording was abandoned. Kenyon continued as an important film player until 1939, and then played television roles successfully during the 1950's.

One thing that *The Home Towners* did was to show film producers that there was a market for domestic situation comedy, and the next decade was to exploit that genre to the fullest. It also showed conclusively that the one-hundred-percent talking feature was here to stay. With only two previous ones at Warner Bros., both of which had more than their share of faults, the talking feature nearly came of age in *The Home Towners*. Critics complained that the players still walked about the sets only in order to reach a vase of flowers or some *objet d'art* masking the presence of a microphone, but the actors were professional and went about their business naturally. Only a carping critic of the medium would know where a microphone might be hidden.

With every production, the talking feature showed more finesse. When one considers that the silent medium was based entirely upon pantomime, it is all the more remarkable that actors and directors could adapt so quickly to the talking feature, which made entirely different demands upon a player. There was more than visual action and reaction; vocal skill was mandatory. The players from the theater who were imported to Hollywood and did not click, failed because they lacked that one thing the silent player had made a part of his performance: action and reaction and expressing thought with the eyes, so often called "the mirror of the soul." With the talking film, listening was now more important than it had ever been because it was coexistent with speech. During the next year, 1929, the new art of the talking film would really reach its first fine budding.

DeWitt Bodeen

HORSE FEATHERS

Released: 1932
Production: Paramount
Direction: Norman Z. McLeod
Screenplay: Bert Kalmar, Harry Ruby, and S. J. Perelman
Cinematography: Ray June
Editing: no listing
Music: Bert Kalmar and Harry Ruby
Running time: 69 minutes

Principal characters:
Professor Wagstaff ....Groucho Marx
Harpo ....Himself
Chico ....Himself
Zeppo ....Himself
Connie Barley .... Thelma Todd
Jennings .... David Landau

Considered by some critics as second only to their masterpiece *Duck Soup* (1933), *Horse Feathers* is one of several classic films in which the Marx Brothers starred. It was their fourth film, and it is a remarkably balanced vehicle designed to exploit the brothers' singular comic virtues while at the same time merging each distinctive *tour de force* into a championship team performance. On the surface are the personalities and comic elements that have been so well remembered by American audiences. Groucho, as Professor Wagstaff, brims with his familiar insults and idiosyncratic romancing as he engages in some of the best anarchic, nonsensical dialogue of his film career. Harpo, whose infamous pockets this time even provide him a hatchet with which to cut in half a deck of cards, storms through his obsessive girl-prodding, slapstick, and gags. Chico, a bootlegger, projects his personal brand of swindling and connivery, and Zeppo, the straight man, portrays a character of more dominance with more screen time than usual. As in all of the films written specifically for the Marx Brothers, the viewer can expect nothing to be considered sacred. Nonsense is the name of the game.

Although inconsistent (as was usual), the plot seems uniquely suited to the Marx Brothers' individual talents. The film opens with Professor Wagstaff assuming the presidency of Huxley College. He accepts the offer in order to save his son, Zeppo, from a helpless infatuation with Connie Bailey (Thelma Todd), a campus widow. Zeppo is not concerned with his affair, however, and worries that his father may not meet the challenge of his new position. There has been a different president at the school each year since 1888, when Huxley last won a football game. Zeppo suggests that only a winning football team can remedy the sagging, infirm college, so Wagstaff goes off to a speakeasy to recruit a couple of athletes with whom he might beef up his team for an upcoming game against Darwin, a rival school. Chico and Harpo, who distribute contraband alcohol, are speak-easy regulars, and Wagstaff mistakenly recruits them for his team; the two real athletes were already recruited by Jennings (David Landau), who works for the Darwin team.

The fast-paced story jockeys back and forth along the paths that the different characters pave, allowing ample time for gags and general nonsense. Groucho tries to straighten out Zeppo's lovelife by paying a visit to the vivacious Mrs. Barley, and promptly attempts to seduce her. "I tell you, you're ruining that boy. You're ruining him. Why can't you do as much for me?" he begs. It is the beginning of a scene that features all four brothers, playing a classic game of hide-and-seek and musical couch. The innocent Zeppo is made a cuckold; Groucho cuts up with puns and his unique doing-one-thing-and-blaming-another routines; Chico swoons in Italian; and Harpo seems to capture the nature of it all by scrambling in and out of the room with a huge block of ice, finally heaving it through an unopened window. The scene also includes Chico and Harpo at their respective instruments, the piano and harp. As always, these musical numbers serve as an interlude to the burlesque, but the effect is achieved with performances that stress style rather than any serious musical interest. Certainly, Zeppo and Groucho's opening number, "I'm Against It," is more original and appealing than the later numbers. Perhaps instinctively, Groucho acknowledges the problem by walking up to the camera and speaking to the audience, "Listen, I have to stay here, but why don't you folks go out for a smoke until this thing blows over?"

Unfortunately, when the brothers separate again the sequences begin to lag and, with the exception of Groucho and Mrs. Barley's "romantic" canoe ride, lose the energy of the earlier scenes. This was not entirely the fault of the Marx Brothers, however; it was a musical comedy convention of the time to tie the film into a tidy, anticlimactic conclusion. The attention in the latter episodes all too deliberately focuses on the subsequent football game, which involves the expected pratfalls that lead to the expected results. The film ends abruptly with a brief scene in which Mrs. Barley marries each of the victorious brothers.

Horse Feathers is a particularly successful film because Norman McLeod, also responsible for *Animal Crackers* (1930), affords the Marx Brothers a relatively free hand to display their special brand of comedy. It transfers onto the screen the best of the personalities that took years of vaudeville and theater to develop. At one end of the spectrum, the leader, Groucho, is a supreme punster and comedian with a mouthful of insults, and Harpo, at the other end, is the champion gag-man who perfected his brilliant stage pantomine methodology on the screen. Their collective personalities provide a unique brand of catharsis for the audience with no punches held back. If they are funny, it is because the barrages of lunacy are cartoonish and absolutely detached. Groucho and Chico's conversational virtuosity penetrates a lavishly nonsensical world, like that of Harpo's, and stays there. The Marx Brothers' "lickety-split" craziness disguises its meaningful commentary. The audience is properly distracted and relieved of the social and political implications that dominate other schools of humor. At the base of the brothers' free-for-all comedy, there is a recognizable idealism. A kind of heroism, in fact, is found in their subversion of authority and in their ability to put themselves in positions of power, where, of course, they can be most destructive to society. When the Marx Brothers are given the screen time to be funny for humor's sake, as they are most of the way through *Horse Feathers*, a memorable piece of comic film history results.

Ralph Angel

THE HOSPITAL

Released: 1971
Production: Howard Gottfried and Paddy Chayefsky Productions in association with Arthur Hiller; released by United Artists
Direction: Arthur Hiller
Screenplay: Paddy Chayefsky (AA)
Cinematography: Victor J. Kemper
Editing: Eric Albertson
Running time: 103 minutes

Principal characters:
Dr. Herbert Bock ....George C. Scott
Barbara Drummond .... Diana Rigg
Drummond .... Barnard Hughes

The Hospital is a crowded, dizzying film, very much in line with Paddy Chayefsky's other work: an institution is dissected by a hero who is both close to the heart of its process and yet, in principle, embodies its opposite. In *The Americanization of Emily* (1964), the hero (James Garner) is a General's aide who preaches to his widowed girl friend the cult of his own very proud cowardice (one's real patriotic duty being, he feels, to avoid combat, stay alive, and perpetuate the species); in *Network* (1976), a formerly rational newscaster (Peter Finch) undergoes a conversion, or breakdown, and preaches on the air against the dehumanizing influence of television.

In *The Hospital*, the institution is a sprawling hospital complex, sparkling amid a section of tenements in New York City. Its hero is the hospital's Chief Resident, Dr. Herbert Bock (George C. Scott), recently divorced, alienated from his children, suffering from impotence, and spiritually bottoming out after having been proclaimed a genius in his early career. The hospital itself is a mess.

In the film's opening moments, a voice drily narrates as an elderly man, complaining of simple chest pains, is admitted to the hospital in the early morning and shuttled from floor to floor, receiving a variety of treatments for a variety of different diseases, each administered in ignorance of the other, until by evening he is dead from the conflicting treatments. "I mention all this," the narrator (Chayefsky himself) tells us, "only to explain how the bed in room 406 became available."

The story that follows is an account of two days in this medical inferno. The bed in question is used by one of the more sexually ambitious interns as a trysting spot to meet one of his girl friends. After they make love, she leaves him sleeping peacefully, and the next morning, he is found dead. He was a diabetic, and a night nurse, mistaking him for the bed's previous tenant, came in while he was still dozing and plugged him into a glucose bottle. Dr.

Bock enters the scene and is given an embarrassed account of all these events. He also hears the story of Drummond (Barnard Hughes), another old man, still alive but comatose, occupying the second bed in room 406: he was brought in for a check-up, in perfect health, and ended up having a kidney needlessly removed in an operation that damaged the other kidney. Bock is, to say the least, flabbergasted. "Where did you train your nurses, Mrs. Christie—Dachau?"

Dr. Bock has been on the verge of suicide, and that night, after a second dead intern has been found, implying murder but having taken place under similarly negligent circumstances, Bock sits in his office getting ready to give himself a fatal injection. He is interrupted by Barbara Drummond (Diana Rigg), the daughter of the old man still alive in 406. She has come to see about taking her father home. Drummond, who was once an eminent doctor himself, underwent a conversion, or breakdown, and now preaches the apocalypse to a tribe of Indians in northern Mexico. Barbara feels he would be better off there, having his kidneys looked after by Medicine Men.

This encounter between Bock and Barbara is the highlight of the film: Barbara, who is very sensual and wears her denim blouse almost totally unbuttoned, talks about her erotic and hallucinogenic experiences with a candor that arouses Dr. Bock in spite of himself; Bock, for his part, makes an impassioned speech, humorously defending his impotence and almost tearfully confessing his helplessness in the face of modern suffering. Barbara is nonplussed by his desire to kill himself. "Well, it's hard for me to take your despair very seriously, Doctor. You obviously enjoy it so much." Bock almost injects himself to prove that he is serious, but ends up smashing the bottle and pouncing on Barbara. The close brush with death seems to have left him potent; by morning he has, as Barbara puts it, "ravished" her three times. They are both very much in love and plan to pack up the old man and go off to Mexico together.

The old man, however, has other plans: he is not in a coma at all, but a self-induced trance, and rises occasionally (Frankensteinlike with his intravenous tubings), unplugging himself in order to prowl the hospital in the uniform of the first dead intern, which has been hanging ignored in his room's closet. It is he who is killing off the hospital staff. By mid-morning he has facilitated the death of a nurse by placing her unconscious on the gurney intended for a fifty-year-old woman: the mistaken identity goes unnoticed by the indifferent staff, and she is given an overdose of anesthesia. When Bock and Barbara catch up with him, he is on his way to dispatch the last physician on his list.

He explains to them that he is doing the Lord's work; he had been a witness to the death of the elderly man so drily narrated at the beginning of the story. The murdered interns and nurse each had a hand in the poor man's demise, and Drummond has been careful in each instance to make himself only the instrument of Divine Will—stopping short of murder but placing his victims in a position where the atmosphere of negligence and incompetence prevailing around the hospital would take its natural course. Bock and Barbara, realizing they have to act fast, get ready to take the old man and flee to Mexico before he attracts any more attention than he already has. However, the patient in the next bed overhears the entire confession.

As it happens, the last victim on Drummond's list, the physician who both removed his kidney and gave the erroneous and fatal diagnosis to the first old man, dies of a heart attack when he hears by telephone that his incorporated Medical Group on Long Island is being investigated by the Security Exchange Commission. The two lovers try to spirit the old man out of the building at this point; in the climactic melee that ensues, a confused staff member puts the name "Drummond" on the death certificate, and Bock, seeing the error, exchanges glances with Barbara but says nothing. Providence seems to have finished the job Drummond started.

They get the old man bundled into a taxi and are about to head for the airport, but Bock stops short of joining them at the last minute. Throughout the story, protesters have been encircling the complex, and now they are swarming into the building itself like a plague of locusts; colleagues of Bock's are abandoning ship, quitting on the spot, and he is pained at the sight. If Bock is married to anything, it is the hospital. "Somebody has got to be responsible, Barbara," he tells her. Although she is not happy about his decision, she nevertheless sees it would be fruitless to object, and leaves with her father. Bock, a healed man, steps back into the center of the chaos.

One of the problems so common to every Chayefsky script that it seems almost a trademark—like the witty dialogue and metaphorical-industrial situation—is that the hero, after tearing the institution apart brilliantly for the entire story, invariably turns around at the last moment and opts for the *status quo*. James Garner, as the General's aide in *The Americanization of Emily*, at his friend Emily's eleventh-hour urging accepts his role as war hero, despite his splendid eloquence of the previous two hours, so as not to let down the boys who are still fighting. Peter Finch as the newscaster in *Network*, after making perfect sense for three-quarters of the picture, does a complete about-face when given the hard sell by an equally witty but far less persuasive character. The backing-off never strikes one as genuine, although Chayefsky is crafty enough that on repeated viewings, the decision seems inevitable. In *The Hospital*, this flaw or idiosyncracy appears in force at the film's conclusion. Chayefsky's script, also a trademark, is for the most part ingeniously written: intricately structured, the dialogue is vivid and believable at the same time that all the characters sound alike. The rest of the ingredients—direction, performance, cinematography, editing—are models of fidelity to the Chayefsky script when they are not simply brilliant.

Arthur Hiller, who also directed *The Americanization of Emily*, does a clean job, is equal to every turn of the story, and keeps the actors moving at a pitch that is both vaudevillian and tragic; this is exactly what the script calls for. There are no obtrusive stylistic flourishes; the overall film has the look and feel of a documentary in its use of seemingly natural light and cuts that impose a tempo on the seemingly "found" workaday environment of a busy hospital. All of this adds to the nightmarish quality of the humor.

George C. Scott is magnificent as Bock. As always, he exudes vitality, even as his character is seemingly disintegrating, and in the manner of any great actor, he makes use of the paradox. His Bock is both coarse and elegant, and Diana Rigg is a sublime counterpart to him. Her role calls for someone who is rather cerebrally sexual, cool even about her appetite, but she brings this quality down to earth with her presence and offsets it with a very physical sensuality. The other performers—Hugh Barnard, the victims, the nurses, and the other doctors—all act with equal ability.

Upon its first release, the critical reaction to *The Hospital* was mixed (Pauline Kael called it "trash" but allowed that it was "funny and lively" and an "entertaining potboiler"), and audiences, either confused about whether to laugh or become depressed about the film's topical plausibility, shied away from it. Still, the film has persisted on late-night television and in rerun houses, entering film history in its own right and taking its place along with the best of Chayefsky's work. The screenplay won an Oscar, and, as with the rest of his films (more obvious here because in *The Hospital* there are more than sixty-seven characters), the script is the star.

F. X. Feeney

HOT MILLIONS

Released: 1968
Production: Mildred Freed Alberg for Metro-Goldwyn-Mayer
Direction: Eric Till
Screenplay: Peter Ustinov and Ira Wallach
Cinematography: Kenneth Higgins
Editing: Richard Marden
Running time: 107 minutes

Principal characters:
Marcus Pendleton .... Peter Ustinov
Patty Terwilliger .... Maggie Smith
Carlton Klemper .... Karl Malden
Willard C. Gnatpole .... Bob Newhart
Caesar Smith .... Robert Morley

Hot Millions is a crime caper, but it should not be dismissed as a nonsensical bit of fluff. It is a cleverly wrought, cosmopolitan comedy in which two of Britain's most accomplished performers skillfully display the broad range of their talents. A distinguished actor and director, Peter Ustinov tapped his writing genius to collaborate with Ira Wallach in creating a character perfectly matching his comic screen *persona*. Ustinov plays Marcus Pendleton, who is about to be released from a term at Wormwood Scrubs prison once he completes the falsification of the warden's tax return. He is a liberal who has been serving time for embezzling from the Central Conservative Office. Although he was caught not by the police but by a computer, he resents computers not for their crime detection but because they have rendered obsolete embezzlers who require books to juggle.

Once he is a free man on the streets of London, Pendleton is faced with the exigencies of finding a job. Our faith in his reformed ways is inspired when he picks up several booklets outlining careers in data processing seemingly in preparation for learning an honest trade. He reads them only to catch the jargon, however; he then poses as a gentleman, wearing a new, bought-on-time pinstripe suit and bowler hat, and gains entry into an elite club to hobnob with the upper classes. At the club, Pendleton astoundingly gleans enough inside information on the hierarchies of computer-based corporations to plot his next move. Robert Morley portrays a renowned British authority on computers, Caesar Smith. As part of his scheme Marcus cunningly persuades Smith to leave for South America to pursue his passion, moths.

The plight of Patty Terwilliger is meanwhile unfolding. Maggie Smith, an actress capable of such deeply dramatic performances as the title role in *The Prime of Miss Jean Brodie* (1969) and well-known as the blasé sophisticate in the play *Private Lives*, here exhibits her versatility playing Patty, a dizzy

London woman with an outrageous Cockney twang. All legs and no brains, she takes a flat in the same seedy rooming house as Marcus but is barely able to support herself because of her inability to hold a job. The dimwitted redhead fails as a meter maid, a bus conductress, and even as an usherette.

Now passing himself off as the computer expert Caesar Smith, Marcus is hired by Carlton Klemper (Karl Malden), president of Ta Can Co, an American industrial conglomerate headquartered in London. The secretary hired for him is, alas, Patty. Nearly as inept as Patty, Marcus bluffs his way through some tight moments, many under the gaze of suspicious Willard Gnatpole (Bob Newhart), Klemper's officious and unctuous right-hand man. Fearful of smudging her dress while coping with the yards of ribbon the typewriter has mysteriously spewed out, Patty one morning greets Marcus in only her slip. When Gnatpole learns of the compromising situation in which she and Marcus have been discovered, his interest in her is immediately aroused. To discourage Gnatpole, she invites Marcus to dinner when Gnatpole can hear her. Her boss reluctantly agrees, although he prefers returning to the office late at night to continue his nefarious investigation of the elaborate hardware.

One night Pendleton is discovered investigating the computer's failsafe system and is delivered to the alarmed Klemper and Gnatpole. His nonchalant tale that he was testing the equipment's security system ingratiates him with Klemper but further alienates the contemptuous Gnatpole, his rival at the office and for the affections of Patty. Marcus perseveres and is finally rewarded with the secret of successfully putting the computer out of operation when he secretly witnesses the company's charwoman warming her tea on one of the computer's hot coils, thus temporarily putting the machine out of function. He is then able to use the computer to his own advantage by programming it to print sheets of checks made out to bogus corporations of which Marcus is the "director." He makes monthly trips to a Paris bar, a Roman barbershop, and a Frankfurt bakery, the locations of these "corporations," to retrieve and cash the checks.

Because they discover that they can play classical music together—Patty on the flute and Marcus on the piano—and because Patty needs a means of support, having been fired by the computer for frequent tardiness, Patty and Marcus tremulously permit the deck of cards to decide their future: the queen of hearts decrees marriage. A dutiful but dotty wife, Patty retrieves the large amounts of foreign currency she finds carelessly left in her husband's suits as she sends them to be dry cleaned. Fearing for Marcus' health, she asks Gnatpole to relieve him of the great deal of foreign traveling he has been doing for the business, unwittingly alerting Gnatpole to the malfeasance.

So that he can collect one last time the checks awaiting him in Europe, Marcus has Patty, now wise to his scheme, detain Gnatpole to delay his investigation of the foreign affairs. Marcus has meanwhile learned of his impending fatherhood and resolves to provide a safe haven for his family in

Rio de Janeiro. He and Patty arrive there soon after Gnatpole discovers elegantly lettered corporate titles on the doors of the bar, barbershop, and bakery. The real Caesar Smith, called back from his moth-hunting expedition to explain to the board the technicalities of Marcus' machinations, is delighted with the embezzler's genius at mastering the system.

The enraged Klemper and Gnatpole, however, cannot press charges against Marcus lest the bad publicity force Ta Can Co stock to nosedive. Unknown to Marcus, Patty invites the two to Brazil and suggests that her husband be forgiven in exchange for one half of the thousands of shares of stock in Ta Can Co's holdings that she has bought these last months with the money she has gleaned from Marcus' suits. She further suggests for him the post of treasurer of the company. His flabbergasted colleagues are only too happy to comply. With the fortune Patty has amassed, the two are able to pursue their dream: Marcus as a flailing conductor of a symphony orchestra and Patty as his first flutist.

Even the most jaundiced critic will succumb to the endearing nuttiness and dizzy logic of this pair. The ease and timing with which they deliver their comic lines and droll asides are astonishingly delightful. Ustinov's facial gymnastics are brilliant and varied, particularly when he is putting on airs. His takes, especially in response to Smith's idiocy, clinch scenes, and director Eric Till swiftly cuts to the consequent action. The smooth composition of the film permits full attention to be focused on the humor.

The screenplay wisely spares us undue preoccupation with the details and tedious techniques of the crime itself. It is through depth of characterization of Marcus Pendleton that criminality is revealed. A man capable of intense concentration and tenacity, he is also highly inventive in coping with either a computer program or an empty-headed woman. If his lack of malice does not redeem him, his love and practice of fine music should temper our judgment of him.

Originally entitled *Hot Millions: Or, a True Tale of Crime and Rascality*, this absurdly funny film is sophisticated enough in its presentation and dialogue to provoke adult laughter, from giggles to guffaws.

Nancy S. Kinney

THE HOUND OF THE BASKERVILLES

Released: 1939
Production: Darryl F. Zanuck for Twentieth Century-Fox
Direction: Sidney Lanfield
Screenplay: Ernest Pascal; based on the novel of the same name by Sir Arthur
  Conan Doyle
Cinematography: Peverell Marley
Editing: Robert Simpson
Running time: 78 minutes

Principal characters:
Sherlock Holmes	Basil Rathbone
Dr. Watson	Nigel Bruce
Sir Henry Baskerville	Richard Greene
John Stapleton	Morton Lowry
Barryman	John Carradine
Dr. James Mortimer	Lionel Atwill
Sir Hugo Baskerville	Ralph Forbes

Sherlock Holmes, the violin-playing, drug-addicted, eccentric but brilliant detective of 221B Baker Street, London, is one of the world's most famous fictional characters. His translation into film was inevitable and continues into the 1970's with such recent offerings as *The Seven Percent Solution* (1976), and *The Adventures of Sherlock Holmes' Smarter Brother* (1976). Not inevitable, however, was the tremendous success of the series of Holmes films which started with *The Hound of the Baskervilles*. These films, running from 1939 through the late 1940's, constituted the most successful series of all time until the exploits of James Bond.

This first film in the series is the only one to make even a pretense of following one of Conan Doyle's original stories. This is understandable, for it is the idiosyncratic character of Holmes which led to the popularity of the stories, not the cleverly concocted exploits Doyle created for his hero. Similarly, the success of this film and the subsequent sequels is indisputably due to the incisive portrait of the detective created by British actor Basil Rathbone. According to one source, Rathbone was the highest paid and most steadily employed freelance actor in the Hollywood of his time. His roles were many and often distinguished, including Murdstone in *David Copperfield* (1935) and the arch villain Guy de Gisbourne in *The Adventures of Robin Hood* (1938). Nevertheless, he will be popularly remembered for his fine performances as Sherlock Holmes.

The Hound of the Baskervilles skillfully incorporates every aspect of the legendary detective: his expertise with disguise; his ever-present pipe, hunting cap, and cape; his scratchy violin performances at odd moments; and his secretive ways and boundless nervous energy. His drug habit is also suggested, albeit obliquely, in the film's last line: "The mystery is unraveled and all parties filled with gratitude." Holmes accepts all the parties' profuse thanks, and as he starts to leave, he turns and says: "Oh, Watson, the needle." At Rathbone's suggestion, Nigel Bruce was chosen to play Dr. Watson; this was a masterstroke of casting. Bruce became as apt a Watson as Rathbone was a Holmes. The contrast and unlikely friendship between the lean, quick, hawklike Holmes and the blustering, rotund, well-meaning Watson are a major appeal of the series.

The plot of *The Hound of the Baskervilles* is pure melodrama, resoundingly unrealistic, filled with red herrings, and thoroughly enjoyable. The current Lord Baskerville has just died mysteriously, and attempts are being made on the life of Sir Henry Baskerville (Richard Greene), the new heir to the estate. Rumors are abroad that the ancient curse of the Baskervilles begun in the time of the evil Sir Hugo Baskerville (*circa* 1650) is at work again. According to the legend, a vicious supernatural hound stalks Hugo's descendants to avenge his murder of a young peasant girl, an event which is effectively presented in the film in the form of a flashback.

The setting for the drama is a blasted, fog-enshrouded heath filled with treacherous quicksand pits. Even in daylight, the heath appears murky, and since most of the action takes place at night, the sense of menace is ever present. The sets for the film have a particularly appropriate gothic quality, and the camera work is quietly effective in the many shadowy, often candle-lit scenes.

Through a combination of brilliant deduction and bold action, Holmes at last uncovers the mastermind behind the present happenings at Baskerville Hall. He is John Stapleton (Morton Lowry), ostensibly a resident of the community, who is actually a distant relative of the Baskervilles. He has plotted the death of Sir Henry so that he will gain the Baskerville inheritance. Before this unexpected denouement, however, the audience's suspicions have been alternately directed to two incidental characters, Barryman the butler and Dr. James Mortimer, played admirably by John Carradine and Lionel Atwill. The plot obviously has a traditional gothic appeal, a fact which perhaps explains why the movie has been remade at least twice.

The Hound of the Baskervilles, however, has a significance beyond that of a gothic mystery. It represents a type of motion picture which has all but vanished from the scene: a professionally filmed, moderately budgeted B-movie designed to please a mass audience. As such, it falls between the most prevalent current offerings of American cinema, which are either high-budget and/or superstar vehicles or less professionally produced amateur efforts which appeal to special audiences.

Susan Karnes Passler

HOUR OF THE GUN

Released: 1967
Production: John Sturges for United Artists
Direction: John Sturges
Screenplay: Edward Anhalt
Cinematography: Lucien Ballard
Editing: Ferris Webster
Running time: 101 minutes

Principal characters:

Wyatt Earp	James Garner
Doc Holliday	Jason Robards
Ike Clanton	Robert Ryan
Virgil Earp	Frank Converse
Morgan Earp	Sam Melville
Andy Warshaw	Steve Ihnat
Pete Spence	Michael Tolan
Frank Stilwell	Robert Phillips
Curly Bill Brocius	Jon Voight

In the annals of the Old West, there are few events more celebrated than the shootout between the Earps and the Clantons at the O. K. Corral in Tombstone, Arizona. Wyatt Earp had made a name for himself as a lawman in the rough cowtowns of Wichita and Dodge City; by the early 1880's, he and his brothers, Virgil, Morgan, and Warren, had gravitated to Arizona Territory, where they became embroiled in a dispute with Ike Clanton, a local patriarch. Matters came to a head on October 26, 1881, when the Earps and their friend Doc Holliday, a dentist turned gambler, drinker, and gunfighter, shot it out with the Clanton gang at the O. K. Corral.

It was a classic Western scenario, and one that has attracted a number of filmmakers. *Law and Order* (1932), *Frontier Marshall* (1939), and *Wichita* (1955) all retold various aspects of the Earp story, as did *The Life and Legend of Wyatt Earp*, a popular television show of the 1950's. The two most notable tellers of the Earp tale, however, were directors John Ford and John Sturges. Ford's version of the Earp/Holliday legend was his magnificent *My Darling Clementine* (1946). Although Ford took more liberties with the facts than did other directors, *My Darling Clementine*, featuring Henry Fonda as Wyatt Earp and Victor Mature as Doc Holliday, is surely one of the finest Westerns of all time.

In 1957, Sturges first addressed himself to the shootout with *Gunfight at the O. K. Corral*, with Burt Lancaster as Earp and Kirk Douglas as Holliday. Both Ford's film and this one, however, concentrated on the development of the relationship between Earp and Holliday (with Ford adding a little romance along the way). These films, like the other versions of Earp's career, ended, for all practical purposes, with the dramatic gunfight.

Ten years after *Gunfight at the O. K. Corral*, Sturges shot what might be considered a sequel to his earlier film. *Hour of the Gun* featured James Garner as Wyatt Earp and Jason Robards as Doc Holliday, and dealt with the aftermath of the gunfight, as the survivors continued their feud. *Hour of the Gun* begins with the gunfight. As the credits appear on the screen, we see two bands of men maneuvering around the Corral. There is no dialogue, although the music on the soundtrack heightens the tension. Guns blaze, and the men inside the Corral fall dead, although several of their allies leave the scene without a fight.

The dead men, of course, are members of the Clanton gang; Ike Clanton (Robert Ryan) is one of those who abandons the field. There is a brief verbal dispute between the victorious Earps and the Cochise County sheriff, Jimmy Ryan (Bill Fletcher), who is on Clanton's payroll, and who attempts to arrest the Earps and Holliday for murder. It soon becomes clear that, whatever the specific incident that led to the showdown, the real battle is for political control of Tombstone, where Virgil Earp (Frank Converse) is the town marshal.

Sturges introduces most of the principals in the film through their testimony at the Earps' murder trial. First to testify is Doc Holliday, who describes his transformation from dentist to gambler thus: "I discovered that there was more gold in people's pockets than in their mouths." Robards' Holliday is a charming rogue with an irreverent disdain for the niceties of society, but he is also intensely loyal to his comrade: "I'd go to hell and back on the word of Wyatt Earp," he says defiantly. Next to testify is Ike Clanton, who suavely describes his hired killers as accountants and stock breeders. Lurking beneath his bland public mask, however, is a man completely without scruples, who has sacrificed his son Billy to try to gain political and economic control of Tombstone, and who is capable of treating his employees with the same contempt with which he treats his enemies.

Wyatt Earp is the last witness to take the stand. He calmly acknowledges his family's grudge (the nature of which is never specified in the film) against the Clantons, but just as calmly—and convincingly—denies that his feelings about the Clantons led him to commit any crime at the O. K. Corral. He and his colleagues were forced to kill the Clanton gang in the line of duty. Indeed, the concepts of duty and respect for the law appear again and again in Earp's statements in the early part of the film, reinforcing his image as a just and dispassionate man. As the film progresses, Sturges reveals that Earp's public image, like Clanton's, masks a darker side of his character. At present, however, this side of Earp is hidden from the audience, and from Earp as well.

As the trial ends, the judge weighs the evidence and finds the Earps and Holliday innocent; but their acquittal only serves to set the stage for more violence. At first, all of the violence comes from the Clantons. Determined

to eliminate his opposition, Ike Clanton orders the ambush first of Virgil and
then of Morgan Earp (Sam Melville). Virgil survives, although he is crippled
for life. Morgan is killed instantly. The two incidents snap something inside
Wyatt, although outwardly he remains calm. He secures an appointment as
federal marshal, with orders to hunt down Curly Bill Brocious (Jon Voight),
Frank Stilwell (Robert Phillips), Pete Spence (Michael Tolan), and Andy
Warshaw (Steve Ihnat), four of Clanton's hired gunmen who were identified
as Morgan Earp's killers. In addition, there is a five-thousand-dollar reward
for each man—if he is captured alive.

The film's perspective then begins to shift to that of Doc Holliday. Sturges
leavens the hunt for the four killers with occasional bits of humor—Holliday's
recruitment of a motley posse of two is priceless—but mainly we watch Holliday as he observes Wyatt Earp being eaten away by the desire for revenge,
to the point that he abandons any attempt to bring the men in for trial. He
simply catches up with them one by one and kills them. The problem, in
Holliday's eyes, is not that Earp kills the men who murdered his brother, but
that he refuses to acknowledge, to himself or to others, that he is killing for
revenge rather than for justice. In each instance, he tricks or goads his captives
into going for their guns, thus maintaining the pretense of shooting them in
self-defense. The audience is gradually persuaded into thinking what Holliday
knew all along: that Earp's actions are hypocritical.

Sturges introduces a subplot about Holliday's declining health—he is dying
of tuberculosis complicated by alcoholism—that takes Holliday and Earp to
a sanatorium in Denver. Watching his friend die slowly shakes Wyatt. He
begins to examine his own life and concludes that Doc was right about his
reasons for killing his brother's murderers: "I don't care about the rules
anymore. I'm not that much of a hypocrite." Word reaches Denver that Ike
Clanton has taken refuge in Nogales, Mexico. Earp determines to hunt him
down, and Holliday, although he fears for Wyatt's sanity if he succumbs to
the impulse to kill Clanton, nevertheless accompanies his friend.

They corner Clanton in Mexico, and in a tense scene, Sturges heightens
the excitement with humor. Holliday: "You got some kind of plan?" Earp:
"Yep." "You want to tell me about it?" "We take whoever gets in our way."
"You call that a plan?" "You got a better one?" "Nope." Visually, the gun
battle is reminiscent of the opening sequence at the O. K. Corral—there is
no dialogue, and the tension is maintained by expert staging and editing.
Inevitably, Earp shoots Clanton down. The film ends back in Denver. The
two friends part, awkwardly at first, and then affectionately. Earp rides back
towards Tombstone, there to pursue a career as a gambler. The dying Holliday
watches silently from the balcony of the sanatorium as his friend departs.

Aside from the unusual plot premise—following the careers of Earp and
Holliday *after* the O. K. Corral—*Hour of the Gun*'s principal charm lies in
the performance of its cast. In truth, the acting in the film ranges from

disappointing to outstanding. Garner, ordinarily a fine, relaxed actor, is surprisingly stiff as Wyatt Earp. In this film, Earp is a man whose sense of justice is confused by a stronger thirst for revenge—the type of role that John Wayne handled well in *Red River* (1948) and *The Searchers* (1956), for example—and Garner simply underplays the part. The result is that the geniality that Garner effortlessly breathes into less complicated characters such as Bret Maverick and Jim Rockford (his two popular television characterizations), is almost entirely missing in Wyatt Earp. Garner's performance is not bad, however; it merely pales next to that of Robards. Robards as Doc Holliday is the complete rascal. Writer Edward Ahnalt clearly saw Holliday as the film's most sympathetic character, a hard-eyed realist with a good heart and a sense of humor, and gave him the best lines. Robards obviously enjoyed the role and made the most of it. His performance is the highlight of the film.

Among the supporting cast, Fletcher as Sheriff Jimmy Ryan and a very young Voight as Curly Bill Brocious—both bad guys—stand out. Ryan is also fine in the role of Ike Clanton, the villain of the film. His Clanton was a truly contemptible man. He even hates his own employees. Ryan's best scene is at the Earp trial where his testimony is so palpably insincere that it is almost funny. Ryan made a career out of performances such as this.

Director Sturges' forte has always been the action film, as witnessed in his greatest successes—*The Magnificent Seven* (1960), *The Great Escape* (1963), and *Joe Kidd* (1972). *Hour of the Gun* is a typical Sturges film in this regard. Its best moments occur in the scenes in which explosive action or the threat/promise of such action occurs. The gunfight at the beginning of the film best exemplifies Sturges' skill. The sequence is filmed without dialogue because there is no need for it. The images on the screen are self-explanatory, and the staging and editing of the scene create a tension that renders words superfluous. It is in the intervals between the action sequences that *Hour of the Gun* occasionally bogs down. The presence of Doc Holliday, easily the film's most engaging character, remedies the situation in some scenes; but there are nevertheless undeniable lulls in the film.

Although imperfect, *Hour of the Gun* is in many respects a fascinating film. Sturges is to be commended for taking familiar characters and following them down unfamiliar paths. In addition to the exciting gunfights and the bravura performance by Robards, Sturges' film is a forerunner of the male bonding sagas that were to dominate American films in the 1970's. Sturges does not emphasize the relationship between Holliday and Earp in the same way that his successors would do eventually, but the dialogue between the two men before the final shootout could have served as the model for the entire script of George Roy Hill's *Butch Cassidy and the Sundance Kid*, produced two years later. Thus *Hour of the Gun* is eminently worth our attention.

Robert Mitchell

THE HOUSE ON 92ND STREET

Released: 1945
Production: Louis de Rochemont for Twentieth Century-Fox
Direction: Henry Hathaway
Screenplay: Barre Lyndon, Charles G. Booth, and John Monks, Jr.; based on the original story of the same name by Charles G. Booth (AA)
Cinematography: Norbert Brodine
Editing: Harmon Jones
Running time: 88 minutes

Principal characters:
Bill Dietrich .... William Eythe
Agent George A. Briggs .... Lloyd Nolan
Elsa Gebhardt .... Signe Hasso
Colonel Hammersohn .... Leo G. Carroll
Johanna Schmedt .... Lydia St. Clair
Charles Ogden Roper .... Gene Lockhart

The House on 92nd Street was the first of the Hollywood "pseudo-documentaries," a successful but brief film cycle that responded to a new interest in realism during the postwar era. The term "pseudo-documentary" relates to the manner in which these films re-create actual, documented events. *The House on 92nd Street* is based on a case history taken from the files of the Federal Bureau of Investigation. It also represents a move away from a studio-created product, and can be placed in the forefront of a trend toward location shooting. Earlier in 1945, Billy Wilder's *The Lost Weekend*, perhaps the most acclaimed film of the year, featured a scene in which Ray Milland walks up New York's Third Avenue trying to pawn his typewriter. Wilder used a hidden camera to film this harrowing scene on location, and critics of the day pointed to its effectiveness in giving the film a documentary feeling. In 1946, Roberto Rossellini's *Open City* was released in the United States, and the critical and financial success of this neorealist classic influenced the trend toward greater immediacy in the Hollywood fiction film. *The House on 92nd Street* also was a critical and financial success, as were subsequent pseudo-documentaries and the realistic, on-location films produced by Mark Hellinger at Universal, including *Brute Force* (1947) and *Naked City* (1948).

The motivating force behind the pseudo-documentary was producer Louis de Rochemont. De Rochemont began his career as a newsreel cameraman and then served as an editor with Pathé's newsreel division. He eventually became head of Time-Life's "March of Time" newsreels, and it was this series that exerted the greatest influence on *The House on 92nd Street*. The "March of Time" films used newsreel techniques to re-create important events of the day. Unlike newsreels as such, which filmed events as they happened, the

"March of Time" series perfected the art of staged documentary, adding a sense of drama to what had really happened. During the war, de Rochemont employed the methods of staged documentary to make several effective non-fiction films glorifying the American serviceman. Twentieth Century-Fox chief Daryl F. Zanuck had been impressed with de Rochemont's work. With studio production costs rising to an all-time high in 1945, Zanuck decided to try location shooting. To this end, he hired de Rochemont to head a production unit within Fox. De Rochemont was asked to apply the techniques of staged documentary to the fiction film. His first effort was *The House on 92nd Street*, followed by *13 Rue Madeleine* (1946) and *Call Northside 777* (1948). All three films were directed by Henry Hathaway. Another important pseudo-documentary produced by de Rochemont's unit was *Boomerang* (1947), directed by Elia Kazan. These films benefited from postwar perambulators which could achieve the same effects as heavier camera cranes, and fishpole microphone booms. This kind of equipment was light and mobile and made on-location filming practically error-free. Moreover, new techniques in film processing enabled studiolike lighting effects to be achieved in the laboratory.

The House on 92nd Street set the tone for the pseudo-documentaries to follow. Its elements include an anonymous narrator whose voice-over not only imparts factual information, but also editorializes. *The House on 92nd Street* combines actual newsreel footage with footage devised by the filmmakers to simulate newsreel footage (achieved by the use of grainy film stock). The film uses locations where actual events took place, including the FBI Headquarters in Washington, D.C., and a beauty parlor and bookstore in New York City. The use of little-known actors instead of stars in key roles adds to the sense of verisimilitude for which the film strives. The characterizations are purposely flat, and the dialogue is rendered in monotone. Later pseudo-documentaries, however, opted for proven box-office stars such as James Cagney in *13 Rue Madeleine*, James Stewart in *Call Northside 777*, and Dana Andrews in *Boomerang*.

The House on 92nd Street interweaves two stories. One concerns the inner workings of the FBI during the war, specifically its attack on enemy spy rings based in the United States. It is this story that employs the majority of the actual documentary footage. At one point, for example, FBI Chief J. Edgar Hoover is seen in his office. The second story takes us "behind the scenes" of the first story, detailing the events involved in "The Christopher Case." This story uses simulated documentary footage, combining it with actual locations and studio sets to produce a conventional spy thriller containing elements of the detective story. The story concerns Bill Dietrich's infiltration of a Nazi spy ring in order to discover the identity of the mysterious "Mr. Christopher," the head of a Nazi spy ring. In typical detective-story fashion, the identity of "Mr. Christopher" is not revealed until the end of the film. The only clue to his identity is the pair of pointed shoes he wears; these are shown in close-up at several key moments in the film. Dietrich (William Eythe) must find out who "Mr. Christopher" is and destroy the spy ring before the Nazis can transmit information about the development of the atomic bomb back to Germany.

The second story is shot in fairly conventional fashion, much in the manner of *film noir* thrillers of the era. The waterfront café sequences, for example, are vaguely expressionistic in tone and impart an aura of menace and foreboding. The spy ring's hideout is filmed in a decidedly *film noir* style as well, notably in the use of heavy shadows which are cast on the walls by Venetian blinds. A hidden room and hints of perverse sexuality complete the melodramatic picture. (Hathaway went on to direct several *film noir* thrillers during the 1940's, notably *The Dark Corner* in 1946 and *Kiss of Death* in 1947.)

The two stories are combined to glorify the FBI, which is shown as an efficient organization totally dedicated to upholding American democracy. In the process, scientific methods of detection are also praised. The film shows us such things as two-way mirrors and devices used to break codes. Ultimately, *The House on 92nd Street* demonstrates how both efficient crime-fighters and ordinary Americans such as Dietrich worked to achieve a common goal—the defeat of the Nazi menace. In general, de Rochemont in these films was concerned with showing American institutions in a good light. In *13 Rue Madeleine*, the Office of Strategic Services is lauded; in *Call Northside 777* it is the news media; and in *Boomerang* it is the American judicial system. This tactic is one not to be found in the Mark Hellinger-produced realist films, which were highly sensationalized in the manner of the journalistic exposé (Hellinger had been a Chicago newspaper reporter during the 1920's).

The pseudo-documentary cycle died out by 1953, when the techniques of staged documentary were appropriated by television. Conversely, Hollywood began to draw upon television-style fictional realism to move in another direction of cinematic depiction. Films such as *Marty* (1955), *A Catered Affair* (1956), and *Bachelor Party* (1957) illustrate this new trend. They examine the lives of ordinary, simple people in much the same way as did the Italian neorealist films, which by this time had successfully penetrated the American film market. De Rochemont grew weary of the increasing "Hollywoodization" of his films—the Zanuck-ordained move toward bigger star names and the distortion of the facts. He became an independent producer in the early 1950's, and while his modest films retained the documentary spirit of *The House on 92nd Street*, they never attained the same level of commercial success.

Audiences and critics of the day responded enthusiastically to the then-unique qualities of *The House on 92nd Street*. The film received an Academy Award for Best Original Story, and it appeared on the Ten Best Films lists of *The New York Times* and *Time*. It was also one of the top money-making films of 1945.

Although today's audiences are accustomed to location filming, hand-held cameras, and the use of factual material as the basis for filmed drama, *The House on 92nd Street* was a radical departure for its day. Its achievement lies in the way it demonstrates that Hollywood could move away from the studio to tell an exciting story (and the film is undeniably exciting, especially in its climactic rescue/raid sequence). Moreover, by using a minimum of glamor and stylization, the film merged documentary and fiction to satisfy a new public demand for realism.

Charles Albright, Jr.

HOUSE OF WAX

Released: 1953
Production: Byran Foy for Warner Bros.
Direction: Andre de Toth
Screenplay: Crane Wilbur; based on a screen story by Charles Belden
Cinematography: Bert Glennon
Editing: Rudi Fehr
Running time: 88 minutes

Principal characters:
Professor Henry Jarrod	Vincent Price
Lieutenant Tom Brennan	Frank Lovejoy
Sue Allen	Phyllis Kirk
Cathy Gray	Carolyn Jones
Scott Andrews	Paul Picerni
Matthew Burke	Roy Roberts
Sidney Wallace	Paul Cavanagh

By the early 1950's in the United States, television presented a threat to the film industry, and cinema producers sought special lures to seduce potential audiences away from their televisions and homemade popcorn and back into the theaters. One of Hollywood's most legendary attempts to recapture its audience was the special effect of three-dimensional cinematography, and the most famous "3-D" film of all is *House of Wax*, a grand and eerie chiller that ironically survives today, on television, as a Grand Guignol classic even bereft of its highly touted 3-D effects.

House of Wax was a remake of Warner Bros.' 1933 *Mystery of the Wax Museum*, an early Technicolor thriller which starred Lionel Atwill as Ivan Igor, victim of a wax museum fire that leaves him with an insane mind and a hideous face. It proved to be one of the 1930's best-remembered horror films, celebrated for the sequence in which ever-screaming Fay Wray attacks Atwill's face, a wax mask, and it cracks, revealing the monstrous effects of the fire. In revamping the film, Warners' gave *House of Wax* a late nineteenth century setting and decided to produce the film in 3-D and stereophonic sound in order to heighten the impact on the audience. Many in Hollywood, including Vincent Price, refused to take the idea of 3-D seriously. Initially, Price took Warners' proposal that he star in *House of Wax* as a joke; a lucrative offer, however, changed his mind. Production began under the direction of Andre de Toth, a one-eyed Hungarian whose handicap prevented him from seeing the final effect of the 3-D shooting. (Toth accepted the situation with rather pretentious stoicism: "Beethoven couldn't hear music either, could he?")

House of Wax tells the grisly saga of Professor Henry Jarrod (Vincent

Price), a sculptor whose entire life is devoted to the historical characters he re-creates in wax. When wealthy Sidney Wallace (Paul Cavanagh) visits him in the museum one evening, Jarrod introduces his characters, all but caressing his masterpiece, Marie Antoinette, to whom he apologizes for betraying her beauty secrets after explaining her construction to Wallace. Wallace is awed by Jarrod's beautiful wax creations and pledges his patronage to continue bigger and better projects; but they never come to pass. Jarrod's partner Matthew Burke (Roy Roberts) is determined to burn the museum and Jarrod's "people" for the insurance. In a thrilling sequence, Jarrod and Burke fight viciously as the museum becomes an inferno and the wax figures, faces, watching the brawl, melt into grotesque forms. While Burke escapes the flames, Jarrod is presumed burned to ashes.

A short time later, a reign of terror begins. Burke, about to wed giggly blonde Cathy Gray (Carolyn Jones in a charmingly comic performance), is murdered by a nightmarish figure with a fire-scarred face, a black cloak, and a broad-brimmed hat, who tosses Burke down an elevator shaft at the end of a rope to suggest suicide. Next, Cathy is slain in her bed and her body is discovered by her roommate, Sue Allen (Phyllis Kirk), who also discovers the black-clad monster in the room. A spine-tingling sequence ensues as the murderer pursues Sue through the fog-shrouded streets, his bestial breathing sounding in the night as the terrified girl seeks refuge at the home of her boyfriend, Scott Andrews (Paul Picerni). Scott has just been engaged as a sculptor to help Henry Jarrod, who reveals that he has escaped the fire, but is now confined to a wheelchair and has lost the use of his hands. Jarrod plans to open a new wax museum with a chamber of horrors which will terrify the patrons.

Jarrod's new museum soon has a gala opening, and Sue attends. There she is deeply upset by the statue of Joan of Arc, which bears a strong resemblance to her dead roommate Cathy. Adding to Sue's uneasiness is the fact that Cathy's body had been stolen from the morgue after her murder. Jarrod, seeing her distressed, glibly thanks her for reacting so deeply to his work, and all the while thinks how much Sue looks like his long-since melted Marie Antoinette. The inevitable soon happens. Sue, searching for Scott, ventures, with the characteristic recklessness of a horror film heroine, into the bowels of the museum, past a swinging devil and guillotine of the shadowy chamber of horrors. As she again passes the statue of Joan of Arc, she is unable to resist and lifts the black wig to reveal Cathy's blonde hair. "You shouldn't have done that, my dear!" says Jarrod, who rises from his wheelchair and begins stalking Sue. Hysterical, she strikes at his face, and the wax cracks, revealing the monster who chased her through the streets on that foggy night.

Meanwhile, police lieutenant Tom Brennan (Frank Lovejoy) has pieced together enough evidence to realize that Jarrod is a maniac who murders his victims and then coats them in wax for display in his new museum. Brennan and his men crash into the museum laboratory just before the crazed Jarrod embalms the naked Sue, who is coyly covered with a coat by Brennan in a touch that greatly amused 1953 audiences. Jarrod is knocked into his own vat of boiling wax and Sue is rescued.

Warner Bros. spared no expense in promoting *House of Wax* at its premiere in the spring of 1953. It was a gala Hollywood event, where the celebrities included Dracula-caped Bela Lugosi holding an ape-suited extra on a leash, and an onslaught of 3-D heralding publicity teasers, such as "SEE Crazed, Lustful Monsters leap from the screen INTO THE AUDIENCE!" In actuality, the special effects that the audience saw through their cardboard glasses were not quite so sensational. Aside from some bric-a-brac thrown into the screen, the most lavish 3-D effects concerned a ball on a paddle and some chorines can-canning their legs into the camera; and, in the final shot, Lovejoy thrusts onto the screen a wax head of Jarrod's assistant Igor, played by 1970's box-office star Charles Bronson. "What hath the Warner Brothers wrought?" demanded an outraged Bosley Crowther of the *New York Times*, lambasting the film for its "savagery," "brutal stimuli," "morbidity," and "idiocies." Yet *House of Wax* proved to be a box-office bonanza, and although not the first of the 3-D films (United Artists' 1953 *Bwana Devil* preceded it by two months), it became the most famous of them all, winning a spot on *Variety*'s Box Office Champions list with a $4.65 million domestic gross ($9.2 million worldwide) and establishing Price as the screen's top purveyor of gothic mayhem.

Despite the success of *House of Wax*, the 3-D craze swiftly extinguished itself. Exhibitors were not enthused about the maintenance of the cardboard glasses, which many patrons tried to sneak out of the theaters, or the need to run both projectors at once, or the dangers of lost picture synchronization, and moviegoers soon became more taken with newly developed Cinema-Scope. Such films as M-G-M's *Kiss Me Kate* (1953) and Hitchcock's *Dial M for Murder* (1954), shot in 3-D, were thus released "flat." In late 1971, *House of Wax* was rereleased in the original 3-D, proving a great curiosity to many film fans.

Even without the 3-D effects and the stereophonic sound, however, *House of Wax* is a sterling chiller, as proven by its perennial popularity on television. It boasts excellent atmosphere, frills of picturesque relief, and most of all, Price's fastidiously wicked performance as the horrific Jarrod. The star is, as *Time* put it, "splendidly clammy" as he lopes and gasps through the foggy streets in pursuit of the heroine, or gleefully informs the bound Sue Allen of her imminent death via boiling wax ("There is a pain beyond pain, an agony so intense, it shocks the mind into instant beauty!"), or suavely offers smelling salts to three young ladies when his Chamber of Horrors proves too much for their corseted stomachs. Price himself has vivid memories of *House of Wax*: "They didn't let us see any of it at Warners' until the entire film had been completed. And when I finally saw it, it scared the hell out of me!" *House of Wax* continues, in the fine tradition of the gothic genre, to frighten audiences as it has ever since its release.

Gregory William Mank

HOW GREEN WAS MY VALLEY

Released: 1941
Production: Darryl F. Zanuck for Twentieth Century-Fox (AA)
Direction: John Ford (AA)
Screenplay: Philip Dunne; based on the novel of the same name by Richard
   Llewellyn
Cinematography: Arthur Miller (AA)
Editing: James B. Clark
Art direction: Richard Day and Nathan Juran (AA)
Interior decoration: Thomas Little (AA)
Running time: 118 minutes

> *Principal characters:*
> Mr. Gruffydd .... Walter Pidgeon
> Angharad .... Maureen O'Hara
> Mr. Morgan .... Donald Crisp (AA)
> Bronwyn .... Anna Lee
> Huw .... Roddy McDowall
> Mrs. Morgan .... Sara Allgood
> Ivor .... Patric Knowles
> Dai Bando .... Rhys Williams

How Green Was My Valley was the last in a distinguished group of human dramas directed by John Ford during the late 1930's and early 1940's, including such films as *Stagecoach* (1939), *Young Mr. Lincoln* (1939), and *The Grapes of Wrath* (1940). This new film firmly established Ford's growing reputation as a successful commercial director. The film, like the novel on which it is based, became an instant popular success.

Richard Llewellyn's novel is a nostalgic remembrance of life in a late nineteenth century Welsh mining town. It is a first-person narrative, told by the aging coal miner Huw Morgan (Roddy McDowall) as he prepares to leave the valley that has been his lifelong home. The novel is essentially a collection of loosely related episodes in the lives of young Huw and his family, relying more on characterization and gentle humor than on a dramatically cohesive plot for its appeal.

The opening fifteen minutes of the film preserve the flavor of the novel almost perfectly. As the offscreen narrator (the adult Huw) begins to reminisce about his past, the audience is introduced in quick succession to young Huw, his older brothers and father (Donald Crisp) who work in the coal mine, his sister Angharad (Maureen O'Hara), and his mother (Sara Allgood). The skillfully assembled sequence establishes the peaceful order of this society in the past: the natural beauty of the valley and surrounding mountains, the community of miners who sing their way to and from work, the loving harmony of the Morgan family, the joyous wedding celebration for Huw's older brother Ivor (Patric Knowles) and his bride Bronwyn (Anna Lee). Employing vigorous narrative images with a minimum of dialogue, the sequence exemplifies one of the film's significant strengths.

The vision of this idyllic existence does not last, however. As the story moves forward, we see the gradual erosion and collapse of the Morgans' former way of life. Greedy mine owners begin to cut the wages of the miners, leading to disputes among them and eventually to a strike. Huw's older brothers angrily disagree with their authoritarian father about the strike and the formation of a miners' union and move out of the family home. Against this background of social and domestic upheaval, twelve-year-old Huw enters adolescence. One winter night Huw takes his mother up the mountainside to a secret meeting of the miners. On their return, mother and son become lost in a storm and nearly freeze to death. During his long convalescence, Huw finds a mentor in Mr. Gruffydd (Walter Pidgeon), the village minister who encourages him in his studies, and later, he attends the National School over the mountain in a neighboring valley. Mr. Gruffydd and Angharad fall in love, but because of his extreme poverty Mr. Gruffydd stoically declines to marry her, and Angharad consequently enters into an unhappy marriage with the mine owner's son. As the black slag heap from the mine spreads over the once-green and beautiful valley, we see the disintegration of Huw's world: his sensitive, musical brother Ivor dies in a mine accident, his other brothers emigrate to find work, his friend Mr. Gruffydd is forced from the valley by vicious gossip linking him with Angharad, and finally Huw's beloved father also dies in the mine.

Although considerable condensation and rearrangement were necessary to give the scenario a manageable length, the screenplay by Philip Dunne adheres to the episodic form of Llewellyn's novel. As a result, the film has a rather loose dramatic structure. Apparently as the result of a decision to cast a single young actor as Huw, the screenplay tends to emphasize the early episodes of the novel, which involve Huw at a younger age. The long section about Huw's difficulties at the National School—the taunting older students and his sadistic bully of a teacher—is included virtually intact in the film, and is one of the most satisfying sequences of the film. However, the young age of the actor is a minor disadvantage in a later episode when Huw as an older adolescent moves in with his sister-in-law Bronwyn in an attempt to take the place of his dead brother Ivor. This has considerable poignancy in the novel, but is merely amusing when played onscreen by a twelve-year-old.

The film benefits from very good actors who go a long way toward making the idealized simple folk of Huw's memory credible. Particularly effective are Donald Crisp and Sara Allgood as Huw's parents, the respective "head" and "heart" of the Morgan household; Crisp won an Academy Award for his performance as Gwilym Morgan. Roddy McDowall gives a memorable performance as the shy, sensitive Huw. In a smaller role, Rhys Williams gives a fine, lusty portrayal of Dai Bando, the professional boxer who teaches Huw to fight and who takes exquisite revenge on the teacher who beat Huw so mercilessly. The international nature of the cast, including as it does American, Irish, and Welsh actors, is responsible for a variety of vocal accents; as a result, the lilting Welsh speech is heard rather unevenly.

How Green Was My Valley is particularly distinguished by its richly detailed visual surface. The art direction was done with painstaking care. An entire mining village—stone houses, chapel, and colliery—were constructed at considerable expense for this film in California's Ventura hills. (This huge exterior set also appeared in several other films of the 1940's.) In fact, the memorable long view of the village, with the row of houses sloping uphill toward the mine at the summit, is the film's visual hallmark. Arthur Miller's superb black-and-white cinematography contributes much to this aspect of the film. His scenes are consistently arranged with care and with strong pictorial composition. In this film the camera itself moves only rarely, and then with clear, dramatic purpose: as Ivor's choir prepares to depart for a royal command performance, the camera pans slightly from the proud but troubled Mrs. Morgan in the foreground to capture a glimpse of two other sons who are leaving home to go abroad.

John Ford's direction of *How Green Was My Valley* confirmed his reputation as a master cinematic storyteller. His perfected narrative technique, weaving together a richly textured fabric of individual images and actions, nearly compensates for the rambling dramatic structure of the screenplay. His control seems to falter only in the film's occasional lapses into sentimentality. These can be partially justified, perhaps, as being inherent in the novel, as well as in the fact that overt sentimentality on the screen was then a more acceptable artistic convention than it is today.

How Green Was My Valley was a successful and highly honored film in 1941. It received Academy Awards in six categories, including Best Picture; but in making this last award, the Academy overlooked Orson Welles's innovative classic, *Citizen Kane*, choosing instead this more conventional and commercial motion picture. Nevertheless, *How Green Was My Valley* endures as a film of great visual beauty, nostalgic charm, and warm human feeling.

David Bahnemann

HOW THE WEST WAS WON

Released: 1963
Production: Bernard Smith for Metro-Goldwyn-Mayer
Direction: Henry Hathaway, George Marshall, and John Ford
Screenplay: James R. Webb (AA)
Cinematography: William H. Daniels, Milton Krasner, Charles Lang, and
  Joseph LaShelle
Editing: Harold F. Kress
Sound: Franklin E. Milton (AA)
Music: Alfred Newman
Running time: 165 minutes

Principal characters:
Lillith Prescott	Debbie Reynolds
Eve Prescott	Carroll Baker
Linus Rawlings	James Stewart
Zeb Rawlings	George Peppard
Cleve Van Valen	Gregory Peck
Roger Morgan	Robert Preston
Jethro Stuart	Henry Fonda
General Sherman	John Wayne
General Grant	Harry Morgan
Charlie Gant	Eli Wallach
Zebulon Prescott	Karl Malden
Rebecca Prescott	Agnes Moorehead
Confederate solider	Russ Tamblyn
Rulie Rawlings	Carolyn Jones
Mike King	Richard Widmark

How the West Was Won is a film gigantic in length, cast, history, screen size, and ambition. It runs for two hours and forty-five minutes, and the list of more than twenty stars is breathtaking. It is one of the last films to have been shot in three-camera Cinerama, which requires a very wide screen and produces wiggly lines where the end frames meet the middle one. What the film ambitiously tries to do, in five loosely interwoven episodes, is depict the conquering of the American West.

The script, for which writer James R. Webb won an Oscar, is imaginative in that it spreads itself over several eras from the early 1800's to long after the Civil War. Its geographical span is most of the continental United States, yet the broad scope of the story still manages to give the audience characters to care about. Lillith Prescott (Debbie Reynolds) and her nephew Zeb Rawlings (George Peppard) are the threads connecting the film's five episodes. Lillith, Zeb, and their families help to open up the Middle Western regions, cross the plains to California and the promise of gold, fight the Civil War, complete the transcontinental railroad, and bring law and order to the new land. Reynolds' character progresses from an unmolded girl to a shrewd old woman. The actress' enthusiasm and indomitable presence buoy up the film; without her, it would have lacked the spirit and poetry a work of this magnitude needs to sustain itself.

Lillith, her sister Eve (Carroll Baker), and their parents (Karl Malden and Agnes Moorehead) move West of civilization to find better farmland. After a quiet ride on an Erie Canal barge, they build their own raft to travel further into the wilderness. The girls' parents are killed on an impressively filmed ride over the perilous rapids. Eve wins the heart of a rough-hewn, freedom-loving mountain man, Linus Rawlings (James Stewart), and the couple settles down to farming. Lillith appears in the next sequence, a few years later, as Lily, the world-weary dance-hall girl. The knowledge that an old admirer has left her a gold mine in California spurs her to join a wagon train headed for the far West. Her adventures along the way include an Indian ambush and proposals of marriage from a straightforward rancher named Roger Morgan (Robert Preston) and a romantic, handsome gambler, Cleve Van Valen (Gregory Peck). She ends up with Cleve and a played-out mine. Never daunted, they decide to try to establish a West coast shipping industry in San Francisco.

In the next sequence, the Civil War is calling young men to arms. Eve's oldest boy, Zeb, follows his father into battle, despite Eve's attempt to ship him off to "Aunt Lil's" in California. In a quick vignette with John Wayne as General Sherman and Harry Morgan as General Grant, Zeb saves the future President's life when a Confederate soldier (Russ Tamblyn) tries to shoot him. Zeb returns to his parents' homestead to find his mother's grave next to the memorial for his father's war death. Expressing the restlessness he has inherited from his father, he leaves the farm to his younger brother and heads West. There, as a scout for the ruthless railroad builders, he witnesses the systematic and merciless removal of Indians from their land. When he protests to the foreman, Mike King (Richard Widmark), he is fired and moves on. Finally, years later, after Marshal Zeb Rawlings vanquishes the enjoyably stereotyped bad guy Charlie Gant (Eli Wallach), he and his wife Julie (Carolyn Jones) and their children settle down with the irascible old Lillith among the dusty buttes and mesas of the Old West.

In addition to the Prescott-Rawlings lineage, there are two other links between the five chapters. One is the narration by Spencer Tracy which occurs at the opening of the movie and at the beginning of each of the five parts. This narration, which is something like a history lecture, is saved from banality only by the power of Tracy's esteemed voice; it is nevertheless an artificial link, which, however necessary to continuity, does not integrate the film as a whole. The other, more unifying connection is the score. The theme music is an upbeat, driving tune that punctuates the movie. Lillith's theme is "I'll

Build You a Home in the Meadow," sung to the melody of the ancient ballad "Greensleeves." With the chorus repeating the words "Come, come, there's a wondrous land, for the open heart, for the willing hand," she sings it as a teenager on the brink of a new life, as a hard-working show-boat trouper, and as an old woman, to her grandnephews. It is a song full of optimism, as performed by Reynolds, who ably embodies in Lillith the resilience of the pioneers. Her energetic rendition of "Raise a Ruckus Tonight" boosts the flagging morale of the wagon train in the hostile hinterland. Other touches, such as banjo music and male choruses singing "Shenandoah" and "Erie Canal," draw on the rich vein of native American music. The M-G-M sound department won an Oscar for its effort.

The film is filled with fine cinematic and dramatic moments. The stampede of buffalo through a rail workers' camp, instigated by angry Indians, and a harrowing train ride during which Zeb defeats his archenemy Gant show the techniques of Cinerama put to excellent use. The acting is, in general, very good. Stewart gives a wonderful, wry portrait of an uncivilized man who allows himself to be tamed by a determined woman. Of the rest, Wayne in a brief role as Sherman, Henry Fonda as a buffalo hunter, and Robert Preston as Lil's earnest suitor offer outstanding performances.

The film had three veteran Hollywood directors, each of whom directed different sections of the film. Henry Hathaway directed the portions dealing with the early move West, the wagon train-gold rush, and the outlaws; George Marshall, those dealing with the railroad; and John Ford, those covering the Civil War. Marshall and Hathaway's segments are competently handled. Although film historians consider Ford to have crystallized the components of the Western genre, his portion of this picture is the least satisfactory. It comes across as contrived, and after the climax of the scene, it simply stops with no denouement. The Civil War episode concerns Zeb's disillusionment in the aftermath of the bloody battle of Shiloh. A Yankee, he meets a deserting Confederate soldier who encourages his anger and frustration. The two happen to overhear Sherman and Grant talking alone, and the Confederate soldier tries to shoot Grant. Zeb instinctively bayonets the boy and prevents the murder. Unfortunately, this part of the film was shot all too obviously on a studio sound stage, a glaring fault in light of the authentic locations of the rest of the movie. Another problem is Peppard, who fails to capture the mood of a young boy tired of war. Ford fails to enhance the melodrama of his portion with the flavor of epic mythology that it needs.

Among the great number of Hollywood Westerns, *How the West Was Won* is an odd case. In spite of its scope, it does not have the power of, for example, Ford's *Stagecoach* (1939); although there is much of quality in it, it will be remembered instead for its quantity. The events it chooses to illustrate are typical, but not archetypal, of the history of the West. In the 1960's, a loss of faith in mythology caused ambivalent attitudes reflected in this film. In one part, for example, the Indians are typical Hollywood villains, while in the next they are the victims of railroad entrepreneurs; the final image is one of assimilation as represented by Zeb's wife, who is an Indian, although she dresses like a white woman. The scholarly, "this is history" tone of *How the West Was Won* prevents it from being one of the last great Western epics. The film was quite popular with the public, perhaps because of its large number of well-known stars; it was the fifth-highest box-office success of 1963. It has attracted a large audience in its television showings, although its considerable length has usually led to heavy editing. Unfortunately, the best aspects of the film—its scenery and sound—have much less of an impact when shown on the small screen.

Stephanie Kreps

HUD

Released: 1963
Production: Martin Ritt and Irving Ravetch for Paramount
Direction: Martin Ritt
Screenplay: Irving Ravetch and Harriet Frank, Jr.; based on the novel *Horseman, Pass By* by Larry McMurtry
Cinematography: James Wong Howe (AA)
Editing: Frank Bracht
Running time: 112 minutes

> *Principal characters:*
> Hud Bannon .... Paul Newman
> Homer Bannon .... Melvyn Douglas (AA)
> Alma Brown .... Patricia Neal (AA)
> Lon Bannon .... Brandon De Wilde

Hud is a Western; but it is a modern Western, examining the manner in which the values of the Old West function in modern society. Essentially a four-character story, the film delineates the conflicts between the values of the nineteenth century and those of the twentieth century, as personified by Homer Bannon (Melvyn Douglas) and his son Hud (Paul Newman). Observing this conflict, and sometimes serving as reluctant participants, are Lon Bannon (Brandon De Wilde), Homer's grandson and Hud's nephew, and Alma (Patricia Neal), the ranch cook.

The film opens in the small town of Thalia, Texas, where Lon is searching for his Uncle Hud. Lon's transistor radio informs the audience that it is 6:00 A.M., and the cafe cook tells Lon that she has seen Hud's pink Cadillac parked down the street. Lon goes to the house and calls for Hud, who comes to the door buttoning his shirt. With a casual farewell to the woman inside, Hud leaves with his nephew just as the woman's husband arrives home. Hud is totally charming, arrogant, and amoral. It is obvious that his seventeen-year-old nephew admires and envies him very much. Hud is everything Lon feels he is not—sexually proficient, mature, capable, and attractive.

At breakfast Homer Bannon explains to Hud why he has sent Lon to find him. The elder Bannon has found a dead heifer and he is concerned. He instructs Hud and Lon to round up the herd while he calls the veterinarian. Homer is a stern, moral man, the exact opposite of his son. Clearly, Homer and Hud are very different role models for Lon, who is torn between the two—the glittering but corrupt uncle, and the cold but principled grandfather.

As they round up the herd and await the vet's diagnosis, Hud argues with his father about the future of the ranch. Hud wants to drill for oil, but Homer believes that oil wells would destroy the ranch and his way of life. The vet announces that the heifer has died of hoof-and-mouth disease, and that the entire herd must be destroyed before others are infected. Hud immediately suggests to his father that he sell the herd in the North before the government finishes the testing. Homer refuses, saying simply that he could not do that to his neighbors. The tensions between the two men intensify as they wait for the final orders to destroy the herd. Lon slowly realizes that Hud is not worthy of his admiration, and he comes to respect his grandfather and the values he represents. Hud tells Lon that he wants to have Homer declared incompetent and take over the ranch himself. Lon is outraged, but incapable of stopping his uncle.

At last the government is ready to destroy the herd. Bulldozers dig huge pits in the ground, and the cattle are herded into them. Cowboys shoot the cattle in the pits, and then the carcasses are limed and buried by the bulldozers. Only the longhorns which Homer has raised as reminders of the Old West remain. Lon tries to persuade his grandfather to save them, at least; but Homer silently walks out with his rifle to kill the steers himself. He returns a broken man, his way of life now only a memory. Meanwhile, Hud, drunk and wild, breaks into Alma's room and attempts to rape her. Lon stops him, but cannot persuade Alma to stay on the ranch. Lon takes her to the bus stop where Hud sees her leaving, and tells her that he will remember her as the one that got away. Alma replies that if he had not been so mean, perhaps she would not have had to leave.

As Lon returns to the ranch, he finds Homer crawling across the road; he has been thrown from his horse. Hud also arrives, and together they try to comfort the old man as he dies. After the funeral, Hud asks Lon to stay on, but Lon is now thoroughly disenchanted with his uncle and walks off the ranch. Hud is briefly shaken by this defection, but then shrugs and opens a can of beer as the film ends.

Homer Bannon is clearly a product of the Old West and of the nineteenth century. A stern, aloof man of principle and morality, he is clearly repelled by his son. Hud has no morals; he is greedy, self-centered, and has no interest in preserving his father's way of life. These might be described as twentieth century attributes, but Larry McMurtry, the author of the novel on which the film is based, has described Hud as a direct descendant of the same era that produced his father. The qualities that Hud exhibits are also qualities that built the great ranches and settled the frontier. Homer represents the best of the pioneer spirit; but Hud is in the pioneer tradition as well. Hud at one point asks his father what he has ever done for him, implying that had Homer been less rigid and more understanding, perhaps Hud would not now be the grasping, egotistical person that Homer finds so disgusting. The two men represent vastly different but equally influential attitudes in the traditions of the West—attitudes which still shape our lives today.

The role of Hud is perhaps Paul Newman's finest characterization. He brings to the part a charisma and a virility that are very attractive. It is difficult to despise the character totally, and it is very easy to understand why both Lon and Alma are so drawn to him. Newman was nominated for but did not receive an Oscar for the role; Patricia Neal did win the Academy Award for Best Actress for her role as Alma. Playing a small part, but one that is very important in softening the pyrotechnics of the male cast, Neal is both dignified and slatternly, motherly and earthy, in a memorable performance. Melvyn Douglas was awarded an Oscar for Best Supporting Actor; James Wong Howe won for Best Cinematography. Howe's camerawork added immeasurably to the film, framing the stark landscape in beautiful images. Martin Ritt, Irving Ravetch, and the art and set decorators were also nominated for awards, but did not win.

Don K Thompson

THE HUMAN COMEDY

Released: 1943
Production: Clarence Brown for Metro-Goldwyn-Mayer
Direction: Clarence Brown
Screenplay: Howard Estabrook; based on the novel of the same name by William Saroyan (AA)
Cinematography: Harry Stradling, Jr.
Editing: Conrad A. Nervig
Music: Herbert Stothart
Running time: 118 minutes

> *Principal characters:*
> Homer Macauley .... Mickey Rooney
> Tom Spangler .... James Craig
> Willie Grogan .... Frank Morgan
> Mrs. Macauley .... Fay Bainter
> Diana Steed .... Marsha Hunt
> Marcus Macauley .... Van Johnson
> Bess Macauley .... Donna Reed
> Tobey George ...., John Craven
> Ulysses Macauley .... Jackie "Butch" Jenkins

The prodigiously prolific William Saroyan made no pretense about being a "literary" writer, but the innocent appeal of many of his stories certainly stems from a poetic bent. He was unabashedly sentimental, with a penchant to recall and wax sentimental about his childhood, which he depicted as a time when everyone was good and there was no caste system. Saroyan was born of Armenian heritage in Fresno, California, in 1908. His early life was spent in an orphanage, and he worked at various jobs including one as a messenger boy for a telegraph office as did the hero in *The Human Comedy*. He began writing at an early age, and his message seemed to be one of cockeyed optimism: all men are created good, and if we laughed and sang a little more there would be fewer problems in the world. A man can hardly be criticized for such sentiments, but many realists have done just that, and *The Human Comedy* as both a film and a book has come in for its share of that criticism.

Saroyan was introduced to M-G-M studio head Louis B. Mayer by musical producer Arthur Freed. Mayer took an immediate liking to the ebullient Saroyan and purchased the story, *The Human Comedy*, for sixty thousand dollars, a sizable sum at that time. Mayer promised he would make Saroyan into another Irving G. Thalberg (the legendary head-of-production at M-G-M in the 1930's) and that he also would direct films. After closer scrutiny of the rambling, episodic story, however, the production and direction were entrusted to veteran Clarence Brown; all Saroyan was given to do was produce and direct a short. Even so, Saroyan took advantage of his mini-mogul status and had a grand piano installed in his office and spent many hours each day in the M-G-M projection room—not viewing what he had shot, but catching up on old M-G-M movies he had missed. He and Mayer later parted company, but the screen version of *The Human Comedy* still remained one of Mayer's favorite films.

It is easy to see how Saroyan's wholesome view of American family life, and childhood especially, appealed to the overly sentimental Mayer, and why the project was given a first-class production with a large cast of capable players drawn from the large M-G-M stock company. The movie dealt with real "folks" and real happenings in their lives, and it touched on the death of young American soldiers with a poignancy extremely significant during those World War II days.

The title, which many intellectuals ridiculed for its pretentiousness, actually refers to the story of one family, the Macauleys, who are comfortably poor and very American. Homer Macauley (Mickey Rooney) is one of four children in the fatherless family in Ithaca, California; he represents any teenager in any town. Marcus (Van Johnson) is his older brother and a private in the Army who is engaged to Mary (Dorothy Morris), who lives next door to the Macauleys and is considered a member of the family already. Homer's sister Bess (Donna Reed) goes to college; five-year-old Ulysses (Jack "Butch" Jenkins) is just an average, cute, freckle-faced boy from anywhere; and Mrs. Macauley (Fay Bainter) is an idealized version of the American mother.

With Marcus in the Army, Homer becomes the man of the household, and with that responsibility comes the obligation to help with the family's finances. To do his share, Homer takes a job as a night messenger boy for the local telegraph office. The office is managed by goodlooking Tom Spangler (James Craig), who is in love with Diana Steed (Marsha Hunt), the daughter of one of the town's wealthiest families. Saroyan makes it clear that although she is rich, Diana is a likable girl. Homer works the nightshift with Willie Grogan (Frank Morgan), one of the oldest telegraphers in the business. Willie is a philosopher and a drinker, and when he has had a few too many, one of Homer's duties is to sober him up. In his job Homer meets people from all walks of life. He learns that, regardless of their station in life, they are all human beings and most are good people. Because it is wartime, the most difficult message for Homer to deliver is the one that reads: "The Department of War regrets to inform you that your son has been killed in action."

During his school days Tom Spangler had been a 220-yard hurdles champion, and Homer sets out to emulate him. He does well with the sport but on the day of the big race, his hopes are shattered when he and his major competitor are told they must stay after school and thus miss the race. The track coach intercedes for the other boy, whom he regards as his most valuable player, and when the teacher learns of this favoritism, she dismisses Homer, who goes on to win the race. Tom congratulates Homer and also tells him that he has met Diana's family, and that they have consented to his and Diana's marriage. Meanwhile, the Macauleys learn that Marcus is to be shipped overseas. Before he goes, he visits his family, bringing along his Army buddy, an orphan, Tobey George (John Craven). The Macauleys welcome Tobey warmly and have hopes that one day he and Bess will marry.

Homer and Bess go to the telegraph office one evening to find Willie slumped over the telegraph machine. Homer assumes Willie has been drinking again but after splashing water on his face with no response, he realizes Willie is dead. He sees a half-finished telegram in the machine and reads it. It is addressed to Mrs. Macauley and it states that Marcus has been killed. Tom arrives to find the boy in despair, and they go off for a walk and to play a few rounds of horseshoes. At the railroad station they see Tobey walking with a limp. Homer goes up to him, and together they walk to the Macauley home where the two enter the house arm in arm. Homer has found a new brother.

The sentimentality of the story cannot be denied, but the theme, for all its naïveté has a universal appeal. It certainly contained a message for America's wartime population, particularly for the mothers of the young boys who were being killed in action. Most critics responded with phrases such as "eloquent and deeply moving," "compassionate with sheer beauty," and "a combination of great charm and tenderness." That certainly was Saroyan's purpose, and the picture proved extremely popular, with Saroyan winning an Academy Award for his screenplay. *The Human Comedy* was also nominated for Best Actor (Mickey Rooney); Best Cinematography (Harry Stradling); Best Direction (Clarence Brown); and Best Picture.

Those critics who did not like the film called it "sentimental goo" and "banal" and said that Saroyan's speeches for many of the characters were not only unspeakable but also came off like sermons. Saroyan's idealism could be at once disarming and irritating, and, particularly in this film, more precise editing was needed to remove some of the preachiness and long-windedness. Such editing would have helped the film show what it meant to show: real people in the honest pursuit of living and sharing the everyday happiness and disappointment that life brings.

The acting in the film raises it far above the level of the usual wartime sentimental story. Members of the cast including Morgan and Bainter give realistic, low-keyed performances, and Rooney gives a remarkably appealing and restrained performance as Homer. It is one of his best, being representative of American boyhood, and not displaying the show-off mannerisms that had become a part of his lighter assignments. Jenkins was a delight—a nonactorish, guileless Ulysses who was adorable without being too adorable, as frequently is the case with child actors.

Ronald Bowers

HUMORESQUE

Released: 1946
Production: Jerry Wald for Warner Bros.
Direction: Jean Negulesco
Screenplay: Clifford Odets and Zachary Gold; based on a story by Fannie Hurst
Cinematography: Ernest Haller
Editing: Rudi Fehr
Running time: 125 minutes

Principal characters:
Helen Wright ....Joan Crawford
Paul Boray ....John Garfield
Sid Jeffers .... Oscar Levant
Esther Boray .... Ruth Nelson
Rudy Boray .... J. Carrol Naish
Gina .... Joan Chandler

After Joan Crawford's remarkable comeback success in *Mildred Pierce* (1945), producer Jerry Wald realized that its very success spelled a real problem: her second comeback vehicle had to provide her with a new kind of role, and the picture had to have as much audience appeal as her first for Warner Bros. That studio did not have a backlog of stories that suited her, and it would have been wrong to put an actress who had just won an Academy Award in a remake of a Bette Davis feature.

However, Wald was planning to produce a remake of Fannie Hurst's story *Humoresque*, which as a silent had been the first picture to win the *Photoplay* magazine Gold Medal. It was to star John Garfield as a poor boy who became a great violinist. The big parts would go to Garfield and to the actress who played his self-sacrificing mother. Then Wald conceived the idea of introducing an entirely new character, a sophisticated woman who would come between mother and son. As Joan Crawford was casually looking over the upcoming projects at Warner Bros., she discovered the new character in *Humoresque* and was interested. Obviously, costarring Crawford with Garfield might mean a box-office bonanza. Screenwriters Clifford Odets and Zachary Gold expanded the new character of Helen Wright, the very rich neurotic who ignores her husband to concentrate on a series of young male protégés. She is near-sighted and wears large-rimmed glasses which she is continually putting on to peer more closely at some man who arouses her interest. She drinks incessantly and has a cutting tongue and a cruel sense of humor.

Crawford was intrigued with the character; she had never had anything like it during her M-G-M days, and playing so self-centered a heroine after all the shopgirls and rich young rebels she had played at M-G-M piqued her interest. There was only one trouble with the part: Helen Wright does not come into the picture until it is nearly a quarter over. The first part of *Humoresque* deals with the boyhood of a young violinist, Paul Boray (John Garfield), who is spurred on to fame in his adolescence through the faith and devotion of his mother. It is not until the boy is grown and becomes a promising young musician that he is summoned to play at a party given by Mrs. Wright (Joan Crawford). She is aware of her guests' interest in his performance, and, putting on her glasses, she moves closer to inspect him. His violin performance is arresting and completely professional, and it draws the plaudits of his audience. Helen tries to cut him down with a belittling remark, but in Paul she has met her match. Ambitious but fiercely independent, he scorns her first words, and they fight a verbal duel. She concedes that the world may soon be divided into two camps: pro-Boray and anti-Boray. "And which side are you on, Mrs. Wright?" he asks.

She has never been so much on the defensive; and she has also never been so attracted. Paul Boray, although considerably younger than she, has a positive belief in himself that fascinates her, and she determines to make herself important in his life. She furthers his career, eventually arranging an audition for him with the conductor of the New York Philharmonic Orchestra. Total opposites, they nevertheless become lovers. Soon she is hopelessly enamored of him; his music comes first in his life, but he does not deny that Helen Wright comes second.

This is not what his mother had planned, however. It was she who first became aware of his interest in music when he was still only a small boy. She had planned, prayed, and "gone without" so that Paul's career as a violinist could advance. She had never dreamed that so hedonistic a force as Helen Wright could come into her son's life. It had now become Mrs. Boray *versus* Helen Wright for the place of honor in Paul's universe.

The introduction of the character of Helen Wright created an entirely new story line in what had been a simple narrative in Fannie Hurst's original story. The wonderful success of the 1920 (silent) *Humoresque* had spawned a whole series of imitative "mother love" pictures, but in this 1946 remake, the character of Paul's mother, Esther Boray, all but disappears as the conflict between Paul and Helen is magnified.

Ironically, what was to have been a starring vehicle for Garfield, and then a costarring feature for Garfield and Crawford, grows into a sympathetic and glamorous starring role for Crawford. She had never been so glamorously gowned by Adrian as she is in this vehicle. Cameraman Ernest Haller photographed her beautifully, and director Jean Negulesco unintentionally favored her in every scene. *Humoresque* becomes Joan Crawford's film, and what had been the struggle of a poor young man to achieve his rightful place in the sun becomes the love story of an aging woman who has every material possession but is obsessed with a great love for a young man who is not in her world and has no need for her except to take what she can offer him toward the advancement of his career.

The picture had begun by adhering faithfully to the narrative Fannie Hurst had written for Frances Marion to adapt to scenario form for the silent screen. Beginning on Paul's birthday, the audience is made acquainted with his humble beginnings. His mother, Esther Boray (Ruth Nelson), sends her husband Rudy (J. Carl Naish) off to buy the boy a suitable present at the novelty story run by Sid Jeffers (Oscar Levant). The father suggests something like a baseball bat, but Paul, whose interest in music has already been aroused by his friendship with a pianist working in his father's store, has eyes only for a violin. Mr. Boray, angered by his son's stubbornness, takes him home with no present. His wife, seeing the disappointed tears of her son, marches downstairs, grabs the day's receipts from the cash register, and undaunted, goes out to buy the violin. That night, when Paul blows out the candles on his cake and opens the gift-wrapped violin, his face is so bright with surprise that his mother knows she has done the right thing. Her satisfaction grows day by day as she sees the intense determination of Paul to master that most difficult of instruments.

So much for the original premise, and, indeed, for Fannie Hurst and the prize-winning scenario of Frances Marion. Once young Paul Boray has grown up to be John Garfield and gone to play as a divertissement for a rich woman's guests, and that woman is Joan Crawford as Helen Wright, it becomes a different kind of *schmaltz*. What had been a story of mother love has turned into an impassioned romance—a love story enacted against a background of beautiful violin music ranging from Dvorak's plaintive "Humoresque" to the "Liebestod" of Tristan and Isolde from Wagner's opera as adapted for the violin by Isaac Stern (who in the film does the actual playing). What had been a drama of the miracle of faith has become a tragedy of a love too impassioned to survive in the modern world.

Paul rises quickly. His promise as a violinist is fulfilled, not because of the sacrifices made by his mother but because Helen Wright directs his life and career. Yet theirs is no happy love story. They argue constantly; he goes on long tours and she cannot accompany him, but must stay with a husband who does not even pretend to love her. Also, she drinks. Her drinking had always been a problem, but now it becomes a vice. Paul has broken with his mother, who is hurt by his open indifference to his family and humble beginnings. Helen's husband, aware of his wife's infatuation for Paul, realizes the truth when her emotion is no longer that of infatuation. She is completely possessed by love, and if not allowed to realize it, will destroy both herself and the man she loves. Helen's husband suggests that she divorce him so that she will be free to marry Paul. Together, they might achieve a mutual happiness; together, she might bring him lasting greatness in his career.

This sets the scene for the finale and Crawford's finest hour. She pays a visit to Paul's mother, who convinces her that marriage with Paul would only ruin him. Paul is soloist that night with the Philharmonic, but Helen does not attend the concert; instead, she goes out to her beach home and listens on the radio. Realizing that there is no hope for the love she had coveted, she takes her last drink, and then, as the "Liebestod" rises in a crescendo of longing, she walks out onto the beach and into the sea, bravely seeking her own resolution to a love that not only cannot be but is destroying the man she loves. This was pure Crawford magic, and the final scene of her trudging against the sea wind in her sequinned gown is one of those moments that is unforgettable. To one who has not seen the picture, it might sound like an imitation of Fredric March's suicide in *A Star Is Born* (1937); but Crawford makes it her own tragic dilemma, resolved with proper Crawford glamour.

Crawford and Garfield were old acquaintances. They had known each other from Group Theatre days, when, as Mrs. Franchot Tone, she had hosted many social gatherings to which Garfield had been invited. They play together effectively, but she often overwhelms him, as many actresses have done with their leading men. This was Garfield's last film for Warner Bros.; it was Crawford's second, leading to *Possessed* (1947) and a second Academy Award nomination.

Still, the role of Helen Wright in *Humoresque* shines as Joan Crawford's best since the brilliant M-G-M days. Oscar Levant maintains that the story of *Humoresque* as Crawford played it was based on a rejected script of *Rhapsody in Blue*, written by Clifford Odets. This may possibly be true, for it indeed reveals little kinship with the Fannie Hurst story or with the Francis Marion scenario for the silent version.

The score of twenty-three classical and seven popular numbers, which brought an Academy Award nomination for Franz Waxman (the score for *The Best Years of Our Lives* won), gives the film a place of honor in the history of film music. Garfield could not play the violin, and extraordinary tricks were employed to make him convincing as a virtuoso. The great Isaac Stern was originally slated to play for Garfield onscreen, wearing a mask of the actor. But this was abandoned after much work, and an even more elaborate device was substituted. In close-ups of Garfield playing, two violinists out of camera range follow the prerecorded Isaac Stern music, one doing the difficult fingering and the other the bowing. The effect is amazingly realistic, at least to the average moviegoer, since Garfield was frequently asked to play the violin at parties after the movie's release.

Larry Lee Holland

THE HUNCHBACK OF NOTRE DAME

Released: 1939
Production: Pandro S. Berman for RKO/Radio
Direction: William Dieterle
Screenplay: Sonya Levien; based on Bruno Frank's adaptation of the novel
  Notre-Dame de Paris by Victor Hugo
Cinematography: Joseph H. August
Editing: William Hamilton and Robert Wise
Art direction: Van Nest Polglase
Interior decoration: Darrell Silvera
Special effects: Vernon L. Walker
Makeup: Perc Westmore
Costume design: Walter Plunkett
Music: Alfred Newman
Running time: 114 minutes

Principal characters:

Quasimodo	Charles Laughton
Esmeralda	Maureen O'Hara
Dom Claude Frollo	Sir Cedric Hardwicke
Clopin	Thomas Mitchell
Pierre Gringoire	Edmond O'Brien
King Louis XI	Harry Davenport
Archbishop	Walter Hampden
Phoebus de Chateaupers	Alan Marshal
Procurator	George Zucco
Beggar	George Tobias
Phillipo	Rod La Rocque
Old Nobleman	Fritz Leiber

There have been three film versions of *The Hunchback of Notre Dame* and one television production. In 1923, a silent version directed by Wallace Worsley starred Lon Chaney as Quasimodo, Patsy Ruth Miller as Esmeralda, Ernest Torrence as Clopin, Tully Marshall as Frollo, and Norman Kerry as Phoebus, and was notable for its lavish sets and for the bravura performance of Chaney in one of his classic roles. A 1957 French version starred Anthony Quinn and Gina Lollobrigida as Quasimodo and Esmeralda. Despite the asset of Technicolor, this version was not as robust as its predecessors and was handicapped by the dubbing in of its English-language release. A British Broadcasting Company television version shown in the United States in 1977, with Warren Clarke in the title role, was well acted but had apparent low-budget production values. Additionally, James Cagney reconstructed a scene from the 1923 version in his film biography of Lon Chaney, *The Man of a Thousand Faces* (1957).

Though some scholars prefer Chaney's version, the critical consensus is that the finest and most memorable film of Victor Hugo's 1831 novel was made in 1939 by RKO, under the direction of William Dieterle, with Charles Laughton playing Quasimodo. Filmed and produced on an epic scale, it was at once an impressive spectacle, a poignant love story, and a masterpiece of the macabre.

The story begins in 1482, during the reign of Louis XI. It is both Epiphany Sunday and the Feast of Fools, and a vast throng of Parisians have turned out for the festivities. There are clowns, tumblers, dancing girls; it is a Brueghelesque carnival of medieval city life. Despite a prohibition against gypsies, a beautiful young gypsy dancing girl, Esmeralda (Maureen O'Hara), has managed to enter the city, hoping to plead with the King for tolerance for her people; in the meantime, she does magic tricks with a trained goat. Nearby, Pierre Gringoire (Edmond O'Brien), a poet and playwright, is trying to produce an allegorical masque of death and retribution, but the mob pays little attention and eventually hoots him down. Instead, the crowd clamors for a contest to elect a Pope of Fools—the person who can make the ugliest face. Numerous contestants are scoffed at, but suddenly the crowd gapes with horror and falls into an awed silence as the grotesque face of Quasimodo (Charles Laughton), the bellringer of Notre Dame cathedral, appears framed through a papier-mâché rose window at the back of the stage. The mob instantly acclaims him the Pope of Fools and crowns him with a jester's cap and bells. Quasimodo, a deformed foundling, has an immense hunchback, a misshapen face with one eye seeming to dangle halfway down one cheek, the other cheek twisted upward with the eye turned outward, a shapeless nose, and a mouth full of ragged teeth. His limbs are twisted and one leg is shorter than the other. Hitherto, he has been a figure of horror in the city, and he is now delighted to be the center of attention and seemingly of admiration. In an imbecilic way, he is enjoying himself immensely until the festivities are interrupted by the stern priest, Dom Claude Frollo (Sir Cedric Hardwicke), who has adopted Quasimodo and who now angrily orders his charge to return to the cathedral. The poor monster is crushed but obeys, holding on to the stirrup of his master's horse and dangling his crown in the other hand as he lurches along.

Though a priest who has taken a vow of chastity, the seemingly ascetic Frollo is a repressed sensualist who has been smitten with lust for Esmeralda. He sends Quasimodo to abduct her, but the hunchback appears as a malevolent apparition to the terrified girl. She flees, but despite his awkwardness, he has a grotesque agility and enormous strength, and he succeeds in intercepting and seizing her. However, the abduction is seen by Captain Phoebus de Chateaupers (Alan Marshal), a handsome gallant, who with his guardsmen succeeds in rescuing Esmeralda and capturing the hunchback.

Meanwhile, Gringoire, the discouraged playwright, having no money and no place to spend the night, accidentally drifts into the Parisian underworld and is suddenly alarmed to find himself in the Court of Miracles, a slum of thieves and beggars, where the lame and blind "miraculously" regain the use of limbs and eyes as they remove the sham deformities they use in their roles as beggars. Gringoire is taken prisoner and led before Clopin (Thomas Mitchell), the king of beggars. Intruders are usually put to death, but Clopin gives Gringoire a chance: if he can successfully pick the pocket of a mannequin spangled with bells and dangling from a rope, he can join them and live. Gringoire tries manfully but loses his balance and grabs the mannequin, which jingles crazily. Clopin is about to pass the sentence of death when Esmeralda, who has entered and observes the scene, takes pity on Gringoire and saves his life by taking him in marriage. Gringoire is enchanted, but she intends the marriage to be in name only, for she has become infatuated with the handsome Captain Phoebus.

Quasimodo, meanwhile, has been taken before a deaf judge. Deafened himself by the tolling of Notre Dame's massive bells, Quasimodo does not understand the judge's questions. Thinking the hunchback is mocking him, the judge sentences him to be bound to a wheel before Notre Dame, flogged, and left in chains at the mercy of the sun and the mob. Frollo refuses to intervene, and Quasimodo is tortured. After the flogging, the mob taunts him and pelts him with debris, but Esmeralda, passing by, takes pity on him. Though he had tried to abduct her only hours before, she braves the hostile crowd and gives him water. In his inarticulate way, he looks at her with adoration.

Frollo continues to burn with lust for Esmeralda, and when he finds her embracing the handsome Phoebus, in jealousy he stabs the captain. Esmeralda is arrested for murder, and because of her magic tricks with the goat, she is tried as a witch. Frollo's frustrated desire has turned to fear and hatred, and he becomes her chief prosecutor. After she confesses under torture, she is sentenced to be hanged in the square before the cathedral, as Gringoire stands by watching in helpless agony. From one of the cathedral towers, however, Quasimodo also watches. His dim brain comprehends the situation, and he begins climbing down the scaffolding of some construction and repair work being done to Notre Dame. Just as the hangman is about to carry out the execution, Quasimodo grabs a rope from the construction, swings down, seizes Esmeralda, and before the startled crowd can stop him, swings back with her into the tower, crying "Sanctuary!"

For the time being, Esmeralda is safe; she finds the misshapen hunchback to be a gentle, sensitive soul who protects her and respects her person. Although deaf, he can speak in a halting fashion, and she comes to sympathize with his loneliness and deformity. He has indeed repaid her for her mercy when he was tortured.

Meanwhile, fearing that the nobles will try to violate sanctuary and carry

Esmeralda off to execution, Clopin assembles an army of beggars and marches to rescue her. Gringoire tries to dissuade him, arguing that the pen is mightier than the sword and that he has written an appeal to the King, but Clopin ignores him. As night falls, his band of vagabonds arrives before the cathedral, but the doors are barred. When they try to force the gates, Quasimodo thinks they have come to kill Esmeralda. In an agony of suspense, he fights them singlehandedly, hurling down upon them a deadly rain of building stones and timbers from the construction. Undaunted, Clopin orders his men to pick up one massive timber and use it as a battering ram. Notre Dame is now under seige, and it looks as if the beggars will win, but Quasimodo lights fires under caldrons of lead intended to repair the roof. When the beggars have almost breached the door, he pours the molten metal into the rain gutters. It runs through the rainspout mouths of gargoyles and drenches the attackers in a deadly downpour, killing Clopin and defeating the beggars. At this point, the King's troops arrive, and Quasimodo realizes to his horror that he has fought the wrong side. Fortunately, however, Gringoire's appeal has reached the King and Louis has granted it, ensuring Esmeralda's safety.

Soon Quasimodo hears the bell that he has told Esmeralda to ring to penetrate his deafness if she is in danger. He clambers towards her eyrie to find that Frollo is pursuing her. Turning against the man who hitherto has been his master, Quasimodo in turn pursues the priest and after a brief struggle lifts him over the battlements and hurls him to his death. In the end, Esmeralda, realizing that she truly loves Gringoire, is carried off with him in triumph, as the forlorn hunchback sits alone among the gargoyles. He embraces one and says, "If only I had been made of stone, like you."

This ending does not follow Hugo's novel, in which Esmeralda is hanged, and her body taken to the charnel house of Montfaucon, where Quasimodo enters the vault and stays with her, embracing her body until he dies of starvation. Only the 1957 French film followed this ending; in the silent version, Esmeralda marries Phoebus, who is not dead after all but only wounded.

Even with some alteration in plot, the success of the story is practically guaranteed, with pageantry, suspense, spectacle, and a virtuoso role for the actor playing Quasimodo. It is, among other things, a variation on the theme of Beauty and the Beast, and part of its magic is a sense of legend. Although there never was a historical Quasimodo, his characterization entered folklore. RKO backed up the story with superlative production values. The sets were immense, and Paris was reconstructed on a vast scale in the San Fernando Valley. To direct, Pandro S. Berman chose William Dieterle, a German expatriate who had worked with Max Reinhardt in Berlin. In Hollywood, Dieterle was Reinhardt's assistant on the 1935 *Midsummer Night's Dream*. He directed a number of outstanding film biographies starring Paul Muni—*The Story of Louis Pasteur* (1936), *The Life of Émile Zola* (1937), and *Juarez*

(1939)—and was later to direct *Dr. Ehrlich's Magic Bullet* (1940), *All That Money Can Buy* (1941), *Tennessee Johnson* (1942), *Kismet* (1944), and *Love Letters* (1945). Leslie Halliwell calls him "all incomparable master of crowd scenes and pictorial composition," qualities particularly notable in his version of *The Hunchback of Notre Dame*.

Cast in the lead was Charles Laughton, who four years earlier had played a memorable Javert in Hugo's *Les Miserables* (1935). As a character, Quasimodo is a living counterpart to the gargoyles adorning the towers of Notre Dame. Lon Chaney had created his own makeup, which, although striking in 1923, now appears crude. RKO turned the job over to Perc Westmore, who covered the left side of Laughton's face with sponge rubber, hid the left eye, and made an artificial socket further down on the cheek. He pulled down one part of the face and pulled up the other. A contact lens gave the relatively normal eye a milky opacity. To make Quasimodo's deafness convincing, Laughton had his ears plugged with wax so that he would not show any reaction to sudden loud sounds. Not only did Laughton wear a hump made of four pounds of foam rubber, but his costume was padded and his torso encased in rubber to project a sense of immense strength. During filming in September, the heat was so great that perspiration sometimes washed away the makeup. Although a stand-in did most of the acrobatic scenes, Laughton's performance was a strenuously physical one: he had to swing on cathedral bells, haul heavy chains, move with a twisted, deformed gait. Although he suffered considerably during filming, he called Quasimodo "Probably one of the greatest parts any actor was ever allowed to play." The role of Quasimodo, having very little dialogue, consists largely of pantomime, with which Laughton managed to convey both terror and pathos. He made no attempt to copy Lon Chaney, observing that "Any actor who understands his stuff always plays to catch the tempo of the moment."

Part of that tempo was the beginning of World War II. The script makes a deliberate parallel between the persecution of the gypsies in the Middle Ages and that of contemporary Jews, and when Laughton was ringing the church bells, he said that he felt he was tolling them for mankind. William Dieterle wrote to Elsa Lanchester in 1968, "When Laughton acted the scene on the wheel, enduring the terrible torture, he was not the poor, crippled creature, expecting compassion from the mob, but rather oppressed and enslaved mankind, suffering injustice . . . ."

Nevertheless, several reviewers complained that the story was an outmoded shocker that, although well put together, should not have been resurrected in 1939. In one sense, *The Hunchback of Notre Dame* is a horror film; yet the monstrous hunchback is actually a kind of gentle person whose exterior ugliness masks his beauty of character. As a human being, he is superior both to the false priest and to the elegant and worldly aristocracy portrayed throughout the film.

The rest of the cast provided Laughton with sterling support. Nineteen-year-old Maureen O'Hara made her American debut as Esmeralda. She had acted with Laughton a year earlier in the British *Jamaica Inn* (1939). The Laughtons had become fond of her, and Charles arranged for her to play in *The Hunchback of Notre Dame*. Later, they made one more film together, Jean Renoir's memorable *This Land Is Mine* (1943). Edmond O'Brien also made his Hollywood debut as Gringoire; his previous work had been on stage with the Mercury Theatre. Although he later became a corpulent actor, O'Brien is almost gaunt as the starving poet, and he projects an idealistic intensity as the romantic hero. Sir Cedric Hardwicke, the saintly Bishop in *Les Miserables*, brings a cold, austere fanaticism to the repressed priest Frollo, while Walter Hampden, renowned for creating Cyrano on the American stage, is quietly effective as his saintly brother. Thomas Mitchell is an energetic, roistering Clopin. Harry Davenport is a curious Louis XI: instead of the traditionally sinister spider king, portrayed brilliantly the year before by Basil Rathbone in *If I Were King*, Davenport's Louis is a kindly, benevolent, grandfatherly monarch. In addition to this excellent supporting cast, thousands of extras swarm all over the film.

It has often been said that 1939 was the greatest year in the history of movies, yet despite its contemporary competition, *The Hunchback of Notre Dame* remains outstanding. John Baxter, in *Hollywood in the Thirties*, calls the film "Dieterle's triumph" and says it "has seldom been bettered as an evocation of medieval life, while Charles Laughton's portrayal of the grotesque Quasimodo makes even that of Lon Chaney seem feeble. The early sequences are of an unbelievable detail and intensity." The Feast of Fools sequence has an immense vitality, but there are equally brilliant sequences throughout. An atmosphere of superstitious fear prevails—from the opening with Gringoire's mystery play on the Dance of Death, through his infernolike descent into the Court of Miracles, and on through the interrogations for witchcraft. Among the unforgettable scenes are the Feast of Fools; the belled mannequin jangling insanely when Gringoire fails his test; Quasimodo on the wheel; the long unbroken shot where he swings from the cathedral to the scaffold and carries Esmeralda back to the church tower, crying "Sanctuary," while Gringoire and Clopin laugh hysterically from joy and the sound track breaks into a hymn of triumph; Quasimodo demonstrating the bells for Esmeralda, first starting them with a kick, then leaping bodily onto the great bell and riding it by its handles, laughing madly while she holds her ears in horror; and the entire episode of the beggars storming Notre Dame. Although Frank S. Nugent, reviewing the film for the *New York Times*, found the cast "expert" but denounced the story as "a freak show" with too many horrors and too much coarseness for his taste, what he calls coarseness is, instead, an energetic vitality. *The Hunchback of Notre Dame* was a huge hit upon release at Radio City Music Hall and subsequently around the country. It currently not only plays on television with some regularity but also has been revived at a number of RKO retrospectives.

Robert E. Morsberger

THE HURRICANE

Released: 1937
Production: Samuel Goldwyn for Goldwyn-United Artists; released by United Artists
Direction: John Ford
Screenplay: Dudley Nichols; based on Oliver H. P. Garrett's adaptation of the novel of the same name by Charles Nordhoff and James Norman Hall
Cinematography: Bert Glennon
Editing: Lloyd Nossler
Special effects: James Basevi
Sound: Thomas T. Moulton (AA)
Running time: 102 minutes

> *Principal characters:*
> Marama ....Dorothy Lamour
> Terangi ....Jon Hall
> Mrs. De Laage ....Mary Astor
> Father Paul .... C. Aubrey Smith
> Dr. Kersaint .... Thomas Mitchell
> Governor De Laage ....Raymond Massey
> Warden ....John Carradine

The tensions that create rich and complex characters and relationships between those characters, though internal in the greatest works of narrative, are the external structural determinants of *The Hurricane.* They take the form of a fundamental nature *versus* culture dichotomy, with the natives, sexuality, passion, freedom, and beauty opposed to law, prison, repression, duty, and honor. The film performs essentially the same ideological function as most of the "South Seas" genre in that it extols the natives for their "primitive" virtues and pits them against the corrupt ones of civilization. The interworkings of the forces of nature and culture are thus externalized and romanticized, and the critique of the white presence in the South Seas is emasculated. It is rather at the level of myth or parable that *The Hurricane* finds its expression, and it performs the myth's function of mediation and reintegration with great beauty and emotional satisfaction.

Like all myths, *The Hurricane* has a narrative past inscribed in its structure, as well as a narrator whose relationship to the myth is both privileged because he was there, and distanced because his involvement was primarily as observer and mediator, rather than as an agent of action. The film opens as a ship in the South Seas passes a desolate island upon which the wrath of God seems to have been visited. Dr. Kersaint (Thomas Mitchell) begins his role as narrator, telling the others that it was once the most beautiful island in the Pacific. The essential movement of the film has already been set forth. How did the island become scorched earth? A dissolve into the past immediately sketches the tensions which will come into conflict to produce the answer.

The European governor, De Laage (Raymond Massey), represents "the law" in his white coat and uncompromising posture. He is contrasted with the natives, Marama (Dorothy Lamour) and Terangi (Jon Hall), whose wedding is celebrated. The couple is identified with smooth freedom of movement, passion, and the trees and flowers of nature, as they run out of the church. Terangi is immediately linked with birds, an imagery which continues through the film. In the next of the series of oppositions, De Laage's wife (Mary Astor) arrives by ship. She is kinder and less formal than her husband primarily because, in terms of archetypes, women are always depicted as being aligned with the nature half of the nature/culture dichotomy, regardless of their cultural identification. Likewise, Marama displays a closer affinity to nature than does Terangi. His wish to wear a uniform cap and be "just like a white man" is the seed of their tragedy. The De Lagges' reserve is contrasted with the sensuality of the newly married couple. Further, Governor De Laage inhibits not only the natives but his own wife as well.

Once this is established, Terangi sails off to Tahiti, already nearly entirely corrupted by the influence of the Europeans, and leaves Marama behind. The best in Terangi, not the worst, will destroy him in this corrupt place. His imprisonment (building on his earlier linking with bird imagery) is determined through tensions constructed in the first sequence. Terangi's passionate nature, which cannot be suppressed, leads to a fight with a white man who disparages a present he has bought for Marama. The injustice which makes this a serious crime begins with the relationship of the governor with the native population. The governor as the agent of the law thus becomes Terangi's jailer, and the structural opposition is made concrete.

Terangi, with more libido than logic, cannot be confined. The visual depiction of the jail is dark and confining, with shadows, chains, and a sadistic warden (John Carradine). Terangi attempts to escape repeatedly, each time enduring savage beatings and suffering a lengthening of his sentence. Governor De Laage, who has more of a sense of honor and duty to the law than to his subjects, continues to carry out the cruelly mechanistic increasing of the sentence, in spite of the counsel of both his wife and the narrator. As a doctor, and because he is somewhat morally weak, Kersaint is closer to the European woman and to the natives than to De Laage. The source of Terangi's need becomes clear in the bird imagery and through a montage of dissolves between Marama and Terangi. His life and its sustenance are tied to his sensuality and to nature. He cannot do otherwise than try to escape, even as they systematically beat him down. The level of opposition and of injustice increases until Terangi escapes again, accidentally killing the sadistic guard. Upon hearing of the escape, the governor swears he will lock Terangi up again, but as the exhausted Terangi paddles his canoe to the island, he brings with him not the logic of the law, but the wrath of God. A hurricane hits the island. One of its first effects is to sweep the legal papers off De Laage's desk. The hurricane destroys everything on the island in one of the most impressive storm sequences on film.

At the same time, in a manifestation of the convergence of the forces of nature, a baby is born and Dr. Kersaint's role as mediator is best illustrated. He is able to give aid because he has not been acting on the side of the "antinature" forces. When the storm finally abates, many people are left alive, but no trees or buildings remain standing. Nature has destroyed the site of European cruelty, although the governor still retains the power of the legal system he represents. He has to give some indication of learning before the tension of the established opposition can relax. This is achieved, in accordance with the archetype, through his wife. Thinking her dead, he is so overjoyed when a canoe brings her to him that he runs into the water to greet her, and having been touched by it and by her, he says he will not pursue Marama and Terangi, who have given her back to him.

The romantic notion that Polynesians (like blacks) are closer to nature, simpler, more childlike, more sensual and musical than others is probably the least attractive aspect of *The Hurricane*. The abundance of destructive stereotypes in the film (the governor, the sadistic warden, and the unbelievably evil corruption of Tahiti) points up the archetypal level of the narrative, rendering it perhaps less dangerous, but no less savory. It is still the Europeans who can learn. They can take on some of the characteristics of the natives without losing their sophistication. The natives, who cannot learn and retain their sensuality, are destroyed by the contact with the developed culture, but not *vice versa*. A European has the role of narrator/mediator who can somehow be in touch with both poles. Further, as a doctor he is the agent of the life born of the storm. These are not agreeable aspects of the film, but at the level of myth *The Hurricane* delineates its task and performs it with amazing clarity, satisfaction, and grace. Despite the simplicity of the binary oppositions, Ford fills the space in between with life and emotional color, and the film is richly successful on that level.

A remake of the film by Dino de Laurentiis appeared in 1979, but it was not successful on either a critical or a financial level.

Janey Place

HUSBANDS

Released: 1970
Production: Al Ruban for Columbia
Direction: John Cassavetes
Screenplay: John Cassavetes
Cinematography: Victor J. Kemper
Editing: Peter Tanner
Running time: 138 minutes

> *Principal characters:*
> Harry .... Ben Gazzara
> Archie ....Peter Falk
> Gus ....John Cassavetes

The director is often the focus of critical comment on film. In many cases, especially European films, the director is also the writer. Even when this is not true, the *auteur* theory (which asserts that in most cases the director is the primary artistic consciousness behind the film, the one who "orchestrates" the creative contributions of others as well as having primary creative responsibility for camera and actor direction) spotlights the director. John Cassavetes is definitely the focus of attention generated by any of his films, but for an additional reason. Cassavetes is first an actor, and besides writing and directing *Husbands*, he is one of the three stars in this film which subjugates everything to acting performance.

In 1968, *Faces*, Cassavetes' highly experimental very personal film, was an unexpected commercial success. It was praised for its superb acting, emotional honesty, and its powerful, direct impact. This success gave Cassavetes a nearly blank check for *Husbands*, which he shot in the same *cinéma-vérité* style. This remains the most interesting element of *Husbands*: the subject matter dates rapidly and the acting begins to look overindulgent, but the style was experimental for 1970, especially in a big-budget commerical film. The film received a great deal of attention when it was in production and after it opened, most of which was centered on Cassavetes and his actors. It was considered an important film, honest, painful, powerful, and direct. Many articles about *Husbands* never reviewed the film at all, but instead interviewed Cassavetes (often with Peter Falk and Ben Gazzara, his costars) or bestowed lavish praise on the spontaneous style and described the actors' technique. Even those reviewers who did not especially like the film had nothing but praise for its fresh, daring style.

Husbands can not really be considered total *cinéma-vérité*. This style was made possible by faster film stocks which made shooting in available light possible and by portable, light sound equipment which made syncronous sound possible even in difficult locations, as well as by the acceptance of the

16mm format which made it economically feasible to shoot a great deal of film. This is necessary when the camera follows the action rather than the action being staged for the camera, and is an essential part of the *cinéma-vérité* aesthetic. The basic goal in *cinéma-vérité* is nonintervention. Used primarily in documentary and news films to give a "you-are-there" feeling, *cinéma-vérité* made it possible to dispense with many of the artificialities of fiction film—studio lights, studio sets, huge bulkly camera, and sound which was created and mixed primarily in postproduction. *Cinéma-vérité* relies on long takes which can follow action in one continuous shot rather than breaking it up into an edited sequence of long shots, medium shots, and close-ups. The technique gives documentary film a veracity, an honesty that greatly increases its power to affect people. Further characteristics of this documentary aesthetic include unscripted situations, use of "real" people (rather than actors), and no extraneous interpretative devices such as mood music, voice-over, or explanatory narrators.

Many clements of this style were readily adaptable to fiction film, where they created the same feeling of honesty and directness. *Husbands* is a scripted film, and all the actors are professionals, but there is a great deal of improvisation which allows the actors to be spontaneous rather than tied to line readings. This method gives their interactions and each individual performance a level of intimacy rarely seen. Scenes are allowed to run as long as they require, and the camera uses both long follow shots and close-ups which are often hastily composed. The working aesthetic is to let the acting dominate by being completely unhampered by the requirements of the shooting, and the technical imperfections which result are easily accepted as a small price to pay for the spontaneity of performances which are created right before the camera. It takes a great deal of film to shoot this way, since many scenes will ultimately not "work," and critical compositions or lines may be missed and have to be retaken. There were regularly two hours of daily rushes on *Husbands*, rather than the usual twenty to thirty minutes. Even in the editing, performance is king, and shots (with a far greater than average percentage of long takes) are arranged to maintain the intensity of the acting.

Husbands is about three men, friends and neighbors in a suburb of New York, for whom the death of the fourth member of their group triggers for each what might be called a "midlife crisis." They go on a two-day binge following the funeral, leaving wives and children behind in a nearly hysterical attempt to demonstrate to themselves that they are alive, free, young, and loved. They tussle like teenagers in the streets, punching each other and laughing; they go to a gym to swim and bounce balls and to a bar to drink and sing in boozy camaraderie, proclaiming their love for one another and then recoiling in embarrassment. Finally they end up vomiting and sick in spirit in a toilet, each afraid of rejection by the others and unable to name their growing anxiety.

Harry (Ben Gazzara) seems the most unstable, accusing the others of putting him down while he nervously puts them down. His marriage is breaking up, and he exhibits more overt homosexual yearnings than the others. He fights violently with his wife when the men briefly return home, then begs the others to go to London with him. They first refuse, then, after finding that they cannot simply resume their normal lives at work, they agree. In London the three behave like loud, abrasive Americans and try to pick up women in an achingly painful series of scenes. They return to their hotel with three women and then crowd awkwardly into one room, clearly reluctant to leave their buddies in this erotically charged situation. Only when Harry begins to cry and the woman he is with takes him off to his own room do they separate. Gus (John Cassavetes) has a violent, sometimes playful, but very neurotic lovemaking session with his tall blonde, and Archie (Peter Falk) has a tender and sad scene with his Chinese girl, who will not talk to him until later, when she runs out into the rain babbling in Chinese. The men regroup; Harry tries to get them to stay with him and three more women, but Gus and Archie finally leave for home. The two part at their neighboring driveways, laden with bags of toys for their kids, wondering what Harry will do "without us." The camera follows Gus into his driveway, where he kneels to hug his daughter and is greeted by his son saying "Boy, are you in trouble!" Finally Gus walks away from the camera around the corner of his house where, presumably, his angry wife waits.

The failure of all three men to communicate or achieve intimacy with anyone, including one another, is painful and powerful, but there is so much self-pity in their attempts and so much self-indulgence in their performances that it is difficult to maintain sympathy for them. Women are routinely trashed in the film, from Gus's hysterical dental patient (shot at an unflattering and vulnerable angle); to Harry's wife (who torments him by declaring she does not love him, demonstrating her greater loyalty to her mother, who seems to live with them, and finally even threatening him with a knife); to the English women (who range from a weird, heavily made-up elderly lady who seems ready to rape Archie); to the generally unattractive and often ridiculous women they pick up. Much of the source of their fear is sexual, and had this fear been expressed in relation to equally physically attractive (all three men are Hollywood-actor handsome) and emotionally appealing women, the film could have achieved a depth and poignancy. The women we see in the film, however, are so clearly deserving of the contempt and hostility they receive that it is difficult to see much emotional honesty in the men's pain.

Husbands looks today like an overlong (138 minutes in which many sequences run on with unintelligible dialogue or none at all), precocious film. The characters seem like spoiled, self-deceptive adolescents insensitive to everything except their own pain. The film remains interesting historically and for its *cinéma-vérité* style, but lacks the emotional honesty for which it was praised when it was released in 1970. Perhaps Cassavetes himself felt that the film could use some revision in style, for he announced in the spring of 1982 that a sequel to the story, using the same principal characters and cast, would be written and directed by him in early 1983.

Janey Place

THE HUSTLER

Released: 1961
Production: Robert Rossen for Twentieth Century-Fox
Direction: Robert Rossen
Screenplay: Robert Rossen and Sidney Carroll; based on the novel of the
  same name by Walter Tevis
Cinematography: Gene Shuftan (AA)
Editing: Dede Allen
Art direction: Harry Horner (AA); set decoration, Gene Callahan (AA)
Running time: 135 minutes

Principal characters:
Eddie Felson	Paul Newman
Sarah Packard	Piper Laurie
Bert Gordon	George C. Scott
Minnesota Fats	Jackie Gleason
Findlay	Murray Hamilton
Charlie Burns	Myron McCormick

With the release of *The Hustler*, director Robert Rossen returned to the kind of institutional corruption which he had studied over a decade earlier in *Body and Soul* (1947) and *All the King's Men* (1949). Similar to those films, *The Hustler* deals with the struggle to reach the top—in this case, the top of the world of pool. Walter Tevis' novel (1959) provided Rossen with the characterization of a skilled, cocky young man, Eddie Felson, whose self-destructiveness changes into a search for value, or "character," as he comes to call it, within that urban sordidness and criminality he can deny but never escape. Rossen, following the example of the European realists, especially uses his decor as the visual extension of the often twisted relationships among the principals. The film's art direction and cinematography both won Academy Awards; and Rossen handles his material with sureness throughout, although at times he lapses into an uncomfortable dreariness or harshness that results from his tight control. *The Hustler* was Rossen's penultimate film (he died in 1966). His last film, *Lilith* (1964), was commercially unsuccessful but has since gained more favor among critics, although *The Hustler*, because of its intensity and naturalistic detail, will probably remain better known.

Fast Eddie Felson (Paul Newman) is a pool hustler, an expert player who, by shooting a mediocre game, traps ordinary players into heavy betting and then wins carefully enough that those opponents fail to see they have been cheated. With his manager Charlie Burns (Myron McCormick) he goes to Chicago to challenge the famous Minnesota Fats (Jackie Gleason), who beats him soundly in a marathon contest. Eddie then meets Sarah Packard (Piper Laurie), a lame, alcoholic tramp attending college, and encounters Bert Gordon (George C. Scott), a gambler who offers to sponsor him; however, he refuses Bert's offer because Bert wants a seventy-five percent share of the winnings. A few days later, Eddie, recognized as a hustler, has his thumbs broken by one of his hustled victims and his friends. Once his thumbs are healed, Eddie and Sarah team up with Bert in Louisville, where Eddie beats millionaire Findlay (Murray Hamilton) at billiards. While there, Sarah, partly because of Bert's control over Eddie, commits suicide at the hotel. Eddie breaks up his association with Bert, then plays Minnesota Fats again, this time winning. When Bert demands his share, Eddie refuses, and, acknowledging Bert's warning that he will never play big-time pool again, walks out on him.

In Rossen's *Body and Soul*, boxer Charlie Davis has to learn to deal with his success; in *The Hustler*, Eddie must learn what he has to do to become truly successful, to graduate from hustler to respected professional. Eddie, as he begins this evolution, has his limitations clearly defined in the thirty-six-hour match with Minnesota Fats. After playing against him for some twenty-four hours, Charlie reports that Eddie had won eighteen thousand dollars, but Fats, although losing the games so far, understands how to win the match psychologically. With Eddie haggard, exhausted, and unsteady from the bourbon he has been drinking straight from the bottle, Fats goes to the men's room, and returns shortly with his hair combed, his face washed, and his clothes straightened, ready to begin anew. The effects of the bourbon and the sight of his now refreshed opponent overwhelm Eddie, who, in the final twelve hours, loses all but a few hundred dollars. Fats victoriously declares the match over.

In time Eddie learns what is necessary to win. Several days after the match with Minnesota Fats, he listens to Bert's carefully worked-out theory on the psychology of winning. Although Bert acknowledges that Fats has "more character in one finger" than Eddie has in his whole body, he still believes Eddie has displayed abundant talent. Fats had simply waited until Eddie lost control. Bert sees Eddie as a compulsive loser, but also a first-rate pool player, one who can learn what he needs to know to become a winner. It remains unclear how Eddie interprets Bert's arrogant rebuff, and not until after he has his thumbs broken does he admit that he needs Bert's help. In the match with Findlay, Eddie plays from a new psychological stance, and the game develops as a slightly modified version of Eddie's match with Fats. For the first part of the night Eddie loses. Findlay plays billiards rather than pool, and the difference between the two games keeps Eddie off balance, especially since his healing thumbs critically affect his shooting ability. Eddie handles himself with caution, however, finding out all he can about Findlay, as well as the game of billiards. Bert thinks he does not know when to quit, but continues to back him reluctantly, finally grasping the importance of Eddie's determination and restored self-esteem. Eddie has seen in Findlay the same carelessness arising from over-confidence that had let Fats beat him, and using it to his advantage, he wins twelve thousand dollars from Findlay.

Much of Eddie's regeneration comes from his relationship with Sarah, who takes him in shortly after his loss to Fats and cares for him while his thumbs are healing. Sarah's lameness from polio becomes an obvious reflection of an inner deformity: she represents an amalgam of various neuroses strengthened by a fully developed sense of self-pity, and has continued to attend college so that her parents will support her and her drinking. Her love for Eddie only manages to break down his devotion to his game while she is still alive; for Eddie, love and its attendant commitments have always meant suffocation. Yet, she communicates to him a notion of probity and of direction, convinced, apparently, that by saving him, she also saves herself. Sarah nonetheless lacks the sanity to integrate into her own life any of the values she attempts to instill in his, particularly the value of loving. She hates Bert for the hold he has over Eddie; it is one that corrupts him further and, to be sure, neutralizes her own influence on him. Eddie must necessarily reject her, for only by playing for Bert can he earn the front money necessary to meet Fats again. As Eddie returns from his match with Findlay, Sarah betrays him, as has Bert, and then slashes her wrists; but before she commits suicide she writes on the mirror in lipstick some of her favorite words—"sick," "perverted," "twisted"—condemning herself along with Eddie and her archenemy Bert.

In his return match with Fats, Eddie plays superbly, the way he did at the beginning of their first encounter, and is thus able to win handily, with Fats finally admitting defeat. The victory over Findlay, the emotional toughening that comes from Sarah's suicide, and the decisive break from Bert exemplify the "character" Eddie has been required to acquire in order to complement his unquestioned talent. Too late he sees the extent and the importance of his love for Sarah. He shoots dispassionately, almost aloofly, lecturing Bert on the necessity of moral awareness. The rematch with Fats becomes more crucial than ever for Eddie because of his newly found motivation and purpose. He must beat Fats, no longer to gain money or glory, but to redeem himself: the game of pool has been translated into a philosophical vehicle for understanding how the drive to win, unchecked by integrity, comes to degrade the human spirit. Bert evinces a wry tolerance for this speech which, after all, serves as Eddie's defense against Bert's earlier criticisms of him as a loser; Bert recognizes, moreover, as he did in the match with Findlay, the advantages brought about by Eddie's will to win, and turns it to his own profit. In time, Fats himself senses that the match is lost.

This film features Paul Newman at the beginning of his stardom, and his characterization of Eddie quietly moves from a brash, rootless hustler to a veteran with some facility for introspection, ever nudging the audience's attention toward the potential under the crude exterior. Yet, the film explores not so much the principal characters themselves as the shifting barriers among them. George C. Scott, who deservedly gained notice three years before in *Anatomy of a Murder* (1959), plays Bert, the entrepreneur who expertly fashions an astuteness born of cynicism and the right percentages. Whatever progress Eddie makes in aligning his goals with his own increasing perception of value, Bert tries to frustrate or destroy; this happens most notably in Findlay's billiard room, where a significant battle develops within the uneasy coalition of Eddie and Bert—a battle for personal identity and control that goes well beyond the money involved. Gleason's characterization of Minnesota Fats is a series of effortlessly posed stills, but the audience never forgets that it is watching Gleason, the comedian, in a dramatic role. The dapper Fats has a muted interaction with Eddie, to whom he remains more a legend than a man, and in the end, he proves to be discreetly sympathetic to Eddie's struggle to free himself from Bert's domination. Sarah's characterization on the other hand, reflects a major flaw in *The Hustler*, as Piper Laurie's self-consciousness with her role makes the power she can muster largely centripetal, even in the best scene outside a pool room, the picnic with Eddie, where he explains to her the elation that comes to him through winning. Most of the fault with Sarah, however, rests in script and direction: she is an obscurely drawn figure, a promising but finally ineffectual blend of a Dostoevskian prostitute and a malformed deranged character of Tennessee Williams. The ponderous middle section of the film suffers from sentimentality, disrupting the carefully executed hardness of the beginning and end. Although Eddie's relationship with Sarah is integral to the plot, it remains awkwardly conceived.

Placing its subject matter of pool aside, although half of the story takes place at a pool table, *The Hustler* works because of the central contest—one in which the young challenger upsets the informally crowned old master whose experience now compensates for his declining power. Rossen's aspirations to convey this contest have on the whole overreached his talents, although his pool room sequences are remarkably expressive. Ably supported by Deedee Allan's editing, Rossen frames a netherworld and its warped inhabitants, drawing out the violence and greed that underlie the competition of the contest. Nonetheless, the film ends with a kind of reconciliation: Eddie is the familiar antihero caught in a menacing, sterile environment; Bert, the confident percentage player who never lets his ego interfere with profits to be taken. Eddie recognizes that Bert, belonging to a gambling syndicate, has the means to destroy him to whatever degree he desires, and that Fats is but one of the stable; but Bert, once again moved by Eddie's determination, permits Eddie to walk away with all the money in his pocket. The fact that Eddie has begun to assume the values of the outside world now saves him, for Bert realizes that Eddie is lost to him forever.

William H. Brown, Jr

I AM A CAMERA

Released: 1955
Production: Romulus Production; released by Distributors Corporation of
    America
Direction: Henry Cornelius
Screenplay: John Collier; based on the play of the same name by John Van
    Druten, adapted from the *Berlin Stories* by Christopher Isherwood
Cinematography: Guy Green
Editing: Clive Donner
Running time: 99 minutes

> *Principal characters:*
> Sally Bowles ....Julie Harris
> Christopher Isherwood .... Laurence Harvey
> Natalie Landauer .... Shelley Winters
> Clive .... Ron Randell
> Fraulein Schneider ....Lea Seidl
> Fritz Wendel .... Anton Diffring

The film *I Am a Camera* begins with a prologue in the form of a publisher's
cocktail party in honor of Sally Bowles (Julie Harris), whose book of reminiscences has just been issued. One of the guests is Christopher Isherwood
(Laurence Harvey), an established writer, and this introduction serves as a
vehicle for Chris's own recollections of the time years before when he had
first known Sally during the early 1930's in Berlin.

During the resulting flashback, Chris is living in Berlin and supporting
himself by giving English-language lessons. He hopes one day to become a
writer and thus justifies his situation of being impoverished in Berlin by
believing that this is giving him an opportunity to observe and experience
life, so that he will eventually be able to use his experiences in his writings.
In one of the initial scenes, Chris explains that his aim as a writer is to be
an impersonal observer. An author must look at life and subsequently be able
to portray it as though he were a camera.

In one of the cabarets typical of the period, Chris and his friend Fritz
(Anton Diffring) meet Sally Bowles, an English girl who is performing there.
It is apparent that Sally does not have great talent as a serious stage performer;
however, she is good-natured and uninhibited. People like her and she enjoys
life. However, Sally is jilted by her lover. When she discovers that he has
gone, in her rage and frustration she goes on a rampage smashing whatever
she can get her hands on. Now stranded in Berlin, Chris befriends Sally and
she subsequently moves into his flat. Both are broke.

Almost at once, however, Sally meets a wealthy American named Clive
(Ron Randell). One of the major sequences in the film occurs at a wild party

thrown by Sally and Clive in the latter's hotel suite. Chris, who has worked himself into a state of exhaustion, has to be dragged from his bed against his will in order to get him to go to the party. As more and more people arrive at the party, Sally is determined to have a good time and forget the preceding weeks of destitution. While the party is going on, several doctors give the semiconscious Chris a series of hydrotherapy treatments. This whole party sequence, composed of the portrayals of unconventional guests and the treatments of the sick Chris, is comparable in incongruity to a Marx brothers' film. When Chris wakes up the next morning, he finds to his surprise that he is feeling fit and cured of what was probably a hangover.

In the weeks that follow, Clive takes Sally and Chris to the races, the theater, the casino, and other entertaining places. He helps them both financially, thus enabling them finally to enjoy themselves. Their newfound life style is in contrast to the situation of the majority of people in depression-ridden Berlin. Clive next proposes to take Sally and Chris on a world tour; Sally starts making preparations and Chris is also willing to go. At this point several scenes are inserted in the film to reveal the extent to which Chris is made more aware of the growing power of the Nazis in his day-to-day business when he discovers that the Nazis are making life difficult for his Jewish student Fritz and his fiancée Natalie (Shelley Winters).

Chris and Sally's life of leisure soon evaporates, however, when a telegram arrives stating that Clive has left Berlin. Although Sally had been counting on Clive's continued help, Chris tells her that she was foolish to expect life to have continued as it recently had. Sally and Chris quarrel, and he orders her to move out. Later, Chris visits Fritz, and, on his way home, becomes involved in a street brawl with some Nazis, an encounter that makes him more aware of the increasing reality of Fascism. When Chris returns to his flat, he finds Sally, who announces that she is pregnant. Chris offers to marry her so that the baby will not be born out of wedlock, but Sally favors an abortion as the best solution. Sally's pregnancy and the couple's lack of money are the stimuli that finally encourage Chris to write an article which is accepted by an editor, who gives him more important assignments. Although Sally now agrees to marry Chris, it is only after Chris gets drunk because of his doubts about the burdens he is assuming, that Sally casually states that she has miscalculated her period and that there is no baby. With their marriage plans dropped, Sally gets an offer to join Clive and become a movie star in Paris. She leaves Berlin and Chris immediately, and the film ends with an epilogue—a return to the same cocktail party with which the film began. Sally is still the same carefree Sally and, of course, broke again. Thus, once more, Chris takes her in.

When British-made *I Am a Camera* was released in the United States in 1955, it was denied the then-important Production Code seal of the Motion Picture Association. A similar fate had happened two years earlier to the film *The Moon Is Blue*. While there is no single daring visual image in *I Am a Camera*, as was the case in the former film, verbal allusions went contrary to the conventions of the time. The dialogue in *I Am a Camera* casually refers to such topics as virginity, sexual intercourse, having a child out of wedlock, abortion, and miscalculated periods of menstruation. However, the characterization of Sally Bowles is so outrageous and Julie Harris' performance so accomplished, that the remarks seem more amusing than shocking. In any case, the film set a precedent by incorporating subjects previously considered taboo into the dialogue of a successful general release film.

I Am a Camera* was intended to be a comedy, and it succeeded. Most of the film's attention is focused on the high-spirited, good-natured, but amoral Sally Bowles. Christopher Isherwood, interpreted by Laurence Harvey, is the cool, impersonal observer who only gets personally involved in life through the efforts of Sally Bowles. However, there is a more serious side to *I Am a Camera*. Since the story takes place in Berlin during the early 1930's, the time and place of the film's action necessarily evoke reflections on the rise of the Nazis, the depression in Germany, and the difficulties increasingly being experienced by the German Jews. While these subjects are peripheral to the main story of Sally and Chris, the intrusion of the real world upon the madcap adventures of Sally Bowles provides contrast and poignancy through its juxtaposition of what we know to be real and that which is make-believe.

The musical *Cabaret* (1972), starring Liza Minnelli, was a remake in color of *I Am a Camera*. While this later version more explicitly covered the topics merely discussed in *I Am a Camera*, the film's emphasis still centered on Sally Bowles—an extravagant but ingenuous personality functioning in a frantic and depraved environment. Once again, the story served both as a superb vehicle for the actress playing Sally Bowles and as a historical commentary on the time and place of the story.

Mark Merbaum

I AM A FUGITIVE FROM A CHAIN GANG

Released: 1932
Production: Hal B. Wallis for Warner Bros.
Direction: Mervyn LeRoy
Screenplay: Howard J. Green and Brown Holmes; based on the story "I Am a Fugitive from a Georgia Chain Gang" by Robert E. Burns
Cinematography: Sol Polito
Editing: William Holmes
Running time: 85 minutes

> *Principal characters:*
> James Allen .... Paul Muni
> Marie Woods .... Glenda Farrell
> Helen .... Helen Vinson
> Pete .... Preston Foster
> Barney Sykes .... Allen Jenkins

I Am a Fugitive from a Chain Gang was a typical 1930's Warner Bros. product and marked the transition from prison to topical films. Following a series of pictures centering around prison life, such as *The Big House* (1930) and *Twenty Thousand Years in Sing Sing* (1933), this film was an attempt to show not only how brutalizing prison life can be, but also how forces within society can conspire unjustly to imprison a man and trap both his body and his spirit.

Mervyn LeRoy initiated the project in 1931 by bringing to Jack Warner's attention a book he had recently read, the autobiography of a man named Robert Burns who had escaped from a Georgia chain gang and was living quietly in New Jersey, a state which had no extradition agreements with Georgia. The book described the incredible tortures and barbaric practices then prevalent in that state. LeRoy was moved by the book and convinced Warner that it would translate into a great motion picture. With Hal B. Wallis assigned as producer and LeRoy as director, the three men arranged to have Burns secretly smuggled into Hollywood to act as technical adviser. Burns was understandably reluctant to leave New Jersey; his life was at stake, since California and Georgia did have an extradition agreement. LeRoy kept the author's presence a secret, however, and Burns provided invaluable assistance, especially to Paul Muni, who was to play the chain gang victim.

Muni had come to films from the stage and had scored a huge success on the screen in *Scarface: The Shame of the Nation* (1932). He still considered himself a man of the theater, and he approached every film role as he did his stage parts—with total immersion of himself into the subject. Muni read everything he could on the prison system and talked with prison guards and other ex-members of chain gangs. He had several meetings with Robert Burns in Burbank, studying the way the real fugitive walked, talked, and breathed. Muni told Burns, "I don't want to imitate you, I want to *be* you"! A replica of a prison camp was built on the Warner Ranch, and all during the back-breaking, brutal work sequences that took place in the prison and in the yard, Muni refused the use of a double. He and several hundred extras playing convicts broke stones with pickaxes in the blazing sun, bringing an intensified element of realism to the film. But more than merely being realistic, this film, made in 1932 at the height of the Depression, was a scathing attack upon a major American institution and reflected a social awareness that was typical of Warner Bros. during the 1930's. No other studio was dealing with real issues at that time. Most films of the period tried to pull American audiences out of the realities of the Depression, while *I Am a Fugitive from a Chain Gang* confronted them with some harsh truths.

The film opens as James Allen (Paul Muni) returns home after World War I intent on avoiding his old factory job and desirous of going into engineering. He is tired of the routine of soldiering and wants to be creative. But family pressures force him into a job in a shoe factory, which he eventually leaves. Allen packs up and leaves home, traveling about the country looking for work. He soon realizes how little qualified he is, trying to compete for jobs when the country is in the midst of a vast wave of unemployment. As he wanders from city to city, Allen becomes an outcast in the country for which he fought, and this fact becomes an important theme of the film. James Allen is always portrayed as a patriotic man who loves his country but to whom his country can offer nothing. Finally, penniless and desperate, he attempts to pawn his war medals, but is shown a whole case of such medals by the pawnbroker. Joining forces with a hobo companion, he enters a dingy road-house. Allen's friend waves a gun at the counterman and demands ham-burgers, for he has no money. The police hear the commotion, enter the restaurant, and arrest Allen, who is sentenced to ten years at hard labor in a chain gang for stealing a hamburger.

In the next section, the imagery is all of confinement—the lock, the fence, the chain. The camera shows the prisoners' faces as those of broken and defeated men devoid of any hope except that of escaping a beating. LeRoy depicts these men as suffering, trapped human beings and the guards as sadistic brutes. Expressionistic camera work is used effectively during the prison scenes, in which the violence is implied rather than directly shown, especially in one sequence in which James Allen is being beaten and only his shadow is shown on the wall, bent over in misery. With the help of a fellow inmate who breaks the chain from his foot on the rock pile, Allen escapes the chain gang with the bloodhounds baying at his heels. He gets away and blends into society. After a fleeting liaison with a rather cheap girl, he goes to work for a Chicago engineering firm.

For five years, Allen works hard and eventually attains a position of prominence, both in the firm and in the community in which he lives. He falls in love with Helen (Helen Vinson), a refined young woman who knows nothing of his past. They are about to be married when Marie (Glenda Farrell), the girl from his past, comes back, having learned of his conviction and escape. Marie threatens to blackmail Allen unless he marries her, which he does. His security is destroyed when Marie later informs on him, in effect wiping out his record of six years as an upstanding citizen. Because of Allen's position in the community, his case becomes a *cause célèbre*, with groups formed to keep him from going back to prison. A deal is made whereby Allen will serve a symbolic ninety days on the chain gang doing easy tasks, and after that, the state will consider his debt to society paid. Allen is suspicious, and justifiably so. No sooner is he back on the chain gang than the brutalization begins anew. Near the breaking point, Allen again escapes, but this time into an America sunk even deeper in the Depression, with no job in sight. He is now a permanent refugee on the fringes of society. At the film's end, he comes back to see Helen, the woman he loves. She sees him outside her house, his face peering out of the black night. As she asks him how he lives, he whispers "I steal!" and disappears back into the darkness.

The ending of the film was almost unbearable for some people in its unremitting despair. LeRoy has written in his autobiography that when Muni's face disappears in the dark, it was because a light had blown out, but that upon seeing the frames, it looked so effective that he retained the take. The film had great emotional impact upon its audiences, and, beyond that, a significant social impact. The nation became collectively offended at the harsh Georgia penal code. Reform committees were formed, letters were written, and editorials composed all over the nation, seeking to force the state of Georgia to change its laws. These efforts were successful, for shortly after the film opened, the Georgia chain gang system was revised. Mervyn LeRoy and Jack Warner, however, were not welcome in the South. They received anonymous letters telling them that if they ever set foot on Georgia soil they would be arrested, or worse. Muni, nominated for an Oscar, was proud of his role in the film, feeling that it was one of his most significant parts.

I Am a Fugitive from a Chain Gang was revived frequently in the 1960's when America was again going through social upheaval. The film now has a new generation of devoted fans, but it is ultimately a product of its time. There has probably never been a bleaker American film. It represents a world devoid of hope and justice, with no relief in sight.

Joan Cohen

I CONFESS

Released: 1953
Production: Alfred Hitchcock for Warner Bros.
Direction: Alfred Hitchcock
Screenplay: George Tabori and William Archibald; based on the play *Nos Deux Consciences* by Paul Anthelme
Cinematography: Robert Burks
Editing: Rudi Fehr
Running time: 95 minutes

    Principal characters:

Father Michael Logan	Montgomery Clift
Ruth Grandfort	Anne Baxter
Inspector Larrue	Karl Malden
Willy Robertson	Brian Aherne
Otto Keller	O. E. Hasse
Pierre Grandfort	Roger Dann
Alma Keller	Dolly Haas

Alfred Hitchcock's *I Confess*, the film immediately following his masterpiece *Strangers on a Train* (1951), was considered to be something of a failure by its director himself. Finding the completed product lacking in humor, an important element in most of his films, he tended to dismiss its importance. Perhaps for this reason, the film is frequently ignored as an integral part of his *oeuvre*. The film is worth analysis, however, if only as a reflection of Hitchcock's own Catholicism. As an *auteur*, Hitchcock did not blatantly illuminate his films with religious symbolism, as was frequently the case with John Ford in his films. In many ways, however, Hitchcock's films do have a religious or at least moral undercurrent. In *I Confess*, one of the major themes of the mystery centers on a priest's moral dilemmas, one of which has a direct bearing on his role as a priest.

The film begins during an attempted robbery when Otto Keller (O. E. Hasse), a caretaker for a local Catholic church, murders a second-rate Quebec lawyer named Vilette. Returning to the church, he confesses his recent crime to Father Michael Logan (Montgomery Clift), who, because of Church law, is unable to divulge information received during confession. Once this fact sinks into the warped mind of Otto, he forgets any thought of going to the police and giving himself up, feeling sure that no one else besides Father Michael will ever know of his crime.

The situation becomes more complex when the local police begin to suspect Father Michael himself of being the murderer. Witnesses in the form of two young schoolgirls testify that they saw a man dressed as a priest leave the murdered man's house on the night of the crime, and Father Michael was also seen at the lawyer's house the next day as the police were beginning their investigation. Other evidence reveals that he had also diverted Ruth (Anne Baxter), the wife of an elected official, away from the scene. With all the circumstantial evidence pointing against him, coupled with his own mysterious silence, the police move to arrest Father Michael for the crime.

In a courageous move, Ruth confesses to the police that she was being blackmailed by the dead lawyer. She reveals that years ago she and Michael were engaged to be married, but World War II began and altered their plans. A lonely Ruth turned to her boss, Pierre Grandfort (Roger Dann), for comfort, eventually marrying him, but never truly forgetting Michael. When he returns home after the war Ruth is there to greet him. She spends the day with him, but conveniently fails to tell him of her subsequent marriage. She is hurt and humiliated when he tells her that he wants to be a priest. They are caught in a sudden rainstorm and forced to spend the night in the garden of a deserted house. Although they were innocent of any adultery, in the morning the owner, a lawyer named Vilette spots the couple and begins to make a scene. Vilette recognizes Ruth as Grandfort's wife, and dismisses the incident as a simple misunderstanding. A short time later, however, Ruth is confronted by Vilette, who asks for money and political influence. If she refuses, the unscrupulous lawyer threatens to tell her husband of his interpretation of the incident in the garden. This blackmail continues until the morning when she meets Michael in front of Vilette's house.

This confession does little more than provide a motive for Father Michael to have murdered the lawyer. He goes to trial, but is acquitted because of lack of evidence. He is branded as a murderer and a poor excuse for a priest by the citizens of Quebec, however, and as he leaves the courthouse he is mobbed by the crowd which has gathered to hear the verdict. Otto's wife, Alma (Dolly Haas), unable to bear the burden of his guilt while the priest suffers silently for a crime he never committed, struggles through the crowd to ask his forgiveness. Otto overreacts to this and shoots his wife while trying to kill Father Michael. He is chased into a hotel and eventually shot by the police in an empty ballroom, where Father Michael goes to him, hears his last confession, and performs the religious rite of *extreme unction* before Otto's death.

I Confess is unlike any other Hitchcock film, with none of the usual fast-paced adventure or suspense associated with the director's more famous films. The audience is aware who the murderer is from the very beginning, so the story's tension must come from watching a man bound by a holy oath, "the seal of the confessional," persecuted for a crime he did not commit. During the late 1940's and early 1950's, Hitchcock was experimenting with the form of film. In *Rope* (1948), produced a few years earlier, he had explored the possibility of shooting a film which gave the illusion of one continuous camera take; in *Strangers on a Train* he experimented with characterization; *I Confess* was an experiment in philosophy.

A large portion of the audience for *I Confess* was not able to understand the religious conviction which allowed a man to be tried for a crime he never committed when he knows who is really guilty. In a real sense *I Confess* becomes an obvious analogy, with Clift's Father Michael taking on a Christlike dimension. The juxtaposition of Clift walking past a sculpture showing Christ dragging his cross to Mount Calvary and the overly sentimental flashback which accompanies Ruth's confession show Hitchcock's predilection for obvious symbolism.

There is a brooding quality to Clift's performance in *I Confess* that can almost be interpreted as an unusual disinterest in the events that affect Father Michael's life. Clift tailored his performance to an emotional level, and in much of the film he is silent, allowing his feelings to be conveyed through expression. The other characters approach their roles less intensely. Karl Malden as police inspector Larrue is effective in his stubbornness to prove the priest's guilt. Baxter is uninspired in her breathy portrayal of Ruth, with the flashback sequence, presented with overdubbed narration, allowing her the most freedom in her otherwise bland characterization.

It is apparent that *I Confess* was adapted from a stage play, since the construction of the dialogue is highly theatrical. Only in a few scenes does Hitchcock manage to break away from the static conversational development of the plot and concentrate on visual aspects of the film. The opening scene, for example, in which Otto murders Vilette and makes his way down the deserted streets of Quebec, is totally expressionistic. Low camera angles, which dominate much of the film, also give a sense of expression to the cinematic quality of the film. Another scene, shot in an actual cloudburst, showing the two former lovers confronting each other in a garden setting, beautifully prefigures the violence which will later cause the final break. The physical action which erupts at the end of the film provides Hitchcock with an opportunity to use the Quebec location cinematography to his advantage. There is an "old world" flavor to *I Confess*, with the atmospheric flavor of Quebec, the religious bias, and the naïve sexual blackmail all seeming out of place in an environment of films desensitized to simple emotions.

I Confess is a controversial film among critics. It is easy to dismiss it as a dull and overblown project directed by an acknowledged master filmmaker, but on the other hand, it also presents a mature Hitchcockian outlook to his much-discussed "wrong-man" theme. This film is one of the few cases in which Hitchcock was willing to allow the material to overshadow the filmmaking. There is a disquieting feeling which accompanies *I Confess*; the film is captivating and involving. Its brilliance rests in its ability to make the Christlike analogy work within the context of a contemporary melodrama.

Carl F. Macek

I COVER THE WATERFRONT

Released: 1933
Production: United Artists
Direction: James Cruze
Screenplay: Wells Root; based on the novel of the same name by Max Miller
Cinematography: Ray June
Editing: Grant Whytock
Running time: 70 minutes

Principal characters:
Julie Kirk .... Claudette Colbert
Joe Miller .... Ben Lyon
Eli Kirk .... Ernest Torrence
McCoy .... Hobart Cavanaugh
John Phelps .... Purnell Pratt
Old Chris .... Harry Beresford

I Cover the Waterfront is an unjustly neglected film that skillfully combines three popular types of cinema: the crime story, the newspaper story, and the romance. It is very loosely based upon elements in the novel of the same name, a collection of sketches about life and newspaper reporting on the waterfront in San Diego, California. The film chronicles the story of a newsman covering the waterfront, but it focuses on only one story he covers, one in which he becomes personally involved.

The opening credits are imaginative, especially in view of the fact that in 1933 most credits were simple white words on a black background. *I Cover the Waterfront*, however, immediately establishes its milieu by showing most of the credits as if they were printed in a newspaper. The three opening scenes then quickly and economically establish all the elements of the narrative. First, Joe Miller (Ben Lyon) arrives at his rundown waterfront room to find a strange man sleeping in his bed. Joe finds that the intruder, McCoy (Hobart Cavanaugh), is an out-of-work journalist who knows one of Joe's old classmates in Chicago. A very short conversation between McCoy and Joe establishes that Joe is discontented with the waterfront, with his job, and with the West Coast, and that he is writing a novel.

Just as Joe is about to go to sleep, he gets a telephone call that shows us why he does not like his job. Having been up all night working on a story, Joe is now ordered by his editor to investigate a report that a woman has been seen swimming nude in a remote cove. Not at all graciously, Joe obeys the order; he discovers that the report is indeed true. He waits on the shore with the young woman's bathing suit until she comes in and then conducts his "interview" with her while she stands behind a convenient shoulder-high rock waiting for him to give her suit to her. He finds that she is Julie Kirk

(Claudette Colbert), the daughter of a man he knows on the waterfront. When Joe reports the story to his editor John Phelps (Purnell Pratt), he lets Phelps (whom he calls a "mental midget") know that he considers it a silly item and that he believes the real story is Julie's father, Eli (Ernest Torrence), whom Joe suspects is smuggling Chinese into the harbor. The editor agrees to let Joe pursue the smuggling story, and the plot of the film is under way: Joe pursues Eli Kirk while falling in love with his daughter, Julie.

We soon see that Joe's suspicions of the old man are well founded. Eli pretends to be a fisherman, but the main cargo his ship carries when it returns to port is human—illegal Chinese immigrants. Joe gets the Coast Guard to stop and search Eli's boat, but Eli has the Chinese man on board bound, gagged, weighted down with chains, and dropped overboard when he sees the Coast Guard boat coming. Later, Joe is talking with Old Chris (Harry Beresford), an old man who drags the harbor bottom for what salvage he can find, when he finds the body of the unfortunate Chinese man. Convinced that this proves Eli's guilt, Joe takes the body (wrapped in canvas) to the editor and wants to print the story, but even though Joe finds that the chain on the body matches the chain on Eli's boat, Phelps is afraid to publish the story until there is more definite evidence.

Meanwhile, we see that Julie is devoted to her father and ignorant of his smuggling activities. Not even the Chinese coat he gives her arouses her suspicions. She does not, however, think her father is flawless. When he is gone one night, she knows exactly where to find him—at a brothel. The filmmakers, incidentally, do nothing to conceal the fact that the establishment is a brothel except to have it referred to as a speakeasy and a boarding house. At the brothel she again meets Joe, who has gone there to see Eli also, hoping to find him drunk and talkative. Although he does not get any information from Eli, Joe does begin a romance with Julie, which is another method he has planned to find out about the smuggling. After they take her drunken father home, Joe and Julie sit and talk in the moonlight. She tells of her love of the waterfront and he of his aversion to it and to the writing he does for the newspaper. He also tells her that he has been trying for five years to write a novel. When he notices that she is wearing a Chinese coat, he adds that item to his store of information on the smuggling case.

McCoy, who has by now become Joe's confidant and sidekick, thinks Joe's interest in Julie is more romantic than professional. He deduces this from the fact that the love scenes in the novel Joe is writing are becoming more believable. Joe, of course, denies this, but we can see his feelings for Julie developing throughout the film.

Also developing is Joe's unraveling of the smuggling story. He finds out from Julie that Eli is going to land at the harbor's Chinese settlement one night, and he alerts the Coast Guard. An officer boards the ship when it lands, but can find nothing illegal until Joe discovers that there is a Chinese inside the body of each of the huge sharks on board. Although Eli is seriously wounded by a Coast Guardsman, he escapes. Joe, however, does get his story, a raise, and a bonus. The headline reads "Chinese Smugglers Exposed— New Version of Jonah and the Whale Uncovered."

Now the feelings of Joe and Julie for each other are reversed. Joe has come to realize that he truly loves Julie but she has found out that she has been used and orders him away when he comes to see her. Then Eli sees Joe and shoots him, and Julie finds that she cannot leave him to die. Since Eli and Julie are ready to leave for the Mexican border in a small boat, they take Joe along. Then Eli, who is still losing strength from his own wound, realizes that Joe must have a doctor and returns to the harbor. "If you love him, he's worth it," Eli tells his daughter just before he dies of the wounds he received earlier. "That's more than I ever was."

We next see Joe returning home from his recuperation in the hospital. He finds the place completely redecorated—cozy and comfortable with clean windows, curtains, and even a fireplace. Then Julie comes in, and he realizes that she has done it all. Joe announces that he has thought of the ending for his novel: the hero marries the girl. "That's a swell finish," Julie says as the film ends.

The two principal interwoven elements of the plot, the newspaper story and the romance, are well handled by the filmmakers. Joe's dedication to doing a meaningful story despite the objections of his editor and his slipping into unethical means (pretending to love Julie) in his obsession with the story are made believable. Equally fascinating is the romance between Joe and Julie, especially as it alternates between flippancy and deeper emotion and as the underlying feelings of the two change, with Joe falling in love despite himself and then Julie finding herself unable to deny her love once she finds out what Joe has done. In the end Julie and Eli both seem to accept Joe's reasoning for what he has done to Eli: "That's my job, and he had it coming to him."

Lyon as Joe and Cavanaugh as McCoy are good, but the outstanding performances in *I Cover the Waterfront* are given by Colbert and Torrence. Indeed, some critics consider Colbert's performance one of the best of her thirty-year career. She is able to display her talent for sophisticated comedy that earned her an Academy Award the next year for *It Happened One Night*, but she also conveys the deeper emotions of a daughter's love for a father who does not deserve it. Torrence's portrayal of the father brings out his greed and cruelty without making him seem a purely evil character.

Also quite important to the overall effect of the film is the nearly documentary style of director James Cruze, which emphasizes darkness and glamorizes almost nothing.

Marilynn Wilson

I MARRIED A WITCH

Released: 1942
Production: René Clair for Paramount; released by United Artists
Direction: René Clair
Screenplay: Robert Pirosh and Marc Connelly; based on the novel *The Passionate Witch* by Thorne Smith, completed by Norman Matson
Cinematography: Ted Tetzlaff
Editing: Eda Warren
Art direction: Hans Dreier and Ernst Fegte
Special effects: Gordon Jennings
Music: Roy Webb
Running time: 76 minutes

Principal characters:
Wallace Wooley .... Fredric March
Jennifer .... Veronica Lake
Daniel .... Cecil Kellaway
Dr. Dudley White .... Robert Benchley
Estelle Masterson .... Susan Hayward
Margaret .... Elizabeth Patterson
J. B. Masterson .... Robert Warwick

Critical opinion of the films of director René Clair has fallen in recent years. Once numbered among the greats, even his best work from the late 1920's and 1930's appears slight beside the more lasting achievements of Jean Renoir and Jean Vigo. His first two films arose out of the *avant-garde*—*Paris Qui Dort* (*The Crazy Ray*), 1923, is whimsical science fantasy, and *Entr'Acte* (1924) is a Dadaistic exercise. The early films shift between lightweight comedy (*The Italian Straw Hat*, 1927; *Le Million*, 1931) and fantasy (*Le Voyage Imaginaire*, 1925; and *Under the Roofs of Paris*, 1930). Never far from the satirical, his considered masterpiece, *A Nous la Liberté* (1932), anticipates Chaplin's *Modern Times* (1936) in its depiction of modern industrialized man. It formerly was held that Clair's hiatus in Hollywood was responsible for his later decline, though much the same thing was also said of Jean Renoir, Fritz Lang, and Alfred Hitchcock. A later generation of critics rightly resurrected the works of these men, while Clair continues to be underestimated. Most nearly approaching Clair's experience in America is that of another European expatriate, Ernst Lubitsch. While Lubitsch, however, particularly in his late works, was making the warmly romantic *The Shop Around the Corner* (1940), the black comedy *To Be or Not to Be* (1942), and the nostalgic *Heaven Can Wait* (1943), Clair contented himself with lightweight whimsy. Lubitsch could shift from the sharply witty to the deeply moving very effectively, while Clair lacked this range. There is something a little too neat about Clair that makes most of the films, however entertaining, seem emotionally shallow.

Clair seemed destined for a certain type of film even before he arrived in America. His first film outside France was *The Ghost Goes West* (1936), made in England for Alexander Korda. After *Break the News* (1938), with Maurice Chevalier, and the uncompleted *Air Pur* (1939), he came to Hollywood at the outbreak of World War II to make his most satisfying film, *The Flame of New Orleans* (1941), a romance which benefits considerably from Marlene Dietrich's exotic presence. The next two films found Clair once again in the familiar vein of fantasy with *I Married a Witch* and *It Happened Tomorrow* (1944), the latter starring Dick Powell as a reporter who is able to get the news a day before it occurs. Finally, he made an efficient, if rather mechanical, adaptation of Agatha Christie's *Ten Little Niggers*, with the title changed to the less offensive *And Then There Were None* (1945).

I Married a Witch, adapted from a tale by Thorne Smith (who wrote *Topper*), had originally been a Preston Sturges project. For whatever reason, Sturges dropped out, and Paramount farmed out the film to an independent production company, although it is easy to see how the elements of political satire in the story might have appealed to Sturges in the first place. The film did make use of a number of Paramount technicians such as Hans Dreier, however, and Paramount released the picture in its theaters.

The story begins with a prologue. In seventeenth century Salem, Massachusetts, we find that two witches, Jennifer (Veronica Lake) and her father, Daniel (Cecil Callaway), are being burned at the stake upon evidence given by one Jonathan Wooley. Although they are immolated and their ashes buried beneath a sturdy oak tree, Jennifer puts a curse on all the male members of the Wooley clan: that they shall each marry the wrong woman. There follow a series of scenes in which a succession of Wooleys, played in various disguises by Fredric March, are henpecked by their shrewish spouses. This leads up to the present, and we see gubernatorial candidate Wallace Wooley about to suffer a similar fate with his fiancée.

During a storm, a bolt of lightning strikes a venerable oak, releasing the corporeal spirits of Jennifer and Daniel. Flying through the air, they come to a nearby house where a party is in progress. There Jennifer sees with satisfaction that her curse is still working, but Daniel scoffs at her, saying, "All men marry the wrong woman." In order to make Wooley truly unhappy, he must fall in love with a woman he cannot have. Thus the seed is planted for Jennifer's revenge. Before that, however, the two witches go in search of some cornfields to ruin, Daniel remarking that "'Tis a good way to limber up."

Having lost their bodies through fire, it is necessary that the ghosts should regain them in like manner. They find a fitting site for Jennifer's rebirth by fire in the Pilgrim Hotel. With the hotel slowly and mysteriously burning from the top floor downward, the inhabitants are evacuated, but the fire department is unable to stop the blaze. Having stopped to watch, Wooley hears screams inside and dashes in to investigate. There follows a slightly risqué scene in which Wooley finds the unclad Jennifer in the smoke-filled rooms. Rather stuffy himself, he is embarrassed by her total lack of shame. He lends her his coat and later puts her in a taxi. Reminiscent of the final shot in *The Flame of New Orleans*, the coat is unceremoniously tossed out the window.

On Wooley's return home he finds, to his surprise, that Jennifer is waiting there for him. Jennifer has no trouble in totally bewitching him by morning. Everything is going according to plan until she drinks the love potion intended for him; now she must prevent his marriage to Estelle Masterson (Susan Hayward). It is upon this marriage that Wooley's political ambitions hinge, as Estelle's father owns a powerful newspaper chain. Jennifer enlists the aid of her father, but he is bent on causing other mischief for the Wooleys. After he disrupts the wedding, he causes further grief for the couple by staging his own fake murder and implicating Wooley. Fortunately, Jennifer is able to trick his spirit into entering a bottle of old New Bedford Rum. With Daniel safely ensconced there, Wooley and Jennifer, now married and entering the governor's mansion, are able to live happily ever after, although in an epilogue their daughter seems to have inherited her mother's former penchant for riding a broomstick.

The dialogue by Robert Pirosh and Marc Connelly is both pointed and witty and its delivery effectively understated. Fredric March is ideally suited for his role as Wallace Wooley. Veronica Lake displays her largely neglected flair for comedy, which was exploited elsewhere only by Sturges in *Sullivan's Travels* (1941). In supporting roles, Susan Hayward, using her bossiness to good effect, is properly nasty as Estelle, while Robert Warwick and Elizabeth Patterson lend comic color to their parts. Robert Benchley is as droll as ever. Standing out, however, is Cecil Kellaway as the charmingly malevolent Daniel.

On the technical side, Clair is ably assisted by Gordon Jenning in his work with special effects. The cinematography of Ted Tetzlaff is at times appropriately low-key. The sets, by Hans Dreier and Ernst Fegte, are authentic. Clair's signature is clearly apparent in the proceedings, but the question remains whether he has anything to say. It often seems that Clair, gliding easily over the surface, is unable to delve into any deeper waters. Expert as he is, he fails to make a truly challenging film. Compared to the more substantial work of Renoir, Clair produces lightweight entertainments which, pleasant as they are at the moment, leave one hungering for more. Yet, if Clair is not to be mistaken for an artist of the first rank, we can still be grateful that he possessed buoyancy and charm, qualities in short enough supply at any time.

Mike Vanderlan

I NEVER SANG FOR MY FATHER

Released: 1969
Production: Gilbert Cates for Columbia
Direction: Gilbert Cates
Screenplay: Robert Anderson; based on his play of the same name
Cinematography: Morris Hartzband
Editing: Angie Ross
Running time: 93 minutes

Principal characters:
Tom	Melvyn Douglas
Margaret	Dorothy Stickney
Gene	Gene Hackman
Alice	Estelle Parsons
Peggy	Elizabeth Hubbard
Norma	Lovelady Powell

I Never Sang for My Father is a disturbing film about the vicissitudes of growing old and about the pain and sense of loss elderly people experience. It also concerns the problems their children experience in trying to help them adjust to roles that are almost reversed: the older person is dependent, while the younger ones have the choices.

Except for a recent trip to California where he met the woman he plans to marry, Gene Garrison (Gene Hackman) has always lived near his parents. When they return from a trip to Florida, he takes up his former relationship with them, visiting them often in the suburbs. His father, Tom (Melvyn Douglas), is forgetful, repetitive, and irascible; his mother, Margaret (Dorothy Stickney), who has had a heart attack, is sweet and patient. When Margaret dies, Tom is left alone, and Gene's sister, Alice (Estelle Parsons), who was banished from the family circle for marrying a Jew, comes East for the funeral. Alice has the courage Gene lacks. Gene always seeks *rapprochement* with his father, whereas Alice knows that this is impossible and warns Gene that he must not sacrifice his life for his father. After a quarrel, Gene leaves his father's house, never to return. His voice on the sound track says that he went to California and that Tom entered a hospital where he died alone. "Death ends a life," Gene says, "but it does not end a relationship which struggles on in the survivor's mind toward some resolution which it may never find."

I Never Sang for My Father is full of pain and regret, of the impossibility of getting close to people and understanding them, and of the gallant effort Gene makes to reach his father. The film is completely verbal, and since the subject matter is so touchy, it is a difficult film to watch; it constantly presents disturbing parallels with one's own life.

The last, extended scene between the two men encapsulates everything scriptwriter Robert Anderson had to relate about his characters. Tom and Gene are in Tom's bedroom, and Tom is looking through old papers and photos and telling Gene the oft-repeated tales of his youth. His father was a drunk who deserted the family, leaving Tom to care for a younger brother and sister. It is understood that the rift between Tom and his father is recapitulated in the relationship between Gene and Tom. Tom reiterates the old litany: how hard his youth was, how, as he says, "I was only tolerated in this house because I paid the bills," and how he worked his fingers to the bone. Tom is a man as full of yearning and sadness as Gene, and it is their tragedy that they never once are able to bridge the emotional chasm that separates them—even on this night when their feelings are exposed as never before. When Gene says that he wanted to love Tom, that he hoped to draw nearer to him, there is such remorse and such understated agony at the missed opportunity that the audience can feel clearly Gene's frustration and thwarted expectations.

Still, there is some evidence of closeness; Tom and Gene embrace when they meet, an act as rare on screen as it is in real life. Gene loves his mother and feels an emotional rapport with her. Tom recalls hearing Gene singing with Margaret—Gene always seemed to be finishing as Tom came into the room. Tom says he wanted to hear Gene sing "When I Grow Too Old to Dream," but he never did. Of course, this is the origin of the title and a perfect metaphor for the relationship between the two men, who are continually on different wave lengths, talking past each other, screaming without being heard.

If Tom has failed in one way with Gene, he has alienated his daughter completely, literally driving her away. Alice sees their relationship clearly and knows that the guilt Gene feels will trap him into staying with Tom instead of marrying Peggy (Elizabeth Hubbard) and living his own life. He cannot face the fact that their relationship is unworkable. Alice is as damaged in her way as Gene is in his. She is bitter, resentful, cut off from her parents, saying she appreciates the lesson Tom taught her—that one has to be tough and accept the fact that one is alone in the world. She is whistling in the dark however, for underneath her bravado she is a frightened child who would very much like to feel close to her father.

The performances are virtually perfect. Douglas had the professional courage to play an unlikable character. Tom is bossy, garrulous, crotchety, and often wrong-headed, but he is also sympathetic and understandable, a real person with mortal dimensions. Douglas plays him on a human scale, not larger than life, but as a man who could be the old "geezer" next door, shouting in frustration when he cannot get his own way. It is a long way from the suave boulevardier he played in *Ninotchka* (1940), but Douglas managed the transition with grace, becoming an elderly character actor of undiminished talent who has won two Oscars since the age of sixty.

In 1970, Hackman was at the peak of his stardom. He had done solid work in *Bonnie and Clyde* (1967) and *Downhill Racer* (1969), and he would soon win an Academy Award for *The French Connection* (1971). Hackman unfortunately burnt his career out through overexposure. He appeared too frequently, sometimes in worthwhile films, but too often in inferior ones. Here he is at his best; his ordinary looks are just right for Gene, and his underplaying (sometimes Hackman can be overly melodramatic) is what is needed for this role. He is expresssive in his frustration at being treated like a child, folding up inside when he cannot make contact with Tom, although the role is not an expressive one. Hackman makes Gene something more than what is written; his naturalism transcends the lapses in Anderson's screenplay, and he gives us a Gene more fully rounded and more thought-out than the one in the script.

Parsons, who played Hackman's wife in *Bonnie and Clyde*, here plays his sister. Parsons is a plain woman, and in *I Never Sang for My Father* she is an aggressive complainer and something of a know-it-all, but she is not on the screen long enough to become annoying. She too feels the ache of estrangement, but she has erected such a protective barrier around her damaged feelings that she is scarcely able to acknowledge the extent of her unhappiness. Parsons gives an even-tempered performance, neither strident nor long-suffering. As a performer she can fall into Method-type acting mannerisms, but here she is sweetly restrained.

If there is any thematic unity to director Gilbert Cates's work, it has to do with the problems of people reaching middle age, as demonstrated in *Summer Wishes, Winter Dreams* (1973), which presented Joanne Woodward as a discontented woman unable to focus on the reasons for her anxiety. Of course, *I Never Sang for My Father* shares *its* subject with an American classic, Eugene O'Neil's *Long Day's Journey into Night*, a play conceived on a far larger scale than Anderson's, and one that by the very nature of its greatness is perhaps less forceful than Anderson's small, intimate drama.

Cates's direction is crude, the lighting is poor, and there is no discernible visual style; yet the film is affecting. It refuses to show a way out of these individuals' dilemmas, to indulge in false reassurances, or even to say that these troubled people can ever hope to find peace. It simply presents them in a realistic, identifiable manner.

Judith M. Kass

I REMEMBER MAMA

Released: 1948
Production: George Stevens and Harriet Parsons for RKO/Radio
Direction: George Stevens
Screenplay: DeWitt Bodeen; based on the play of the same name by John
   Van Druten and on the book *Mama's Bank Account* by Kathryn Forbes
Cinematography: Nicholas Musuraca
Editing: Robert Swink
Running time: 119 minutes

   Principal characters:
   Mama .... Irene Dunne
   Katrin .... Barbara Bel Geddes
   Uncle Chris .... Oscar Homolka
   Papa .... Philip Dorn
   Mr. Hyde .... Sir Cedric Hardwicke
   Mr. Thorkelson .... Edgar Bergen
   Aunt Trina .... Ellen Corby
   Doctor Johnson .... Rudy Vallee
   Florence Dana Moorhead .... Florence Bates
   Jessie Brown .... Barbara O'Neil

RKO producer Harriet Parsons was so enchanted with *Mama's Bank Account*, Kathryn Forbes's book of stories about a Norwegian family living in San Francisco around 1910, that when she learned her studio had bought the film rights, she immediately asked studio executives to assign the production to her, which they did.

When a treatment was approved and the screenplay written, preproduction plans began, but were brought to a sudden halt when composers Richard Rodgers and Oscar Hammerstein bought the dramatic rights to *Mama's Bank Account* from RKO and signed John Van Druten to dramatize and direct it for the theater. Wisely, the studio retained the rights of first refusal on buying back the film rights after the play's premiere, and the new version was to be called *I Remember Mama.* When the play which Van Druten fashioned opened on Broadway under the auspices of Rodgers and Hammerstein and was an immediate success, RKO eventually acquired the film rights to the property again. This new success of the story made many producers interested in it, but Parsons remained firm in her desire to produce the new film herself, and eventually studio executives acquiesced and assigned her to the project again.

The film was to be a big-budgeted special with a long shooting schedule. There were certain problems in adapting the play to the screen which had not existed when the story basis had been a series of short stories. First, much of the action had to move from inside the house onto the streets of San

Francisco, where the company was to go for exterior location shots. There were, furthermore, two censorship problems in the story, not censorable in the theater, but definitely so on the screen: in the hospital sequence in which Arne, the little nephew, has had surgery for a malformed leg, Uncle Chris could not teach the boy to say "Damn!" when the pain became bad and "God damn!" when it became very bad; and Uncle Chris's longtime mistress, Jessie Brown, had at some point to become his legal wife or be separated from him. These matters were taken care of satisfactorily, with Uncle Chris teaching Arne to say something harmless in Norwegian; and before Uncle Chris dies, he confesses to Mama that years ago Jessie and he were married, but he never wanted the aunts to know because they had been so mean to her.

Irene Dunne, who was a youthful-looking fifty at the time, was the favorite for the role of Mama, but, although she loved the role, she realized that playing a mother of four growing children and changing her physical appearance to conform to character might keep her from that point on in character roles. She had director approval, however, and finally agreed to accept the part of Mama if one of five directors whose names she proposed was given the assignment. George Stevens, back in Hollywood after a longterm service in the Army overseas, was one of the directors listed, and he accepted the assignment as his first after his discharge. He wanted certain changes in the screenplay, so an entirely new version was written to his specifications.

I Remember Mama is more than a mother-love narrative; it is a simple family story with Mama an understanding matriarch, the ever-present lead. The focal character, however, is the "I" of the title; she is the oldest daughter, Katrin (Barbara Bel Geddes), who wants to be a writer. The picture fades in on her in her attic studio (her "boudoir," as she calls it) where she is writing the story of her family, and her voice over the scene narrates the action that opens the story outside the frame. Although Papa (Philip Dorn) is a hard-working carpenter, providing the means of support, it is first and foremost Mama who runs the family, who is its heart and its very life. Every Saturday night when Papa brings home his salary for the week, the family, father, mother, three daughters, and a son, all gather around the kitchen table, and as the weekly expenses are itemized, Mama counts out the sums in cash for which the money is to be spent—even the little things, such as ten cents for a new notebook. The children hover anxiously, watching Mama as she adds the items and then smiles in satisfaction, saying, "Is good. We do not have to go to the bank."

When Lars, the oldest child and the only son, confesses that he would like to go on to high school, each member of the family commits proudly to sacrifices so that he may go. Christine and Dagmar, the youngest sisters, promise to take on new chores that will bring in pennies; so does Katrin; Lars himself will take on an early paper route; Papa will give up tobacco for his pipe; and Mama will do without a new coat for the winter. Thus Lars's going on to high school becomes more than a possibility; it will be a fact. The family stays together because they help one another, which was once the way of the American family.

Mama has three sisters, and the aunts are frequent visitors. Mama also has an older brother known as Uncle Chris (Oscar Homolka), a rough-going character who runs a ranch in Ukiah, and who sometimes arrives without warning in his automobile, bringing boxes of oranges and good fresh food. He also brings with him Jessie Brown (Barbara O'Neil), known to the aunts as "that woman," who sits quietly in the car and waits while Uncle Chris concludes his cyclonic visit inside with Mama. On one occasion it is he who bundles up Mama, carrying little Dagmar, who is very ill with a mastoid, and drives them to the hospital for surgery.

The hospital sequence evokes both tears and laughter, bordering on sentiment that does not spill over into sentimentality. Mama, denied entry to the ward where Dagmar lies in postoperative recovery, contrives a scheme for entering the ward. She takes over for a scrubwoman, and, scrubbing her way past the watchful nurses on duty, gets into the forbidden ward, assures Dagmar that there is nothing to fear, and softly sings an old Norwegian lullaby so that not only her child but also all the children in the ward go peacefully to sleep.

I Remember Mama is a story of little things which, in time, become the most important, the best-remembered events in a family's life. In the end it is Mama who gets Katrin's manuscripts to a visiting authoress at the Fairmont Hotel in San Francisco and makes a deal with the lady so that Katrin eventually is represented by an agent. When the word comes that Katrin's story has been accepted and a check is enclosed, Katrin turns the check over to Mama and asks her to put it in the bank. With honest embarrassment, Mama confesses that she has never been inside a bank; there is no bank account; it had been a myth so that the children would not feel afraid and be insecure. By Scandinavian thrift the family has survived over adversity, and if Mama has been forced into deception to give her family a feeling of security, it is a kindly lie that can be forgiven, for the family has come of age, and they possess the one security that money will never buy—lasting love.

At a time when audiences were surfeited with big films on big postwar subjects, the simplicity and nostalgic charm of *I Remember Mama* also captured their fancy. It had its premiere, along with a big Easter stage show at Radio City Music Hall in New York City, where it ran for more than a month, earning excellent notices and public approval. When Academy Award time came, cinematographer Nick Musuraca and four of the cast members garnered nominations. Dunne received her fifth and last nomination as Best Actress, and she has stated that *I Remember Mama* and *Love Affair* (1937) are her two favorite roles. *I Remember Mama* is still shown in retrospectives. A true period piece, it has never dated, and audiences have never tired of laughing and crying, of living and remembering with Mama.

The popularity of the film version of *I Remember Mama* led to a very successful television series called *Mama* which was based on Forbes' stories. The series ran from 1949 to 1956, and starred a more maternal looking "mama" in the person of actress Peggy Wood. The series, in fact, has been credited with starting the family situation comedy genre which has been a staple of television ever since.

The most recent resurrection of the story came in the late 1970's. The Scandinavian actress Liv Ullman starred in a very short-lived version of the story which was produced on the Broadway stage as a musical. Unfortunately the charm and timelessness of the story could not salvage a mediocre musical score.

DeWitt Bodeen

I WALKED WITH A ZOMBIE

Released: 1943
Production: Val Lewton for RKO/Radio
Direction: Jacques Tourneur
Screenplay: Curt Siodmak and Ardel Wray; based on an original story by
 Inez Wallace and the novel *Jane Eyre* by Charlotte Brontë
Cinematography: J. Roy Hunt
Editing: Mark Robson
Art direction: Albert S. D'Agostino and Walter E. Keller
Sound: John C. Grubb
Music: Roy Webb
Running time: 68 minutes

Principal characters:
Wesley Rand .... James Ellison
Betsy Connell .... Frances Dee
Paul Holland .... Tom Conway
Mrs. Holland .... Edith Barrett
Dr. Maxwell .... James Bell
Jessica .... Christine Gordon
Alma .... Teresa Harris
Calypso singer .... Sir Lancelot
Carrefour .... Darby Jones

In *The Bad and the Beautiful* (1952), Hollywood producer Jonathan Shields (Kirk Douglas), the film's fictional protagonist, comes into his own with a little sleeper called *The Curse of the Cat Men*, in which horror is suggested rather than shown. Anxious to move on to bigger things, he is openly scornful of his next assignment, *The Son of the Cat Men*. The real Val Lewton, whose own success with *Cat People* (1942) inspired that section of the later film, was in actuality the temperamental opposite of Shields. He might not have wanted his next film to be called *I Walked with a Zombie*, but the title was his only compromise. He was happy to make modestly budgeted films, created with loyal and valued collaborators of his choosing under conditions of maximum freedom. Although another of his subsequent productions was christened *The Curse of the Cat People* (1944) by the studio, it involves neither curses *nor* cat people, being a work, much admired by child psychologists, about a lonely child and her imaginary playmate. Lewton's central preoccupation was the relationship between death and life, and he used the horror genre to approach this subject with resolute seriousness. If his first three films, *Cat People*, *The Leopard Man* (1943), and this film, remain his best, this may be attributed to the presence of director Jacques Tourneur, who realized Lewton'a ideas with uncommon visual acuity and poetic suggestiveness, humbly contributing a few ideas of his own.

Tourneur's expressiveness is best displayed in *I Walked with a Zombie*, an enchanting film possessed of a subtlety at odds with the conventions of its genre and a beauty which might be described as otherworldly. Tourneur believed in the supernatural, and while the narrative action often seems susceptible to rational explanation, ultimately it escapes the rational and demands of us that we scorn reason, embracing elusive truths which initially seem fanciful. The opening image and voice-over narration beautifully establish the work's mood and are immediately evocative of how the film elicits an openness of response. The distant figures of two women, later to be identified as Betsy (Frances Dee) and Jessica (Christine Gordon), are seen walking in long-shot along a beach beneath a tranquil sky barely disturbed by drifting white clouds. Betsy speaks her narration quietly and sensibly. "I walked with a zombie. It sounds funny, I know. A year ago I didn't even know what a zombie was. . . ."

That image, seemingly a fragment of Betsy's consciousness as she recalls the events of the story, never appears again. Her voice assures us that the story will be subjectively related, but the image objectifies her. The heroine, whole and alive, she is at the same time identified as the companion of Jessica, a zombie, dead within a continuing physical existence. In this manner, death and life walk hand in hand throughout the film, metaphorically coexisting as determining factors of the destinies of the characters. Further, Betsy's control of the narrative proves to be illusory. Midway through the film, the voice-over narration stops, following Betsy's conscious recognition that she has fallen in love. Verging on the mysterious and unexplainable, the film must finally reject Betsy as a reasonable observer and absorb her into its ambiguous texture, pointedly at the moment when her emotions conquer her cultivated good sense.

Betsy is a Canadian nurse, sent to the island of St. Sebastian in the West Indies to take employment in the home of the owner of a sugar cane plantation, Paul Holland (Tom Conway). Paul's wife, Jessica exists in a state of what her doctor (James Bell) explains as a form of paralysis which has left her mind empty of thought and emotion, although her physical movements are unrestricted. The cause of her condition is mysterious, although several explanations are ultimately offered. It develops that Paul's half-brother Wesley Rand (James Ellison), now a hard-drinking wastrel, had been in love with Jessica, and the two had planned to run away together. That night, an encounter between husband, wife, and lover had resulted in Jessica's helpless state. Paul and Wesley's mother (Edith Barrett) later admits that she feels some of the responsibility for what happened, and her two sons each share her guilt. Betsy attempts to be dispassionate in her dealings with the family, but Paul's kindness and sensitivity arouse her sympathy, and, ultimately, her love. At this point, she resolves to do everything possible to cure Jessica, and her efforts include a nocturnal visit to a voodoo ceremony. Jessica remains a zombie, and Betsy is certain that Paul, although he shares her love, will never be free. Voodoo intervenes, and Wesley, in a trance, kills Jessica and carries her body, now as lifeless as her mind, into the ocean, dying himself. Paul and Betsy are united, and a chant spoken by the islanders warns that life should be spent with the living, while the dead should be left with the dead.

The thrust of the work is to affirm that people who have the capacity for living (Paul and Betsy) should not linger on the spectre of death, however morally conscientious their motives might be, and that a man like Wesley, seeking oblivion through drink and without the will to resume his life positively once Jessica is lost to him, belongs to the world of death and rightfully gives himself to it. Wesley, however, is no less sympathetic than the other characters, and Jessica, a haunting presence throughout the story, is treated as being deserving of compassion in spite of the seeming meaninglessness of her continued existence. The resolution in death of this couple's love occurs in the same sea upon which Betsy had gazed as her love for Paul was born, and this connection is symptomatic of the disturbing complexity with which the concept of death is imbued throughout the film. In the garden of the Holland home is a statue of St. Sebastian which the blacks call T-Misery. It had formerly been the figurehead of a slave ship, and it is the legacy of both the white and black characters who inhabit the island to remember that slavery somberly colors the island's history. For this reason, the blacks still rejoice when someone dies and weep when a baby is born. The telling effect of historical memory on the lives of the characters is thematically linked to the family history and to the "death" of Jessica.

This detailed context for an intimate story permeates the texture of the work, providing substance for its pervasive tone of melancholy and its twilight atmosphere. It is characteristic of the Tourneur-Lewton films (although not those Lewton made with others) for tragic episodes of historical oppression to be woven into events of the present. Similar motifs, the source of superstition and fantasy from which outsiders such as Betsy initially disengage themselves, are vital to *Cat People* and to the final collaboration, *The Leopard Man* (1943). *I Walked with a Zombie*, however, most thoroughly assimilates these past associations into its narrative. Slavery is implicitly linked to the state of living death embodied by Jessica. The imposing figure of Carrefour (Darby Jones), the black guardian of the crossroads, is also a zombie, and it is he who implacably follows Wesley to the sea in the climactic sequence and carries Jessica's body back to the house. Another black character, the calypso singer (Sir Lancelot), provides a narrative voice as authoritative as Betsy's. His song relates to her the history of the Rand-Holland family. The character's wry sense of humor and the song's gay and lilting melody contrast affectingly with the gentle resignation of the characters and the plaintiveness which typify Tourneur's rendering of the story.

Experience of the film reveals it to be very elaborate, but its story is quite simple. Nuance and detail, superficially incidental but essential to the film's philosophical tendencies, endow the narrative flow with a richness at once complementary to the lucidity with which it develops characters and describes events and unexpected in a film running only sixty-eight minutes. The intricacy of lighting, gracefulness of camera movement, and care taken in the art direction and editing testify to the flair of Lewton, Tourneur, and their colleagues for utilizing careful preparation and ready imagination to the best advantage. The artistry achieved in the film on a brief shooting schedule deserves to be envied by the makers of countless films not suffering from restraints of time and budget. The nonstar cast also contributes to this impression, especially the lovely Dee, a sadly underrated actress, as the idealistic but naïve Betsy, and Teresa Harris as Alma, a black servant who persuasively argues the superiority of voodoo over Christian medicine. Tourneur's contribution to the playing of his films is a very distinctive one. He encourages his actors and actresses to speak very quietly and to be dramatically restrained so that our attention to them becomes keener. While eerie and unsettling, sequences rooted in fear and the inexplicable are not handled for shock effect, making it difficult to relate *I Walked with a Zombie* to what is commonly thought of today as the horror genre. Its screenplay owes as much to romantic novels, especially Charlotte Brontë's *Jane Eyre*, which suggested the outline of the story. Critic Robin Wood, an ardent and insightful admirer of the film, was quite perceptive when he chose to describe it as a poetic fantasy.

Tourneur's style disdains scare tactics at the same time that it demonstrates an imposing respect for the supernatural. This stylistic individuality is discernible throughout the film, as Tourneur characteristically approaches every scene by seeking its overall mood rather than attempting to isolate and emphasize specific dramatic elements. He is most comfortable with long shots and camera movements which minimize the significance of particular actions and maximize the relationship of those actions to connected actions. This directorial attitude is of crucial importance in sequences that are primarily visual, most impressively that of the journey through the cane fields to the voodoo ceremony. This sequence introduces a new setting to the film, a world traveled at night which is strange and foreboding. Alternations of black and white, which extend from the costumes of the two women to the contrast of their pale faces with that of the silent Carrefour who materializes with disquieting suddeness in their path, provide an evocative link to unstated themes of the island's tragic racial history and the life-death symbiosis which governs the lives of all the central characters. The series of swift and graceful tracking shots which follow as Betsy resolutely leads Jessica through the rows of discreetly rustling cane vividly enhances the impression that the heroine is bravely venturing forth into a perilous unknown. Like her own emotional needs of which she is only semiconscious, the voodoo ceremony into which she and Jessica emerge is a half-comprehensible and half-frightening alien world. It is the strategy of the sequence to encourage the ambiguity of these impressions. Calm and assured, Tourneur invites tentative acceptance of the mysterious truths of the world he evokes, not oppressively but with a gentle magic.

Blake Lucas

I WANT TO LIVE!

Released: 1958
Production: Walter Wanger for Figaro, Inc. Production; released by United
  Artists
Direction: Robert Wise
Screenplay: Nelson Gidding and Don Mankiewicz; based on newspaper ar-
  ticles by Ed Montgomery and letters of Barbara Graham
Cinematography: Lionel Lindon
Editing: William Hornbeck
Sound: Gordon E. Sawyer
Music: John Mandel
Running time: 120 minutes

Principal characters:

Barbara Graham	Susan Hayward (AA)
Ed Montgomery	Simon Oakland
Peg	Virginia Vincent
Henry Graham	Wesley Lau
Emmett Perkins	Philip Coolidge
Jack Santo	Lou Krugman
Bruce King	James Philbrook
District Attorney	Bartlett Robinson

I Want to Live! is a film which defies easy classification. It is both a documentary type of drama about the conviction and subsequent execution of
Barbara Graham in the gas chamber at San Quentin on June 3, 1955, and
a damning indictment against capital punishment. It is also the story of a
woman, a petty thief, prostitute, perjurer, forger, loyal friend, and loving
mother, who was, according to a psychiatrist, neither a drug addict nor a
person capable of physical violence. Until her execution, she maintained her
claim of innocence. The controversy over Barbara Graham's guilt or innocence did not die with her in the San Quentin gas chamber, but will continue
as long as the question of what constitutes cruel and unusual punishment
remains unanswered.

Figaro, Inc., the company which produced this grim but compelling drama,
had previously produced such outstanding films as *The Barefoot Contessa*
(1954) and *The Quiet American* (1958) for release by United Artists. *I Want
to Live!* was produced by Walter Wanger, whose production credits include
Smash-Up (1947)—a film for which Hayward received an Academy Award
nomination—and directed by Robert Wise, who counts among his credits
such films as *Run Silent, Run Deep* (1958) and the film biography, *Somebody
Up There Likes Me* (1956). The screenplay by Nelson Gidding and Don
Mankiewicz is based on newspaper and magazine articles by the Pulitzer

Prize-winning journalist Edward S. Montgomery, one of the leading criminal investigative reporters in the nation. Additional sources of reference were the actual court transcripts and Barbara Graham's personal letters written during her term of imprisonment. These letters, sent mostly to a friend, Sharon Stone, provide a harrowing account of a condemned person's mental anguish.

Director Robert Wise chose the cast for the film carefully. He selected Susan Hayward to portray Barbara Graham based on her unsettling but totally realistic performances in the films *Smash-Up*, *My Foolish Heart* (1949), *With a Song in My Heart* (1952), and *I'll Cry Tomorrow* (1955). All of these films dealt with the personal tragedies and ordeals suffered by slightly less than respectable principal characters, and each performance resulted in an Academy Award nomination for Hayward. For his supporting cast, Wise chose proven actors, but none who had the status to overshadow the principal lead or provoke enough recognition to detract from the stark realism and atmosphere of the film.

This drama, filmed in black and white to heighten its overall documentary feeling, is divided into roughly two parts. The staccato tempo through the first half is established by a progressive jazz rhythm which was arranged by John Mandel, one of the foremost composers of jazz, and performed by the well-known Gerry Mulligan combo. This was the first time jazz had ever been used to score an entire film, and the music serves to embellish the film's realism. Using a fast-cut, cinemagraphic style that complements Mandel's beat, Lionel Linden's constantly moving camera pans and captures the changeability and seediness of the San Francisco tenderloin district, an area frequented by Barbara Graham.

Barbara is a contradictory and complex woman who spent much of her childhood in foster homes and reform schools. She speaks with a slangy "jive" vernacular that reinforces her image of being street-wise and tough. Yet, this image does not accurately reflect the total woman, for the letters written to her counsel and friends while she was imprisoned reveal a highly literate, sensitive, philosophic side of her personality.

After serving a prison sentence for perjury, Barbara marries bartender Henry Graham (Wesley Lau) and has a child by him. Graham turns out to be a hopeless drug addict. Pressed by both the responsibility for her child and a lack of excitement in her life, Barbara becomes involved with two petty crooks, Emmet Perkins and Jack Santo, with whom she had worked before. Perkins is played by Broadway actor Philip Coolidge; Santo is played by Lou Krugman, a veteran television actor.

Then, on the night of March 9, 1953, Mrs. Mabel Monahein, an elderly widow, is beaten to death in her Burbank, California, home during an attempted robbery. An underground figure, Bruce King (James Philbrook), claims he was present at the scene of the crime, turns state's evidence, and directs the police dragnet to the hideout of Barbara and her associates. The crime is first revealed to the audience when the police close in on the trio's hideout in Lynwood, California. Although the murder is not depicted in the film, the details of King's testimony are strongly suspect, which Edward Montgomery's investigation later confirms.

The scene depicting the capture of the three suspected murderers reveals much about Barbara Graham's defiance and spirit; it raises the question of her innocence as well. While searchlights bathe the hideout in a pitiless glare, a curious but uneasy crowd gathers; inside, Barbara calmly fixes her makeup. Some long minutes after the surrender of her partners, she emerges from the beleaguered building; a burlesque bump and defiant toss of her head leave little doubt about her contempt and disdain for all concerned. The first half of the film sets the stage for the harrowing second half, for now the march to the gas chamber begins. The tempo becomes solemn, dirgeful, inexorably beating out the seconds, minutes, and hours of Barbara Graham's final days. Under Wise's masterful direction, Susan Hayward vividly portrays the changes that take place in Graham's personality as she draws closer to the horror of the death chamber. She has appeared as the tough, flippant B-girl and the disdainful, suspected murderess. Now, as she languishes in first one jail and then another anxiously awaiting the correction of justice that does not come, tormented by the knowledge that her two-year-old son will soon forget her, we see her plunged into the depths of terror and despair, praying for a death that will finally end her mental anguish.

Only a few voices are raised in Graham's behalf: her staunch and loyal friend, Peg (Virginia Vincent); the psychiatrist who is convinced she was incapable of physical violence; and reporter Ed Montgomery (Simon Oakland). Montgomery, after labeling her "Bloody Babs" during the trial, interviews her numerous times on death row and becomes convinced of her innocence.

Hayward has the power to involve her audience so profoundly that the question of Barbara Graham's guilt or innocence becomes secondary. Stunned by the horror of what is happening, the audience watches helplessly as the state's legal machinery grinds blindly toward the execution of justice. Time and again reprieves are granted, then ground to dust. The execution is set for 10:00 A.M. on June 3, and Barbara is outwardly calm, prepared to face her death. Twice that morning, the execution is postponed as her lawyers desperately maneuver to save her life, one stay coming as she stands at the door to the gas chamber. At 11:12 A.M., after all maneuvers have failed, the final phone call comes, and at 11:34 A.M. the cyanide pellets drop into the solution of sulphuric acid.

Under Wise's taut direction, the suspense and anguish of Barbara Graham's last few days mount to a point of unbearable intensity. The film, which earned Susan Hayward a well-deserved Academy Award as Best Actress, also received Academy Award nominations for Best Director, Best Screenplay, Best Black and White Cinematography, and Best Sound Direction. Following her unforgettable performance in *I Want to Live!*, Susan Hayward, before her untimely death in 1975, went on to appear in a number of other fine films.

D. Gail Huskins